Literature
and Science

Forthcoming titles in
ABC-CLIO's

Science and Society: Impact and Interaction
Series

The Environment and Science, Christian C. Young

Exploration and Science, Michael S. Reidy, Gary Kroll, and Erik M. Conway

Imperialism and Science, George N. Vlahakis, Isabel Maria Malaquias, Nathan M. Brooks, François Regourd, Feza Gunergun, and David Wright

Literature and Science

Social Impact and Interaction

John H. Cartwright and Brian Baker

ABC-CLIO

Santa Barbara, California • Denver, Colorado • Oxford, England

Library of Congress Cataloging-in-Publication Data

Cartwright, John H., 1953-
    Literature and science : social impact and interaction /
    John H. Cartwright and Brian Baker.
        p. cm. — (Science and society)
    Includes bibliographical references and index.
    ISBN 1-85109-458-X (hardback : alk. paper) — ISBN 1-85109-463-6 (ebook)
1. Science and literature. I. Baker, Brian, 1969– II. Title.
III. Series: Science and society (Santa Barbara, Calif.)

    PN55.C39 2005
    809'.9336—dc22

                                                                2005000977

09 08 07 06 05   10 9 8 7 6 5 4 3 2 1

This book is also available on the World Wide Web as an eBook.
Visit abc-clio.com for details.

ABC-CLIO, Inc.
130 Cremona Drive, P.O. Box 1911
Santa Barbara, California 93116-1911

This book is printed on acid-free paper.
Manufactured in the United States of America

JHC: To Margaret

BB: To Deniz, Sophie, and baby

Contents

Series Editor's Preface

T he discipline of the history of science emerged from the natural sciences with the founding of the journal *Isis* by George Sarton in 1912. Two and a half decades later in a lecture at Harvard Sarton explained, "We shall not be able to understand our own science of today (I do not say to use it, but to understand it) if we do not succeed in penetrating its genesis and evolution." Historians of science, many of the first trained by Sarton and then by his students, study how science developed during the sixteenth and seventeenth centuries and how the evolution of the physical, biological, and social sciences over the past 350 years has been powerfully influenced by various social and intellectual contexts. Throughout the twentieth century the new field of the history of science grew with the establishment of dozens of new journals, graduate programs, and eventually the emergence of undergraduate majors in the history, philosophy, and sociology of science, technology, and medicine. Sarton's call to understand the origins and development of modern science has been answered by the development of not simply one discipline, but several.

Despite their successes in training scholars and professionalizing the field, historians of science have not been particularly successful in getting their work, especially their depictions of the interactions between science and society, into history textbooks. Pick up any U.S. history textbook and examine some of the topics that have been well explored by historians of science, such as scientific racism, the Scopes trial, nuclear weapons, eugenics, industrialization, or the relationship between science and technology. The depictions of these topics offered by the average history textbook have remained unchanged over the last fifty years, while the professional literature related to them that historians of science produce has made considerable revision to basic assumptions about each of these subjects.

The large and growing gap between what historians of science say about certain scientific and technological subjects and the portrayal of these subjects in most survey courses led us to organize the Science and Society series. Obviously, the rich body of literature that historians of science have amassed is not regularly consulted in the production of history texts or lectures. The authors and editors of this series seek to overcome this disparity by offering a synthetic, readable, and chronological history of the physical, social, and biological sciences as they developed within particular social, political, institutional, intellectual, and economic contexts over the past 350 years. Each volume stresses the reciprocal relationship between science and context; that is, while various circumstances and perspectives have influenced the evolution of the sciences, scientific disciplines have conversely influenced the contexts within which they developed. Volumes within this series each begin with a chronological narrative of the evolution of the natural and social sciences that focuses on the particular ways in which contexts influenced and were influenced by the development of scientific explanations and institutions. Spread throughout the narrative readers will encounter short biographies of significant and iconic individuals whose work demonstrates the ways in which the scientific enterprise has been pursued by men and women throughout the last three centuries. Each chapter includes a bibliographic essay that discusses significant primary documents and secondary literature, describes competing historical narratives, and explains the historiographical development in the field. Following the historical narratives, each book contains a glossary, timeline, and most importantly a bibliography of primary source materials to encourage readers to come into direct contact with the people, the problems, and the claims that demonstrate how science and society influence one another. Our hope is that students and instructors will use the series to introduce themselves to the large and growing field of the history of science and begin the work of integrating the history of science into history classrooms and literature.

—*Mark A. Largent*

Acknowledgments

The authors are happy to acknowledge the help of a number of people who read sections of this work and offered their advice. Thanks are due to Chris Walsh, who read chapters five and seven and made many valuable comments. Derek Alsop generously shared his enthusiasm for the eighteenth century and gave useful commentary on chapter four. Thanks are due to Graham Atkin, who carefully examined and improved chapter two; and thanks also to Emma Rees, who expertly commented on chapter three and was right in persuading one of the authors to give more space to Margaret Cavendish.

The authors, John Cartwright and Brian Baker, would also like to thank their respective departments, Biological Sciences and English, at the University of Chester for the opportunity to adjust their timetables to enable the work to progress. Although we acknowledge the beneficial input of our colleagues, all errors that may be found here are our own.

We would also like to thank the editorial team at ABC-CLIO, and in particular an anonymous copy editor who, as well as improving the readability and clarity of the work, made some kind remarks about its content that gave us a final burst of energy to cross the finishing line.

We must also acknowledge the valuable help of the library staff at the University of Chester who are never less than efficient and organized at procuring books and articles not in stock. Finally, special thanks to Angela Bell and Gary Martin of graphic services for their artistry and professionalism in assisting with several diagrams in this book.

Preface

Writing a book that claims to offer a historical survey of science and literature may seem to some an undertaking that is either bold or foolish, or both. One reason is that each of those terms has multiple meanings, meanings that, to make matters worse, have shifted over time. Even the very idea of a sharp distinction between the literature of science and other literature stems, in part, from the rise of empirical science in the seventeenth century and the need felt by its protagonists to prescribe for themselves a more precise language and to distance their deliberations from other forms of writing. Some scholars in the humanities today would place great emphasis on the idea that separation of these terms is both a cultural construct and an artifact of scholarship, preferring instead to see both as parts of a more basic level of culture open to theoretical analysis. It is important, then, to clarify at the outset how we propose to interpret this task, to reveal our assumptions on how these words can be read, and to make clear what we try to achieve and, just as importantly, what we do not try to achieve.

The words *science* and *scientist* only acquired their modern meanings relatively recently. The word *scientist*, for example, did not come into use until 1833 when, at a meeting of the British Association for the Advancement of Science (BAAS), the poet Samuel Taylor Coleridge objected to the word *philosopher* to describe the activities of the BAAS members and someone at the meeting suggested "scientist." A year later the word "scientist" first appeared in print in a review of Mary Somerville's book *On the Connexion of the Physical Sciences* by the Victorian polymath William Whewell. In this review Whewell (who coined many scientific words such as anode, cathode, and ion) considered alternative terms for scientists such as *nature-pokers* and *nature-peepers*, which (we may be relieved to know) he rejected. Even so, the term *scientist* did not catch on until near the end of the century. Similarly, before the early nineteenth century the word *science* meant disciplined knowledge. So when Thomas Jefferson wrote to the English chemist Joseph Priestley in 1800, he listed those "sciences" that interested him as "botany, chemistry . . . commerce, history, ethics, law, arts, fine arts." Most of the topics in his list would not fall under the heading of science today. Before the 1830s, the physical sciences fell under the heading natural philosophy.

Another question to face is what activities in the past qualify for the term that we now (with conscious regard for the anachronism) apply the label *science*. On the whole, we have taken a pragmatic approach to this. Hence, in the early chapters we have discussed astrology and alchemy, since they were then regarded as sciences even though today they would not qualify. We have eschewed technology as belonging to a different type of enquiry. Similarly, the practice of medicine, with its own rich history, is only touched on here and there—although it is covered in the early chapters on medieval and renaissance science and literature since medical practice in this period drew upon a wider worldview that encompassed astronomy and astrology. As "science," then, we have tended to concentrate on the natural sciences that now fall in the area of physics, astronomy, biology, geology, and chemistry.

The word *literature* can also sustain a variety of interpretations. We have chosen here to concentrate on fictive and imaginative writing—plays, poems, and novels—rather than biographies, travel writing, or other forms of nonfiction. For reasons of space and of expertise, we have focused on literature in English, from Europe and from North America. Practically, this means a main focus on British literature with some reference to European texts, particularly in the early chapters, and on literature of the United States, particularly in the twentieth-century chapters toward the end of this volume. As will become clear, the connection between science and culture is a problematic one, and the final chapters investigate this problem in detail. Because it is such a troublesome area, concentration on literature in English enables the book to bracket off problems of translation and cultural difference to a large degree. The connection between science and the literature of postcolonial states in Africa, for instance, would be another very large and important subject, but would involve a consideration of political, cultural, and ethical issues for which there is no space in the project at hand. We are also conscious of the problem of the "canon" in this book: that we have traced the connection between science and "great works" of literature, to the exclusion of minority voices. We hope we have addressed this as far as possible within each chapter, but the focus upon the Gothic and science fiction in chapters eight, nine, and ten will, we hope, give some insight into the links between science and popular genres.

At the onset it is important to be clear that we are not aiming to be anything near comprehensive in our treatment of the field of science and literature. To even attempt this would be beyond the expertise of two authors and in such a short book would leave nothing but a list of brief references or an unreadable route map of the terrain. Instead, we have chosen to focus upon authors, periods, and topics that we think would be interesting to the reader and at the same time reveal something significant about the interactions between science and literature in the period under study. Some readers may be surprised, therefore, at aspects of science or famous authors left out. For example, we have not dealt with biotechnology in the twentieth century or George Eliot in the nineteenth, both of which would deserve mention, had we but space enough and time. Our task is to be representative, not comprehensive.

This brings us of course to the most troublesome and problematic word in our title: *and*. For in that simple conjunction a multitude of assumptions and biases must reveal themselves. Yet the word *and* is necessary since, unlike the history of or the philosophy of science, the subject we are here exploring is not simply a matter of looking at one type of enquiry through the lens of another. Instead, we are exploring the interactions between both activities as well as their mutual grounding in a common historical context. Consequently, we have tried to go beyond a mere mechanical cataloging of "influence," such as characterized the early emergence of this field in the 1940s, where scientific allusions in literature were documented and literature shown to be influenced by science, with science treated as the independent variable. We have aimed at detailing a richer catalogue of interactions.

The critical approach of this volume is broadly historical in emphasis, though we have tried to include as much detailed textual analysis as we can in each of the chapters. We do not place this book in any particular "school" of criticism or endorse a particular theoretical approach. While it would be incorrect for us to assume a position of critical neutrality with regard to our approach, we have tried to be as broad and flexible as possible in the range of critical responses we bring to bear. In general, however, it could be said that the approach of this book fits with recent critical writings on the relationship between science and literature, which foreground the historical and cultural landscape at the time of production of the text. We have tried to make this book as accessible as we can, and while some technical and critical language is used, we have avoided a critical idiom that would alienate some readers while indicating too rigid a theoretical set of assumptions on our part.

For the general reader, one problem with some recent writing on science and literature has been a tendency of scholars to adopt a narrow chronological focus or to specialize in one or two authors. In addition, much work on the subject has been concerned with deeply theoretical issues and marked therefore by methodological self-consciousness and reflexivity. Necessary as these approaches are, in this book we have aimed to provide a work that has been informed by theory and is usable in the classroom but also one that is accessible and interesting to the intelligent general reader.

The narrative framework of this book is historical, but it would also have been possible to treat the relationship between science and literature thematically. For those readers who may warm to this approach, it may be useful to list some of the themes that will emerge as the chapters unfold.

1. Where writers use scientific images and metaphors for literary effect or as explanatory devices. Science here is seen as part of an unquestioned intellectual framework. This is particularly the case with Chaucer and Dante examined in chapter one.

2. Where writers use their medium (especially extended verse) to didactically convey scientific findings. One well-known example of this is the scientific verse of Erasmus Darwin explored in chapter four.

3. Where science is rejected, derided, or lampooned. Satire has long been one of the standard ways in which writers have responded to what they have regarded as scientific hubris. It is particularly found in seventeenth- and eighteenth-century writing. It is a rather broad category and ranges from the view of the scientist as a foolish and impractical amateur to the romantic perception of scientists as cold, inhuman, and sinister.

4. Where scientific ideas and discoveries provide an intellectual challenge requiring accommodation and negotiation by the author. An obvious example of this might be John Donne's reaction to the new philosophy that called "all in doubt" in the seventeenth century. This category is particularly apt for our discussion of the effect on literature of advances in geology and evolutionary biology in the nineteenth century.

5. Where science is celebrated as an indication of divine power or human achievement, the results of scientific inquiry embraced, and their implications explored. This is where the scientist is painted as a hero. It is particularly found in the attitude of some eighteenth-century poets to the awesome achievements of Newton. It can also be found in the tradition of natural theology (or physico-theology) that grew up in the seventeenth century, where scientific findings were celebrated in literature as further evidence of God's munificence and authority.

6. Where science is represented in a mythic or religious framework. Mary Shelley in her most famous work, *Frankenstein*, saw herself describing the story of "a modern Prometheus" who, unlike the original, brought gifts of questionable value. Similarly, many treatments of science and scientists fall into the category of the Faust myth: the overreacher who brings ruin on himself and others. This motif can also be found in the figure of Captain Ahab in Melville's *Moby-Dick*, whose overreaching and self-destructive quest to kill the White Whale is narrated in diabolical terms.

7. Where science becomes a means of exploring our world through the rigorous extrapolation of other worlds from scientific concepts. This approach is particularly common in science fiction, where imagining other worlds is often a way of thinking about our own—by imagining other worlds, beings, or social organizations, we throw into relief the assumptions we bring to the "naturalness" of our own culture and society.

8. Where scientific paradigms are used to explore cultural and social forces, or to imagine societal change or breakdown, such as in the widespread use of the scientific concept of "entropy" in twentieth-century literature as a metaphor for social dislocation.

9. Where literary forms and conventions have provided means for scientists to think through their own problems in interpreting nature. Gillian Beer's work on Darwin is a classic example of this. This category is especially important, since it shows science as affected by and responsive to literature. It is a controversial one, since some scientists see it as a step toward the argument that science is merely a social construct. This subject is explored in chapter twelve.

These themes appear throughout the volume and provide an alternative way of approaching the subject that complements the chronological survey offered in the first ten chapters. In the last two chapters we examine the idea of a conflict between scientists and literary scholars ranging from Snow's sketch of the Two Cultures in 1959 to the more recent science wars of the 1990s.

Medieval Cosmology and European Literature: Dante and Chaucer

John Cartwright

In the opening line of the novel *The Go Between*, by L. P. Hartley, we read that "the past is another country; they do things differently there." The analogy is particularly apt when we consider the European Middle Ages. Thinkers then did not make the same distinctions between science and literature that we do today. For them *science*, or rather *natural philosophy*, was seen as part of a much larger world picture, a world picture that by the end of the thirteenth century wove together physical, philosophical, and theological components. In such a universe the moral dimension was never very far away. God had created the world and had assigned man a natural place and duties within it; failure of humans to carry out their defined role was, therefore, unnatural and by definition immoral. Understanding this worldview today is no easy task: the assumptions, beliefs, and modes of reasoning that underpinned it are so different from our own that it requires considerable effort for us to begin to see the world through medieval eyes. But the effort is worth it. Writers of the late Middle Ages documented a natural world that to them was rich in metaphors and allegories set out by God to delight and instruct, a numinous and poetic world full of meaning and purpose, where every object was a symbol of some higher level of reality. When we make the effort to appreciate this mindset, the fact that it proved factually wrong on most counts seems a small price to pay for the aesthetic pleasure gained.

Aristotelian Cosmology

A convenient starting point to explore this strange landscape is the realization that thinking in the Middle Ages was shaped by two great authorities: the authority of the Church and the authority of texts. Virtually every writer of the period based his or her views, as far as possible, on earlier authors. Classical sources and manuscripts were held in a reverence akin to that bestowed on the bones of saints and fragments of the true cross.

The main source of ideas about the natural world came from the translation of Greek and Arabic texts that took place with renewed vigor in the twelfth and thirteenth centuries. These texts comprised the output of Greek and Roman poets and philosophers, and later, Arabic commentaries. Initially, the thought of the pagan Greek philosophers did not sit easily with Christian theology. In 1210, Aristotelian science was rigorously condemned and excluded from the curriculum at the University of Paris, then Europe's main center of scientific learning. By around 1270, however, Christian scholars such as Thomas Aquinas reconciled Aristotelianism with Christian doctrine. A generation after Thomas's death, his philosophical compromise—a philosophical tour de force that managed to harmonize sacred and secular paths to truth—became the official doctrine of the Church. Thomas Aquinas was made a saint in 1323. From then until about 1600, this combination of Greco-Roman and Arabic scholarship formed the basis of the European university curriculum.

In Aristotelian physics the earth was held to be a sphere sitting inside a much larger but likewise spherical universe. The earth lay at the exact center of the cosmos, and other celestial objects—the planets and the stars—revolved around it. The orbit of the moon divided the cosmos into two distinct areas. From the center of the earth to the sphere of the moon was the terrestrial or sublunary realm. Here change was incessant: things moved about, rivers ran downhill, smoke rose upward, clouds drifted across the sky, man tilled the fields and then lay beneath. In contrast, the region above the sphere of the moon was a changeless realm where celestial objects whirled around on a fixed, unchanging course.

Aristotle held to the view that the fundamental stuff of the sublunary world was *prime matter*. In itself, prime matter was thought to be inert and to possess no properties. However, four qualities could adhere to prime matter to raise it to the level of a sensible element or substance: hot, cold, dry, and moist. Now a body cannot be simultaneously hot and cold; nor can it be moist and dry. But it can be hot and moist, cold and dry, and so on. It is the possible combinations of these four qualities that give rise to the four elements as shown in Table 1. In this theory the ordinary objects of the world were regarded as mixtures of two or more elements. Crucially, Aristotle's theory allowed an explanation of change to be conceived. When water is heated, for example, and turns to an "air" or vapor, this can be understood as the heat from fire driving out the "cold" in the water; so instead of cold and wet defining water we now have hot and wet defining a vapor or air.

**TABLE 1: COMBINATION OF THE FOUR BASIC QUALITIES
GIVING RISE TO FOUR ELEMENTS**

Combination of properties	Resulting element
Cold and dry	Earth
Cold and wet	Water
Hot and dry	Fire
Hot and moist	Air

Change of place in the sublunary realm could be partly understood in terms of Aristotle's *doctrine of natural place*. In this view, the world below the moon was structured into four concentric regions or proper places. Moving from the moon downward we have fire, air, water, and finally earth. If objects were left to themselves, they would naturally gravitate to their respective spheres: earthy objects would move downward and fiery objects would move upward. Change occurs because the circular motion of the spheres above (starting with the outer-most sphere—the primum mobile) is communicated downward and (especially through the motion of the sun) stirs up the matter on earth. The movement of the sun rising at dawn, for example, evaporates water, turning it into the airy state and so raises it upward.

In this way we have a theory for the rising and falling of objects. A stone falls because it contains predominantly earth, earth belongs at the center of the cosmos, and so the object, in longing to return to its proper place, falls down-ward. For an Aristotelian, a stone taken to the surface of the moon should fall back to earth, not down onto the moon. The heavier the object, the greater the longing to return, and so the faster it falls.

Above the sphere of the moon things were very different. One of the most obvious features of the superlunary realm was its changelessness. Although the stars move across the night sky in an east to west direction, they remain in the same positions relative to each other. The constellation of Orion that we see today looks much the same as in Aristotle's time. Common sense suggested that whereas objects on earth moved in straight lines toward their proper place, celestial objects, like the stars that make up the constellations, move in circular paths around the earth. It followed that celestial objects could not be made up of the four elements found on the earth; otherwise they would move to their proper place. A further problem was that since terrestrial motion, in Aristotle's view, was due to objects moving to their proper place (or being pushed out of it), it was difficult to see why celestial objects should move at all if they were already where they should be. Consequently, Aristotle assigned a fifth element, the ether, to the material that made up the heavens. Change in these ethereal layers was impossible since ether did not possess the properties (hot, cold, moist, dry) of

Schema præmiſſæ diuiſionis.

EMPIREVM   HABITACVLVM

Decimūm Coelūm   Primū Mobile

Nonū Coelūm   Criſtallinūm

Octauūm   Firmamentū

COELV ♄ SATVRNI

♃ IOVIS

♂ MARTIS

☉ SOLIS

♀ VENERIS

☿ MERCVRII

☾ LVNÆ

COELVM   DEI

ELECTORVM   ET OMNIVM

DE CIRCVLIS SPHAERAE.
CAP.III.

B

Woodcut of the universe taken from Peter Apian's Cosmographia *(1539). Note the sequence of elements rising above the earth followed by one sphere for each planet. Beyond the sphere of stars there is a crystalline sphere, the primum mobile, and then the Empyrean—the abode of God and all the elect (saints). This view of the universe was essentially Aristotelian with a few added Christian elements. (Peter Apian/Corbis)* earthly matter. Similarly, lightness and heaviness had no meaning there: motion was uniform and circular and eternal. Any signs of changes that did appear to take place in the sky, such as phenomena we now call shooting stars and comets, could not logically belong to the region above the moon. Instead they were assigned to the sublunary realm and were thought to be atmospheric phenomena. The common root of the word *meteor* (a shooting star or fragment of matter entering the earth's atmosphere) and *meteorology* (the study of the weather) still echoes this view, even though now we know that meteors and meteorites do not originate in the earth's atmosphere.

Beyond the moon lay the planets, the stars, and the prime mover. The prime mover was needed to explain the movement of the stars and planets around the earth. Aristotle held to a common-sense view of the physics of motion: that if a thing moved it needed a force to push or pull it to keep it going. If a horse stopped pulling a cart, the cart stopped moving. Since celestial objects constantly move there must be some source of force to keep them all moving around the earth. To account for the fine detail of how these objects appear to behave to earth-bound observers, Aristotle borrowed the concentric spheres concept of two Greek mathematicians, Eudoxus of Cnidus and Callipus of Cyzicus. He modified these essentially geometric schemes to give them a sense of physical reality. As a result, Aristotle's universe required some fifty-five spheres to carry around the stars and the seven planets (Moon, Mercury, Venus, Sun, Mars, Jupiter, and Saturn). In practice, translations of Aristotle that became available to medieval Europe typically simplified this scheme to some eight or nine spheres. The figure is typical of the popular conception of Aristotle's world.

The other conception of the structure of the universe above the sphere of the moon available to medieval astronomers was the series of models given by Claudius Ptolemy (ca.100–170 A.D.) in his great book *The Almagest* (ca.140 A.D.). In this system, the order of the planets stretching from the moon to the primum mobile is the same. The difference was that Ptolemy explained the puzzling motion of the planets using *epicycles* and *deferents*. According to Ptolemy's model, each planet ran on an epicycle, the center of which ran around a larger wheel called the deferent. The earth sat somewhere near the center of the deferent. For professional astronomers and astrologers, Ptolemy's scheme had numerous advantages: it could, for example, forecast eclipses and conjunctions (the time when planets appear very close together in the sky) with an accuracy that was remarkable, considering that we now regard the whole construction as false.

Appendix A gives a brief account of how the schemes of Aristotle and Ptolemy stand in relation to the observations that were available to the ancient and medieval observers. This appendix will help the reader understand the incorporation of astronomical concepts into literature, from medieval times up to the seventeenth century, and especially in the work of Dante and Chaucer.

Dante and The Divine Comedy

The influence of Dante Alighieri (1265–1321) on world literature has been enormous. His most famous and influential work, *The Divine Comedy*, has been in print and studied continuously for the last 500 years. The story opens on Good Friday 1300 (or possibly 1301). We read how, over the next few days, Dante is led, first by the Roman poet Virgil and then by his beloved Beatrice, on a dazzling journey from the surface of the earth down to the depths of hell, from hell to the summit of purgatory, and from there up to the heights of heaven—a fantastic journey across the entire medieval universe. The regions visited correspond to the divisions of the work into three books or *cantica: Inferno* (Hell), *Purgatorio* (Purgatory), and *Paradisio* (Paradise). The universe of Dante was closed, compact, thoroughly Aristotelian, and, compared to modern notions, of relatively recent origin. Passages in canto twenty-six of *Paradisio*, for example, suggest a date of creation at about 5198 B.C.

In the first part of their journey, Virgil and Dante make their way down to the center of the earth toward hell. Hell is described as a steep conical pit containing successive layers of sinners—the sins getting worse as they approach the center. At the exact center lies Satan, once one of the brightest of the angels an now reduced in hell to immobile misery. His fall from heaven to the center of the earth ("farthest from High Heaven's all-moving gyre" [*Hell*, 129]) created an impact crater and a corresponding mountain (Purgatory) on the other side of the earth. As Virgil and Dante pass through the exact center of the earth, they find themselves climbing up the legs of Satan, since they have passed through what we now call the center of gravity or, in Dante's words, "the point passed by / Toward which all weight bears down from everywhere" (*Hell*, Canto 34, l. 109).

Purgatory is described as a gigantic, stepped mountain, upon whose various ledges reside repentant sinners. At the top of Purgatory sits the earthly paradise of Eden, once the home of Adam and Eve before their expulsion. After the Fall, man's habitation was moved to the northern hemisphere. At the summit of Purgatory Dante feels a breeze caused by the turning of the celestial spheres that lie immediately above (Canto 28, l. 103).

The next stage of his journey is recounted in the third part of *The Divine Comedy*, *Paradisio*. Dante moves through the spheres of the heavens with his beloved Beatrice as his guide. Rising through the sphere of fire, so bright that "day seemed joined to day" (Canto I, l. 61), Beatrice gazes on the eternal wheels

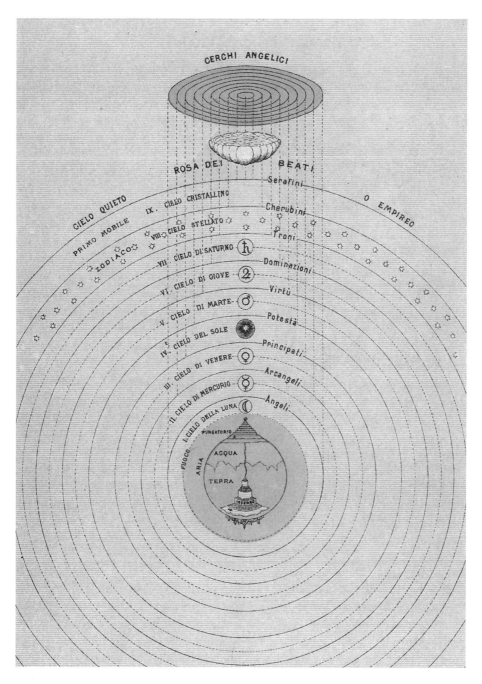

The universe according to Dante. Each sphere above the central earth is associated with departed souls appropriate to the qualities of the planet. Before he meets God Dante beholds the Snow-White Rose of Paradise, consisting of the nine orders of angels circling around God. These same angels are also the intelligences that help move each sphere. Dante ascends into the sphere of the fixed stars through his birth sign, Gemini. (Mary Evans Picture Library)

Dante Alighieri (1265–1321)

Dante was born in Florence in 1265 under, as he tells us, the sign of Gemini and hence between 21 May and 20 June. Dante was both a politician and a poet. Intellectually he was a product of the profound synthesis of Christian theology and Greek philosophy that had been achieved just ten years before his birth. Politically, his life was shaped by conflict within the Italian peninsula and civil strife with Florence itself.

Dante, Allegory of the Divine Comedy and City of Florence *by Domenico di Michelino. In the foreground stands Dante holding his work* The Divine Comedy. *To one side Florence is depicted, and on the other is a vision of hell. Behind Dante, human figures try to ascend purgatory. At the top of the picture are the spheres of the planets leading up to Paradise. (David Lees/Corbis)*

For most of the Middle Ages there were rival claims to power and influence in the area now occupied by the nation of Italy. The encroachment of the mainly German Holy Roman Empire was resisted by a papal alliance of city-states. Also, within Florence itself, a particularly nasty series of feuds started some fifty years before Dante was born. At this time, there were two rival clans in Florence, the Uberti, later called the Ghibellines, and the Donati, later called the Guelfs. In 1260 the Guelfs were defeated at the battle of Montaperti (see *Inferno* Canto X and Canto XXXII), but in 1266, a year after Dante's birth, a combined force of Guelfs and French and papal armies defeated the Ghibellines at Benevento and effectively expelled them forever from Florence. So Dante grew up in a city full of postwar pride, and the Florentines routinely compared their own city-state with that of Rome and those of the ancient world. Dante was passionate about his attachment to Florence, and at one level his masterpiece, *The Divine Comedy*, is about the tortured history of that city.

From about 1290 to 1301 Dante held a series of important public offices. During this time Florence had once again become a divided city with two factions of the Guelfs, the Whites and the Blacks, vying for supremacy. Initially, Dante's political career prospered. In 1295 he occupied a seat on the People's Council; in 1297 he was given the title of *poeta fiorentino* in the esteemed guild of apothecaries; and in 1300 he was appointed as one of the city's six priors. Soon after this, however, despite his original membership of the Guelf party (the party of papal power), Dante began to

and Dante begins to hear the music of the spheres. The notion that the spheres emit music but that mortals rarely hear it goes back to the thought of Pythagoras and Plato. The idea reappears in Macrobius's commentary on Cicero's *Dream of Scipio (Somnium Scipionis)*. In fact Cicero's dream provides a model for both Dante and Chaucer in their tours across the medieval cosmos.

oppose the secular and territorial ambitions of Pope Boniface. To further his aims, Boniface formed an alliance with the exiled Black Guelfs and the French throne. In 1301 Dante was chosen as an emissary from Florence to Rome to gauge the Pope's intentions. While he was in Rome, the troops of Charles Valois and the exiled Blacks entered Florence and seized power.

In January 1302 Dante was summoned to appear before the new Florentine government. Knowing that he would almost certainly be imprisoned, he declined to appear, and on March 10, 1302, Dante and fourteen other White Guelfs were condemned to death by burning. Dante remained exiled from his beloved home city of Florence for the rest of his life. In his years of exile Dante wrote his most famous work, *The Divine Comedy*, begun around 1308 and finished just months before his death in 1321.

In the third book of *The Divine Comedy, Paradisio*, Dante introduces the character of Beatrice as his guide through the spheres up to paradise. The relationship between Dante and the real life Beatrice Portinari is surprising. Dante's lifelong love for Beatrice began on May Day 1274, when at the tender age of nine he was taken to a children's party given by the Florentine banker Folco Portinari for his daughter Beatrice, who was then just eight years and five months old. Beatrice, as Dante tells us in his work *La Vita Nuova* (The New Life), was wearing a dress of "decorous and delicate crimson, tied with a girdle." From the moment he caught sight of her his life was transformed. He describes the moment in terms of an inner voice saying to him, "Behold the God who is stronger than I and who in coming will rule over me" (*La Vita Nuova*, II, 1.19). The modern mind will have difficulty accepting that a nine-year-old boy could fall in love with a girl aged eight. In his poetry, however, Dante describes various levels of the theme of love. At one level, it is a version of courtly love such as celebrated by the troubadours of southern France, where men express their masculinity by respecting a woman who is unobtainable. At another, Dante's love of Beatrice is an expression of the love for the Virgin Mary. At yet another level, Beatrice is the embodiment of love itself, a love that guides Dante to his salvation, and a love that governs the universe and moves the stars.

In reality, Dante and Beatrice only met five times, and there was nothing sexual in their encounters. Beatrice married Simone dei Bardi, another banker, when she was just thirteen. When he was about twenty years old, Dante was led into an arranged marriage with Gemma Donati, with whom he had two sons and a daughter. Dante never mentions his wife in his poetry. In 1290 Beatrice died, aged just twenty-four. Following her death, Dante began a massive program of reading and study that was to culminate in *The Divine Comedy*.

As Dante and Beatrice move through the planetary spheres, souls descend from the Empyrean (where they all reside) to greet them. The souls descend to that sphere most appropriate to their earthly life. Hence in the moon's sphere— the moon being a symbol of inconstancy—Dante and Beatrice meet Piccarda dei Donati, sister of Corso Donati, who took religious vows but then renounced them when pressed to marry. Moving upward, Dante describes Mercury as "this shy star, / masked by another's rays from mortal eye," accurately reflecting the fact that Mercury is rarely seen since it is so close to the sun. Venus is also always observed close to the sun, and Dante captures this poetically with "the star that gazes amorous-eyed / Now on the sun's nape, now upon his brow" (Canto 8, l. 12). The nape and brow refer to the observational fact that sometimes Venus is seen rising in the morning before the sun, looking at the sun's "brow," and sometimes seen setting after the sun in the west and therefore following it and looking at its "nape." In the third sphere of Venus Dante and Beatrice meet the lovers, in the sphere of Mars the warriors.

As they move through the spheres of the Sun, Mars, Jupiter, and Saturn, the beauty of Beatrice grows ever more radiant. Dante and Beatrice then rise rapidly to the sphere of fixed stars. They enter at the "heaven of the twain" (Canto 22, l. 111) meaning the constellation of Gemini, Dante's birth sign. From this vantage point Dante looks down on the seven planets and realizes he is now in a position to understand their motions:

> How their positions changed, to me was clear.
> All seven being display'd I could admire
> How vast they are how swiftly they are spun.
> (Canto 22, l. 148)

In this sphere St. Peter examines Dante in the Christian faith. Dante replies:

> One God, eternal, sole, my creed doth know,
> Mover of Heavens, being Himself unmoved;
> Loving desiring Him around they go.
> (Canto 24, l. 130)

Here Dante equates God with the prime mover that moves the heavens by desire. At last Dante moves to the primum mobile and Beatrice gives a description of its significance and function as a place from where "as from its starting point, all movement wills." It is a heaven which "has no other 'where' / Than the Divine Mind," a circle whose "motion takes no measurements from other spheres beneath." (Canto 27, l. 106)

The Divine Comedy offers a picture of the universe that is a mixture of physical cosmology and spiritual allegory. Sometimes Dante sacrifices philosophical consistency for poetical effect. In the *Inferno*, for example, he describes a great river (Cocytus) that flows downward toward the center, where it enters a lake frozen by the beating of Satan's wings. A strict Aristotelian would have argued, however, that water should flow upward to its proper place above the sphere of the element earth. Elsewhere, Dante takes care to ensure that his journey through the universe is scientifically plausible. Hence, when he is at the top or Purgatory and ready to ascend into the spheres of the aether, he is aware that as a mortal being composed of the four elements he will be unable to rise upward, since all these elements belong to the sublunary sphere. He gets round this problem by the neat device of experiencing a purgation of all his earthly sins. In effect, he is transformed to a prelapsarian state of a being without original sin. So, relieved of this burden, he is lifted upward by the love he bears for God to the source of this love, and he rises as fast as a lightning bolt falls. The solution achieved is thereby both physically and poetically satisfying.

In general terms though, the distinction that we hold today between allegory and an objective factual account would not have been so strong to Dante. The medieval mind thought and understood analogically. Understanding the deeper significance of surface appearances was a way of understanding God's providence and his design of the universe. It is significant that each of the three books of *The Divine Comedy* ends with the word "stars," and Dante has continual recourse to astronomical imagery throughout. For Dante, the stars were symbols of beauty and perfection; the fact that they were unchanging yet visible and capable of influencing human affairs providing a metaphor for the divine mind.

Beatrice is the proper guide through the spheres since she herself is a symbol of divine love. In the *Vita Nuova* (New Life) (ca. 1290), a book in which Dante describes the progress of his love for Beatrice, great emphasis is placed on the number nine. At their first encounter they are both in their ninth years, they meet again nine years later at the ninth hour of the day; even the date of her death can be seen in multiples of nine (1290, and $90 = 10 \times 9$). Most extraordinarily, he lists in order the sixty most beautiful women in Florence, and Beatrice comes out, as might be guessed, in ninth place. Dante offers two explanations for this identification of the number nine with Beatrice (*Vita Nuova*, 29). One is that the square root of nine is three, and three is the number of the Trinity, source of all miracles. The second reason advanced is that according to Ptolemy there are nine heavens (Moon, Mercury, Venus, Sun, Mars, Jupiter, Saturn, the firmament, and the primum mobile). The heavens are moved entirely by love, so Beatrice becomes a symbol of Aristotle's prime mover, the unmoved agency that sets all else in motion through desire.

In the ninth heaven of paradise, appropriately enough, Dante bids farewell to Beatrice. As his final guide, there appears St. Bernard, the Abbot of Clairvaux (1091–1153) who prepares Dante to meet God. In his final vision, Dante in "a flash" understands how the human and divine are conjoined in God. At this point he observes that

My will and my desire were turned by love
The love that moves the sun and the other stars.
(Canto 33, l. 145)

And these are the last words of *The Divine Comedy*.

Chaucer

Another major figure in European literature that appeared in the fourteenth century was Geoffrey Chaucer. Chaucer and Dante had much in common: both were deeply versed in philosophy and science, and both wove scientific concepts into their poems. They also shared the view that their universe was geocentric in a physical sense but profoundly theocentric in a moral one. Both held the central ambition of showing that their world was orderly and planned. Nevertheless, there were important differences in their work. In *The Divine Comedy*, we are carried along on a tour of the universe and meet en route the damned and the saved according to Dante's austere and sometimes peculiarly private judgment. In Chaucer's world, especially in *The Canterbury Tales*, we meet flesh and blood humans gently probed by Chaucer with an affectionate irony and humor allowing us, the readers, to judge their moral worth by their own words and actions.

Chaucer and Astrology

As we have seen, in reading Dante the stars are never very far away. The same is true of Chaucer, but in his case the stars are more precisely described and their influence more carefully delineated according to that typically medieval system of ideas, astrology. Something of a revival in astrology occurred in the thirteenth century. One influential and popular source was Guido Bonatti's *Liber astronomicus*. Dante came down hard on Bonatti and placed him in the eighth circle of hell with his head on his shoulders backward, a symbol of his inability to see ahead (*Inferno*, Canto 20). But whatever Dante's motives, there is no doubt that he held to the view that the configuration of the stars had an impact on human affairs (see *Purgatorio* 20, l. 13–15, and *Paradisio* 27, l. 144–148).

In the Middle Ages the study of astrology was divided into two branches: natural astrology and judicial astronomy. Natural astronomy predicted the motions of the heavenly bodies and made comments on their effect on the weather; judicial astrology, named for the "judging" of favorable or inauspicious conditions, purported to foretell individual destiny on the basis of celestial signs.

Of these branches, judicial astronomy was more controversial; with its suggestion that human will is not totally free, it excited the suspicion of the church.

According to astrological theory, each of the seven planets had its own peculiar influences and properties. Mars, for example, was the planet of iron; it inclined men to war (hence the adjective martial). On the whole, Mars exerted a baneful influence and was given the title the Lesser Infortune (*Infortuna Minor*). But worse than Mars was the malevolent planet Saturn, the Greater Infortune, or *Infortuna Major*. Saturn was associated with the metal lead and seen as a cold, dull, and heavy planet—the harbinger of misfortune and disaster. In a particularly powerful passage in *The Knight's Tale*, Chaucer describes how Saturn, in a dark and chilling speech, sets about the death of one of the characters in the story:

> "My deere doghter Venus," quod Saturne,
> "My cours, that hath so wyde for to turne,
> Hath moore power that woot any man.
> Myn is the drenching in the see so wan;
> Myn is the prison in the derke cote;
> Myn is the strangling and hanging by the thote.
> I do vengeance and pleyn correction,
> Whil I dwelle in the signe of the leoun.
> And myn be the maldyes cold,
> The derke treasons, and the castes olde
> (l. 2453–2468)

Other planets are more kindly. Jupiter is the *Fortuna Major* and brings luck, good fortune, and peace. The sun is the planet of gold and produces wisdom and generosity. Venus, like Jupiter, is a lucky planet; called the *Fortuna Minor*, her influence inclines people to good looks and an amorous nature. Mercury is a changeable planet; its influence is favorable with good planets and malevolent with evil ones. It is the planet of knowledge and wisdom. The nearest planet to the earth, the moon, is associated with silver and is a symbol of inconstancy.

The precise influence of a planet, however, depended crucially on what sign of the zodiac it was in or passing through. The different signs had different properties, and different parts of the body were thought to be under the influence of specific signs. Aries, for example, was a hot and dry sign and was linked with the head and face.

The medieval astrologers that Chaucer studied also divided the celestial sphere into a series of "houses." Houses were fixed regions of sky; at any one time six were above the horizon and six below. Through these houses moved the

Geoffrey Chaucer (ca. 1360–1400)

Like Dante, Geoffrey Chaucer led a double life as a poet and public servant. Although the exact date of Chaucer's birth is uncertain, it is known that he was the son of a successful London wine merchant. In 1357 he entered the court of Edward III and in 1359 accompanied the English army in an expedition against France. Chaucer was captured near Reims and held prisoner until March 1360, when his ransom was paid—the king himself contributing sixteen pounds. Between 1369 and 1386 Chaucer took part in a number of important diplomatic missions. Some of his destinations are unknown, but the most decisive to his literary career must have been his visit to Italy in 1372, when he visited the city-states of Genoa, Pisa, and Florence. It is likely that in Florence he met Petrarch (1304–1374) and Boccaccio (1313–1375), a humanist scholar and Dante's biographer.

English poet and writer Geoffrey Chaucer riding a horse. From a manuscript copy of The Canterbury Tales. *(Getty Images)*

Up to his death in 1400, Chaucer undertook further diplomatic missions abroad and held a number of significant and lucrative posts in England. Apart from his literary output, his professional career as courtier, diplomat, civil servant, Controller of Customs, and Clerk of the King's works earned him favors from three monarchs (Edward III,

signs of the zodiac, the zodiacal constellations (not the same thing as the signs), and the planets. The first house was thought to be especially important, since the heavenly bodies present in that house at a person's nativity were held to have a strong influence on their destiny. This house was a region of sky 30 degrees (hence two hours worth of movement and one twelfth of the celestial sphere) below the eastern horizon. For a person to be born under Aries meant that the sign of Aries lay just two hours below the eastern horizon at the time of birth.

All Arians were not the same, however, since the planets wandered through the houses and signs of the zodiac and produced a different pattern every day of the year. One of the most explicit and famous of Chaucer's uses of this system is in the section of *The Canterbury Tales* known as the *Wife of Bath's Prologue*. *The Canterbury Tales* describes a gathering of pilgrims on their way to the shrine of St. Thomas à Becket at Canterbury. To pass the time, each pilgrim tells a tale or two. The Wife of Bath, or "Alisoun" as she is called, describes the taking of her fifth and last husband, Jankyn, when she is aged forty and he just twenty. In this scene she attributes her personality to astrological influences:

Richard II, and Henry IV) and showed him to be a highly intelligent and resourceful individual.

Chaucer lived through some of the great events of his time: the Black Death, the Hundred Years War between England and France, and the Peasants' Revolt. He read fluently in Latin, French, and Italian; was a competent astronomer and mathematician; and read widely in the sciences. His work for the state must have brought him into contact with virtually every sector of society and supplied rich material for his art.

Not much is known about Chaucer's private life. Around 1374 he married Philippa, possibly one of the queen's ladies. In 1390 he wrote one of the earliest scientific textbooks in the English language, the *Treatise on the Astrolabe*. It was once thought that book was written for his son "little Lewis," but it now seems likely that it was written for the son of his friend Lewis Clifford.

The Canterbury Tales, generally regarded as his finest work, was begun about 1387 but never finished. There are twenty-four tales in all, although this represents only a quarter of the projected work. Here Chaucer paints an assembly of characters with all their virtues, faults, and foibles laid bare. The tone is often ironic, but the cynicism is usually gentle, friendly, and tempered by affection for humankind. *The Canterbury Tales* provides a marvelous insight into the customs and beliefs of the various layers of English society in the late Middle Ages. Perhaps his greatest contribution to culture was to show the artistic possibilities of the English language and to elevate it to an acceptable medium for communication. If we list the factors—social, economic, and cultural—that led to English becoming the global language that it is today, the poetry of Geoffrey Chaucer must be among them.

"Gat-toothed I was, and that becam me weel;
I hadde the prente of seynt Venus seel.
And help me god, I was a lusty oon . . . .
For certes, I am al Venerien
In felinge, and myn herte is marcien.
Venus me yaf my lust, my likerousnesse,
And Mars yaf me my sturdy hardinesse.
Myn ascendent was Taur, and mars thereinne.
Allas! allas! That ever love was sinne!
I folwed ay myn inclinacioun
By vertu of my constellacioun;
That made me I coude noght withdraw.
My chamber of venus from a good felawe.
Yet have I Martes mark upon my face,
And also in another privee place."
(*Canterbury Tales, The Wife of Bath's Prologue*, l. 603–620)

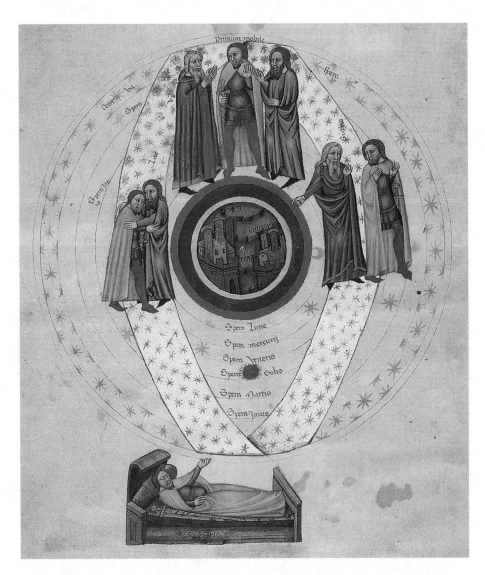

The frontispiece to a fourteenth century manuscript of Macrobius's commentary on the Dream of Scipio. Macrobius was a Neo-Platonist who lived around 400 A.D. His most significant work was Somnium Scipionis (Dream of Scipio), *a commentary on Book VI of Cicero's* Republic. *Publius Cornelius Scipio Africanus is shown at the bottom of the picture dreaming of his voyage through the spheres of heaven where he meets the souls of the departed (in this picture his father and grandfather). Macronius's work heavily influenced Dante and Chaucer, and set a model for a type of science fiction dream writing—where the narrator travels through space—that lasted into the eighteenth century. (The Art Archive / Bodleian Library Oxford / The Bodleian Library)*

For a long time it was a matter of some contention as to whether the horoscope described for herself by Alisoun was historically valid (in the sense that it represented a real alignment of planets and signs) or, like the story, a work of fiction. A convincing argument for the former is given by the historian John North, who, following an earlier suggestion by Hamlin, argues that the birth of the fictional Wife of Bath could be dated to a real horoscope of 6 February 1342 (North, 1988). A sketch of this horoscope is given in the figure on page 18. Such a horoscope would place the planets as follows:

POSITIONS OF THE PLANETS IN THE ZODIACAL SIGNS IN THE PROJECTED HOROSCOPE OF CHAUCER'S *WIFE OF BATH*

Planet:	Saturn	Jupiter	Mars	Sun	Moon	Venus	Mercury
Sign:	Capricorn	Scorpio	Taurus	Aquarius	Aquarius	Pisces	Pisces

The evidence for this is that the passage tells us that Taurus was in the ascendent and Mars was "thereinne." It was Mars that gave her a red face and excess sexual energy and left marks upon her face and also another private place. She also has the "prente of seynt Venus." These marks are not simply figurative expressions; it was thought by astrologers that real marks would be left on the body. The imprint of Venus is strengthened by the fact that Taurus, the sign supposedly ruled by Venus, is in the ascendant.

It is important to note that the signs were also places of *exaltation* (enhanced power) and *dejection* (reduced power) of the planets. Significantly, Pisces was the sign of the exaltation of Venus and the dejection of Mercury. This is observed in the Wife's prologue: "And thus, God woot, mercury is desolat / In Pisces, wher Venus is exaltat" (l. 703–704). It was Venus that gave the Wife her lust and licentiousness. The horoscope shown here would make Alisoun forty in 1382, and in that year Mercury was in the same house as Venus, symbolizing (since Mercury is the sign of clerks, of which Jankyn was one) the marriage of the Wife to her last husband.

We have already noted that the influence of a planet varied according to the sign in which it was found. In addition, each hour of the day was supposed to be under the special influence of one of the seven planets. In this case, however, the hours were not divided equally into sixty minutes but were the *hours inequal* of astrology. In this system, each day was divided into twelve hours of daylight and twelve hours of night, even though it is only at the equinoxes that this is actually the case (see Appendix A). Thus, each of the twelve *hours inequal* of daylight in winter when days are short must be of shorter absolute duration than the hours of summer when the sun is above the horizon for much longer. As these *hours*

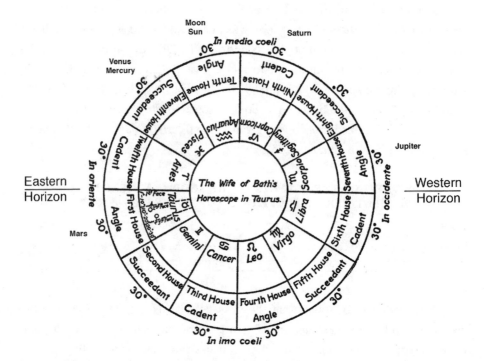

The projected horoscope of the Wife of Bath. The diameter left to right represents the eastern and western horizons. At the top of the circle we have the meridian. The whole circle is divided into twelve houses of 30° each. If we imagine this figure to be stationary, then the signs of the zodiac pass through these houses as the celestial sphere turns. (Courtesy of John Cartwright)

inequal unfold, so the seven planets in order govern them. The planet that gives the day its name always rules the first hour of the day. The next planet down, moving toward the earth, then rules the next hour. After the hour of the moon, the sequence begins again with Saturn (Table 3).

The Humours

It was thought that the planets also had a major influence on a person's physiological and psychological makeup. In Chaucer's time, a person's temperament was interpreted in terms of the theory of humours. The concept of humours and the belief that they played a major role in health and disease goes back to the earliest Greek medical texts. By 340 B.C., the unknown author of the Hippocratic treatise "On the Nature of Man" presented a well worked-out theory of four humours (bile, phlegm, blood, and black bile) linked to the four elements pro-

TABLE 3: DAYS OF THE WEEK AND THE *HOURS INEQUAL*

The first hour of each day is special to the planet of the day's name. For the hours that follow, each planet exerts its influence in sequence until the first hour of the next day, when the ruling planet again identifies the day

Hour	Saturday	Sunday	Monday (Lundi)	Tuesday (Mardi)	Wednesday (Mercredi)	Thursday (Jeudi)	Friday (Vendredi)
1	Saturn	Sun	Moon	Mars	Mercury	Jupiter	Venus
2	Jupiter	Venus	Saturn	Sun	Moon	Mars	Mercury
3	Mars	Mercury	Jupiter	Venus	Saturn	Sun	Moon
4	Sun	Moon	Mars	Mercury	Jupiter	Venus	Saturn
5	Venus	Saturn	Sun	Moon	Mars	Mercury	Jupiter
6	Mercury	Jupiter	Venus	Saturn	Sun	Moon	Mars
7	Moon	Mars	Mercury	Jupiter	Venus	Saturn	Sun
8	Saturn	Sun	Moon	Mars	Mercury	Jupiter	Venus
9	Jupiter	Venus	Saturn	Sun	Moon	Mars	Mercury
10	Mars	Mercury	Jupiter	Venus	Saturn	Sun	Moon
11	Sun	Moon	Mars	Mercury	Jupiter	Venus	Saturn
12	Venus	Saturn	Sun	Moon	Mars	Mercury	Jupiter
13	Mercury	Jupiter	Venus	Saturn	Sun	Moon	Mars
14	Moon	Mars	Mercury	Jupiter	Venus	Saturn	Sun
15	Saturn	Sun	Moon	Mars	Mercury	Jupiter	Venus
16	Jupiter	Venus	Saturn	Sun	Moon	Mars	Mercury
17	Mars	Mercury	Jupiter	Venus	Saturn	Sun	Moon
18	Sun	Moon	Mars	Mercury	Jupiter	Venus	Saturn
19	Venus	Saturn	Sun	Moon	Mars	Mercury	Jupiter
20	Mercury	Jupiter	Venus	Saturn	Sun	Moon	Mars
21	Moon	Mars	Mercury	Jupiter	Venus	Saturn	Sun
22	Saturn	Sun	Moon	Mars	Mercury	Jupiter	Venus
23	Jupiter	Venus	Saturn	Sun	Moon	Mars	Mercury
24	Mars	Mercury	Jupiter	Venus	Saturn	Sun	Moon

posed earlier by Empedocles of Akragas (c.490–435 B.C.) and endorsed by Aristotle (see figure).

These humours were thought to be real bodily fluids. Phlegm described any whitish or colorless secretion (except semen and milk) and was thought to be manufactured by the brain. Yellow bile was found in the gallbladder, although, like black bile and blood, it was produced in the liver. Blood held a special significance in humoural theory. Blood flowing in the veins was thought to be a mixture of pure humoural fluid and lesser quantities of other humours. It was the particular balance of humours in an individual that was responsible for their physical and psychological state. The theory of humours was endorsed and elaborated by the Roman physician Galen (c.130–200 A.D.). Galen's numerous medical texts dominated Western medicine up to the renaissance.

The term *complexion* described an individual's combination of humours. In the Middle Ages this term had a far deeper meaning than the modern sense of facial coloring. When Chaucer says of the Franklin "his complexioun he was

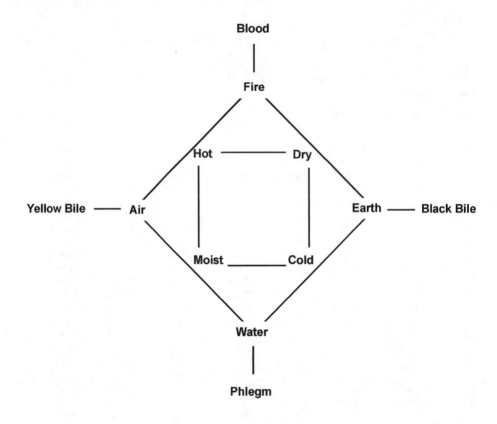

Diagram of the four humours and their association with the four elements. (Courtesy of John Cartwright)

sangwyn," he means something much more than asserting he had a rosy face. He means that the Franklin was a sanguine man: he loved food and drink, was given to laughing and singing, was gracious, and was probably fond of bright clothes. In modern parlance we might call him a *bon viveur*:

> Of his complexioun he was sangwyn
> Wel loved he by the morwe a sop in wyn;
> To lyven in delit was evere his wore,
> For he was Epicurus owere sone.
> (*Canterbury Tales*, l. 333–336)

Chaucer uses many of these stock astrophysiological categories to describe his pilgrims. Table 4 shows how predominance of the various humours gave rise to personality types.

The grafting of the humour theory onto other branches of learning was typical of the medieval mind's quest for unity and interconnectedness. By the time

TABLE 4: THE HUMOURS IN RELATION TO TYPES OF PERSONALITY

Humour	Planet governing humour	Type	Attributes
Blood	Jupiter	Sanguine	Hearty and merry. Enjoys singing, dancing, good food, and bright clothes.
Phlegm	Moon and Venus	Phlegmatic	Slow, heavy, and sleepy. Rather indolent and dull-witted. Tends to like green.
Yellow bile	Mars	Choleric	Full of ire, foolish, malicious, and deceitful. Tends to like black or gray cloth.
Black bile	Saturn	Melancholic	In Middle Ages, unstable and "neurotic." Did not acquire its modern meaning of soulful, introverted, and sad until the sixteenth century.

of Chaucer, the humours were linked with parts of the body, the elements, the seasons, the signs of the zodiac, and the planets. Nothing could move in the heavens above without it affecting something else down below. The theory's effect on medical science must have been at best to render treatment ineffective and at worst dangerous.

Chaucer's Doctor of Physic

Armed with Galen's books on anatomy and the theory of humours, the medieval medical practitioner could offer three basic types of treatment: diet, surgery, and medicine. Major surgery in the form of deep incisions and amputations was left to surgeons and barbers. Minor surgery, such as cautery (application of a hot instrument to the body) and bloodletting, and the prescription of healing substances were the province of the physician. In the *General Prologue* to *The Canterbury Tales*, Chaucer provides in just forty lines a marvelous description of just such a physician: his Doctor of Physic. The tone is wonderfully ironic and the content rich enough to paint a detailed picture of a medieval doctor.

> With us ther was a Doctor of Physik
> In al this world ne was ther noon hym lik,
> To speke of physik and of surgerye
> For he was grounded in astronomye. (l. 411–414)

The Physician is a "Doctor," which means he has won a degree from a university medical school. What is surprising to the modern mind is that the doctor is praised for his grounding in astronomy, not something that is part of modern medical training. Such knowledge, however, was essential for medieval physicians and was part of the whole doctrine that the human body was in some way a microcosm of the world at large, a view, as we shall see in the next chapter, that survived well into the sixteenth century. We are further informed that:

> He kept his pacient a ful greet deel
> In houres by his magyk natureel.
> Wel koude he fortunen the ascendent
> Of his ymages for his pacient.
> He knew the cause of everich maladye,
> Were it of hoot, or coold, or moyste, or drye,
> And where they engendered, and of what humour.
> He was a verray, parfit praktisour:
> The cause yknowe, and of his harm the roote,
> Anon he yaf the sike man his boote. (l. 415–424)

Here we need to realize that the precise influence of the planets on health depended on their position in the zodiac. In addition, it was the configuration of the heavens at the moment of birth that determined a person's physical constitution, their "humour," and hence their predisposition toward certain ailments and diseases. Diagnosis and treatment were further complicated by the fact that it was important to know the position of the star signs and planets at the time of onset of the disease and at the time the physician visits to offer treatment. Knowledge of this timing had to be accurate to within an hour since, as we have already seen, the *hours inequal* come under the varying influence of the seven planets. Furthermore, it was held that in each six-hour period of each day, one of the four humours was dominant: blood from midnight to six A.M.; choler from six A.M. to noon; melancholy from noon to six P.M.; and phlegm from six P.M. to midnight. On top of this, the strength of the humoural influence depended on the phase of the moon, it being greatest when the moon was full. Each season of the year (and conveniently there are four) had affinities with each of the humours. Summer, for example, a hot and dry season, is associated with the element fire and the humour of choler. So for every individual, although the disposition of their humours was partly determined at birth, subtle and ever-changing influences are brought to bear on the body each hour of the day, each day of the week, and each season of the year as the celestial machinery grinds away overhead. No wonder the medieval doctor needed training in astronomy. This is the essence of Chaucer's remark that he kept "his pacient a ful greet deel / In houres by his magyk natureel." Here natural magic refers to the acceptable science of the day, astrology, as opposed to black magic or necromancy.

The lines "Wel koude he fortunen the ascendent / Of his ymages for his pacient" are amongst the most difficult in the passage. The most probable interpretation is that to "fortunen" the images refers to the practice of placing engraved images of favorable zodiacal signs on appropriate positions on the body of the patient. This procedure stemmed from the belief that all objects fashioned by man bear the imprint of the constellation reigning at the time of manufacture and retain this celestial energy with them until they are destroyed. In a typical clinical encounter the physician might produce a small disc of gold, manufactured, for example, as the sun was entering Aries and so engraved with the sign of the Ram, and place this on a patient's head to cure a fever. The passage continues:

> Ful redy hadde he his apothecaries
> To sende hym drogges and his letuaries.
> For ech of hem made oother for so wynne-
> Hir frendshipe nas nat newe to bigynne.
> We knew he the olde Esculapius,
> And Deyscorides, and eek Rufus,
> Olde Ypocras, Haly, and Galyen, . . .
> Of his diete mesurable was he,
> For it was of no superfluitee,
> But of greet norissyng and digestible.
> His studie was but litel on the Bible. (425–438)

So far, Chaucer's physician seems to know his stuff; he has studied sound authorities, ancient and modern, is versed in astrology, and understands humour theory. Chaucer also tells us he is well connected and organized: his apothecaries are on hand to send him drugs and "letuaries" (medical powders mixed with honey or syrup). Moreover, his relationship to the apothecary is tried and tested: "Hir frendshipe was nat newe to bigynne." The learned physician also looks after himself with nourishing food and avoidance of excess ("superfluitee").

But there are a few careful phrases where Chaucer destroys what illusion we may have about the integrity of the learned doctor. We find, for example, that there was none to match him for speaking of physic and surgery. Perhaps the physician is a little too fond of his own voice or is all bombast and no substance. Chaucer's readers would also understand that his long-standing arrangement with apothecaries is designed to ensure that they both share the exorbitant profits charged for drugs containing cheap or useless ingredients. In a curious line, Chaucer tells us that he little studied the Bible. We could read this to mean that the pious physician is too busy with good works for such reading; more likely, we are to note that he is a godless man. Indeed, medieval theologians eyed physi-

cians, with their study of pagan and heathen authors, with some suspicion. The
end of the section is most revealing:

> In sangwyn and in pers he clad was al,
> Lynded with taffeta and with sendal;
> And yet he was but esy of dispence
> He kepte that he wan in pestilence.
> For gold in phisik is a cordial
> Therefore he lovede gold in special.
> (*General Prologue* l. 411–444)

The physician, then, is wealthy and fashionable: even for a pilgrimage he is
clad in clothes of red (sangwyn) and blue (pers or Persian blue) lined with
expensive thin silk. He is not, however, overgenerous with his wealth: he is "esy
of dispence," in other words reluctant to part with money he has gained from disease (pestilence). Gold was supposed to be a useful remedy (in its drinkable
form it was called *aurum potabile*), but in reality it simply bumped up the price
of medicine for no medical benefit. Unsurprisingly, this physician especially
loved gold.

Alchemy

Another of the medieval sciences that Chaucer incorporates into *The Canterbury Tales* is alchemy. The possibility of transmuting one element into another,
a premise of alchemy, was lent support by Aristotle's system of matter. Looking
back at Table 1, we see that if the quality of coldness were to be expelled from
earth and replaced with heat, then the element of earth would be transformed
into fire. Similarly, if heat displaces coldness from water it will turn into air; such
a process is observed when water is evaporated by heating and so turns into the
vaporous or airy state.

Alchemy was initially conceived as a means of perfecting both life and matter, but despite the serious intentions of its foundation, it became a refuge for
scoundrels and tricksters. Several medieval texts, including William Langland's
Piers Plowman and Chaucer's *The Canon's Yeoman's Tale* make fun of alchemy
and show how the greed it encouraged leads to the undoing of the gullible.

In the *Prologue* to the *The Canon's Yeoman's Tale*, the Yeoman (servant of
the Canon) describes his experiences of alchemy with the Canon. His account
reveals a disturbed mind. At the start of the tale itself he expresses self-disgust
for wasting his time on a worthless pursuit that has left him penniless:

Sixteenth-century copper engraving by Stradanus of alchemists in a workshop. (Christel Gerstenberg/Corbis)

That slidynge science hath me maad so bare
That I have no good, wher that evere I fare;
And yet I am endetted so therby,
Of gold that I have borrowed.
(l. 732–735)

On the other hand he describes alchemical procedures and apparatus with such gusto and enthusiasm that it is clear he is reluctant to give it up entirely.

Alchemists recognized seven metals, associated with the seven planets as discussed earlier, and four spirits: mercury, arsenic, sal ammoniac, and brimstone. The hope was that the four spirits, together with the heat from a charcoal furnace, would cause the baser metals to ascend the scale of perfection and reach gold. When the host asks the yeoman why he has a strange color, the yeoman explains that it comes from blowing the fire:

I am so used in the fyr to blowe
That it hath changed my colour, I trowe.
(l. 666–667)

Later the Yeoman observes that alchemists can usually be known by their sulphurous (brimstone) smell:

> And everemore, where that evere they goou,
> Men may hem knowe by smel of brymstoon.
> For al the world they stynken as a goot.
> (l. 884–886)

Notice here how the demonic associations of goat and brimstone serve to link alchemy with the devil. Indeed, several scholars (e.g., Gardner, 1967) have suggested that the mysterious canon that appears with the yeoman and then rapidly departs is probably the devil himself in clerical disguise.

The self-portrait of the yeoman spills over into his tale proper when he describes how another canon uses alchemical trickery to fool a young chantry priest into parting with his money. Having witnessed a trumped-up demonstration of the production of gold, the priest pays forty pounds for the secret of the process, only to find the canon disappears with his money.

The detail that Chaucer invests into his description of the canon and his yeoman suggests that he may have had a particular alchemist in mind. There was a canon at Windsor, one William Shuchirch, known to have practiced alchemy. It is possible that Chaucer is satirizing this individual and may even have been a victim of alchemical fraud himself. Chaucer was not the first, nor was he the last, to expose the fraudulent practices of alchemists. The surprising aspect of Chaucer's treatment of alchemy is that at the end of the play, Chaucer defends true alchemy as a pursuit in search of spiritual truth rather than material gain.

In 1403, shortly after Chaucer's death, a statute was passed prohibiting the "multiplication of metals." Nevertheless, medieval and renaissance monarchs generally did not reject the possibility of transmutation; rather they sought to control it for their own ends.

Although modern science has shown that on most points medieval notions about cosmology, astrology, medicine, and alchemy were false, the whole system withstood the turbulence of the Renaissance and the Reformation remarkably well. Alchemy did not fade from the minds of serious scientists until the end of the seventeenth century, and even the theory of humours was still in use in the 1650s. Even today, astrology, although discredited by modern science, still has a popular following. Newspapers and magazines contain horoscopes. Indeed, for a period in the 1980s Ronald Reagan, the head of the most powerful and scientifically advanced nation on earth, was advised by his wife on the basis of astrological forecasts.

In the next chapter, as we peer into the minds of writers in the Elizabethan renaissance and examine their assumptions about the natural world, we can observe the familiar medieval framework still largely intact. We can also detect, however, a whole new series of cultural tensions, both destructive and creative, that were eventually to bring the whole edifice of medieval thought crashing down and help prepare the way for the modern world.

Bibliographic Essay

For an introduction to the medieval world picture that formed the backcloth to both Dante and Chaucer, C. S. Lewis's *The Discarded Image* (Cambridge: Cambridge University Press, 1964) remains a classic. Chapters three and four in this book compliment the material in this volume by presenting and discussing the sources that medieval authors relied upon so heavily. A sound general work giving the social and intellectual context to the development of science from classical times to the late Middle Ages is David Lindberg's *The Beginnings of Western Science* (Chicago: University of Chicago Press, 1992). For early Greek science, G. E. R. Lloyd is one of the soundest authorities, and his *Early Greek Science: Thales to Aristotle* (New York: Norton, 1970) provides an excellent introduction. For the physical sciences in the Middle Ages, the work of Edward Grant is highly recommended. A useful start is his *Physical Science in the Middle Ages* (London: John Wiley, 1971). For a detailed examination of the changing influence of Aristotle on medieval scientific thought, see Grant's *The Foundation of Modern Science in the Middle Ages* (Cambridge: Cambridge University Press, 1996).

For an introduction to spherical astronomy in a historical context, E. Rogers's *Astronomy for the Inquiring Mind* (Princeton NJ: University of Princeton Press, 1968) is superb and a model for how history and science can be combined. Anyone who wishes to pursue the material in Appendix A further is advised to consult this work.

Many translations of Dante's *Divine Comedy* carry an introduction that gives details of Dante's cosmology and footnotes that help elucidate the scientific background to selected passages. A particularly useful version is that edited by Dorothy Sayers and Barbara Reynolds (London: Penguin, 1962) The three separate volumes carry helpful diagrams, and the Appendix of *Paradise* carries an essay on astronomy. M. A. Orr's *Dante and the Early Astronomers* (London and New York: Kennikat Press, 1913) surveys early Greek and Arabic astronomy and elucidates Dante's use of astronomical terms. For a more modern treatment see Alison Cornish's *Reading Dante's Stars* (New Haven CT: Yale University Press, 2002). Cornish extends the scientific decoding offered by Orr to argue that the use of stellar imagery demands a variety of interpretations. Perhaps the best modern analysis of the curious mixture of realism and symbolism in Dante's work is *Dante: Philomythes and Philosopher* (Cambridge: Cambridge University Press, 1981) by Patrick Boyde. The author gives a solid overview of Aristotelian and medieval views on the natural world and shows how Dante was both a lover of myth (philomythes) and a philosopher, and that therefore science and poetry are blended as one. One drawback to the book is that most of the quotations are in the original Italian, so many readers will also need a translation at hand. A highly readable account of Dante's life is provided in *Dante, a Life* by R. W. B. Lewis (New York: Viking/Penguin, 2001). Lewis weaves together Dante's personal experiences and his writings.

A valuable short introduction to the science of Chaucer's day is to be found in M. W. Grose's *Chaucer* (London: Evans Brothers, 1967); chapter three is given over to the various branches of medieval science. One of the most ambitious and comprehensive treatments of Chaucer's astronomy is John North's *Chaucer's Universe* (Oxford: Oxford University Press, 1988). North takes great pains to weigh the different interpretations of astronomical and astrological references in Chaucer's works. He tends to argue that Chaucer's horoscopes related to real events and enable dates for the composition of his works to be deduced. For a slightly more skeptical view of what historical astronomy can be read into Chaucer, see Hamilton Smyser's *A View of Chaucer's Astronomy* (*Speculum* 14, No. 3, July 1970). Smyser does come to the conclusion, however, that Chaucer did believe in astrology. A pioneering work in documenting scientific references in Chaucer is *Chaucer and the Medieval Sciences* by Walter Curry (rev. ed., London: Allen and Unwin, 1960). Curry takes a number of Chaucer's works in turn and elucidates the scientific concepts used. Clear and short expositions of the various branches of science in Chaucer are given in James Winny's "Chaucer's Science" in M. Hussey, A. C. Spearing, and J. Winny: *An Introduction to Chaucer* (Cambridge: Cambridge University Press, 1965). An accessible introduction to Chaucer's use of alchemy is given in a short article, "Geoffrey Chaucer and Alchemy," by Frederic Walker (*Journal of Chemical Education* 1932, vol. 9, pp. 1378–1385), in which the author gives an abridged translation of *Canon's Yeoman's Tale*.

Going beyond alchemy and Chaucer to consider the impact of chemistry more generally is Robert Ward's "What Forced by Fire: Concerning Some Influences of Chemical Thought and Practice upon English Poetry" (*Ambix*, vol. 23, part 2, July 1976, pp. 80–95), an article that contains some useful references and quotations. For a wider coverage of alchemy, see Stanton Linden's *Darke Hierogliphicks: Alchemy in English Literature from Chaucer to the Restoration* (Lexington: University of Kentucky Press, 1996). This is an excellent work for the treatment of alchemy in literature from about 1380 to 1700. For an even more general work, but equally rewarding, consult *From Faust to Strangelove* by Roslynn Haynes (Baltimore and London, John Hopkins University Press, 1994). This book is valuable additional reading for the whole of this volume, and Haynes provides a masterly treatment of the differing perceptions of the scientist in English literature from the Middle Ages to the twentieth century.

Science and Literature in the Elizabethan Renaissance

John Cartwright

In the winter months of 1563 the aldermen of Stratford upon Avon called upon their chamberlain, one John Shakespeare, to perform a strange and, to him no doubt, a melancholy task. His instructions were to procure workmen, scaffolding, and pots of whitewash, assemble in the town's Guildhall Chapel, and cover over the religious paintings on the walls. They were the usual images that once adorned the walls of medieval churches all over Catholic England: saints, Christ in judgment, scenes of heaven and hell, and the murder of Thomas Becket. We recall that it was the pilgrimage to the shrine of Thomas Becket that had inspired Chaucer's *Canterbury Tales*. Now these images were being erased from history.

The Council of Stratford were carrying out an order that had emanated from Elizabeth I. Soon after her accession to the throne in 1558, she issued an injunction across England for "the removal of all signs of idolatry and superstition from places of worship" (Wood, 2003, p. 8). The process was part of a broader movement that had its roots forty years earlier, when Elizabeth's father, Henry VIII, attempted to divorce his first wife, Katherine of Aragon, and marry Anne Boleyn. The Pope (Clement VII) declared Henry's divorce to be illegal; in response, Henry took steps that changed British culture forever: he closed and largely demolished the monasteries, opposed the authority of the Roman Catholic Church in England, and set himself up as both head of state and head of the Church, a position held by British monarchs ever since. The Reformation in England had started, and the nation was on its way to becoming Protestant.

The Reformation itself was a product of numerous forces at work in Europe that were tearing apart the Christian faith. The great Dutch humanist scholar Erasmus (1466–1536), for example, while remaining a loyal Catholic, criticized the sale of pardons and religious relics by Church authorities. The German theologian Martin Luther (1483–1546), incensed at the corruption of the

Church, went one step further and refused to submit to papal authority, pinning to the chapel door in Wittenburg in 1517 his defiant "Ninety five theses against the sale of Papal Indulgences." Luther, like Henry VIII, was eventually excommunicated from the Catholic Church. The Reformation caused a profound dislocation in European thought and belief, and the fault lines still stand. In the sixteenth century it led to a new questioning of the old Catholic and scholastic certainties; the place of heaven and hell, the nature of man and the physical world, the relationship between man and God were all up for renegotiation.

The European imagination was further stimulated by the impact of classical learning that had lain dormant in monasteries and Arabic libraries for centuries. Ever since the expulsion of the Moors from Spain in the thirteenth century, allowing whole libraries of Arabic books and Arabic translations of classical texts to fall into Christian hands, there had been a small but steady flow of Greek and Roman texts into Western Europe. In 1453 Constantinople, already in decline, finally fell to Islam, and the Byzantine Empire—that last remnant of Christianized classical culture that had held on in Eastern Europe—was extinguished. As scholars fled, they carried further evidence of classical culture to the West. What was once a trickle became an irresistible flood, and the impact on the European mind was enormous, consolidating that decisive break with the medieval world that we call the renaissance.

Whereas the Protestant reformers turned to scripture for their hopes of salvation, the humanists looked for their intellectual guidance in the works of classical antiquity. A Renaissance humanist of particular importance to the development of Elizabethan thought was Michel de Montaigne (1533–1592). In the 1570s and 1580s Montaigne wrote a series of essays that explored a wide variety of human experiences: friendship, cannibalism, fashion, sexuality, nudity, and the effect of his growing impotence in later years—to name but a few. The crucial word here is *explore* or *assay*, for Montaigne approached his topics without preconceptions and without constantly referring to established doctrine. Montaigne did not always feel the need to bring God into the question, nor did he worry, as did so many medieval thinkers, about personal salvation. Montaigne displayed a skepticism toward established belief and turned his relativistic questioning on his own culture.

Back in Stratford we know that the desecration of images in the Guildhall Chapel was completed before the end of 1563, for in the following January John Shakespeare recorded in his account book "item payd for defaysing ymages in the chappell." It seems that on this occasion his heart was not in his work, for the paint was applied only thinly and the workmen left all the stained glass in place, though it, too, should have been removed. We also know that at the time his wife was pregnant, for in April of 1564 she gave birth to a son, William Shakespeare. Like his father's, William's imagination drew upon the symbols and customs of the Old Catholic Faith, declining but still vivid in rural Warwickshire. But William grew up in a period of economic, political, and intellectual transition, on the very cusp of history, as one religious and philosophical system gave way to another. Consequently, his work became a mirror of the times and will be drawn upon later in this chapter.

By the middle years of the sixteenth century, then, the intricate and coherent medieval worldview was under siege on all sides. Even Aristotelian cosmology, that bastion of certainty for the previous thousand years, came under threat from developments in astronomy and natural philosophy.

Natural Philosophy

The first assaults on Aristotelian cosmology came from the mainland of Europe. In 1543, Copernicus published his "On the Revolution of the Heavenly Spheres," a book that placed the sun at the center of the cosmos and the earth as a planet revolving around it. Initially, Copernicanism was slow to take hold. Even otherwise radical thinkers such as Martin Luther and Francis Bacon (see chapter three) rejected it as too speculative and lacking a common-sense foundation. But by 1610 this "revolutionary" notion (the very word takes its current connotations from precisely this book) had found strong champions in the form of Johannes Kepler and Galileo, and it was the telescopic observations of the latter that helped secure its victory.

Several of the natural philosophers in sixteenth-century England were attracted to the Copernican hypothesis. In 1556, Robert Recorde (1510–1558), a Fellow of All Souls Oxford and physician to Queen Mary, published *The Castle of Knowledge*. The book was written to serve as a textbook on mathematics and astronomy for artisans, but Recorde uses this opportunity to both explain and commend the system of Copernicus. Other scholars sympathetic to the Copernican cause included William Gilbert (1540–1621), physician to Elizabeth and author of an important book on magnetism, and the enigmatic mathematician and astronomer Thomas Harriot (1560–1621).

Disenchantment with Aristotelian cosmology was also precipitated by a remarkable series of celestial phenomena observed across the skies of Europe from 1572 to 1604. The first of these was a new star seen in the constellation of Cassiopeia. The star, often visible before sunset and even outshining Venus, blazed brightly for about seventeen months and then disappeared from view in 1574. For the Elizabethans there were two questions to be faced, one metaphysical and the other scientific: what did the star signify, and where in space was it

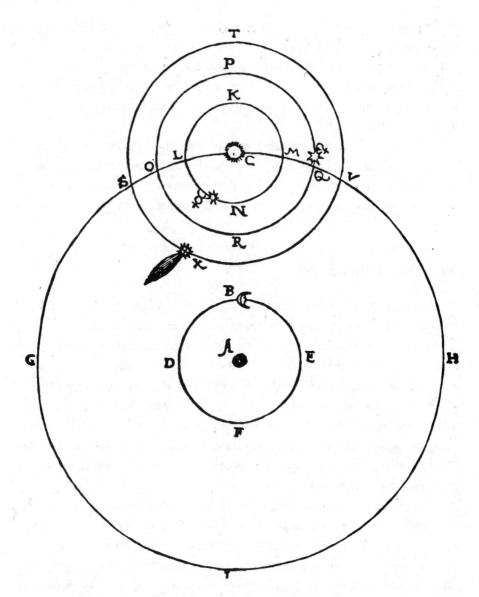

The Great Comet of 1577. Measurements by Tycho Brahe showed that it must be above the sphere of the moon. Phenomena such as these helped cast doubt on the Aristotelian system. Here Tycho shows the comet in orbit about the sun as the sun orbits the earth. From Tycho Brahe, De Mundo aetherei recentioribus Phaenomensis, *1588. (Image Select / Art Resource)*

located? On the former, the star generated all sorts of apocalyptic fears and hopes, including the idea that it prophesied the victory of the Catholic Church over the Protestant reformers. On the latter, numerous astronomers, including Thomas Digges (1546–1595) in England and Tycho Brahe (1546–1601) in Denmark, examined the position of the star, found its parallax to be vanishingly small, and concluded that it must be too far away to belong to the sublunary sphere. Faith in Aristotelian cosmology began to weaken, since such things should not occur above the sphere of the moon.

The next shock came in 1577, when a comet was observed moving across the western skies of Europe. Tycho Brahe, then working on the island of Hveen off the coast of Denmark, established that this phenomenon was also occurring above the sphere of the moon but closer than the firmament. Comets could no longer be regarded as atmospheric phenomena. Again, not only should there have been no change above the moon, but the moving comet was blasting its way through the crystalline spheres on which the planets were reputed to move.

Despite these puzzling celestial events and support from some leading figures such as Galileo and Kepler, the Copernican hypothesis spread slowly in Britain and did not trouble the consciousness of playwrights and poets until the early decades of the seventeenth century. In "Orchestra, or, a Poem on Dancing," written by the lawyer, politician, and poet John Davies (1569–1626), for example, the earth stands still and the Copernican debates are dismissed as a side issue:

> Only the earth doth stand for ever still,
> Her rocks remove not nor her mountains meet;
> (Although some wits enrich with learning's skill
> Say heav'n stands firm and that the earth doth fleet
> And swiftly turneth underneath their feet):
> Yet, though the earth is ever steadfast seen,
> On her broad breast hath dancing ever been. (l. 351–357)

Even the greatest poet of the age, William Shakespeare, shows little awareness or interest in the achievements or concerns of the astronomers. The character of Berowne in *Love's Labour's Lost* is not too impressed by the value of astronomy:

> Study is like heaven's glorious sun,
> That will not be deep-search'd with saucy looks
> Small have continual plodders ever won
> Save base authority from other's books.
> These earthly godfathers of heaven's lights
> That give their name to every fixed star
> Have no more profit of their shining nights
> Than those that walk and wot not what they are.
> (Act I, scene i, 84–91)

Here then we face a puzzling feature of Elizabethan England. Despite the fact that the theology of medievalism was under attack from the Protestant reformers, its philosophy from the humanists, and its cosmology from the astronomers, the outlook of the poets and playwrights on the physical world remained remarkably conservative. It was largely a medieval view of nature, albeit one under great pressure, that underpinned the most creative period that English literature has known.

Elizabethan Commonplaces

It was in the middle years of the twentieth century that scholars realized that to appreciate Elizabethan literature more deeply, some understanding of the mind-set of assumptions about political order, hierarchy, the nature of man, and cosmology was needed. A landmark work in this respect was E. M. Tillyard's *Elizabethan World Picture*, first published in 1943. Tillyard documented the cluster of medieval ideas, as well as renaissance modifications, that formed a background to thought in the Elizabethan age. He argued that this worldview was taken for granted by most educated people, such that many expressions of it were in the form of commonplaces: standard allusions, turns of phrase, and reference points that may seem puzzling to the modern reader but would have been instantly recognizable to educated Elizabethans. We now realize that many of these assumptions were under great strain. Some of them are detailed below.

The Great Chain of Being

The concept of a Chain of Being was a way of setting objects in their proper place and emphasizing the order, unity, and richness of God's creation. The chain was all-inclusive and stretched down from God to the smallest particle of inani-

**TABLE 5: CLASSES AND PRIMATES FORMING PART
OF THE GREAT CHAIN OF BEING**

Class	Primate
Humans	King or Sovereign
Beasts	Lion
Planets	Sun
Fish	Dolphin
Trees	Oak
Flowers	Rose
Stones	Diamond
Metals	Gold
Elements	Fire

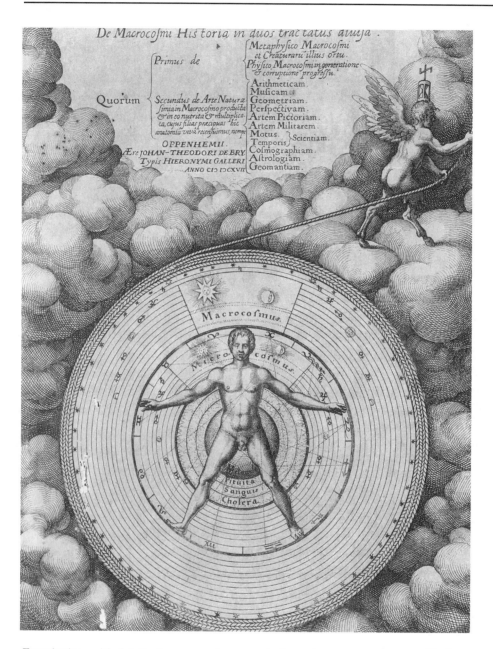

Frontispiece with detail of man as microcosm to the universe or macrocosm. The four humours (sanguine, phlegmatic, choleric, and melancholic) are also shown. From Utriusque Cosmi Historia, *1617–1624, by Robert Fludd, 1574–1637, English physician and mystical philosopher. (The Art Archive / Dagli Orti)*

mate matter. The idea was first expressed in Plato's *Timaeus* and was developed by Aristotle. It remained an influential idea right up to the end of the eighteenth century. Although the chain was really a continuum of microscopic differences, objects could be broken down into classes. Within each class, there existed a *primate* or chief kind. Lists of the primates of each class vary from source to source, but Table 5 shows a typical compilation.

The idea of primates helps us understand the potency of certain passages in Shakespeare's plays. In *Richard II*, for example, we have the scene where Henry Bolingbroke (the future Henry IV) is in the process of deposing the rightful monarch, Richard II. Richard is cornered in a castle as Bolingbroke approaches with his troops. The majesty of the sovereign is conveyed by Bolingbroke himself:

> Bolingbroke: Methinks King Richard and myself should meet
> With no less terror than the elements
> Of fire and water . . .
> Be he the fire, I'll be the yielding water . . .
> See, see, King Richard doth himself appear,
> As doth the blushing discontented sun
> From out the fiery portal of the east.
> York: yet looks he like a king: behold his eye,
> As bright as is the eagle's . . . (Act III, scene iii, l. 56–71)

Later, when Richard is in captivity (Act V, scene i), his queen compares him first to a rose, and then later to a lion, the king of beasts. In these passages the king, chief among men, is compared to other primates in the chain of being: fire, the sun, the lion, the rose, and the eagle. The notion of a primate of each class helps otherwise puzzling allusions become clearer. In *Antony and Cleopatra*, for example, after Antony's death Cleopatra praises his virtues with the line:

> his delights
> Were dolphin like, they showed his back above
> The element they lived in.
> (Act V, scene ii, l. 88–90)

The point being made is that Antony, at least to Cleopatra's eye, enjoyed his pleasures but was not a slave to them. Just as the dolphin is the king of fishes, since it exists halfway out of its own element (water) and spends some time in a higher element (air), so Antony always, in the midst of his delights, retained his awesome stature, existing above the normal elements that men reside in.

In the Chain of Being, man occupied a pivotal position, his nature being somewhere between the base appetites of the beasts and the spirituality of angels. Hamlet gave one of the most famous expressions of this notion:

> What a piece of work is a man! How noble in reason! How infinite in faculty!
> In form and moving how express and admirable; in action how like an angel;

in apprehension how like a god; the beauty of the world, the paragon of animals. (*Hamlet*, Act II, scene ii, l. 322–325)

This precarious position of man on the chain was held to even in the eighteenth
century. Alexander Pope (1688–1744), in his *An Essay on Man* (1732–1734), calls
it the "isthmus of a middle state" where man

> hangs between; in doubt to act or rest;
> In doubt to deem himself a god or beast;
> In doubt his mind or body to prefer.
> (Epistle ii, l. 7–9).

Astrology

On the subject of judicial astrology, the Elizabethans faced the same problem as
their medieval counterparts: how to reconcile freedom of the will and personal
responsibility with astrological determination. Their answer was basically the
same: the stars influence but do not totally determine behavior. A humorous and
rather subtle use of astrology appears in *Twelfth Night*, when Sir Toby Belch
encourages the foolish Sir Andrew Aguecheek:

> Sir Toby: I did think by the excellent constitution of thy leg it was formed
>   under the star of a galliard.
> Sir Andrew: Ay,'tis strong . . .shall we set about some revels?
> Sir Toby: What shall we do else? Were we not born under Taurus?
> Sir Andrew: Taurus: that's sides and heart.
> Sir Toby: No, sir, it is legs and thighs. (Act I, scene iii, l. 145–151)

The humor here is double layered. The rather stupid Andrew Aguecheek is
wrong, since the sign of Taurus is associated with the neck and throat, but Sir
Toby continues with the buffoonery by enticing him to dance by suggesting legs
and thighs. The initial reference to Taurus as the sign of revelry may be correct
in the sense that neck and throat could also refer to drinking. Shakespeare was
probably aware of the proper ascriptions of the zodiac signs, but here, as elsewhere, astrology is no longer treated with the seriousness that would have been
common in the Middle Ages. There were even satirical works, such as a pamphlet written by Thomas Nashe in response to some failed predictions made by
Richard Harvey titled "Wonderfull strange and miraculous Astrological prognos-
tication for this year of our Lord God 1591." The author is given as "Adam Foul-
waether, Student in Asse-tronomy." Astrology is becoming a suspect science.

Despite signs of waning confidence in astrological prediction, many European courts of the period had their consultant astrologers. Queen Elizabeth is known to have consulted the astronomer, astrologer, and mathematician John Dee. Dee was a transitional figure, half mystical and half rationalist. He was clearly an accomplished mathematician—he suggested ways for determining stellar parallax—but at the same time claimed some remarkably implausible experiences in communicating with the spirits of the dead. The historian A. L. Rowse thinks it likely that Shakespeare had Dee in mind when he composed the exchange between Hotspur and the Celtic leader Glendower in the play *Henry IV*. Glendower claims that at his birth the "font of heaven was full of fiery shapes, / Of burning cressets" and "the huge foundation of the earth / Shaked like a coward." To which Hotspur replies "it would have done at the same season, if your mother's cat had kittened." The exchange continues, and as Glendower grows more furious he claims, "I can call spirits from the vasty deep" and Hotspur retorts that "Why, so can I so can any man; / But will they come when you do call for them?" (Act III, scene i, l. 14–40.)

Analogical Thinking and the Correspondences

In the exchange between Hotspur and Glendower above, Hotspur rebuffs Glendower's claims about the significance of earthquakes at the birth of Glendower by giving a naturalistic explanation. He suggests that the earth shook because:

> oft the teeming earth
> Is with a kind of colic pinch'd and vex'd
> By the imprisoning of unruly wind
> Within her womb.
> (Act II, scene i, l. 30–34)

The explanation uses an analogy between the human body and the frame of the earth. To the modern mind it hardly counts as an explanation, but renaissance writers attached far more efficacy to the power of analogical reasoning than we do today. It was a habit of mind that the Elizabethans inherited from the Middle Ages, and they saw analogies and correspondences everywhere: between the planets and the metals; between the political state and the human body; between the cosmic and the social. It was as if every plane of existence was a reflection of another plane and somehow connected to it. Bodies have blood vessels and surface hair, for example, just as the earth has rivers and grassy fields. It was, moreover, a satisfying mode of thought, since it gave the impression of simultaneously understanding the world aesthetically and philosophically.

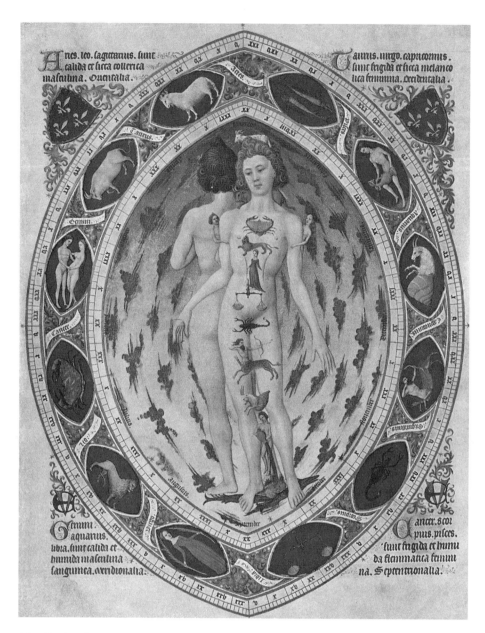

The Zodiac Man. This beautiful illustration comes from the Tres Riches Heures *of the Duke of Berry, illuminated by the Limbourg brothers around 1413. It shows how different zodiacal signs were associated with different parts of the human body. (Bettmann/Corbis)*

Hierarchy and Degree

A justly famous passage that reveals volumes about Elizabethan thinking and illustrates the serious retention of medieval concepts is Ulysses's speech on degree in *Troilus and Cressida*. The Greek army stands before Troy, dismayed at its failure to defeat the Trojans, and Ulysses gives a speech emphasizing the importance of leadership and deference to rank:

> The heavens themselves, the planets, and this centre,
> Observe degree, priority, and place,
> Insisture, course, proportion, season, form,
> Office, and custom, in all line of order;
> And therefore is the glorious planet Sol
> In noble eminence enthron'd and spher'd
> Amidst the other, whose med'cinable eye
> Corrects the ill aspects of planets evil,
> And posts, like the commandment of a king,
> Sans check, to good and bad. But when the planets
> In evil mixture to disorder wander,
> What plagues and what portents, what mutiny,
> What raging of the sea, shaking of earth,
> Commotion in the winds! Frights, changes, horrors,
> Divert and crack, rend and deracinate,
> The unity and married calm of states
> Quite from their fixture! O, when degree is shak'd,
> Which is the ladder of all high designs,
> The enterprise is sick! How could communities,
> Degrees in schools, and brotherhoods in cities,
> Peaceful commerce from dividable shores,
> The primogenity and due of birth,
> Prerogative of age, crowns, sceptres, laurels,
> But by degree, stand in authentic place?
> Take but degree away, untune that string,
> And hark what discord follows! Each thing melts
> In mere oppugnancy: the bounded waters
> Should lift their bosoms higher than the shores,
> And make a sop of all this solid globe;
> Strength should be lord of imbecility,
> And the rude son should strike his father dead.
> (Act I, scene iii, l. 85–115)

It is almost certain that the comparisons in the passage between social hierarchies and the state of nature were to be taken as objective realities and not only as metaphor. Notice how degree permeates the whole of creation: from planets, to royalty, primogeniture, the elements, seniority by age, and domestic order. We find the same exposition in Elyot's *The Book Named the Governor* (1531), where Elyot notes "in everything is order, and without order may be nothing stable or permanent; and it may not be called order except it do contain in it degrees, high and base, according to the merit or estimation of the thing that is ordered" (*Governor*, Book I, quoted in Rollins and Baker, 1954, p. 107).

Throughout Shakespeare, order in the political state is routinely compared to order in the heavens. The monarch could be like the sun or the primum mobile. The cosmic and terrestrial planes worked in sympathy so that events at the celestial level—comets, meteors, eclipses, and the like—could presage momentous events on earth. Similarly, a calamity at the social level could bring out the heavens in sympathy. As Richard II is deposed, for example, a Captain says:

> 'Tis thought the king is dead: we will not stay.
> The bay trees in our country are all wither'd
> And meteors fright the fixed stars of heaven,
> The pale-faced moon looks bloody on the earth. . . .
> Rich men look sad and ruffians dance and leap.
> (Act II, scene iv, l. 7–11)

In *Hamlet* the appearance of the ghost prompts Horatio to comment on the nature of such signs:

> A little ere the mightiest Julius fell,
> The graves stood tenantless and the sheeted dead
> Did squeak and gibber in the Roman streets;
> As stars with trains of fire and dews of blood,
> Disasters in the sun; and the moist star
> Upon whose influence Neptune's empire stands
> Was sick almost to doomsday with eclipse.
> (Act I, scene i, l. 128–134)

The "disasters in the sun" are probably sunspots, and the moon looks bloody or sick because during an eclipse of the moon it does not disappear entirely from view but darkens to a dull red color as red light refracted through the earth's atmospheres continues to illuminate it.

The Elements

As noted in chapter one, the four-element theory of the Greeks was not really challenged until the seventeenth century, so Elizabethan writers regularly incorporated the theory in their work. Cicero had suggested that the soul is air and fire, hence Cleopatra's claim at the point of her death that "I am fire and air; my other elements / I give to baser life" (Act V, scene ii, 288–289). In sonnets forty-four and forty-five, Shakespeare plays with the notion that his love causes the separation of the four elements. When he is apart from his lover, the elements of fire and air fly out toward the loved one, leaving earth and water behind; but these heavy elements induce a melancholy relieved only when fire and air return. In *Henry V* the Dauphin praises his horse: "He is pure air and fire, and the dull elements of earth and water never appear in him"(Act III, scene vii, 22–23). As with astrology, it seems that the usage of the four-element theory is at times more figurative than technically accurate.

The Age of the World

Elizabethan thoughts on the age of the earth were similar to those of Dante. It was generally understood that the earth was created at some finite point in the past (and was not infinite as Aristotle supposed), and that one day the whole experiment of Creation would be wound up and put away with the Second Coming of Christ and the Last Judgement. There had been a Golden Age, that of Greece and Rome, and things thereafter were in decline. At the start of *Timon of Athens* (Act I, scene i, 3–5) we find that the notion that the world is wearing out is "well known"; in *As You Like It*, Rosalind notes that "the poor world is almost six thousand years old" (Act IV, scene i, 83).

It was also believed that the fallen nature of the world had left its mark on the ecliptic. We noted in chapter one how Dante suggested that the obliquity of the ecliptic (the fact that the sun moves on a line at 23.5 degrees to the celestial equator) was designed by God to enable the seasons to take place. In *As You Like It* we find reference to a different interpretation. The Duke living in exile finds himself in a wood and tries to cheer up his followers:

> Here feel we but the penalty of Adam,
> The season's difference; as the icy fang
> And churlish chiding of the winter's wind.
> (Act II, scene i, l. 5–7)

Adam's curse, as Genesis tells us, was that sustaining life would be hard work, but here Shakespeare seems to have added something about the "season's difference." It was once thought that prior to Milton no other writer had made the seasons part of Adam's punishment. In *Paradise Lost* Milton details the natural consequences of original sin and suggests:

> Some say, he bid his angels turn askance
> The poles of the earth twice ten degrees and more
> From the sun's axle; they with labour push'd
> Oblique the centric globe.
> (Book X, l. 668–671)

Milton notes rightly that the seasons result from a tilting of the ecliptic with respect to the celestial equator (see chapter one). With Shakespeare, however, it seems likely that he read Arthur Golding's translation of Ovid's *Metamorphoses*, printed in 1567, and drew from it the same notion that The Fall ushered in the seasons. Hence there is a barren period of winter when food must be stored. In Genesis 3:19 Gabriel tells Adam the bad news about the reality of the seasons and a barren period of hard work: "In the sweat of thy brow shalt thou eat bread."

Medicine

The training of the Tudor physician, like his medieval forebears, still consisted almost entirely of textual study of the works of Galen and the Hippocratic Corpus. Quacks and cheats were still in evidence, and the College of Physicians was established in 1518 as a way of regulating the profession. Marlowe's Faustus in his opening soliloquy calls "Galen come" before dismissing physic in favor of necromancy. Falstaff in *Henry IV* part two claims to have read Galen (Act I, scene ii, l. 133).

In Tudor literature, the humours are treated as metaphors for types of personality as well as real fluids. The dominant humour revealed itself in facial coloring. Melancholy lent a sallow (yellowish) pallor. In *Romeo and Juliet* the Friar remarks to Romeo: "what a deal of brine / Hath washed thy sallow cheeks for Rosaline" (Act II, scene iii, l. 73–74). And in *Twelfth Night*, when Viola describes her imaginary sister, she says she has a "green and yellow melancholy" (Act II, scene iv, 114).

Medical treatment still relied on phlebotomy as an almost invariable remedy. Shakespeare makes use of astrologically timed blood letting as a cure for excess choler in Richard's speech to this troublesome subjects:

Wrath-kindled gentlemen be ruled by me,
Let's purge this choler without letting blood,
Forget, forgive; conclude and be agreed,
Our doctors say this is no month to bleed.
(Act I, scene i, l. 152–157)

Shakespeare's daughter Susanna married a Stratford physician, John Hall. Shakespeare seems to have trusted Hall, and many of his references to physicians paint them in a positive light.

Music of the Spheres

The idea that that the spheres emitted music as they turned was still a common notion in the sixteenth century. As noted in chapter one, the idea was popularized by Macrobius in his commentary on Cicero's *Dream of Scipio*. Macrobius even gives a reason why ordinary mortals cannot hear the music: they are earth-bound and the soul is a long way from its home in the upper spheres. There are numerous references to celestial music in Elizabethan literature. The most famous expression of the idea that humans living in the sublunary realm of corruption and decay are deaf to this music is found in *The Merchant of Venice*, where Lorenzo addresses Jessica:

Lorenzo: Sit Jessica. Look how the floor of heaven
Is thick inlaid with patines of bright gold.
There's not the smallest orb which thou behold'st
But in his motion like an angel sings,
Still quiring to the young-eyed cherubins.
Such harmony is in immortal souls;
But whilst this muddy vesture of decay
Doth grossly close it in, we cannot hear it.
(Act V, scene i, l. 54–61)

Satire

Some aspects of the Elizabethan world picture were taken for granted and employed relatively uncritically. But some practices, especially magic and the occult, were viewed with suspicion. Often the state and the Church strongly opposed such activities, but they had a strong popular following. One example, which we met in chapter one, was alchemy. It is in the Elizabethan period that we find the most extensive satirization of alchemy in the form of Ben Jonson's *The Alchemist*, first performed by the King's Men in 1610.

Jonson was born about 1572 in London. He received some education at Westminster school, but being too poor for university, he worked for a time for his stepfather and was thereafter self-educated. He came to prominence in 1598 by writing and producing *Every Man in his Humour*, a play that Shakespeare is known to have acted in and one that satirizes the snobbish aspirations of status seekers. *The Alchemist* is probably Jonson's greatest play—one of the few of his works still performed. It is a play about greed above all else, and the alchemical dream of transmutation provides an ideal vehicle to expose human folly and avarice.

In the play, Lovewit, the master of the house in which the play is set, flees from an epidemic of the plague and leaves his house in the charge of his servant Face. The latter, conspiring with Subtle, the alchemist, and Dol Common, Subtle's consort, proceed to use the house to outwit the gullible by promising them the philosopher's stone. This mythical stone was initially thought to be the substance capable of turning base metals into silver and gold. As alchemy evolved it aquired greater powers including that of granting eternal life. Various characters are taken in until a gamester called Surly finally exposes the fraud.

It is likely that Jonson based his play on the activities of Simon Forman (1552–1611) and John Dee. Forman was a notorious astrologer, occultist, and physician working in London at the same time as Shakespeare and Jonson. His copious records inform us of his love of the theatre and his experiments in casting horoscopes and raising spirits. He also left notes on his numerous amorous encounters. He seems to have treated one Emilia Bassano, a prime candidate for the "dark lady" mentioned in Shakespeare's sonnets.

Many in Jonson's original audience would have also remembered the strange case of Dr. John Dee and Edward Kelly, and both these characters are mentioned in the play (Act II, scene vi and Act IV, scene i). Dee was a mathematician, astrologer, and mystic who impressed Queen Elizabeth. He was duped, however, by Edward Kelly, a crooked lawyer who, even before meeting Dee, had had his ears cut off for forging coins. Kelley persuaded Dee that he could summon up spirits and that he had found the philosopher's stone at Glastonbury. Eventually Kelly died in prison, when the patience of Emperor Rudolph II of Prague, to whom Kelly had promised alchemical wealth, ran out.

In *The Alchemist*, Jonson shows considerable understanding of alchemical theory and procedures. The central target of the play is not alchemy as such, but the human greed that corrupts everything. In exposing folly, Jonson is harder on the victims than the perpetrators. Just as alchemy fails to transform anything, so

Ben Jonson (1572–1637)

In many ways Ben Jonson was larger than life. He was tall of stature, arrogant, quarrelsome, and drank excessively. In his own day some regarded him as a finer dramatist than Shakespeare, although history has not endorsed that verdict. He is now chiefly remembered for his caustic satires aimed at a variety of targets: the Puritans who despised the theater, greedy social climbers, the gullible, and the tricksters who preyed on them.

The colorful and turbulent life of Jonson began in London on June 11, 1572. His father, a clergyman, died shortly after his birth, and, after schooling, Jonson was apprenticed to his stepfather in the building trade. After a brief spell in the army, he returned to London to pursue a career in the theater. His first steps in his new profession were inauspicious. In 1597, he performed in a lost satiric comedy called the *Isle of Dogs*, but the play so incensed the authorities that Jonson and two other actors were flung into prison. He was released, only to land in trouble again a year later when he killed a fellow actor, Gabriel Spenser, in a duel. He was placed on trial for murder and only escaped the gallows by pleading the "benefit of clergy" (his father had been a priest).

Ben Jonson (1572–1637). Jonson was Shakespeare's friend and rival. He possessed a great store of classical learning and had firm views about the function of poets and dramatists. His greatest plays, such as The Alchemist, *are satires exposing human frailties. (Library of Congress)*

too the characters remain unredeemed. Subtle and Dol escape (albeit without their gains), but Dapper, Drugger, Mammon, and the other gulls endure their losses and their humiliation. For Jonson's artistic intentions, alchemy was the ideal vehicle, since it was a system of thought that by the early seventeenth century was looking increasingly moribund. A particularly instructive section of the play is the exchange between the clever Subtle (the alchemist) and the skeptical Surly (Act II, scene iii). Subtle explains to Surly that Nature breeds gold in the earth from "remote matter." When pressed to explain what remote matter is, Subtle replies:

> It is, of the one part,
> A humid exhalation which we call
> Material liquida or the unctuous water.
> On th'other part, a certain crass and viscous
> Portion of earth, both which, concorporate,

He was branded on the thumb and released. During this spell in prison he converted to Catholicism, only to convert back to the Anglican Church twelve years later.

In 1598 Jonson received critical acclaim with one of his earliest plays, *Every Man in his Humour*, a play in which Shakespeare played the leading role. The work was a great success and established Jonson's satirical style. The play was a "comedy of humours," meaning that the characters represented a certain type or temperament (humour). His next play, *Every Man out of his Humour* (1599), was less successful but confirmed Jonson's reputation as a moralist and social realist. He exposed and ridiculed the human failings of his age, driving home the moral of his plays (unlike Shakespeare) in a rather didactic style.

In 1604 he took part in a production of another satirical comedy called *Eastward Ho*. The Scottish faction at the court of the new monarch, James I, found this play so offensive that he was again placed in prison and threatened with the loss of his ears and nose. He was released unmolested, though, and eventually regained favor with the king. He later wrote a series of masques to entertain the court and was appointed court poet.

Probably his greatest plays were *Volpone*, first published in 1607, and *The Alchemist* of 1610. Both plays expose human greed and folly. In *The Alchemist* Jonson shows a deep awareness of alchemical principles. His main target, however, was not alchemy itself, though Jonson may have had reservations about the ethics of manipulating nature, but the greedy and credulous personality types it attracted.

Jonson's later works were disappointing. His reputation was such, however, that he was the center of attention and served as mentor for a group of writers, including John Donne, Walter Raleigh, William Shakespeare, and Walter Herrick, that met regularly at the Mermaid Tavern in London. He died in 1637 and is buried in Westminster Abbey under a stone slab engraved with the words "O Rare Ben Jonson."

Do make the elementary matter of gold
Which is not yet propria materia,
But common to all metals and all stones.
For where it is forsaken of that moisture
And hath more dryness, it becomes a stone.
Where it retains more of the humid fatness,
It turns to sulphur or the quicksilver
Who are the parents of all other metals.
(Act II, scene iii, l. 142–154)

The passage here shows how alchemy drew upon Aristotelian notions of qualities and elements (watery or vaporous exhalations and earthy exhalations) and a later view that two "principles," mercury and sulphur, were responsible for all metals. "Remote matter" is that primary stuff that, when acted upon by the qualities of hot, dry, moist, and cold, gives rise to the elements. Subtle then explains that Nature operates slowly to perfect matter and turn it into gold and suggests that this is quite feasible, since life can spontaneously generate from the carcasses of animals:

> Beside, who doth not see in daily practice
> Art can beget bees, hornets, beetles, wasps,
> Out of the carcasses and dung of creatures.
> (Act II, scene iii, l. 142–173)

Surly sees through the obfuscating fog of language, however:

> What else are all your terms,
> Whereon no one o' your writers 'grees with other?
> Of your elixir, your lac virginis,
> Your stone, your medicine, and your chrysosperm
> Your sal, your sulphur and your mercury
> Your oil of height, your tree of life, your blood,
> With all your broth, your menstrues, and materials
> Of piss and egg shells.
> Would burst a man to name.
> (Act II, scene iii, l. 181–198)

It is clear that Jonson held the over-elaborate language of the philosophers in contempt. Jonson, like Shakespeare, was philosophically conservative and resented the pseudo philosophical thinking inherent in alchemy and its pretensions to manipulate nature to satisfy human greed.

Breaking Boundaries

Renaissance scholars were also responsible for questioning the assumptions that had underpinned political authority in the Middle Ages. In the sphere of political science, Machiavelli was the most famous and shocking exponent of a new secular and empirical approach to politics that broke with medieval traditions. Nicolo Machiavelli (1469–1527) was a Florentine politician and author whose name has since become synonymous with cynical statecraft. In his book *The Prince* (1513), he advocated the separation of politics and ethics, something that Greek thinkers such as Aristotle had laboured hard to show were inseparable. Machiavelli suggested that the successful political operator should use cunning and deceit to achieve political ends without too much concern with moral restraints or the means used. The Elizabethans viewed Machiavelli with awe and fascination. Here was someone who put the state before religion, a thinker who feared neither God nor the devil but would serve both if necessary to further his ambition. Machiavelli provided intellectual approval for an individualism released from the bonds of religion that was both frightening and exhilarating. Although he was roundly condemned in public, in private many read him and pondered on his message.

Marlowe's Faustus

Machievellian type figures often lent themselves to tragedy, since their over-reaching (hubris) was inevitably brought down by a fall (nemesis). One could overreach in terms of grasping for power, as in the case of Marlowe's Tamburlaine or Shakespeare's Macbeth, or in the search for forbidden knowledge, as in the case of Marlowe's Faustus.

Christopher Marlowe (1564–1593) was the son of a prosperous Canterbury shoemaker. He studied at the Kings School, Canterbury, and then Corpus Christi College, Cambridge. It is possible that he was a government agent, and his early and mysterious death in a tavern at Deptford, ostensibly over an unpaid bill, may have had political causes.

The central character of Marlowe's *The Tragical History of Doctor Faustus* is based on a real historical figure, one Johannes Faustus, who was a strolling scholar and reputed magician practicing in Germany between 1510 and 1540. An English translation of a German work describing the life of the real Faustus appeared in print in 1592, and it was on this book—*The Historie of the damnable life and deserved death of Doctor Iohn Faustus*—that Marlowe based his play. The play was performed at the Rose Theater in the 1590s but only published in 1604, after Marlowe's death.

The opening chorus of the play tells us what to expect: Faustus is a man of humble origin who through his own efforts acquires great learning; he is proud and arrogant, however, and his overweening ambition precipitates his downfall. The play paints a vivid picture of a new renaissance type: the natural philosopher casting aside traditional restraint and dabbling in dangerous and forbidden knowledge. In many ways the figure of Faustus is symbolic of the new humanist learning that is impatient with the stale intellectual fodder of the Middle Ages. As Faustus says:

> Philosophy is odious and obscure
> Both law and physic are for petty wits

Christopher Marlowe (1564–1593)

Christopher Marlowe was born the same year as William Shakespeare in Canterbury, England, and was the son of a successful shoemaker. Toward the end of 1580 he

entered Cambridge University and received the degree of bachelor of the arts in 1584 and his master of the arts in 1587. However, the latter award was placed in jeopardy by his frequent absences from the university. It is likely that Marlowe spent the time in Rheims among Catholics who were plotting the overthrow of Elizabeth's Protestant rule. The degree was granted, however, after the intervention of the crown authorities, suggesting that Marlowe was engaged in government business of a secretive nature. Shortly after leaving Cambridge, he achieved success as a playwright with his *Tamburlaine the Great*. This play helped secure the place of blank verse in Elizabethan drama.

English dramatist Christopher Marlowe (1564–1593) in the only known portrait of him. Marlowe helped establish blank verse as a medium for Elizabethan plays. In the character Faustus he established an archetype for the portrayal of scientists. (Hulton Archive/Getty Images)

Marlowe seems to have had a fiery temperament, and he dressed and behaved extravagantly. In 1589 he was involved in a sword fight during which a friend of his, Thomas Watson, killed another man. According to at least two of his associates, Thomas Kyd and Richard Baines, Marlowe was also wont to scorn religion and express atheistic views. In two of his plays, *Tamburlaine* and *The Jew of Malta*, Christians are presented as treacherous and hypocritical. However, the reliability of the testimony of Kyd and Baines is debat-

Divinity is basest of the three
Unpleasant, harsh, contemptible, and vile;
'Tis magic, that hath ravished me.
(Act I, scene i, l. 105–109)

The downfall of Faustus is that he wants to become more than a man: he craves knowledge and power to the extent that he is prepared to enter into a terrible bargain with Satan: his own soul in return for knowledge and power. Faustus enjoys his side of the deal. He calls forth the emissary of Satan, Mephistopheles, to question him on astronomy; and, in scenes that would have delighted his Protestant audience (thankful of a recent deliverance from the Spanish Armada of 1588), he plays tricks on the Pope, flies through the air, and enjoys the sensuous delight of kissing Helen of Troy.

able; Kyd was arrested in 1593 and claimed under torture that heretical documents in his possession belonged to Marlowe.

On May 30, 1593, a few days before he was due to give evidence before the Privy Council in the face of charges of heresy, Marlowe visited Dame Eleanore Bull's tavern on the outskirts of London to meet three rather shady companions: Frizer, an agent of the spymaster Thomas Walsingham, a swindler called Nicholas Skeres, and another spy called Robert Poley. The official account of what followed is that a quarrel broke out over the payment of the bill; then Frizer, acting in self defense, stabbed Marlowe over his right eye, causing his death. Perhaps we will never know the exact circumstances surrounding his death. One interpretation is that Marlowe was provoked into a fight so that he could be killed before he appeared before the Privy Council and possibly give evidence against men of some power.

Marlowe is known as the author of *Faustus, Tamburlaine the Great, The Jew of Malta, Edward II, Dido Queen of Carthage, The Massacre at Paris*, and the unfinished long poem "Hero and Leander." Marlowe's characters often combine a Machiavellian approach to politics, a disdain for established conventions, and a thirst for scientific knowledge and power. He placed blank verse firmly on the Elizabethan stage and set a path that Shakespeare would follow with remarkable results. The lines he wrote in *Tamburlaine* are a fitting tribute to the man and the characters he created:

Our souls, whose faculties can comprehend
The wondrous Architecture of the world,
And measure every wand'ring planet's course,
Still climbing after knowledge infinite,
And always moving as the restless spheres,
Will us to wear ourselves and never rest.
(Part I, Act II, scene vii, l. 21–26)

But Faustus has to deliver his part of the pact, and his final soliloquy, as Lucifer and Beelzebub come to claim his soul, is the most moving of the play. As the soul of the screaming Faustus is pulled down to hell, he calls out first for Christ and then to God and notes how "Christ's blood streams in the firmament." The final chorus drives home the moral of the play and instructs the audience to "regard his hellish fall / Whose fiendful fortune may exhort the wise / Only to wonder at unlawful things" (Epilogue, 5).

Marlowe's *Faustus* was, in so many respects, a groundbreaking piece of work, yet there are still medieval elements in the cosmology it describes. Marlowe, unlike Shakespeare, studied at university and in 1584 was awarded his B.A. degree. Highly educated, well traveled, and widely read, he must have been aware of the debates surrounding Copernicanism and the contemporary challenges to Aristotelian cosmology. Yet, when Faustus, having bargained away his

The Tragicall History of the Life and Death

of *Doctor Faustus.*

Written by *Ch. Marklin.*

LONDON,
Printed for *Iohn Wright*, and are to be fold at his fhop
without Newgate, at the f....of the
Bibl. 1616.

An illustration of the 1616 cover to The Tragicall History of the Life and Death of Doctor Faustus *by Ch Marklin (sic). The author was actually Christopher Marlowe. Faustus is shown conjuring spirits and a devil is rising from a trap door. (Getty Images)*

soul, quizzes Mephistopheles about the true structure of the heavens, he receives
a reply that Dante would have recognized some 300 years earlier:

> **Faustus:** Come Mephistopheles, let us dispute again,
> And reason of divine astrology.
> Speak, are there many spheres above the moon?
> Are all celestial bodies but one globe
> As is the substance of this centric earth?
> **Mephistopheles:** As are the elements, such are the heavens,
> Even from the moon unto the empyreal orb,
> Mutually folded in each other's spheres,
> And jointly move upon one axle-tree,
> Whose termine is term'd the world's wide pole;
> Nor are the names of Saturn, Mars, or Jupiter
> Feign'd, but are erring stars.
> **Faustus:** But have they all
> One motion, both situ et tempore?
> **Mephistopheles:** All move from east to west in four and twenty hours
> Upon the poles of the world, but differ in their motions
> Upon the poles of the zodiac.
> **Faustus:** These slender questions Wagner can decide:
> Hath Mephistopheles no greater skill?
> Who knows not the double motion of the planets?
> That the first is finish'd in a natural day;
> The second thus: Saturn in thirty years,
> Jupiter in twelve, Mars in four, the sun, Venus and Mercury
> In a year, the moon in twenty-eight days. These are
> Freshmen's suppositions. But tell me, hath every sphere a
> Dominion or intelligentia?
> **Mephistopheles:** Ay
> **Faustus:** How many heavens or spheres are there?
> **Mephistopheles:** Nine: the seven planets, the firmament and the
>   empyreal heaven.
> (Act VI, l. 33–61)

In describing an essentially unmodified medieval model of the universe,
Marlowe may have simply been emphasizing what a poor return ("freshmen's
suppositions") Faustus received for his deal. On the other hand, Marlowe had to
give a picture that would have been familiar to his audience. In 1592–1593 when
the play was written, it was not clear what the new discoveries indicated about

the structure of the heavens. For Marlowe's artistic intentions, the medieval view would suffice.

The lasting cultural significance of the play is that in the character of Faustus Marlowe provided a metaphor (and hence the adjective "Faustian") for irresponsible meddling in the arcane arts that science has struggled to shake off ever since. It is an image that we will meet again in the guise of Mary Shelley's Dr. Frankenstein (chapter five). The charge is that, like Faustus, scientists trespass across traditional and divinely set moral boundaries in their insatiable search for knowledge and power, and in so doing bring damnation on themselves and those around them. Science becomes irresponsible and diabolical instead of liberating. Yet for all this, the picture Marlowe gives is deeply ambiguous. Faustus is something of a hero; he dares to challenge the existing order, and at his demise we are invited to feel some sympathy with his suffering.

Lear and the World Breaking Up

In *King Lear* we find Shakespeare exploring different conceptions of nature current at the end of the English Renaissance. In an influential study of 1948, John Danby argued that two meanings of nature emerge from the play: the conventional and orthodox view of Cordelia, Lear, and Gloucester, and the more brutal and calculating view of Edmund. The orthodox view, that of Chaucer and the Middle Ages, held that custom and morality were rooted in natural law. It was natural and ordained by God that children owed loyalty to their parents, that subjects owed allegiance to their monarchs, and that bonds between humans should be based on custom and birthright. As we saw in Ulysses's speech on degree, order and hierarchy in society are features consonant with the natural world and part of the unchallengeable fabric of the universe.

If the values of the feudal order were based on bonds of loyalty, then measuring and quantifying belong more appropriately to a post-feudal world of mercantile capitalism and empirical rationalism. In asking his three daughters how much they love him so he can compare their answers, Lear makes the fatal mistake of wanting to measure that which cannot be measured. Following Lear's grave error, Gloucester's bastard son Edmund reveals a quite different concept of nature. In a speech that would have shocked the audience, Edmund questions the customs that deprive bastards of the birthright given to legitimate sons:

> Thou, Nature art my goddess; to thy law
> My services are bound. Wherefore should I
> Stand in the plague of custom, and permit

The curiosity of nations to deprive me,
For that I am some twelve or fourteen moonshines
Lag of a brother? . . .
Now gods stand up for bastards.
(Act I, scene ii, l. 1–7)

As Danby aptly notes: "No medieval devil ever bounced on to the stage with a more scandalous self announcement" (Danby, 1948, p. 32). Edmund espouses the ethics of detached individualism and empirical rationalism. To modern post-Enlightenment minds his complaint (although not his evil intentions) will probably seem quite reasonable: customs are to some degree arbitrary and why should bastardy be equated with illegitimacy and baseness? The villainy of Edmund therefore is not the usual tension between reason and the passions. Edmund is a rationalist through and through, but his assumptions about the workings of the natural world are fundamentally different from those of the Lear camp.

As Lear's kingdom is broken up and Edmund works his Machiavellian tricks, Gloucester looks for causes:

> Gloucester: The late eclipses in the sun and moon portend no good to us: though the wisdom of nature can reason it thus and thus, yet nature finds itself scourged by the subsequent effects. Love cools, friendships fall off, brothers divide . . . the king falls from bias of nature.

To which Edmund replies to himself:

> Edmund: This is the excellent foppery of the world, that when we are sick in fortune, often the surfeit of our own behaviour, we make guilty of our disasters the sun, the moon, and the stars; as if we were villains of necessity, fools by heavenly compulsion, knaves thieves and treachers by spherical predominance, drunkards liars and adulterers by an enforced obedience of planetary influence; and all that we are evil in, by a divine thrusting on . . . . My father compounded with my mother under ursa major; so that it follows I am rough and lecherous. Tut! I should have been that I am had the maidenliest star in the firmament twinkled on my bastardising. (Act I, scene ii)

Shakespeare himself could be irreverent with astrological notions as we have seen, but he leaves their direct repudiation and the assertion of complete self-control to the voice of his villain. For Edmund the Machiavellian, man exists on a plane outside inert nature; people, like things, can be manipulated, and he sets out to do just this. Edmund suggests a new vision of nature that was already taking root in the late sixteenth century and one that Thomas Hobbes and Rene

Descartes more fully expounded in the next. In this view, nature is not a normative principle, a source and guidance for moral action. For Hobbes the natural
state of man is brutish and bestial. In this new vision the medieval consensus is
broken, the compact between reason, nature, God, and the social order falls
apart. In *King Lear*, Shakespeare presents us with a stark commentary of the
breakdown of the medieval world. The supernatural assumptions of the Middle
Ages seem vanquished forever: madness becomes not possession but an internal
derangement; evil is not a malevolent spirit but man's inhumanity to man.

King Lear was probably written in the year 1605. On November 5 of that
year an inspection of the vaults underneath the Houses of Parliament revealed
vast quantities of gunpowder placed there by Jesuits to destroy King James I and
his ministers. The plotters, many of whom would have been known to Shakespeare, were hunted down and brutally executed. This was a decisive point in the
politics of the Reformation, and the anti-Catholic feeling that followed the failed
attempt (still celebrated by the British today with the burning of bonfires) symbolized another break with the Old Faith.

In philosophy, too, the cozy medieval world was receding rapidly. In the
year of *King Lear* and the gunpowder plot, Francis Bacon published his
Advancement of Learning, in which he proposed to clear away "the rubbish of
ages" and set philosophy on a new track. The direction this track led is explored
in the next chapter.

Bibliographic Essay

The story of John Shakespeare and his effacing of the images in the Guildhall
Chapel of Stratford was drawn from Michael Wood's *In Search of Shakespeare*
(London: BBC Worldwide, 2003). A good introductory work for students wishing
to discover more about the breakdown of the feudal order, the renaissance, and
the Reformation is *The Foundations of early Modern Europe 1460–1559* (New
York: Norton, 1994) by Eugene Rice and Anthony Grafton. This work covers the
economic expansion of Europe, the effect of the opening up of the New World,
the impact of printing, the rise of science, and the religious debates of the period.

A seminal early work on Elizabethan beliefs about the natural and social
worlds is E. M. W. Tillyard's *Elizabethan World Picture* (London: Chatto and
Windus, 1943). The book has a heavy emphasis on Shakespeare and covers the
great chain of being, the cosmic dance, and the microcosm and macrocosm.
Another influential text is Arthur Lovejoy's *The Great Chain of Being* (Cambridge, MA: Harvard University Press, 1971, first published 1936).

A book that gives details of the philosophical context to Shakespeare's thought and endeavors to locate the sources he used is John Hankin's *Backgrounds of Shakespeare's Thought* (Hassocks, Sussex: Harvester Press, 1978). For a profound and highly condensed treatment of this same theme see "Shakespeare and the Thought of His Age" by W. R. Elton in *A New Companion to Shakespeare Studies*, edited by K. Muir and S. Schoenbaum (Cambridge: Cambridge University Press, 1971). The Arden edition of Shakespeare's plays is thorough and provides plenty of footnotes to explain allusions and difficult terms.

An important work on the philosophic traditions behind Elizabethan literature is Hardin Craig's *The Enchanted Glass* (Oxford: Basil Blackwell, 1950). C. S. Lewis's *The Discarded Image* (Cambridge: Cambridge University Press, 1964) is relevant to this chapter as well as chapter one. For a broader treatment of the historical context of English renaissance literature, see *The Chorus of History* (London: Blandford Press, 1971). Chapter five of this volume lumps together science, exploration, and the Reformation. A collection of essays entitled *Shakespeare's England: An Account of the Life and Manners of his Age* (Oxford: Oxford University Press, 1916) contains a useful chapter titled "Astronomy and Astrology," by E. B. Knobel.

Many modern editions of the drama of the period, such as Marlowe's *Faustus* and Jonson's *The Alchemist*, give introductions that provide further material on the philosophical context of the ideas covered in the plays. The editions consulted in preparing this chapter were *Tamburlaine* (Manchester and New York: Manchester University Press, 1981), edited by J. S. Cunningham; *Faustus*, edited by John D. Jump (London, Methuen: 1962); and *The Alchemist* (Manchester and New York: Manchester University Press, 1997,1967), edited by F. H. Mares. For an account of Simon Forman and his rise to fame and notoriety, consult *The Notorious Astrological Physician of London: Works and Days of Simon Forman* (Chicago and London: Chicago University Press, 2001), by Barbara Howard Traister. For a series of recent essays on the role of astrology and alchemy in this period, it is worth consulting *Secrets of Nature: Astrology and Alchemy in Early Modern Europe* (Cambridge MA and London: MIT Press, 2001), edited by W. R. Newman and A. Grafton.

For a wider perspective on the science of this period, see Marie Boas's *The Scientific Renaissance 1450–1630* (London: Collins, 1962) and *The Rise of Scientific Europe 1500–1800*, edited by D. Goodman and C. Russell (London: Hodder and Stoughton, 1991). For another discussion of the relationship between Protestantism and natural science, it is instructive to consult Peter Harrison's *The Bible, Protestantism and the Rise of Natural Science* (Cambridge: Cambridge University Press, 1998). Harrison argues for a close connection between the problems of biblical interpretation and the methodology of modern science. For further information on the great comet of 1577, it is worth consulting chapter twelve ("Tycho Brahe and the Great Comet of 1577") of *The Great Coperni-cus Chase* (Cambridge: Cambridge University Press, 1992) by Owen Gingerich. The first few chapters of *The Cambridge Illustrated History of Astronomy* (Cambridge: Cambridge University Press, 1997), edited by Michael Hoskin, provide a beautifully illustrated introduction to the astronomy of the Middle Ages and the sixteenth and seventeenth centuries.

A particularly interesting source for Tudor medicine is Harriet Joseph's *Shakespeare's Son-in-Law: John Hall, Man and Physician* (Hamden, CT: Archon Books, 1964). This book contains a facsimile of the second edition of Hall's *Select Observations on English Bodies* (1679). John Hall married Shakespeare's daughter Susanna and together they inherited his house. Hall left his observations and thoughts about treatment as notes that were later published and are to be found in this volume.

Science and Literature in Seventeenth-Century England

John Cartwright

Affecting the Metaphysical

In 1631, the dean of St. Paul's Cathedral in London had an "excellent" and "exemplary" death, at least according to his biographer Isaac Walton. Knowing he was dying, the dean put on his death shroud and had his portrait painted with his face turned to the east, "from whence he expected the second coming of his and our saviour Jesus." Once finished, the portrait remained at his bedside until he died on March 31. Soon after his death, a marble sculpture based on the picture was commissioned and placed in the cathedral. The old cathedral of St. Paul's burned down in the great fire of 1666, but remarkably, the statue survived and was placed in Wren's new cathedral, where the effigy of the dean, otherwise known as John Donne, still stands in the south transept.

John Donne was born to Catholic parents in 1572. The early years of the seventeenth century were difficult for Donne in terms of both his domestic life and his struggle to express his Christian faith. In many ways Donne is a microcosm of the tension between faith and reason that emerged in the seventeenth century and the journey made by many from Catholicism to Protestantism. As a Catholic, Donne's early education would have brought him into contact with the *Summa Theologica* of Aquinas. This work, unfinished at the death of Aquinas in 1274, argued that human reason could, by and large, successfully comprehend the world. Against this confident assumption, which had underpinned medieval thought for centuries, the renaissance had thrown up a revival of classical skepticism, stemming from the Greek philosopher Pyrrho of Elis and his disciple Empiricus, which suggested our sense perceptions may be unreliable. Donne was caught up in this skepticism and it affected him deeply. He knew reason was limited but desperately hoped it would prove compatible with his faith.

John Donne (1572–1631)

John Donne was born to Roman Catholic parents in 1572. At the age of twelve he left London to study at Oxford. He remained there for three years and then moved to Cambridge for a similar period. As a Catholic he would have been unable to receive the formal award of his degree, since this entailed taking an oath of allegiance to the Protestant Queen Elizabeth. Sometime in the 1590s, however, he converted to Anglicanism and later in life was awarded, by royal mandate and against some opposition, a doctor of divinity degree from Cambridge.

John Donne (1572–1631). Donne was an Anglican dean and poet. Many of his poems display a technical brilliance in the use of scientific imagery. His writings reveal a tension between reason and faith. Ultimately Donne appears skeptical about the virtues of the new sciences. (Michael Nicholson/Corbis)

In 1601, he secretly married Anne More without her father's consent. Anne was just sixteen, and her father did all he could to ruin Donne. He ensured that Donne was dismissed from his employer, Sir Tomas Egerton, and he even had Donne imprisoned while trying, without success, to annul the marriage. The next few years were hard, and Donne relied upon the charity of relatives and noble patrons to support his family. Gradually, Donne drifted toward the Anglican Church. In 1610 he published an attack on Catholicism called *Pseudo-Martyr* that so impressed the king that he insisted that Donne enter the ministry. He was ordained in 1615 and rose quickly, so that by 1621, aged forty-nine, he was made dean of St. Paul's, where he remained until his death. He proved to be a sensational speaker and a favorite of both James I and Charles I. He delivered his last sermon, the appropriately titled "Deaths Duel," on February 25, 1631, a month before his death.

Most of Donne's poetry was never published in his lifetime, so dating its composition is difficult. His poems usually involve some form of conceit, that is, an extended metaphor that draws parallels between ostensibly dissimilar subjects. He draws his imagery from diverse fields such as alchemy, astronomy, medicine, exploration, philosophy, and politics. He seems to have written his love poems to please himself, a mistress, or a small circle of friends. The poems are not always consistent in their philosophy of love and attitude to women, but Donne's lovers tend to celebrate both the spiritual and physical aspects of love. His versatile and innovative verse was admired by W. B. Yeats and T. S. Eliot. Two poems published in his lifetime were *The First Anniversary* and *The Second Anniversary*. In the first of these he laments the spiritual death of humanity, the signs of decay in the contemporary world, and the lack of connection with God. In the second, Donne reasserts his faith as the route to eternal life. Donne read widely and was aware of the scientific discoveries of his day. He uses science to provide the imagery for his poems, but fundamentally he always treats scientific knowledge as inferior to religious faith.

John Donne is now known as the prime exemplar of the metaphysical poets. Strictly, the term *metaphysics* refers to the study of first principles, in particular, the nature of being (ontology) and how we know (epistemology). It examines fundamental questions about the nature of reality. Scientists tend to avoid metaphysical questions since they are difficult, if not impossible, to answer using empirical methods. The metaphysical poets wrote about non-material problems such as the existence of the soul, the nature of goodness, and the idea of God. Metaphysical poetry, which included the work of George Herbert, Henry Vaughan, and Andrew Marvell, was much admired in the twentieth century for its originality, its clever use of paradoxes, puns, and conceits. At the time such poetry was not part of a self-conscious grouping. Indeed, the epithet "metaphysical" began life somewhat later as a term of rebuke. John Dryden in his "Discourse on Satire" (1693) wrote of Donne that:

> He affects the metaphysics, not only in his satires, but in his amorous verses, where nature only should reign, and perplexes the mind of the fair sex with nice speculations of philosophy. (Quoted in Bewley, 1966, p. xii)

It is the ingenious use of ideas in Donne that appeals to a modern audience. In one of his best known short poems, "A Valediction: Forbidding Mourning," for example, he writes to his wife telling her not to weep while he is away. In nine short verses he compares their parting to the last breath of a dying man, "As virtuous men pass mildly away"; to the refinement and beating out of gold leaf, "Like gold to airy thinness beat"; and to a pair of stretching compasses that remain together as they are parted. He also throws in a discussion on earthquakes, "Moving of th'earth brings harms and fears"; the precession of the equinoxes, "trepidation of the spheres"—a complicated motion of the celestial sphere; and, borrowing from Aristotle's physics, the impermanence of mere "Dull sublunary lovers' love / (Whose soul is sense)."

"A Valediction" is remarkable for the number of metaphors or metaphysical "conceits" crammed into a small space; in other poems Donne often takes a metaphor and plays with it in an extended fashion. Donne's prolific recourse to scientific images from geography, cosmology, and astronomy might suggest at first glance that he relishes the new knowledge that science and exploration were providing. Yet the use of scientific imagery is always subservient to a deeper poetic purpose. One gets the feeling that Donne is not overawed by new discoveries and is even factually inconsistent in his references. In "Elegie XIX Going to Bed," he tries to persuade his mistress to take off her clothes and let him explore her body as colonists explore America: "O my America! My new found land." Yet in "A Valediction: Of Weeping" he refers to workmen making a terrestrial globe, and he misses out on the new continent of America ("discovered" over a hundred years earlier!) and reverts to a Ptolemaic geography of just three continents. For Donne, the inconsistency is less important that the celebration of his passion.

The World's Decay

Despite such odd oversights, we know that Donne kept abreast of developments in natural philosophy. Soon after the appearance of the new star in Cassiopeia in 1572, two more stars appeared in the first decade of the seventeenth century: one in the Swan in 1600, and another in Serpentarius in 1604. Both of these, together with a long discussion of their significance and rival interpretations, were described by Kepler in *De Stella Nova* (1606). Then in 1609 Galileo turned his newly improved telescope on the heavens. His remarkable observations—revealing, among other things, mountains on the moon, spots on the sun, and four new planets orbiting around Jupiter—were reported in his book *The Starry Messenger* of 1610. It is clear that Donne read both Galileo's and Kepler's works.

The year 1610 also witnessed the sad death of Elizabeth Drury just before her fifteenth birthday. Elizabeth was the daughter of Sir Robert Drury, an aristocratic courtier with a large fortune. At the time, Donne was still seeking patronage, and the death of Elizabeth led him to write a number of verses in her honor. In "A Funeral Elegie," Donne compares the mystery of the girl's short life and death with the appearance and disappearance of the new stars:

> But, as when heaven looks on us with new eyes
> Those new stares every Artiste exercise,
> What place they should assign to them they doubt
> Argue, and agree not, till those stares go out.
> ("A Funeral Elegie," l. 167–170)

It is significant here, as elsewhere, that Donne notes how the philosophers "argue and agree not." This theme is repeated in two of his most difficult works, "The First Anniversary" (1611) and "The Second Anniversary" (1612). The death of Elizabeth may have supplied the occasion for the works, but the subtitle of the first shows that Donne had a much wider agenda: "An Anatomy of the World Wherein, By occasion of the untimely death of Mistress Elizabeth Drury, the frailty and the decay of this whole world is represented." In effect, Donne uses the event to discuss everything he thinks is wrong and worrying at the time.

The two "Anniversaries" were among the very few of Donne's poems to be published in his lifetime. One of the most interesting passages, as far as Donne's attitude to science is concerned, is found in "The First Anniversary":

> And now the springs and summers which we see
> Like sons of women after fifty be.
> And new philosophy calls all in doubt,
> The element of fire is quite put out;
> The sun is lost, and the earth, and no man's wit
> Can well direct him where to look for it.
> And freely men confess that this world's spent,
> When in the planets, and the firmament
> They seek so many new; they see that this
> Is crumbled out again to his atomies.
> 'Tis all in pieces, all coherence gone;
> All just supply, and all relation:
> Prince, subject, father, son, are things forgot.
> For every man alone thinks he hath got
> To be a Phoenix, and that then can be
> None of that kind, of which he is, but he.
> ("First Anniversary," l. 203–218)

Despite references to new scientific discoveries, this is a deeply conservative, pessimistic, and quasi-medieval viewpoint. Indeed, Stephen Toulmin (1990) calls Donne one of the voices of the "counter renaissance." In the lines above we see the poet bemoaning the poor weather and harvests of the early seventeenth century as another sign of the world wearing out. The "new philosophy" he refers to is both Copernicanism and the work of people like Galileo, Kepler, and Tycho. We also know that Donne had read *De Subtilitae* (1551) by Jerome Cardan, in which he questioned whether there really was a sphere of fire overhead as the Aristotelians had supposed. On this subject, Kepler had also made the point (obvious to the modern mind) that if there were a region of fire, how come starlight seemed to pass through it unaffected. Hence, for Donne, the element of fire is "quite put out." Copernicus moved the sun to the center and redefined the earth as a planet and so to Donne they both seem "lost." We also have reference to observations on the new stars of 1572, 1600, and 1604, as well as Galileo's work with the telescope of 1609 that had revealed the Milky Way to consist of thousands of stars hitherto not seen separately.

Donne is also concerned with the revival of atomism. In the poem he moves to express concern that old values that bonded together prince and subject, father and son are crumbling in face of a new individualism. Donne's pessimism carries over to the whole of astronomy, ancient and new, as the following lines show:

> We think the heavens enjoy their spherical,
> Their round proportion embracing all
> But yet their various and perplexed course
> Observ'd in diverse ages, doth enforce
> Men to find out so many eccentric parts.
> Such divers downright lines, such overthwarts,
> As disproportion that pure form: it tears
> The firmament in eight and forty shares,
> And in these constellations then arise
> New stars, and old do vanish from our eyes.
> ("First Anniversary," l. 251–260)

The tearing of the firmament into forty-eight parts dates from the time of Ptolemy, as does the use of "eccentric parts" to account for the strange motion of the planets (see chapter one and Appendix A). The new stars are again those observed by Tycho and Kepler, but the old that "do vanish" are probably those in Tycho's catalogue of stars, where he listed a total of 777 stellar objects compared to the 1,022 of Ptolemy. In the lines that follow this extract, Donne goes on to note how the sun is impaled in a zodiac of twelve constellations and how the precession of the equinoxes is another sign of the world's decay. The significant point in this list of woes is that most of them are nothing to do with the new science; these are ancient observations and conventions. This tends to confirm that for Donne it was not just the new science that called all in doubt but that the very use of reason to solve nature's puzzles was deeply problematic.

"The Second Anniversary" (1612) lends weight to this view. About halfway through this poem, Donne, almost gleefully, lists several medical and biological problems that were unsolved in his day:

> Know'st thou how the stone doth enter in
> The bladder's cave, and never break the skin?
> Know'st thou how blood which to the heart doth flow,
> Doth from one ventricle to the other go?
> And for the putrid stuff, which thou dost spit,
> Know'st thou how lungs have attracted it?
> . . .
> Why grass is green, or why our blood is red
> Are mysteries which none have reach'd unto

In this low form poor soul, what wilt thou do?

When wilt thou shake off this pedantery?

Of being taught by sense, and fantasy?

Thou look's through spectacles; small things seem great

Below; but up unto the watchtower get,

And see all things despoil'd of fallacies.

("Second Anniversary," l. 270–295)

Clearly, Donne is no modernist. For an experimental philosopher, the movement of the blood, the formation of gallstones, mucus in the lungs, the greenness of grass, and the redness of blood would all be problems to be solved. In Donne's own lifetime, William Harvey had demonstrated the circulation of the blood, and with 400 years of science behind us we could now confidently answer Donne on all these points. One suspects, though, that Donne would be unimpressed: however glittering their surface appearance, Donne's poems are deeply infused with a medieval sense of the futility of human endeavor. Why trouble ourselves with the natural world when in heaven and the next life (the "watchtower") all will be revealed? Renaissance skepticism had shown that human reason was a limited tool and Donne's response was to abandon scientific rationality altogether and take refuge in faith, something that remained immune to his skeptical mind.

The Redemption of Natural Philosophy

The climate of ideas in Britain in the opening years of the seventeenth century (putting aside the interminable theological disputes that raged across Europe) was marked by three systems of thought: Aristotelian scholasticism, Renaissance humanism, and occultism. The nascent practice of natural philosophy, struggling to find its feet, did not fit easily into any of these categories. The curriculum of the universities was still dominated by Aristotelian orthodoxy, which, despite having been reanimated in the rest of Europe by the Counter Reformation, was still essentially an ossified system of ideas. The humanism of Montaigne and his followers led to a skepticism about absolute knowledge, which, however laudable for its tolerance, tended to encourage a gentlemanly preoccupation with style over substance. Moreover, the humanists tended to press for the recovery of the lost learning of the ancients rather than the generation of new knowledge. Occultism involved the esoteric pursuit of mystical analogies between man and the cosmos, and the search for magical powers that would give its practitioners power over nature. It had affinities with the Neoplatonism that

Francis Bacon (1561–1626)

Francis Bacon was a philosopher, lawyer, politician, and essayist. He is a rare example of someone who exerted an enormous influence over the direction of scientific

inquiry without himself practicing science. He was born in London, the younger son of an eminent government official, Sir Nicholas Bacon. He studied at Cambridge from 1573 to 1575 and there quickly acquired a distaste for Aristotelian philosophy, the staple fare of universities until well into the seventeenth century. Following the sudden death of his father, Bacon turned to a career in the law and by 1582 was made a barrister. Early in his career he had offended the ruling monarch Elizabeth I, but with her death in 1603 and the accession of James I, his career began to flourish. He secured preferment by somewhat obsequiously courting the favors of the rich and powerful. He became solicitor general in 1606, and in 1618 he was made a peer and Lord Chancellor. In 1621, he was made Viscount St. Albans, but then, at the pinnacle of his career, he fell into disgrace. He was accused by

Portrait of Francis Bacon (1561–1626), philosopher and Lord Chancellor. (Historical Picture Archive/Corbis)

his enemies of accepting bribes, found guilty, and forced to resign. After a short spell in prison (the Tower of London) and a hefty fine, Bacon withdrew from public life and concentrated on his writings.

Bacon's major intellectual contribution was to set out a grand plan for the reform

resurfaced in Renaissance Europe and was used to provide a whole panoply of pseudoscientific explanations of natural phenomena. We have already observed how astrology and alchemy were part of this mentality and were regarded with a mixture of fascination and distrust. Such systems of thought were hardly fertile soil for the emergence of the empirical sciences.

Into this inauspicious atmosphere, stepped the lawyer, politician, philosopher, and essayist Francis Bacon (1561–1626). In 1605 he published *The Advancement of Learning*, in which he convincingly challenged the medieval conception that natural science was somehow forbidden knowledge (Bacon was writing, we recall, only nine years after the first production of *Dr. Faustus*, and only a year or so after Marlowe's text appeared in print). He did this by arguing that God had revealed himself through two kinds of books: The Book of Words (i.e., the Bible) and The Book of Works (the natural world). It was obvious to Bacon that a natural world created by God could not be solely the province of of natural knowledge and justify the role of the new sciences. He hoped to set out his ambitious blueprint in a monumental work to be called *The Great Instauration*. The whole work was never finished, but several parts were set in place. In 1605, he wrote *The Advancement of Learning* and an expanded Latinized version (part of *The Great Instauration*) called *De Augmentis Scientiarum* appeared in 1626. In this work, Bacon classified the various branches of learning and, most importantly, separated out the scientific study of the natural world from religion and mysticism. Having charted his fields of study, Bacon laid out his view on the proper method of inquiry in the natural sciences in his *Novum Organum* of 1620. In this same work, numerous drafts for which were written between 1608 and 1620, Bacon attacked scholasticism and analyzed the errors of reasoning that humans tend to display. In contrast to the deductive reasoning of the scholastics, Bacon advocated a science based on induction: the careful amassing and examination of factual evidence. His last work of interest here is *The New Atlantis*, published posthumously in 1627. The work is a utopian vision of what a community of scientists bent on securing the public good might look like. It was parodied in the eighteenth century by Jonathan Swift (see chapter four).

Ironically, one of the few experiments that Bacon ever attempted led to his death. While traveling on a cold day in March 1626, he wondered whether cooling meat would delay putrefaction. He stopped his carriage, purchased a hen, and stuffed it with snow. He was shortly seized with a chill and died of bronchitis a few days later.

Modern philosophers have found fault in Bacon's philosophy of science, but that is not the real point. Bacon's lasting influence, and one that stretched well beyond the seventeenth century, was to give the fledgling sciences a sense of direction, purpose, and respectability. His vision of a human future dominated by natural science has proved remarkably prescient.

Satan. It followed that the study of nature was consistent with and not contrary to the study of religion. Understanding the natural world only served further to reveal the munificence of the Creator. In this way, Bacon legitimized the pursuit of science as a wholesome activity and, just as importantly, separated it from the study of religion and allowed its autonomous development.

He titled another of his major works the *Novum Organum* (1620) signaling that this was going to replace the *Organum*, a medieval compilation of Aristotle's writings. In this book, Bacon classified the errors into which human reasoning tended to fall, the so-called Idols. One of these was the "Idol of the Marketplace," or the tendency of language to lead reason astray. Words often did not correspond to reality, he said, and empty abstractions often led philosophers into fruitless verbal debates. This distrust of language struck a chord with many seventeenth-century scientists, as we shall see later. The *Novum Organum* is rightly famous for Bacon's account of what should be the proper rules of scientific inquiry: the inference of general laws from masses of carefully controlled observations, the so-called inductive method.

One of Bacon's major objections to Aristotelianism was that it had produced no useful works to benefit mankind. The scholars were, he said, like spiders that produced cobwebs out of their own substance. For Bacon, it was a moral imperative that human beings should recover the dominion over nature that they had lost at the Fall. To restore this dominion, Bacon advocated the state funding of research centers where individuals would work cooperatively on promising projects for the "relief of man's estate." In *The New Atlantis* (1627), Bacon gave a fictionalized idea of what he had in mind. A party of European travelers chances upon the mythical island of Bensalem. They find here that research is carried out in Solomon's House by some thirty-six academicians working in groups on a variety of experiments. To allay fears that science might be a godless activity, Bacon made his Bensalemites model citizens: devoutly Christian and resolutely chaste. The purpose of Solomon's House is explained to the visitors: "The End of our Foundation is the Knowledge of Causes, and the Secrett Motions of Things; And the enlarging of the bounds of the Humane Empire, to the Effecting of all Things possible" (quoted in McKenzie, vol. 2, 1960, p. 43).

It is noteworthy that Bacon's scientists work cooperatively and altruistically for the common good. This effectively distanced science from the secret practices of the occultists and challenged the Faustian image of the lone scientist who tries to comprehend all but inevitably fails. Science thereby becomes Promethean and not Mephistophelean. The good Baconian scientist knows he added his bit to the common stockpile of useful knowledge.

The activities taking place in Solomon's House are remarkable to the extent that they anticipate the technology that science did deliver in the centuries that followed. Hence, in Bacon's projected research island we have the genetic engineering of plants and animals, zoological gardens, robots, telephones, refrigerators, weather observation towers, and all sorts of flying machines. Bacon also seems to forecast the existence of submarines and cinemas: "Wee have Shipps and Boates for Going under water, and Brooking of Seas. Wee have also Houses of Deceits of the Senses; Wher we represent all manner of Feats of Jugling, False Apparitions, Impostures and Illusions" (quoted in McKenzie, 1960, p. 44).

On many points, Bacon turned out to be wrong. His proposed inductive method was not the best advice to give physical scientists and neglected the important role of hypotheses and conjectures. He also failed to anticipate the important role mathematics had to play in the construction of theories and laws. Surprisingly for an original thinker, he also rejected or ignored some of the key innovative ideas of his age, such as Gilbert's work on magnetism, Copernicus's heliocentric theory, and Harvey's work on the circulation of the blood (even though Harvey was his own physician). What Bacon did achieve, however, was to lend the pursuit of science, and empirical crafts and industries outside the universities, enormous credibility. His image of the scientist as the public servant motivated only by the disinterested pursuit of truth influenced subsequent writers such as H. G. Wells. His dream of an organized scientific body for the pursuit of scientific research bore fruit some forty years after his death in the form of the Royal Society.

The Royal Society

The Royal Society is the longest-running learned scientific society still in existence, and was one of the first to be founded. With its elected membership, regular meetings, and a published journal, the early Royal Society set a pattern for the practice of science that continues today. Its formation after the Restoration of the monarchy in 1660 can be traced to a number of earlier meetings of natural philosophers in London and Oxford. In 1579, a wealthy merchant named Thomas Gresham died and left instructions in his will for the founding of a college. The result was Gresham College in London, finally established in 1598. Meanwhile, another group of philosophers gathered around John Spacey Wilkins (1614–1672) at Oxford and formed an Experimental Philosophy Club at Wadham College. Around 1658, some members of Wilkins group moved to London, and, on November 28, 1660, they formally established the Royal Society for the Improving of Natural Knowledge. In that same year, the monarchy was restored. Charles II took a keen interest in science and granted the society its Royal Charter in 1662. Many early members of the Royal Society were not professional scientists in the modern sense—science as a vocation hardly existed—instead, the society drew its support from the ranks of the aristocracy, clergymen, and men of letters.

The vision of Francis Bacon inspired the work of the Royal Society in three main respects: the emphasis on experimentation, the open communication of results nationally and internationally, and the search for useful applications of natural knowledge. Their indebtedness to Bacon is reflected by Thomas Sprat in his *History of the Royal Society of London* (1667):

> I shall onely mention one great Man who had the true Imagination of the whole extent of this Enterprize, as it is now set on foot, and that is Lord Bacon. In whose Books there are every where scattered the best arguments that can be produc'd for the defence of experimental philosophy. (Sprat, 1667, p. 35)

Thomas Sprat (1635–1713). Sprat's History of the Royal Society *is an invaluable source of information about the motives of the early Fellows. It is particularly instructive about their ambitions to reform philosophy and the English language. (Getty Images)*

The frontispiece of Sprat's *History* shows a figure of Charles II, Lord Viscount Brouncker, the first president, and Lord Bacon, called the "Artium Instaurator." The poet Abraham Cowley (1618–1667) wrote an "Ode to the Royal Society" that was also printed in Sprat's book. In it, he compares Bacon to Moses, who led mankind from the wilderness of ignorance. Interestingly, he also praises

Bacon for the liberation of knowledge from mere words, a theme later taken up by Sprat and itself an important milestone in the relations between science and literature. Not everyone agreed, however, that Bacon's path led to the Promised Land, and as the experimental philosophers discussed their strategies for the reform of knowledge, so the satirists took note.

Satire and the Virtuosi

Soon after its formation in 1662 the Royal Society attracted suspicion and ribaldry from a variety of writers, but none more flamboyant and eccentric than Margaret Cavendish, the duchess of Newcastle. The duchess was something of a celebrity of her times, famous for her good looks and her extravagant dress, and notable for her eclectic writing.

Margaret Cavendish was one of the few women of the day to be invited (at her own insistence) to the otherwise all-male preserve of the Royal Society (the first women Fellows were not elected until 1945). Her visit took place on May 30, 1667. Also in attendance, amid an unusually full gathering of Fellows eager to witness the spectacle, was Samuel Pepys, the diarist and later president of the Royal Society. Pepys was not overly impressed by the duchess and her "antic" dress but noted her admiration of the several fine experiments that had been especially performed for her. These included Robert Boyle weighing air by evacuating a large vessel, Robert Hooke demonstrating the wonders revealed by the microscope, and an experiment on a large loadstone.

The mixed feelings of fascination and skepticism that Fellows such as Pepys and John Evelyn recorded in their reaction to the duchess seem to have been reciprocated by Cavendish's attitude to the new sciences. A year before her visit in 1666 she had published *Observations upon Experimental Philosophy* and, bound with it into a single volume, her *Description of a New Blazing World*, the latter being the first work of science fiction featuring a woman as a central character. *Blazing World* is a parody of the genre of travel writing where the voyager chances upon a utopian new world. Cavendish may have had in mind Bacon's *New Atlantis*, since in both works the traveler is caught in a storm and in the new worlds subsequently discovered, one of the main priorities of the state is scientific research. But unlike the *New Atlantis*, in Cavendish's world the heroine (remarkably like the author) can exercise her intelligence and exert political power. In this light, one reading of *Blazing World* is to see Cavendish as offering an alternative way of comprehending nature, different in many respects to Bacon's highly masculinized ideal of science as the subjugation of feminine nature for practical purposes.

Margaret Cavendish (1623–1673)

Margaret Cavendish (neé Lucas) was born in 1623 into a wealthy gentry family in the English county of Essex. In the 1640s tensions grew between the king and parliament, and as royalist sympathizers finding their position uncomfortable in their home county, the Lucas family moved to Oxford to join the king's court. Margaret became maid of honor to Queen Henrietta Maria, the Catholic wife of Charles I.

The civil war between the royalists and the parliamentarians lasted from 1642 to 1649 and ended with the execution of Charles I and the abolition of the monarchy. In the midst of the conflict, Margaret Lucas fled with the queen in 1644 to Paris. In 1645,

she met and later married William Cavendish, marquis of Newcastle. The couple lived in exile over the next fifteen years, during which time Margaret received informal lessons in science and philosophy from her husband and his brother Sir Charles Cavendish.

Margaret Lucas (later Cavendish), c. 1650. In her lifetime Margaret Cavendish was an aristocratic celebrity. Many of her male contemporaries dismissed her scientific writings as eccentric and confused. More recently, feminist scholarship has restored her reputation as someone alert to the restricted role of women in the seventeenth century, who, through her writings, explored alternative approaches to natural philosophy. (Photo by Edward Gooch/Hulton Archive/Getty Images)

In the story, a merchant sailor kidnaps a maiden, but before he can violate her the ship is blown toward the North Pole, where all the crew freezes, leaving only the heroine alive. The lady now voyages to a new world, whose pole adjoins that of the earth, which is populated by animal-human hybrids. Soon she becomes empress of this new land and establishes an academy where, for example, the bear-men are the experimental philosophers, the ape-men the chemists, and the bird-men the astronomers. She questions her virtuosi on such matters as why there are spots on the sun, why the sea is salty, and what causes the wind, but is disappointed that they disagree so much. In her exasperation at the astronomers she

> began to grow angry at their telescopes, that they could give no better Intelligence; for, said she, now I do plainly perceive, that your Glasses are false Informers and instead of discovering the Truth, delude your senses; Wherefore I Command you to break them. (*Blazing World*, in Bowerbanck and Mendelson, 2000, p. 170)

In 1660 the monarchy was restored (Samuel Pepys began his diary) and the Cavendish family returned to England for the marquis to reclaim his estates. The marriage of William and Margaret was childless, and without the distraction of children Margaret concentrated on her writing. Between 1653 and her death in 1673 she produced over a dozen volumes of poetry, plays, letters, and scientific treatises. In 1665, William Cavendish was made duke of Newcastle, and so Margaret became a duchess. In 1667, she published a biography of her husband.

Early commentators on her literary output, such as Samuel Pepys, were dismissive. In his diary entry of March 18, 1668, Pepys thought her biography of William Cavendish "ridiculous" and that it "shews her to be a mad, conceited, ridiculous woman, and he as asse to suffer her to write" (quoted in Nicolson, 1965, p. 113). Virginia Woolf thought her to be "noble and Quixotic" but also "crack-brained and bird-witted."

More recent commentators have viewed the duchess in a more sympathetic light. Marjorie Nicolson thought Margaret's biography of her husband to be "of real importance in the history of English literature and one of the earliest psychological biographies in our language"(Nicolson, 1965, p. 114). Many now see the writings of Cavendish, for all their florid exuberance and twists of ideas, worth exploring from a feminist standpoint. Sylvia Bowerbank and Sara Mendelson, for example, see the duchess as satirizing the self-interested and male-dominated nature of seventeenth-century scientific debate, and regard her as part of an attempt to "resist the hegemonic claims of early modern science to interpret nature" (Bowerbank and Mendelson, 2000, p. 26)

The empress is persuaded that the telescopes should be preserved, however, since the astronomers actually enjoy disputing and without them would have nothing else to do.

In the story we read of the empress denying the existence of a vacuum and also questioning the value of new instruments such as the microscope. Interestingly, the evacuation of a chamber to produce a vacuum and the revealing power of the microscope were two of the several demonstrations arranged for Cavendish's entertainment during her visit to the Royal Society, suggesting the possibility that one of the Fellows had read *Blazing World.*

Blazing World cites many opinions and notions of the natural philosophers, usually to ridicule them. Until recently, most modern readers tended to conclude that either the duchess had not understood the ideas she mocked, or had countered them with something even more implausible. One of her major biographers, for example, thought *Blazing World* to be a "confused ridiculous fancy" with "ludicrous situations" and tedious "quasi-philosophical disquisitions," a work that as "either narrative or speculation . . . is quite hopeless"

(Grant, 1957, p. 208). There is now, however, a Margaret Cavendish Society dedicated to exploring her specifically female contribution to the science writing of the period. Once dismissed as "mad Madge," the academic reputation of the duchess is now perhaps higher than ever. Her work is seen as offering a feminine counterpoint to the male-dominated science of the period and a critique of contemporary philosophers such as Hobbes and Descartes.

A more successful satirist than Cavendish, commercially speaking, was Thomas Shadwell, whose *The Virtuoso* appeared on the London stage in 1676. For the next hundred years the figure of the virtuoso became a familiar one in English literature. The term *virtuoso*, which had come into use early in the seventeenth century, was originally applied to gentlemen of wealth and leisure who collected Greek and Roman antiquities—people whom we today would call antiquarians. As fascination with the natural world grew, so the interests of the virtuosi evolved to encompass the collection and study of natural curiosities such as shells, eggs, exotic stones, and minerals. Indeed, the Royal Society had its own cabinet of curiosities called the Repository until it handed it over to the British Museum in 1779. Eventually the term virtuoso came to denote an amateur scientist.

The central character of Shadwell's play is Sir Nicholas Gimcrack, the virtuoso par excellence, who, we are told, has spent £2,000 on microscopes, telescopes, and air pumps, and has spent twenty years studying the nature of "lice, spiders, and insects" (Act I, scene ii, 241). Gimcrack's first appearance (Act II, scene ii) shows him lying on a table learning to swim by imitating the motion of a frog in a basin of water beside him. Nicholas Gimcrack is joined by Bruce, Longvil, and Sir Formal. The conversation unfolds as follows:

> Longvil: Have you ever tried in the water sir?
> Sir Nicholas: No, sir but I swim most exquisitely on land.
> Bruce: Do you intend to practice in the water sir?
> Sir Nicholas: Never, sir. I hate the water. I never come upon the water sir.
> Longvil: Then there will be no use of swimming.
> Sir Nicholas: I content myself with the speculative part of swimming; I care
>   not for the practice. I seldom bring anything to use; 'tis not my way.
>   Knowledge is my ultimate end.
> Bruce: You have reason sir. Knowledge is like virtue, its own reward.
> Sir Formal: To study for use is base and mercenary, below the serene and
>   quiet temper of a sedate philosopher.
> (Nicolson and Rodes, eds., 1966, *The Virtuoso*, l. 78–90)

As the play unfolds several targets of the satire emerge: the trivial nature of the subject matter of the investigations, the expense of the equipment, the uselessness of the results, the exaggeration of the findings, and the neglect by the virtuoso of the welfare of his own family. Furthermore, the prescriptions Gimcrack offers his patients are worthless. In effect, Gimcrack has turned his back on his fellow man. His niece Miranda says of him that he is "one who has broken his brains about the nature of maggots, who has studied these twenty years to find out the several sorts of spiders and never cares for understanding mankind" (Act I, scene ii, 11–13). Sir Nicholas is actually proud of this: he boasts that he has traveled over Italy but took no notice of its culture 'Tis below a virtuoso to trouble himself with men and manners. I study insects" (Act III, Scene iii, 86–89).

It would be hasty, however, to read *The Virtuoso* solely as an attack on the Royal Society, or the College as it was sometimes called. In passing, Lady Gimcrack, the virtuoso's wife, says "he is a rare mechanic philosopher. The College indeed refused him. They envied him." In addition, Gimcrack is condemned for his moral failings (he is a pompous hypocrite) as well as for his scientific pursuits.

Gimcrack may not have been respectable enough for the College, but Shadwell clearly drew upon the activities of Society members to paint his picture of the virtuoso. Sir Nicholas claims that he has spent whole days and nights looking through a microscope inside the eggs of ants (Act II, scene ii) and twenty years "compiling a book of geography for the world in the moon" (Act II, scene i, 242). He once carried out a blood transfusion from a sheep to a man: the sheep died but the man lived, and thereafter "he had wool growing on him in great quantities, and a Northamptonshire's sheep's tail did soon emerge or arise from his anus or human fundament" (Act II, scene ii, 193–194). All these concerns reflect the practice of science in the period and especially the experiments carried out by Hooke, Boyle, and other scientists in the Society. Reports of transfusions from animals to humans appear in the diary of Samuel Pepys and were reported in the *Philosophical Transactions of the Royal Society* (see Nicholson, 1966). Robert Boyle (1627–1691) performed a number of experiments on air: he showed that sound could not travel through a vacuum, and that in the absence of air, a lightweight object, such a feather, fell as fast as a heavy one. Boyle's gifted assistant was Robert Hooke (1635–1703). In 1665, aged twenty-nine, Hooke published *Micrographia*, a record of his observations with a microscope, which contained sixty beautifully drawn plates of his observations. Several of these show flies and fleas (see illustration p. 78), and one shows a head louse clutching a human hair. Shadwell's Gimcrack also experiments with air: he employs people all over the country to collect and bottle air. He has a collection of air bottles to open at his pleasure as others would open wine (Act IV, Scene iii, 256). It looks likely that the character of Gimcrack was based largely on Robert Hooke. Having heard of the play's success, Hooke went to see it himself on June 2, 1676. His dairy entry for that evening refers to "Dammed Doggs. Vindica me deus. (God grant me revenge). People almost pointed" (quoted in Jardine, 2003, p. 322).

A fly from Hooke's Micrographia. *The concern of scientists such as Hooke with insects and other small creatures provided a source of amusement for satirists such as Shadwell, whose character Nicholas Gimcrack is based on the work of Robert Hooke. (Library of Congress)*

The obvious question is why the satirists chose the virtuosi and the Royal Society as the butts of their jibes. Weighing air and using microscopes are now standard activities in schools, and blood transfusions have saved countless lives. Part of the answer is that the virtuosi were easy prey: they were (although Boyle and Hooke did not fall into this category) essentially enthusiastic dilettantes who tended to collect and hoard curiosities indiscriminately. The other problem was that early members of the Royal Society expected too much from both the method of induction and the ability of the new science to deliver the technological wonders of Bacon's dream. The difficulty with Baconian empiricism is that, at least in the early stages of any branch of science, it is not always clear which facts will prove significant and which are unrewarding. With the benefit of hindsight we can see that the fascination of the early members with the unusual, monstrous, and even macabre was not to be productive. Among the earliest accounts of the activities of the Royal Society published in their journal we have, for example, "An Account of a Dog Dissected by Mr Hook," "Experiments on a Stone called Oculus Mundi Made by Dr Goddard," "A Discourse proving from Experiments that the larger the wheels of a Coach are the more easily they are drawn over stones lying in their way," "Experiments of keeping Creatures many hours alive by blowing into the Lungs with Bellows," and "An account of a large praeternaturall Glandulose Substance found between the Pericardium and Heart of an Ox." No wonder then that the cultivated wits found such studies both ludicrous and disgusting.

The other sin of the new science, as perceived by its detractors, was its association with Puritanism. It was an American scholar, Robert Merton, who, in 1938, suggested that there was an affinity between the ethos of science and such Puritan values as self-restraint, delayed gratification, orderliness, thrift, hard work, and simplicity. It is true that Christian theology was always at the back of Bacon's program; his advocacy of studying nature directly, without going through ancient texts and tired authorities, appealed to the egalitarian instincts of the Puritans. The Puritan ideal of the "priesthood of all believers," which entitled all believers to interpret scripture (hence bypassing the Episcopal elite), also ran parallel with the idea of the scientific study of nature using fresh observations and a mind purged of classical and medieval dogma. Such affinities were quite self-conscious, as Sprat noted in his *History:*

> That the Church of England will not only be safe amidst the consequences of a Rational Age, but amidst all the improvements of Knowledge, and the subversion of old Opinions about Nature and new ways of Reasoning thereon. This will be evident, when we behold the agreement that is between the present Design of the Royal Society, and that of our Church in its begin-

ning. They both may equal claim to the word Reformation; one having compass'd in Religion, the other purposing it in Philosophy. They both have
taken a like cours to bring this about; each of them passing by corrupt
copies, and refereeing themselves to the perfect originals for their instruction; the one to Scripture, the other to the large Volume of the Creatures"
(Sprat, 1667, pp. 370–371)

So why should the possible link between science and Puritanism be a cause
of the attack on science by the literary intelligentsia? Part of the answer lies in
the fact that during the interregnum (the period between Charles I and Charles
II, 1649–1660, when the Puritan Oliver Cromwell reigned as Lord Protector and
the only time in British history when England was a republic) the Puritans had
tried to modify the curriculum at Oxford. Puritan dons received preferment, and
an attempt was made to displace the humanities in favor of applied scientific
research such as gardening and optics. Much more damaging, however, was the
fact that when in power the Puritans had closed the theatres in London on the
grounds that they encouraged immorality. Dramatists scarcely needed any more
provocation. It is hardly surprising then that Thomas Sprat feared that the
raillery of the "wits" (poets and dramatists: "this pleasant but unprofitable sort
of men") would jeopardize the whole enterprise of science. He acknowledges
that these "terrible men" inspire a "dread of their power," but argues that they
should: "behold that their interest is united with that of the Royal Society; and if
they decry the promoting of experiments, they will deprive themselves of the
most fertile Subject of Fancy" (Sprat, 1667, p. 417).

Reading Sprat, one senses the same anxiety over presentation, image, and
media coverage that besets modern politicians. The perceived concordance
between the new science and Puritanism helps explain Samuel Butler's
(1612–1680) mock heroic poem *Hudibras* (in three parts, 1663, 1664, and 1678).
In this work, Butler lumps together a whole series of ideas and movements that
he finds reprehensible. As a royalist, Butler had no time for the self-righteous
Puritans, with their inner lights and convictions that led to the beheading of the
monarch. He sees a link between the enthusiasm of the Puritans, occultism, and
scientific experimentalism. The new light and the new science are both to be
scorned. Hence the main character of the poem, Sir Hudibras, is a "Presbyterian
true blew" and is, like Sir Nicholas Gimcrack, absorbed in impractical schemes
and useless knowledge:

For he by Geometrick scale
Could take the size of Pots of Ale
Resolve by Sines and Tangents straight

If Bread or Butter wanted weight;
And wisely tell what hour o'th'day
The Clock does strike by Algebra.
(Part 1, canto 1, 121–126)

Charles II was delighted with the work and is said often to have carried it with him.

In another poem, *The Elephant on the Moon,* Butler presents a group of astronomers peering at the moon through a telescope. They are amazed to see a battle scene on its surface—involving of all things an elephant—and they plan the publication of their findings. A servant then points out that the elephant may be just a mouse trapped in the tube. They open the telescope and out falls the mouse and various insects. The astronomers then discuss how best to suppress their error. The moral of Butler's tale is to expose the hypocrisy of philosophers who claim to seek truths but are more interested in their own fame. The message is that instruments such as the telescope become useless if the users are morally blind. Butler obviously planned an even more caustic satire on seventeenth-century science since there survives an incomplete fragment of a poem called *A Satire on the Royal Society* where he tried to mock the irrelevance of such things as measuring wind and weighing air. Weighing air was obviously a wide source of amusement, since Samuel Pepys records in his diary (1st Feb 1663/4) laughing with Charles II over the same subject.

Science and the Language of Literature

Satire does not always imply any fundamental incompatibility between the worlds of science and literature—merely that one has fallen short of expectations in some way. Chaucer satirized the alchemists but still held to the assumptions of his age about the nature of matter and the role of celestial influences. In the seventeenth century, however, we observe a parting of the ways between the literature of science and other literature. It may be that a schism between the two worlds was inevitable. After all, poetry is fundamentally about thought and feeling, and science, as it evolved after the seventeenth century, is supposed to be only about thought applied to the external world. The route that science took finally led to the modern scientific paper, itself a marvelous exercise in the excision of all individuality and feeling that could cloud the issue of objective truth. But before this path could be followed, the practitioners of science had to purge the English language. Again, Thomas Sprat's *History of the Royal Society* (1667) is instructive here. Sprat openly declares that the mingling of poetry with philosophy is a grave error and they should be kept resolutely apart. The society will avoid these errors, he says, since: "to accomplish this they have endeavour'd to separate the knowledge of Nature from the colours of Rhetorick, the devices of Fancy, or the delightful deceit of fables" (Sprat, 1667, p. 62).

As Sprat clears the table for a reformation in philosophy, he attacks "the luxury and redundance of speech" as shallow and unprofitable: "of all the Studies of men, nothing may be sooner obtain'd, than this viscious abundance of Phrase, this trick of Metaphors, this volubility of Tongue, which makes so great a noise in the World" (Sprat, 1667, p. 112). Sprat says he has almost despaired of curing this but that the Royal Society has set in place a remedy:

> a constant Resolution, to reject all the amplifications, digressions and swellings of style: to return back to the primitive purity, and shortness, when men deliver'd so many things, almost in an equal number of words. They have exacted from all their members a close, naked, natural way of speaking ... preferring the language of Artizans, Countrymen, and Merchants, before that of Wits, or Scholars. (Sprat, 1667, p. 113)

It is clear that Sprat is reflecting the views of the whole Society and not just his own since the *History* was written at the instigation of the Society and members approved it when it was completed. In fact three years earlier, at a meeting of the Society on December 7, 1664, a committee was formed to examine and improve the English language. On this committee, of over twenty members, sat John Dryden, John Evelyn, Sprat himself, and Edmund Waller, although nothing substantial resulted.

This seeming derogation of the role of the poet did not deter poets from eulogizing the Royal Society and its members. Abraham Cowley, for example, little read today but in his time one of the most esteemed poets of his generation, was at his best in such works as "Ode on Mr Harvey" and "Ode to the Royal Society." He even wrote an ode to the materialist philosopher Thomas Hobbes. Once, he said, mankind lay in ignorance and feared "Fancies, ghosts and every empty shade," but then "Great Hobbes appeared, and by plain reason's light / Put such fantastic thoughts to shameful flight" (*On Mr Hobbes and his writings*).

Thomas Hobbes (1588–1679) was part of the Cavendish circle and, like Margaret Cavendish, he was a royalist who spent some years with the court of the future Charles II in exile in Paris. His greatest political work was *Leviathan* (1651). For Hobbes, only a powerful central state (the Leviathan) could ensure that man did not revert to his natural state of egoism and competitive selfishness. The separation of matter and spirit that Descartes had argued for was taken one step further by Hobbes, who regarded spirit as nonexistent.

Milton

John Milton (1608–1674) did share with Bacon and Hobbes a distaste for medieval scholasticism; but unlike them, Milton pinned his hopes on salvation rather than experimental philosophy or a powerful state. His theological outlook explains his treatment of science. Indeed, his life's creed, and his greatest work, *Paradise Lost*, stand in direct contradiction of Hobbes's materialistic atheism. In contrast to Hobbes's moral relativism and his advocacy of the subordination of both the individual and the Church to the monarch, Milton restated the doctrine of the Fall: it was disobedience to God that led to the fall of both Satan and Adam, but man could find redemption in Christ.

From an early age, Milton seemed conscious that he was destined to become a poet, and he prepared himself for his vocation. He graduated from Cambridge in 1632 and returned to his father's house in Buckinghamshire to continue his long program of self-study. In 1638, having already published a few minor poems, Milton left for a European tour—the traditional way a gentleman completed his education. He traveled for fifteen months through France and on to Italy, and returned in 1639. During his travels, he met a number of important European scholars, including Galileo. By the time they met, Galileo was nearly blind and had been under house arrest since 1633 in his villa just outside Florence. Galileo's crime against the Holy Catholic Church had been to advocate the Copernican system in his book *Dialogue Concerning the Two Chief World Systems* (1632). Galileo's trial of 1633, and the insistence by the Inquisition that Galileo retract his belief in Copernicanism (an instruction given persuasive force by showing Galileo the instruments of torture), has become a major landmark in the study of the relations between science and religion, or science and political authority, depending on the perspective. Milton recorded his meeting with Galileo in his "Areopagitica" (1644), a pamphlet championing freedom of the press: "There it was that I found and visited the famous Galileo grown old, a prisoner to the Inquisition, for thinking in astronomy otherwise than the Franciscan and Dominican licensers thought" (in Griswold 1873, p.166).

Milton was obviously aware of the political significance of Galileo's imprisonment and also understood the scientific importance of his work. In *Paradise Lost* Milton refers to Galileo's use of the telescope as part of a description of the moon (Book I, 287–289). The importance of Galileo for Milton, however, is not as a great scientist who had made a major step in understanding the real structure of the universe, but rather as a martyr in the cause for free speech and thought against a climate of religious and political dogma.

It is Milton's Puritan conscience that determined his treatment of science in *Paradise Lost* (1667). He began this work around 1658, by which time he had

John Milton. Milton's most famous poem, Paradise Lost, *employs a vast canvas of space only conceivable after the Copernican Revolution. Despite visiting Galileo when the scientist was under house arrest, Milton still places his poem in a geocentric framework. (Bettmann/Corbis)*

lost his sight and was obliged to dictate his verse to his wife and daughters. In composing this work, Milton faced an almost insoluble dilemma. By the middle of the seventeenth century most intellectuals were coming round to accept that the Copernican hypothesis accorded with reality, and that the earth really did revolve on its axis in orbit around the sun in a heliocentric universe. But Milton was composing a religious story: the rebellion of Satan, the fall of man, the expulsion from Eden, and the hope of salvation through Christ. His ambitious intention was, as he said at the start of *Paradise Lost,* to "assert eternal Providence / And justify the ways of God to man" (Book I, 25). For this purpose, the medieval view of the cosmos—the package deal of a fallen world at the center of a closed, finite universe that was theologically, metaphysically, and scientifically consistent—was obviously more conducive to his artistic intentions. Milton's dilemma then was this: to accept the views of the astronomers and so find new ways of imaginatively adapting the Christian story to a heliocentric universe—thereby possibly alienating some of his readers who may not yet have accepted Copernicanism; or to frame his poem in a Ptolemaic setting and risk the whole work looking archaic and medieval. His solution, not an altogether satisfactory one, was to keep the Ptolemaic framework but update it aesthetically by conveying the vastness of space that the new cosmology entailed. As a further prop to his archaic structure, he inserted a section arguing that cosmological theories and disputations are not that important anyway.

It is in Book VIII where rival cosmologies are discussed. Here Adam quizzes Raphael (an angel sent down to Eden to warn Adam that Satan is on the loose) about the motion of celestial objects. Adam wonders why the earth remains stationary with everything revolving around it, when, given the enormous distances to the planets and the stars, this must entail immense speeds of movement to enable them to complete their diurnal rotations. Adam suggests that moving the earth would have been a much simpler solution to the need to give the earth day and night and the seasons, and wonders

> How nature wise and frugal could commit
> Such disproportions, with superfluous hand
> So many nobler bodies to create,
> Greater so manifold, to this one use,
> For aught appears, and on their orbs impose
> Such restless revolution day by day
> Repeated, while the sedentary earth,
> That better might with far less compass move,
> Served by more noble than herself, attains
> Her end without least motion.
> (VIII, l. 25–35)

Raphael replies that he does not blame Adam for asking such questions but suggests that Adam should not trouble himself with such thoughts and should content himself with admiring the appearances:

whether heav'n move or earth,
Imports not, if thou reckon right; the rest
From man or angel the great Architect
Did wisely conceal, and not divulge
His secrets to be scann'd by them who ought
Rather admire.
(VIII, l. 70–73)

In the next lines Milton may reveal his impatience with the complexities of Ptolemaic astronomy, since the "great Architect" looks on with amusement at the disputations of the astronomers:

he his fabric of the heav'ns
Hath left to their disputes, perhaps to move
His laughter at their quaint opinions wide
Hereafter, when they come to model heav'n
And calculate the stars, how they will wield
The mighty frame, how build, unbuild, contrive,
To save appearances; how gird the sphere
With centric and eccentric scribbled o'er,
Cycle and epicycle, orb in orb.
(VIII, l. 77–84)

Raphael then describes the Copernican system: "What if the sun / Be center to the world and other stars dance around him," but concludes:

Whether the sun predominant in heav'n
Rise on the earth, or earth rise on the sun . . .
Solicit not thy thoughts with matters hid,
Leave them to God above . . .
heav'n is for thee too high.
(VIII, l. 160–172)

At this point Adam gives up and accepts that he really ought only to seek useful knowledge.

This is virtually the only place in any of Milton's works where he confronts Copernican cosmology, and only to dismiss it. Milton does, however, exploit aesthetically the vastness of space that the astronomers were unveiling. The universe in *Paradise Lost* is not infinite—in the poem God marks it out with a pair of compasses—but it stretches across a canvas of space never before seen in literature. Unlike Dante, Milton places hell outside the earth, but when Satan looks down from its gates the earth is not even visible. Instead he sees

> a dark
> Illimitable Ocean, without bound
> Without dimensions, where length, breadth, and highth
> And time and place are lost. (Book II, l. 892–894)

When Raphael flies from heaven to earth (and Raphael tells Adam that he is not slow) it takes him all morning, a "distance inexpressible / By numbers that have name"(VIII, 113). Even Adam knows that in comparison to the universe the earth is tiny: "this earth a spot, a grain, / An atom, with the firmament compared"(VIII, l. 18). Hence when Mammon, one of the rebel angels siding with Satan, falls from heaven, his trajectory is dramatic:

> from morn
> To noon he fell, from noon to dewy eve,
> A summer's day; and with the setting sun
> Dropt from the Zenith like a falling star.
> (I, l. 742–745)

Yet intellectually, the compromise that Milton aims to achieve between the old and new frameworks is surely unconvincing. A digression telling Adam not to meddle and to be "lowly wise" does nothing to further the narrative. The journeys in space taken by Satan and the other angels are breathtaking, but ironically only conceivable in the light of the new astronomy, the main conclusion of which (heliocentrism) Milton rejects. The poetic use of astronomy is, therefore, inconsistent with his world picture. In Book VII, for example, where Milton describes the creation of the world, he notes how the sun acts as a source of light for the moon and the other planets. In passing he incorporates Galileo's discovery of the phases of Venus: "And hence the morning planet gilds her horns" (VII, l. 366). The term "horns" of Venus (the morning planet because it is often seen in the morning in the eastern sky before daybreak) refers to the crescent shape that Galileo observed through his telescope. Like the moon, the planet Venus passes through phases, but the phases observed are impossible in an Aristotelian or Ptolemaic framework. Milton's engagement with science appears all the more strange in light of the fact that he was a close friend of the Royal Society's first secretary Henry Oldenburg and was also for a time a tutor of Boyle's nephew.

Overall, in contemplating Milton's treatment of science, one is tempted to agree with A. E. Housman who, writing three hundred years later on the subject of food and drink, observed:

> Oh many a peer of England brews
> Livelier liquor than the Muse,
> And malt does more than Milton can
> To justify God's ways to man.
> ("A Shropshire Lad," LXII, *Collected Poems*, Jonathan Cape, London, 1939)

The Earl of Rochester

Someone who would have probably agreed with Houseman's view of the vindicating power of drink was John Wilmot, second earl of Rochester (1647–1680). Wilmot was a notorious rake and libertine who, in Johnson's words, "blazed out his youth and health in lavish voluptuousness." For a time he was attached to the court of Charles II, but frequently involved in long sessions of drunkenness and debauchery, he died worn out at age thirty-three. He wrote frankly about sex, and his explicit satires and lyrics can still shock a modern audience. A 1926 collection of his verse was destroyed by the New York Customs before it could enter America.

Like skeptics before him, Wilmot realized that reason is an unreliable guide to certainty, but unlike Donne, he eschewed religion in favor of atheism. He took refuge in a life of hedonism, and a world-weary cynicism pervades his verse. His most accomplished and serious poem is probably "A Satyr against Mankind" (1675). He dismisses reason as destructive of the true light of nature, the senses:

> Reason, an ignis fatuus in the mind,
> Which leaves the light of nature, sense, behind.
> (l. 12–13)

Books and philosophy only prolong the agony of human life:

> Books bear him up awhile and make him try
> To swim with bladders of philosophy.
> (l. 20–21)

In the end, old age and senescence bring reason crashing down: "Huddled in dirt, the reasoning engine lies, / Who was so proud, so witty, and so wise"(l. 29–30).

Wilmot's life and work represent one trajectory that logically follows from skepticism. His ideas and behavior stand in stark contrast to both the Puritanism of Milton and the distrust of the bodily senses expressed by the earlier metaphysical poets. For Shakespeare's Hamlet, a beast was something that "wants discourse of reason"; for Wilmot, it was better to be a beast, since they obey rather than deny the senses that nature designed for them. Fittingly, Wilmot's portrait hanging in the National Gallery London shows the earl crowning his pet monkey with a poet's laurels. If reason can't be trusted, one might as well honor the actions of a monkey.

At the opening of the seventeenth century there were many who questioned whether the counterintuitive ideas of Copernicus could really be true. In the middle years many laughed at the strange experiments and activities of the amateur scientists of the Royal Society. But by the end of the century, one scientist above others had placed his indelible stamp on the content and methodology of European science. He showed that the heliocentric system was the only one to make physical sense, he made major breakthroughs in mathematics, and his work consolidated the direction of astronomy and physics for the next two centuries. His genius and austere gravitas also raised him above the contempt of the satirists. His name was Isaac Newton, and his achievements are explored in the next chapter.

Bibliographic Essay

Although published some time ago, Basil Willey's *The Seventeenth Century Background* (London: Penguin, 1962) still effectively captures the impact of the revolution in thought brought about by Bacon, Descartes, Locke, and Hobbes and its impact on authors such as Browne, Milton, and Glanvill. For a short, readable, and clear account of Bacon's work, see Anthony Quinton's *Francis Bacon* (Oxford: Oxford University Press, 1980). For more substantial biographies, consult *Francis Bacon* (Princeton, NJ: Princeton University Press, 1999) by Perez Zagorin and *Hostage to Fortune: The Troubled Life of Francis Bacon* (New York: Farrar, Straus, and Giroux, 2000) by Lisa Jardine and Alan Stewart.

An excellent account of the rise of science in Europe over this period is David Goodman's and Colin Russell's *The Rise of Scientific Europe 1500–1800* (London: Hodder and Stoughton). The book, a set text for an Open University course, is student friendly and well illustrated. For an account of Bacon's philosophy in the wider context of the history of the philosophy of science, see John Losee's *A Historical Introduction to the Philosophy of Science* (Oxford: Oxford University Press, 1992). For a short, concise, and highly informed account of the scientific revolution, see Steven Shapin's *The Scientific Revolution* (Chicago: University of Chicago Press, 1998).

There is a useful chapter called "Literature and Science" by C. J. Horne in Boris Ford's (ed.) *The New Pelican Guide to English Literature 4, From Dryden to Johnson* (London: Penguin). A masterly account of magic, occultism, witchcraft, and astrology and its decline in this period is given in Keith Thomas's *Religion and the Decline of Magic* (London: Penguin). Douglas Bush devotes a lengthy chapter to "Science and Scientific Thought" in his book *English Literature in the Earlier Seventeenth Century* (Oxford: Clarendon Press, 1945). Bush conveys the atmosphere of the period admirably and is especially good on the works of Bacon, Hobbes, Robert Burton, and Thomas Browne. A lucid account of the way the increased size of the universe revealed by astronomy in this century impacted on poetry is given by Margaret Byards in "Poetic Responses to the Copernican Revolution," *Scientific American*, June 1977. A short chapter on science and literature in this period is provided in the well-illustrated book by A. G. R. Smith, *Science and Society in the Sixteenth and Seventeenth Centuries* (London: Thames and Hudson, 1972).

Pioneering work on the relationship between science and literature in the seventeenth century was done by Marjorie Hope Nicolson. Her *The Breaking of the Circle* (Evanston, Illinois: Northwestern University Press, 1950) is a collection of her lectures on the subject. The whole book is relevant to this chapter. Chapter three examines Donne's *Anniversary* poems with great clarity. Not all scholars agree that the "shee" of these poems is the Virgin Queen Elizabeth, but Nicolson did much to restore the literary reputation of these two poems. Those interested in the reception of natural philosophy and the activities of the Royal Society as recorded in Pepys's diary are advised to consult Marjorie Nicolson's *Pepys's Diary and the New Science* (Charlottesville: University of Virginia Press, 1965).

A very fine and closely detailed analysis of Donne's poetry in relation to science is given in Charles Coffin's *John Donne and the New Philosophy* (New York: Humanities Press, 1958). For a more recent treatment of John Donne's work see John Carey's *John Donne: Life, Mind and Art* (London: Faber and Faber, 1981). Chapter eight on "The Crisis in Reason" gives a good account of Donne's skepticism. A clear and accessible account of the intellectual and scientific background to Donne's work is given in chapter three ("The Intellectual Background") of James Winny's *A Preface to Donne* (Longman: London, 1970). Robert Ellrodt provides a useful analysis of the response to science by the Metaphysical Poets, taking into account what he sees as several crucial factors (utilitarianism, intellectual curiosity, and the tensions between faith and reason), in "Scientific Curiosity and Metaphysical Poetry in the Seventeenth Century," *Modern Philology* 61, 1963–1964, pp. 180–197. Stephen Toulmin gives a thought provoking account of the rise of modernism, drawing lessons for today, and seeks to reemphasize the role of Montaigne compared to Descartes, giving a valuable account also of the counter renaissance, in *Cosmopolis* (Chicago: University of Chicago Press, 1990).

A good starting point for the life and work of Margaret Cavendish is Douglas Grant's *Margaret the First* (London: Rupert Hart-Davis, 1957), although Grant finds little to admire in Cavendish's grasp of science. Recently, Cavendish's *Grounds of Natural Philosophy* has been reprinted, edited, and introduced by Colette V. Michael (West Cornwall, CT: Locust Hill Press, 1995). A selection of Margaret Cavendish's writings, together with an editorial introduction that celebrates her originality, is *Paper Bodies: A Margaret Cavendish Reader*, edited by Sylvia Bowerbank and Sara Mendelson (Peterborough, Ontario: Broadview Press, 2000). Interested readers are also advised to consult the web site of the Margaret Cavendish Society, http://marcav.web.brockport.edu, where they will find plenty of links and suggestions for further reading.

A good background to Milton's life and work is provided by a volume edited by John Broadbent called *John Milton: Introductions* (Cambridge: Cambridge University Press, 1973). It contains a clear and well-structured chapter on "Milton and Science" by W. Reavley Gair. A far more detailed treatment of the physical world in which Milton lived and his use of and attitude toward science—scholarly yet accessible to the general reader—is Lawrence Babb's *The Moral Cosmos of Paradise Lost* (East Lansing: Michigan State University Press, 1970).

For an account of the virtuoso in English literature that goes beyond Shadwell's treatment to consider treatments in the eighteenth century, see the article by Daniel McCue, "Science and Literature: The Virtuoso in English Belles Lettres," *Albion* 3, 1971, pp.138–156. An excellent text of Shadwell's *The Virtuosos*, together with commentary that effectively discusses the scientific context and allusions of the play is that edited by Marjorie Nicolson and David Rodes, *Thomas Shadwell, The Virtuoso* (London: Edward Arnold, 1966)

A facsimile of Sprat's *History of the Royal Society* was edited by Jackson I. Cope and Harold W. Jones (London: Routledge Kegan and Paul, 1958) and is well worth consulting. Sprat's own style is a pleasure to read. For a more detailed analysis of the effect of the Royal Society on the English language and on literary criticism, see two excellent chapters by Richard Foster Jones: "Science and Criticism in the Neo-Classical Age of English Literature" and "Science and English Prose Style in the Third Quarter of the Seventeenth Century," both of which are to be found in Richard Foster's (ed.) *The Seventeenth Century* (Palo Alto, CA: Stanford University Press, 1951).

Two recent biographies of Robert Hooke are Lisa Jardine's *The Curious Life of Robert Hooke: The Man Who Measured London* (London: Harper Collins,

2003) and Stephen Inwood's *The Man Who Knew too Much: The Inventive Life of Robert Hooke 1635–1703* (London: Macmillan, 2002). Those wishing to learn more about how Robert Boyle reconciled his science and theology are advised to consult *A Free Enquiry into the Vulgarly Received Notions of Nature by Robert Boyle*, edited by E. B. Davis and M. Hunter (Cambridge: Cambridge University Press, 1996). This work is a reprint of Boyle's attempt to converge science with the biblical doctrine of creation and so to deny that nature had any purposive wisdom of her own.

For a sophisticated analysis of how late seventeenth-century natural philosophers saw themselves engaged in recovering the epistemological acuity of a pre-lapsarian Adam, see Joanna Picciotto's "Experimentation and Paradisial Return" in Cynthia Walls (ed.), *The Restoration and the Eighteenth Century* (Malden, MA: Blackwell Publishing, 2005).

Science and Literature 1680–1790

John Cartwright

In the closing decades of the seventeenth century the Royal Society had lapsed into a moribund state. Its finances were unsound, nonscientific members (clergymen, gentlemen, men of letters, virtuosi, and antiquarians) greatly outnumbered practicing scientists, and many papers in *Philosophical Transactions*, its official organ, described projects that were foolish and impractical. Records show that meetings often degenerated into a preoccupation with trivia, such as one in 1699, when the vice president informed the gathering that the best time to smell flowers was in the morning—or another in 1702, when Sir John Hoskins entertained those who had bothered to turn up with news of a Gloucestershire woman who had finally succeeded in poisoning her husband with arsenic, having tried "Sow-bread, Nightshade, mad-nips, Spiders and Toad without effect." For a time it looked as if the learned body had outlived its usefulness.

But then, in 1703, Isaac Newton was elected president and set about a program of reform. By the time he was elected, he was the preeminent scientist in Britain and perhaps the whole of Europe. His presence lent enormous status and prestige, and his efficient, albeit authoritarian, style rescued the society from bankruptcy. More generally speaking, we may say that Newton more than any other individual rehabilitated the image of science and the scientist and largely rescued it for the rest of the century from the "raillery of the wits" that Thomas Sprat so feared. Although, as we shall see later in chapter five, a few Romantic writers criticized Newton and his methods, the praise he drew from the poets in the eighteenth century was more fulsome than that given to any other scientist before or since.

"Of Newton, to the Muses Dear"

The versification of Newton's achievement began as soon as his work was published. For the frontispiece to Newton's *Principia* (1687), the Astronomer Royal,

Isaac Newton (1642–1727)

In 1705, at a formal ceremony in Trinity College Cambridge, Queen Ann conferred a knighthood on Isaac Newton. Although the honor was as much for Newton's politics as his scientific achievement, it was a significant moment, and for Newton, son of a humble and illiterate farmer from rural Lincolnshire, a great personal triumph. The ceremony was performed in the same college where over forty years earlier he began university life as a subsizar—a poor student who paid his way by performing menial tasks for other members of the college.

Isaac Newton (1642–1727). Newton's achievements drew fulsome praise from the poets. (Library of Congress)

Isaac Newton was born in a farmhouse near the town of Gratham in the county of Lincolnshire on Christmas day 1642. His birth was premature: his mother recalled he could fit at birth into a quart pot, and he was not expected to survive. His father, a yeoman who could not sign his own name, had died three months before his birth. The young Newton was raised initially by his mother and then, after his mother remarried and moved away when he was three, by his grandmother and uncle. It may be the denial of his mother's attention during those crucial early years of life that explains the troubled psyche he displayed all his life.

His long life divides quite neatly into three parts associated with different areas of Britain and different phases of his life: his childhood and youth in Lincolnshire, his studies and academic career at Cambridge, and his work as civil servant and elder statesman of science in London.

He entered Cambridge University in 1661 and graduated with his B.A. in 1665. Later that year there was an outbreak of plague in Cambridge and the university was closed. As a consequence, Newton returned to his Woolsthorpe home and stayed there until 1667. Over these two years he made extraordinary breakthroughs in mathematics and physics: he developed integral calculus, or "fluxions" as he called it; performed experiments on white light by refracting it through a prism and showing its compound nature; began thinking about a new design for a refracting telescope; and began his work on the operation of gravity.

He returned to Cambridge in 1667, and two years later his tutor Isaac Barrow recognized the ability of his former student and resigned his professorship to make way for the young Newton to occupy his chair. In 1671, Newton made a model of his refracting telescope, which, although only just over six inches long, was found to be superior to a refracting telescope of six feet. On the basis of this achievement and an account of his researches into the composition of white light, he was elected Fellow of the Royal Society in 1677.

In 1684, Edmund Halley approached Newton to ask his advice on what orbit a planet would follow if acted upon by a force that varied as the inverse square of the distance from the sun. Halley was staggered when Newton replied that he had begun thinking about this matter in the 1660s and had mathematically demonstrated that it would be elliptical. Halley eventually persuaded Newton to write up his work on this and related subjects, and his thoughts finally appeared in July 1687 in a single volume entitled *Philosophiae Naturalis Principia Mathematica* (the mathematical principles of natural philosophy), one of the most important books ever written. The book consists of three parts: *The Motion of Bodies*, in which Newton laid out his concept of force and demonstrated the nature of elliptical orbits; *The Motion of Bodies in Resisting Mediums*, in which in he discussed the force of friction; and *The System of the World* where, in magisterial style, Newton applied his laws of motion and ideas about gravity to explain the motion of planets, the orbit of comets, and the motion of the moon and the tides.

Newton's original work in the physical sciences began to wane after 1687, although he was still involved in revising his ideas, preparing new editions of *Principia*, and writing up his earlier thoughts on optics. After *Principia*, Newton pursued other nonacademic career interests. Between 1689 and 1690, for example, he was elected as Member of Parliament for Cambridge University—although he never made a speech. In 1693, he suffered a complete mental breakdown. Various theories have been proposed as the cause, including mercury poisoning during his alchemical researches, overwork, the stress of controversy with other scientists such as Hooke, and the loss of an intimate friendship with the brilliant but unstable young Swiss mathematician Fatio de Duillier. He recovered, and in 1695 he was appointed to the prestigious post of warden of the Royal Mint, becoming master of the mint in 1699. He was made president of the Royal Society in 1703 and was reelected to this position every year until his death in 1727.

In 1704, he published his second major scientific work *Optiks*, a book that was to prove as influential on literature as *Principia*. In this work, Newton reported on his work on refraction carried out in the 1660s, outlined his corpuscular theory of the nature of light, and added a section on scientific methodology.

In most science textbooks Newton is recognized and remembered for his pioneering work in mechanics, mathematics, astronomy, and optics. Yet we now know that Newton spent much of his time involved in alchemical and theological research and wrote about half a million words (about four books the size of this one) on each of these subjects, most of which were never printed. Modern historians of science now see his natural philosophy and his alchemical and theological inquiries as complimentary aspects of his own search to understand the mind of God and God's intentions for this world, to reconcile, in effect, the Book of Nature with the Book of Scripture.

The summation of his work in the physical sciences is sometimes called the Newtonian Synthesis, since he took the various ideas about cosmology, matter, and motion proposed by the likes of Galileo, Copernicus, Kepler, and Descartes, rejected some, modified others, and set astronomy and physics on a new unified basis.

As a human being Newton appears to have been cool and aloof. Although he enjoyed the company of the rich and famous, his own tastes were modest, even ascetic. He rarely joked, never formed a close attachment to a woman, and confessed near the end of his life that he had never "violated chastity." Newton died on March 20, 1727, and was given a state funeral at Westminster Abbey.

Edmund Halley, added an ode (in Latin but translated for the English edition) that set the tone for much verse that was to follow. Halley advised readers to:

> Learn ye the potency of the heaven-born mind
> Its thought and life far from the herd withdrawn!

He also called upon heroes of the past to :

> Come celebrate with me in song the name
> Of Newton, to the Muses dear; for he
> Unlocked the hidden treasures of Truth . . .
> Nearer the gods no mortal may approach.

Edmund Halley was one of the few people living who would have understood the mathematics of *Principia* (which Newton had written in Latin and made deliberately difficult to avoid wrangles with those who only had a "smattering of mathematics") and appreciated the monumental significance of the work. But there were other reasons for the apotheosis of Newton, such as the support his physics (and metaphysics) lent to a particular conception of God, the perceived usefulness of his ideas, and the fact that he was British and could therefore be celebrated as an example of national achievement. In David Mallet's *The Excursion* (1728), for example, Newton is "Britain's justest pride, / The boast of the human race," and for James Thomson he is "Britain's Boast."

As a riposte to the satirists, scientists could at last point to the predictive power of Newtonian mechanics as a perfect example of putting theory into practice: Newton's ideas could be applied to problems in ballistics and hydrostatics, his theory of tides was an important addition to naval science, and his lunar tables were an important step toward the determination of longitude, one of the central problems of the day. The wits had also been highly amused by the enormously long telescopes that astronomers were forced to construct if they wanted to avoid the problem of chromatic aberration. Johannes Hevelius (1611–1682), for example, used a 150-foot-long telescope supported by ropes and pulleys. Newton's invention of the reflecting telescope enabled shorter telescopes to be constructed more easily and at lower cost—another example of sound practical science. One spectacular vindication of Newtonianism came in 1758, when Halley's comet returned, just as predicted by the application of Newtonian mechanics.

Above all, Newton provided an image and role for the Creator that the poets found appealing, and even if they could not understand the mathematics the metaphysics was clear enough. Newton transformed the image of the scien-

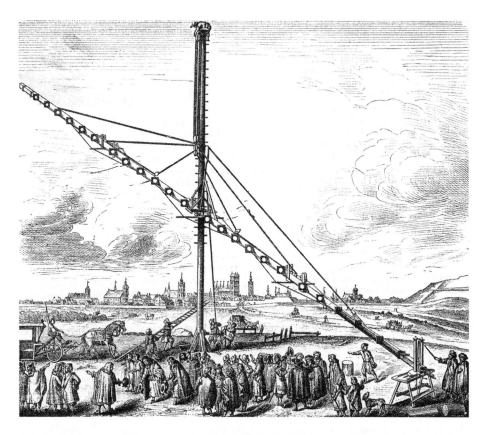

The long telescope of Johannes Hevelius (1611–1687). The problem of spherical aber-
ration meant that in the seventeenth century only lenses of low radius of curvature
could provide really reliable images; but this entailed increasing the length of any tel-
escope. This one is 150 feet long. The construction had to be kept lightweight to avoid
disturbance by winds. In reality such telescopes were difficult to use and their appear-
ance was a gift for the satirists. (Bettmann/Corbis)

tist from someone who dabbles in forbidden knowledge to the wise man who
lays out God's laws, a priest of nature rather than a magician. In this way, Newtonianism provided one of the main pillars of support for what has been called
the "divinization of nature"—a view of the world, allied to Deism, that suggests
that God's mind lies behind the laws of nature and the behavior of all objects on
earth and beyond.

In 1690, two books appeared that helped consolidate this way of thinking.
One was John Locke's *Essay Concerning Human Understanding*, and the
other was Robert Boyle's *The Christian Virtuoso: Shewing that by Being*
Addicted to Experimental Philosophy a Man is rather Assisted than Indis-
posed to be a Good Christian. The two men were friends, and their books were
complementary. The first brought philosophy into alignment with science, and

the second showed the consistency between science and religion. The title of Boyle's work speaks for itself; it was an essay showing the conformity between empiricism and the Christian faith. Boyle died in 1691 (the same year that John Ray (1627–1705) published a similar work entitled *The Wisdom of God Manifested in the Works of Creation*, but left in his will provision for a series of lectures (thenceforth called the Boyle lectures) aimed at stemming the rise of heresy and atheism in England. In the years 1711–1712 William Derham delivered these under the title of *Physico-Theology, or, A Demonstration of the being and Attributes of God from the Works of His Creation*. *Physico-Theology* became an apt name for a whole tradition of theorizing and a mental outlook that found consistency between scientific principles, natural laws, and the existence of a Creator.

In the *Essay* Locke is concerned with epistemology, or how we come to acquire knowledge, and his answer is that sensation is the key route. The real physical universe, in this view, consists of particles in motion. It is these particles and emanations from them (e.g., light) that impact upon our senses to induce in us ideas about the external world. Our ideas of "primary qualities" such as "solidity, extension, motion, or rest" are qualities that objects really do possess; they are out there in the world. Ideas of secondary qualities, however, such as color, sound, and taste, are not in the objects themselves but merely in the organism receiving the sensation. Locke laid the basis, therefore, for an empirical philosophy of knowledge. The mind becomes a blank slate, like a sheet of "white paper, void of all characters, without any ideas." We born with such minds, and what we know derives primarily from experience.

Eighteenth-century science not only helped buttress a certain type of religious belief, but also facilitated a whole new interpretation of the effect of the Fall. In 1684, the English version (the previous had been in Latin) of Thomas Burnet's *Sacred Theory of the Earth* appeared. Burnet proposed the highly unlikely theory that the current irregular shape of the earth, with its mountains, chasms, gorges, and ravines, was the result of original sin and the flood that God sent as punishment. The original prelapsarian earth, he argued, was wonderfully smooth: "it had the beauty of youth and blooming Nature, fresh and fruitful, and not a wrinkle, scar or fracture in all its body; no Rock nor Mountain, no hollow caves, nor gaping Channels, but even and uniform all over" (quoted in Macklem, 1958, p. 7). This book, which perhaps just sixty years earlier would have been greeted with some sympathy, was now highly criticized. Newton had written letters to Burnet explaining his reservations with the ideas when he read the Latin text published earlier in 1681. Following the English version, about thirty tracts appeared over the next twenty years attacking Burnet's basic premise. They proposed instead the idea that God had intended from the outset that the earth should be as it is now, or at most that it's shape resulted from some naturalistic event such as the passing by of a comet. John Ray and John Keill (Savilian Professor of Astronomy at Oxford) both suggested that the features of the earth were part of an original divine purpose: mountains, for example, were necessary for the production of various plants and metals, they bounded nations and empires, were the source of rivers and streams, they directed "inland winds," and provided pleasant prospects from their summits. The response to Burnet reveals the development of a new mindset and the falling from favor of the idea that the physical structure of the world bears the signs of disorder that followed from original sin. In the future, the earth and the heavens would both become symbols of divine order intended from the beginning.

The most authoritative imprimatur granted to this way of thinking came from Newton. In the "General Scholium" of the second edition of *Principia*, Newton wrote:

> This most beautiful system of the sun, planets, and comets, could only proceed from the counsel and dominion of an intelligent and powerful Being. And from his true dominion it follows that the true God is a living, intelligent and powerful being. (*Principia*, vol. 2, Motte's trans., p. 544–545)

In preparing this edition, Newton allowed the brilliant young mathematician Roger Cotes to suggest improvements in presentation and add a preface that assessed the significance of the whole work. Cotes was speaking for a whole generation of scientists, when he observed that:

> Without all doubt this world, so diversified with that variety of forms and motions we find in it, could arise from nothing but the perfectly free will of God directing and presiding over all . . . Newton's distinguished work will be the safest protection against the attacks of atheists. (*Principia*, vol. 1, Motte's trans., p. xxxii–xxxiii)

Although Newton struggled in several places to identify the origin of the force of gravity, he was adamant that it required an agency continually acting. Moreover, the precise placing of the planets, with speeds perfectly calculated to keep them in their orbits, pointed to a cause "very well skilled in mechanics and geometry." To accept Newton's metaphysics involved accepting the rejection of a distinctive sublunary realm with laws peculiar to itself. God had laid out the laws of motion that bound the earth and the farthest stars to his will.

The event that generated a dramatic efflorescence of scientific poetry was the death of Sir Isaac Newton in March 1727. By June of that same year, James

Thomson (1700–1748) completed his "To the Memory of Sir Isaac Newton." He gives fulsome praise for the scientist's work on gravity and cosmology:

> O unprofuse magnificence divine!
> O wisdom truly perfect! Thus to call
> From a few causes such a scheme of things.
> (l. 68–70)

Newton is "first of men" and "our philosophic sun" who with "awful wing pursued / The comet through the long elliptic curve" (l. 76–77). Thomson also celebrates his work on the spectrum:

> Even light itself, which every thing displays,
> Shone undiscovered, till his brighter mind
> Untwisted all the shining robe of day.
> (l. 96–98)

Over the course of the poem, Thomson alludes to Newton's work on the solar system, comets, the orbit of the moon, the tides, the motion of sound, and the composition of white light. The achievement of the poets dwindles in comparison:

> Did ever poet image aught so fair,
> Dreaming in whispering groves by the hoarse brook?
> (l. 120)

Newton, who thought less of the poets than they did of him and once called poetry a "kind of ingenious nonsense" (quoted in Abrams, 1971, p. 300) probably would not have disagreed.

The most influential of Thomson's works was *The Seasons*, the first part of which, *Winter*, appeared in 1726 and the final complete edition in 1746. Between these years Thomson continually made revisions and gradually inserted more science. In common with much verse of his century, the whole work treats nature as a manifestation of the glories of God. In the poem's final form, the season most instructive of Thomson's attitude to science is summer. This section begins with a celebration of the sun and the "strong attractive force" that keeps the whole heliocentric universe revolving. He expresses joy at the fullness of creation, the vastness of the Chain of Being:

> Gradual from these what numerous kinds descend,
> Evading even the microscopic eye!

Full Nature swarms with life.
(l. 287–289)

Shortly after, he argues that God created these myriad forms, often invisible, for a deeper purpose:

Let no presuming impious railer tax
Creative Wisdom, as if aught was formed
In vain.
(l. 318–320)

He concludes *Summer* with a description of comets, object that once caused "guilty nations" to tremble, but that science can now explain, which are welcomed by the enlightened philosophers:

But, above
Those superstitious horrors that enslave
The fond sequacious herd . . .
the enlightened few,
Whose godlike minds philosophy exalts,
The glorious stranger hail.
(l. 1711–1716)

The Seasons brought Thomson the fame and recognition he craved, and his work is a useful illustration of that long tradition, so easily overlooked in the post-Romantic era, of poets offering panegyrics to science and natural philosophy.

Pope and the Essay on Man

When Alexander Pope planned the publication of the four epistles of the *Essay on Man*, he was mindful of the fact that several critics had mauled his previous work. So between 1733 and 1734 he issued this, his finest work, anonymously, then sat back and enjoyed the spectacle of his enemies praising it handsomely. Pope's *Essay* is, in effect, a theodicy: an effort to, as he said, "vindicate the ways of God to man" (Epistle I, l. 16). In laying out his argument Pope draws upon notions commonly encountered in eighteenth-century thought, such as the great chain of being, the principle of plenitude, and the idea that this world was the best of all possible worlds. As Arthur Lovejoy noted, "Next to the word 'Nature' the Great Chain of Being was the sacred phrase of the eighteenth century"(Love-joy, 1961, p. 184), and Pope embraces it enthusiastically:

> Vast chain of being, which from God began,
> Nature aethereal, human, angel, man,
> Beast, bird, fish, insect! what no eye can see
> No glass can reach! From Infinite to thee,
> From thee to Nothing.
> (l. 237–241)

Such lines recall Thomson's earlier version of this theme, "The mighty Chain of beings, lessening down / From infinite Perfection to the Brink / Of dreary Nothing" (*Summer*, 1727 ed., l. 283–286), and Pope may have had *The Seasons* in mind. The principle of plenitude states that God has filled his entire creation with living things, and there are no gaps or breaks in the chain, only subtle gradations from one type to another. As Pope says, this chain is so fixed that to break one link would be to introduce universal confusion:

> From Nature's chain whatever link you strike,
> Tenth or ten thousandth, breaks the chain alike.
> The least confusion but in one, not all
> That system only, but the whole must fall.
> Let Earth unbalanc'd from her orbit fly,
> Planets and Suns run lawless thro' the sky,
> Let ruling Angels from their spheres be hurl'd.
> (*Essay*, l. 245–253)

The passage is reminiscent of the speech of Ulysses in Shakespeare's *Troilus and Cressida* (see chapter two); the difference now is that post Copernicus the earth is in orbit around the sun—although somewhat anachronistically the orbits of the planets are still ruled by angels.

Pope argues that humans should not think of natural disasters such as tempests, earthquakes, and plagues as products of evil; such a view comes only from man's limited apprehension of the greater whole. In Pope's flirtation with Deism, he views all these as part of a universal order, God's master plan:

> All partial Evil, universal Good;
> And spite of Pride, in erring Reason's spite,
> One truth is clear, "Whatever IS, is RIGHT."
> (292–294)

The world Pope inhabited is sometimes called the age of optimism, a time when numerous European thinkers accepted that they lived in the best of all possible worlds. This should not be taken to mean that all eighteenth-century thinkers were cheerful types without a care in the world. They knew the world to be full of bad things, but, they reasoned, this was inevitable to ensure that the world was filled with variety, and any other arrangement would be worse. Indeed, the very fact that Creation is filled with living things (the principle of plenitude) explains why they are imperfect. God, of necessity, must have created creatures different from himself, and these, therefore, could not be perfect. Similarly, differences between creatures must entail differences in degrees of perfection. Hence, each creature is given faculties and powers appropriate to its position. It would be foolish for men to complain that they are not more wise or good since they are made to fit their station in the grand scheme of things. They are superior beings who occupy a higher rung in the ladder of creation. Hence Pope's observation:

> Why has not man a microscopic eye?
> For this plain reason, man is not a fly.
> (Epistle I, l. 193–194)

Since God filled out creation with myriad creatures, it follows that they were not created solely for the use of humans. Many of them were either too small or (in the case of beings on other planets) too distant for humans to see, so it would be absurd to suppose these were there simply for man's benefit. Rather, God created them to connect the chain of being and fill his world:

> While Man exclaims, "See all things for my use!"
> "See man for mine!" replies a pamper'd goose;
> And just as short of Reason he must fall,
> Who thinks all made for one, not one for all.
> (*Essay*, III, l. 45–48)

In the Second Epistle, Pope addresses the curious middle state of man: half angel, half beast, torn between reason and passion, between humility and pride. To Pope, humans stood at a nodal point between physical and incorporeal beings. The passage on the middle state of human existence shows Pope at his best:

> Know then thyself, presume not God to scan;
> The proper study of Mankind is Man.
> Plac'd on this isthmus of a middle state,

A being darkly wise, and rudely great:
With too much knowledge for the Sceptic side,
With too much weakness for the Stoic's pride,
He hangs between; in doubt to act, or rest,
In doubt to deem himself a God, or Beast;
In doubt his Mind or Body to prefer,
Born but to die, and reas'ning but to err; . . .
Sole judge of Truth, in endless Error hurl'd
The glory, jest, and riddle of the world!
(Epistle II, l. 1–18)

In this same epistle, Pope also passes judgment on Newtonian science. Pope had been enthralled by the new astronomy when he heard it expounded by William Whiston at a series of coffeehouse lectures At the same time, however, he had been drawn into a circle of satirical writers: the so called Scriblerus club, which included Jonathan Swift and John Arbuthnot, whose target, through the imaginary writings of one Martinus Scriblerus, included science. These various influences led Pope to both praise Newton and remind his readers that even a Newton is subject to the limitations of human knowledge and has his place on the endless chain:

Superior beings, when of late they saw
A mortal Man unfold all Nature's law,
Admir'd such wisdom in an earthly shape,
And shew'd a NEWTON as we shew an Ape.
Could he, whose rules the rapid comet bind,
Describe or fix one movement of his mind?
(Epistle II, l. 31–36)

This passage is not so much an attack on Newton per se but rather on those who have deified him. The idea of "Superior beings" that "shew'd a Newton" means that Newton is to an angel of higher intelligence as an ape is to man. In other words, even a Newton is part of a scale of excellence and has his limitations. That Pope greatly admired Newton's achievement is shown by the epitaph of just two lines that he wrote following the scientist's death:

Nature and Nature's Laws lay hid in Night
God said, Let Newton be! And All was Light.

Pope was less kind to other scientists. In *The Dunciad*, a long mock-epic satire in which Pope attacks his rivals, critics, and enemies and lumps them together as products of a general "Dullness" taking over the world, he places among these dunces Fellows of the Royal Society (FRS). Pope suggests such people waste their talents studying inconsequential things:

> O! would the Sons of Men once think their Eyes
> And Reason giv'n them but to study Flies.
> (Book IV, l. 453–454)

Similarly, although scientists are not his main target throughout the satire, he complains of those who obtain titles for dull work, men who:

> Impale a Glow-worm, or Vertù profess,
> Shine in the dignity of FRS
> (l. 569–570)

Jonathan Swift

A satirist even less kind to science than Pope was Jonathan Swift, a doctor of divinity and an Anglican dean. Swift demonstrated his satirical skills in *The Tale of a Tub* (1704) and *The Battle of the Books* (1697), attacking divisions in the Christian Church and the hubris of modern scholars and enthusiasts, but he channeled his most savage satire against science (and a good many other things) into Part III of *Gulliver's Travels* (1726). The book is in four parts: Part I, *A Voyage to Lilliput;* Part II, *A Voyage to Brobdingnag;* Part III, A *Voyage to Laputa;* and Part IV, *A Voyage to the Country of the Houyhnhnms.*

In the *Voyage to Laputa*, Gulliver lands on a desolate island. Wondering how he is to survive, he notices another circular island floating toward him. In due course he is hauled up to this floating land mass and there meets the Laputans. The chief preoccupation of these people seems to be mathematics and music. Their ears are specially adapted to hear the music of the spheres, but they are so lost in abstract contemplation that they have to employ servants (flappers) to periodically beat them about the mouths and ears with a bladder on a stick whenever it is necessary for them to speak or listen. Swift here is probably parodying Locke's theory of sensations as outlined in *Essay Concerning Human Understanding* (1690), where it is suggested that all knowledge must come from sense impressions. Gulliver is then led to meet the king and finds him deeply absorbed in a mathematical problem. He is then given some food:

Jonathan Swift (1667–1745)

Jonathan Swift was an Irish author and journalist who rose to become dean of St. Patrick's Cathedral in Dublin and one of the most accomplished writers of prose in the English language. He spent his life between England and Ireland, writing poetry, satirical pamphlets, and books.

He was born in Dublin to English parents—Ireland at the time being ruled from London. His father died before he was born. When he was four, his mother took up residence in England and left her son in the care of his uncle in Ireland. From schooling in Kilkenny he moved to Trinity College, Dublin. He seems to have neglected his studies and failed his papers in natural philosophy and mathematics. He was awarded a degree by "special favour." In 1689 his mother obtained employment for him as secretary to Sir William Temple at Moor Park in Surrey, England. Swift worked here for the next ten years and, taking advantage of a magnificent library, his talents as a writer began to show. In 1695 he sought and obtained ordination as a priest in the Church of Ireland, the Irish branch of the Anglican Church. In 1699 Temple died and Swift returned to Ireland, taking on a series of ecclesiastical posts. In 1701 Trinity College made him a doctor of divinity.

Portrait of Jonathan Swift, drawn by John Thurston and engraved by Alfred Warren. Jonathan Swift (1667–1745), an Anglo-Irish satirist and clergyman, has sometimes been called a critic of modernity since in A Tale of a Tub *and* Gulliver's Travels *he satirized many aspects of scientific rationality and modern learning. (Michael Nicholson/Corbis)*

In 1704 he published two books: *The Tale of a Tub*, a satire on religion, and *The Battle of the Books*, an attempt to justify the superiority of ancient learning over modern, revealing the first inkling of his animosity toward science that was to appear in *Gulliver's Travels*. Both books secured his reputation as a satirist and wit. In 1708 Swift met Joseph Addison and Richard Steele and published the *Bickerstaff Papers*, a

We had two courses, of three Dishes each. In the first Course, there was a shoulder of Mutton cut out into an Aequilateral triangle; a piece of Beef into a Rhomboides; and a Pudding into a Cycloid. (p. 135)

The king, concerned at Gulliver's shabby appearance, orders that he be fitted with a new suit. But the tailor took his measurements in a strange fashion:

He first took my Altitude by a Quadrant, and then with Rule and Compasses described the Dimensions and Outlines of my whole Body, all which he entered upon paper, and in six days brought me my clothes very ill made, satirical attack on an astrologer called John Partridge. In 1714, he teamed up with Alexander Pope, John Gay, and John Arbuthnot to found the Scriblerus Club, with the intention of writing to denounce and combat the spread of pedantry and bad taste.

Swift always hoped that the government would recognize his talents and reward him with an English bishopric. But the best offer he received was the deanery of St. Patrick's Cathedral in Dublin. He never really liked Ireland and was often contemptuous of its people, although he did champion the interests of ordinary Irish people in the face of economic oppression from England.

He visited London again in 1726, this time carrying the manuscript of *Gulliver's Travels*, his best-known work. The book, a devastating parody of travel narratives, was written, as he said, to "vex" people and not "divert" them, and was published anonymously later that year. It is ironic that the book as children's literature now causes more diversion than vexation, something far from the intentions of its author. In 1735, a collected edition of his works appeared, but by this time his health was deteriorating. For most of his life he suffered from Menieres Disease, a condition causing dizziness and nausea. By 1738, he was slipping into senility, and following a stroke he was declared insane in 1742.

Although Swift mercilessly exposed human vice and folly, he also had a tender, playful, and charitable side to his personality. His letters to his dear friend Esther Johnson ("Stella"), for example, are touching. Swift also donated a sizeable portion of his income to charity and provided funds after his death to help found St. Patrick's Hospital for Imbecility. He could also mock himself as he did in *Verses on the Death of Dr. Swift*, written in 1731. The final lines are both moving and funny in their anticipation of his own fate and his death in Ireland in 1745.

> He gave the little wealth he had
> To build a house for fools and mad;
> And show'd by one satiric touch,
> No nation wanted it so much.
> That kingdom he hath left his debtor,
> I wish it soon may have a better.

and quite out of shape, by happening to mistake a Figure in the Calculations. (p. 136)

Similar mistakes are made in the people's buildings: "Their houses are very ill built, the Walls Bevil, without one right angle in any Apartment; and this Defect ariseth from the Contempt they bear to practical geometry" (p. 137).

Swift would have been aware of the attempts of the Royal Society to reform language (see chapter three), and as a writer would probably have resented this. Unsurprisingly, he portrays the Laputans as destitute of understanding in anything but mathematics and music: "Imagination, Fancy, and

Invention, they are wholly strangers to, nor have any Words in their language by which those ideas can be expressed" (p. 138).

Swift was also no doubt enraged by Thomas Sprat's advocacy of returning to a "close, naked, natural way of speaking" when "men delivered so many things, almost in an equal number of words" (Sprat, 1667, p. 113; see also chapter three) and possibly by John Wilkins's *An Essay toward a real Character and a Philosophical Language* (1668), since a scheme for doing away with words entirely appears in this voyage. We are told how

> An expedient was therefore offered, that since Words are only Names for things, it would be more convenient for all men to carry about them such Things as were necessary to express the particular Business they are to discourse on. (p. 157)

The only problem with his scheme, Gulliver notes, is that people who have a lot to say (the sages) have to employ servants to carry large sacks of these object-words as they move around.

In general, the Laputans are not a happy people since they live in a constant state of anxiety about the possibility of a series of celestial calamities:

> that the earth by the continual approaches of the Sun towards it, must in course of time be absorbed or swallowed up. That the face of the sun will by degrees be encrusted with its own effluvia, and give no more light to the world. That the earth very narrowly escaped a brush from the tail of the last comet . . . and that the next, which they have calculated for one and Thirty years hence, will probably destroy us. (p. 138)

They sleep uneasily in their beds and "When they meet an acquaintance in the morning, the first question is about the Sun's health, and what hopes they have to avoid the stroak of the approaching comet" (p. 139).

As the American scholar Marjorie Nicolson showed (see bibliographic essay), these fears are parodies of some serious scientific concerns of Swift's day. In *Principia* (Book I, sections VII and VIII), Newton considered the possibility of the earth slowing down in space but concluded that the effect was small. The "effluvia" on the face of the sun are sunspots, and *Philosophical Transactions* often carried accounts of such phenomena and their possible cause and meaning. Robert Hooke, for example, speculated that such spots indicated that the sun's fiery matter was being consumed. The comet that the Laputans live in dread of is probably Halley's, which the public expected back about 1757 (with a period of seventy-five years since Halley first observed it in 1682) but which

(1)   Numb. 1.

PHILOSOPHICAL
TRANSACTIONS.

Munday, March 6. 1665⁴⁄₅.

The Contents.

An Introduction to this Tract.   An Accompt of the Improvement of
Optick Glasses *at* Rome.   *Of the Observation made in* England,
of a Spot in one of the Belts of the Planet Jupiter.   *Of the motion of
the late* Comet *prædicted. The Heads of many New Observations
and Experiments, in order to an Experimental* History of Cold;
together with some Thermometrical *Discourses and Experiments.
A Relation of a very odd Monstrous* Calf.   *Of a peculiar* Lead-
Ore *in* Germany, *very useful for Essays. Of an Hungarian Bolus, of the same effect with the* Bolus Armenus. *Of the New* American *Whale-fishing about the* Bermudas. *A Narative concerning
the success of the* Pendulum-watches *at Sea for the Longi-
tudes ; and the Grant of a* Patent *thereupon. A Catalogue of the
Philosophical Books publisht by* Monsieur de Fermat, *Counsellour at*
Tholouse, *lately dead.*

The Introduction.

Hereas there is nothing more necessary for promoting
the improvement of Philosophical Matters, than the
communicating to such, as apply their Studies and
Endeavours that way, such things as are discovered or put in practise by others ; it is therefore
thought fit to employ the *Press*, as the most proper way to
gratifie those, whose engagement in such Studies, and delight
in the advancement of Learning and profitable Discoveries,
doth entitle them to the knowledge of what this Kingdom, or
other parts of the World, do, from time to time, afford, as well

A   of

professional astronomers calculated would return in 1758, when it did. Swift published *Gulliver's Travels* in 1726, so thirty-one years from this date brings us close to the expected date. Philosophers at the time (e.g., William Whiston) had speculated about the effect of a comet coming close to the earth.

The Laputans also use a short telescope (possibly an allusion to Newton's reflecting telescope) and with it make a remarkable discovery:

> They have likewise discovered two lesser stars, or satellites, which revolve around Mars, whereof the innermost is distant from the centre of the primary planet exactly three of his diameters, and the outermost five; the former revolves in the space of ten hours, and the latter in twenty one and a half; so that the squares of their periodical Times are very near in the same proportion with the cubes of their distance from the centre of Mars which shows them to be governed by the same law of Gravitation, that influences the other heavenly Bodies. (p. 144)

A quick calculation with Swift's figures shows that he made these satellites conform to Kepler's Third Law, which in modern form states that R^3/T^2 = a constant for any orbiting system, where R = distance of moon from planet (or planet from sun) and T = orbital period. This is not especially remarkable since the mathematics is not complex. What is extraordinary is that the two moons of Mars were not observed until August 1877 by Asaph Hall at the U.S. naval observatory in Washington, D.C. Yet Swift, writing in 1726, anticipates their discovery by 151 years. In addition, although the orbital periods are not exact, they are remarkably close for a complete guess (Table 6).

The probable explanation of this coincidence is that Swift had come across some writings of Kepler, where, misinterpreting a cryptic communication from Galileo about Saturn, the astronomer had supposed Mars might have two moons. Moreover, there did seem to be a pattern at work, since at the time, Mercury and Venus were thought to have no moons, the earth one, and Jupiter four. If Mars were to be assigned two moons, then this would give a pleasing sequence (0124) of a doubling of moons for each planet from the sun. It is also reasonable to suppose that Swift placed them close to Mars since they had not been observed in his time, and arbitrarily chose three and five diameters for the distance away. The orbital periods would then have been fixed in accordance with Kepler's Law (Table 6).

After his instruction in astronomy, Gulliver is lowered from the floating island to the larger, earth-bound island of Balnibarbi, where he is escorted to the Grand Academy of Lagado. This section is so amusing and pertinent to our study that it is reproduced in the primary sources section at the end of this volume. The

TABLE 6: SWIFT'S REMARKABLE ANTICIPATION
OF THE TWO MOONS OF MARS

Attribute	Swift in *Gulliver's Travels*	Modern Observations
Number of moons	Two	Two
Distance from Mars of inner moon (Phobos)	Three times diameter, which gives 13,600 km	6,000 km for Phobos
Distance from Mars of outer moon (Deimos)	Five times the diameter, which gives 27,200 km	20,100 km for Deimos
Rotational period of inner	10 hours	7 hours and 39 minutes
Rotational period of outer	21 hours 30 minutes	30 hours

academy is a satirical portrait of the Royal Society, in particular the sort of research institution that Bacon envisaged in *The New Atlantis*. Here researchers are engaged in attempts to turn ice into gunpowder, extract sunbeams from cucumbers, turn excrement back to food, and other improbable activities. Many of Swift's absurd projects can be traced to actual reported experiments. The idea of extracting sunbeams from cucumbers may refer to the work of Stephen Hales, the clergyman amateur scientist who collected the "airs" or gases given off from a whole range of heated vegetables and speculated on the penetration of sunlight into plants. The experiment of the astronomers who construct a combined weathercock and sundial is even closer to the mark, since Sir Christopher Wren designed an automatic wind recorder in 1666 by linking together a weathercock, a clock, and a pencil.

What does the Laputa episode reveal about Swift's attitude to science? At first sight it would seem obvious: Swift is opposed to the enterprise of science and belittles its usefulness. To some extent Swift had already declared his colors in *The Battle of the Books* (an examination of the ancients-versus-moderns debate), in which he showed more sympathy for ancient learning than new ideas. But what Swift seems to object to specifically is the importation of the scientific method to areas where it does not belong. He rejects the atomistic conception of language where words are merely things in a one-to-one correspondence— hence the ludicrous spectacle of scholars carrying sacks of objects. Elsewhere in the academy Gulliver meets a "projector" who has developed a mechanical device for writing books by jumbling words together until something makes sense. Generally, Swift seems to be rejecting abstraction where practical reason applied on a moral basis would be better.

Likewise, Swift is scornful of attempts to bring precision and mathematical certainty to subjects where practical wisdom or prudence would be more appropriate. So the Laputans miscalculate his clothes, their houses are badly built, and their political system is in a mess. Swift here is echoing Aristotle's famous lines in his *Nicomachean Ethics:* "It is the mark of an educated mind to accept just that exactitude in any subject that the nature of the matter permits" (quoted in Patey, 2002, p. 380).

Scientists may take some comfort from the fact that Swift was even more critical of politicians. A fitting note on which to end here is Swift's voice of the king of the Brobdingnags in Gulliver's second journey :

> And he gave it for his opinion, that whoever could make two ears of corn, or two blades of grass, to grow upon a spot of ground where only one grew before, would deserve better of mankind, and do more essential service to his country, than the whole race of politicians put together. (Part II, Chap vii, p. 113)

It is too difficult to resist the observation that in the centuries that followed Swift, this is precisely what science has done.

Nature Poems: Scientific and Moral

Generally, poets of the second half of the eighteenth century viewed science more sympathetically than Swift, and what might be called the scientific nature poem, often in the style of Pope, became a common genre for the rest of the century. The standard pattern for this kind of verse was first the reminder to readers of the wonders of nature—the size and scale of the universe and the myriad living forms as revealed by the microscope—followed by a reflection on this as a sign of God's power and diligence, and of the lowly state of man. A typical example is Mary Leapor's *The Enquiry*, first published in 1748. The poem is written in the style of Pope, a poet she greatly admired, and Leapor includes a conventional statement on the Chain of Being and an expression of amazement at the new life forms revealed by the microscope:

> How near one Species to the next is joined,
> The due Gradations please a thinking mind;
> And there are Creatures no eye can see,
> That for a Moment live and breathe like me.
> These we can reach—and may we not suppose
> There still are Creatures more minute than those.
> (l. 36–44)

An Experiment on a Bird in the Air Pump *by Joseph Wright of Derby (c. 1767). A means for removing air from a sealed container was initially developed by Otto von Guericke of Magdeburg (Germany). It was improved by Hooke and Boyle and became a popular piece of equipment in the eighteenth century. Some scientists, such as James Ferguson, used such equipment to show that in the absence of air animals died. Derby effectively captures the moral ambiguities surrounding scientific experimentation. The experimentalist is about to reintroduce air into the jar to demonstrate that air is needed for life. The scientist has an almost manic gaze into the distance, while the figure in the foreground seems concerned only with recording the mathematical details. The only spectators concerned about the bird's suffering are the children. The idea of the natural virtue of children was a foreshadowing of the Romantic conception of the child to be developed later by Rousseau and Wordsworth. (National Gallery Collection/Corbis)*

She goes on to imagine that drops of water on a leaf may contain "whales" that live just "half a day." Leapor spoke with more truth than perhaps she knew, for she fell prey to one of these invisible microscopic life forms and died of measles in 1746, aged just twenty-four.

Night Thoughts

A major poem of this period is Edward Young's melancholic *Night Thoughts*, a work admired by continentals, such as Diderot and Robespierre, and much reprinted during the eighteenth century. The poem, once thought to be a literary masterpiece, is now generally regarded as rather gloomy and ponderous. The work was originally published as nine separate poems (each corresponding to a night of thinking), and these were published between 1742 and 1745. The first poem followed the death of Young's wife in 1741, an event that plunged him into a brooding melancholy and led him to reflect upon life and death.

In *Night Thoughts*, Young argues a case for the immortality of man, the superiority of the Christian faith, and the lowness of the merely sensual life. The final night thought (the ninth) is called *The Consolation*, and here Young conducts a "moral survey of the nocturnal heavens." The heavens carry a moral message, since the "stars teach as well as shine" (1230) for "'Tis Nature's system of Divinity" (l. 644). Like Pope, Young is quite content with the idea that other beings (above man in perfection) may exist:

> What read we here?—Th' existence of God?
> Yes; and of other beings, man above;
> *Natives of ether! Sons of higher climes!*
> (l. 657–659)

Then, like Dante, Chaucer, and Donne before him, Young ventures on an imaginary "dream journey" through the spheres, only now the distances are immense. He travels so far that the sun becomes invisible:

> O nature's Alps I stand,
> *And see a thousand firmaments beneath!*
> A thousand systems! As a thousand grains!
> (l. 1750)

Here then, as elsewhere, we have the eighteenth century reply to Donne's lament that philosophy calls forth doubt. Astronomy now teaches piety:

> Devotion! Daughter of Astronomy!
> An undevout astronomer is mad.
> (l. 773)

A similar imaginary experience is found in *A Summer Evening's Meditation* by Anna Laetitia Barbauld (1743–1825). Barbauld (née Aikin) was encouraged in her writing by Joseph Priestley, a tutor at the Warrington Academy in northwest England, where her father taught. The poem, although not published until 1773, seems to have been inspired by Young. Barbauld imagines herself journeying from the earth, past the moon, beyond Mars, Jupiter, and Saturn, and then (since at the time no planets beyond Saturn were known) moving among the stars:

> I launch into the trackless deeps of space,
> Where, burning round, ten thousand suns appear,
> Of elder beam; which ask no leave to shine
> Of our terrestrial star, nor borrow light
> From the proud regent of our scanty day; . . .
> Here must I stop
> Or is there aught beyond.
> (l. 83–91)

The Didactic Poem

It is not a huge leap from the philosophic poem that uses science as part of a broad canvas to preach a moral message about the position of man in the universe, to poetry whose very purpose is to celebrate the results of scientific research. Hence, toward the end of the eighteenth century, the didactic scientific poem comes to prominence—an experiment that had, however, little lasting effect on science or literature. Many such poems were written during this period, but the best known are those written by Erasmus Darwin, physician, poet, and grandfather to Charles Darwin. In 1789 Darwin published *The Loves of the Plants*, a work of nearly 2,000 verses explaining the sex lives of hundreds of different plants based on the Linnean system of classification. In 1791 this was reprinted as part II of *The Botanic Garden* and another work, *The Economy of Vegetation* added as part I. His stated aim in *The Loves of the Plants* was to

> Inlist Imagination under the banner of Science; and to lend her votaries from the looser analogies, which dress out the imagery of poetry, to the stricter ones which form the ratiocination of philosophy. (Quoted in McNeil, 1986, p.184)

To appreciate Darwin's achievement we need to examine his social affinities, ideological outlook, and the social context of America and Europe in the 1790s. Darwin was a central figure in the Midlands Enlightenment. His social circle included inventors, writers, philosophers, and entrepreneurs who shared his liberal beliefs and who provided the intellectual driving force behind the Industrial Revolution. This group met formally in a gathering called The Lunar Society of Birmingham, and its members included the manufacturer Mathew Boulton

(1728–1809), the engineer James Watt (1736–1819), the industrial chemist James Kier (1735–1820), the potter Josiah Wedgwood (1730–1795), and the chemist, philosopher, and theologian Joseph Priestley (1733–1804).

The outlook of this group was radical and socially progressive. They favored the abolition of slavery, were sympathetic to the American Revolution, and supported (in its early stages) the French revolution. Darwin's poetry reflects his affinities with these causes as well as the forces of industrialization. In *The Loves of the Plants*, for example, we are given a joyous picture of the mechanized carding and spinning of cotton:

> With wiry teeth revolving cards release
> The tangled knots, and smooth the ravell'd fleece;
> Next moves the iron hand with fingers fine,
> Combs the wide card, and forms the eternal line;
> Slow, with soft lips, the Whirling can acquires
> The tender skeins, and wraps in rising spires.
> (Canto II, l. 95–101)

For Darwin, the heroes of the day, justly celebrated in his verses, were the freethinkers and the entrepreneurs. People such as the engineers Thomas Savery and James Bridley, the industrialist Richard Arkwright, and the scientist and political reformer Benjamin Franklin. This mingling of descriptions of the sex lives of plants with paeans for the captains of industry may seem odd until we realize that this was part of a coherent epistemological stance to encompass the working of nature, matter, and organic life under one framework. This project of showing the continuity between matter and mind was to be continued in a more coherent fashion by his grandson Charles. The program logically entailed an account of the origin and development of life, and Erasmus obliges here also. He envisions the creation of the universe as a series of explosions and replaces the Genesis myth with a pagan notion of "Love Divine" calling forth life from inert matter. He also seems to have accepted ongoing spontaneous generation—reporting that he had observed tiny animacules or "eels" appearing in a sealed vessel of flour and water. He suspected that humans had evolved from simpler life forms but was unable to provide a mechanism. He also knew that creatures were adapted to their environment and that reproduction produced surplus individuals that were culled by competition—"One great Slaughter House the warring world" was how he described organic nature—but he was unable to connect the two.

The Botanic Garden was a huge success on both sides of the Atlantic. By the end of the 1790s four editions had been published in London, and in 1798 in New York the scholar and freethinker Dr. Elihu Hubbard Smith (1771–1798)

"The New Morality" by James Gillray. This is a satirical print attacking the radical ideas of Erasmus Darwin (shown as an ape carrying a basket on his head labelled "Jacobin plants" stand around as pamphlets issue from the "Cornucopia of Ignorance.") and others. Joseph Priestley, Gilbert Wakefield, Coleridge, and Southey. The socially progressive ideas of the Lunar industrialists and Enlightenment radicals came under attack as Britain drifted into war with revolutionary France. (Courtesy of The British Library)

issued an American edition. *The Loves* brought Darwin fame, and he often crowed to his friends how much he earned from the royalties. Horace Walpole thought it the "most delicious poem on earth." William Wordsworth, Samuel Coleridge, and Humphrey Davy were, for a time, equally impressed.

Toward the end of the century, however, both literary taste and the political atmosphere were on the turn. In 1797, as the war against Napoleon fared badly and the French occupied a good part of Europe, a conservative backlash was inevitable. To boost morale and combat subversive views, a magazine called *The Anti-Jacobin* was founded, published by George Canning (then undersecretary of state for foreign affairs and later prime minister), John Frere, and George Ellis. Darwin was an obvious target, and in 1799, a poem appeared called *Loves of the Triangles*. The poem was a wicked and funny parody of *The Loves of the*

Plants, aiming to "enlist the Imagination under the banner of Geometry" and claiming that humans had risen to their current state from the cabbages of the field. The poem also poked fun at Darwin's playful eroticism. Suddenly Darwin was linked with the French revolution, irreligious views on evolution, and sexual immorality—all dangerous forces that threatened to undermine the social order. Two months later the same magazine published Gillray's cartoon (shown page 117) called "New Morality, an attack on the radicalism of Darwin, Priestley, Wakefield, Southey, and Coleridge."

Although Darwin shrugged off these insults and carried on writing *The Temple of Nature* (published in 1803, one year after his death), he must have felt that opinion was turning against the philosophy of enlightened social reform that he and his Lunar friends had espoused. In 1798 Wordsworth and Coleridge published their *Lyrical Ballads*, in which they stated their rejection of the "gaudiness and inane phraseology of many modern writers" (and hence neoclassical verse) in favor of, as they said in the 1800 edition, "the real language of men." Only a few years later William Blake would attack the very things that Darwin praised: the science of Newton, Bacon, and Locke, and the "cogs tyrannic" of industrial progress. But this subject belongs to the next chapter.

Bibliographic Essay

A classic single volume on this period is William Powell Jones's *The Rhetoric of Science* (London: Routledge and Kegan Paul, 1966); this book was used to help assess the significance of the physico-theological theme in poetry and the shift to natural history after about 1760. The book is especially valuable in identifying little-known works of this period. An excellent brief introduction to the phenomenon of the Enlightenment is given by Roy Porter, *The Enlightenment* (London: Palgrave, 2001). Porter provides a good account of the European context of this movement. An examination of science as part of the cultural context for literature of this period is ably given by James Sambrook in *The Eighteenth Century: The Intellectual and Cultural Context of English Literature 1700–1789* (London and New York: Longman, 1993). The first chapter of this work is entitled "Science," and Sambrook accords it the importance it deserves. There is also a useful chapter ("Science") by G. S. Rousseau in *The Context of English Literature: The Eighteenth Century*, edited by Pat Rogers (London: Methuen, 1978). Rousseau gives a good treatment of medicine and psychology (not covered in this chapter) and ends with an annotated list of further reading.

The edition of *Gulliver's Travels* used in this chapter was *Jonathan Swift's Gulliver's Travels*, edited by Albert J. Rivero (New York and London: Norton,

2002). This edition has the advantage of the full text as well as a series of critical commentaries at the end. The chapter by Douglas Lane Patey, "Swift's Satire on Science and the Structure of Gulliver's Travels," is especially useful. The source used for some of Swift's own writings and memoirs of Marinus Scriblerus was *Satires and Personal Writings of Jonathan Swift*, edited by W. A. Eddy (London and New York: Oxford University Press, 1962). Two articles are particularly useful in helping trace the source of Swift's ideas. The first is "The Scientific Background of Swift's Voyage to Laputa" by Marjorie Nicolson and Nora Mohler in *Annals of Science* 2, 1937, pp. 299–334. The second, which places Swift in a wider context and considers all three of Gulliver's voyages, is "Swift and Natural Science" by George Potter in *Philological Quarterly*, vol. 20, no. 2, April 1941, 97–118, Andrew Varney also provides a good treatment of *Gulliver's Travels*, *The Spectator*, and Thomson's *Seasons* in chapter seven, "Science and Nature" of his *Eighteenth Century Writers in Their World* (New York: St. Martin's Press, 1999). Varney captures the impact of science on eighteenth-century writers and offers a good analysis of Swift's attitude toward science as well as the new concept of nature in eighteenth-century verse.

For some of the details about Newton's life, Frank Manuel's *A Portrait of Isaac Newton* (New York: Da Capo Press, 1968) was consulted. There are, of course, numerous biographies of Newton; this one offers a more psychological portrait than most. An English translation of Newton's *Principia* is available, edited by Florian Cajori (Berkeley and Los Angeles: University of California Press, 1962). Cajori added a commentary to Andrew Motte's 1729 translation. This version contains Halley's poetic ode at the start, together with Cotes's important preface to the second edition.

For a discussion of the profound change in the concept of natural law and conceptions of the Fall, *The Anatomy of the World: Relations between Natural and Moral Law from Donne to Pope* by Michael Macklem (Minneapolis: University of Minnesota Press, 1958) is a useful volume. This work provides a thoughtful treatment of the contrast between Donne's *Anatomy of the World* and Pope's *Essay on Man*. It also provides material to judge the significance of Thomas Burnet's *Sacred Theory of the Earth*. The edition of Pope's *The Dunciad* used in this chapter was edited by James Sutherland (New Haven, CT: Yale University Press, 1965). A good edition of Pope's *Essay on Man* is that edited by Maynard Mack (Newhaven, CT: Yale University Press, 1970). For some of the sources of scientific ideas available to Pope, it is worth reading *This Long Disease My Life: Alexander Pope and the Science* by Majorie Nicolson and G. S. Rousseau (Princeton, NJ: Princeton University Press, 1968). This book provides an interesting medical history of Pope together with discussions on his views on other sciences.

A useful anthology of verse for this period is *Eighteenth-Century Poetry: An Annotated Anthology* (Oxford: Blackwell, 1999), edited by David Fairer and Christine Gerrard. This volume is especially useful for women writers such as Anna Barbauld and Mary Leapor. A reading of Erasmus Darwin that places him firmly in a political context is Maureen McNeil's article "The Scientific Muse: The Poetry of Erasmus Darwin" in *Languages of Nature*, edited by Ludmilla Jordanova (London: Free Association Books, 1986). McNeil shows Darwin to be a champion of the ideology of industrialization, but also goes further to contrast Darwin with William Blake. For a fresh and lively treatment of the whole Lunar movement see Jenny Uglow's *The Lunar Men* (London: Faber and Faber, 2002). Uglow adds new vistas to this well trodden path in a readable yet scholarly volume.

An interesting examination of the relationship between the language used by eighteenth-century poets and the language of science is given by John Arthos in *The Language of Natural Description in Eighteenth Century Poetry* (London: Frank Cass, 1966). Arthos suggests (in his thesis first published in 1949) that many features of poetic language in this period can be related to the scientific need for a fixed language. A short and instructive summary of this theme and the broader one of the role of metaphor in scientific and poetic language is given by Donald Davie in *The Language of Science and the Language of Literature 1700–1740* (London and New York: Sheed and Ward, 1963).

Though there was insufficient space in this chapter to cover the interesting attitude of Samuel Johnson, readers are encouraged to consult *Samuel Johnson and the New Science* (Madison, Milwaukee and London: University of Wisconsin Press, 1971).

The Touch of Cold Philosophy: The Response to Science in Romantic Literature 1790–1840

John Cartwright

Unweaving the Rainbow

In terms of the relationship between perception and reality, the rainbow is an interesting phenomenon. Looking at one, it is tempting to imagine that there is a bow "out there" that walking toward we could touch. In reality, of course, the bow recedes as fast as we approach since it only exists in our minds. Two people looking at a rainbow are seeing different bows, since each is created uniquely for and by the spectator. Sunlight refracts through raindrops into the eyes of each person and the brain is convinced that there is a semicircular band of light hanging in the sky. There is a nice paradox here: the rainbow exists in the mind, but not only in the mind since we cannot just invent a rainbow. One feature of Romantic thought, as we shall see, was the search for an understanding of how the mind constructs reality. Hence, the rainbow becomes particularly interesting in this respect. The more so since both scientists and poets have had much to say on the subject. In this chapter we will examine the attempt of Romantic writers to forge a new kind of epistemology, a theory of knowledge that rejected the passive and mechanical role assigned to the mind by eighteenth century thinkers and asserted instead the essential creativity of the human imagination.

In his *Optiks* (1704), Isaac Newton gives a marvelously succinct and elegant explanation of how rainbows are formed (Book One, Part II, Proposition IX, Problem IV). Others before him had suspected that it had something to do with sunlight passing through raindrops, but it took Newton's genius to realize that the colors we see were already in the light from the sun (and not added to it by the water). It took his mathematical ability to show how, and in what direction, the rainbow is thereby formed.

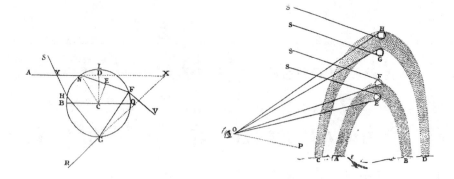

Two diagrams from Newton's Optiks *(4th Edition, 1730, p. 170 and 173). The circle shows the path of a ray of light incident onto a raindrop at A emerging at G to give one of the colors of the rainbow. The rainbow diagram shows how the eye perceives each bow thereby formed. The lower bow arises from one internal reflection; the higher and fainter bow from two. (Courtesy of John Cartwright)*

In a piece of elegant reasoning, Newton proceeds from the laws of refraction and reflection to show that two rainbows will be formed, one corresponding to a single internal reflection in the raindrop, and the other to two reflections. The former will be the brighter, and the violet portion (the lower) will stand at an angle of 40 degrees to the angle of the sunlight (POE in the figure) and the red at 42 degrees (POF). The higher bow will be fainter and the angles of the colors will be 51 degrees for the red (POG) and 54 degrees for the violet (POH) at the top. The colors will be observed at precisely these angles, and so a bow results, since these are the positions where the angles can be found (imagine the angle POE as a pair of compasses sweeping out a line in the sky). Needless to say, these angles correspond precisely to the positions in which rainbows are actually observed—a wonderful confirmation of the power of theoretical reasoning.

Newton's account then must surely represent an intellectual triumph: another puzzling phenomenon of nature brought within the circumference of human reason, another case of science freeing humankind from the tyranny of superstition. After Newton's death, many poets celebrated his achievement. As noted in chapter four, the praise of James Thomson (1700–1748) was particularly fulsome. In "To the Memory of Sir Isaac Newton" (1727), for example, Thomson lauds Newton for explaining the rainbow, versifies the spectral sequence (red, orange, yellow, etc.), and notes "How just, how beauteous the refractive law." Similarly, Mark Akenside, in "The Pleasures of the Imagination" (1744), writes that the rainbow was never so pleasing "as when first / the hand of science pointed out the path / In which the sun beams . . . fall on the wat'ry cloud." He even goes on to explain in verse how each reflects from the interior of the raindrop.

By the early nineteenth century, however, a different outlook prevailed among British poets. Whereas Thomson and Akenside met science on its own ground—celebrating an objective account of the formation of the rainbow—William Wordsworth's response was deliberately personal and emotional: "My heart leaps up when I behold / A rainbow in the sky." An episode that neatly illustrates this changed temper is that of a dinner party held at the house of the painter Benjamin Haydon on the December 28, 1817. Haydon had gathered together William Wordsworth, Charles Lamb, John Keats, and Tom Monkhouse, and the group dined in front of Haydon's unfinished painting "Christ's Triumphant Entry into Jerusalem"—a painting into which Haydon had placed portraits of Newton (depicted as a believer), Voltaire (a skeptic) and Wordsworth. At some point in the evening, as Haydon recalled, Charles Lamb

> in a strain of humour beyond description, abused me for putting Newton's head into my picture—"a fellow" he said "who believed nothing unless it was as clear as the three sides of a triangle." And then he and Keats agreed he has destroyed all the poetry of the rainbow by reducing it to the prismatic colours. It was irresistible to resist him and we all drank "Newton's health and confusion to mathematics." It was a delight to see the good humour of Wordsworth giving in to all our frolics. (Quoted in Thomas and Ober, 1989, p. 29)

This changed attitude toward Newton, as least in the minds of Lamb and Keats, reveals an important strand in Romantic thought. By the time Keats drank to the toast, some were beginning to feel that science had somehow destroyed the mystery that fed the poets' imagination. Eighteenth months after the dinner party, Keats wrote up his reservations about Newtonian science in the poem *Lamia* (1820). The crucial passage is:

> Do not all charms fly
> At the mere touch of cold philosophy?
> There was an awful rainbow once in heaven;
> We know her woof, her texture; she is given
> In the dull catalogue of common things.
> Philosophy will clip an Angel's wings,
> Conquer all mysteries by rule and line,
> Empty the haunted air, and gnomed mine-
> Unweave a rainbow, as it erewhile made
> The tender-person'd Lamia melt into a shade.
> (Part 2, 229–238)

Again the contrast with Thompson is instructive. For Thomson, it was Newton who was "awful" (as in full of awe rather than bad) and possessed the "sage instructed eye" that understood the origin of the bow while, in contrast, the ignorant swain foolishly runs to catch the bow that only fades away before him.

The visionary poet William Blake also harbored distrust of scientific rationality. He objected to Locke's model of the mind as blank slate (or *tabula rasa*) that remains passive while experience leaves its mark. Instead he asserted the essential creativity of perception, as when he considered what we "see" when the sun rises:

> "What," it will be Question'd, "When the Sun rises do you not see a round disk of fire somewhat like a Guinea?" O no, no, I see an Innumerable company of the Heavenly host crying "Holy, Holy, Holy is the Lord God Almighty." I question not my Corporeal or Vegetative Eye any more than I would Question a Window concerning a Sight: I look thro it & not with it.
>
> (From "A Vision of the Last Judgment," in *Blake's Poetry and Designs*, Johnson and Grant, 1979, p. 416.)

Blake railed against what he viewed as a unified threat to the imagination and to the humane life: Locke's sensationalist epistemology, Newton's mechanical laws of nature, materialism, atomism, and industrial capitalism. His own answer to the problem of perception and reality was the suggestion that the poet apprehended eternal verities (and did not slavishly imitate nature as the empiricists supposed) through the inspection of innate ideas. In his annotation on a book by the artist Joshua Reynolds he wrote: "Innate ideas are in Everyman, Born within him; they are truly Himself. The man who says we have No Innate Ideas must be a Fool and a Knave" (quoted in Keynes, 1966, p. 459).

Just nine years after *Lamia* was published, the American poet Edgar Allan Poe echoed the same sentiments as Keats but with more bitterness in his sonnet "To Science" (1829):

> Science! true daughter of Old Time thou art!
> Who alterest all things with thy peering eyes.
> Why preyest thou thus upon the poet's heart,
> Vulture, whose wings are dull realities?
> . . .
> Hast thou not torn the Naiad from her flood,
> The Elfin from the green grass, and from me
> The summer dream beneath the tamarind tree? (l. 1–4, 12–14)

The complaint of Keats and Poe seems to be twofold. Firstly, that science demolishes belief in myths and fairy lore, and secondly, that by explaining a complex and beautiful phenomenon, such as the rainbow, the aesthetic experience attending it is somehow destroyed. The modern response to Keats might be that the first is no bad thing and the second complaint is a fallacy. The modern response to Blake is that in some ways he was right in suspecting the mind was creative in perception, and that the empiricists of the eighteenth century were wrong when they supposed that the human mind is totally constructed afresh by the experience of each individual. But a coherent account of this had to wait for the philosophy of Kant, explored later in this chapter, and the evolutionary biology of Darwin, explored in chapter seven.

Misguided or astute, the views of Keats, Blake, and Poe are products of a change of sensibility that occurred over the years 1780–1830 and come under the heading of the Romantic revolution, a complex phenomenon that we need to explore.

The Romantic Revolution—Context and Characteristics

The Romantic revolution in literature and the arts (occupying roughly the period between 1790 and the 1830s) coincided with other profound changes in culture and society that were taking place in Europe and America. In 1776 the American Declaration of Independence from Britain was an event heralding democratic reform and self-government, a government, moreover, to be founded on a constitution without hereditary legislators. The year 1776 also saw the publication of Adam Smith's *Wealth of Nations*, a remarkably prescient economic text in which Smith foresaw the power and potential of industrial capitalism and the free market. As Smith was writing, there were signs that Britain herself was moving from an agrarian economy, with its levers of power in the hands of the landed gentry, to an industrial-capitalist democracy. If Britain provided the model and driving force for economic change, then the French revolution provided the images, ideas, and vocabulary for political reform that both inspired and terrified other nations.

Although virtually all scholars agree that there was a Romantic movement and that it is easy enough to spot a Romantic artist or piece of work, Romanticism was not a single coherent creed. Pinning down a list of its defining characteristics is more difficult. In very general terms, Romantic thinkers were in revolt against many of the norms, conventions, attitudes, and values of the Enlightenment. The result was a profound dislocation in thought. More abstractly, we might say that following the Romantic revolution the Western mind became bifurcated, leading to a dislocation between the sciences and the humanities that has been with us ever since (see chapter eleven). The following table shows some of the contrasts between the Enlightenment and Romantic outlooks.

TABLE 7: CONTRASTING ENLIGHTENMENT AND ROMANTIC PERSPECTIVES

Note that compiling lists and tables always invites exceptions. It should be borne in mind that this is an illustrative and not definitive list.

The Enlightenment or The Age of Reason c. 1680–1780	Romanticism c. 1780–1830
Epistemology	
Atomistic and reductionist	Holistic
Knowledge to be sought through experience and reason. Distrust of emotions. Truths to be tested.	Knowledge attained through imagination. Truth should be ennobling and sublime. Personal feelings important.
The mind can grasp reality by attending carefully to sensations.	The mind is active in shaping reality. The mind illuminates the world.
Ontology	
General laws that define a single reality. The truth is out there and can be uncovered.	Multiple realities, different perspectives valued. Truths are created.
Nature	**Nature**
Nature as an object for experimentation and technological mastery. The laws of nature a sign of God's plan.	Nature as sacramental, a source of mystery, revelation, and moral guidance. A longing for a time of lost unity between man and nature.
Function of art and artist	
Writing must conform to conventions such as the balance and symmetry. Special poetic diction favored. Literature to illustrate general truths and normalities of human life. Wit is prized.	Art as important link between the natural and spiritual worlds. Cult of individual artist. Art creates realities; does not simply record them. Writing to capture the flow of ordinary experience through everyday language. Rejection of commercialism. Art for art's sake. Artist as hero, often misunderstood and alienated from conventional society.
Key Metaphors	
Machine	Organism
Mind as mirror	Mind as lamp
Human Mind	
Best understood by examining sense perception and cognition. Strong feelings to be controlled.	Importance of subconscious, emotion, imagination, and inspiration. Drug-induced visions important. Concern with both the noble and heroic side of human nature as well as the darker side.
Mind of adult superior to child. Children valuable since they can be socialized and matured into adults.	The insights of children valued. Children can grasp truths that adults have forgotten or have become immured against.

TABLE 7: CONTINUED

Note that compiling lists and tables always invites exceptions. It should be borne in mind that this is an illustrative and not definitive list.

The Enlightenment or The Age of Reason c. 1680–1780	Romanticism c. 1780–1830
Social progress and social structures	
Optimistic view of progress through science, technology and education.	Belief in perfectibility of man through radical social reform.
Past civilizations and their cultures valued for their historical interest. Modern civilization an advance on predecessors, hence division of post-classical European history into Dark Ages, Middle Ages, and Enlightenment.	Ambivalence towards modernity. Respect for medievalism as time of spiritual growth. Past cultures as repositories of collective wisdom
Carefully regulated human institutions can improve people. Fondness for neat, fixed social hierarchies where each knew their place.	Suspicion of human institutions. Elevation of the nobility of the child and people in traditional cultures–the "noble savage" concept. Retreat from urban civilization to search for wisdom among people living simple lives. Freedom to move across social boundaries and conventions valued.
Theology	
Reason more important than revelation; the latter must be justified by appeals to former. Deism. Disparagement of medieval superstitions and concern with the supernatural. Temporary alliance in eighteenth century between science, poetry, and religion.	Skeptical of orthodox Church hierarchies, but experimented with alternative mystical religions, e.g. Gnosticism, pantheism. God as a numinous creative force.
Exemplars	
Francis Bacon, John Locke, Isaac Newton (as perceived), Francois-Marie Voltaire, Marquise de Châtelet Denis Diderot, Sophie Volland, Marquis de Condorcet, Antoine Lavoisier, Elizabeth Montagu, Thomas Paine, Mary Wollstonecraft, Ben Franklin, Joseph Priestley.	Jean Jacques Rousseau, Goethe, Emmanuel Kant, William Blake, William Wordsworth, Elisabeth Oakes-Smith, Mary Shelley, Lucy Aikin, Anna Letitia Barbauld, Ralph Waldo Emerson, Henry David Thoreau, Nathaniel Hawthorne, Edgar Allen Poe, Walt Whitman, Casper David Friedrich, Joseph Mallord Turner, Ludwig van Beethoven.

Romantic Epistemologies

Wordsworth

William Wordsworth, in his youth at least, had a much more open-minded view of Locke and Newtonian science than William Blake. At Cambridge Wordsworth would have encountered both the epistemology of Locke and its direct rival Neo-platonism. The Cambridge Platonists compared the spirit of man with the candle of the Lord. In other words, the human mind first illuminates the world in order

William Wordsworth (1770–1850)

William Wordsworth was born on April 7, 1770, at Cockermouth in the English Lake District, an area that subsequently became strongly identified with his name and work. His mother died in 1778, and his father sent him away to the grammar school in the nearby town of Hawkshead. The school gave Wordsworth a solid foundation in the classics, mathematics, and science. He thrived at this school (despite the death of his father in 1783) and was successful enough to enter Cambridge University in 1787. His achievement at Cambridge was unimpressive, but he did receive a degree in 1791.

Portrait of William Wordsworth. Wordsworth's attitude toward science is quite complex. Generally he distrusted the use of scientific rationalism and empiricism where he thought they did not belong, such as accounting for the moral sense and the role of the imagination. (Library of Congress)

In 1790 Wordsworth made the first of several visits to France and was there for the celebration of the anniversary of the fall of the Bastille. He returned there again in November 1791 and became a passionate supporter of the French revolution. On his second visit he also fell in love with, and had a child by, Annette Vallon, the daughter of a surgeon in Orleans. Financial problems forced Wordsworth to return to England in 1792, and he did not see Annette or their child again until 1802.

On his return to England, Wordsworth was confused, divided, and disillusioned. He had been sickened by the sight of mob violence in Paris, but when England declared war on France in 1793, he was still enough of a republican to feel that his own country was declaring war on liberty itself. This was a radical phase in Wordsworth's life: he detested the idea of kingship, aristocratic privilege, and the unequal distribution of wealth. He also befriended other radicals such as William Godwin, Mary Wollstonecraft, and Thomas Paine. In 1793 Wordsworth walked from the south coast of England northwest to Bath and Bristol and then onwards past Tintern Abbey and through the Wye valley to North Wales.

In 1795 Wordsworth met a fellow poet, Samuel Taylor Coleridge, and an instant friendship began. Two years later the two were living close together in Somerset and planning to transform the writing of poetry. Their first collaborative work, *Lyrical Ballads*, was published on October 4, 1798. In the same year, the two poets and Dorothy Wordsworth (William's sister) set off for Germany, the aim being to learn German and, in the case of Coleridge, to study German philosophy. The visit was a success for Coleridge but less so for the Wordsworths, who spent a cold and miserable winter there.

In 1799, William and Dorothy returned to Britain and settled at Dove Cottage in Grasmere in the Lake District. Coleridge returned from Germany in 1800 and moved to Keswick to be near the Wordsworths. The second edition of *Lyrical Ballads* appeared in 1800 with a preface discussing the nature of poetry and its relationship to science. A third edition with an expanded preface appeared in 1802 (see biographical insert on Davy). Also in 1802 there occurred a temporary peace in the war between Britain and France, the Peace of Amiens, and this enabled Wordsworth to return to France and meet again Annette and their daughter Caroline. He returned to England after only one month but not before leaving his daughter financially secure. In October he married his childhood friend Mary Hutchinson, much to Dorothy's dismay.

By 1804 Wordsworth had completed his *Ode: Intimations of Immortality* and had written a great deal of *The Prelude*. As the title implies, *The Prelude* was intended as just that, a prelude to a much larger work, a philosophical poem dealing with man, nature, and society to be called *The Recluse*. This larger work was to be in three parts, but only *The Prelude*, part of part one (also called *The Recluse)* and the second section, *The Excursion*, were finished.

Wordsworth's steady drift toward conservatism and away from the radical beliefs of his youth was given additional impetus when he heard that on November 2, 1804, Napoleon crowned himself emperor in the cathedral of Notre Dame, Paris (snatching the crown at the last moment from the Pope, who had been summoned from Rome to perform the ceremony). Napoleon, the champion of the republic had become just another tyrant. This same event caused Beethoven to violently scratch out the dedication of his third symphony to Bonaparte and to call it the *Eroica* instead.

In 1813, Wordsworth and his family moved to Rydal Mount in the Lake District, where he spent the rest of his life. By the 1820s Wordsworth has lost virtually all of his youthful radicalism and disappointed the younger Romantics. He even campaigned for the Tories in the 1820 elections. He also seemed to protest against what now seemed quite reasonable reforms, such as the emancipation of the Irish Catholics, the education of women, the spread of mechanics institutes (centers of education for the working classes), and the abolition of capital punishment.

Wordsworth's response to science in his writing is quite complex. He celebrates mathematics and Newtonian physics as examples of certitude that the human mind can take pleasure in. But he detests science (and any form of reasoning for that matter) that undermines religious belief or does not respect the moral dimension of life. Wordsworth is distrustful of the pursuit of material gain and the "false utilitarian lure" ("Sonnet on the Projected Kendal and Windermere Railway"). One of his strangest pronouncements on the relationship of poetry to science was made in the 1802 preface to *Lyrical Ballads*, when he said:

> If the time should ever come when what is now called Science, thus familiarised to men, shall be ready to put on as it were, a form of flesh and blood, the Poet will lend his divine spirit to aid the transfiguration.
>
> This can only be understood in relation to Davy's claims about the potential of chemistry as a subject that will improve the human condition and moreover bind the different sections of the community together. Hence poetry and science can walk together if they serve some greater purpose.

William Wordsworth *(cont'd)*

William Wordsworth *(cont'd)*

In his later years his moralizing tendencies shaped his attitude to science. In the poem "To the Planet Venus" (1838), for example, he grudgingly accepts that science has given us increased knowledge but regrets the lack of a corresponding moral development:

> True is it Nature hides
> Her treasures less and less—Man now presides
> In power, where once he trembled in his weakness;
> Science advances with gigantic strides;
> But are we aught enriched in love and meekness?
> (l. 5–9)

Similarly, in Sonnet XIV, composed during the summer tour of 1833, he realizes that science has dispelled many myths but again falls back on the claim that reason will always reach a wall that only faith can surmount:

> Desire we past illusions to recall?
> To reinstate wild Fancy, would we hide
> Truths whose thick veil Science has drawn aside?
> No,—let this Age, high as she may, instal
> In her esteem the thirst that wrought man's fall,
> The universe is infinitely wide;
> And conquering Reason, if self-glorified,
> Can nowhere move uncrossed by some new wall
> Or gulf of mystery, which thou alone,
> Imaginative Faith! canst overleap.
> (l. 1–10)

Following the death of the poet Robert Southey in 1843, Wordsworth was made poet laureate. He died on April 13, 1850.

to perceive it. The passive mirror of Locke is replaced by the creative illumination of a candle or a lamp.

In 1793 William Godwin's *Political Justice* appeared, and Wordsworth read it eagerly. The book was written in the wake of the opening stages of the French revolution and conveyed the hope that the American and French revolutions were heralding a new era of world peace, progress, and social justice. The crucial premise of Godwin's philosophy was the belief that humans could be persuaded by reason to act for the general good of mankind if their actions could be guided by the rational utilitarian principle of maximizing total happiness rather than by irrational emotions.

By around 1796 both Wordsworth and Coleridge became interested in the ideas of the Scottish philosopher David Hartley. Whereas Godwin emphasized the importance of reason in guiding right conduct, Hartley stressed the importance of environment. Hartley was a strange mixture: a materialist, a determinist (then called a "necessitarian"), a moral philosopher, and a Christian. He had studied Locke at Cambridge, and he set about combining Locke's theory of sensations with Newton's ideas about vibrating particles. His conclusions were set forth in *Observations on Man, his Frame, his Duty and his Expectations* (1749), in which he gave a physiological account of the origin of ideas in the brain. In essence, Hartley's system was an early form of what was resurrected in the twentieth century as behaviorism—an approach that supposes that there are no natural inclinations, innate ideas, or drives, but that the content of our brains is due to the association of one experience with another. Hartley imagined that as external objects impressed themselves on our sensory organs, so vibrations were carried by nerves to the brain, where further vibrations are set up. Each new vibration is then modified by those already present. In this way Hartley hoped to give a purely mechanical account of the working of the mind. Our moral sense was not innate but "factitious," that is, acquired by the association of pleasure with certain actions and objects. We are led to virtuousness, however, by the fact that God in his benevolence designed the world so that good actions would give rise to pleasurable sensations.

Hartley's doctrine appealed to radicals such as Joseph Priestley and Samuel Taylor Coleridge, since it suggested that humans were capable of spiritual perfectibility as long as they were raised under the right social conditions and so acquired the right habits of mind. For radicals such as Coleridge and Wordsworth, the appeal of this blank slate model of the mind, advanced by Locke and developed by Godwin and Hartley, was obvious. If people are what experience dictates, then royalty and the hereditary aristocracy can claim no innate wisdom or merit. This model also could be used to oppose slavery, since slaves are not born inferior. The blank slate model of human nature has had an enduring and similar appeal ever since. Priestley said the book influenced him more than any other, apart from the Bible; Coleridge had his own portrait painted holding the book and named his son Hartley. Hartley's influence can be seen at work in that defining text of the Romantic movement, *Lyrical Ballads*.

Lyrical Ballads *(1798)*

The year 1798 is a chronicler's delight, an *annus mirabilis*. In this year Thomas Malthus's *Essay on Population* appeared—a work designed to show that the basic laws of population growth and food supply must always undermine any hopes of fundamental social reform such as that sprang from the thinking of French and English radicals. In Ireland, English forces crushed a rebellion of some 100,000 peasants, led by Wolf Tone, who were seeking home rule. Across the English Channel, the French were busy assembling an invasion force. In America, Congress passed The Sedition Act and The Alien Act, the former making it a criminal offence to criticize government officials, and the latter enabling the summary deportation of dangerous revolutionaries such as French or Irish immigrants. This was also the year that Godwin published *Memoirs of the Author of The Rights of Woman*, a frank but affectionate account of the life of his wife, the feminist author Mary Wollstonecraft, who had died the year before while giving birth to their daughter Mary Wollstonecraft Godwin, later Mary Shelley. Finally, *Lyrical Ballads*, a collection of poems by Wordsworth and Coleridge, was published on October 4, 1798. The authors withheld their identity because, as Coleridge (then regarded as a dangerous revolutionary) said later, "Wordsworth's name is nothing—to a large number of persons mine stinks."

The influence of Hartley and Godwin can be readily recognized in several of the poems in *Lyrical Ballads*. In *Lines Written a Few Miles above Tintern Abbey*, for example, written when he revisited that spot in 1798, Wordsworth recalls his previous experiences of visiting the scene and comments on the effect of his sensations (i.e., his communion with nature) on his moral development:

> I have owed to them,
> In hours of weariness, sensations sweet,
> Felt in the blood, and felt along the heart,
> And passing even into my purer mind
> With tranquil restoration:—feelings too
> Of unremembered pleasure; such perhaps
> As may have had no trivial influence
> On that best portion of a good man's life;
> His little, nameless, unremembered acts
> Of kindness and love.
> (l. 27–36)

Notice how Wordsworth has modified the scheme of Hartley, whereby sensations pass as vibrations along nerves to the brain, to the more poetical blood and heart. In the preface to the second edition of *Lyrical Ballads*, Wordsworth was open about his view that "our continued influxes of feeling are modified and directed by our thoughts, which indeed are representatives of our past feelings." He went on to observe that his poetry will work upon those in a "healthful state of association." Hence his rejection of the worn out and gaudy stock poetic diction of the eighteenth century that had lost "any art of association to overpower."

Wordsworth's rejection of Godwin's optimistic rationalism is to be found in two poems in *Lyrical Ballads:* "Expostulation and Reply" and "The Tables Turned." In the preface to the second edition of *Lyrical Ballads*, Wordsworth tells us that the poems "arose out of a conversation with a friend who was somewhat unreasonably attached to modern books of moral philosophy." The friend was William Hazlitt (who visited Wordsworth at Alfoxden in Somerset, Southwest England, in June 1798) and the philosopher Godwin. To the suggestion in "Expostulation and Reply" that the poet ought to spend more time learning from the books of past masters—"Up! Up! and drink the spirit breath'd / From dead men to their kind"—the poet replies that "One impulse from the vernal wood" can teach more about "moral evil and of good" than all the sages. There follow two lines that are easily misconstrued to represent Wordsworth's view on the whole of science:

> Our meddling intellect
> Misshapes the beauteous form of things:-
> We murder to dissect.

We meet a similar sentiment in "A Poet's Epitaph," written in 1799 and included in the second edition of *Lyrical Ballads*, where the dead poet imagines different types of people approaching his grave:

> Philosopher! a fingering slave,
> One that would peep and botanise
> Upon his mother's grave?
> . . .
> A Moralist perchance appears;
> . . .
> A reasoning, self-sufficing thing,
> An intellectual All-in-all!

Yet the crucial point here is that Wordsworth is not dismissing the whole of science but the application of science to matters where he thinks it does not belong, in this case the rationalist account of human morality. Hence, he also rejects, where it does not belong, bookish learning more generally; in "The Tables Turned," he says, "enough of Science and of Art / Close up those barren leaves."

Ultimately, Wordsworth found the explanation of the moral sense in the schemes of Locke, Hartley, and Godwin unconvincing. For these thinkers, individuals came, through experience, to associate pleasure with some actions and pain with others. There were, therefore, no specifically moral motives; humans were essentially egoists who eschewed pain and sought pleasure—something Wordsworth felt to be untrue. Wordsworth also identified another problem. If a good action is that which promotes general happiness, then to act morally would require a full calculation of the positive and negative effects of every action. In *The Prelude* (1850) he describes the despair to which this utilitarian calculus had led:

> demanding formal proof,
> And seeking it in everything, I lost
> All feeling of conviction, and, in fine,
> Sick, wearied out with contrarieties,
> Yielded up moral questions in despair.
> (Book XI, l. 301–305)

Interestingly, after this crisis Wordsworth turned toward mathematics for the "employment of the enquiring faculty" and the "clear and solid evidence" that it supplied (X, l. 902–905)

Kant's Revolution

Around 1800 Coleridge grew out of Hartley's associationism, finding it incapable of explaining the creative aspects of perception and imagination. Instead, he turned briefly to the idealism (the idea that it is mind that constructs the world and not the other way round) of George Berkeley and thence to the transcendentalism of Immanuel Kant. In his *Critique of Pure Reason*, Kant suggested that the mind is not born as a blank slate but is in some way primed for experience, containing a priori schemas into which experience is organized. These schemas, such as space and time, are antecedent to experience and enable us to make sense of an otherwise confusing mass of sensory data. Kant's skill lay in steering a path between the pure rationalism of Descartes (the idea that the structure of the world can be deduced through the exercise of reason) and the naïve empiricism of Locke and his followers. Hence, his view that concepts without percepts are empty, but percepts without concepts are blind.

Kant famously compared his break with the empiricism of the eighteenth century with the "first thoughts of Copernicus," leading later commentators to suggest that he had effected a "Copernican revolution" in philosophy. What Coleridge found in Kant was a set of ideas that enabled him to challenge what he thought were the unsatisfactory philosophies of British empiricism, utilitarianism and Cartesian dualism. For Coleridge, Cartesian dualism had dismembered nature by separating mind and matter so categorically, and utilitarianism and empiricism threatened to displace God from the center of the moral life.

In both their writing careers, Wordsworth and Coleridge seem to debate the merits of empiricist and transcendentalist approaches to understanding the human mind. In his *Immortality Ode* (1804), Wordsworth explored the Platonic idea that the mind at birth is already equipped with perceptual categories capable of recognizing the universal "forms." Plato had developed a theory that the world of everyday objects is just an expression of the more fundamental reality of Forms or Ideas. Hence a beautiful object is beautiful because it contains the essence of beauty, which exists separately. We are equipped to recognize these forms in ordinary objects due to the preexistence of the soul, during which time it was exposed to the transcendental realm of pure forms. Some of the experience of the forms, but not all, we have forgotten:

> Our birth is but a sleep and a forgetting:
> The Soul that rises with us, our life's Star,
> Hath had elsewhere its setting,
> And cometh from afar:
> Not in entire forgetfulness,
> And not in utter nakedness
> (l. 59–64)

It is the memory of these forms in the child that provides the answer to the creativity of perception:

> Thou best Philosopher, who yet dost keep
> Thy heritage, thou Eye among the blind,
> That, deaf and silent, read'st the eternal deep,
> Haunted for ever by the eternal mind.
> (l. 111–114)

Wordsworth continued to debate with himself the tension between the passive and creative mind until his conversion to orthodox Christianity in 1814.

Wordsworth and Newton

In later life Wordsworth's response to the natural sciences was framed by his overriding religious concerns. In *The Excursion* (1814), for example, he is unflattering about contemporary scientists. He speaks of them as "ambitious spirits" who "regulate the moving spheres, and weigh / The planets in the hollow of their hand," people who "dive rather than soar." He questions whether they might prove to be "a degraded race" and suggests that "Oh! There is laughter at their work in heaven" (Book IV, l. 947–956). Some fifteen years later, in August 1829, Wordsworth was taken to task by his friend William Rowan Hamilton, a leading mathematician and astronomer, for such derogatory remarks. According to Hamilton's sister, Wordsworth defended himself by saying that he was only attacking those scientists who were concerned with "a bare collection of facts for their own sake or to be applied merely to the material uses of life," adding that he "venerated" those scientists like Newton who had the effect of "elevating the mind to God." Perhaps feeling chastised by Hamilton, when in 1837 Wordsworth came to revise the 1803 edition of *The Prelude*, he added two lines to an otherwise rather neutral description of the statue of Newton he could see from his room during his undergraduate days at Cambridge. They are the last two lines of the following extract and have become justly famous:

> And from my pillow looking forth by light
> Of moon or favouring stars, I could behold
> The Antichapel where the statue stood
> Of Newton with his prism, and silent face,
> The marble index of a Mind for ever
> Voyaging through strange seas of Thought, alone.
> (Book III, l. 58–63)

Newton is one of the few scientists whose concepts informed Wordsworth's verse. In *The Prelude*, for example, he refers to "Newton's own ethereal self" (Book III, l. 267). The adjective is apposite, since it was Newton himself who speculated about the nature of the aether (supposedly an imponderable fluid filling all space) and compared it to the omnipresent spirit of God (see chapter four). It seems likely that Wordsworth had this concept in mind when he wrote "Lines Written a Few Miles above Tintern Abbey," noting how he has felt a

> presence that disturbs me with the joy
> Of elevated thoughts; a sense sublime
> Of something far more deeply interfused,
>
> . . .
>
> A motion and a spirit, that impels
> All thinking things, all objects of all thought,
> And rolls through all things.
> (l. 95–103)

Wordsworth's use of scientific language is sparing, yet when he does use it, the effect can be powerful. A Newtonian frame of reference lies behind the second verse of the enigmatic Lucy poem "A Slumber Did My Spirit Seal" as the brutal finality of death is described:

No motion has she now, no force;
She neither hears nor sees
Rolled round in earth's diurnal course
With rocks and stones and trees.

The use of concepts borrowed from physics and astronomy, such as "motion," "force," and "diurnal" emphasizes the undeniability of death and links it to cosmic processes. More generally we can detect the universe of Newton and the astronomers in various places in Wordsworth. The Lucy poems make reference to the stars, the "sinking" moon, the "descending" moon, the rolling of the earth, and the cycles of life and death ("Lucy's race was run"). In *The Prelude* also we have the sense of a mighty universal frame carrying all along. We read of

the Solitary Cliffs
Wheeled by me, even as if the earth had roll'd
With visible motion her diurnal round.
(Book I, lines 484–486)

And later we have the phrase "the great system of the world / Where man is sphered and which God animates." The *System of the World* is the title of Book III of Newton's *Principia*.

Mary Shelley's Frankenstein

In 1815, the 13,000 foot volcano Tambora on the island of Sumbawa in Indonesia erupted, and between April 7 and 12 disgorged between thirty-seven and one hundred cubic miles of dust and ashes into the atmosphere. It was possibly the largest explosion in recorded history. The dust encircled the globe and, by blocking out sunlight, was responsible for a marked drop in temperature the following year, so much so that 1816 became known as the year without a summer. In America and Europe crops froze and failed; the temperature in Madison County, New York, dropped below freezing every month of the year; in June seven inches of snow fell in New York; and in Europe food riots were widespread. As the weather worsened, a group of exiles from Britain spent a wet and gloomy sum-

Mary Shelley (neé Godwin) (1797–1851)

Mary Shelley was the daughter of two of the most notorious and influential intellectual rebels of the late eighteenth century: William Godwin and Mary Wollstonecraft. In the 1790s, Godwin became famous as a leading theoretical interpreter and supporter of the American and French revolutions. His *Enquiry Concerning Political Justice*

(1793) influenced for a time Wordsworth and Coleridge. Mary Wollstonecraft was a writer and political theorist whose most famous work, *A Vindication of the Rights of Women* (1792), became a major source of inspiration for the feminist movement. Although Godwin dismissed the institution of marriage as an absurd convention, when Mary became pregnant in 1797 the two were married to confer legitimacy on their future child. On August 30 that year Mary Godwin was born. Tragically, complications followed the birth and eleven days later Mary Wollstonecraft died of puerperal fever.

Portrait of Mary Shelley. Mary Shelley was the daughter of Mary Wollstonecraft and William Godwin. She eloped with Percy Shelly and in 1818 completed her most famous work, Frankenstein. In this novel Mary Shelley provided a lasting and critical image of the scientist unleashing uncontrollable forces. Painting by R. Rothwell. (Archivo Iconografico, S.A./Corbis)

William was left to raise his daughter alone. They became particularly close, and in an intellectual atmosphere, he encouraged Mary in her attempts at writing. Their home was a center of radical intellectual discussion, and visitors included Wordsworth, Coleridge, the chemist Humphrey Davy, and the American politician, adventurer, and later vice president Aaron Burr.

In 1812 the young aristocrat Percy Bysshe Shelley, recently expelled from Oxford, visited the Godwin household. Other visits followed, and although Shelley was married, he and Mary (then only sixteen) formed an intense attachment. Godwin forbade the liaison, and so in 1814 the two eloped to France, accompanied by Claire Clairmont, Mary's stepsister.

Mary and Percy were destined to spend only eight years together. Over this time Mary gave birth to four children: a premature daughter who died in 1815, a boy William born in 1816 who died of malaria in 1819, Clara born in 1816 and who died from dysentery in 1818, and finally Percy Florence born in 1819 and the only child to survive to adulthood. The year 1816 was a tragic and momentous year for the Shelley household. In the summer, Mary began writing *Frankenstein,* and before it was complete, news arrived of the suicide of Fanny Imlay (Mary's half sister and daughter of Mary Wollstonecraft by the American officer Gilbert Imlay), to be followed in December by the drowning of Harriet Shelley, Percy's first wife.

Given the events surrounding the conception of *Frankenstein*, it is hardy surprising that it is a Gothic work exploring the themes of creation of life, parental abandonment, and death. At the end of the novel the monster says, "I, the miserable and the abandoned, am an abortion to be spurned at, and kicked, and trampled on."

In 1822 further tragedy unfolded: Mary nearly lost her life as she hemorrhaged from a miscarriage and was only saved by Percy immersing her in an ice cold bath. Later that year, Percy was drowned in a sailing accident. Mary then had to rely on her writing to support herself. She produced a number of other works: *Valperga* (1823), *The Last Man* (1826), *The Fortunes of Perkin Warbeck* (1830), and two domestic romances, *Lodore* (1835) and *Falkner* (1837). Mary resisted the temptation to marry again, writing to one suitor, "Mary Shelley shall be written on my tomb." She died in London in 1851.

Soon after the publication of *Frankenstein*, the story, like the monster itself, acquired a life of its own beyond the powers of Shelley to control; and, like the monster, it was often misunderstood. The London playwright Richard Brinsley Peake began a trend that many would follow. In his play of 1823, *Presumption*, instead of a sensitive and well-read creature mistreated by his creator, the monster became a speechless brute killing without remorse. Peake's play was performed around Britain and in 1825 traveled across the Atlantic to open at New York's Park Theatre. In the twentieth century the image of the monster out of control was used as a political metaphor. In 1824, for example, the British Foreign Secretary George Canning compared the emancipation of slaves to letting loose a Frankenstein creation. Conversely, the Massachusetts senator and abolitionist Charles Sumner compared the Southern Confederacy to "the soulless monster of Frankenstein" (quoted in Lederer, 2002, p. 35).

The twentieth century witnessed numerous film adaptations of the story. The one to leave the most enduring image perhaps was that released in 1931 by Universal Studios, starring the then little-known actor Boris Karloff as the monster. Again, the film was a distortion of Mary's intention. The monster kills not because of the suffering he has endured from humans around him but because he has been given the brain of a criminal.

The endurance of the Frankenstein myth into the twenty-first century is in some ways hardly surprising. We can read a lot in *Frankenstein*, because Shelley ransacked science, literature, and her own experiences to pour a great deal into the novel. In essence, amid the multiplicity of themes she explored in the work, she put her finger on the central paradox of modern science: how can humankind control a science that is powerful to the point of explaining and manipulating human life itself? This dilemma continues to resonate in the modern mind. Indeed, many of the products of twentieth century science, such as nuclear power, genetically modified food ("Frankenstein foods"), cloning, and genetic engineering make the questions that Mary Shelley raised more pertinent than ever.

mer on the shores of Lake Geneva, walking, sailing, and entertaining indoors. A chance remark by one of them that they should each tell ghost stories led to two of the most famous works of horror fiction ever written: John Polidori's *Vampyre* and, more significantly for our purposes, Mary Shelley's *Frankenstein.*

The full party consisted of Lord Byron, his personal physician Polirdori, Mary Godwin (soon to become Mary Shelley), Percy Shelley, the Shelleys' baby son William, and Mary's stepsister Claire Clairmont. The presence of this group of celebrities caused a sensation, and tourists lined up on the other side of the lake with telescopes trained on the Villa Diodati, hoping to catch a glimpse of the notorious group. Following Byron's suggestion one evening that they each compose a ghost story, Mary tells us that she had difficulty in devising a story until she sat in a conversation between Byron and Shelley at which she was "a devout but nearly silent listener"—she was, we recall, only eighteen years of age. The poets talked

> of experiments of Dr Darwin. who preserved a piece of vermicelli in a glass case, till by some extraordinary means it began to move with voluntary motion. Perhaps a corpse would be re-animated; galvanism had given token of such things. (*Frankenstein*, p. 357)

That night Mary Shelley, who only a year before had lost her first child, suffered a nightmare in which she saw a scientist —the "pale student of unhallowed arts"—creating life from death. She woke realizing that she had her ghost story; as she said, what had terrified her would terrify others. In due course, Mary extended her short story to the length of a novel, and it was published anonymously as *Frankenstein or The Modern Prometheus* in 1818. The work has had a profound effect on the perception of science and scientists, and it is worth examining the plot, the scientific basis, and the enduring significance of this influential novel.

The story opens with Victor Frankenstein relating his life story to an English explorer, Robert Walton, who has rescued him somewhere in the icy wastes of the Arctic. Victor describes his happy childhood and the dying wish of his mother, Caroline, that he marry his cousin Elizabeth. But Victor delays his marriage and moves away to university, where he becomes enthralled by the creative potential of chemistry. He devotes himself to study and neglects his own health and his friends. Eventually he finds his goal in life: to create a living creature from parts gathered from the corpses of the dead. Using a spark of electricity, Frankenstein succeeds, but when he views the monster he has created (who, significantly, has no name), he falls ill. The monster escapes and secretly attaches himself to a poor family from whom he learns to speak and to read. Finding himself shunned and pilloried because of his grotesque appearance, the monster searches out his creator, Victor Frankenstein, and demands that he make a female companion. Victor reluctantly agrees, but, worried that the two might breed a race of devils, he destroys his half-finished creation. The monster is so enraged that later, in a sexually charged scene, he kills Elizabeth on the night she is wedded to Victor. The story ends with the monster, having witnessed the death of his creator aboard Walton's ship, striding out to die somewhere near the North Pole.

The sources on which Mary Shelley based her ideas about science are fairly well established. Victor's enthusiasm for chemistry has strong parallels with the promising role Humphrey Davy ascribed to chemistry in his famous introductory lecture given at the Royal Institution on January 21, 1802. The role of electricity in *Frankenstein* is also important. In the 1750s, Benjamin Franklin (it is claimed) demonstrated the electrical nature of lightning with his famous kite experiment—an experiment repeated by Victor in the book. In *Prometheus Unbound*, Percy Shelley, always enthralled by the study of electrical phenomena, associated electricity with love, light, and life. We may recall Thomas Jefferson Hogg's (Percy Shelley's roommate) description of Shelley's room at Oxford:

> Books, boots, papers, shoes, philosophical instruments, clothes, pistols, linen, crockery, ammunition, and phials innumerable, with money, stockings, prints, crucibles, bags, and boxes, were scattered on the floor and in every place; as if the young chemist, in order to analyse the mystery of creation, had endeavoured first to re-construct the primeval chaos . . . An electrical machine, an air pump, the galvanic trough, a solar microscope, and large glass jars and receivers, were conspicuous amidst the mass of matter. (Quoted in Kipperman, 1998)

Both Mary and Percy Shelley probably subscribed to a view that electricity was somehow rejuvenating. Early in the novel the young Frankenstein's curiosity is aroused when he witnesses a bolt of lightning split an oak tree. He then notes that his father "Constructed a small electrical machine, and exhibited a few experiments; he made also a kite, with a wire and string, which drew down that fluid from the clouds" (p. 70).

That electricity should be so linked with life was quite in keeping with scientific notions of the day. In the 1780s Luigi Galvani, working at the University of Bolgna, noticed that the leg of a dead frog twitched if touched by a metal scalpel in a room where an electrostatic generator was operating. Further experiments showed that it twitched when the scalpel was in contact with a different metal—a discovery that led his fellow countryman Alessandro Volta (1745–1827) to

Biography: Humphrey Davy (1778–1829)

Humphrey Davy was born into a family of small landowners on December 17, 1778, in Cornwall, Southwest England. His formal education ended when he was sixteen, and afterwards he was virtually self-taught. In 1794 his father died, and to help support his family he became apprenticed to a surgeon and apothecary named Bingham Borlase. Sometime in 1795 he read Antoine Lavoisier's *Elements of Chemistry* in the original

Portrait of Humphry Davy. Humphry Davy was a friend to Wordsworth and Coleridge and an amateur poet himself. (Library of Congress)

French and began to repeat the experiments described and devise new ones. Davy also struck up a friendship with Gregory Watt, the tubercular son of the famous engineer James Watt. Through him, he came to know of the work of Thomas Beddoes at the newly founded Pneumatic Institution of Bristol. Dr. Beddoes was a former lecturer in chemistry at Oxford University who was forced to resign because of his radical politics and support for the French revolution. Beddoes set up his institution in the belief (now seen to be mistaken) that the various gases discovered in the previous two decades by Joseph Priestley and others might prove useful in the treatment of respiratory diseases such as tuberculosis. Beddoes was an impressive character. He was in touch with James Watt, Erasmus Darwin, and the Wedgwood family. He also read German and was one of the first to introduce Kant's ideas to Britain. Through correspondence with the Davy, Beddoes became impressed by the fledgling chemist and offered

him a position as an experimental researcher, a post that Davy accepted.

During his time at Bristol, Davy inhaled all manner of dangerous gases, including (in modern parlance) methane, carbon dioxide, nitrogen, hydrogen, and even nitric oxide and carbon monoxide, and survived to record his observations. It was his work on nitrous oxide (NO), published in 1800, that brought him fame and recognition. The gas had been discovered by Priestley in 1772, and Davy noticed that it produced an intoxicating effect, so he named it laughing gas. Quite a craze for imbibing this gas grew up, and it became something of a recreational drug for chemistry students in the nineteenth century (and is occasionally still used illicitly in this way). Davy also predicted that it might prove useful as an anaesthetic, although it was not used for this purpose until 1846.

In 1799 Davy was introduced to the poet Coleridge, and the two struck up an instant friendship, having alike an interest in science and poetry. He and Coleridge both contributed poems to Southey's *Annual Anthology* for 1799. In 1800 Wordsworth and Coleridge moved up to the Lake District (Northwest England), entrusting to Davy the task of correcting the proofs of the second edition of their *Lyrical Ballads*. It was this edition that contained the famous preface by Wordsworth where he noted the "contradistinction" between poetry and science, something that Davy was to remember two years later.

The scientific work of Davy also caught the attention of Benjamin Thompson (Count Rumford of the Holy Roman Empire), a colorful American Tory who spied for the British in the American revolution and later married Lavoisier's widow. Thompson needed a new professor of chemistry at the recently formed Royal Institution in London, and Davy was duly appointed. It was here that he did his most important work and, through his popular lectures, ensured the success of the institution itself. On January 21, 1802, he delivered a lecture introducing a course of further lectures in chemistry. He spoke of the potential of chemistry to improve human welfare and made claims for his science that look very much like a reply to Wordsworth's 1800 preface to *Lyrical Ballads*. When Wordsworth rewrote the preface for the 1802 edition he, in turn, responded to Davy's lecture and went out of his way to consider how science and poetry might work together:

> If the labours of Men of Science should ever create any material revolution, direct or indirect, in our condition, and in the impressions which we habitually receive, the Poet will sleep then no more than at present, but he will be ready to follow the steps of the Man of Science. (Preface to *Lyrical Ballads* in Owen and Worthington Smyser 1974, p. 606)

In 1806, Davy began a series of spectacular experiments in electrochemistry using the newly invented voltaic cell to pass electricity through a whole range of substances. In 1807 he electrolyzed compounds of the alkali metals and identified two new elements: potassium and sodium. He also analyzed oxymuriatic acid (hydrogen chloride) and refuted Lavoisier's claim that all acids must contain oxygen. In 1812 he published *Elements of Chemical Philosophy* and later that year was knighted. Over the years 1813–1815 he traveled across Europe with his new wife and his young protégé, Michael Faraday. On his return, he devised his famous miner's lamp to prevent gas explosions underground. In principle, the lamp should have improved safety, but mine owners used it to dig even deeper mines involving greater risks, and its effect on the rate of accidents was not as dramatic as hoped.

Up to about 1812 Coleridge followed Davy's work with much interest. Here was a scientist investigating phenomena that provided an alternative approach to the soulless and mechanical picture of the universe associated with the Newtonians. Coleridge attended Davy's 1802 course of lectures and took notes, looking, as he said, to improve his stock of metaphors. Coleridge was still a radical at this time, and in his notebook entry on witnessing Davy's experiments on chlorine and nitrogen peroxide records he writes, "If all aristocrats [were] here, how easily Davy might poison them all" (quoted in Coburn, 1973, p. 53).

Eventually, however, as Davy retracted his earlier opposition to Dalton's atomic theory and enjoyed the social life of a minor celebrity, Coleridge grew disaffected with his former friend, noting in 1812 that "Alas, Humphrey Davy has become Sir Humphrey Davy and an Atomist" (quoted in Coburn, 1973, p. 60).

In 1820 Davy became president of the Royal Society, where he took much delight in the formal paraphernalia of ceremonies. By now fame seems to have affected his demeanor, and he became something of a snob. Davy was a brilliant chemist. But perhaps because of the distractions of office and the various demands placed on him by manufacturers looking for profit-enhancing applied science, his work amounts to a series of brilliant fragments rather than the foundation of a new system. There is much truth, therefore, in the remark that his greatest discovery was Michael Faraday, a chemist and physicist who succeeded him as director of the Royal Institution in 1824 and went on to unify the study of electricity and magnetism.

develop the first electric battery (the "Voltaic pile") created by suspending two different metals in a dilute solution of acid.

Galvani's nephew, Giovanni Aldini, also created a sensation when he showed that the limbs of all manner of dead animals jolted when electrified. One notable occasion occurred on January 17, 1803, when, during a visit to Britain, Professor Aldini, applied galvanic electricity to the corpse of an executed murderer, one Thomas Forster. In an account published later that year, Aldini described how when wires were attached to the ear and mouth of the dead criminal, "the jaw began to quiver, the adjoining muscles were horribly contorted, and the left eye actually opened" (Aldini, quoted in Mellor, 1987, p. 304). One observer, a Mr. Pass, went home so shocked that he died shortly afterwards, his death ascribed by *The Newgate Calendar* to the fright induced by witnessing the experiments.

Aldini may have contributed to the image of the scientist that Mary Shelley drew up in *Frankenstein*. Indeed, as Aldini himself noted, the aim of his researches was to "continue, revive, and, if I may be allowed the expression, to command the vital powers" (Quoted in Sleigh, p. 220). Shelley does not go into detail about exactly how Frankenstein created his monster. The crucial passage when the monster finally is given life reads:

> It was on a dreary night of November, that I beheld the accomplishment of my toils. With an anxiety that almost amounted to agony, I collected the instruments of life around me, that I might infuse a spark of life into the lifeless thing that lay at my feet. . . . I saw the dull yellow eye of the creature open; it breathed hard, and a convulsive motion agitated its limbs. (p. 84–85)

In the 1818 text of *Frankenstein* Mary Shelley is remarkably terse in her description of the details of how Victor breathes life into his monster. We are told it is a "filthy process," but it is only later, in her 1831 Preface, that she suggests electricity may have been involved. Indeed, there are some readings of the text that suggest the creation process Mary originally had in mind was a type of in vitro fertilization with the life principle that Victor discovered added to a soup of embryonic parts. His revulsion at his creation could then represent Mary's own postnatal depression after her difficult pregnancies. It has even been suggested that the yellowness of the monster (he had "yellow skin" and a "dull yellow eye") may be Mary's experience of viewing jaundice in her own new-born children (see Sutherland 1996).

Ultimately, however, the scientific veracity of Frankenstein's methods are of less importance than the fact that in this work Mary Shelley provides an image and metaphor for the nature of science and its effects that have haunted think-

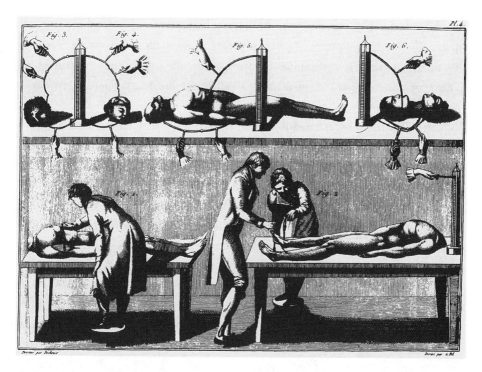

A plate from Aldini's work on galvanism (1803) showing the application of electricity to cadavers. Experiments such as these caused a sensation and probably provided the inspiration for Mary Shelley's Frankenstein. *(Courtesy of The Bakken Library, Minneapolis)*

ing ever since. So complete has the identification of the effects of science (the monster) with its creator (Victor) been, that Frankenstein is commonly thought to be the monster—an impression not too far from an interpretation that sees the monster as a projection of Frankenstein's own personality, his alter ego.

The power of the novel has many dimensions. At one level Frankenstein is the familiar Faust figure, the overreacher who meddles in forbidden knowledge, only to bring ruin upon himself. Victor is also like Prometheus: someone who brings what he thinks is a benefit to mankind, only to suffer as a consequence. Shelley also emphasizes the unwholesome aspects of Victor Frankenstein's blinkered scientific rationalism by describing how his obsessions are detrimental to his own health. He becomes physically emaciated, emotionally disturbed, and cuts himself off from the company of friends who could have proffered good advice.

Significantly, whereas previous attacks on scientific hubris from the likes of Thomas Shadwell, Samuel Butler, and Jonathan Swift concentrated on the failure of science or at best the triviality of its findings, Shelley examines the ethical consequences of success. Frankenstein's creation is a product of genius, but its scientist creator is blind to the effects of his work on his creation—the monster has feelings like ordinary mortals—and those around him. Furthermore, by running away and lapsing into a "nervous fever" as soon as the monster comes to life, he tries to disavow responsibility for the monster's escape. Hence the novel is also seen as a critique of the attempt to ethically disengage scientific research from its consequences.

Possibly the most interesting dimension to the novel, however, is Shelley's feminist analysis of the scientific approach as practiced by Frankenstein. In the seventeenth century, Francis Bacon, consciously or not, spoke of science and nature in highly gendered terms. He wrote, for example, of putting nature "on the rack and extracting her secrets" and claimed, "I am come in very truth leading you to nature with all her children to bind her to your service and make her your slave." In the eyes of the new philosophy, nature is portrayed as a passive female to be corrected and brought into service. The effrontery of this masculine bias may have struck Shelley at the onset of writing her story, when she heard her future husband, Percy Shelley, and Byron talking about the electrical generation of life. A year before, Mary had lost her first child and later had troubled dreams of reviving his dead body by the fire. Her confinement with her second child, William, now just one year old, had also been difficult. It is likely, then, that the thought of bypassing the female role in the creation of life would have shocked her. This reaction supplies another dimension to Frankenstein's crime: the creation of life without the involvement of any feminine activity. Pursuing this line, it also begins to look as if the monster is a substitute for the natural child Frankenstein should have had by marrying Elizabeth, a marriage he continually defers. In places Victor seems to relish the prospect of becoming a surrogate father through science:

> A new species would bless me as its creator and source; many happy and excellent natures would owe their being to me. No father could claim the gratitude of his child so completely as I should deserve theirs. (*Frankenstein*, MacDonald text, p. 82)

Frankenstein has not only transgressed natural boundaries of life and death, he has also attempted to usurp the role of women. The theme of the violation of nature by science is also illustrated by the fact that the monster kills (having possibly raped) Elizabeth on her wedding night. When Victor discovers her, "She was there, lifeless and inanimate, thrown across the bed, her head hanging down, her bloodless arms and relaxed form flung by the murderer on its bridal bier" (p. 218).

It is important to realize, however, since this is central plank of Shelley's argument, that the monster is not intrinsically evil. Indeed, for a horror story,

Boris Karloff, Basil Rathbone, and Bela Lugosi in a scene from the 1939 Universal Pictures production Son of Frankenstein. *Screen adaptations of Mary Shelley's story tended to simplify the character of Frankenstein and ignore the fact that he was sensitive and intelligent but mistreated by those around him. (Bettmann/Corbis)*

Frankenstein is surprisingly secular; there are no ghosts, nothing supernatural, no divine retribution. Shelley dedicated the novel to her father, William Godwin, someone who stressed the formative influence of social experience on the molding of character and rejected a religious basis to morality. It is significant then, that the monster initially learns human kindness from the De Lacey family and reads some sound liberal texts. But then he is mocked and rejected: children shriek, women faint, and people throw stones at him. As the monster says when he confronts his maker: "I was benevolent and good; misery made me a fiend. Make me happy, and I shall again be virtuous." In short, the monster behaves badly because he is unloved. The importance of social influences on character for Shelley provides an answer to a question often posed about Victor's creation: why assemble parts from lots of dead bodies when one would presumably suffice? But if Victor had simply brought to life a single body it would have to carry with it its personality at death. Shelley needed a completely new creation to work her theme. Sadly, this social dimension to the novel was neglected in the numerous stage and film adaptations that followed its publication, where the monster is invariably depicted as born clumsy and dull witted.

Although primarily European in origin, the Romantic movement quickly became a transatlantic phenomenon. It traveled well, for the emphasis on nature found a resonance with the New World view that the American landscape had a spiritual quality. Romantic writing, and especially the philosophy of Kant, also appealed to the New England transcendentalists, who were conducting their own debates about the active power of the mind: Emerson, for example, was heavily influenced by Coleridge, Carlyle, and Kant. These subjects are explored in the next chapter.

Bibliographic Essay

A good edition of *Lyrical Ballads* is that edited by R. L. Brett and A. R. Jones (London: Methuen, 1978). This text provides a useful introduction and the famous prefaces to the two editions. Geoffrey Durant's *Wordsworth and the Great System* (Cambridge: Cambridge University Press, 1970) shows how the outlook of Wordsworth on the natural world was strongly influenced by Newtonianism. He shows clearly that the relationship between Wordsworth and science was not simply one of antithesis. For a close textual analysis of Wordsworth's attitude to Newton himself see *A Mind For Ever Voyaging* by W. K. Thomas and Warren U. Ober. The book looks carefully at the various literary sources of Wordsworth's ideas, culminating in an examination of the famous "mind for ever voyaging" section of *The Prelude*. A highly important paper that considers the relationship of Wordsworth to the British empiricist tradition of Locke, Hartley, Godwin, and Mill is Fred Wilson's "Wordsworth and the Culture of Science" in *Centennial Review*, 1989, 33, 4, pp. 322–392. Wilson convincingly describes Wordsworth's disillusionment with Godwin's rationalistic morality and how the poet's response influenced John Stuart Mill.

For a survey of Romantic ideas on creativity and especially the epistemology of the British Romantic poets, an essential guide is M. H. Abrams's *The Mirror and the Lamp* (Oxford: Oxford University Press, 1953). A book that deals explicitly with Wordsworth's struggles with empiricism and transcendentalism is *Wordsworth and Philosophy: Empiricism and Transcendentalism in the Poetry* by Keith Thomas (Ann Arbor, MI: UMI Research Press). For a close and subtle analysis of the views of Wordsworth, Davy, and Coleridge on the scientific method, it is worth consulting chapter two of Jonathan Smith's *Fact and Feeling: Baconian Science and the Nineteenth–Century Literary Imagination* (Madison: University of Wisconsin Press, 1994).

For views on William Blake, see "William Blake Rejects the Enlightenment" by Jean H. Hagstrum, in Northrop Frye's *Blake: A Collection of Critical Essays* (New Jersey: Prentice Hall, 1966). Someone who argues that Blake had a more favorable attitude to Locke than is commonly supposed is Steve Clarke in his essay "Labouring at the Resolute Anvil: Blake's Response to Locke" in Blake in the 90s, edited by S. Clark and D. Worrall (London: Macmillan Press, 1999).

For an interesting examination of events around the year 1798, a remarkable year in many ways, see *1798: The Year of Lyrical Ballads* (New York: St. Martin's Press, 1998), edited by Richard Cronin. For more information of the relationship between Coleridge and science, a useful start can be made with Trevor Levere's essay, "The Lovely Shapes and Sounds Intelligible: Samuel Taylor Coleridge, Humphrey Davy, Science and Poetry" in *Nature Transfigured*, edited by John Christie and Sally Shuttleworth (New York: St. Martin's Press, 1989). This concept can then be extended with a reading of Mark Kipperman's article "Coleridge, Shelley, Davy, and Science's Millennium" in *Criticism* Summer 1998, Vol. 40, No. 3, pp. 409–436. Another valuable article by Levere that focuses on Coleridge's interest in chemistry and points to the importance of Thomas Beddoes is "Coleridge, Chemistry, and the Philosophy of Nature," *Studies in Romanticism*, 1977, Vol. 16, pp. 349–379. The relationship between Davy and the various prefaces to *Lyrical Ballads* is dealt with by Roger Sharrock in "The Chemist and Poet: Sir Humphrey Davy and the Preface to the Lyrical Ballads," *Notes and Records of the Royal Society* 17 (1962) 44–59. For a view of how Romantic notions may have affected science itself, see D. M. Knight's "The Physical Sciences and the Romantic Movement," *History of Science* 9 (1970) 54–75. For a thorough account of the relationship between Wordsworth and geology, and one that discusses the nature of science-literary relations more generally, see John Wyatt's *Wordsworth and the Geologists* (Cambridge: Cambridge University Press, 1995).

A feminist analysis of *Frankenstein* together with a useful discussion of the scientific sources is to be found in Ann Mellor's "Frankenstein: A Feminist Critique of Science" in *One Culture* (Madison: University of Wisconsin Press, 1987), edited by George Levine. For a variety of perspectives on *Frankenstein*, plus a useful introductory chapter on the ambiguities in the heritage of this novel, consult *The Endurance of Frankenstein* (Berkeley: University of California Press, 1974), edited by George Levine and U. C. Knoepflmacher. For the relevance of the Frankenstein myth to modern biology, it is worth consulting Jon Turney's *Frankenstein's Footsteps: Science, Genetics and Popular Culture* (New Haven, CT and London: Yale University Press, 1998). A serviceable edition of Shelley's *Frankenstein* is that edited by D. L. Macdonald and Kathleen Scherf, *Frankenstein or the Modern Prometheus* (Letchworth: Broadview Literary Texts, 2001). This volume presents the 1818 text and helpful commentaries. Charlotte Sleigh in "Life Death and Galvanism," *Studies in History and Philosophy of Science Part C: Studies in History and Philosophy of Biological and Biomedical Sciences* vol. 29, no. 2, September 1998, 219–248 provides an interesting analysis of the sources behind the Aldini link to Mary Shelley. For a well-illustrated account of the background to the creation of *Frankenstein*, the use of the story in film, and its contemporary relevance, see *Frankenstein: Penetrating the Secrets of Nature* by Susan Lederer (New Brunswick, NJ: Rutgers University Press, 2002), a book written to accompany a National Library of Medicine Exhibition.

6

Nineteenth-Century American Literature and Science: Problems of Analogy

Brian Baker

The Analogical Method

"Very like a whale"—that is how the elderly Polonius, attempting to humor Hamlet, describes a cloud in the sky. In Shakespeare's *Hamlet*, Polonius is being teased by the young Prince, who jokes that he can see the forms of different beings in the insubstantial, ever-changing bodies of the clouds. But notice how Polonius responds. Warily he says, "Very like a whale," not that it is indeed a whale. It is shaped like a whale, it has a relationship to the shape of a whale, but it is not a whale. Likeness does suggest similarity between two separate things, but strangely, it also signifies that those things are not identical.

Describing likeness of appearance, or describing an unknown natural object in terms of another known object or thing, was a common tool for the natural scientists of the late eighteenth and early nineteenth centuries. The philosopher William James (1842–1910), elder brother of Henry James, defined knowledge as "an ultimate relation between two mutually exclusive entities." This use of analogy was central for those who were seeking to expand the boundaries of scientific knowledge, for the world has often been understood in terms of relationships, correspondences, and analogies, as was noted in chapter two. It is no coincidence that Herman Melville (1819–1891) quotes Polonius's speech in the opening "Extracts" section of *Moby-Dick* (1851). Melville's great, compendious novel—one that both imitates encyclopedic organization and questions the whole idea of scientific knowledge and classification—is centrally concerned with the human in encounter with the natural and how knowledge of the world is gained. Ahab's demonic quest for the white whale is a quest in search of knowledge as well as of revenge, and in its "circumnavigation" retraces the path of the great voyages of "discovery" of the seventeenth and eighteenth centuries.

Despite the colonialist framework of many of these voyages, most were accompanied by at least one botanist, "natural philosopher," or "man of science," whether professional or amateur. These Natural Philosophers' desires and energies (and perhaps their quests) were directed toward finding out new knowledge, new species, or new "races" of human beings rather than new territories to be claimed and used for colonial expansion. Many were unattached to academic life (the professionalization of science and the rise of the research university had yet to happen), and in fact many were clergymen. Some were members of learned bodies such as London's Royal Society or the Royal Geographical Society, which attempted to collate, discuss, and distribute such knowledge among a fairly select body of like-minded natural philosophers. (The break with other branches of "philosophy" was also yet to happen.) Some, like Charles Darwin, whose voyage on the *Beagle* was made possible by his private income, were independently wealthy men whose material comfort allowed them to lead lives devoted to the study of the natural world.

The essential point to grasp about analogy is that the process is not neutral. In attempting to draw likeness between different objects, the natural scientists of the late eighteenth and nineteenth centuries imported their own set of assumptions about the world into their description. If we suggest that a thing is like another thing, then several inferences can be drawn. To take an example, let us say that "an antelope is like a deer." Firstly, for the analogy to make sense we would have to know what a deer is. Secondly, we would have to appreciate why the comparison is being drawn: what is important about a deer that might provide us with some idea of what an antelope is without having seen one? Important things about a deer may be: it is a four-legged mammal living on land, it is herbivorous, it lives in herds, it is often found in woodlands. These are only assumptions, of course, about what "an antelope is like a deer" suggests, but the analogy will guide us toward these assumptions. Thirdly, within a particular community of knowledge (such as biology, or here, zoology) an analogy will rely upon more specialist knowledge and will indicate a rather more detailed likeness. The deer-antelope analogy might suggest the social structure of the herds or the pattern of reproduction, or might take account of migration patterns.

The key point is that analogies work within defined bodies of knowledge, and we must be inside that knowledge to decode the analogy. Within those bodies of knowledge will also be assumptions about the world. For the botanist, a foundational assumption must be that the natural world is a knowable, material thing, and that by close study, description, and analysis we can understand its workings. But what if the world, or thing, or event that the scientist sees and describes does not tally with his or her assumptions? What if something inexplicable occurs, or something utterly unknown is encountered? Either he or she must dismantle all of the structures of knowledge that have formed the way the world has been understood and its workings interpreted (such as in a branch of science like biology), or there must be recourse to analogy. If it is not something we can understand, it might be *like* something we do understand. The unknown, the threatening "other," is then brought within the realms of the known.

Changes in Nineteenth-Century Science

In the natural sciences, the understanding of life on earth was becoming much more systematic and less anecdotal (the province of the amateur) by the end of the eighteenth century. Great biologists such as Georges Cuvier in France (also quoted in the "Extracts" section of *Moby-Dick*), through amassing great collections of specimens from all over the world, were able to formulate systems of classification for the natural world. The Swedish biologist Carl von Linné, better known by his Latin name, Linnaeus, published his *System Naturae* in 1758, which introduced the zoological names and classification system that form the basis for the one in use today. Cuvier suggested that animal life should be classified into four groups or *embranchements*, namely the "vertebrates," the "molluscs," the "articulates" (such as insects), and the "radiates" (such as starfish).

Not all of these classification systems were in agreement, however; in fact, the whole set of assumptions on which they were based differed widely, and differs from our own understanding of the natural world, one which we might call "post-Darwinian." The *Origin of Species* was published in 1859, and the impact of "evolutionary theory" (in all its forms, not simply that of Darwin) will be explored in the next chapters. But before Darwin, and even after, there was great debate about how the natural world should be understood.

By the early nineteenth century, the idea that nature conformed to a great "chain of being" (see chapter two), with each species in its own cosmological pigeonhole and "man" at the very top, was being challenged by such classification systems as those of Linnaeus and Cuvier. The Chain of Being suggested that, according to the Bible, God had created the earth and all natural life upon it, and that each took its place in the order of creation. The correspondence or relationship each species had to another reflected the great design of its Creator. By definition, although there may be some cosmic pigeonholes unfilled (because humans had not discovered this species yet), none had disappeared, for why should God have created an animal only to destroy it? Many of the early natural philosophers and botanists were Anglican clergymen, and their faith shaped the way in which the evidence of the natural world was interpreted. Even professional academics were constrained by the assumptions of the Christian faith: professors at British universities such as Cambridge and Oxford were ordained ministers of the church. For them, as for William Paley (1743–1805), whose *Natural Theology, or Evidences of the Existence and Attributes of the Deity, Collected from the Appearances of Nature* (1802) celebrated nature as bearing the signature of the divine hand, experience and encounter with nature was a spiritual undertaking. Nature in all its diversity and profusion did not compromise their faith, but complemented their appreciation of creation.

American Nature and Spirituality

Paley's manner of thinking in "natural theology," and its understanding of nature as spiritual, influenced the way American nature was represented, particularly among American transcendentalists like Ralph Waldo Emerson (1803–1882) and Henry David Thoreau (1817–1862). We can also see its traces in the burgeoning conservation movement of the later nineteenth century. Praiseworthy though this desire to preserve the "natural wonders" of North America may be, the spiritual idea of an American "wilderness" is one filtered through representations in art and literature.

As the North American continent was "opened" through the nineteenth century, the idea of westward expansion took on the missionary aspects of the colonial settlement of America itself. America becomes (in Henry Nash Smith's phrase) the "Virgin Land," the new Eden to be explored, inhabited, and owned by a chosen people—not the Native Americans, but white settlers. The American landscape became venerated as a place of particular spiritual significance and the symbol of a particular kind of American national identity—not one tainted by the history and sins of Europe, but one built afresh in an untainted New Found Land. This contrast of American innocence, youthfulness, and vigor with European experience, sin, and decline can be found in much American art and culture of the nineteenth century.

The American landscape, as represented in landscape art, became empty of human life in the nineteenth century, a vast spectacle of natural wonders to be consumed by gallery crowds back east, or, as in the novels of James Fenimore Cooper (1789–1851), a testing ground for the white woodsman in harmony with American nature. The most important of these landscape artists was Frederick Edwin Church (1826–1900), whose *Niagara* of 1857 was a huge success when exhibited. By the time Church painted the falls, it had already become the most represented natural wonder in American cultural life and by the 1850s attracted over 60,000 tourists a year. Church edits the tourists out and portrays the water thundering over the falls as an awe-inspiring spectacle devoid of human life, framing a moment of direct communion between spectator and nature in its most powerful guise. By the 1860s Church had become the most prominent American artist, and his vision of the American landscape as God's Creation places him in direct lineage to Paley and the transcendentalists. His detailed observation of plants, animals, geology, and atmosphere successfully linked the tools of scientific description with a vision of the harmonious order of Creation made immanent in the American landscape.

Moby-Dick *and Classification Systems*

If nature is seen to be spiritual, then it should not be exploited; but if "man" has dominion over the earth, should we not use its resources as we see fit? Melville's *Moby-Dick* (1851) returns to this issue. Though concerned with Captain Ahab's voyage in search of revenge on the white whale, the novel is narrated by another, who announces himself in one of the most arresting opening lines of any fiction: "Call me Ishmael." But this is not in fact the beginning of the novel. This phrase occurs at the start of chapter one ("Loomings"), but is preceded by two other sections, "Etymology" and "Extracts." While "Extracts" quotes from a variety of literary, scriptural, and scientific texts that mention the whale (or Leviathan), the "Etymology" section foregrounds what the creature is called, in a variety of languages. "Call me Ishmael," call the creature "whale": what meanings, what knowledge is imparted in a name?

As I showed above, the modern Linnean system of naming, and thereby placing species within a field of knowledge, predates *Moby-Dick* by nearly a hundred years. Melville, however, by imitating the linguistic and taxonomic habits of encyclopedias, brings into question the whole idea of classification. This is particularly evident in chapter thirty-two, "Cetology," where the narrator suggests a system of classification of whales based on bookbinding sizes (folio, octavo, and duodecimo). In a joking footnote, the narrator acknowledges that quarto is more properly the next size smaller than folio, but "the bookbinder's Quarto volume in its diminished form does not preserve the shape of the Folio volume, but the Octavo volume does." Although Melville exposes the seeming absurdity and arbitrariness of classification systems, it does have a self-contained logic. The folio-octavo-duodecimo classification preserves the element of likeness between the types of whales and does suggest a relationship in size, shape, and scale. It is a half-joking use of analogy. Ironically, the whales themselves become books, just as the subtitle of *Moby-Dick* is *The Whale.* The text parodies systems of knowl-

Herman Melville (1819–1891)

Herman Melville was born in New York to a prosperous merchant family, but following the failure of his business in 1832, Melville's father declined into madness and died when his son was only twelve. Leaving school at fifteen, Melville worked to support his family, but his departure from formal education was the spur for his own program of diverse reading. Melville read the King James version of the Bible, other writings from the seventeenth century, and a wealth of technical, anthropological, and historical studies, all of which he drew upon in his later writings.

Melville's development can be understood in terms of two influences, his experience of the sea and his own self-education. He was to say of himself that the sea was his Harvard or Yale. At nineteen years of age, Melville shipped to Liverpool, England, and this trip taught him much about the cruelties of authority on board ship and the camaraderie of the "hands." Later, in 1841, he sailed aboard the *Acushnet* on a whaling voyage to the South Seas. These journeys had a major bearing on his early works, such as the semiautobiographical *Typee* (1846) and *Omoo* (1847), *Redburn* (1849) and *White-Jacket* (1850).

Melville, author of Moby Dick, *based his most famous novel on his early experiences of life on board whaling ships. He suffered from critical neglect in his day, and even gave up novel writing after the commercial and critical failure of* The Confidence Man *(1857). (Corbis)*

Typee is an early indication of Melville's concerns. He was particularly worried about the impact that white (American) "civilization" had upon nature, and in *Typee*, this contrast is organized around the experiences of an American sailor on a Polynesian island. In his greatest work, *Moby-Dick* (1851), this opposition becomes Captain Ahab's demonic quest for the white whale. Unfortunately, Melville's dramatization of the conflict between human and nature reached few ears. *Moby-Dick* was a commercial failure, as were his subsequent novels up to *The Confidence Man* (1857). From then Melville turned to poetry, and it wasn't until 1924 that *Billy Budd, Sailor* was finally published from his manuscript papers. Melville died virtually forgotten, and his reputation was not revived until the twentieth century. From this later perspective, Melville has been reassessed as a "classic" American writer, and *Moby-Dick*, in particular, an encyclopedic novel that criticizes and encapsulates many mid-nineteenth-century American attitudes and values.

edge and their claims to truth while suggesting that the white whale itself is somehow unknowable, mysterious, occult.

Moby-Dick: *Analogy, Anatomy, and Autopsy*

Perhaps it would be naïve to read *Moby-Dick* simply as a novel about whaling, or even about the relationship between humans and nature. It is, though, a novel about knowledge. In a long sequence of chapters that begins with chapter sixty-one, "Stubb Kills a Whale," the novel offers a detailed description of the process of rendering the killed and captured sperm whale into the precious oil that is the economic rationale for the voyage. To begin, they strip the skin from the whale's carcass:

> Now as the blubber envelopes the whale precisely as the rind does an orange, so it is stripped off the body precisely as an orange is sometimes stripped by spiralizing it. For the strain constantly kept up by the windlass continually keeps the whale rolling over and over in the water, and . . . the blubber in one strip uniformly peels off the line called the "scarf," simulta-neously cut by the spades of Starbuck and Stubb, the mates.

Notice the use of analogy here: the whale is like an orange, once again describing the unknown in terms of the known. The analogy reduces the act of killing and butchering the whale to a domestic size, masking any moral qualms we might have about the act itself. In chapter seventy, "The Sphynx," the whale is beheaded; in chapter seventy-four, "The Sperm Whale's Head—Contrasted View," the head is described in anatomical detail. While these descriptions do provide a detailed insight into the process of whaling in the mid nineteenth cen-tury (and later chapters concentrate on the technical and industrial processes at work on the *Pequod*), they are, symbolically, a fragmenting of the whale into its constituent parts, making the mysterious Leviathan knowable through exact description.

It is through anatomy that the whale becomes known, and this emphasis reflects medical developments in the early nineteenth century. Dissection of corpses was, in the eighteenth century, seen as the best way of understanding disease, partly because the modern medical practice of diagnosing illness from its symptoms was widely unknown. Perhaps the most explicit demonstration of this doctrine comes from Xavier Bichat's *Anatomie générale* of 1801:

> What is the value of observation, if one does not know the seat of the dis-ease? You can take notes for twenty years from morning to evening at the

sickbed on diseases of the heart, lung, and stomach, and you will reap nothing but confusion. The symptoms, corresponding to nothing, will offer but
incoherent phenomena. Open a few corpses, and immediately this obscurity,
which observation alone would never have removed, will disappear.

The autopsy, following swiftly on from death, was, in Bichat's rhetoric, the
only true path to understanding the body. In life, the bodily symptoms were confused, incoherent, obscure—because their source was not visible. In death, however, the body becomes open to the knife and the observation of the doctor.

Anatomy and analogy were two vital tools for the natural scientist and the
doctor in the nineteenth-century, and one would often be used to correct the mistakes of the other. In *Moby-Dick*, the body of the whale becomes knowable
because it is taken apart, made into the fragments of knowledge (about the skin,
the head, the eyes, the oil) that can then be set down in the form of the encyclopedia. As *Moby-Dick* makes clear, this kind of knowledge is also a kind of violence. It is also precisely the kind of knowledge that Ralph Waldo Emerson, in
his essay "The American Scholar," first given as a speech in 1837, suggests should
be refused. In that essay, Emerson suggests that narrow specialization has come
to characterize knowledge of the world, and he advocates a return to self-reliant,
independent, and full engagement with the experiences of life. The "American
Scholar" is a whole human being who embraces life, rather than fragments
knowledge and experience into compartments or classifications. We find a similar impulse in Thoreau's *Walden*.

Nature and the Transcendentalists

Henry David Thoreau's *Walden* (1854), which is a key text of the transcendentalists, commemorates the two years and two months he spent living in a cabin
on Walden Pond—land owned by his friend Ralph Waldo Emerson. In the form
of a year's passage—human life allied to the cycle of the seasons—*Walden* offers
the reader an example of the good life constituted by simplicity, solitude, self-
reliance, and personal freedom, particularly freedom from the possessions and
material ambitions of the "civilized" world. In the opening chapter, "Economy,"
Thoreau outlines the necessary and sufficient conditions of life at Walden Pond,
mainly consisting of food, clothing, and shelter. To enumerate his simple economy, Thoreau famously included lists of building materials, foodstuffs, and
incomings and outgoings. As in the American rhetorical tradition of nature versus civilization, simplicity versus luxury, innocence versus corruption, Thoreau
finds moral value away from the life of the towns and cities, and finds recourse

in an ideal and indeed transcendental vision of natural harmony. As in Emerson's "The American Scholar," Thoreau puts forward his ideal of "scholarly" or "philosophical" engagement with the world:

> None can be an impartial or wise observer of human life but from the vantage ground of what we should call voluntary poverty. Of a life of luxury the fruit is luxury, whether it is agriculture, or commerce, or literature, or art. There are nowadays professors of philosophy, but not philosophers. Yet it is admirable to profess because it was once admirable to live. To be a philosopher is not merely to have subtle thoughts, nor even to found a school, but so to love wisdom as to live according to its dictates, a life of simplicity, independence, magnanimity, and trust. It is to solve some of the problems of life, not only theoretically, but practically. The success of great scholars and thinkers is commonly a courier-like success, not kingly, not manly. They make shift to live merely by conformity, practically as their fathers did, and are in no sense the progenitors of a noble race. But why do men degenerate ever? What makes families run out? What is the nature of the luxury which enervates and destroys nations?

This long quotation pinpoints the anxiety that lies behind the search for the simple life, an anxiety centered on manliness, vigor, and nobility—the attributes of Natty Bumppo, in James Fenimore Cooper's *Leatherstocking* series. Natty Bumppo is an idealized American, at home in the wilderness, courageous, resourceful, and generous. Most of all, he is unpretentious, noble, and vigorous, a new type of man wholly suited to American life and untainted by Europe or "civilization." He is at one with nature, and in fact, embodies its moral value. In *The Last of the Mohicans*, Bumppo might claim a moral kinship with Chingachcook, the last of the Mohican tribe, but his assertion of racial difference signifies that Bumppo (and by extension his stock) is the man of the future, and that the Native American is soon to be consigned to the past. As the United States developed into a large, powerful, and industrial modern state, novelists such as Cooper, and the landscape artists of the nineteenth century, indicate that in the path to the future, it is the white (settler) community that will prevail. The indigenous peoples will perish in a pseudo-Darwinist competition for resources. Natty Bumppo, ironically, is at once the man of the future and the repository of the values of the past.

Thoreau's *Walden* is also an attempt to rediscover that which has been lost, the simplicity of life in tune with nature. In a Walt Whitman (1819–1892) poem collected in the 1891–1892 *Leaves of Grass* (a collection of poetry much revised, added to, and amended since its first publication in 1855), we find the same suspicion of book-learning, and the same elevation of an unmediated communion

Henry David Thoreau (1817–1862)

Henry David Thoreau, a man who sought harmony in life, was born in an aptly named place: Concord, Massachusetts. Thoreau tried his hand at many occupations but never settled at any one (even that of writer), a source of amusement and complaint among both family and friends. He is most famous as the author of *Walden* (1854), a long essay based on his time in a cabin at Walden Pond. It sets forth his transcendentalist views on nature and living the "good" and moral life. Thoreau was

Essayist Henry David Thoreau, friend of Ralph Waldo Emerson and key Transcendentalist writer, sought spirituality through experience of Nature, most famously in his account of living for two years in the woods, Walden (1854). (Library of Congress)

educated at Harvard, and soon became the friend (and admirer) of Ralph Waldo Emerson, the leading thinker of transcendentalism, and in fact spent some time living with Emerson as a handyman. Ironically, Thoreau's reputation now eclipses that of his friend and mentor.

Thoreau described himself as a "mystic, a transcendentalist, and a natural philosopher," but where his contemporary Charles Darwin was to use a model of "economy" to investigate the workings of evolution, Thoreau used the same idea to offer a vision of harmony and self-sufficiency, a life away from the materialism and corruption of the urban and "civilized" world. Like Darwin, Thoreau went through a long period of thinking and rewriting before his experiences and vision of nature were expressed in a form he was happy to see published. Thoreau epitomized the virtues of Emerson's "American Scholar," combining learning in a range of fields with practical experience and moral sense. Sadly, Thoreau died young, from tuberculosis. Most of his works were published after his death, but his calls for (and personal commitment to) nonviolent resistance to unjust laws, the abolition of slavery, and a much less exploitative relationship between humans and nature have had a long-lasting influence on American thought and literature. His writings on nature can be seen in a lineage from William Paley's *Natural Theology* (1802), but in Thoreau's hands, understanding nature as having a profound spiritual and moral value leads not to seeing God's signature in the shape of the world, but all humanity's responsibility for its preservation.

with the natural world. In "When I Heard the Learn'd Astronomer," Whitman attends an astronomy lecture, where he is told about the cosmos and is "shown the charts and diagrams, to add, divide, and measure them," but sitting in the lecture room and being told about the great cosmos rather than experiencing it brings on a kind of nausea:

How soon unaccountable I became tired and sick,
Till rising and gliding out I wander'd off by myself,
In the mystical moist night-air, and from time to time,
Look'd up in perfect silence at the stars. (ll.5-8)

Notice how Whitman exhibits the same avoidance of second-hand learning, the same desire to experience nature in solitude, the same sense of completeness ("perfect silence") found in the moment of communion. It is nature experienced in its fullest sense that provides spiritual comfort for Whitman, and in which his vision of humanity and nature finds its fulfillment. In "I Sing the Body Electric," also from *Leaves of Grass*, Whitman celebrates bodies and the love of bodies, and again expresses this in an image of bodily sharing: "The armies of those I love engirth me and I engirth them," a paradoxical kind of double spiritual enclosure, where each holds or contains the other within it. Section eight of the poem lists the parts of the body (male, for it includes "man-root"), from head down to heel, and identifies the soul with the body:

O I say these are not the parts and poems of the body only, but of the
    soul,
O I say now these are the soul! (l. 163–164)

"The Body Electric" is not the muscular impulses identified by Galvani, nor the "magnetic influence" of Poe's "The Facts in the Case of M. Valdemar," which this chapter will look at shortly, but a spiritual vitality, the human expression of the wonder of life found everywhere in Whitman's poetry. The electric body is profoundly material as well as sacred, and love for it is both carnal and transcendent, doing away with any distinction between human and nature, body and soul, the material world and the divine. Nature is not a church in which to worship; all life, all experience is to be embraced. In its inclusiveness, its vibrancy, and its energy, Whitman's poetry is where we truly find the voice of the "American Scholar."

Science and Religion: The Way to Hell

One of the ironies of *Moby-Dick* is, of course, that all that fragmented knowledge (the kind that Emerson rejects as non-American) and Ahab's obsessive quest for the whale leads only to doom and self-destruction. *Moby-Dick* suggests that the quest for the ultimate knowledge of the whale may, in fact, be satanic. Ishmael sees "wraiths" boarding the *Pequod* in Nantucket, and Stubb, the second mate, speculates that Fedellah (Ahab's harpooner) is "the devil in disguise." Most importantly, the whole enterprise of whaling is cast in a demonic light in chapter ninety-six, "The Try Works," and here the *Pequod* becomes a floating factory, and a hellish one at that.

> As they narrated to each other their unholy adventures, their tales of terror told in words of mirth; as their uncivilized laughter forked upwards out of them, like the flames from the furnace; as to and fro, in their front, the harpooners wildly gesticulated with their huge pronged forks and dippers; as the wind howled on, and the sea leaped, and the ship groaned and dived, and yet steadfastly shot her red hell further and further into the blackness of the sea and the night, and scornfully clamped the white bones in her mouth, and viciously spat round her on all sides; then the rushing *Pequod*, freighted with savages, and laden with fire, and burning a corpse, and plunging into that blackness of darkness, seemed the material counterpart of her monomaniac commander's soul.

Once again we find analogy: the hellish ship, cloaked in blackest night, becomes the symbol of Ahab's demonic soul, but also of human technology and industry run amok in nature, consuming and destroying as it goes. The contrasting moral values associated with nature and civilization in texts like *The Last of the Mohicans* here become something far more complicated and disturbing: the relationship between human and nature may lead to the destruction of both. *Moby-Dick*'s depiction of industry, consuming both nature and those who pursue it, was taken up by Upton Sinclair (1878–1968) and Jack London (1876–1916) in the early twentieth century with an avowedly socialist purpose. In Sinclair's *The Jungle* (1906), a fictional exposé of the meat-packing factories of Chicago, industry becomes that which oppresses and eventually destroys its "working men." In *The Jungle* and *The Octopus*, which focuses on the railroads, the titles indicate a perversion of natural processes, where the brutal competition of capitalism exceeds even that of Darwin's natural selection.

Melville, when reviewing *Mosses from an Old Manse* (1846), his friend Nathaniel Hawthorne's second volume of stories, appreciated the "power of blackness" to be found in them. This blackness was probably located in recurrent ideas of sin and damnation in Hawthorne's stories, his narratives of Puritan morality such as "Young Goodman Brown" (1835) and *The Scarlet Letter* (1850), for which he is now most famous. Hawthorne (1804–1864) himself identified his fictions as romances rather than novels, allowing himself "a certain latitude" in the depiction of life. His stories, therefore, tend toward the allegorical and symbolic.

Hawthorne was initially attracted to the ideals of the transcendentalist movement, founded by Ralph Waldo Emerson and Henry David Thoreau, themselves heavily influenced by Samuel Taylor Coleridge, William Wordsworth, and German Romantic writing. It seems, however, that Hawthorne's Puritan upbringing, especially his exposure to the ideas of John Calvin, disposed him to reject transcendentalist ideals. For Hawthorne, Calvin was right—"In Adam's fall we sinned all," and there is evil in the heart of everyone that cannot be expunged by social reforms. *The Scarlet Letter*, the first work to bring Hawthorne any success, was published in 1837. The plot is set in the seventeenth century, where Puritan zealots have established a dour and repressive theocracy, where civil laws are based on strict religious principles, in the town of Boston. The central characters are Hester (an adulteress), Roger Chillingworth (the husband), and a Puritan minister called Arthur Dimmesdale, who has fathered a child with Hester while Chillingworth was in Amsterdam. The Puritan elders have punished Hester by forcing her to wear a scarlet letter "A" embroidered on her breast.

It is in the character of Chilingworth that we can discern Hawthorne's distrust of scientific rationalism; his very name suggests a lack of compassion. Chillingworth is a physician who has studied at a German university and has learned the use of herbs and natural magic from the New England natives. His medical knowledge is of a rather sinister kind, however, and he is conscious of the power it gives him to find out who has committed adultery with his wife:

> I shall seek this man, as I have sought truth in books; as I have sought gold in alchemy. There is a sympathy that will make me conscious of him. I shall see him tremble. I shall feel myself shudder. . . . Sooner or later he must needs be mine.

Chillingworth proceeds to identify and destroy the adulterer Arthur Dimmesdale. He tracks his victim mercilessly until he is caught, pinned, and wriggling like a collector's specimen. He pretends to try to heal Dimmesdale, who is suffering from psychosomatic stress, but instead uses his powers to weaken his patient. As the plot unfolds, Chillingworth takes on a diabolical aspect:

> Now there was something ugly and evil in his face . . .According to the vulgar idea, the fire in his laboratory had been brought from the lower regions, and was fed with infernal fuel; and so, as might be expected, his visage was getting sooty with the smoke.

Elsewhere the symbolism is even more direct, and he is compared with Satan and diabolical agents. In some ways, then, Chillingworth is also a Faust-like figure, someone who has intellectual gifts that have been diverted to ignoble ends. Hawthorne's image of the heartless scientist is found in his other works, such as the short stories "The Birthmark" and "Rappaccini's Daughter."

In some stories, most notably "Rappaccini's Daughter" (1846), Hawthorne used fiction to criticize what he felt to be the misguided or malevolent intentions behind scientific method, which treats nature in isolation and reproduces that isolation in the scientist and in others. "Rappaccini's Daughter" features, at the center of its narrative, one Giovanni Guasconti, who travels from southern Italy ("very long ago") to study at the University of Padua. There he takes rooms that overlook a walled and isolated garden where he sees a beautiful young woman tending some rather strange flowers and plants. On talking to a professor of medicine at the university, he is told that it is the garden of a Dr. Rappaccini and Beatrice, his daughter. Rappaccini, he learns, has a grim reputation:

> But as for Rappaccini, it is said of him—and I, who know the man well, can answer for its truth—that he cares infinitely more for science than for mankind. His patients are interesting to him only as subjects for some new experiment. He would sacrifice human life, his own among the rest, or whatever else was dearest to him, for the sake of adding so much as a grain of mustard seed to the great heap of his accumulated knowledge.

Ignoring the professor's warnings, Giovanni becomes increasingly infatuated with Beatrice and is eventually shown a secret entrance into the garden. Though he woos her successfully, the narrative reveals that Giovanni has been the victim of a nasty experiment by Rappaccini, one first visited on his daughter. Giovanni had noticed "an analogy between the beautiful girl and the gorgeous shrub that hung its gemlike flowers over the fountain," but the shrub, like all the flowers in the garden, is poisonous. The analogy holds true: Beatrice (also the name of Dante's beloved in his *Divine Comedy*) is herself the embodiment of poison, and her charms are fatal. The allegory, of course, has to do with the Garden of Eden and loss of innocence, but this is a polluted, man-made version of the garden:

> there had been such commixture, and, as it were, adultery, of various vegetable species, that the production was no longer of God's making, but the monstrous offspring of man's depraved fancy, glowing with only an evil mockery of beauty. They were probably the result of experiment.

The knowledge that Giovanni seeks, embodied in Beatrice, is fatal to him (he, too, becomes an embodiment of poison) and to his beloved: when she takes an "antidote," she dies. Like Ahab, Giovanni Rappaccini is destroyed by the desire to know and to possess. His attempt to protect his daughter and to make her "as terrible as thou art beautiful," only increased her isolation, prevented her from loving, and precipitated her death. The scientist becomes a monster, his cold intellect preventing him from understanding that human contact, and above all, love, is the only thing that can nourish.

Science, Non-Science, and Nonsense: The Case of Edgar Allan Poe

Edgar Allan Poe (1809–1849) was also very interested in science and the scientist, although some of his stories and "essays" assume the form of the tall story or "put-on." In Poe's "The Facts in the Case of M. Valdemar" (1845), the story seems to have the status (as the title suggests) of a scientific report or paper, explaining some strange or newly discovered phenomenon. Poe, as is well known, was a great hoaxer, and in part this story is a put-on—and a successful one at that. Like "Von Kempelen and His Discovery" (1849), the last story Poe wrote before his death, "M. Valdemar" was taken by many readers as a factual account. The narrator of the story is a mesmerist who is called to the bedside of his friend Ernest Valdemar, who is on the threshold of death, and places the dying man into a trance. Mesmerism, an early and rather dubious forerunner of hypnosis, provides evidence of a growing nineteenth-century interest in "sciences of the mind" that were to culminate in Sigmund Freud's psychoanalytical theories. Also associated with mesmerism was a hypothesis of magnetic attraction or influence between organic bodies, which Poe in this story calls "magnetic influence" but is elsewhere called "animal magnetism." In the story, the narrator makes "passes" over the inert, dying body of Valdemar to assert his "clairvoyant" influence:

> As I approached M. Valdemar I made a kind of half effort to influence his right arm into pursuit of my own, as I passed the latter gently to and fro above his person. In such experiments with this patient I had never perfectly succeeded before, and assuredly I had little thought of succeeding now; but to my astonishment, his arm very readily, although feebly, followed every direction I assigned it with mine. I determined to hazard a few words of conversation.

This idea of "magnetic" influence is also found in *Moby-Dick*, where Ahab "magnetises" Starbuck's will and forces him to be an unwilling participant in the quest. There, as here, it has overtones of dark magic or the occult. In "M. Valdemar" we are at the edge of science, in the borderlands of the unexplainable, where known organic processes can be suspended by force of the mind. The distinction or division between body and mind, or perhaps body and soul—one that

Edgar Allan Poe, literary hoaxer and writer of poetry and Gothic stories, whose influence on American literature and subsequent horror fiction is profound. (National Archives)

is at the core of Captain Ahab's torment—is expressed in the literal disembodiment of Valdemar's voice. This projects directly from his blackened and protruding tongue by seemingly supernatural means. The narrator returns to the body some seven months after the original suspension, and in response to his question, the tongue utters the chilling sentence: "For God's sake!—quick!—quick!—put me to sleep—or, quick!—waken me!—quick!—I say to you that I am dead!" "Quick," of course, can mean "alive" as well as "fast" (as in the phrase "the quick and the dead"). Which one is Valdemar? Is he dead, still alive, or something in between? As the narrator releases the body from the trance, it "absolutely rotted away," and the processes of decay, which had been seemingly held back by mesmeric intervention, overcomes Valdemar like a flood. Finally, on the bed "there lay a nearly liquid mass of loathsome—of detestable putridity." And there the tale ends. The dash in that last sentence, almost a gulp of nausea, also indicates the holes in the explanation of this strange event.

What are the facts in this case? Is Valdemar's state the result of mesmerism or some other unexplained process? We are left with no "case," no deduction, no explanation. "The Facts in the Case of M. Valdemar" calls up the form of the scientific case-study, only to expose its limits. Like *Moby-Dick* and the *encyclopaedia*, "M. Valdemar" expresses a profound suspicion of scientific explanation and provides plenty of room for the occult, the mysterious, and the inexplicable.

In other texts, Poe is equally skeptical. "Maelzel's Chess-Player" (1836) is a journalistic exposure of a "mechanical" chess player that in fact hides a thoroughly human operator; "Some Words with a Mummy" (1845) describes how a revived Egyptian mummy revels in the discomfort of a group of pompous professional men, systematically undermining any delusions of "human progress."

Conclusion

This chapter will end by turning to Samuel Clemens, better known as Mark Twain (1835–1910), without whom no survey of nineteenth-century American literature would be complete. As the nineteenth century progressed, humanity was dethroned from its position in the "great chain of being." From being the steward of God's Creation, human beings came to understand with far greater clarity their place in the earth's long, fascinating history, and through science, to see more clearly the processes that have shaped, and still shape, life on earth. Some may have found this new role a diminishment, but in the move from assuming dominion over the earth to learning a proper respect for it, much more was gained than lost. However, the result of this change can be confusion. Here is Mark Twain:

> Man has been here 32,000 years. That it took a hundred million years to prepare the world for him is proof that that is what it was done for. I suppose it is, I dunno. If the Eiffel Tower were now representing the world's age, the skin of paint on the pinnacle-knob at its summit would represent man's share of that age; and anybody would reckon that that skin was what the world was built for. I reckon they would, I dunno.

"I dunno," says Twain. This seems now a profoundly modern phrase. Does it betray confusion, an inability to comprehend the new knowledge that had begun to influence popular thinking by the beginning of the twentieth century? Is there a change from certainty to uncertainty? If there is, we still have analogy to fall back on. Notice how Twain uses analogy here, and not an analogy drawn from nature, as in scientific analysis earlier in the century. It is the Eiffel Tower, one of the late nineteenth century's most famous achievements in engineering, which serves as the model for geological time. The process of drawing the unknown, or incomprehensible, into a knowable and familiar scale by use of analogy is the same as it was a century before, but the way of explaining has changed, because the world had changed. In the twentieth century, the acceleration in the pace of change in science and technology would become more radical still, and the United States would be at the forefront of these developments.

Bibliographic Essay

Critical writing on science and literature has tended not to focus on American literature of the nineteenth century, and conversely, the traditions of criticism of American literature tend not to investigate any connection to science. Recently, however, relevant source material has been published in Literature and Science in *Nineteenth Century: An Anthology*, edited by Laura Otis (Oxford: Oxford University Press, 2002). American literature has been studied (in the last sixty years) through myth and symbol, such as in Henry Nash Smith's *Virgin Land: The American West as Symbol and Myth* (Cambridge, MA and London: Harvard University Press, 1950); through the American reliance on Romance rather than realist modes of fiction, as in Richard Chase, *The American Novel* (New York: Doubleday, 1957); through violence and the frontier, as in Richard Slotkin, *Regeneration Through Violence: The Mythology of the American Frontier, 1600–1860* (1973) (University of Oklahoma Press, 2000); and more recently, through concentration on issues of race and gender. British critics have focused either on the connections between Romantic or Victorian writing and science, for which see Peter Morton, *The Vital Science: Biology and the Literary Imagination 1860–1900* (London: George Allen and Unwin, 1984), or on the literary metaphors that influenced the scientific writings of Darwin and others. For this, see Gillian Beer, *Open Fields: Science in Cultural Encounter* (Oxford: Oxford University Press, 1996). Therefore, the connections made in this chapter have been diverse and have largely been produced through the representations of nature in American literature, or occasionally the representation of the scientist.

Edgar Allan Poe has become a much more widely discussed and admired writer in the last thirty years, when detective, gothic, and fantastic fiction gained a kind of academic and critical acceptance. His short stories, which date from the 1830s and 1840s, are reprinted in several collections. References to "The Facts in the Case of M. Valdemar" (1845) and "Some Words with a Mummy" (1845) are taken from *Edgar Allan Poe, Selected Tales* (Oxford and New York: Oxford Classics, 1980). For a detailed overview of the critical reception of Poe, see the four volumes of Graham Clarke, *Edgar Allan Poe: Critical Assessments* (Mountfield, East Sussex: Helm Information, 1991). For the relationship between Poe and science, see Peter Swirski, *Between Literature and Science: Poe, Lem and Explorations in Aesthetics, Cognitive Science, and Literary Knowledge* (Montreal: McGill-Queens University Press, 2000). Nathaniel Hawthorne and Herman Melville, friends in life and now seen as American "classics," have both been the focus of much critical writing. The edition of Melville's *Moby-Dick* used in this chapter (first American edition, New York: Harper's, 1851) is the widely available British Penguin edition (London: Penguin, 1987). For Hawthorne's stories, collections cited are *Mosses from and Old Manse* (1846) (Columbus: Ohio State University Press, 1974) and *The Snow Image* (1852) (Columbus: Ohio State University Press, 1974), from which "Rappacini's Daughter" (1846) is taken. For Melville's and Hawthorne's connection to science and problems of analogy, see Sharon Cameron, *The Corporeal Self: Allegories of the Body in Melville and Hawthorne* (Baltimore and London: Johns Hopkins University Press, 1981). Conference papers given by Sam Halliday and Peter Massender at the 2002 British Association of American Studies conference, held at St. Anne's College, University of Oxford, have also had an influence on the shape of this chapter. For the transcendentalists, Ralph Waldo Emerson's essay "The American Scholar" (1837) is collected in *English Traits, Representative Men and Other Essays* (London: J. M. Dent, 1908); Henry David Thoreau's *Walden* (1854) is widely available.

For general surveys of American literature in the period, see Peter Conn, *Literature in America: An Illustrated History* (London and New York: Guild, 1990) and Marcus Cunliffe, *The Literature of the United States* (Harmondsworth: Penguin, 1982). Or for a more personal approach, see Tony Tanner, *The American Mystery: American Literature from Emerson to Delillo* (Cambridge: Cambridge University Press, 2000). For the connection between American landscape art and nature in literature, Robert Hughes's *American Visions: The Epic History of Art in America* (London: Harvill, 1997) is highly informative and very readable. Daniel Boorstin, *The Americans: The National Experience* (London: Phoenix, 2000) is a very lively and readable survey of American culture and society in the period and has also proved a very useful source of information.

The *Fontana History of Science* series can be recommended for its wide-ranging and detailed surveys of developments in the history of science. For a concise history of the natural, biological, and environmental sciences, Peter J. Bowler, *The Fontana History of The Environmental Sciences* (London: Fontana, 1992) is an excellent and accessible reference work. For medical science in the nineteenth century, see Roy Porter, *The Greatest Benefit to Mankind: A Medical History of Humanity from Antiquity to the Present* (London: Fontana, 1999), and W. F. Bynum, *Science and the Practice of Medicine in the Nineteenth Century* (Cambridge and New York: Cambridge University Press, 1994). For more general overviews of the history of science and its institutions, see R. C. Olby, G. N. Cantor, J. R. R. Christie, and M. J. S. Hodge, eds., *Companion to the History of Modern Science* (London and New York: Routledge, 1990); A. E. E. Mackenzie, *The Major Achievements of Science* (New York: Simon and Schuster, 1973), which also features some useful extracts from primary scientific writings; and Lewis Pyenson and Susan Sheets-Pyenson, *Servants of Nature: A History of Scientific Institutions, Enterprises and Sensibilities* (London: Fontana, 1999). For detailed, polemic, and highly entertaining essays on evolutionary theory, see Stephen Jay Gould, *Ever Since Darwin* (London: Penguin, 1980); and for keen insights into the geological theories of Charles Lyell and others, see Stephen Jay Gould, *Time's Arrow, Time's Cycle: Myth and Metaphor in the Discovery of Geological Time* (London: Penguin, 1990).

Those Dreadful Hammers: Geology and Evolution in Nineteenth-Century Literature

John Cartwright

Geology Comes of Age

In the Middle Ages it was a common belief in Christendom that the earth would last for 6,000 years after the moment of Creation. This conclusion was based on a typically medieval argument: since God created the world in six days and, according to Peter, "one day is with the Lord as a thousand years," then by analogy the world should last the same length of time. Setting the precise time for Creation, and hence determining how long was left, proved more difficult. The rise of Protestantism renewed interest in literalist interpretations of scripture, and Luther and his followers turned to the early books of the Bible for an authentic record of historical and geological events. By the seventeenth century a consensus emerged that four millennia must have elapsed before the birth of Christ. The most famous of all chronologies, which was often added to the standard English Bible and has been quoted with amusement ever since, was that calculated by Archbishop James Usher and published in 1650 in *The Annals of the Old Testament, Deduced from the First Origin of the World.* Usher set the date of Creation at October 26, 4004 B.C. By this reckoning the world should have ended on October 23, 1996 (or 1997, if we take into account the absence of a zero in the B.C./A.D. system).

Even in the eighteenth century many realized that Usher was wide of the mark and that to ascertain the age of the earth, science was a better guide than biblical scholarship. A revised estimate of the earth's antiquity was prepared by the French naturalist G. L. Leclerc, Comte de Buffon, who outlined his speculations in his *Histoire naturelle*. Buffon thought that the earth began as a fragment chipped off the sun by a colliding comet. So by experimenting on cooling spheres and comparing them with the imagined cooling of the earth from its molten state, in 1774 he estimated the earth to be about 75,000 years old. The problem now, of course, became reconciling this number with Mosaic cosmogony—the account of the origin of the world as given in the first five books of the Bible (the Pentateuch) attributed to Moses. Buffon proposed that the six days of creation as mentioned in Genesis should not be taken as six days of twenty-four hours each—after all, day and night themselves were only established on the third day. Rather they should be interpreted as epochs of indefinite length. In this way a biblical "day" could be 1,000 or even 35,000 years—a solution seized upon by creationists ever since.

In Victorian Britain, geology was a popular science, and many of its practitioners, such as Adam Sedgwick and William Buckland, were ordained clergymen who had no doubt that geology and scripture would prove to be in harmony. The orthodox found some temporary comfort in the "catastrophist" theories brought into prominence by the Frenchman Georges Cuvier (1769–1832), who was struggling with the problem of how to explain masses of huge bones that were turning up in Europe and America (especially at Big Bone Lick, Kentucky). In 1796 he wrote a paper "Notes on the Species of Living and Fossil Elephants," followed in 1812 by *Essay on the Theory of the Earth.* In these works Cuvier advanced the notion that the earth periodically experienced a series of global catastrophes—Noah's Flood being the most recent—during which the surface of the earth was remolded and whole species were wiped out. The earth was then repopulated by survivors or, as Cuvier's supporters suggested, fresh creations.

Any incipient conflict between science and religion was also kept at bay by the continuation of writings in the tradition of natural theology, a mindset that can be traced back to the seventeenth century and to the writings of Bacon and Boyle. Creation is God's book of works; therefore, by studying nature we can read signs of God's active hand. One leading advocate of this line of reasoning in the late eighteenth century was William Paley (1743–1805), whose *Natural Theology, or Evidences of the Existence and Attributes of the Deity, Collected from the Appearances of Nature* (1802) was required reading for Cambridge undergraduates. As touched on in the previous chapter, Paley used an analogical argument to argue from the appearances of nature to the existence of a benign Deity. In *Natural Theology,* he reasons as follows:

> In crossing a heath, suppose I pitched my foot against a stone and were asked how the stone came to be there, I might possibly answer that for anything I knew to the contrary it had lain there forever; nor would it, perhaps, be very easy to show the absurdity of this answer. But suppose I had found a watch upon the ground, and it should be inquired how the watch happened

to be in that place, I should hardly think of the answer which I had given before, that for anything I knew the watch might have always been there. Yet why should not this answer serve for the watch as well as for the stone? Why is it not as admissible in the second case as in the first? For this reason, and for no other, namely, that when we come to inspect the watch, we per-ceive—what we could not discover in the stone—that its several parts are framed and put together for a purpose . . . . The inference we think is inevitable, that the watch must have had a maker . . . who comprehended its construction and designed its use.

This is the famous "argument from design" to prove the existence of God that was so influential in the early nineteenth century. If the world is like a watch, then the watch cannot construct itself: it must have a designer or a creator. Paley infers this from its complexity and purpose. The world, or Creation, in Paley's terms, is infinitely complex and diverse by comparison, yet also showing signs of purpose; therefore, the presence of an infinitely powerful creator is implied. Most people—the Scottish philosopher David Hume being one notable exception— were convinced by Paley's argument. One such was the young Charles Darwin studying at Cambridge in his early twenties. Looking back over his life he said:

In order to pass the BA examination, it was also necessary to get up Paley's *Evidences of Christianity*, and his *Moral Philosophy*. The logic of this book (*Evidences*) and, as I may add, of his *Natural Theology*, gave me as much delight as Euclid. I did not at that time trouble myself about Paley's prem-ises; and taking these on trust, I was charmed and convinced by the long line of argumentation. (Darwin, 1929, p. 22)

Ironically, it was Darwin who, more than any other, finally demolished Paley's reasoning.

In Britain, a notable follower of Cuvier was the Oxford geologist William Buckland (1784–1856). In his inaugural address at Oxford entitled *Vindiciae Geologicae: or The Connection of Geology with Religion Explained*, Buckland affirmed his belief in the reality of Divine Creation followed by the Flood and repudiated any attempt to separate geology from religion. Following Buckland there grew up a whole school of catastrophist thought that sought to reconcile scripture and geology using the idea of a whole series of divinely directed cata-clysms in the earth's past.

The geologist who more than any other finally managed to extricate geol-ogy from both natural theology and scriptural authority was Charles Lyell (1797–1875). Lyell was strongly influenced by the work of the Scottish Enlight-enment chemist, farmer, and geologist James Hutton (1726–1797), who argued

"The Great Day of His Wrath" (c. 1852), by John Martin. Martin (1789–1854) made his name as a painter of cataclysmic scenes, drawn largely from biblical stories, in which mankind is overwhelmed by the vengeful power of God. In keeping with cata- strophic geology, Martin supposed that God had interfered violently in the earth's past. By the end of the nineteenth century such catastrophic accounts of earth history had been challenged by the uniformitarian geology of Lyell and his followers. (Tate Gallery, London / Art Resource, NY)

that the earth's surface features could be explained by a seemingly endless cycle of erosion, sedimentation, and uplift. The process was slow but unrelenting, revealing, as he said, "no vestige of a beginning,—no prospect of an end." Lyell's most famous work, *Principles of Geology*, published in three volumes in 1830–1833, took this theme to greater depth. Lyell firmly agreed with Hutton that the earth was exceedingly old and that processes we can observe now (weath- ering, sedimentation, and so on) were the same as those acting in the past—a position known as uniformitarianism. The crucial point was that if there had been no convulsions as the catastrophists supposed, then these slow, uniform forces must have acted over immense periods of time to shape the earth into the features (mountains, valleys, cliffs) we can now observe. The earth must be mil- lions not thousands of years old. *Principles of Geology* greatly influenced Dar- win, who took the first volume with him when he set out on the *Beagle* in 1831, collecting the second volume in Montevideo in 1832 and the third in Valparaiso in 1834. Later this work was to provide the timeframe he needed to accommo- date his theory of evolution by slow, gradual changes.

"Pegwell Bay—A Recollection Oct 5th 1858," by William Dyce (1806–1869). In the foreground stand several figures dwarfed by the cliffs behind. In the sky hangs Donati's comet, which was visible in daylight at the time. The comet was first observed in June of 1858 by the Italian astronomer Giovanni Battista Donati (1826–1873). The painting suggests the immensity of both space (comet) and time (cliffs). Interestingly, Tennyson would in his 1889 poem Parnassus *refer to his two "terrible muses": astronomy and geology. The melancholy tone of the painting raises questions about the brevity and significance of human life. (Tate Gallery, London / Art Resource)*

As geology exposed the abyss of time, so that of space was being further extended by developments in astronomy. In 1831, the same year Darwin set sail on the *Beagle*, the Scottish astronomer Tomas Henderson (1798–1844) made the first measurement of the distance to the nearest star, alpha centauri. The answer was a staggering 24,000,000,000,000 (24 trillion) miles—over a quarter of a million times farther than the distance to the sun. Two paintings illustrate the changing mood of Victorian Britain in this period: John Martin's "The Great Day of His Wrath" (1852) and William Dyce's "Pegwell Bay." In Dyce's painting, small human figures wander on a desolate foreshore in front of layers of rock accumulated over aeons of time as a comet passes overhead. The paintings also seem to voice two cultural perspectives: Martin's apocalyptic scene belongs to the Romantic era, a sublime illustration of the power of God, while Dyce's melancholic scene seems to reflect Victorian uncertainty and feelings of insignificance.

In 1845 Buckland was appointed dean of Westminster, by which time he realized that his attempts to accommodate geology to scripture had failed. By now he had, like most geologists, renounced the whole idea of a deluge and accepted that the earth was much older than biblical chronology suggested.

Lamarck and Chambers

The revolution in geology initiated by Lyell provided favorable ground for evolutionary theories to take root. Before the 1840s the notion that species were not fixed ("the transmutation hypothesis") was chiefly associated with Erasmus Darwin and the French naturalist Jean-Baptiste Lamarck (1744–1829). Lamarck believed in the progressive transformation of species according to a mechanism known as the inheritance of acquired characteristics. As individual animals strove toward some goal (birds pecking into deeper crevices or wading into deeper water, for example) so their physical characteristics changed and, crucially, these changes were then inherited by their offspring. So, in the cases above, over time birds' beaks or legs grew longer. By this means species gradually modified themselves and new species emerged. Instead of a fixed chain of being (see chapter two) Lamarck imagined the whole of creation to be moving upward like some giant escalator, with spontaneous generation supplying new life at the lower end.

Lamarck published these speculations in his *Philosophie zoologique* of 1809 and was promptly ridiculed by Cuvier. In Britain his reception was mixed. In the aftermath of the Revolution, where the ruling elite of France had been deposed by a movement from below, the idea of the transmutation of species smacked of French radicalism, and the few naturalists who were attracted to the idea kept their heads down. Someone less cautious was the Edinburgh book dealer Robert Chambers (1802–1871). Chambers was a self-taught amateur scientist, and in 1844 he published his own synthesis of ideas from geology and biology titled *Vestiges of the Natural History of Creation*. The book was a national sensation, and it both shocked and enthralled the reading public. It went through four editions in the first six months alone, yet all the editions up to Chambers's death were published anonymously. When his future son-in-law asked him why he never owned up to his authorship, Chambers is said to have pointed to his house and eleven children and said, "I have eleven reasons." The fact that Chambers's firm was a leading publisher of Bibles made the matter even more sensitive.

Chambers argued that two great laws could explain the mysteries of nature: gravitation for the inorganic realm and the law of development for plants and animals. For all its faults, the book was remarkably insightful on the significance of, for example, the unity of structure between different species (homologous structures suggest common descent) and the gradation of animal forms in the fossil record. Chambers even recognized the importance of variation, so crucial to Darwin's later theory. On this point Robert and his brother William had their own evidence, since they were born fully hexadactyl, that is, they had six digits on both their hands and feet.

What fascinated the reading public was Chambers's idea that humanity was not static: humans had evolved from simpler creatures and they would go on evolving to higher forms. In addition, although Chambers used such terms as the "Almighty Conception," the "Great Father," or the "Eternal One," it was clear that God was being relegated to a vague, deistic first cause who had set out a divine plan of progression and left animals to it. Alarmed at its popularity, Hugh Miller wrote a repost called *Footprints of the Creator.* The more conservative members of the Anglican establishment were less polite. Adam Sedgwick, Cambridge don and Darwin's former tutor, thought Chambers's book was a product of the frail intellect of a woman (privately he suspected Byron's daughter Ada Lovelace) and called it a "filthy abortion" that would "undermine the whole moral and social fabric"(Desmond and Moore, 1991, p. 321).

This ferocious response was one of the reasons Darwin delayed publication of his own ideas until 1859. Even Thomas Huxley, who championed Darwin's version of evolution so enthusiastically, was dismayed that Chambers offered no mechanism to explain how animals were driven to progress other than that it was God's plan. In his savage review he called the book "pretentious nonsense." With hindsight, however, it appears that Chambers's book did have the singular function of drawing the theological fire upon *Vestiges* so that when Darwin's *Origin of Species* appeared in 1859, a less hysterical reaction was forthcoming. But even by the 1850s, the more liberal theologians were softening and could entertain the idea of a divinely directed sequence of transmutation.

For one thinker, however, *Vestiges* only confirmed the implications obviously inherent in the direction geology and biology were heading. It was this man's honesty in recording his anxieties that made him popular with scientists and the lay public alike. It also secured his fame; his name was Alfred Tennyson.

Tennyson

Alfred Tennyson (later 1st Lord Tennyson) was born in 1809, the same year as Darwin and the same year that Lamarck first advanced his evolutionary hypothesis in his *Philosophie zoologique.* Throughout his life he maintained a steady interest in science. When he died in 1892 Huxley claimed that he was "the first poet since Lucretius who has understood the drift of science." Like Darwin, he would have encountered the influence of Paley's *Natural Theology* at Cambridge. When they appeared in print, Tennyson also eagerly seized upon Lyell's *Principles* and Chambers's *Vestiges.*

The impact of these ideas is recorded in perhaps his finest poem, *In Memoriam*, a confessional elegy written over the years 1833–1849. The poem charts Tennyson's attempt both to come to terms with the death in 1833 of his dear and brilliant young friend Arthur Henry Hallam and, in parallel, assess the implications for his Christian faith of the ideas stemming from the new sciences of biology and geology. The personal and the ideological run in tandem as he charts his progress on both levels from grief and despair to acceptance and reconciliation.

Early on in the poem Tennyson expresses his fears about the lack of meaning in an indifferent universe.

> O Sorrow, cruel fellowship,
> O Priestess in the vaults of Death,
> O sweet and bitter in a breath,
> What whispers from thy lying lip?
> "The stars," she whispers, "blindly run." (Section 3, l. 1–5)

This theme of a directionless universe governed by purposeless mechanical laws, a "hollow form" with stars blindly moving about, pervades the whole work. Sections 55 and 56 are perhaps the most penetrating and philosophically interesting in the entire poem. Here Tennyson confronts directly the implications of geological time, the extinction of species, and the immense suffering that lies at the heart of natural processes. First, he offers the conjecture that the very wish for immortality is evidence of an internal apprehension of a Creator God.

> The wish, that of the living whole
> No life may fail beyond the grave,
> Derives it not from what we have
> The likest God within the soul?

But if this is the case, why is nature so wasteful and indifferent to the suffering of individuals?

> Are God and Nature then at strife,
> That Nature lends such evil dreams?

So careful of the type she seems,
So careless of the single life;
That I, considering everywhere
Her secret meaning in her deeds,
And finding that of fifty seeds
She often brings but one to bear. (Section 55, l. 1–12)

In section 56 Tennyson advances the argument by noting how species ("types") themselves become extinct, the implication also being that there is no such thing as spirit—it is just another name for a physiological process such as breathing:

So careful of the type?' but no.
From scarped cliff and quarried stone
She cries, 'A thousand types are gone:
I care for nothing, all shall go.
'Thou makest thine appeal to me:
I bring to life, I bring to death:
The spirit does but mean the breath:
I know no more. (Section 56, l. 1–8)

Then Tennyson considers the irony of human endeavour: our noblest goals may prove to be pointless and our ultimate fate to become just another fossil:

Man, her last work, who seem'd so fair,
Such splendid purpose in his eyes,
Who roll'd the psalm to wintry skies,
Who built him fanes of fruitless prayer,
Who trusted God was love indeed
And love Creation's final law—
Tho' Nature, red in tooth and claw
With ravine, shriek'd against his creed—
Who loved, who suffer'd countless ills,
Who battled for the True, the Just,
Be blown about the desert dust,
Or seal'd within the iron hills? (Section 56, l. 9–20)

Finally, the terrifying conclusion is that human ethics is an aberration: the brutality of gigantic creatures of the past (the "dragons" or dinosaurs) was at least in harmony ("mellow music") with the natural order. The overall effect is crushing: individuals perish, humanity is doomed, and our very value system is invalid by naturalistic standards:

> No more? A monster then, a dream,
> A discord. Dragons of the prime,
> That tare each other in their slime,
> Were mellow music match'd with him.
> (Section 56, l. 21–24)

It would seem impossible to crawl out from such a slough of despair, and Tennyson only does so by resorting to faith and that very Victorian notion of progress. To counter his doubts about the future of humanity as a whole, he turns Chambers's idea that the grand law of development would eventually lead to "a nobler type of humanity which shall complete the zoological circle on this planet and realize some of the dreams of the purest spirits of the present race" (*Vestiges*, p. 278). Indeed, the idea that evolution was somehow directional and that humanity could with exertion improve itself was a grain of comfort that many found in evolutionary ideas before and after Chambers. The key statement of this idea by Tennyson appears in the highly important section 118. He relates how the earth began from "fluent heat" and then gave rise to man, who is but a "herald of a higher race"(l. 14). He looks forward to a time when humans will evolve past their sensual (the "faun") and subhuman (the ape and tiger) past:

> Arise and fly
> The reeling Faun, the sensual feast;
> Move upward, working out the beast,
> And let the ape and tiger die.
> (Section 118, l. 25–28)

Similarly, in the epilogue he imagines that his sister on her wedding night (Cecilia Tennyson was married in October 1842) will conceive a child that will be another step toward that "crowning race" where humans will be

> No longer half-akin to brute,
> For all we thought and loved and did,
> And hoped, and suffer'd, is but seed
> Of what in them is flower and fruit . . . (Epilogue, l. 132–135)

To complete his reconciliation to the death of Hallam and finally confront the concerns raised in section 55, Tennyson also has to believe in the immortality of the individual soul. The problem, of course, for the scientifically minded Tennyson was that there is scant scientific evidence for the survival of individual personality after death. Tennyson gets round this by abandoning any rational attempt to derive the existence and attributes of God and falls back on faith. With his faith restored, Tennyson can then accept that Hallam lives on somehow. Indeed it becomes possible for him to identify Hallam with one of the "purer spirits of the present race" that Chambers had identified. From the point of view of scientific naturalism, it is hardly convincing. What is significant, however, is a section that typifies the changed relationship between science and theology. Tennyson finally rejects the argument from design so commonly employed by preceding thinkers (such as Paley). The structure of a bird's wing or an insect's eye can no longer, by analogy with a watch, be regarded as irrefutable evidence of the great artificer. Instead, we must search within:

> I found Him not in world or sun,
> Or eagle's wing, or insect's eye;
> Nor thro' the questions men may try,
> The petty cobwebs we have spun:
> If e'er when faith had fall'n asleep,
> I heard a voice "believe no more"
> And heard an ever-breaking shore
> That tumbled in the Godless deep;
> A warmth within the breast would melt
> The freezing reason's colder part,
> And like a man in wrath the heart
> Stood up and answer'd "I have felt." (Section 124, l. 5–16)

So in the end Tennyson resorts to faith and intuition.

In Memoriam was published on June 1, 1850, and instantly secured Tennyson's reputation as an interpreter of his age. On June 13 of that year he was married to Emily Sellwood after a frustrating twelve-year engagement. In the same year, as if on cue, Wordsworth died, leaving vacant the laureateship. The queen appointed Tennyson poet laureate on November 13.

The immediate popularity of *In Memoriam* seems to derive from the fact that many thought it voiced their own doubts and yet proved an adequate resolution to the tensions it had identified between science and faith. When Tennyson visited Queen Victoria in 1862, shortly after the death of her husband, Prince Albert, she informed him that: "next to the Bible 'In Memoriam' is my comfort" (quoted in Ross, 1973, p. 100). Agnostics, too, admired the work, perhaps because it did not simply fall back on scriptural authority, and possibly because Tennyson recognized the sincerity of the doubters when in section 96 he noted:

> There lives more faith in honest doubt,
> Believe me, than in half the creeds.

In the twentieth century, fewer people thought that Tennyson's solution was convincing. T. S. Eliot, for example, called it a great religious poem not because of the quality of its faith but because of the quality of its doubt.

In the middle of the nineteenth century, many felt like Tennyson that the old certainties were being swept away and that a new basis, or none at all, must be sought for religious faith. One particularly heartfelt lament came from the writer and art critic John Ruskin. Writing to his friend Henry Acland in 1851, he complained that his beloved science, geology, was destroying his faith and his peace of mind:

> You speak of the Flimsiness of your own faith. Mine, which was never strong, is being beaten into mere gold leaf, and flutters in weak rags . . .. If only the Geologists would let me alone, I could do very well, but those dreadful Hammers! I hear the clink of them at the end of every cadence of the Bible verses. (Cook and Wedderburn, 1909, vol. 36, p. 115)

And this we may recall from a man who published papers on geology and was a member of the Geological Society.

The poet A. E. Housman, near the end of the century, used an equally vivid metaphor—one of disinheritance—to describe the impact of the great ideas of the age:

> man stands today in the position of one who has been reared from his cradle as the child of a noble race and the heir to great possessions, and who finds at his coming of age that he has been deceived alike as to his origin and his expectations. (1892 in Ricks, 1980, p. 272)

By this time, however, Housman was reflecting on more than just the challenge to biblical chronology by the geologists' hammers. He had in mind new views about the origin and antiquity of humans as established by Darwin and his followers.

Darwin and The Origin of Species

When *In Memoriam* (1850) was completed, Charles Darwin was already a respected gentleman of science and had published pioneering work on coral atolls, volcanic islands, and barnacles. What he had not done, alarmed perhaps by the reception of *Vestiges*, was to publish his ideas on the transmutation of species that he had worked on since 1838. In 1858 he was forced into print by the receipt of a letter from Alfred Russel Wallace outlining ideas very similar to his own. A joint paper, by Wallace and Darwin, was read before the next gathering of the Linnean Society on July 1 of that year. One year later, in November 1859, Darwin published *On the Origin of Species by Natural Selection*. It was an instant success, and a second edition was planned for January 1860. Since that time the book has never been out of print.

The two crucial features of the *Origin* were the primacy of the mechanism of natural selection and the absence of teleology. Although Darwin retained a role for Lamarckian inheritance, he also noted how blind chance through the survival of those individuals with favorable but randomly acquired variations could modify, shape, and bring into being whole species. The chance nature of the occurrence of such variations and the fact that it was simply reproductive success that ensured their survival (i.e., natural selection) meant that the whole of the living world was not heading in any particular direction. One could not infer an artificer from creation because the parts of plants and animals, however complex, were not designed.

Although Darwin did not explicitly deal with the evolution of humans in the *Origin* (leaving this, as we shall see shortly, to 1871) the implications were clear enough and provoked an immediate response. The reaction of Darwin's old friend and tutor the Reverend Adam Sedgwick was typical of orthodox conservative clergymen. Darwin sent Sedgwick a personal copy of *Origin* in 1859. Sedgwick replied in a letter to him, that

> I have read your book with more pain than pleasure. Parts of it I admired greatly; parts I laughed at till my sides were almost sore; other parts I read with absolute sorrow. 'Tis the crown and glory of organic science that it does through final cause link material to moral . . . You have ignored this link; and if I do not mistake your meaning, you have done your best in one or two pregnant cases to break it.
>
> Were it possible (which thank God it is not) to break it, humanity, in my mind, would suffer a damage that might brutalize it, and sink the human race into a lower grade of degeneration than any into which it has fallen since its written records tell us of its history. (Sedgwick to Darwin, November 24, 1859, in Burkhart and Smith, 1997)

Charles Darwin (1809–1882)

Charles Darwin was born in Shrewsbury on February 12, 1809, the same day as Abraham Lincoln and the same year as Tennyson and the future British prime minister William Ewart Gladstone. Darwin's father was an overpowering and successful local doctor, his mother a member of the wealthy Wedgwood family, and his paternal grandfather the pioneering doctor, poet, and natural philosopher Erasmus Darwin. The Darwin household was liberal minded and freethinking, both the Darwins and the Wedgwoods, for example, abhorred slavery. In 1818, Charles attended the local boarding school but failed to impress his tutors. His father despaired and noted that "You care for nothing but shooting, dogs and rat catching, and you will be a disgrace to yourself and all your family." (Desmond and Moore, 1991, p. 20)

Charles Darwin from a photograph taken by Elliot and Fry, London, c. 1875. Darwin exerted a lasting influence over virtually every area of Victorian thought, including literature. His explanation of how species change through time broke once and for all with the tradition of natural theology and the teleological idea that nature is imbued with some transcendent purpose. (Courtesy of John Cartwright. Source: Francis Darwin, 1902, The Life of Charles Darwin, Lonson: John Murray.)

In 1825 Darwin was sent to the cosmopolitan city of Edinburgh (then the center of the Scottish Enlightenment, the "Athens of the north") to study medicine. Here Darwin met Robert Grant (1793–1874), a radical francophile expert on marine life and sponges, and follower of Lamarck. By 1826 Darwin had become disaffected with his medical studies and in 1827 enrolled at Cambridge to take a B.A. degree, with the intention to later qualify for Holy Orders. Here he came under the influence of the botanist the Reverend John Henslow. He also amassed a sizeable collection of beetles. In this period Darwin recalled that he was most impressed by William Paley's *Evidences of Christianity*, and like many others accepted the watchmaker analogy: just as a watch implies a watchmaker, so the manifest appearance of design in the natural world implies a Creator.

Darwin obtained his degree in 1831, and to brush up his geological skills he began a geological tour of north Wales with the Reverend Adam Sedgwick. Acting on advice from Henslow, Darwin then embarked on a five-year voyage as gentleman companion to Captain FitzRoy of the *Beagle*. He set sail from Plymouth on the south coast of England in 1831.

He returned in 1836 and later reflected that this voyage had been the most important event in his life. He stepped ashore not as an evolutionist but as someone who had observed the geographical distribution of species, had become converted to Lyell's uniformitarian geology, and was puzzling about where species came from. In

July 1837 he opened the first of his many notebooks on transmutationism. A decisive moment in the formation of Darwin's ideas came in October 1838, when he read Malthus's *Essay on Population*. Darwin realized that the over-fecundity of nature leads to struggle and competition over scarce resources, and that variations that help in this struggle would tend to be preserved. In 1838 he proposed to his cousin Emma Wedgwood and they were wed in 1839.

In 1842 the Darwins moved from London to the sleepy hamlet of Down, about sixteen miles southwest of the city. Here Darwin brooded over his great insight and amassed evidence to support his case. In 1844 he wrote a 200-page sketch of his theory and placed it in the care of his wife with instructions to publish if he were to die. After Wallace's letter arrived in 1858, Darwin was finally forced into print and the result was *The Origin of Species* of 1859. His next great work was *The Descent of Man and Selection in Relation to Sex* of 1871, in which Darwin outlined his other major contribution to understanding selection mechanisms, sexual selection. He followed this in 1872 with *The Expression of the Emotions in Men and Animal*, a book in which Darwin extended his belief in the continuity between animal and human minds. His last work was *The Formation of Vegetable Mould through the Action of Worms*, published in 1881. Typically, rather than pontificating on grand themes, as many thinkers are wont to do near the end of their lives, Darwin returns to a humble subject. He was always fascinated by the action of worms, whose tiny actions over long periods of time (like natural selection itself) could bring about great changes. Darwin died on the April 19, 1882, and was later buried in Westminster Abbey. His place of burial indicates the extent to which his ideas were by then accepted by the establishment. The fact that an agnostic (Darwin lost the last remnants of his Christian faith around 1851) should be so honored also points to the power of the emerging scientific elite.

Of the three great thinkers born in the nineteenth century who had a massive influence over the twentieth, Darwin, Marx, and Freud, it is now only the reputation of Darwin that remains unscathed. Indeed, not only is there a "Darwin industry" in the history of science, but contemporary evolutionists have revived Darwin's ideas as applied to human behavior, and Darwinian psychology has become one of the most vigorous sciences of the last twenty years.

The American philosopher Daniel Dennett captured the importance of Darwin when he said, "If I were to give an award for the single best idea anyone has ever had, I'd give it to Darwin, ahead of Newton and Einstein and everyone else. In a single stroke, the idea of evolution by natural selection unifies the realm of life, meaning and purpose with the realm of space and time, cause and effect, mechanism and natural law." (Dennett, 1995, p. 2) In essence, Darwin provides a naturalistic answer to those age-old questions that have befuddled metaphysicians for generations: where did we come from, and why are we here? The answer to the first is a long line of primate then mammalian and animal ancestors, stretching back, ultimately, to the first organisms of the pre-Cambrian. The answer to the second is that it is a tendency of genes to make copies of themselves. Darwin, therefore, abolished teleology and purpose from the universe of natural science, and that is why his ideas were discomforting to his contemporaries, as they are to us today.

A marble statue of English naturalist Charles Darwin by Sir J. E. Boehm at its unveiling at the Natural History Museum, London, on June 9, 1885. The unveiling of this statue was an event of enormous symbolic importance and in attendance were earls, lords, the Archbishop of Canterbury, and the Prince of Wales. (Photo by Rischgitz/ Getty Images)

Sedgwick was of course right in noting that Darwin had severed the material and moral worlds and had sought to banish teleology from the life sciences. Taking Darwin seriously meant no longer looking to nature for a source of moral guidance. In a Darwinian world, Wordsworthian nature as a benevolent teacher that "never did betray the heart that loved her" is a laughable absurdity. The Darwinian revolution posed a far greater challenge for faith than the science of the seventeenth century. Newtonian mechanics at least provided a convenient metaphor to conceive God: that of the lawgiver and supreme watchmaker. But at the root of evolutionary theory lay chance, waste, and suffering; what image of God could be reconciled with this? Moreover, if there really is a loving personal God and humans are his chosen species, why did he take so long in getting round to creating us? We now turn to one writer who explored the imaginative opportunities this severance provided: Thomas Hardy.

Thomas Hardy (1840–1928)

Man's Place in Nature

Hardy responded to the tensions between science and religion by dismissing the concepts of the latter (sin, redemption, a loving creator) as long-standing products of self-deception. In his early poems and novels Hardy presents an image of nature as something indifferent to the hopes and suffering of ordinary mortals. In the poem "Hap" (1866), for example, he depicts natural forces as "purblind Doomsters" that meet out bliss and pain quite randomly. In "At a Bridal" nature is the directionless "Great Dame" who cares not what type of creatures live. In his moving poem "The Impercipient" he describes sitting at a cathedral service contemplating his own lack of faith and his alienation from the throng of believers around him:

> That faith by which my comrades stand
> Seem fantasies to me
> And mirage-mists their Shining Land.

The poem "Nature's Questionings," published in *Wessex Poems* in 1898 but possibly written much earlier, sums up this early phase of Hardy's thinking. The poem presents in turn a number of conceptions of the Creator: he is some "Vast Imbecility" that framed the world in jest and left it to "hazardry"; or some "Automaton" mechanically blind to human feelings; possibly it is a "Godhead dying downward, brain and eye now gone"; finally he wonders if there is after all

Thomas Hardy (1840–1928)

Thomas Hardy was born in 1840 in a thatched cottage in the hamlet of Higher Brock-hampton in the English country of Dorset. His father was a master mason, builder, and

amateur musician; his mother had been a domestic servant but was fond of books and instilled in Hardy a love of the English countryside. By the age of sixteen Hardy was helping his father with architectural drawings. Showing some talent in this direction, he soon moved to London as an architect's apprentice. There he began writing poems, but publishers rejected his early efforts. Later he commented to a friend that he would never have written prose if he could have earned his living as a poet.

In 1870, while planning the restoration of a church at St. Juliot in Cornwall, he met and fell in love with Emma Glifford, the sister-in-law of the local vicar. In his youth Hardy himself had been religious: he taught at Sunday school, for example, and mastered Greek in order to read the New Testament. Ironically, by the time he met Emma, his reading of Darwin, Huxley, and Spencer had confirmed him as a agnostic.

Photograph of Thomas Hardy (1840–1928) taken around 1890. Hardy was deeply read in the works of Darwin, Huxley, and Spencer and profoundly influenced by them. Unsurprisingly then, Hardy rejected Christianity and explored through his work the role of humans in the natural order newly envisioned by science. His conclusions were often grimly pessimistic. (Bettmann/Corbis)

His first novel, *Desperate Remedies* (1871) met with critical indifference. His reputation took off, however, with *Under the Greenwood Tree* (1872) and *A Pair of Blue Eyes* (1872). The success of *Far from the Madding Crowd* (1874) meant that Hardy could marry Emma, give up his architectural work, and concentrate on writing. Major novels followed, including *The Return of the Native* (1878), *The Mayor of Casterbridge* (1886), and *Tess of the d'Urbervilles* (1891). His last novel, *Jude the Obscure* (1896), landed him in a maelstrom of critical distaste. The public thought it to be an attack on the institution of marriage (the Bishop of Wakefield solemnly burned his copy), and Emma thought it would be read as a reflection of their, by now, strained marriage. In disgust, and now financially secure, Hardy turned from novels to his first love, poetry. *Wessex Poems* (1898) was the first of a number of volumes that followed (containing some 1,093 poems in all), many of which dated back to the 1860s. In November 1912, Emma died, prompting the grief-stricken and guilt-ridden Hardy to write some of his most exquisite and poignant

some "high Plan betides" of "Evil stormed by Good." To these four alternatives the agnostic Hardy replies "No answer I."

In the last phase of his career Hardy developed the idea that the ethical evolution of humanity will eventually make the world a better place, a stance he verse: *Poems 1912–13.* In 1914 Hardy married his secretary, Florence Dugdale.

Hardy himself was in no doubt about his intellectual mentors: on two occasions, separated by thirteen years, he proffered the same list: Darwin, Huxley, Spencer, Comte, Hume, and Mill. Having lost his faith, he did not, like Tennyson or Arnold, begin a struggle to ascertain what was left that could be believed, or try to assemble his thoughts into some alternative coherent system. Rather, he explored through prose and verse what human existence is like in a universe irredeemably drained of cosmic significance.

Hardy's novels convey a strong sense of fatalism and suggest that human will is not free but fettered by circumstances, environment, and even heredity. Modern critics usually feel that the use of coincidence and accidents is overdone. The Victorian reading public tolerated his critique of the problems of the rural poor and the stifling effect of class divisions. It was less welcoming, however, of his religious scepticism and his criticism of the divorce laws and conventional sexual mores.

It is easy to see Hardy's gloomy view of the universe as the final realization of the impact of nineteenth century science. But Hardy is not simply content to endorse and apply the scientific worldview. He is also critical of its detached objectivity, its cold rationality, and its disdain of folklore and traditional ideas. Thus Henry Knight, in *A Pair of Blue Eyes* and Swithin St. Cleeve in *Two on a Tower* are both arch rationalists and detached observers. For Hardy, their detachment is not the result of the Romantic vision of the outsider (the artist as hero), but rather the result of their awareness of the immensity of space and time and the insignificance of human affairs. In the end though, they are shown to be emotionally deficient. They are not malevolent or wicked in the sense of Hawthorne's Chillingworth, but the insensitivity inherent in an unconstrained scientific outlook untouched by human sympathy is exposed. Similarly, Angel Clare in *Tess* is supposedly a freethinker, but he realizes too late the absurdity of his emotional attachment to irrational social conventions about sexuality.

When Hardy died in 1928, fate had in store one final bizarre twist. His expressed wish was to be buried in Stinsford Churchyard where lay his parents, his sister, and his first wife, Emma. One of his executors, however, thought that the nation had a greater claim on his body. Eventually a grisly compromise was settled: his heart for the churchyard, and the rest of his body for the nation. Accordingly, his heart was removed by a surgeon and placed in a biscuit tin. In due course the cremated remains of the rest of his body were placed in poets corner in Westminster Abbey, and his heart was interred in the grave of Emma in Stinsford. A rumor circulated after the funeral, however, that the urn buried at Stinsford did not contain the real heart, but that a cat called Cobby had eaten it as it lay on the kitchen table awaiting the undertakers. One legend has it that the cat was buried instead. Whatever the truth behind this macabre tale, the term *Hardyesque* seems an appropriate adjective.

calls "evolutionary meliorism." He tried to assert the dignity of man without appealing, as Tennyson did, to a transcendent God lying outside of nature. Indeed, he seems to suggest that the only center of ethical consciousness in the world lies in humans. So in the poem "God's Education" he upbraids God for stealing away the life of a young lady and asks him if he is keeping her some-where else. God replies that he is not and routinely throws away lives carelessly. The poet responds:

> Said I: 'We call that cruelty-
> We your poor mortal kind'
> He mused: 'The thought is new to me
> Forsooth, though I men's master be,
> Theirs is the teaching mind.

For Hardy, ethical awareness is both our curse (since it makes us aware of cos-mic injustice or rather indifference to our values) and a weapon to chastise the universe.

Having ditched Providence, Hardy, as Gillian Beer said, had to "find a scale for the human, and a place for the human within the natural order" (Beer, 2000, p. 235). One informative illustration of Hardy's effort in this direction is the famous (and literally "cliff-hanger") coastal scene in his novel *A Pair of Blue Eyes*, where Henry Knight (a rationalist and amateur geologist) slips on the edge of a cliff (probably Beeny Cliff in north Cornwall) and is hanging on for his life with the sea and rocks 700 feet below. As he contemplates his fate he notices a fossil embedded in the cliff staring out at him:

> It was a creature with eyes. The eyes, dead and turned to stone, were even now regarding him. It was one of the early crustaceans called Trilobites. Separated by millions of years in their lives, Knight and this underling seemed to have met in death. It was the single instance within reach of his vision of anything that had ever been alive and had had a body to save, as he himself had now.
>
> The creature represented but a low type of animal existence, for never in their vernal years had the plains indicated by those numberless slaty layers been transversed by an intelligence worthy of the name . . .. He was to be with the small in his death. (p. 252–253)

Interestingly William Buckland, the creationist geologist, had chosen the com-pound eye of the trilobite with its many lenses all set in perfect alignment with one another as a supreme example of the operation of a "Creative Intelligence." But there are no such comforts for Knight: he hangs there contemplating oblivion on an individual level just as the trilobite experienced it individually and as a species. Hardy, like Darwin, has reunited man with nature, but the injustice of it all pains:

> Knight, without showing it much, knew that his intellect was above the aver-age. And he thought—he could not help thinking—that his death would be a

> deliberate loss to earth of good material; that such an experiment in killing
> might have been practiced upon some less developed life. (p. 256)

There is an irony in this scene directed against the cold rational detachment of Knight. He prides himself on his rationalism and objectivity, but when facing his own oblivion he is as concerned about his fate as any country yokel that he looks down on. Hardy also located his characters in the natural order through their sexuality, and here he was influenced by Darwin's theory of sexual selection, the subject of the next section.

Hardy and Sexual Selection

If references to humans are few in the *Origin*, then, likewise, the other main plank of Darwin's whole program, sexual selection, is only touched on in two pages. Darwin announced his views on both these matters, however, in 1871, when he published *The Descent of Man and Selection in Relation to Sex*, his most important work after *Origin*. In typical fashion, Darwin arrayed a vast assemblage of evidence to show that humans were similar in kind to other primates. No quarter was spared: our moral codes, our ethical sense, our sense of beauty were all explicable by reference to their survival value. To complete his project, however, he needed to introduce a new principle of selection. In the *Origin* he had defined natural selection as the process that ensures that those features of an animal that give it a competitive edge in the ordinary trials of life (such as sharp eyes for finding food and camouflage to avoid predation) are preserved. But he was obviously struck by the features of some animals that appear maladaptive: the gorgeous plumes and colors of some bird species being the classic example. What could be the survival value of these ostentatious and costly appendages? His theory of sexual selection provided an answer to this.

Darwin realized there were two components to sexual selection: intra-sexual selection, or competition between members of one sex (usually males) to gain access to the other; and inter-sexual selection where one sex does all it can (through behavior and appearance) to impress the opposite sex. The former mechanism was relatively uncontentious; it was the latter that excited the most curiosity and had the most imaginative appeal. In the common case where females choose from a selection of males, Darwin supposed that over time, female choice had driven males to extraordinary lengths to impress their consorts: colorful plumage, extravagant ornaments, and complicated courtship displays. As Darwin noted:

The males are almost always the wooers; and they alone are armed with special weapons for fighting with their rivals. They are generally stronger and
larger than the females, and are endowed with the requisite qualities of
courage and pugnacity. They are provided, either exclusively or in a much
higher degree than the females, with organs for vocal or instrumental music,
and with odoriferous glands. They are ornamental with infinitely diversified
appendages, and with the most brilliant or conspicuous colours, often
arranged in elegant patterns, whilst the females are unadorned. . . . It cannot
be supposed, for instance, that male birds of paradise or peacocks should
take such pains in erecting, spreading, and vibrating their beautiful plumes
before the females for no purpose. (Darwin, 1874, p. 938)

Hardy exploits these insights in *Tess of the D'Urbervilles* and *Far from the
Madding Crowd*. In *Tess* the sound of Angel Clare on his harp draws Tess toward
him. As she approaches she walks through a garden teeming with life and sexually charged sensations. Tess walks in a trance, drawn by her sexuality into the
natural order of things and toward the displaying male:

She went stealthily as a cat through this profusion of growth, gathering
cuckoo-spittle on her skirts, cracking snails that were underfoot, staining
her hands with thistlemilk and slug-slime, and rubbing off upon her naked
arms sticky blights which, though snow-white on the apple-tree trunks,
made madder stains on her skin; thus she drew quite near to Clare, still
unobserved of him.

  Tess was conscious of neither time nor space. The exaltation which she
had described as being producible at will by gazing at a star, came now without any determination of hers; she undulated upon the thin notes of the second-hand harp, and their harmonies passed like breezes through her, bringing tears into her eyes. The floating pollen seemed to be his notes made
visible. (*Tess of the D' Urbervilles*, p. 118)

As Darwin noted, males who can excite females through some elaborate
performance or display are not necessarily those best adapted to other aspects
of life. In terms of flying around and avoiding predators, for example, the peacock would be far better off without its absurd train. But for some deeper func-
tional reason, and Darwin was uncharacteristically unclear about this, females
are attracted to such traits. This surely is the implication in the seduction of
Bathsheba by Sergeant Troy in *Far from the Madding Crowd*, published just
three years after Darwin's *Descent* appeared. As a farmer, Troy is incompetent;
he is also an irresponsible philanderer. He wins the affections of Bathsheba,
however, by his sword play. Dressed in his scarlet uniform he gives Bathsheba a
display of his skills:

Never since the broadsword became the national weapon had there been more dexterity shown in its management than by the hands of Sergeant Troy, and never had he been in such splendid temper for the performance as now in the evening sunshine among the ferns with Bathsheba. . . .

Behind the luminous streams of this aurora militaris, she could see the hue of Troy's sword arm, spread in a scarlet haze over the space covered by its motions, like a twanged harpstring, and behind all Troy himself mostly facing her; sometimes, to show the rear cuts, half-turned away, his eye nevertheless always keenly measuring her breadth and outline, and his lips tightly closed in sustained effort. Next, his movements lapsed slower, and she could see them individually. The hissing of the sword had ceased, and he stopped entirely. (*Far from the Madding Crowd*, p. 204)

Troy's actions are like some courtship display, where the male provides a show of skills to impress the coy female, hoping that it will provide him with a mating opportunity. The setting of the scene in a woodland clearing amid ferns reinforces the point that Hardy's characters have been relocated in the natural order.

Hardy and August Weismann

Hardy was hardly alone in finding Darwin a pivotal figure in nineteenth-century thought, but what is extraordinary is that Hardy adhered to an unadulterated form of Darwinism that was only fully vindicated in the 1920s. Whereas after about 1870 many of his contemporaries turned away from natural selection and stressed the greater importance of Lamarckian mechanisms, Hardy was remarkably perceptive in recognizing early on the enormous importance of the work of August Weismann (1834–1914), a German biologist who taught zoology at the University of Freiburg. Up to about 1882 Weismann accepted Lamarckian inheritance, but then he realized that during the development of an individual, the sex cells that go on to make sperm or eggs are separated and isolated early on from the rest of the body's cells (somatic cells). Weismann linked this observation with the ideas of the Belgian cytologist Edouard van Beneden, who in 1883 argued that hereditary information is strung out in some way along the chromosomes in cells. Combining these insights, Weismann advanced his famous germ plasm theory of herediy which states that only the "germ plasm" is passed from generation to generation and the information contained in this germ line is unaffected by the experiences of each individual. Put in modern terms, information flows from genotype to pheonotype but not the other way round. In a material world, it is not the soul but the germ line that is immortal. To convince his critics, Weismann cut off the tails of a family of mice for twenty-two generations, removing in all 1,592 tails. Yet each generation showed no signs of producing mice with shorter tails; environmental influences had no effect on the germ line; Lamarckian inheritance failed to work. Actually, all Weismann had to do was point to the practice of male circumcision among orthodox Jews. It is an operation practiced since biblical times yet still needs to be performed anew on each male child.

It is known that Hardy was reading Weismann's *Essay on Heredity* around 1890, as he was putting the finishing touches to *Tess of the d'Urbervilles*. Hereditarian motifs figure throughout this novel. In the very opening scene, the parson, an amateur genealogist, informs the rural laborer John Durbeyfield (Tess's father) that he belongs to a distinguished ancestry: "There have been generations of Sir Johns among you, and if knighthood were hereditary . . . you would be Sir John now" (p. 2). As the dialogue moves on, John Durbeyfield becomes reduced to a "you," a representative of a type, part of a germ line. Hence when John asks where his ancestors are buried, he is told "At Kingbere-sub-Greenhill: rows and rows of you in your vaults" (p. 3).

Weismann's ideas fitted neatly with Hardy's fatalistic pessimism. In *Tess*, the fate of the characters is partly determined by their germ line. For example, Hardy describes her as "an almost typical woman, but for the slight incautiousness of character inherited from her race" (p. 86). The only modicum of hope in the entire novel is revealed in the last climactic scene, when Angel Clare and Tess rest at Stonehenge as they flee from the authorities, Tess having killed her seducer, Alec D'Urberville. Tess suggests to Clare that he should marry her sister Liza-Lu: "She has all the best of me without the bad of me; and if she were to become yours it would almost seem as if death had not divided us" (p. 388).

So the germ line marches on. In the last paragraph of the book, after the rising flag of Wintoncester gaol announces the death by hanging of Tess, Clare and Liza-Lu walk away like Adam and Eve to a new future:

> "Justice" was done, and the President of the Immortals, in Aeschylean phrase, had ended his sport with Tess. And the d'Urberville knights and dames slept on in their tombs unknowing. The two speechless gazers bent themselves down to the earth, as if in prayer, and remained thus a long time, absolutely motionless: the flag continued to wave silently. As soon as they had strength they arose, joined hands again, and went on. (p. 392)

But even here, paradise is not regained. Hardy's readers would have been aware of the fact that, as a result of a much-disputed Act of Parliament passed in 1835 (and not reformed until 1906), it was illegal for a man to marry his deceased wife's sister. It was a quite irrational piece of legislation based on a passage in

Leviticus, and, unlike the prohibition of incest, is one that has no foundation in biology. Even at the last Hardy reminds us of the tensions between biology, belief, and social customs.

Thoughts about heredity also help elucidate Hardy's musings on ancestry in two notable poems, "Pedigree" (1916) and "Heredity" (1917). In "Heredity," Hardy contemplates the germ line (the "immortal replicators" as the contemporary biologist Richard Dawkins would say) manifesting itself in each generation:

> I AM the family face;
> Flesh perishes, I live on,
> Projecting trait and trace
> Through time to times anon,
> And leaping from place to place
> Over oblivion.
> . . . that is I;
> The eternal thing in man,
> That heeds no call to die.

In "The Pedigree" Hardy imagines the force of all his ancestors acting on him, determining his thoughts and movements until he thinks his own identity a sham:

> I am the merest mimicker and counterfeit
> Though thinking I am I
> And what I do I do myself alone.

Epilogue: Evolutionary Epistemology

In chapter five we examined how the Romantics struggled with the problem of the mind's construction of reality. The theory of Locke, and his "associationist" followers such as Hartley—that each individual mind builds up knowledge of the world from scratch, including its emotional and moral sense—always had its problems. Blake, Wordsworth, and Coleridge found it unlikely and not in accordance with their own experiences. Wordsworth, in the "Intimations" ode, even flirted with the Platonic notion of the prior existence of the soul and its exposure to the immortal forms to explain how the mind can make sense of experience. It was evolutionary theory that enabled scientific naturalism to sort out this riddle. Even as Wordsworth was alive and writing, Darwin mused to himself in his secret notebooks that:

> Plato . . . says in *Phaedo* that our "imaginary ideas" arise from the pre-exis-
> tence of the soul, are not derivable from experience.—read monkeys for pre-
> existence. (Darwin, 1838, quoted in Gruber, 1974, p. 324)

In the same notebook he also realized that the problems Locke grappled
with were explicable by examining our near relatives among the great apes: "He
who understand baboon would do more toward metaphysics than Locke" (Darwin, 1838, quoted in Gruber, 1981, p. 243). Darwin had realized that the brain at
birth is not a formless heap of tissue; neither does it carry a recollection of eternal verities associated with an immortal soul. The brain enters the world already
structured by the effects of a few million years of natural selection having acted
upon our primate and hominid ancestors. Its data processing mechanisms are a
priori, as Kant suspected, but only prior to individual experience, not to experience as a whole. In a few jottings, Darwin had cut through the philosophical disputes between Kantian idealism and Lockean empiricism—a dispute revived in
the mid-nineteenth century by debates between J. S. Mill and William Whewell,
the former advocating an inductive view of knowledge in the manner of Locke
and the latter espousing a Kantian position. In 1838, however, these were dangerous thoughts, and Darwin did not reveal them again in published form until 1871.

Someone who propounded his own similar evolutionary epistemology independently of Darwin was the philosopher and sociologist Herbert Spencer
(1820–1903). Even before Darwin published his *Origin*, Spencer was attempting to
build a philosophy of knowledge on the unifying principle of evolution. In his essay
of 1852, "A Theory of Population Deduced from the General Law of Animal Fertil-
ity," he introduced the famous phrase "survival of the fittest." It was this phrase
that Darwin borrowed from Spencer and used in his fifth edition of the *Origin*. As
well as clinging to Lamarckian notions of heredity since shown to be false,
Spencer's reputation has also suffered from his association with social darwinism—a view of social progress that advocated allowing nature to take its course at
the social level through minimal state intervention and welfare aid. By allowing the
feeble to perish and the fittest to survive, the future strength of the species could
be fostered—a rather hideous idea and one explored in the next chapter.

Bibliographic Essay

The edition of *In Memoriam* used for this chapter was that edited by Robert H.
Ross (New York and London: W. W. Norton, 1973). This edition contains some
valuable critical material including two essays by Eleanor Mattes on the impact
of geology and *Vestiges* on Tennyson's mind. For a highly detailed analysis of the

intellectual context of *In Memoriam*, one that is sensitive to how cultural influences occur, consult Susan Gliserman's "Early Victorian Writers and Tennyson's In Memoriam: A Study in Cultural Exchange" in *Victorian Studies*, March 1975 and June 1975.

A good analysis of the development of geology in the nineteenth century and how this vexed the Victorian mind is given by Dennis Dean in "Through Science to Despair: Geology and the Victorians" in *Victorian Science and Victorian Values* (New Brunswick NJ: Rutgers University Press, 1985), edited by James Paradis and Thomas Postlewait.

Tess Cosslett in her *The Scientific Movement and Victorian Literature* (New York: St. Martin's Press, 1982) discusses the reaction to science by both Tennyson and Hardy. She also shows how the cliff scene in Hardy's *A Pair of Blue Eyes* was probably suggested by an essay by Leslie Stephen called "A Bad Five Minutes in the Alps." A riveting account of Darwin's life is given by Adrian Desmond and James Moore in their *Darwin* (London: Michael Joseph, 1991). A longer and highly praised account is given by Janet Browne in two volumes: *Charles Darwin: Voyaging* and *Charles Darwin: the Power of Place* (London: Pimlico, 1985 and 2002, respectively).

An excellent survey of the impact of scientific ideas on the literary imagination in the nineteenth century is J. A. V. Chapple's *Science and Literature in the Nineteenth Century* (Macmillan: London, 1986). The book is provided with a careful analysis of a whole range of extracts and quotations and a helpful introduction and general discussion about science and literature in this period.

For a clear discussion of the emergence of Darwinism, one of the best short accounts of the scientific and philosophical issues (as opposed to the social) is Ernest Mayr's *One Long Argument* (London: Penguin, 1991). This book is especially good on highlighting Darwin's anti-Platonism and the importance of Weismann's work.

For a good discussion on Lamarckian inheritance and the importance of Weismann's work in Victorian fiction, Peter Morton's *The Vital Science: Biology and the Literary Imagination 1860–1900* (London: George Allen and Unwin, 1984) is essential reading. For a clear account of Hardy's "evolutionary meliorism" see J. O. Bailey's "Evolutionary Meliorism in the Poetry of Thomas Hardy," *Studies in Philology*, 1963, 569–587. For a convincing account of how Hardy through his poetry gradually established his reaction to a natural world without a belief in any transcendent authority, see John Roland Dove's excellent article, "Thomas Hardy and the Dilemma of Naturalism," (1967), *Die Neuren Sprachen* 16, 253–268. The editions of Hardy used in chapter seven were *Tess of the D'Urbervilles* (London: Penguin, 2002), *A Pair of Blue Eyes* (London, Macmillan, 1926).

The best account available of the reception of *Vestiges* is given by James Secord's incredibly thorough work, *Victorian Sensation* (Chicago and London: University of Chicago Press, 2000). A good starting point to explore the impact of Darwinism on literature is to consult "Darwinism and Literature," which is chapter twenty-two of David Oldroyd's *Darwinian Impacts* (Milton Keynes: Open University Press, 1980). The chapter contains a quick survey of numerous literary figures, but the voluminous references provide a key to further secondary and primary works.

A by now classic work on the relationship between Darwin and literature, showing how Darwin incorporated literary devices into his writing, is Gillian Beer's pioneering *Darwin's Plots* (Cambridge: Cambridge University Press, 1983 and 2000). For a clear discussion on how the new science of the nineteenth century affected attitudes toward nature and particularly the process of observing the natural world, consult chapter eleven, "Nature and Science," of Bernard Richards's *English Poetry of the Victorian Period* (London and New York: Longman, 1988).

Darwin's Gothic: Science and Literature in the Late Nineteenth Century

Brian Baker

Darwin and "Progress"

D arwin's theory of evolution had, as described in the last chapter, a somewhat turbulent reception, and even within his own field of natural history,
was not fully accepted until some sixty or seventy years later. However, it
did have a very strong impact, in somewhat altered form, in other areas. Perhaps
the most important was in the social and political field. In later versions of Darwinian evolutionary theory, and particularly in that of Herbert Spencer, progress
and evolution are synonymous. Darwin himself made no such claims. He was more
interested in investigating the process by which species diversity was produced
than suggesting that such a process was progressive in any way. Although he did
not state this explicitly in *The Origin of Species* (1859), Darwin made no claims
that human beings were in any way exempt from natural processes at work everywhere. "Man" therefore stood not above nature, but was a part of it. If the Galapa-
gos finches had been produced by a natural process that could be investigated and
understood, then so had "man." We were no different from any other species. Our
closest relatives, the great apes, were then seen as our immediate ancestors (a mistaken view, for in the Darwinian model, both *homo sapiens* and primates are
derived from a common ancestor very far back in time).

The established Church in Britain found theories of *progressive evolution*
more congenial to their teachings than Darwin's *natural selection*, because they
suggested that history (natural and human) led up to this point of attainment.
History was therefore teleological, meaning that it had an endpoint in sight, that
it had meaning and direction. Looking back, then, various developments could
be seen as anticipations of what we have now. This is a cosmological version of

what has been called "the Whig version of history," a coinage that suggests that when history is seen and understood from a certain perspective, it is revised or selected (in a circular way) to validate the perspective from which it is seen. The Whig version of evolution was "progress." Progress was very important to the Victorians; it informed many of their social and industrial projects, and it had highly moral overtones. If we see history as progressive, where we are now is more developed, more civilized, and more sophisticated than anything that came before. But why should history move in one direction? Why should we see ourselves as the end point of all that went before?

Herbert Spencer and Social Darwinism

Such questions did not trouble Herbert Spencer. A popularizer of evolutionary thinking, Spencer liked to draw parallels between species and society, mapping an uncomplicated model of Darwinian evolution from the biological world directly onto the social world. It was Spencer, not Darwin, who coined the phrase "survival of the fittest," and in his hands "fittest" became not best adapted, but strongest. In Spencer's system of Social Darwinism, the cultural organization of society directly corresponded to its intellectual, psychological, or "mental development" (judged, of course, by the standards of Europeans like Spencer). This connection of biological and social should be seen in the context of a long nineteenth-century scientific debate about race, particularly deriving from anthropometrical (human measurement) surveys taken around and after the American Civil War. Africans were seen by this science, pervaded by implicit or explicit racist assumptions, as "less evolved" than Europeans. Aboriginal Australians and "Hottentots" were still further removed from European/ Caucasian "development" or "civilization." Evolution was also seen as taking place between the human "races" (ethnic groupings understood as species), which were in direct competition with each other. As Europeans and white North Americans constrained within their own versions of the Whig version of history, Social Darwinists assumed that the Caucasian "race" was the most highly developed, or the most evolved. Africans or Australians were further back along the evolutionary chain, in a sense the "ancestors" of the Caucasian "race" (and thereby also closer to the great apes). Therefore, according to this version of Darwinism, the Caucasians would win the evolutionary battle, and others would necessarily perish. Natural selection had "proved" the Caucasian "race" to be the fittest, a view that provides a fine rationale for racism, imperialism, and even slavery. But why see the different races as different "species?" Why should not *homo sapiens* all together be subject to evolutionary pressures (environment, scarcity of resources, competitor species)? Why should humans survive at all?

The Time Machine

The tension between these three questions informs one of the most interesting texts produced by late Victorian culture (and this is a time that produces many of the recurrent myths of the twentieth century), a text where time, history, evolution, and politics converge in the crucible of fantastic literature. The text is H. G. Wells's *The Time Machine* (1895). Narrated largely by the unnamed Time Traveller (whose audience is a group of professional men), *The Time Machine*'s story focuses on the genius inventor-scientist who builds his time machine and hurtles into the future, to the year 802,701. The machine itself is a Rube Goldberg device, a delicate frame like a bicycle, which contains bars of nickel, ivory, and a "rock crystal," which in combination allow the machine to move through time. The Time Traveller himself explains the "theory:" "'Scientific people,' proceeded the Time Traveller [. . .], 'know very well that Time is only a kind of Space.'" Time is the "Fourth Dimension," and here is the Time Traveller's explanation at greater length:

> It is simply this. That Space, as our mathematicians call it, is spoken of as having three dimensions, which one may call Length, Breadth, and Thickness, and is always definable by reference to three planes, each at right angles to the others. But some philosophical people have been asking why three dimensions particularly—why not another direction at right angles to the other three?—and have even tried to construct a Four-Dimensional geometry. Professor Simon Newcomb was expounding this to the New York mathematical Society only a month ago.

Professor Newcomb is a refugee from the "real" world (ours), brought in by Wells to add some scientific authenticity to this rather woolly pseudoscientific explanation. The Time Traveller's discovery allows him to move about in time as though it were Space, completely neutral and without effect upon it. Wells's conception of time is far from that which causes later science-fiction writers to think in terms of paradox and altered histories. For them, the movements of Time Travellers in time will have their own consequences. This static or spatial conception of time suggests that Wells is writing from a strictly empiricist scientific standpoint (and his skeptical audience are themselves only in part convinced by demonstrations and proof: a flower from the future). Heisenberg's Uncertainty Principle, which argues that the presence or position of the scientific observer itself has an effect upon the results, is some thirty years into the

Herbert George (H. G.) Wells (1866–1946)

Born just after the end of the American Civil War, H. G. Wells died soon after the end of the Second World War, and the span of his life marks the construction of a world that we would recognize as truly modern. Wells's scholarship to the Normal School of Science, awarded in 1884, was the turning point in his life and formed his later career. There, Wells came under the influence of Thomas Henry (T. H.) Huxley, the most prominent advocate of Darwin's evolutionary theories. Huxley, known as "Darwin's Bulldog," was a role model for Wells, perhaps because he was a scientist whose position of eminence gave him an authority not only in matters of science, but more generally in late Victorian culture and society. Wells spent a year studying comparative anatomy with Huxley and eventually took a degree in zoology. After an accident that damaged his kidneys, however, he turned his attention to writing.

H. G. Wells, science fiction writer, thinker, anticipator of the future, and major public figure. Wells did a great deal in the late nineteenth and early twentieth centuries to promote and popularize scientific understanding. (Library of Congress)

His first book was a textbook on biology written for high-school pupils, but he achieved fame with the publication of *The Time Machine* in 1895. An immediate success, it was followed by *The Island of Dr. Moreau* (1896), *The Invisible Man* (1897), *The War of the Worlds* (1898), and many others. These "scientific romances" ensured Wells's fame and are his most enduring popular success, but all of them are informed by the scientific thinking of the day. Unlike the earlier Jules Verne, Wells was always more interested in the social and material effects of science and technology than encouraging wonder at new gadgets and technology. This social focus had a strong bearing on Wells's interest in utopias and utopian writing, and many of his utopian works (such as *A Modern Utopia* of 1905) are visions of a future society organized in terms of science, reason, and order.

Wells became an important cultural figure like his mentor, Huxley. As a popularizer of scientific ideas, a famous writer and broadcaster, and a social critic and anticipator of the future, Wells's influence was strong (such as in his hugely popular *The Outline of History* of 1920 and *A Short History of the World* of 1922). Always an independent and sometimes controversial presence, Wells was someone who truly attempted to bridge the gap between the "two cultures" of science and arts, and whose "scientific romances" remain as fresh and as readable today as they were when they were published.

future —our future. The next chapter will look at Stephen Baxter's 1995 "official sequel" to *The Time Machine*, called *The Time Ships*, with regard to his rather different conception of time.

The Time Machine *and Evolution*

That the Traveller ends up in the year 802,701 also indicates the vast passages of time required by Lyell's uniformitarian geology and Darwin's theory of "natural selection." *Time* as a concept had expanded by 1895, had become something far more cosmological in scope. Travelling these millennia also allows Wells to bring to bear the evolutionary mechanism with regard to human beings, extrapolating from the world of 1895 to this far-flung future. The class division Wells saw in the 1890s—the wealthy, leisured bourgeoisie and the laboring, oppressed proletariat—become the ancestors of two "species of Man." One, privileged, pampered, protected from the "harsh grindstone" of competition and selection, evolves into the Eloi, a dainty race of childlike beings who are unable to fend for themselves. The other, downtrodden and industrial, are forced underground and evolve into the Morlocks, a technically adept race of pallid, ugly, and predatory beings. Notice here that, like Herbert Spencer, Wells too connects the biological with the social, makes social class into species. Here is the Time Traveller's realization of the true state of affairs of this future earth:

> The gradual widening of the present merely temporary and social difference between the Capitalist and the Labourer, was the key to the whole position. . . . in the end, above ground you must have the Haves, pursuing pleasure and comfort and beauty, and below ground the have-nots; the Workers getting continually adapted to their conditions of labour.

The spatial metaphor, above-below ground, stands for a relationship of power between the classes. The Traveller finds out that the power relationship of his time has been inverted in the far future: where the Haves above ground once ruled and lived from the labor of the Have-nots, in 802,701 the Morlocks are in control and keep the Eloi as a form of cattle.

The analogies between biology and society are central to *The Time Machine*, but earlier scientific "discoveries" in the field of physics had an impact not only on Wells's vision of the far future, but also on Darwin's theory itself. William Thomson, later known as Lord Kelvin, an eminent scientist working in the field of physics, is most famous for his formulation of the Second Law of Thermodynamics in 1851, which posits that all energy flows in the universe will eventually equalize, leading to stasis, uniformly distributed heat, and the extinction of all life. Taken up by science fiction writers in the twentieth century, this becomes "entropy," a process of dissolution and decay leading to the "Heat Death of the Universe." Thomson's Second Law of Thermodynamics also has a bearing on Wells's imagination in *The Time Machine*, particularly the end of the text, in the chapter called "The Further Vision." The Time Traveller journeys to the end of the earth, comes to see a faraway beach, roamed by a "monstrous crab-like creature," and looks about him.

> All trace of the moon had vanished. The circling of the stars, growing slower and slower, had given place to creeping points of light. At last, some time before I stopped, the sun, red and very large, halted motionless upon the horizon, a vast dome glowing with a dull heat, and now and then suffering a momentary extinction.

He moves on in time and finally sees a "round thing, the size of a football perhaps, or, it may be, bigger, and tentacles trailed down from it; it seemed black against the weltering blood-red water, and it was hopping fitfully about." The Traveller has come to the end of things, the final retrogressive evolution. Humans have evolved, or de-evolved, to this tentacled football, a bleak vision indeed of humanity's future and of its current pretensions.

The Time Machine *and Race*

While the scenario of *The Time Machine* is clearly drawing upon evolutionary theory to extrapolate a cautionary myth about Wells's own contemporaneous society and subjects "Man" to fluctuations of natural selection, some rather disturbing crosscurrents appear in the text. The Eloi, for instance, while appearing "very beautiful and graceful creatures," are "on the intellectual level of one of our five-year-old children." They lack concentration, are unable to maintain either their surroundings or culture, and as the prey of the Morlocks, are clearly the losers in the evolutionary survival race. And *race* here is the key word. Wells's representation of the Eloi fits all too neatly with prevailing nineteenth-century conceptions of non-European, non-"civilized" races. John S. Haller Jr., in *Outcasts from Evolution*, describes this attitude, as shown in his quotations from Herbert Spencer's own writings:

> The semicivilized nations, "characterized by a greater rigidity of custom," were less capable of modifying their ideas and habits to present or future

experiences. Marked by an early precocity and arrested mental development at puberty, they soon relaxed into a relatively automatic nature, incapable of responding to stimuli in other than a reflex-response pattern. Just as an infant showed small persistence in any one thing (wanting an object then abandoning it for something new), so the inferior races exhibited resistance to "permanent modification." Lacking intellectual persistence, "they [could not] keep the attention fixed beyond a few minutes of anything requiring thought even of a simple kind." Intensity of any sort produced exhaustion. (Haller 1995, p. 127)

The Eloi, in their demeanor and behavior, show that they are not a well-adapted species. They have de-evolved, and this is demonstrated through their individual characteristics: they are "arrested" at a childhood stage—a word used often in racial theories in the nineteenth century. The intellectual development (or lack of development) of the individual is seen as an index of the cultural development of the "race," and the childishness of the Eloi proves their inferiority. The "Negro" in the United States was similarly represented as "childlike," because it positioned African culture as inferior or nonexistent, and was similarly seen as facing imminent extinction. There are several ironies here. While the Time Traveller professes to "loathe" the Morlocks, and his identification with the Eloi extends to his love of Weena, a female Eloi, the representation of the two species in fact places the Morlocks closer to the Victorians of the Traveller's world, and to the Traveller himself. Morlocks and British Victorians are both industrial and industrious, logical, and they are both (the Morlocks obscenely) white. The Traveller's loathing of the Morlocks is really a self-loathing, and his identification with the Eloi an identification with the non-Caucasian "others" who were deemed to have lost the Social Darwinist race.

Theories of Degeneration

An alternative explanation is that the Time Traveller's attitude toward the Morlocks may be a manifestation of late-Victorian culture's imperial anxieties. Britain in the last three decade of the nineteenth century was wracked by invasion fears, and by worries about the "declining stock:" that the country was no longer breeding "sons fit for Empire." Like the racism-inflected anthropometric surveys that seemed to support the "decline" of non-Caucasian "races" in the United States, a series of reports on the dwellers of Britain's urban centers seemed to suggest that they were becoming weaker, less physically developed, more prey to "vice." In a word, they were becoming degenerate. Degeneration theories of the late nineteenth century, ones that argue for evidence of a "retrogressive evolution," are the inverse image of Darwin's evolutionary theory, and they expose fears of the "decline of the West" mirrored in some scientific writings.

E. Ray Lankester, a curator of the British Museum, in 1880 published *Degeneration: A Study in Darwinism*, which highlighted what seemed to be the problems of an evolutionary theory that did not include the element of progress. Lankester outlines the evidence for processes of natural selection that led not to greater complexity, but to simpler, "less evolved" forms. Lankester's key example is the tapeworm, which has evolved according to Darwin's theory to fit a particular niche, but this evolution is from a more complex form to a less complex one and ends in the form of a parasite. Degenerationist theorists often drew upon parasitology for their examples, and Lankester's conclusions echo those of the Social Darwinists. Connecting biology to society, he suggested that "a contented life of material enjoyment accompanied by ignorance and superstition" is the evolutionary fate of those who degenerate. It is easy to see how clearly *The Time Machine* fits into the concerns of its era: the Eloi have lives of "material enjoyment," but they are a degenerated species, locked into a parasitic relationship with the Morlocks. It also becomes apparent how a moral judgment is introduced into Lankester's analogy: why should the tapeworm be held up as an example of "degeneracy" when the species has, through natural selection, reduced its complexity to the level it needs to survive in a certain environment? Further complexity is superfluous to its survival. The tapeworm is a success story rather than a symbol of "degeneration."

Theories of decline have an obvious cultural significance in a High Imperial Britain that is becoming progressively more anxious about its grip on its empire and the growing power of competitor nations (such as the unified Germany and the United States). Perhaps Britain would not be the winner in the geopolitical evolutionary race; or perhaps, as in *The Time Machine*, the "Golden Age" (the title of chapter five) of Empire is illusory, the cultural high-water mark has already been reached, and a long, slow decline is about to set in. This is certainly the approach of Max Nordau's *Degeneration*, first published in 1893 but not translated into English until 1895—the year of publication of *The Time Machine*. Nordau's text used the evolutionary mechanism to again suggest social decline, arguing that the stress and speed of modern (that is to say, nineteenth-century) culture induced a kind of hysteria. Nordau's book intersects with theories of heredity, with "inheritance" of characteristics from generation to generation, and for him, the emphasis is on the inheritance of debility. Nordau's use of "retrogressive evolution" demonstrates virulent anti-modernity, and he especially hated the "decadent" aesthetes of the 1880s and 1890s. His book was, however, a great popular success, transmitting these pseudobiological concepts

Racist anthropology of the nineteenth century tried to demonstrate the "inferiority" of some races by demonstrating their closeness to "inferior," nonhuman species. Similar ideas can be found in "degenerationist" writings of the period. (Leonard de Selva/Corbis)

across European culture. *Degeneration* is a reactionary book that prizes tradition in culture above all else and characterizes any innovation as degenerate. His description of modern artists is very revealing:

> Degenerates lisp and stammer, instead of speaking. They utter monosyllabic cries, instead of constructing grammatically and syntactically articulated sentences. They draw and paint like children, who dirty tables and walls with mischievous hands. They confound all the arts, and lead them back to the primitive form they had before evolution differentiated them. Every one of their qualities is atavistic.

The word *atavistic* was used by the Italian doctor and criminologist Cesare Lombroso to denote the "criminal type" and means the recurrence of "lower" behavioral or physical traits in "higher" forms (the return of the "primitive"). Notice how, like the racist medical scientists of the nineteenth century, Nordau characterizes "degeneracy" as both "retrogressive evolution" and as "arrested childhood:" "they draw and paint like children" and lead the arts back to a "primitive form." The same analogies between biology, race, and evolution that informed the racist assumptions of the American anthropometrists and the theories of the Social Darwinists are seen here with their attendant anxieties almost entirely undisguised.

Cesare Lombroso's Criminal Man

Lombroso's work had a profound effect on European theories of crime and was a strong influence on Nordau's *Degeneration*. Lombroso was a devotee of photography, and he amassed huge files of photographs of the faces of criminals. These he blended together to create "types" of criminals, so that the police (or anyone who read his book) could identify a criminal at a glance. Lombroso, then, defined crime not as an act, but as form of innate physiological debility. In his *Criminal Man* (*L'uomo Delinquente*) of 1876, Lombroso advanced the theory that criminality was biologically determined from birth, and that the "criminal type" was innately predisposed to violence. In *Criminal Man According to the Classification of Cesare Lombroso*, written in 1911 by his daughter and collaborator Gina Lombroso Ferraro, we find a highly recognizable characterization of "criminal man":

> The criminal instincts common to primitive savages would be found proportionally in nearly all children, if they were not influenced by moral train-

Cesare Lombroso (1835–1909)

Cesare Lombroso was born within the Jewish community in Verona to a prosperous family whose fortunes began to fail as he grew up. He studied medicine at Pavia, and after obtaining his degree, was a volunteer doctor in the newly created Italian national army. Although he went on to be an internationally famous doctor and scientist, Lombroso's temperament always pointed him toward engagement with the social and political realities of nineteenth-century Italy.

Lombroso became familiar with the work of Charles Darwin during the 1860s, but like Darwin himself, Lombroso was largely a product of earlier evolutionary theories, notably those of Lamarck. This influence can be seen in the balance between biological and environmental factors that can be found in his work. Like Herbert Spencer, Lombroso adapted an evolutionary mechanism to the study of social forces, and eventually came to a biological (and deterministic) explanation of a social phenomenon: in this case, crime and "criminal man." Italian variants of Darwinist theories of evolution stressed the elements of struggle and became part of the bedrock for Lombroso's theories of crime as "atavism" (derived from the Latin word *atavus*, meaning "ancestor"). Lombroso's ideas suggested that the temporal direction of the evolutionary mechanism could, in some cases, be transgressed or reversed. Lombroso argued that

Cesare Lombroso, Italian physician and criminologist, who understood "criminal types" to be degenerate throwbacks to pre-civilized times. (Bettmann/Corbis)

"criminal man" was a "throwback," a being whose biological development and moral sense was representative of an earlier stage of human evolution. Along with these "born criminals," he identified other types, such as the "insane criminals" (who turn to crime through some kind of moral trauma, emphasizing the environmental factor), or the "criminaloid" (involved in less serious crimes).

Lombroso, it could be argued, was a product of his turbulent times. An advocate of a modern, secular, and rational Italian state, Lombroso argued that science should be a part of the social and political fabric, and advocated a science that assumed a central role in the development of the new Italian nation. His cataloguing of criminal types, the pages of photographs of "faces of criminality" in *L'uomo delinquente* (1876), was in part a practical attempt to do just that. His "scientific" criminology attempted to bring order where there had been disorder (after Italian unification in 1860, there was major social disruption in the form of strikes, riots, demonstrations, and a high level of crime). In an Italy that had recently been unified, Lombroso's investigations into the causes of crime (which also veered into anthropometry, craniometry, and even phrenology) perhaps found more simple and comprehensible answers in biology and heredity than in complex social and political factors. Ironically, for a man who thought science to be intimately connected with the social and political world, Lombroso's work now expresses far more about the cultural assumptions of late-nineteenth-century Italy (and European science) than it can ever offer as a valid tool for analyzing the causes of criminal behavior.

ing and example. . . . This fact, that the germs of moral insanity and criminality are found normally in mankind in the final stages of his existence, in
the same way as forms considered monstrous when exhibited by adults frequently exist in the foetus, is such a simple and common phenomenon that
it eluded notice until it was demonstrated clearly by observers like Moreau,
Perez, and Bain. The child, like certain adults, whose abnormality consists
in a lack of moral sense, represents what is known to alienists as a morally
insane being and to criminologists as a born criminal, and it certainly resembles these types in its impetuous violence.

The "criminal," then, is analogous to the child in its "moral insanity:" its ethical sense has been "arrested" at a pre-adult stage. Notice how the passage uses
a biological example—the development of the individual from foetus to adult—
to explain its point about the persistence of undeveloped traits into adulthood.
(This notion is derived from what is called in biology *neoteny*, the persistence of
bodily organs beyond a stage where they have biological use.) As in the language
of Social Darwinism, the biological development of the individual is crudely
mapped onto assumptions about the social development of "civilization" (the
equivalence between "criminals," "children," and "primitive savages"). Lombroso's main point about "criminal man" is that he represents a type of being further back along the evolutionary chain (like children and "savages"), a survivor
or "throwback" from a time where civilization had not developed its moral codes
against crime. Lombroso's use of "retrogressive evolution" theories leads him to
suggest that the mutation required of natural selection will occasionally produce
degenerate beings, ones that in all respects are the siblings of "primitive man."
This process is known as *atavism*.

Atavism and Dracula

The idea of atavism was pervasive in the late nineteenth century, and police
forces across Europe developed files of "mug shots" of criminals to be able to
identify the "criminal type." A version of this atavistic type is Count Dracula, as
portrayed in Bram Stoker's *Dracula* (1897). Count Dracula is himself a version
of the degenerate, the Transylvanian aristocrat who has de-evolved into a parasitic being, feeding on the blood and life of others. The vampire in this text is the
embodiment of Otherness: non-European, able to shift shape and identity, of
predatory sexuality, unnaturally long-lived, and strange and threatening in facial
expression and behavior. Jonathan Harker's description of the Count resembles
the cataloguing of Lombroso's physiognomy:

His face was a strong—a very strong—aquiline, with high bridge of the thin nose and peculiarly arched nostrils; with lofty domed forehead, and hair growing scantily round the temples, but profusely elsewhere. His eyebrows were very massive, almost meeting over the nose, and with bushy hair that seemed to curl in its own profusion. The mouth, so far as I could see it under the heavy moustache, was fixed and rather cruel-looking, with peculiarly sharp white teeth; these protruded over the lips, whose remarkable ruddiness showed astonishing vitality in a man of his years. For the rest, his ears were pale and at the tops extremely pointed; the chin was broad and strong, and the cheeks firm though thin. The general effect was one of extraordinary pallor.

Notice how the description struggles to express the extreme strangeness of the figure: "peculiarly" is used twice in the passage, "very" twice, and "remarkable," "astonishing," "extremely," and "extraordinary" once each. If he had read Lombroso, like Professor Van Helsing, Harker would have been able to identify the Count's true nature from this description of Dracula's face alone: it clearly expresses his criminality and his degeneration. Van Helsing, the Dutch adversary of Dracula, explains to his skeptical ally, Dr. Seward, the relationship between Dracula and the theories of "criminal man:"

The criminal always work at one crime—that is the true criminal who seems predestinate to crime, and who will of none other. The criminal has not full man-brain. He is clever and cunning and resourceful; but he be not of man-stature as to brain. He be of child-brain in much. Now this criminal of ours [Dracula] is predestinate to crime also; he, too, have child-brain. . . . The Count is a criminal and of criminal type. Nordau and Lombroso would so classify him, and *quâ* criminal he is of imperfectly formed mind.

Notice how childhood, criminality, and degeneration all come together, once again, in Van Helsing's speech. Ultimately, Dracula can be defeated because he is not a supernatural monster; he is the last descendant of a demonstrably inferior race. The "Crew of Light," a tough group of rational adults (most of the time), will be able to destroy a mere "child-brain."

Degeneration and Sherlock Holmes

The face of Dracula is very similar to that of another "higher degenerate" (a figure of genius produced by degenerative social processes, a type identified by Lombroso), Professor Moriarty, arch-criminal and nemesis of Sherlock Holmes. Moriarty is described like this: "He is extremely tall and thin, his forehead domes out in a white curve, and his two eyes are deeply sunken in his head." The "domed forehead" refers to another branch of anthropometric medical science of the nineteenth century, that of "craniometry." The leading proponent of this "science" was Paul Broca (1824–1880), a French scientist of Huguenot background. He invented several instruments with which to measure skulls and also derived the "cephalic index," which is "the breadth of the head above the ears expressed in percentage of its length from forehead to back." The bigger the brain case, the argument ran, the more powerful the brain. Broca conceived of three standards of the "cephalic index," in descending order: the *brachycephalic*, the *dolichocephalic*, and the *mesocephalic*. Moriarty, like Holmes, is brachycephalic, although Moriarty, clearly a disciple of Broca, greets his adversary with the comment "You have less frontal development than I should have expected." As with many of these measuring scales, when applied more generally, racist assumptions intrude. When measured, Africans, "Hottentots," and Aboriginal Australians were found to have skulls with smaller cranial capacity. Therefore, in the crude equivalence of brain size with intelligence, they must be "less developed" intellectually and culturally. As in Lombroso's analyses of facial characteristics, what can be observed on the outside is assumed to be a clear indicator of what is inside.

In the Holmes stories, however, larger skull size does not necessarily equate with a developed moral sense. Colonel Moran, the degenerated aristocrat and former tiger-hunter who tries to assassinate Holmes in "The Empty House," is "an elderly man, with a thin projecting nose, a high, bald forehead, and a huge grizzled moustache." Moran is in the pay of Moriarty and resembles him physically as well as morally. Holmes himself is a version of the scientist, whose method is empirical and deductive. He observes first, then deduces the events from what he sees. A cataloguer like Lombroso, Holmes has made empirical and comparative analyses of (among other things) types of cigar ash, the mud of London's streets, and the history of criminal cases across Europe. Although Holmes is a version of the scientist as empiricist, in some later stories he does offer theories on crime and criminality, which are always inflected by the thinking of the late nineteenth century. In "The Empty House," the story that reintroduced Holmes after his "death" at the Reichenbach Falls, for once Holmes becomes the prey rather than the predator, stalked by the aforementioned Colonel Moran. Once the tables have been turned, and Moran captured, Holmes offers Watson the following explanation of the man's crimes:

> There are some trees, Watson, which grow to a certain height and then develop some unsightly eccentricity. You will see it often in humans. I have a theory that the individual represents in his development the whole pro-

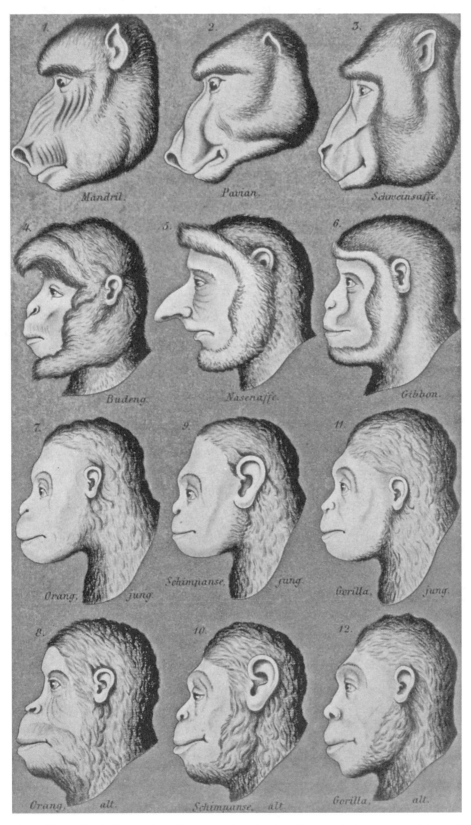

Ernst Haeckel's studies, such as the comparison between human and nonhuman here, fed into the racial anthropology of the nineteenth century. (National Library of Medicine)

cession of his ancestors, and that such a sudden turn to good or evil stands for some strong influence which came into the line of his pedigree. The person becomes, as it were, the epitome of the history of his own family.

Holmes neglects to mention that his "theory" rests upon the same assumptions we saw in Nordau, Lombroso, and in the history of nineteenth-century interpretations of evolution. The basis of Holmes's version is in Ernst Haeckel's analysis of the development of the fetus: noting what appear to be residual gill-slits in the neck of the human fetus, Haeckel suggested that the development of the individual (ontogenesis) recapitulates the development of the species *in utero* (phylogenesis). Holmes suggests that the individual recapitulates the development of the family, another reading of the biological back onto the social.

Thomas Hardy's Tess of the d'Urbervilles

The biological metaphor of the family line being like a tree is commonplace enough but echoes another passage about lineage and descent from an earlier novel. In Thomas Hardy's 1891 novel *Tess of the d'Urbervilles*, the female protagonist is Tess Durbeyfield, the daughter of the foolish John Durbeyfield, who claims descent from an aristocratic line. Ironically, Durbeyfield is correct:

> Parson Tringham had spoken truly when he had said that our shambling John Durbeyfield was the only really lineal representative of the old d'Urberville family existing in the country, or near it; he might have added, what he knew very well, that the Stoke-d'Urbervilles were no more d'Urbervilles of the true tree than he was himself. Yet it must be admitted that this family formed a very good stock whereon to graft a name which sadly wanted such renovation.

The Durbeyfields, then, are also degenerated aristocrats, and the parson approves of a "renovation" of the line. However, this leads only to disaster for Tess: seduced by her "Cousin" Alec d'Urberville, her entire life is blighted by the connection. While Hardy often seems to suggest that it is the impersonal hand of fate that destroys his protagonists, in *Tess of the d'Urbervilles* there are hints that it is the ancient and degenerate line of blood itself that "infects" Tess's character. After marrying Angel Clare, a well-meaning but somewhat hypocritical and priggish young man, Tess is taken to one of her "ancestral mansions," a former d'Urberville house. There we find evidence of the d'Urberville character:

[Angel Clare] looked up, and perceived two life-sized portraits on panels built into the masonry. As all visitors to the mansion are aware, these paintings represent women of middle age, of a date some two hundred years ago, whose lineaments once seen can never be forgotten. The long pointed features, narrow eye, and a smirk of the one so suggestive of merciless treachery; the billhook nose, large teeth, and bold eye of the other, suggesting arrogance to the point of ferocity, haunt the beholder afterwards in his dreams. [. . .] The unpleasantness of the matter was that, in addition to their effect on Tess, her fine features were unquestionably traceable in these exaggerated forms.

Tess's fate is written in her own physiognomy, and her ultimate end predetermined by the degenerated and rather unpleasant nature of her forebears. Although writing in a much more naturalistic vein than other writers considered in this chapter, Hardy is still influenced by Lombrosian theories of degeneration and of physical evidences of "moral insanity."

Reversion and "The Creeping Man"

In a much later story, "The Creeping Man" (published in the last collection of Holmes stories, *The Case-Book of Sherlock Holmes* of 1927), Conan Doyle returns to the idea of reversion or recapitulation. Called to investigate the strange behavior of Professor Presbury of "Camford University," Holmes and Watson discover that a strange ape-like creature, the "Creeping Man" of the title, has been disturbing the household of the professor. When Holmes finally discovers the (barely credible) truth, the reader is transported into the world of Gothic fiction: the "creeping man" is the professor's "Hyde," an atavistic being manifested by a strange drug. Holmes explains all: the professor's behavior has been caused by a late love affair, which made the middle-aged man desire his youth once more. Sending to a certain A. Dorak in the East End of London, the professor received a vial of an elixir of youth, a serum of "black-faced Langur." The effects transformed him not into the image of his youthful years, but into an atavistic version of his primeval forebears. Holmes spells out the moral of the story in tones remarkably similar to Wells or Nordau:

The highest type of man may revert to the animal if he leaves the straight road of destiny. [. . .] There is a danger here—a very real danger to humanity. Consider, Watson, that the material, the sensual, the worldly would all prolong their worthless lives. The spiritual would not avoid the call of something higher. It would be the survival of the least fit. What sort of cesspool may not our poor world become?

Sir Arthur Conan Doyle (1859–1930)

It was often said of Sir Arthur Conan Doyle that he felt overshadowed by his greatest creation, the master detective Sherlock Holmes. This is true to the extent that Conan Doyle tried unsuccessfully to "kill off" Holmes in "The Final Problem," collected in *The Memoirs of Sherlock Holmes* (1894), an attempt that was doomed to failure. Through public demand, he was forced to bring Holmes back

Sir Arthur Conan Doyle, creator of Sherlock Holmes. Conan Doyle was also the author of adventure yarns such as The Lost World, *which imagined the survival of prehistoric creatures into the present day in remote lands. (Hulton-Deutsch Collection/Corbis)*

for *The Hound of the Baskervilles* (1902) and further series of short stories. The last, *The Case-Book of Sherlock Holmes* (1927), was published a mere three years before Conan Doyle's own death.

The massive and long-lasting fame of Sherlock Holmes has obscured both Conan Doyle's other writings and the facts of his life. Born in Edinburgh, Scotland (where a statue of him still stands), the son of an unsuccessful architect and nephew of a well-known illustrator, Conan Doyle attended a Jesuit college and then trained as a doctor at Edinburgh University. Edinburgh was then the foremost of British universities in the matter of medical training and had close links to continental Europe, particularly French schools of advanced scientific thinking. In 1885, Conan Doyle graduated and practiced for a while as a doctor. But soon, needing to add to his income and fill his empty hours, Conan Doyle began to write. The first story he wrote featured a certain Mr. Sherrinford Holmes and his sidekick, Dr. Ormond Sacker, in a detective story called "A Tangled Skein." After some rethinking, and several rejections by publishers, "A Study in Scarlet," the first story of Sherlock Holmes and Dr. Watson, was published in 1887.

The scientific training Conan Doyle received at Edinburgh was put to good use in the Holmes stories. The detective's deductive and analytical methods are derived from advanced medical thinking in the mid-nineteenth century and are, in a sense, a portrait of the eccentric research scientist following his own obscure paths of knowledge. Conan Doyle kept himself up-to-date on current medical, political, and other issues of the day, all of which find their way into the Holmes stories. Strangely, for an author who created the ultimate rationalist and materialist, in his later years—after the death of his son in the First World War—Conan Doyle became heavily involved in spiritualism, believing in the possibility of communication with human souls in the "afterlife." Perhaps we can most charitably see this as an attempt to solve the most enduring mystery of all: that of life and death.

Holmes's take on evolution derives from Spencer; his phrase "the least fit" has distinct moral overtones. Against evolution as progress—"the straight road of destiny," "something higher"—is placed the spectre of degeneration into mere sensualism (like Wells's Eloi) or corruption (the "cesspool"). "The Creeping Man," like *The Time Machine*, uses an evolutionary metaphor as a stark warning to its reader but here seems much more reactionary: if one strays from the path of evolutionary progress, the consequences will be dire. This story may also be a kind of reply to another text that features transformation and atavism, written some forty years before. In "The Creeping Man," a letter, sent from Prague explains the truth of the "serum" and reveals something else: there is another recipient. "I have one other client in England, and Dorak is my agent for both." Who is this mysterious client? Could it have been a certain Dr. Henry Jekyll?

Strange Case of Dr Jekyll and Mr Hyde

Robert Louis Stevenson's *Strange Case of Dr Jekyll and Mr Hyde* (1886) introduces another of the recurrent figures of twentieth-century popular culture. Henry Jekyll is a version of the scientist as transgressive experimenter, and like Frankenstein and Moreau, his research takes place in isolation. There is much play in the text with doors, windows, and locked rooms, and it is not until the final part of the narrative, "Henry Jekyll's Full Statement of the Case," do we really understand what Jekyll's experiments have found. What we discover, of course, is not an external and empirically provable result, but a transformation of the scientist himself into his dark, atavistic Other. Like Professor Presbury in "The Creeping Man," Jekyll uncovers the primitive within, and Hyde displays all the furious violence of Lombroso's "criminal man." He is first reported mowing down a little girl on foot, "trampl[ing] calmly over the child's body and [leaving] her screaming on the ground." Hyde, as is usual in these fictions, physically displays the mark of his "primitiveness" or lack of development. He was "pale and dwarfish, he gave an impression of deformity without any nameable malformation, he had a displeasing smile, he had borne himself to the lawyer with a sort of murderous mixture of timidity and boldness," and what's more, like the Morlocks, he produces a reaction of "disgust, loathing and fear" in the narrator. Hyde is, of course, Jekyll's psychological double, his alter ego who satisfies all Jekyll's repressed or unacknowledged desires. *Strange Case* is innovative in that it places the dangerous Other not outside, like Dracula (who wants to get in but can be combatted by the forces of light), but inside the scientist himself. Stevenson's conception of the psychological basis of atavistic desire aligns him with developments in psychiatry and psychology in the late nineteenth century.

Stevenson's narrative of dual identity and bodily transformation has, like other Gothic icons such as Frankenstein's monster and Dracula, entered the popular imagination. (Getty Images)

Although Sigmund Freud was yet to exert his influence upon the world (and upon literature), other investigators of human psychology and human sexuality, notably Krafft-Ebing's study *Psychopathia Sexualis* (1894), were beginning to develop a new understanding of human behavior. *Strange Case* seems to anticipate some of Freud's ideas: repression of the unconscious, the return of repressed desires in other forms, a battle between a controlling "Superego" and a desiring "Id." Where other texts of the period crudely connect the biological mechanism of evolution onto the social world, *Strange Case of Dr Jekyll and Mr Hyde* internalizes the conflict between self and Other, the "civilized" and the "primitive," suggesting that they are really one and the same.

Conclusion

By the time of Conan Doyle's "The Creeping Man," the imaginative impact of Darwinism, evolutionary theory, and degeneration discourse upon culture in general and literature in particular was on the wane. As discoveries in the field of physics became popularly understood, a rapid market grew for a kind of fiction that would explain and explore these new ideas and possible technologies. Drawing upon the technological wonders of Verne rather than the speculations of Wells, by the 1920s this new form of *science fiction* had been born and was rapidly developing. We shall look at its recurrent themes and concerns in the next chapter.

Bibliographic Essay

The critical literature on the links between science and literature in the late Victorian period is a rich and growing one. A good anthology of source material from the period is *Literature and Science in the Nineteenth Century: An Anthology,* edited by Laura Otis (Oxford: Oxford University Press, 2002). Peter Morton's *The Vital Science: Biology and the Literary Imagination 1860–1900* (London: George Allen and Unwin, 1984) is an early entry in the field, but is still very useful. Gillian Beer's *Open Fields: Science in Cultural Encounter* (Oxford: Oxford University Press, 1996) and *Darwin's Plots: Evolutionary Narrative in Darwin, George Eliot and Nineteenth Century Fiction* (London: Routledge and Kegan Paul, 1983) offer very interesting readings of nineteenth-century scientific writings as literature. Darwin's theory of natural selection is first stated in *The Origin of Species* (1859) (Philadelphia: University of Pennsylvania Press, 1959). For histories of the rise of Darwinism, the influence of Lyell's uniformitarian geology, and the challenges to the theory of natural selection, see Peter J. Bowler, *The Fontana History of The Environmental Sciences* (London: Fontana, 1992) and Stephen Jay Gould, *Ever Since Darwin* (London: Penguin, 1980) and *Time's Arrow, Time's Cycle: Myth and Metaphor in the Discovery of Geological Time* (London: Penguin, 1990).

The "scientific romances" of H. G. Wells are widely available. The critical work on the science fiction of Wells is relatively strong. See Bernard Bergonzi, *The Early H. G. Wells: A Study of the Scientific Romances* (Manchester: Manchester University Press, 1961); Patrick Parrinder, *Shadows of the Future: H. G. Wells, Science Fiction and Prophecy* (Liverpool: Liverpool University Press, 1995); John Batchelor, *H. G. Wells* (Cambridge: Cambridge University Press, 1985); Mark Hillegas, *The Future as Nightmare: H. G. Wells and the Anti-Utopians* (New York: Oxford University Press, 1967). With regard to his technological utopianism, see Krishan Kumar, *Utopia and Anti-Utopia in Modern Times* (New York and Oxford: Blackwell, 1987). Peter Morton's *The Vital Science* and Kelly Hurley's *The Gothic Body: Sexuality, Materialism, and Degeneration at the Fin de siècle* (Cambridge: Cambridge University Press, 1996) have chapters considering *The Time Machine* and degenerationist theories.

For degeneration and its influence on literature, see Hurley, *The Gothic Body: Sexuality, Materialism, and Degeneration at the fin de siècle* (Cambridge: Cambridge University Press, 1996); William Greenslade, *Degeneration, Culture and the Novel 1880–1940* (Cambridge: Cambridge University Press, 1994); Robert Mighall, *A Geography of Victorian Gothic Fiction: Mapping History's Nightmares* (Oxford: Oxford University Press, 1999); Daniel Pick, "'Terrors of the Night': Dracula and 'Degeneration' in the Late Nineteenth Century" in *Reading Fin de siècle Fictions*, ed. Lyn Pykett (London and New York: Longman, 1996); and Daniel Pick, *Faces of Degeneration: A European Disorder, c.1848–1918* (Cambridge: Cambridge University Press, 1993). For the theories of Cesare Lombroso, see Pick, *Faces of Degeneration;* for further information and the work of his daughter, Gina Lombroso Ferraro, see the excellent supplementary material in Robert Louis Stevenson, *Strange Case of Dr. Jekyll and Mr Hyde* (1886), edited by Martin A. Danahay (Peterborough OH: Broadview, 1999). For the racial aspects of nineteenth-century anthropological science, see John S. Haller, Jr., *Outcasts from Evolution: Scientific Attitudes of Racial Inferiority 1859–1900* (1971), 2nd edition (Carbondale and Edwardsville: Southern Illinois University Press, 1995). A good selection of primary texts on degeneration, science, and imperialism is available in Sally Ledger and Roger Luckhurst, eds., *The fin-de-siècle: A Reader in Cultural History 1880–1900* (Oxford: Oxford University Press, 2000).

The primary texts referred to in this chapter also include Bram Stoker, *Dracula* (1897) and Thomas Hardy, *Tess of the d'Urbervilles* (1891), both of which are widely available in popular paperback editions; Max Nordau, *Degeneration* (1895) (Lincoln: University of Nebraska Press, 1993); and E. Ray Lankester, *Degeneration: An Essay in Darwinism* (London: Macmillan, 1888). For further insight into *Strange Case of Dr Jekyll and Mr Hyde* and its relationship to theories of sexuality in late Victorian culture, see Stephen Heath, "Psychopathia Sexualis: Stevenson's Strange Case," *Critical Quaterly*, 28:1–2, Spring/Summer 1986, 93–108.

The Sherlock Holmes stories have been collected in a wide range of editions, some of which are in single-volume format, some in the original collections of stories. "The Final Problem" is collected in *The Adventures of Sherlock Holmes* (London: Wordsworth, 1992), which reproduces facsimilies of the original stories from *The Strand* magazine. These stories were first collected in *The Adventures of Sherlock Holmes* and *The Memoirs of Sherlock Holmes*. "The Empty House" was published in *The Return of Sherlock Holmes* (1905) (London: Penguin, 1981); "The Creeping Man" in *The Case-Book of Sherlock Holmes* (1927) (London: Penguin, 1951). For the connection between Conan Doyle and theories of degeneration, see William Greenslade, *Degeneration, Culture and the Novel 1880–1940* (Cambridge: Cambridge University Press, 1994).

9

Themes in Science Fiction

Brian Baker

This chapter will look at the genre of literature that seems to deal most explicitly with science, and even bears its name, *science fiction*. Some histories of science fiction (known to fans as SF) trace the genre back to classical times, before what we would understand as "science," although others, such as the British SF writer Brian Aldiss, see it as a distinctly modern form. Aldiss argues that science fiction's oldest forebear is Mary Shelley's *Frankenstein* (1818), and this is certainly true in terms of a recognizable scientist. However, several other forms of literature feed in to what we would today recognize as science fiction, and two of these have classical founding texts. Plato's *Republic* is often cited as one of the inaugural works of utopian literature; it is discussed in a section on utopias and dystopias (or anti-utopias) later in this chapter. The other strand that influences science fiction, particularly in its early texts in the eighteenth and nineteenth centuries, is the *voyage imaginaire* or fantastic journey. The earliest known work of this type is by Lucian of Samosata, who wrote in Roman times. *His True History*, a tall tale of sea monsters and wild adventures, in its knowing and ironic title acknowledges that it is partly a put-on and partly a journey of the imagination, rather than one of reality. Another much later devotee of the hoax and put-on, Edgar Allan Poe, would also write "tall" sea–stories in "A Descent into the Maelstrom" and "The Narrative of A. Gordon Pym" (1838). The latter certainly had an influence upon the French writer Jules Verne, who we will turn to shortly.

It is little wonder that Lucian of Samosata set his tale of wonder and imagination aboard ship. The Roman Empire encompassed Western and Southern Europe, Northern Africa, and the Middle East. It circled the Mediterranean Sea, which can be translated as "the sea in the middle of the land" but also might describe "the sea in the middle of the World." For the Romans, the limits of their empire defined the limits of the "known world," and so a fantastic sea voyage would be a journey to the "space outside" that world. For us, of course, such a journey involves going not to the "space outside" of civilization, but to "outer space."

The sea is the location for these journeys because it represents the unknown, and therefore the space of possibility and imagination. If you don't know what lies outside the door, you can imagine it. (Horror fiction and film work this way, too.) In science fiction, the unknown may take many shapes or forms, whether it is "outer space" itself, alien life forms, scientific problems, or technological inventions and the possible impact of any such innovation. In *The Science in Science Fiction* (1990), Robert Lambourne, Michael Shallis, and Michael Shortland suggest six ways in which science plays a key role in science fiction.

1. Using science to provide a description of a real but relatively unfamiliar environment, the description being based on scientific information available at the time of writing.

2. Using science to provide a description of an imaginary environment that is as consistent as possible with established facts and principles.

3. Using a piece of scientific information as the basis of a puzzle.

4. Using science to justify the existence of devices or processes.

5. Using the scientific process itself or using a credible scientific setting for a story.

6. Using science peripherally, to justify a device or process, or to provide a generally scientific background.

Most science fiction is covered by classification number two, as the "imaginary" element would seem to mark out science fiction from other forms of writing that use scientific principles in some way. Classification five is also usually present in what is called "hard" science fiction, which has a consistent scientific rationale behind its inventions or imagined scenarios. Science fiction is particularly suited to imagining the unknown because of its cultural connection with "discovery" and with "new" modes of understanding.

The Fantastic Journey

Jules Verne's *Journey to the Centre of the Earth* (1864) places the scientist at the very center of a voyage of discovery. The novel is narrated by the skeptical and irresponsible nephew of one Professor Liedenbrock, who is a rather unpredictable and irritable German academic and scientist. Liedenbrock, who comes across a Runic message accidentally slipped between the pages of a medieval manuscript, eventually decodes the directions to an entrance to a passageway to the earth's core. The whole novel is dependent upon a conception of a hollow earth that would certainly have been scientifically disproved by the mid-nineteenth century: so much for Verne's scientific plausibility. The three travelers—Liedenbrock, his nephew, and the Icelandic guide Hans—descend through and beneath the crust of the earth and discover not tectonic plates (the theory of continental drift was not proposed by Wegener until 1912), nor vulcanism, nor even a core of molten rock, but a *Mare Internum*, a subterranean sea. The narrator stresses the alienness of this world and his incapacity to comprehend or describe it. As in other literary and scientific texts we have seen, he then resorts to analogy:

> I gazed upon these wonders in silence. Words failed me to express my feelings. I felt as if I was in some distant planet—Uranus or Neptune—and in the presence of phenomena of which my terrestrial experience gave me no cognisance. For such novel sensations, new words were wanted; and my imagination failed to supply them. I gazed, I thought, I admired, with a stupefaction mingled with a certain amount of fear.

His choice of an astronomical analogy serves to emphasize the very inability of analogy to deal with this scene of wonder, for the surface conditions (let alone conditions "in" the planets) of both Neptune and Uranus would have been obscure to nineteenth-century observers. It is not scientific description or understanding Verne privileges here: it is a sense of wonder.

What the travellers find under the earth is a world whose development has been arrested at a prehistoric stage. Liedenbrock and the narrator discover gigantic mushrooms and shrubs, and speculate that "the sea contains none but species known to us in their fossil state, in which fishes as well as reptiles are the less perfectly and completely organised the farther back their date of creation."

Perhaps we should excuse Verne and blame his translator (he was notoriously ill-served by both publishers and translators), but here an understanding of evolutionary mechanisms is hopelessly confused. To begin with, the concept of the underground sea depends upon the dubious foundation of a catastrophic event that ruptured the earth's surface and allowed the prehistoric oceans to enter its hollow interior; then, for the idea of "fossil" fishes swimming in the sea to make sense, it is necessary to presume that while evolution took its course upon the surface of the Earth, the evolutionary process was held in suspension below. It would be perfectly consistent with evolutionary theory for prehistoric species to evolve differently to those on the surface (indeed, considering Darwin's concepts of adaptation, mutation, and natural selection, this would have been the consequence of such a catastrophe). However, there is no evidence of any understanding of that in *Journey to the Centre of the Earth;* as an explanation, the novel suggests that below ground, "ages seem no more than days." The long quotation above also conflates evolution with progressivist conceptions of evolution that accommodated both Christian teleology and the legacy of the Great Chain of Being—the idea that prehistoric species are "less perfect."

"Man" is, of course, at the top of this Great Chain, and ultimately Liedenbrock and his nephew encounter a "monstrous," troglodytic version of humanity itself:

> at a distance of a quarter of a mile, leaning against the trunk of a gigantic kauri, stood a human being, the Proteus of those subterranean regions, a new son of Neptune, watching this countless herd of mastodons. [...] His head, huge and unshapely as a buffalo's, was half hidden in the thick and tangled growth of his unkempt hair. It most resembled the mane of the primitive elephant. In his hand he wielded with ease an enormous bough, a staff worthy of this shepherd of the geologic period.

This "man" is both closer to the animal kingdom (the resemblance to the buffalo and elephant) and further away, seeming near-heroic in stature, as the reference to the Greek myth of Proteus implies. Liedenbrock had previously stumbled across the skulls of such "men" and had been pleased to notice that their "facial angle" was close to ninety degrees, unlike "the Negro countenance and [...] the lowest savages." Here we see the traces of the racial anthropology of the nineteenth century, whose racist assumptions are exposed in the analogy between "Negro" and "savage" as beings of a lower order. Liedenbrock is certain that the skulls are ancestors of "the white race, our own," which perhaps explains the reference to Proteus and to the heroic stature of the mastodon-shepherd. Strangely, neither Liedenbrock nor his nephew attempt to make contact with this being. Rather, they flee the "horrible monster" in terror and revulsion. When confronted with the racial Other, like H. G. Wells's Time Traveller and the Morlocks, they perhaps cannot face the fact of the essential similarity between the observers and observed rather than the difference that racial anthropology tried to maintain.

Although the "scientific romances" of H. G. Wells have passed into pop-cultural myth, and characters like the Invisible Man have become archetypes, it was really Jules Verne whose influence was most felt in the early development of science fiction. His emphasis on technology and wonder at the expense of character marked the path for the pulp magazine short stories of the 1920s. Glamorous, mysterious outsider-figures such as Verne's Captain Nemo, from *20,000 Leagues*

Under the Sea (1869–1870), provided a fantasy of the scientist-inventor as adventurer that obscured the real, complicated process of scientific advance and discovery. It was a fantasy, however, that the readers of such magazines as Hugo Gernsback's *Amazing Stories* (which began in April 1926, the first issue of which carried stories by Wells and Poe, as well as Verne) found easy to believe in. Perhaps this is because the readership was almost certainly young men who had a strong practical, if amateur, interest in science or technology, and who liked to identify with adventurers and explorers.

Gernsback, the editor who coined the term *science fiction*, insisted on scientific accuracy in the stories he published. As Brian Aldiss describes them, these stories "were built like diagrams, and made clear like diagrams, and stripped of atmosphere and sensibility" (Aldiss, 1973, p. 211). They were often also accompanied by diagrams. These stories, which provided the templates for dozens of other pulp magazines and science fiction writers, followed Verne's pattern: fast-paced adventures centered on the invention of a technological device or an extrapolated scientific principle that allowed wonder full rein. However, once science fiction entered the 1930s—Gernsback had lost control of *Amazing Stories* in 1929—the possibilities of science fiction were expanded and explored.

Evolution and Humanity

The early master of the form of *space opera* was E. E. "Doc" Smith—"Doc" because he held a Ph.D. Smith's science fiction operated on the largest scale imaginable and is full of the staples of the subgenre: faster-than-light ships, horrific super-weapons, and superhero characters. FTL (faster-than-light) ships are now a staple of a certain kind of science fiction that requires a broad canvas and the kind of narratives that transport its characters across unthinkable distances. These have been dubbed (a little less than kindly) *space opera*. FTL ships are a kind of Nautilus that ignores the scientific impossibility of any material substance traveling faster than the speed of light (186,000 miles per second). As Stephen Hawking explains, Einstein's famous equation $E = mc^2$ (E is energy, m is mass, and c is the speed of light) postulates that there is a fundamental equivalence of mass and energy. Because of this:

> the energy which an object has due to its motion will add to its mass. In other words, it will make it harder to increase its speed. For example, at 10 per cent of the speed of light an object's mass is only 0.5 percent more than normal, while at 90 per cent of the speed of light it would be twice its normal mass. As an object approaches the speed of light, its mass rises ever

more quickly, so it takes more and more energy to speed it up further. It can in fact never reach the speed of light, because by then its mass would have become infinite and by the equivalence of mass and energy, it would have taken an infinite amount of energy to get there. For this reason, any normal object is forever confined by relativity to move at speeds slower than the speed of light. Only light, or other waves that have no intrinsic mass, can move at the speed of light. (Hawking, 1988, pp. 23–24)

FTL ships are impossible objects, then, purely elements of the imagination. They are a generic convention, however, without which the science fiction canon (let alone the history of science fiction film) would be greatly diminished. Doc Smith's "Lensman" series started with the serialization of the first volume, *Triplanetary*, in 1934 and sets in train a vast, galaxy-wide conflict between two opposing races of beings: the Arisians, descended from humanoids, the defenders of freedom and civilization, and explorers of the "limitless possibilities of the mind;" and the Eddorians, intruders into "our" universe, "intolerant, domineering, rapacious, insatiable, cold, callous and brutal," non-humanoid totalitarians who attempt to crush any species that does not resemble its own obsession with "P-O-W-E-R!!" The halting and turbulent development of the human race is explained through Eddorian influence, which is combated by the positive influence of the Arisians. This galaxy-wide struggle is played out in microcosm on earth, which accounts for the fall of various "civilizations," both mythic and historical (including Atlantis and Rome) and the twentieth-century's two World Wars. What is of most interest here is E. E. Smith's implicit use of an evolutionary dynamic to explain the development of the Arisians (they went through "all the usual stages of savagery and barbarism" on the way to enlightenment). However, this fails to explain the "rise-and-fall" pattern of the "civilizations" Smith uses to depict moments of potential in human evolution. The Eddorians are a necessary fictional device to explain humanity's failure to exhibit proper evolutionary "progress."

The same pattern can be found in Arthur C. Clarke's much later *2001: A Space Odyssey* (1968). A curious paradox is built into the narrative of this novel. It seems to describe the evolution of humanity from Neolithic times to the birth of interplanetary travel. The novel *2001* begins, however, with proto-human beings on the verge of extinction. Clarke's evolutionary mechanism, the "battle for existence," is indeed red in tooth and claw, but it is humanity's very lack of these offensive weapons that seems to spell their eventual doom: "The man-apes of the veldt were [neither swift or fierce], and they were not flourishing; indeed, they were far down the road to extinction." It is at this point that we find another intervention from an alien (and incomprehensibly more advanced) intelligence, in the shape of a "rectangular slab" that a tribe of man-apes stumbles across, and

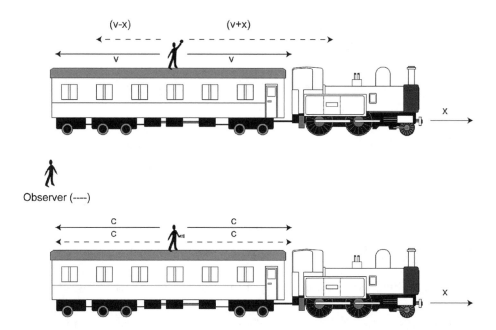

The constancy of the speed of light. If a person standing on a moving train (velocity x) throws a stone with velocity v either in the direction of, or opposite to, the direction the train moves, then the velocity of the stone relative to an observer on the ground is either (v+x) or (v-x), respectively.

The person on the train, however, would measure the velocity of the stone relative to him or her as just v in either direction. On the other hand, if a person were to shine a beam of light from a moving train both the person on the train and the observer at rest would agree that the velocity is the same ($c = 3.0 \times 10^8 \ ms^{-1}$), whatever the direction of the beam. This constancy of the speed of light for all observers, a fundamental premise of special relativity, means that we can no longer think of space and time as separate entities. (Drawn by A. Bell and G. Martin; adapted from Frank Ashall, Remarkable Discoveries [Cambridge: Cambridge University Press, 1994], p. 72)

that encourages them to manipulate tools: "the very atoms of his simple brain were being twisted into new patterns." The central hominid, "Moon-Watcher," learns from this "twisting" to use a sharp stone to kill an unsuspecting warthog, and he understands from this point that he and his tribe need never be hungry again. He is set on the road to survival and to dominion over all, through his "P-O-W-E-R!!" Clarke's vision of human evolution is, then, that civilization and human use of instruments is inexplicable in terms of natural selection or any kind of evolutionary mechanism. Indeed, he stresses in *2001* that human beings are singularly ill-equipped to win the "battle for survival." Although this conception nicely de-centers human beings from the evolutionary narrative (for "our" intelligence is really the product of "alien" tinkering with hominid brains), it also runs directly counter to Clarke's own avowed interest in the exploration of space and the structure of the novel as a whole.

Science Fiction and Time

Here let us return to H. G. Wells, and to *The Time Machine.* Wells drew upon work already done in the fields of dynamics and electromagnetic theory to explain the imaginative possibility of traveling through time, but we must remember that he was writing ten years before Einstein's Special Theory of Relativity, and nearly twenty years before the General Theory of Relativity. As Stephen Hawking argues,

> Before 1915, space and time were thought of as a fixed arena in which events took place, but which was not affected by what happened in it. This was true even of the special theory of relativity. Bodies moved, forces attracted and repelled, but time and space simply continued, unaffected. It was natural to think that time and space went on forever.
>
> The situation, however, is quite different in the general theory of relativity. Space and time are now dynamic quantities: when a body moves, or a force acts, it affects the curvature of space and time—and in turn the structure of space-time affects the way bodies move and forces act. Space and time not only affect but are affected by everything that happens in the universe. (Hawking, 1988, p. 38).

Wells's *The Time Machine* certainly corresponds to Hawking's suggestion of a kind of rupture in scientific understanding in the early years of the twentieth century. As we saw in the previous chapter, the Time Traveller explains the theoretical side of time traveling as follows: "'Scientific people,' proceeded the Time Traveller [. . .], 'know very well that Time is only a kind of Space. Time is the 'Fourth Dimension.'" He goes on:

> It is simply this. That Space, as our mathematicians call it, is spoken of as having three dimensions, which one may call Length, Breadth, and Thickness, and is always definable by reference to three planes, each at right angles to the others. But some philosophical people have been asking why three dimensions particularly—why not another direction at right angles to the other three?—and have even tried to construct a Four-Dimensional geometry.

In *The Time Machine*, space and time are "fixed," both static worlds to be explored. The Traveller is even unable to save Weena, the Eloi with whom he has fallen in love, in the text—that possibility only comes after the end of Wells's novel. It is interesting, however, that Wells only imagines travel into the future. Travel into the past might have resulted in one of several time-paradoxes that later science fiction writers have explored in some detail. Essentially, though, the Time Traveller seems to be able to move about in time without major disturbance either to the path of evolution (presumably his arrival in 801,702 did not cause the final "Further Vision") or to historical time. If we take further the metaphor of time as space, then for *The Time Machine*, time is an empty room. The Traveller can move about in it, observing and interacting with it, without disturbing its fabric. We might make the analogy here to a scientific method that understands the process of scientific experimentation and discovery empirically: that there are absolute measures and a stable body of scientific knowledge, without any need to problematize the role of the scientist/observer or the act of observing.

When he published the "official sequel" to *The Time Machine* in its centenary year of 1995, the British science fiction writer Stephen Baxter was able to incorporate twentieth-century scientific developments into his fictional framework. *The Time Ships* has an entirely different conception of time, in which the Traveller does not move about an empty room of time, but his very act of travelling changes the nature of the world. The novel begins where Wells's narrative ended, with the Traveller on his way back to save Weena from the Morlocks. However, when he gets to 801,702 he discovers a very different earth and very different Morlocks. His act of time travel has changed history, and the Morlocks are now a highly intelligent and technologically advanced species who have encased the sun in a huge sphere in order to capture and use its energy. Earth, in 801,702, is a dark, dead playground for Morlock children. Eventually the Traveller is shown around the Morlock world by one Nebogipfel, a very human kind of Morlock, who then accompanies the Traveller on further adventures in time and space. *The Time Ships*, as well as being a time-travel story, also verges onto the science fiction subgenre of the "alternate history," a "what if?" form that takes a key moment in human history and then extrapolates an alternative outcome. The Traveller, Nebogipfel, and a younger version of the Traveller (nicknamed "Moses") all find themselves in an alternative 1938, where the First World War never ended and London is encased in a vast dome of concrete. There they have a conversation about the world they find themselves in:

> I said bluntly, "But look here—let's suppose I perform some simple experiment. I will measure, at some instant, the position of a Particle—with a microscope, of an accuracy I can name. You'll not deny the plausibility of such an argument, I hope. Well, then: I have my measurement! Where's the uncertainty in that?"

"But the point is," Nebogipfel put in, "there is a finite chance that if you were able to go back and repeat the experiment, you would find the particle in some other place—perhaps far removed from the first location . . ." [. . .]

"It's like this," Moses said. "Suppose you have a Particle which can be in just two places—here or there, we will say—with some chance associated with each place. All right? Now take a look with your microscope and find it here . . ."

"According to the Many Worlds idea," Nebogipfel said, "History splits into two when you perform such an experiment. In the other History, there is another you—who has just found the object there, rather than here."

Rather than the single time-track traversed by the Time Traveller in Wells's story, here the world divides into an infinitely proliferating multiplicity. Baxter's extrapolations are based upon the Uncertainty Principle of Werner Heisenberg. In 1926, the German physicist Heisenberg proposed a theory that would have a major impact upon how science understood the very nature of scientific experimentation and observation. To predict the future position and velocity of a particle, he proposed, you need to be able to measure its present position and velocity very precisely. The best way of doing this is to shine light upon the particle, as the light will be scattered when it hits the particle. To measure accurately, the scientist would need to use light of a short wavelength, as the distance between the crests on the wavelength will determine the accuracy of the measurement (the shorter the better). However, in 1900 another German scientist, Max Planck, had suggested that light is only emitted in a certain form, which he called *quanta*. (This is the derivation of the phrase "quantum physics.")

According to Planck's hypothesis, the scientist wishing to shine light on the particle could not use some arbitrarily small amount of light: the minimum is one "quanta." The shorter the wavelength of this quanta, the more energy it will have, so when this quanta of light hits the particle, it will disturb the position and velocity of the particle in a way that cannot be predicted. Therefore, the very act of trying to determine the velocity and position of the particle will cause a change in both velocity and position. Measurement, or experimentation, is not a neutral process; in observing, the observer changes what is observed. Quanta also introduce the element of unpredictability, or uncertainty, into science. Newton's mechanical universe of force and reaction, or cause and effect, was no more. Another element of Heisenberg's theory is that light, a waveform, behaves like particles (it is emitted in quanta), and particles behave like waves (because their position is not fixed but "smeared out" among a probability distribution).

What the travelers in *The Time Ships* have been doing is creating new worlds every time they move about in time, but the theory suggests that any moment of decision or choice will result in a split. (We can find this idea stated most elegantly in the short story "The Garden of Forking Paths" by the Argentinian writer Jorge Luis Borges, collected in *Labyrinths*.) In *The Time Ships*, the philosophical and scientific conception of travel in time is entirely different to *The Time Machine*, and the problems and paradoxes explored in more detail. What we discover at the end of the story is that it is the Traveller himself who delivers the strange, green element to his younger self, brought from the end of time. This kind of causality-paradox is one of the recurrent motifs of time-travel science fiction.

The classic form of the causality paradox is given by Nebogipfel soon after the discussion about the Many Worlds theory. He says:

> Look: suppose you had returned through time with a gun, and shot Moses summarily. [. . .] So there we have a classic Causality Paradox in its simplest terms. If Moses is dead, he will not go on to build the Time Machine, and become you—and so he cannot travel back in time to do the murder. But if the murder does not take place, Moses lives on to build the machine, travels back—and kills his younger self. And then he cannot build the machine, and the murder cannot be committed, and—

Another version of this is that the traveler in time goes back to kill his own father, which means he can never then be born, so cannot travel back to kill his father, so will be born, and so on. This type of paradox is also central to two of the classic science fiction short stories of the twentieth century: Robert Heinlein's "By His Bootstraps" (1945) and "All You Zombies" (1959).

Baxter's *The Time Ships* ends in a manner clearly indebted to the cosmic imagination of Arthur C. Clarke and his forebear, Olaf Stapledon, the author of the cosmological fictions *Last and First Men* (1930) and *Star Maker* (1937). The Traveller and Nebogipfel end up in earth's far future, where humanity has become extinct and their "children" are a species of mechanical entities with God-like intelligence called Constructors. The Constructors have gone as far as they can in altering the physical universe, so decide to remake the cosmos from the beginning on their preferred (or "optimal") pattern. The Traveller and Nebogipfel, like the narrator of *Star Maker*, leave their material bodies and achieve a cosmic vision of creation. But even here, the strange nature of time is emphasized:

> Since this Universe was infinitely old—and Life had existed here for an infinitely long time—there was no beginning to the benign cycle of Life's maintenance of the conditions for its own survival. Life existed here because the

Werner Heisenberg (1901–1976)

Few scientific careers can have been as controversial as Heisenberg's, both within the scientific community and in the wider world. If nothing else, the story of Werner Heisenberg's life indicates that far from being an "ivory tower" endeavor, even theoretical physics is bound up with politics and with history.

Heisenberg's father was a professor of Greek Philology at the University of Münich, and in his childhood young Werner found both mathematics and languages interesting. In his teenage years, however, Heisenberg became increasingly fascinated by developments in physics (he read Einstein's work on relativity in his own time) and began to study theoretical physics at the University of Münich in 1920. Heisenberg quickly achieved the status of star pupil and gained his doctorate in the space of three years (then a record). Heisenberg went on to study with, and debate with, the leading physicists of the time: Max Born, Niels Bohr, Wolfgang Pauli, even Albert Einstein. Heisenberg studied at key centers of excellence with regard to theoretical physics: at Göttingen (where, after World War II, he would return as director of the Institute for Physics); at

Nobel laureate Werner Heisenberg, best known for his work on quantum physics and the "Uncertainty Principle." (Bettmann/Corbis)

Münich, and in Copenhagen with Bohr, where his facility for languages—his Danish was fluent—was a major advantage.

In the mid 1920s, Heisenberg embarked on a series of researches, on which his scientific fame—and his 1933 Nobel Prize for Physics—rests. In 1925, he published a breakthrough paper on particles and observation, which led the way to quantum mechanics, and in 1927 he published the paper that contained the theorems and mathematics for his "Uncertainty Principle," which was hotly contested by both Bohr and Einstein. Heisenberg's principle again concerns observation and particles of light. He argued that the act of observation itself has a direct effect on the scientific phenomena being observed—and that light could therefore appear as both particle or wave

universe was viable; and the universe was viable because Life existed here to manage it . . . and on, an infinite regression, without beginning—and without paradox!

Baxter's novel ends where *The Time Machine* ends, with the Traveller about to embark on a journey to save Weena, but where Wells's text offered the "Further Vision" of terminal time, of a degenerated earth slowing to an entropic halt, Baxter suggests a circular and perpetual universe, where the paradoxes (the subject of a long-standing, and unresolved, scientific conundrum). He also suggested that the more precisely the observer attempted to determine the velocity of a particle, the less precise could be the determination of the position of the particle—and vice versa. An element of uncertainty was therefore built into the act of scientific experimentation and observation. Heisenberg's paper split the community of theoretical physicists until the Austrian Erwin Schrödinger—the author of a rival theory of the same phenomena—proved that their theories, though arrived at independently, were in fact mathematically the same.

It was Heisenberg's subsequent career, however, that brings into focus the relationships between science and politics, science and ethics. The Nazi party came to power in Germany in 1933, and unlike many of his colleagues, Heisenberg stayed in Germany throughout their time in power, even during the Second World War. In fact, Heisenberg's eminence in theoretical physics meant that when the Nazis wanted to develop nuclear fission—which had first been discovered in Berlin—it was Heisenberg whom they chose to direct the program. Possible explanations have been put forward to exonerate him, or explain his involvement, and they partly rest on the comparative failure of the Nazi nuclear weapons program. First, and most generously, it has been suggested that Heisenberg accepted a role in the program to sabotage it from within; second, and less charitably, that Heisenberg's comparative weakness at experimental, laboratory physics meant that he was ill-equipped to succeed; and third, that the Nazi military strategy in fact privileged aircraft and rocket programs to the comparative neglect of the nuclear program.

He was captured by the British, and after the war he returned to West Germany and became a major figure in the new federal republic, working very hard to assure that science had a key role to play in the reconstruction of Germany. He was also internationally active in the science community, until his retirement in the early 1970s. History, however, continues to question Heisenberg's reputation. In 1941, he traveled to Copenhagen to discuss matters with his old colleague Niels Bohr. Though their debates have been shrouded in controversy, Bohr was so troubled by what Heisenberg had to say that it ended their friendship. This meeting is the subject of Michael Frayn's highly praised play *Copenhagen*. Whatever his reasons or his true role, Heisenberg's reputation has been, and will continue to be, tainted by his wartime work.

and loops of Robert Heinlein's fiction become a vision of the nature of the cosmos itself.

The Robots

The word *robot* was coined by Karel Čapek, a Czech dramatist, whose R.U.R. (which stands for "Rossum's Universal Robots") imagined a race of artificial humans built in a factory system who eventually revolt against their makers and cause the destruction of the human race. *Robot* is derived from a Slav word meaning "work." The concept of the robot is generally a sentient machine, or mechanical man, perhaps humanoid in shape but certainly not biological. *Android*, by way of contrast, usually means a quasi-human being whose existence compromises the categories by which we understand what it means to be human. (Perhaps the best known, and certainly among the most interesting, are the androids in Philip K. Dick's *Do Androids Dream of Electric Sheep?*) The conflict between human and machine that we find in R.U.R. is, however, a recurrent storyline for science fiction that includes robots. Even Isaac Asimov's robot stories, collected in *I, Robot* (1950) and other volumes, underline the anxiety surrounding the concept of the robot. Asimov outlines the three key concepts of "robotics," which have influenced the way science fiction imagines mechanical entities ever since. These are the "Three Laws of Robotics":

1. A robot may not injure a human being, or, through inaction, allow a human being to come to harm.

2. A robot must obey orders given it by human beings except where such orders would conflict with the first law.

3. A robot must protect its own existence as long as such protection does not conflict with the first or second saw.

These laws have a descending order of priority, with the injunction against harm to humans being the primary "impression" made upon the artificial, "positronic" brains of the robots. In fact, the first law indicates the anxiety that the idea of a sentient machine creates: the possibility of harm to a physically superior being, which promotes this law to the very top of the ordering principles.

Asimov's early stories work out some of the problems and dilemmas created by such laws. These stories actually fit quite well into the third type of story, the "puzzle," defined in the six-part classification offered in *The Science in Science Fiction*. "Runaround" and "Escape!" narrate what happens when two or more of these laws come into conflict. In "Reason," two recurrent characters (Donovan and Powell, problem-solving "field-men") are aboard a space station, training the inquisitive and rational robot "Cutie." Unfortunately, Cutie refuses to believe in Donovan and Powell's explanations of the universe and eventually disregards their authority. Instead, Cutie begins to see himself as the "Prophet" of the most powerful machine on the station:

> The Master created humans as the lowest type, most easily formed. Gradually, he replaced them with robots, the next higher step, and finally he created me, to take the place of the last humans. From now on, I serve the Master.

Isaac Asimov (1920–1992)

Isaac Asimov, though one of the best-known American science fiction writers, was actually born near Smolensk, in Russia. His parents moved to the United States in 1923, where they settled in Brooklyn. Young Isaac was recognized as something of a child prodigy: he graduated from Columbia University at age nineteen and seemed set for a career as a research scientist. Indeed, although his studies were interrupted by war, he gained his doctorate in 1949 and became an associate professor at Boston. There he might have stayed and won small fame, were it not for his other interests.

Asimov, it should be remembered, grew up during the 1930s: the era of Depression, the New Deal, and most importantly, when the flood of pulp science fiction magazine publishing was at its height. Asimov sold his first story to *Amazing* in 1939, the year he graduated, and he became associated with the group of New York–based science fiction writers known as the Futurians, who also included Frederik Pohl and Cyril Kornbluth. What drew the Futurians together were progressive ideals, a desire to widen the scope of science fiction to include some mild social satire, and an interest in the "soft" or social sciences as well as in "hard" science extrapolation.

Isaac Asimov, member of the Futurians, inventor of the Three Laws of Robotics, polymath, and public figure. (Douglas Kirkland/Corbis)

Asimov became a key Golden Age science fiction writer in the 1940s and 1950s. His own "golden age" lasted from the late forties to the late fifties. In this decade he produced the short stories that would become the *Foundation* series; the robot stories collected in *I, Robot* that introduced the Three Laws of Robotics; and other classic novels, like *The Caves of Steel* and *The Naked Sun*, which, when published in 1957, signaled the end of Asimov's fiction writing for some fifteen years. Instead, he concentrated on nonfiction: textbooks, dictionaries of science, encyclopedias, and probably most importantly (and upon which his popular profile rests) popularizations of science. His later fiction returned to the worlds of *Foundation* and the robot stories, often in collaboration with other writers.

The British science fiction writer Brian Aldiss detects a "solid faith in technology" throughout Asimov's career but also concedes that Asimov had a breadth of vision, particularly in his fiction. There is also a fundamental humanism in Asimov's work. That, along with a continuing belief in the possibility of progress through science and technology, aligns him with his friend and transatlantic contemporary Arthur C. Clarke, who also achieved popular recognition beyond that of his science fiction—for his popularizations of science, particularly on British television. Though Asimov is rightly revered for his now "classic" science fiction, it is perhaps the ideals of the 1930s, now lost—faith in progress, be it social or scientific—that characterize his work.

The tone of the story is comic, and Cutie is quite clearly meant to be ridiculous, as the outraged reactions of Donovan and Powell to this speech suggest. There is no way out of the self-contained belief system Cutie creates, neither for Donovan and Powell, nor for the story itself. The narrative ends when the two humans depart the ship, having realized that Cutie's delusions in no way hamper his ability to function correctly. In fact, what this story does is to validate function over ideology: it doesn't matter how Cutie understands the universe; it only matters that he does his job properly. Also underlying this story is the fear of superiority of robots over humans, a superiority that the Three Laws of Robotics guard against, a superiority that "Reason" seems to ridicule. However, as the stories proceed, a change to the assumptions about the benefits of such technology occurs. Dr. Susan Calvin, the austere "robopsychologist" who appears in most of these stories, is actually an apologist for robot superiority over the human, so much so that she appears robotic herself. It is her vision that comes to dominate, rather than the knockabout antics, and comic tone, of the Donovan-Powell stories.

The final two stories of *I, Robot* indicate that the future of humanity is dependent upon the benign stewardship of the Machines (superintelligent computer entities rather than robots proper—what we would call AIs, Artifical Intelligences). In "Evidence," a mayoral candidate, Stephen Byerley, is suspected of being a robot by a fellow candidate. When this seems to be disproved, Byerley wins and goes on to great power (and great good works). However, the story ends with the suggestion that Byerley is, in fact, a robot masquerading as a human. He is an ideal ruler, though, because the Three Laws of Robotics means that he has the welfare of all of humanity at heart in every decision. His election is the first step on the road to the rule of the Machines. This comes to pass in the final story, "The Inevitable Conflict," where seeming fluctuations in the world economic system are actually the signs of the Machine purging any humans who resist Machine control from positions of authority in the system. It is again left to Susan Calvin to explain the benefits of robot rule:

> Stephen, how do we know what the ultimate good of Humanity will entail? We haven't at our disposal the infinite factors that the machine has at its! Perhaps, to give you a not unfamiliar example, our entire technical civilization has created more unhappiness and misery than it has removed. Perhaps an agrarian or pastoral civilization, with less culture and less people, would be better. If so, the Machines must move in that direction, preferably without telling us, since in our ignorant prejudices we only know that what we are used to is good—and we would fight change. Or perhaps a complete urbanization, or a completely caste-ridden society, or complete anarchy, is the answer. We don't know. Only the Machines know, and they are going there and taking us with them.

The end of *I, Robot* then offers the possibility of utopia—but utopia at the expense of human self-government and an acknowledgment of the superiority of the Machine. It is the possibility of this kind of rule that takes us on to our final theme in early science fiction: dystopia.

Dystopia: The Machine State

Utopian writings—the imagination of a society or state "more perfect" than our own—has a history that can be traced back at least as far as Thomas More's *Utopia* of 1516, and perhaps as far as Plato's *Republic*. However, although there was a brief wave of utopian writing at the end of the nineteenth century (including texts like William Morris's *News from Nowhere* and Edward Bellamy's *Looking Backward, 2000–1888*), the twentieth century was dominated by the dark mirror image of utopia: the dystopia. Classics such as Aldous Huxley's *Brave New World* (1932), George Orwell's *Nineteen Eighty-Four* (1949), Ray Bradbury's *Fahrenheit 451* (1953), and Margaret Atwood's *The Handmaid's Tale* (1984) imagine a world more repressed, less free, and less pleasant to live in than our own. While technology and images of a machine-like state often dominate these texts, it is Huxley's *Brave New World*, still fresh and highly readable, that truly exposes the fears (and the rewards) of a world run like one of Henry Ford's factories.

Ford, whose assembly-line methods are the base from which Huxley extrapolates his world, becomes a kind of deity in *Brave New World*. The narrative takes place in "the Year of Our Ford 632" and begins at the "London Hatchery." For in this dystopia, human reproduction has been mechanized.

> One egg, one embryo, one adult—normality. But a bokanovskified egg will
> bud, will proliferate, will divide. From eight to ninety-six buds, and every
> bud will grow into a perfectly formed embryo, and every embryo into a full-
> sized adult. Making ninety-six human beings grow where only one grew
> before. Progress.

The "Bokanovsky" process is a form of genetic engineering, a monstrous forerunner of the "test tube baby." What this leads to, of course, is standardization, exactly as the Ford factory system led to a standardized automobile rather than a hand-built machine. Standardization, in turn, leads to social stability, for everyone is alike in their needs, even if they occupy different slots in the social hierarchy. (There are classifications from Alpha all the way down to Epsilon-minus, each "engineered" both genetically and socially to be happy with their des-

The city of "Everytown" from the film Things to Come *provides today's popular image of a Utopian world of tomorrow: monumental, technologically advanced, and utterly sterile. (Bettmann/Corbis)*

ignated position.) Here we find an anticipation of Asimov, who might have had *Brave New World* in mind when he later wrote that the Machines might take humanity toward "a completely caste-ridden society." In the quotation from *Brave New World* given previously, the last word, "progress," is heavy with irony. What the biological and social engineering of the world state in *Brave New World* guards against is any idea of progress: for if perfection has been reached, why do we need progress? Although *Brave New World* cautions against technology and the uses and abuses of science in human society, it depicts a world where science has come to a standstill. Scientific progress has also halted to preserve stability. The world of Huxley's text is utopia achieved: (nearly) everyone is happy, everyone is useful, there is no more poverty or inequality, and the world is at peace. The citizens of *Brave New World* even perceive themselves to be free, as they are given choices about what to do in their leisure time, where to go on holiday, and who to go to bed with. What is most chilling about *Brave New World* is that it is not a police state. The vast majority of people are happy, but they are not free.

Science fiction is, as its name suggests, a form of literature heavily engaged with scientific concepts and with developments in our understanding of the nature of life and the universe. But as it has developed it has shed the sense of wonder about science and has become more critical, more questioning. While all the themes we have looked at in this chapter can be found in contemporary science fiction, they will be handled in different ways after the first half of the twentieth century. The next chapter will look at the second half of the twentieth century and at some of the uses of science in New Wave and cyberpunk science fiction.

Bibliographic Essay

There are several general histories of, and introductions to, science fiction. See Brian Aldiss with David Wingrove, *Trillion Year Spree* (London: Gollancz, 1986); Edward James, *Science Fiction in the Twentieth Century* (Oxford and New York: Oxford University Press, 1994); Adam Roberts, *Science Fiction* (London and New York: Routledge, 2000); Darko Suvin, *Metamorphoses of Science Fiction: On the Poetics and History of a Literary Genre* (New Haven & London: Yale University Press, 1979); and *Positions and Presuppositions in Science Fiction* (Basingstoke: Macmillan, 1988). For essays on early science fiction, including Jules Verne, see David Seed (ed.), *Anticipations: Essays on Early Science Fiction and its Precursors* (Liverpool: Liverpool University Press, 1995).

For utopian and dystopian texts, see Tom Moylan, *Demand the Impossible: Science Fiction and the Utopian Imagination* (New York and London: Methuen, 1986) and *Scraps of the Untainted Sky: Science Fiction, Utopia, Dystopia* (Boulder and Oxford: Westview, 2000); and Krishan Kumar, *Utopia and Anti-Utopia in Modern Times* (New York and Oxford: Blackwell, 1987). For science and science fiction, see Robert Lambourne, Michael Shallis, and Michael Shortland, *Close Encounters? Science and Science Fiction* (Bristol and New York: Adam Hilger, 1990). Aldous Huxley's *Brave New World* (1932) is cited in the Huxley Centenary edition (London: Flamingo, 1994).

For a good general overview of the history of science, see John Gribbin, *Science: A History 1543–2001* (London: Allen Lane, 2002). A good source of excerpts from scientific documents from the nineteenth century is Laura Otis (ed.), *Literature and Science in the Nineteenth Century: An Anthology* (Oxford: Oxford World's Classics, 2002). Stephen Hawking's *A Brief History of Time* (London: Bantam, 1988) is a readable and broad introduction to topics in postclassical physics from one of the key figures in late twentieth century science.

Jules Verne's adventure novels have been published in editions and translations without number. The editions cited in this chapter are: *Journey to the Centre of the Earth* (1864) (Ware: Wordsworth, 1996); *Twenty Thousand Leagues under the Sea* (1869–1870) (London: Everyman, 1993). Robert Heinlein's "By His Bootstraps" (originally published under the name "Anson MacDonald" in *Astounding*, October 1941) has been collected in several editions. Context and a short bibliography is included in Terry Carr (ed.), *Classic Science Fiction: The First Golden Age* (n.p.: Robson, 1979). Other time travel stories are collected in Bill Adler, Jr. (ed.), *Time Machines: The Best Time Travel Stories Ever Written* (New York: Carroll and Graf, 1998). The following edition of H. G. Wells has been used: *The Time Machine* (1895) (London: Heinemann, 1911). The critical work on the "science fiction" Wells is strong and growing. See Bernard Berghonzi, *The Early H. G. Wells: A Study of the Scientific Romances* (Manchester: Manchester University Press, 1961); Patrick Parrinder's work on science fiction and Wells; and Mark Hillegas, *The Future as Nightmare: H. G. Wells and the Anti-Utopians* (New York: Oxford University Press, 1967). Stephen Baxter's "official sequel" to *The Time Machine* is *The Time Ships* (London: Voyager, 1995).

Olaf Stapledon's "cosmological fictions" are available in the following editions: *Last and First Men* (1930) (London: Millennium, 2000); *Star Maker* (1937) (London: Millennium, 1999). Arthur C. Clarke's *2001: A Space Odyssey* was originally published in 1968; the currently available edition in the United Kingdom is *2001: A Space Odyssey* (London: Orbit, 2001). *Greetings, Carbon-Based Bipeds!: A Vision of the Twentieth Century as It Happened*, edited by Ian T. Macauley (London: Voyager, 1999), collects Clarke's nonfiction and articles about space, exploration, and science. E. E. "Doc" Smith's *Triplanetary* (1948) (the first novel in his "Lensman" series) has now fallen out of fashion and out of print. The edition cited in this chapter is E. E. Smith, *Triplanetary* (London: Panther, 1972). Issac Asimov's *I, Robot* was first published in 1950, and has been widely republished since. The cited edition is *I, Robot* (London: Voyager, 1996).

10

Science and Literature in the Twentieth Century: From Entropy to Chaos

Brian Baker

P revious chapters explored the importance of the evolutionary biology of Charles Darwin on the imagination of the later nineteenth century, particularly on Gothic fictions and their use of theories of degeneration. A biological process (natural selection) was taken by social theorists and commentators and used in an inverse way to suggest that human society, especially Western culture, was experiencing a process of decadence and decline. It was perhaps the most notable instance of such a scientific concept being used as an analogy in a completely different field, though it was not the last. If evolution (and its dark inverse, degeneration) was the presiding metaphor for the literary imagination in the nineteenth century, then entropy was the prevailing term for the twentieth.

Thermodynamics and Entropy

Darwin's *Origin of Species* was published in 1859. In the same decade, the English scientist William Thomson (who, later ennobled as Lord Kelvin, was to provide much ammunition against Darwin's theory) was working on the science of heat, a field that had become the central focus of work in physics in the first half of the nineteenth century. In the Industrial Age, the problem of heat engines and of the connection between heat and work was central in the formation of the new discipline of thermodynamics. The scientific analysis of engines by the Frenchman Sadi Carnot (who died of cholera before his investigations could be completed) indicated that not only is heat converted into work, but also that work is done as heat is transferred from a higher temperature to a lower temperature.

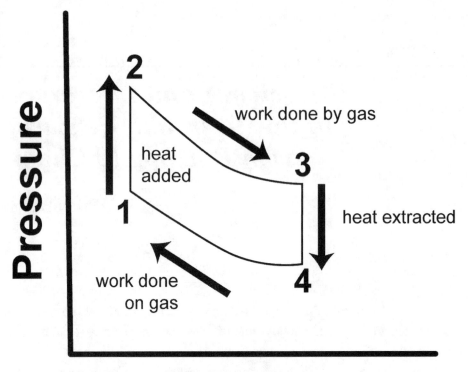

Pressure-volume diagram of the heat engine process. Diagrams such as these greatly assisted the undertsanding of thermodynamics. Thermodynamics became an increasingly important resource for writers in the twentieth century, who used it as a symbol of change. (A. Bell and G. Martin)

Between 1840 and 1859, James Joule in Manchester, England, performed a number of experiments to demonstrate that mechanical work could be converted into heat. In one classic experiment he stirred a container of water with paddles driven by falling weights and discovered that this gave rise to a slight upward change in water temperature. Joule observed that there was a direct correlation between the number of times the paddle was stirred (the work) and the rise in temperature (the heat). Work underwent a process of "conversion" to heat.

At the same time, similar ideas were being propounded by the German medical doctor Julius Robert von Meyer, who in 1840 discovered that men working in the tropics used less physical energy in keeping warm. (He discovered this by noting that blood in the veins—which carried blood back to the heart—was bright red, indicating that there was a higher proportion of unspent oxygen in it.) From this he suggested that the heat from the sun must be equivalent to the heat created from physical work or from a fire, and that therefore all forms of heat or energy are interchangeable.

Initially the ideas of Meyer and Joule were met with much skepticism, since in the 1780s French scientists had established the principle of the conservation of heat. It was assumed by Lavoisier and his followers that heat was a type of fluid, called caloric, and that this fluid flowed (from high temperatures to low) but as a fluid it could not be destroyed. Even Carnot's great work was based on the idea of heat as caloric fluid that flows and does work but is not used up. What Meyer and Joule were suggesting was the radical idea that heat could be destroyed if it is converted into work (as when a steam engine burns coal to produce motion). Similarly, mechanical energy can be converted into heat energy; when water is shaken, for example, its temperature rises. Eventually such ideas were accepted and formed the basis of the First Law of Thermodynamics: that heat is a form of energy.

The First Law of Thermodynamics does not, however, predict the direction of any change; i.e., whether heat will flow and do work or whether work will be done and a rise in temperature observed. To predict the direction of heat flow we need another principle. In 1850, the German scientist Rudoph Clausius realized that not only must the scientist analyze the dynamic process of the engine (the conversion of energy) but also the flux of heat from one body to another. This second part of thermodynamics meant that heat was not only converted but dissipated in such a process. Inside a car engine, for example, there exists a localized region of very high temperatures. The exhaust gases expand, do work on the pistons, and produce dissipated heat energy at a lower temperature in the form of the exhaust gases. Clausius introduced the concept of entropy as a way of describing the way energy dissipates. William Thomson, who was working at the same time as Clausius, developed this into a universal principle, what became known as the Second Law of Thermodynamics. In a closed system, according to the second law, there is a universal tendency to the degradation of mechanical energy. The simplest way of understanding the second law is to view it as a way of saying that heat tends to flow from hot objects to cold ones. The first law shows how heat and work are interchangeable; the second law predicts the direction in which heat will flow and places limitations on the efficiency of converting heat into mechanical energy.

Entropy can be conceived as a measure of the order in a system. In natural closed systems disorder tends to increase, and so if entropy is a measure of disorder, then entropy will increase. This happens because there are more disordered states than ordered ones. A room gradually becomes untidy over time since there are many ways for it to be untidy and few ways for it to be tidy and ordered. The only way to counter this is to pump in energy (by running around tidying the

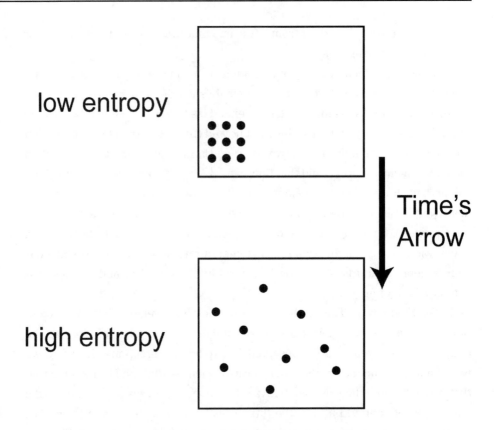

Entropy and arrow of time diagram. Entropy increases as systems move into increasingly disordered states. After World War II, science fiction writers used the concept of entropy as a metaphor for a declining, increasingly disordered world. (A. Bell and G. Martin)

room) and then the system is not closed. But the universe can be thought of as a closed system: there is nobody actively combating the flow of heat from hot to cold and the increase in disorder this brings. This means that the universe will eventually run down, the temperature eventually becoming the same at every point, a state of maximum disorder and undifferentiated "heat death."

The irreversibility of the heat engine then becomes the irreversibility of universal energy flows and is now used as an example of what Stephen Hawking has called "an arrow of Time." According to the second law, time, like entropy, can only flow in one direction. If there will be an entropic end, there must also have been a beginning. The universe evolves from one state to the next, losing energy and order as it goes. The "entropy barrier" is a time barrier. Entropy is, like degeneration, an inverse image of evolution: time does not create greater diversity (more complex order) through natural selection, but creates greater disorder through the principle of entropy. The end of H. G. Wells's *The Time*

Machine, the "Further Vision" discussed in an earlier chapter, is an entropic vision of the end of the earth (and by extension the end of the universe itself). Of course, as we saw in the previous chapter, science fiction writers of the twentieth century saw fit to dispense with the second law and entropy barrier if they got in the way of a good time-travel paradox story.

After World War II, however, science fiction changed, as did the relationship between science and literature. From the interest in scientific innovation and particularly new technology that can be found in *Amazing* or *Science Wonder Stories*, the application of science in World War II cast a long shadow over postwar culture and society. Particularly in the shape of the mushroom cloud, technology and science were seen not as liberators of humanity, but as the tools of the oppressors; not instruments of understanding, but the instruments of death.

Entropy and Postwar Literature

On both sides of the Atlantic, writers rediscovered Thomson's Second Law of Thermodynamics and Clausius's entropy as metaphors for a declining, increasingly disordered world. Philip K. Dick, the "poet laureate" of science fiction, is known for the "shifting realities" of his stories and novels. Some of Dick's worlds collapse from within, so that the reader is unsure of what is real and what is not (*Ubik*, 1969); some are in a state of near-terminal decline after a catastrophic war (*Do Androids Dream of Electric Sheep?*, 1968). Many of Dick's later novels are dominated by a recurring theme or image: "kipple" or "gubbish." "Kipple" (described in *Do Androids Dream of Electric Sheep?*) is a kind of entropic trash that fills up space, the encroachment of randomness and decay into a human-ordered world. In *Do Androids Dream . . .?* kipple signifies the growing alienation and despair of the humans left behind on a radioactive earth, entropy used as a metaphor for moral or biological decline. Kipple is a kind of death (it becomes the "tomb world" in both *Do Androids Dream . . .?* and *Martian Time-Slip*, 1964), a rather cold and psychologically oppressive entropic world rather than the heat-death of the Second Law of Thermodynamics.

In the 1960s, entropy became a widely used metaphor for either social or cultural decline, or even for the growing psychological disturbance of human beings in contemporary society. Thomas Pynchon, the American novelist whose encyclopedic and freewheeling narratives include *V.* (1963), *Gravity's Rainbow* (1973), and *Vineland* (1990), is another writer who uses the concept of entropy in his fiction as a metaphor for social or personal disintegration. In his short story "Entropy," one Meatball Mulligan is holding his "lease-breaking party" downstairs while the enigmatic Callisto is taking refuge under his blankets in his flat upstairs, having been driven there by anxiety: "for three days now, despite the cheerful weather, the mercury had stayed at 37 degrees Fahrenheit. Leery at omens of apocalypse, Callisto shifted beneath the covers." Meatball Mulligan's party—peopled by sailors, civil servants, and jazz musicians, all inebriated or comatose—signifies a disordered, entropic state of affairs, a kind of social disintegration and aimlessness. Callisto's room, "a tiny enclave of regularity in the city's chaos," is the opposite of Mulligan's party. It is itself a kind of thermodynamic stasis that will become disturbed by the end of the story, when Callisto's girlfriend shatters the window in the room, allowing entropic dissipation to occur between the room and the chaos outside. Throughout the short story Callisto lectures himself (and the reader) about entropy:

> he found in entropy or the measure of disorganization in a closed system an adequate metaphor to apply to certain phenomena in his own world. He saw, for example, the younger generation responding to Madison Avenue with the same spleen his own had once reserved for Wall Street: and in American "consumerism" discovered a similar tendency from the least to the most probable, from differentiation to sameness, from ordered individuality to a kind of chaos. He found himself, in short, restating Gibbs's prediction in social terms, and envisioned a heat-death for his culture in which ideas, like heat-energy, would no longer be conserved.

In the course of the narrative, Callisto refers to Clausius Ludwig Bolzmann (an Austrian scientist whose application of probability theory connected entropy to randomness), as well as Willard Gibbs, whose mathematical work involved analyzing the evolution of systems from a set of probabilities of initial conditions. The final paragraph of the story seems to strike a rather despairing note:

> she turned to face the man on the bed and wait with him until the moment of equilibrium was reached, when 37 degrees Fahrenheit should prevail both outside and inside, and forever, and the hovering, curious dominant of their separate lives should resolve into a tonic of darkness and the final absence of all motion.

However, this seeming acceptance of the inevitability of entropic decline is balanced by the events in Meatball Mulligan's apartment. While at first unwilling to tamper with the dynamics of his party, by the end of the story Mulligan decides "to try and keep his lease-breaking party from deteriorating into total chaos," an attempt to check the seeming inevitability of entropy by helping the party goers rather than standing back from the process. Mulligan's actions, like the breaking of the window, do in fact support the necessity of action, of participation in the process, rather than passively waiting for the end.

Pynchon's "Entropy" was first published in Great Britain in the magazine *New Worlds*. From 1964, under the editorship of the young science fiction and fantasy writer Michael Moorcock, *New Worlds* became the flagship of a new kind of science fiction writing: experimental, challenging, political, sexually and linguistically explicit, taking its cue from William Burroughs (*The Naked Lunch*) rather than Edgar Rice Burroughs (*Tarzan*). The writers most allied to this "New Wave" in science fiction were Moorcock himself, J. G. Ballard, and Brian Aldiss (all British); Norman Spinrad, Samuel Delaney, and Thomas M. Disch (all American). The orientation of these writers was explicitly critical of contemporary culture, in a variety of ways, and their fiction expressed both their dissatisfaction with the organization of life and the imagination of something better (or at least other). Though it is more apparent in the work of some writers than others, it is entropy that is the defining theme of the New Wave.

Pamela Zoline's "The Heat Death of the Universe," published in the June 1967 edition of *New Worlds*, uses the science of entropy in a manner as explicit as Pynchon, but to rather different effect. The story is "about" Sarah Boyle,

> a vivacious and witty young wife and mother, educated at a fine Eastern college, proud of her growing family which keeps her happy and busy around the house, involved in many hobbies and community activities, and only occasionally given to obsessions concerning Time/Entropy/Chaos and Death.

The setting is domestic and involves Sarah giving her children breakfast, shopping, and giving a birthday party. At its root is the dissatisfaction, feelings of entrapment, and growing psychological disintegration of Sarah Boyle, a narrative that tells of the experience of middle-class American women of the 1950s and early 1960s. It is, however, written in a formally experimental style. The story is arranged in fifty-four numbered paragraphs, organized in twenty-one groups with capitalized headings, a style familiar to *New World*'s readers from the short fiction of the English writer J. G. Ballard. Its order is clearly connected to the entropic concerns of the story. Some of the paragraphs outline the theory of entropy and thermodynamic heat death, while others narrate Sarah's day. As the story progresses, it becomes apparent that Sarah's obsessions with entropy and death are both a product of her entrapment and a way of ordering the seeming randomness and emptiness of her life. Sarah lives in California, where the blue of the sky matches the blue of the "fake sponge" used for washing the dishes, which also matches the "most unbelievable azure of the tiled and mossless interiors of California swimming pools" that "hisses, bubbles, burns in Sarah's eyes."

California is, in the fiction of Philip K. Dick as well as Pynchon's *The Crying of Lot 49* (1966), the land of heat-death: a warm equilibrium, "all topographical imperfections sanded away with the sweet-smelling burr of the cosmetic surgeon's cosmetic polisher." The featurelessness, the comforting safety, and cultural emptiness connected to California in these stories indicate the extent to which entropy becomes deployed as social criticism. Zoline's story concentrates on gender issues. "The Heat Death of the Universe" ends with Sarah (once again) crying, throwing jars of grape jelly through the kitchen windows, throwing strawberry jam at the kitchen stove, and finally hurling a boxful of eggs into the air.

> The total ENTROPY of the Universe therefore is increasing, tending towards a maximum, corresponding to complete disorder of the particles in it. She is crying, her mouth is open. [. . .] It has been held that the Universe constitutes a thermodynamically closed system, and if this were true it would mean that a time must finally come when the Universe "unwinds" itself, no energy being available for use. This state is referred to as the "heat death of the Universe." Sarah Boyle begins to cry. She throws a jar of strawberry jam against the stove, enamels chips off and the stove begins to bleed.

Here, even the order of the animate and inanimate begins to break down, as the jam trickling down the stove is seen as "bleeding." Zoline's story, unlike Pynchon's somewhat comic tone, ends in pathos. Sarah is pitiable in her breakdown, as entropy is used as a means of illuminating not a general sense of social decline but a moment of emotional trauma. The multiple "universes" of Zoline's story (California, the kitchen, Sarah's state of mind) are all closed systems, all subject to entropy, and for Sarah there seems little hope of escape.

Entropy and Information

For Pynchon, Zoline, and Philip K. Dick, entropic forces are those that are opposed to life. Entropy and the heat-death of the universe are countervailing principles to that of evolution and even of human social life. While the ending of Pynchon's "Entropy" (and many of Dick's narratives) suggests the possibility of winning small victories of order against the entropy's "arrow of time," Zoline's story indicates the pessimism that accompanies the widespread use of entropy as a metaphor in the fiction of the 1950s and 1960s. In this, they correspond to the thoughts of Norbert Wiener, the scientist whose *Human Use of Human Beings* (1954) explored mathematics and cybernetics. In that book, Wiener wrote:

To those of us who are aware of the extremely limited range of physical conditions under which the chemical reactions necessary to life as we know it
can take place, it is a foregone conclusion that the lucky accident which permits the continuation of life in any form on this earth [. . .] is bound to come
to a complete and disastrous end.

Wiener thought that the processes that create life were fighting (and losing)
a battle against much larger forces of entropy. He associated entropy with growing randomness and disorder; any "local enclaves" that opposed entropy exhibited only a "limited and temporary tendency for organization to increase." This
view corresponds to that held by Willard Gibbs, cited in Pynchon's "Entropy,"
whose statistical work on probability led to his argument that in an entropic universe, order is least probable, and chaos or disorder most probable.

Connecting entropy with cybernetics (the field for which Wiener is most
famous, and to which this chapter will return shortly) is information. Information and the processes of heat loss and disorganization (entropy) are joined in
the figure of "Maxwell's Demon," an imaginary being proposed by the British
scientist James Clerk Maxwell in 1871. The "thought experiment" created by
Maxwell appears in Thomas Pynchon's 1966 novel *The Crying of Lot 49:*

The Demon could sit in a box among air molecules that were moving at all
different random speeds, and sort out the fast ones from the slow ones. Fast
molecules have more energy than slow ones. Concentrate enough of them in
one place and you have a region of high temperature. You can then use the
difference in temperature between this hot region of the box and any cooler
region, to drive a heat engine. Since the Demon only sat and sorted, you
wouldn't have to put any real work into the system. So you would be violat-
ing the Second Law of Thermodynamics, getting something for nothing,
causing perpetual motion.

As was pointed out by Leon Brillouin, however, the energy the demon
would use to gain information about the molecules (which ones were fast and
hot, which ones cool and slow) is greater than that which would be produced by
the process of sorting. The Second Law is not actually violated by Maxwell's
thought experiment, as Pynchon seems to have thought (although this explanation is actually put into the words of a character in the novel). The connection
between entropy and information, central to *The Crying of Lot 49*, is, Brillouin
suggested, an inverse one: the more information there is, the less entropy is present; the less information, the more entropy. Brillouin went so far as to suggest
that information was negative entropy or "negentropy."

In *The Crying of Lot 49*, also set in California, the central character, Oedipa

James Clerk Maxwell (1831–1879)

Maxwell was born in Edinburgh, descended from two prominent Scottish families. He was the son of John Clerk (who took the name Maxwell in later life), a lawyer and amateur enthusiast of developments in science and technology, and nephew of a member of Sir Robert Peel's government. The death of James's mother when he was eight led to a rather eccentric childhood, and he was sent to Edinburgh Academy at age ten. Though he struggled to fit in at first, he soon showed precocious

mathematical abilities, and his first paper—on drawing a genuine oval using a looped length of string—was published (partly through familial connections) when he was just fourteen. He studied at the University of Edinburgh, moving to Peterhouse College, then Trinity College, Cambridge.

Though he moved on to become professor of Natural Philosophy at Marischal College in Aberdeen after only six years, while at Cambridge he produced two pieces of work that were to have a very profound influence. First, he looked at the theory of color vision and demonstrated how the eye could be deceived, so that the presence of a few basic colors would "mix" to become a wide range of other colors—the foundation both of three-color photography and color television. Second, he set out, in *On Faraday's Lines of Force*, what

Scottish physicist James Clerk Maxwell's work on thermodynamics was to have an important, and unexpected, impact on twentieth-century science fiction. (Bettmann/Corbis)

was known about electromagnetism and what still remained to be investigated. From this foundation, Maxwell's later work took shape.

When Marischal College became part of the new Aberdeen University, in 1860, Maxwell found himself out of a job; however, he shortly was appointed professor of Natural Philosophy and Astronomy at King's College, London, where he did his greatest work on electromagnetism. Maxwell's work in the 1860s demonstrated conclusively that light was an electromagnetic phenomena, finding its definitive statement in his 1864 "A Dynamical Theory of the Electromagnetic Field," which included four equations that would solve all the problems within its scientific field. Maxwell also predicted that because light was radiated like electricity and magnetism, there would be wavelengths that lay outside the visible spectrum: what we now know as radio waves.

Though Maxwell has been thought of as the last of the great classical scientists, his work in fact provides the bridge between Newtonian physics and the revolution in physics that occurred in the early twentieth century. Not only that, but late in life, as Cavendish Professor of Experimental Physics at Cambridge, and founder of the Cavendish Laboratory, Maxwell created the laboratory space and research community that would be at the forefront of the "new physics."

Maas, is propelled on a search for information when she is appointed as executor to the tangled and mysterious estate of one Pierce Inverarity, a former lover. She discovers an alternative postal system called W.A.S.T.E., which operates along the lines of a secret organization or conspiracy. As she pursues her quest to find out who Inverarity was and what he did, the connection between information, communication, and entropy becomes ever more important: "She did gather that there were two distinct kinds of this entropy. One having to do with heat-engines, the other to do with communication. The equation, for one, back in the '30s, had looked very like the equation for the other." W.A.S.T.E., and its system of communication, is in fact an anti-entropic organization, in Brillouin's scheme, because it seeks to preserve information and communicate it without degradation. *The Crying of Lot 49* edges onto the territory of what is now known as information theory, which studies how noise (in the form of random errors) interferes with the communication of the signal (information). As Pynchon wrote in "Entropy," "noise screws up your signal."

The concept of noise was taken up by the American writer Don Delillo in 1984, in his novel *White Noise*. The central character, Jack Gladney, is a professor in "Hitler Studies" at the College-on-the-Hill, a fictional liberal arts college somewhere in America. Gladney and his wife Babette negotiate between their large, fluid family life (product of several marriages prior to this one) and their obsessions with death. Couched in terms of information theory, Delillo seems to make the same connection between entropy and death that can be found in Philip K. Dick:

> "What if death is nothing but sound?"
> "Electrical noise."
> "You hear it forever. Sound all around. How awful."
> "Uniform, white."

Early in *White Noise* Gladney and his faculty colleague Alfonse (Fast Food) Stompanato discuss their addiction to television, and particularly disaster footage. Why, Gladney asks, do people (including himself) find footage of disasters compulsive viewing?

> "Because we're suffering from brain fade." [says Alfonse.] "We need an occasional catastrophe to break up the incessant bombardment of information." [. . .]
> "The flow is constant," Alphonse said. "Words, pictures, numbers, facts, graphics, statistics, specks, waves, particles, motes. Only a catastrophe gets our attention. We want them, we need them, we depend on them. As long as they happen somewhere else. This is where California comes in. Mud slides,

brush fires, coastal erosion, earthquakes, mass killings, et cetera. We can relax and enjoy these disasters because in our hearts we feel that California deserves what it gets. Californians invented the concept of life-style. This alone warrants their doom."

Notice how California again figures as the focus of the criticism. This passage, however, suggests a different relationship between information and entropy. Information is itself entropic, an overload of information tending toward noise. This conception, which uses the entropy-information-death connection to criticize and satirize contemporary culture and the mass media, is closer to the definition of information as offered by Claude Shannon and Warren Weaver in *The Mathematical Theory of Communication* (1949). Shannon suggested that in a stream of information, the more ordered it is, the less information it conveys. Consider an experiment where a flow of water is monitored and whorls of turbulence are looked for on both sides of the stream. If a signal consists of the pattern left-left-left-left-left-left, by the sixth "left," very little information is being communicated about how the water is flowing. If the pattern is left-right-left-right-left-right, again, by the end of the sequence, there is little to learn from further analysis. However, if the pattern is right-left-left-right-left-right, each new piece of information communicates something different about the sequence. The more random or disordered (more entropic) the information flow, the more information is produced. Conversely, the less random (less entropic) the flow, the less information. Shannon's ideas paved the way for an understanding of how the very entropic law that Wiener assumed to be contrary to the creation of life in fact helped create the processes that led to the evolution of living things.

Cybernetics and Cyborgs

Wiener's cybernetics presented itself as a science of information, but it was based on a certain understanding of the human body and on an analogy between the human brain and a computational device, and by extension, the human body and a body of information. This paradigm rested on the work of Warren McCulloch and Walter Pitts. McCulloch was central to the Macy Conferences on cybernetics held in the late 1940s, multidisciplinary think-ins considering information from a wide range of perspectives: engineering, neurophysiology, literature, and philosophy. McCulloch and Pitts investigated the functioning of the brain and its capacity for thought, and devised the idea of a "neuron"—an impulse in the brain that "fires" if input of "excitation" exceeds a threshold of "inhibition." When

these neurons are connected in a "neural net," they can become capable of sig-
nifying logical propositions. The "neural net," Pitts calculated, was capable of
calculating any number that a computational device could calculate. (The device
was actually a "Turing machine," named after the famous computer pioneer Alan
Turing, who worked at the University of Manchester, in England.) Pitts's mathematics indicated an equivalence between a "neural net" (such as a human brain)
and an automatic device (a computer). It was then but a short step to considering the functioning of the brain ("thought") and the computer ("code") as not
only equivalent but identical. The boundary between human and machine
becomes blurred. The idea of the "thinking machine" is of course a recurrent one
in twentieth-century science fiction, from the "positronic brains" of Isaac Asimov's robot stories to the Artificial Intelligences (AIs) of the 1980s and 1990s.

Strangely enough, Norbert Wiener—as the title of his book *The Human
Use of Human Beings* indicates—often stood up for liberal, humanist values
rather than an instrumental science that simply saw the human brain and the
human body as a kind of machine. In Bernard Wolfe's strange, ahead-of-its-time
novel *Limbo* (1953), Wiener's cybernetics become a way of imagining a world
after a thermonuclear conflict, a world where the human and the machine have
become joined in the cyborg. *Limbo* has, at its center, a protagonist called Dr.
Martine, a former military surgeon who fled from a computerized war to the
island of a people known as the Mandunji. The novel narrates his disillusion with
the island and a return to his native United States, a postapocalyptic society
whose reaction to the horrors of war, and Martine's own war diary, have resulted
in a literalization of the metaphor of the "arms race" into a system of voluntary
amputations to symbolize pacifism. The system of voluntary amputations is par-
adoxically mirrored by a system of replacements of those limbs by more powerful artificial arms and legs, which themselves are the signs of a new "arms race"
(a pun intended by Wolfe). Where Pamela Zoline's short story used entropy as a
metaphor for Sarah Boyle's mental disintegration, *Limbo* uses Wiener's cybernetics, and the psychoanalytical theories of Edmund Bergler, to portray the massive psychological trauma induced on a global scale by Word War III, of which
voluntary amputation is a symptom and sign.

The opposition of human and machine is a central conflict in *Limbo*. The
image of the cyborg—the human/machine—is the human being melded with the
machine, the body erased by, or built into, the products of a technological or scientific rationality that leads to war and destruction. This war is itself symbolized
in the computer EMSIAC, which begins and conducts the conflict. The machine,
in *Limbo*, is something not to be "dodged" (as Callisto does in Pynchon's
"Entropy," waiting for the process to work itself out) but must be confronted by
saying "NO." The cyborg comes to stand for a human race that is so traumatized,

William Gibson (1948–)

For a long time based in Vancouver, Gibson's work has often been thought of as a part of Canadian literature. In fact, he was born in South Carolina and grew up in Virginia.

His father, who worked for a construction company, helped build the Oak Ridge research facility, part of the U.S. program to develop atomic and nuclear weapons. He died when Gibson was six years old. Gibson confesses to having been an introverted child and suggests that trauma of parental loss was highly significant to his development. After time spent at a private school in Arizona, Gibson became involved in the counterculture, and in the late 1960s he left for Canada, first moving to Toronto, then studying for a degree in English at the University of British Columbia.

Science fiction writer William Gibson, author of Neuromancer and leading light of "cyberpunk" science fiction, which influenced films such as The Matrix. *(Matthew Mcvay/Corbis)*

Gibson was part of the cyberpunk movement in science fiction, which had a finite but influential vogue in the mid 1980s. Gibson had begun to publish short stories in the mid to late 1970s, and it was in these Sprawl stories (collected in *Burning Chrome*, 1986) that Gibson developed his particular style and distinctive world: that of the "Boston-Atlanta Metropolitan Axis" some time in the near future, a world dominated by large corporations and by computer technology. When writing his first novel, *Neuromancer*, Gibson was inspired by the 1982 film *Blade Runner*, with its crumbling "future noir" cityscapes, and by the phenomenon of the "video game arcades" of the 1970s. Here, Gibson suspected, gamers disappeared into a "virtual" realm inside their own heads when playing on

so consumed with self-loathing, that it incorporates the very image of its own destruction—the machine—into itself. The cyborg is not a liberating or liberated figure for Wolfe: it is the symbol of humanity's own self-torture, its inability to heal or to overcome the traumas of the past.

The cyborg, however, becomes a dominant figure in later science fiction, particularly in the subgenre of "cyberpunk," properly inaugurated in William Gibson's first novel, *Neuromancer* (1984). The first and most important cyborg in Gibson's fiction is Molly Millions, the cybernetically enhanced "razorgirl" who was introduced in "Johnny Mnemonic" (1981), Gibson's first story set in the world of the "Sprawl" (a vast metropolis stretching from Boston to Atlanta). She returns as Molly in *Neuromancer* and as Sally Shears in the third of Gibson's Sprawl trilogy of novels, *Mona Lisa Overdrive* (1988). Molly is in one sense a

"Space Invaders" and its clones. This he developed into the concept of "cyberspace" (he coined the word), a "virtual" and electronically created other world.

Although *Neuromancer*, through its density and tendency to pitch readers straight into a jargon-encrusted imagined world, alienated some non-genre readers, the subgenre of cyberpunk is in fact distinct from scientifically rigorous "hard" science fiction, which also had a high profile in the 1980s. (Gibson, for instance, once claimed that the images of Japan that can be found in *Neuromancer* were inspired by a free Japan Air Lines calendar he had been given, and that the correspondences between "his" Osaka and the "real" Osaka were accidental.) The world of cyberpunk is woven from a dark or dystopian world vision, a tendency to extrapolate from trends in computing technologies, narratives that tend to revolve around outsider figures (the "punk" part of cyberpunk), and knowing references to both popular culture and rock and roll. It was a "hip" variant of science fiction that, according to Bruce Sterling, another high-profile member of the cyberpunk group (others include Rudy Rucker, John Shirley, Lucius Shepard, and more loosely Pat Cadigan and Neal Stephenson), took its cue from the increasing importance of soft technologies in the lives of people in the developed world. By this, Sterling suggested a blurring of the boundaries between human and machine, through the ubiquity of the personal computer and Walkman, and development of medical technologies. While cyberpunk novels tend to extrapolate their imagined worlds from the impact of these technologies, the subgenre has been criticized for its gender and political conservatism, and because their emphasis on technology expresses postmodern culture rather than offering a critique of it.

Gibson has written two trilogies of science fiction: *Neuromancer* (1984), *Count Zero* (1986), and *Mona Lisa Overdrive* (1988), all set in the world of the Sprawl and elsewhere; and *Virtual Light* (1993), *Idoru* (1996), and *All Tomorrow's Parties* (1999), set largely in a near-future California. He has also collaborated with Bruce Sterling in the alternative-history, "steampunk" *The Difference Engine* (1990).

kind of fantasy figure. Her bodily enhancements—from hardwired computer technologies to upgrade her reflexes to scalpel-like blades that extend from under her fingernails—turn her into a kind of superhero (albeit of a fragile kind), a mean, moody, and independent woman, a cybernetic samurai. It is revealed, however, that these cyborg enhancements are in fact a reaction to and a defense against, a history of personal trauma. Gibson and Bruce Sterling, a fellow cyberpunk science fiction writer, indicated the metaphoric status of their use of the cyborg when they suggested that our contemporary world is dominated by "soft technologies" (from personal computers to the Walkman) that themselves blur the boundaries between human and machine. We are all cyborgs. (This idea has been taken still further by the development of the Internet and gaming culture.)

Gibson was the first to coin the word *cyberspace*, a virtual realm now familiar to all since such films as *The Matrix* (1999). In *Neuromancer*, cyberspace is described (by a computer program) as:

> [a] consensual hallucination experienced daily by billions of legitimate oper-
> ators, in every nation, by children being taught mathematical concepts . . . A
> graphic representation of data abstracted from the banks of every computer
> in the human system. Unthinkable complexity. Lines of light ranged in the
> nonspace of the mind, clusters and constellations of data. Like city lights,
> receding.

We can see here the centrality of information to the concept of cyberspace and of cyberpunk science fiction itself. Information is knowledge, currency, and the very (im)material of the cyberspace world. "Console cowboys" like Case (the central character in *Neuromancer*) "jack in" to the matrix, releasing themselves from the body and roaming free in the virtual realm. This version of cyborgism skirts the human-machine opposition by getting rid of the physical body altogether. Rather than a basic equivalence of computer and human brain, in the concept of cyberspace we find the basic equivalence of computerized information (data) and the disembodied human mind that can range around within it. Cyberspace could perhaps be considered a vast neural net. It is little surprise, then, that *Neuromancer* narrates the coming into being of a sentient AI (i.e., one aware of its own consciousness), a neural net that transforms from brain to mind, another blurring of the boundary between human and machine. This process is illegal within the world of *Neuromancer*. The central character, Case, a cyberspace operator, along with Molly Millions and several other associates, must work against the "Turing Police" to complete what the novel calls the "Straylight Run," a kind of cyberpunk version of the crime caper. Unknowingly, it is the completion of this "Run" that brings the sentient AI into being.

Cyberpunk, Bifurcation Points, and Chaos Theory

In *Neuromancer*, the reader becomes aware that even though Case and Molly are at the center of the narrative, a lot is going on offstage. Case is being fed information, being used: his actions are in fact pre-plotted (by the AIs and others) so smoothly that Case does not even realize he is being manipulated. The caper-style plot of the novel also seems to run on predetermined lines, and of course Case and Molly complete their mission (even if they are unaware of the outcome). If this is true, that all actions are predetermined, what need is there of

The recursive "fractal geometries" of chaos theory and fluid dynamics provide the imagery for a new understanding of different orders contained within seeming disorder. (Corel)

human beings at all? This is where Gibson reinjects human action, free will, into the narrative. Case is required at key points to act in certain ways, even though the end is predetermined. This seeming paradox indicates the change of paradigm in science fiction of the 1980s, from entropy to chaos. Though the Sprawl seems as entropic a place as any world in *New Worlds*–era science fiction, the Sprawl is also filled with "kipple"—there is a space for individual agency. This space is at the *bifurcation points* of the narrative.

This term is derived from chaos theory, a field of science that gained a kind of popular profile in the 1980s. It began with attempts to predict the weather. Edward Lorenz, a research meteorologist who tried to model "toy weather" on his computer, discovered that although there seemed to be an unpredictability about weather systems, there were in fact patterns and repetitions to be found. These were not exact, but they suggested that within seeming disorder, there was a form of order. (In "Entropy," Pynchon had suggested that "the cosmologists had predicted an eventual heat-death for the universe [. . .]; the meteorologists, day-to-day, staved it off by concentrating with a reassuring array of temperatures." This suggestion of a "negentropic" pattern occurring within a cosmic system of entropy today seems farsighted.) Similarly, Ilya Prigogine, who was awarded the Nobel Prize for Chemistry in 1977, has suggested that in "far-from-

equilibrium" thermodynamic systems (where a state of disorder exists), a new
state of order can be produced, what Prigogine has called a *dissipative structure*. As suggested above in the work of Shannon and Weaver, Prigogine suggests
that without transgressing the Second Law of Thermodynamics, order can be
produced out of chaos. Bifurcation points (jumps to different orders and structures) occur when thermodynamic systems reach a threshold in stability where
the fluctuations within the system cause a "branching" into different possible
states, depending upon the nature of the "perturbation."

In *Neuromancer*, Case's intervention at these bifurcation points causes the
AIs Neuromancer and Wintermute to combine into a new sentient being. In
Count Zero (1986) and *Mona Lisa Overdrive*, this moment is itself called "When-
It-Changed," an indication of the leap to a new kind of order. In the fictions of the
Argentinian writer Jorge Luis Borges, particularly in "The Garden of Forking
Paths," these branches in order become branchings in time and reality: each
moment of choice or decision becomes a new world. This idea lies behind the
science fiction subgenre of the "alternative history."

Back to the Future: The Difference Engine

In their 1990 collaboration, *The Difference Engine*, Gibson and Sterling conceived a nineteenth-century Britain where Lord Byron was prime minister,
where Charles Babbage's Difference Engine is reimagined as a proto-computer,
the Age of Steam accelerating early into the Information Age. The central character, Mallory, is a palaeontologist who meets many of the famous personages of
the nineteenth century in recognizable (and not-so recognizable) guises. Benjamin Disraeli, British prime minister and novelist, is turned into a hack writer,
but Gibson and Sterling put into his mouth their most explicit indication of the
centrality of chaos to their fiction:

> Disraeli waved his smouldering pipe. "There tumults of the mind, when like
> the great convulsions of nature, all seems anarchy and returning chaos; yet
> often, in those moments of vast disturbance, as in the strife of nature itself,
> some new principle of order, or some new impulse of conduct, develops
> itself, and controls, and regulates, and brings to an harmonious consequence,
> passions and elements which seem only to threaten despair and subversion."

The Difference Engine is a knowing and parodic fiction, and the whole
novel collapses in on itself in the end as the narrative is revealed to be a story
that the Difference Engine (or some kind of Artificial Intelligence) tells itself as

a precursor to an act of self-recognition: another coming to sentience, another crossing of the human-machine boundary. Like the literary and language games Lewis Carroll plays in *Alice's Adventures in Wonderland* and *Through the Looking Glass*, we are not sure whether we are dreaming the Red King or he is dreaming us, whether the novel is writing the Difference Engine or the Difference Engine is writing the novel. By 1990, fiction and its treatment of science had come very far from the nineteenth century, yet *The Difference Engine* returns—quite properly—to the scene of the initial discoveries and debates that produced twentieth-century fiction's enduring use of thermodynamics and the metaphor of entropy. In the bifurcation point and the dissipative structure, science (and science fiction) seems to have found a way out of the determinism and despair of the entropic universe, but for *The Difference Engine*, the victory is hollow. What happens to free will when we are all the figments of a machine's imagination?

Bibliographic Essay

Entropy in science fiction is the focus of Colin Greenland's excellent *The Entropy Exhibition: Michael Moorcock and the British "New Wave" in Science Fiction* (London: Routledge and Kegan Paul, 1983), and there are also chapters on entropy fiction and Thomas Pynchon in Tony Tanner's wide ranging analysis of post–World War Two American fiction, *City of Words: American Fiction 1950–1970* (London: Jonathan Cape, 1971). For criticism on Thomas Pynchon, see David Seed, *The Fictional Labyrinths of Thomas Pynchon* (Basingstoke: Macmillan, 1988); John Digdae, *Thomas Pynchon: Allusive Parables of Power* (Basingstoke: Macmillan, 1990); and Harold Bloom (ed.), *Thomas Pynchon* (New York: Chelsea House, 1986). For a more general analysis of the connection between American literature and science, see John Limon, *The Place of Fiction in the Time of Science: A Disciplinary History of American Writing* (Cambridge: Cambridge University Press, 1990).

For a good general overview of the history of science, with chapters on the development of thermodynamics, see John Gribbin, *Science: A History 1543–2001* (London: Allen Lane, 2002). A good source of excerpts from scientific documents from the nineteenth century is Laura Otis (ed.), *Literature and Science in the Nineteenth Century: An Anthology* (Oxford: Oxford World's Classics, 2002). Stephen Hawking's *A Brief History of Time* (London: Bantam, 1988) is a readable and broad introduction to topics in post-classical physics from one of the key figures in late-twentieth-century science. Ilya Prigogine and Isabelle Stengers, *Order Out of Chaos* (London: Flamingo, 1985) offers a more theoretical and mathematical overview of the development of dynamics and thermodynamics, along with key chapters on dissipative structures and bifurcation points. James Gleick's *Chaos* (1988; London: Vintage, 1998) is a popular and accessible introduction to the science of chaos that also places chaos theory within broader subject areas such as thermodynamics and information theory. For entropy and communication theory, see Claude Shannon and Warren Weaver, *The Mathematical Theory of Communication* (Urbana: Illinois University Press, 1949).

For cybernetics and the Macy Conferences, see Norbert Wiener, *The Human Use of Human Beings: Cybernetics and Society* (Garden City NY: Doubleday, 1954); and N. Katherine Hayles, *How We Became Posthuman* (Chicago and London: University of Chicago Press, 1999), which also features chapters analyzing key works of science fiction that deal with cybernetics. For this also see Patricia Warrick, *The Cybernetic Imagination* and David Porush, *The Soft Machine: Cybernetic Fiction* (NewYork: Methuen, 1985). For the connection between Prigogine and cyberpunk, see Porush, "Prigogine, Chaos and Contemporary Science Fiction," *Science Fiction Studies* vol. 18, number 55, November 1991. For theoretical and critical analyses of cyberspace, see Michael Benedikt (ed.), *Cyberspace: First Steps* (Cambridge MA and London: MIT Press, 1991). For critical essays on cyberpunk science fiction, including William Gibson and Bruce Sterling, see Larry McCaffrey (ed.), *Storming the Reality Studio* (Durham NC: Duke University Press, 1991); George Slusser and Tom Shippey (eds.), *Fiction 2000: Cyberpunk and the Future of Narrative* (Athens: University of Georgia Press, 1992); Brian McHale, *Constructing Postmodernism* (London: Routledge, 1992); and key science fiction journals *Science Fiction Studies*, *Foundation*, and *Extrapolation*.

Primary texts for science fiction vary enormously, and Philip K. Dick in particular has been reprinted in many editions. There is no standard collected works, as one might imagine. This chapter has used the following editions: *Do Androids Dream of Electric Sheep?* (London: Grafton, 1969); *Martian Time-Slip* (London: Gollancz, 1990). For further background and analysis of Dick, see Samuel J. Umland (ed.), *Philip K. Dick: Contemporary Critical Interpretations* (Westport CT and London: Greenwood Press, 1995); R. D. Mullen et al. (eds.), *On Philip K. Dick: 40 Articles for Science Fiction Studies* (Terre Haute: TH-SFS, Inc., 1992); and Lawrence Sutin, *Divine Invasions: A Life of Philip K. Dick* (1989) (London: Paladin, 1991).

Thomas Pynchon's "Entropy" is collected in *Slow Learner* (1984) and can also be found in Nina Bawm et al. (eds.), *The Norton Anthology of American Literature*, 6th edition (New York: W. W. Norton, 2002). Pynchon's 1966 novel, *The Crying of Lot 49* (London: Picador, 1979) was also cited in this chapter. Pamela Zoline's "The Heat Death of the Universe" was first published in *New Worlds* magazine, number 173, July 1967. It was collected in Michael Moorcock (ed.),

New Worlds: An Anthology (London: Flamingo, 1983), and more recently in *The Heat Death of the Universe and Other Stories* (Kingston NY: McPherson, 2002). Jorge Luis Borges, *Labyrinths* (Harmondsworth: Penguin, 1970), and *Ficciones* (New York: Grove, 1962) both contain "The Garden of Forking Paths." Bernard Wolfe's *Limbo* (1952) (New York: Carroll and Graf, 1987) was also published in Britain, by Penguin, as *Limbo 90* in a shortened version.

Don Delillo's 1984 novel *White Noise* has been widely reprinted; this chapter cited the London: Picador, 2002, edition. William Gibson's "Johnny Mnemonic" is collected in *Burning Chrome* (London: Grafton, 1988). The following editions of his "Sprawl" trilogy were used: *Neuromancer* (1984) (London: Voyager, 1995); *Count Zero* (1986) (London: Grafton, 1987); *Mona Lisa Overdrive* (1988) (London: Grafton, 1988). Gibson's collaborative novel with Bruce Sterling is *The Difference Engine* (1990) (London: Gollancz, 1991).

11

The Two Cultures Debates

John Cartwright

Two Cultures: An Anatomy of a Cultural Divide

Over the previous ten chapters we have noted how the realms of science and literature in their common historical contexts have enjoyed a lively exchange of ideas. The exchanges have taken many forms, including satire, mutual admiration, and sometimes antagonism. At first glance it would appear to be a love-hate affair. But the relationship has deeper dimensions. Writers have been quick to exploit the literary potential of new scientific ideas and have shown themselves especially skilled at expanding on their consequences and implications. It is also worth repeating that the very boundaries between science and literature shift and weaken as we travel back earlier than the eighteenth century. In this chapter we now focus on the idea that these two activities are somehow irreconcilably opposed in goals and methodology. It may seem that the previous chapters invalidate such a conception, but there is a level of abstraction at which in several historic periods the sense of a fundamental opposition has been felt and aired. We can detect five such episodes. In their shorthand descriptions, they are:

- The *Battle of the Books* in the seventeenth century
- The Romantic revolution of the late eighteenth and early nineteenth centuries
- The Arnold-Huxley debate in the second half of the nineteenth century
- The Two Culture debate (Snow and Leavis) of the 1960s
- The Science Wars of the 1990s (and beyond)

We have already met the first two in previous chapters and so they will only be given a brief treatment here. This chapter will concentrate on the Huxley-Arnold debate of the nineteenth century and the Two Cultures concept explored by C. P. Snow and others in the 1960s. The last of these, the so-called Science Wars, is left until the next chapter.

The Battle of the Books

Some of the earliest expressions of a literary mistrust of natural philosophy occurred in the seventeenth century, just as the new sciences were asserting themselves against a decaying scholasticism and a still vigorous Renaissance humanism. It is tempting to think that renaissance scholars should have welcomed the birth of science as a creature after their own heart: an activity ambitious to break out of the confines of a suffocating medievalism. To a degree this was true, and there are parallels between, for example, the revival of naturalism and the use of perspective in Renaissance art and the concern of empiricist natural philosophers to see the world afresh and not through the texts of the ancients. But in scholarship there were also important differences. Renaissance humanists were not primarily concerned with seeking new knowledge of nature and new systems of inquiry; their priority was to rescue what had been discovered, thought, and written down by the philosophers and poets of ancient Greece and Rome and then lost during the Dark and Middle Ages (indeed, this very concept of a golden age of classical civilization followed by a collapse into the Dark Ages was an invention by Renaissance historians). A clash of this rescue operation with scientific empiricism could have been avoided if the scholars kept to literature, but inevitably the recovery, translation, and exegesis of classical texts led to the classification and comprehension of natural objects along the lines of ancient thought—lines that were often misleading or simply wrong. To be sure, the natural philosophers of the seventeenth century were usually trained in Latin and Greek and quoted ancient sources respectfully, but they were bound to view askance the renaissance humanist tradition of producing compendia of the observations of worthies such as Aristotle and Pliny without any reflection on whether they were accurate or could be improved upon.

The debate that grew up around this clash of temperaments was conceived in terms of the Ancients versus the Moderns. In 1690 the English diplomat Sir William Temple (1628–1699) wrote an essay called *Of Ancient and Modern Learning* and so set off this lively controversy. Temple belittled modern science and doubted, for example, the truths of the discoveries of Copernicus and Harvey. William Wotton, a minor Anglican cleric, published an effective reply to Temple's rather ill-informed essay in the form of a book, *Reflections upon Ancient and Modern Learning* (1694). In reviewing English and European Science, Wotton came down clearly on the side of the moderns, concluding that "the extent of knowledge is at this time vastly greater than it was in former ages."

Temple's secretary in the 1690s was that master of English prose Jonathan Swift. Swift called this debate a "squabble" and parodied it in his satire (completed in 1697 and published in 1704) titled "A Full and True Account of the

Battle Fought Last Friday Between the Ancient and Modern Books in St James's Library." In Swift's story, all would have been well in the library if the books had been shelved separately, but the librarian placed them together, with Descartes next to Aristotle, and Plato next to Hobbes; the results were explosive.

Like those of his employer, Swift's sympathies are obviously with the ancients. In an extended metaphor he compares the moderns to a spider and the ancients to a bee. The spider is fat, self-satisfied, and has spun a complicated mathematical web. The web represents modern learning, but it is learning only produced from the spider's own entrails. The bee, on the other hand, is criticized by the spider for only foraging indiscriminately among other people's insights (visiting both flowers and nettles) and creating nothing new. Swift's reply is through Aesop, who prefers the bees since they produce honey and wax:

> Whatever we have got, has been by infinite labour, the search and ranging through every corner of nature: the difference is, that instead of dirt and poison, we have rather chose to fill our hives with honey and wax, thus furnishing mankind with the two nobles of things, which are sweetness and light. (Gould 151)

Swift's metaphor for humane learning is a good one, and Matthew Arnold later adopted the metaphor "sweetness and light" in his defense of classical culture, an essay titled *Culture and Anarchy* (1869). Interestingly, Bacon in *The Advancement of Learning* had also appropriated the bee, but this time as an emblem of modern science. It was the dogmatic reasoning of the scholastics that he compared to the work of the spider, both producing fine webs but of no substance. Modern scientists tend to feel that Bacon was nearer the mark.

In later works, Swift also seems to attack the pride of those who claim privileged access to truth. In the seventeenth century there occurred a profound shift in the epistemology of natural knowledge. The scholastic philosophy of the Middle Ages, criticized by the New Philosophy, tended to reason that once a phenomenon had been named it was virtually explained. But naming an effect, however latinized the label, does not explain it. Saying that opium induces sleep because of its soporific qualities, for example, is both circular and uninformative. In tackling this mode of thinking, one step taken by philosophers such as Descartes and Locke was the separation of primary and secondary qualities. The mind cannot directly apprehend real essences; it must infer from sensations what forces, mechanisms, and substances might be at work. Swift is aware of this shift but feels that although the new sciences have purported to abandon occult qualities and pseudo explanations, in reality they are smuggled in the back door. This explains Swift's attack on Newton's theory of gravitational attraction in both *The Tale of a Tub* and *Gulliver's Travels*. Shortly after leaving Laputa, Gulliver visits the little island of Glubbdubdrib, populated by sorcerers who can call up the spirits of the dead. Gulliver asks to see Descartes, Gassendi (a French astronomer and mathematician who advocated atomism), and Aristotle:

> I then desired the Governor to call up Descartes and Gassendi, with whom I prevailed to explain their Systems to Aristotle. This great philosopher (i.e., Aristotle) freely acknowledged his own mistakes in natural philosophy, because he proceeded in many things upon Conjecture, as all men must do; and he found, that Gassendi and the Vortices of Descartes were equally exploded. He predicted the same fate to Attraction, whereof the present Learned are such zealous asserters. He said that new systems of Nature were but new fashions. . . . and even those who pretended to demonstrate them from mathematical principles, would flourish but a short period of time. (*Gulliver's Travels*, p. 168)

This passage shows that Swift was capable of more than a mere burlesque of experimentation (see chapter four). He suggests that the status of science is a series of conjectures that come and go, remarkably similar to Popper's concept some centuries later. Karl Popper (1902–1994), an Austrian-born philosopher, argued that the dynamism and reliability of science is accounted for by the two great processes of conjectures and refutations. Scientists advance ideas of a conjectural nature, some of which are then refuted (and hence rejected) by experimental falsification. Thus science progresses by eliminating bad ideas in favor of good ones. Swift suggests that Newton's concept of attraction was flawed, however precise the mathematics, since it was not a complete explanation because the origin of the gravitational force remained obscure. The source of the force of gravity clearly worried Newton himself, and he tried several explanations, none of which were entirely satisfactory. The problem was that the inverse square law of gravitational attraction involved action at a distance, and in mechanical science, how could one object influence another without touching it? For this reason Christiaan Huygens, Gottfried Leibnitz, and followers of Descartes dismissed the notion as a return to medieval occult qualities of sympathy and antipathy. Naming a force and describing it mathematically do not account for its origin. Swift's complaint against science then is it that it involves this contradiction.

The Romantic Revolution and Varieties of Truth

As we saw in chapter four, tensions between humane literature and the new sciences were muted in the second half of the eighteenth century by Enlightenment optimism, the divinization of nature, and the growth of natural theology. The universal orderliness that science endorsed was generally welcomed by artists and theologians alike who could see scientists as emphasizing the beauty of God's works. The truce, however, failed to hold. Part of the reason was that following the scientific revolution, the very quality of beauty tended to be seen as a secondary rather than primary quality. Consequently, aesthetics had to shift from the realm of ontology to epistemology. This brought into question once again the relationship between truth and beauty.

The fault lines between science and poetry that opened up in the Romantic period, explored in chapter five, left an interesting legacy in the form of rival conceptions of truth. Wordsworth in the Preface to *Lyrical Ballads* (1802) desired to replace the inadequate "contradistinction of Poetry and Prose" by the "more philosophical one of Poetry and matter of Fact or Science." By such means the Romantics further cemented the separation of matters of feeling from matters of fact, assigning the former to poetry and the latter to science. But poetry, conceived as mere feeling and emotion, had already aroused the hostility of people such as Plato, John Locke, and Jeremy Bentham, who thought that poetically inflamed passions could only bring detriment to the clear exercise of reason (Plato, for example, would have banished poets from his ideal state, only allowing them to return when they learned to sing hymns to the gods or praise virtuous men).

The challenge to literature, therefore, in the Romantic era and beyond, was to identify what type of truths poetry did convey. A number of possibilities were explored. Blake, for example, suggested that poetry had access to a reality transcending the world of sense. An alternative was Keats's idea that truth is about successfully initiating an emotional experience: "I am certain of nothing but of the holiness of the heart's affections and the truth of imagination" (quoted in Abrams, 1971, p. 315). In several letters he equates beauty with truth: "What the imagination seizes as Beauty must be truth" (November 22, 1817); "I can never feel certain of a truth but from a clear perception of its Beauty" (December 31, 1818). There is also the well-known ending of "Ode on a Grecian Urn," where the urn tells us that "Beauty is truth, truth beauty,—that is all / Ye know on earth, and all ye need to know."

Another response was to suggest that poetry was neither true nor false, since it exists simply to excite feelings and thoughts for aesthetic contemplation. This view, revived in the nineteenth century, had been espoused before. Sir Philip Sydney in his Apology for Poetry (published posthumously in 1595), for example, observed that "Of all writers under the sun the poet is the least liar; . . . Now for the poet he nothing affirmeth, and therefore never lieth."

In the wake of Romanticism, one thinker who was deeply conscious of the need to reformulate conceptions of truth in religion and the arts was Mathew Arnold. Arnold saw parallels between the rival claims of science and religion (over such things as prominence in the curriculum, sources of guidance for civilized life, and claims about the natural world) and the more general relationship between science and the humanities, and literature in particular. In the face of discoveries in geology, advances in evolutionary biology, and German higher criticism (the work of people such as D. L. Strauss and L. Feuerbach), Arnold realized that the time-honored factual and historical basis for traditional Christianity was failing. Arnold's strategy for rescuing Christianity was to accept that it could no longer depend on the literal historicity of the Bible, and to argue instead that religion contained poetic truth: "the strongest part of our religion today is its unconscious poetry" (quoted in Daiches, 1972, p. 448). The lines of demarcation then become clear: science is assigned to dealing with factual truths about the world, and poetry is aligned with religion to capture emotional, aesthetic, and moral truths—a realm of imaginative discourse no longer to be troubled by any factual correspondence to the natural world. Furthermore, because of their special qualities, both religion and poetry could still claim a central place in preparation for a civilized life.

The crucial feature of this alignment, and one that underwrites much of the subsequent history of the relations between science and literature, is that if religion is saved as poetry then poetry takes on the hue and respectability of religion. Correspondingly, literary critics become the new priests of culture responsible for tracing out the "great tradition" (the phrase coined by the Cambridge critic F. R. Leavis) and entrusted with the task of sorting out the genuine prophets from the fake, the canon from the apocrypha.

The Huxley-Arnold Debate

By the late nineteenth century most scientists were quite happy to see religion relinquish its hold over cosmology (the Catholic Church, for example, had already lifted its ban on all the works of Copernicus, Kepler, and Galileo by 1835) and were content to see poetry and literature exploring moral truths, leaving the natural world free for empirical enquiry. The question now remained as to what type of education, scientific or literary, was best for training young minds. Over the years 1868–1883 there occurred a fascinating exchange of views between those two cultural giants of the Victorian era in Britain, Thomas Henry Huxley and Matthew Arnold, on this very issue. Broadly speaking, Huxley was asserting the value of science for a balanced education while Arnold insisted on the centrality of languages (Greek and Latin) and belles lettres. The

Thomas Henry (T. H.) Huxley (1825–1895)

Huxley, in the later nineteenth century most famous as "Darwin's bulldog," was born into an unexceptional family, though his descendents—which include the novelist Aldous Huxley and scientists Julian (Sir), Andrew, and Francis—proved to be almost as exceptional as their forebear. His father was a mathematics teacher in Ealing (in western outer London), at a school where the young Huxley was to obtain his only formal schooling: for only two years, ending at the age of ten, when the family moved to Coventry. Huxley was one of the great autodidacts: he taught himself science, philosophy, history, and German, and at the age of fifteen went to Charing Cross Hospital in London to begin a medical apprenticeship.

Like Charles Darwin, however, it was a series of long sea voyages that made Huxley into the great public figure he became. As Lieutenant Huxley, he shipped with HMS *Rattlesnake* on a voyage to Australia and New Guinea, in the role of assistant ship's surgeon. Like the Stephen Maturin of Patrick O'Brien's seafaring novels, Huxley used his time on board to further his knowledge in "natural philosophy," studying marine invertebrates and sending his findings back to England. His work led to his election to the Royal Society and the award of their Gold Medal.

Thomas Henry Huxley (1825–1895). Photograph taken about 1875 by Elliott and Fry, Portman Square, London. (Source collection of J. Cartwright)

This was the first, but by no means the last, honor bestowed on Huxley. On leaving the navy, he found a position at the Royal School of Mines in 1854; in 1861 he received an honorary degree from the University of Breslau; in 1879, from Cambridge; and six more up until 1893. Although known as "Darwin's bulldog," Huxley was not, in fact, a wholehearted supporter of Darwin's theory of natural selection. He was indeed the most powerful advocate for evolution, but was critical of some aspects of Darwin's theory (which partly led to the revisions and qualifications to the *Origin of Species* toward the end of the nineteenth century) and also rejected "progressionist" evolutionary theories, as well as those of Lamarck.

Huxley was not a great innovator in science like Darwin; he was a great organizer, and perhaps most of all, a great advocate for science and a scientific education. His debates with Arnold, and with Archbishop Wilberforce, are landmark events in British nineteenth-century culture. Rarely since has there been a scientist who achieved Huxley's eminence, or whose social and cultural ideas have been given such weight. Particularly in the field of education, where his ideas still inform the way children are taught, T. H. Huxley's legacy is powerful indeed.

combatants addressed the subject on numerous occasions, but two of the key speeches and subsequent essays were Huxley's address titled "Science and Culture," given on October 1, 1880, at the opening of Sir Josiah Mason's Science College in Birmingham, and Arnold's Rede lecture given at Cambridge on June 14, 1882, titled "Literature and Science," a lecture subsequently revised for his American tour of 1883.

In reality Arnold and Huxley had much in common (both shared in common a distrust of the factual claims of organized religion), and the debate was both cordial and good humored. However, their differences were deep: Huxley was a scientist, utilitarian, and champion of an emerging scientific meritocracy; Arnold was a poet and humanist, less concerned with the material fabric of life than the ends to which life should be directed.

In his "Science and Culture" lecture Huxley agrees with the conditions laid down by Sir Josiah Mason for his new science college—that it should not deal with party politics and theology and not provide "mere literary instruction and education." Huxley then continues to assert the importance of science as part of a balanced liberal education, criticizing the pretensions of the humanists (with classicists especially in mind) that literature is the real route to culture. He notes "for the purpose of attaining real culture, an exclusively scientific education is at least effectual as an exclusively literary education." He then hits out at those scholars who cling to medieval ways of thinking:

> Scholarly and pious persons, worthy of all respect, favour us with allocu-
> tions upon the sadness of the antagonism of science to their medieval way
> of thinking, which betray an ignorance of the first principles of scientific
> investigation, an incapacity for understanding what a man of science means
> by veracity, and an unconsciousness of the weight of established scientific
> truths, which is almost comical. (Huxley, 1880, p. 1448)

To those who look to classical Greece and Rome as a basis for culture, he points out that this heritage also contained the development of the scientific method—letting slip his view that science is the sole method to reach truth:

> We cannot know all the best thoughts and sayings of the Greeks unless we
> know what they thought about natural phenomena . . . . We falsely pretend
> to be the inheritors of their culture, unless we are penetrated, as the best
> minds among them were, with an unhesitating faith that the free employ-
> ment of reason, in accordance with scientific method, is the sole method of
> reaching truth. (Huxley, 1880, p. 1448)

Huxley appreciates, however, the value of literary studies and is aware of the perils of narrow scientific specialization:

> Nevertheless, I am the last person to question the importance of genuine literary education, or to suppose that intellectual culture can be complete without it. An exclusively scientific training will bring about a mental twist as surely as an exclusive literary training. The value of the cargo does not compensate for a ship's being out of trim. (Huxley, 1880, p. 1449)

Arnold's response was delivered before a crowded audience in the Cambridge Senate House on June 14, 1882. The talk was modified and given again during his 1883 American Tour. In the latter version he considers that the dynamism of the United States has made the question of education acute:

> The question is raised whether, to meet the needs of our modern life, the predominance ought not now to pass from letters to science; and naturally the question is nowhere raised with more energy than here in the United States. (Arnold, 1882, p. 1430)

He then examines again his view of culture that "to know ourselves and the world" we need "to know the best which has been thought and said in the world." He clarifies his view of what knowing a nation's literature means:

> Literature is a large word; it may mean everything written with letters or printed in a book. Euclid's *Elements* and Newton's *Principia* are thus literature. All knowledge that reaches us through books is literature . . . . By knowing modern nations, I mean not merely knowing their belles lettres, but knowing also what has been done by such men as Copernicus, Galileo, Newton, Darwin. (Arnold, 1882, p. 1432)

But Arnold's very next point, although designed to show his agreement with the scientist, reveals his own rather limited perception of what science is about. He praises science for supplying facts—"we must all admit that in natural science the habit gained of dealing with facts is a most valuable discipline"—but he never seems to appreciate that science also employs imaginative conjectures and hypotheses, devises systems, makes predictions, has a grandeur and sublimity of its own, and contributes to the illumination of the human condition. Hence, in his speech at Eton (1879) in championing the values of a classical education (Greek and Latin), he speaks ironically of science that tells us only the "diameter of the sun and moon," and in his 1882 Rede lecture, he disparages

Matthew Arnold (1822–1888)

Educated at Rugby School (where he was the son of the headmaster) and Balliol College, Oxford, Matthew Arnold was a poet, educator, essayist, and one of the foremost thinkers and cultural critics of his age. His education could not have been more different from his great contemporary, T. H. Huxley. Arnold was one of the "establishment," whose values, however, led him to be highly critical of British culture and society in the Victorian period.

In 1858, after a considerable career as a poet, Arnold became professor of Poetry at Oxford, but ironically, except for *New Poems* of 1867 (which contains his most famous, "Dover Beach"), he only published prose after this time. This was no retreat to the ivory tower: Arnold continued to be very active in the field of education and was highly critical of the state of British schooling at the time. He advocated a kind of education that would expose all citizens to (his most famous phrase) "the best which has been thought and said in the world," a vision of the importance of "culture" and an attack on what Arnold saw as the materialism and utilitarianism of Victorian life.

The poet and critic Matthew Arnold (1822–1888). Photograph c. 1860, taken by Elliott and Fry, Portman Square, London. (Source: collection of J. Cartwright)

Arnold's idea of a cultured society is a moral one, but a humane one. The values he saw embodied in the "great" works of literature, a liberal, tolerant humanism, may seem out of place in contemporary society and have been understood as antithetical to science. However, though he was an eminent Victorian, with all that phrase entails, his outlook was European rather than narrowly nationalistic, and he advocated objectivity both in the criticism of literature and in everyday life in order to avoid prejudice and "Philistinism." In fact, in his continuing role as a reformer of education, Arnold visited France and other continental European countries in order to report on their education systems and to change British education for the better. As with Huxley, it has been rare since the Victorian period for anyone in his field to achieve the gravity, and eminence, of Matthew Arnold.

someone who knows that the moon is "two thousand one hundred and sixty miles in diameter" but has no feeling for poetry.

More significantly, Arnold thought that science lacked a conception of or a concern with human experience, and this neglect provided a continuing and vital role for poetry. Literature, "humane letters," could provide an account of human nature and satisfy the longing for beauty and right conduct. Science provided knowledge, but after a time, such knowledge would prove "unsatisfying, wearying," since it did not touch on these matters. Overall, a person given a choice would fare better studying literature than science. According to Arnold, as science advances and dispels the mist of superstition, the need for literature increases:

> the importance of humane letters in a man's training becomes not less but greater in proportion to the success of modern science in extirpating what it calls "medieval thinking." (Arnold, 1882, p. 1438)

In essence, Huxley and Arnold represent two sides of a neo-Kantian division of knowledge. On one side lies a concern for facts and on the other a concern with values. Interestingly, Arnold thought one of the main functions of literature was to enable people to accept the burden of the results of science.

In the end, Huxley and Arnold agreed to differ and remained good friends. Looking back, however, we can see them as representatives of wider tendencies at work. Arnold was intent on securing a normative role for the humanities in the face of the relentless growth of science. Huxley was a champion of the emerging scientific meritocracy and the self-made entrepreneurs of industrial Britain. The group to which Huxley belonged, which included the physicist John Tyndall and the social philosopher Herbert Spencer (see chapter eight), wanted to forge a new secular society based on the scientific understanding of nature. A culture based on science had to displace that based on religion, and to do so, religious claims had to be dismissed as false and the clerical and literary elite ousted from positions of influence. This was the manifesto announced by Tyndall in his famous "Belfast Address," given at the Meeting of the British Association for the Advancement of Science at Belfast in 1874. Tyndall's proposed solution was a demarcation: science to explain the natural world and the humanities to inform and nourish our moral life and to satisfy our spiritual yearnings.

This demarcation at the end of the nineteenth and beginning of the twentieth centuries coincided with the establishment of science and literature as separate university subjects taught by specialist professionals. Professional scientists were also to be increasingly found in corporate and industrial contexts. In very general terms, communication between the two domains was limited and strained. In literature, many writers styled themselves "modernists," and like their Romantic forebears, they often expressed fear, distrust, or indifference toward the increasing cultural prestige of science and the material changes brought about by its technological applications. Such tensions came to a head in the famous "Two Cultures" debate initiated by C. P. Snow.

C. P. Snow and Two Cultures

We noted above how Arnold outlined his major thoughts on science and literature in his Rede lecture at Cambridge in 1882. In 1959, C. P. Snow gave his own Rede lecture on a similar theme: "The Two Cultures and the Scientific Revolution" but came to very different conclusions.

Charles Percy Snow (1905–1980) was that rare combination of scientist, novelist, and civil servant. He studied for a degree in chemistry and then later acquired a doctorate in physics from Cambridge, becoming a Fellow there in 1930. Over the following years he became a university administrator and, when World War II broke out, a scientific advisor to the British government. He published his first novel in 1932, followed by an eleven-volume sequence collectively titled *Strangers and Brothers*. Although popular in his own lifetime, his novels are little read today.

Snow's Rede lecture was published as a slim volume, *The Two Cultures*, in 1959. Much to Snow's surprise, the book became a sensation on both sides of the Atlantic, and a lively, and at times ill-tempered, debate ensued. The main thrust of Snow's argument, drawing deeply on his own experience as novelist and scientist, was that culture had become polarized into two camps: scientists and technologists on the one hand, and literary intellectuals and humanistic scholars on the other. The tragedy of this polarization was that the two groups "had almost ceased to communicate at all" (Snow, 1993 edition, p. 1). His characterization of the two groups was sketchily done and simplistic. He painted the scientists as progressive, left-of-center modernizers with a natural sympathy for the poor in underdeveloped nations and a desire to do something to improve things. In contrast, he saw literary intellectuals as reactionary and backward-looking individuals, proud of their ignorance of science and contemptuous of science-driven economic growth. As he said: "If the scientists have the future in their bones, then the traditional cultures respond by wishing the future did not exist" (p. 11). But scientists also had their faults; by neglecting great literature they had become "self-impoverished" (p. 14).

Whatever the deficiencies of Snow's argument, the subsequent response showed that he had clearly hit a nerve. Mountains of commentary followed, some sympathetic and some critical. The most outrageous, bitter, and personal attack came from one of those university literary intellectuals that Snow had chastised, the English critic F. R. Leavis. The written response from Leavis was *Two Cultures? The Significance of C. P. Snow*. The ferocity of its contents (its ad hominem style indicated even in its title) was such that Leavis's publishers had to check with Snow that he would not sue before they published. Leavis concluded that Snow was actually of no significance, claiming that "not only is he

Charles Percy (C. P.) Snow (1905–1980)

C. P. Snow was born and educated in Leicester, where he studied science at Leicester University College (now a university). Like T. H. Huxley, he was a "provincial," and like Huxley, he achieved positions of some prominence. For Snow, his training as a scientist (he took a Ph.D. in physics at Cambridge) led to a position at the heart of British government: he served as a scientific advisor during World War II and continued as an eminent civil servant, becoming parliamentary secretary to the Ministry of Science and Technology in 1964.

He is most famous, of course, for the Rede lecture he gave in 1959, *The Two Cultures and the Scientific Revolution*. The controversy this lecture aroused, which suggested that in Britain (and particularly in British academia) science and the arts no longer communicated, was highly ironic. Snow, as well as being a scientist and civil servant, was also a novelist of some standing. He had published his first novel in 1934 and constructed a long sequence of novels under the title *Strangers and Brothers*. One of these, *The Corridors of Power* (1963), has since slipped into British political language when describing the machinery of governmental power.

Portrait of Charles Percy Snow (1905–1980), English author, physicist, and diplomat. Undated photograph. (Bettmann/Corbis)

Like Matthew Arnold, whose remedy for the ills of Victorian Britain was reform in education, Snow advocated a change in how the British were educated to overcome the debilitating effects of the "two cultures." This phrase, which has also achieved a kind of currency in thinking about British culture and society, draws upon the rhetoric of Matthew Arnold, who used "culture" to mean "the best that has been thought and said," but inverts it, by indicating it was not the humanist scholar but the forward-thinking scientist who held the reins of progress. Snow's lecture, which was itself attacked from within English academia, perhaps signals the point at which "Arnoldian" values ceased to hold sway.

not a genius, he is intellectually as undistinguished as it is possible to be. He doesn't know what he means and doesn't know he doesn't know (Leavis and Yudkin, 1962, p. 28).

Leavis was incensed that Snow should assert the superiority of scientific over humanistic culture. He did make some telling points, but his piece was renowned for its invective and personal abuse. He claimed, for example, that "The Two Cultures exhibits an utter lack of intellectual distinction and an embarrassing vulgarity of style" (Leavis and Yudkin, 1962, p. 30), asserting that

Snow was completely ignorant of literature, the nature of civilization, and the "history of the Industrial revolution" (p. 28). He thought the standard of Snow's essay pitiful:

> the argument of Snow's Rede lecture is at an immensely lower conceptual
> level than any I myself, a literary person, should permit in a group discussion
> I was conducting, let alone a pupil's essay. (p. 34)

In some ways Leavis's attack backfired, since many were moved to denounce his intemperate language and express sympathy for Snow. The Snow-Leavis debate looked for a time like a re-run of the dichotomy that has so often surfaced in Western civilization: the Utilitarian Snow versus the Romantic Leavis, Bentham versus Coleridge, Huxley versus Arnold.

Snow's essay stimulated debate on a number of key questions that exposed the weaknesses in Snow's argument. For example, were there two cultures or more? Was it accurate to use the professional activities and proclivities of an elite (the university dons and writers that Snow mixed with) as a proxy for the culture consumed by the mass of ordinary people? Was Snow describing the real state of Western culture or the narrow parochialism of a class-conscious English establishment? Could one really use the reactionary prejudices of a few modernist writers (Ezra Pound, William Faulkner, Wyndam Lewis) to categorize the whole of literary or "traditional" culture? In reality, Snow's essay was full of sweeping generalizations, a naïve faith in science, and a rosy-eyed (but inaccurate) estimation of the efficiency of Soviet science and economic planning.

Despite its limitations, the phrase "two cultures" survives in the language, but the sense of Snow's work that is now often forgotten is the political and economic aspect of his message. Snow admitted that the lecture had almost been given a different title: "Before I wrote the lecture I thought of calling it 'The Rich and the Poor,' and I rather wish that I hadn't changed my mind" (Snow, 1993, p. 79).

Indeed, Snow's argument is as much about his belief that traditional culture is not helping the world's poor as lamenting the fact that literary types do not understand thermodynamics or that scientists do not read enough Dickens. His view was that practical-headed scientists with "the future in their bones," and with a natural sympathy for the poor, would be the ones to spread the scientific and industrial revolutions to where they are needed. He was passionate about this, even if one of his more precise predictions has failed to transpire:

> This disparity between the rich and the poor has been noticed. Most acutely
> and not un-naturally by the poor. Just because they have noticed it, it won't
> last for long. Whatever else in the world we know survives to the year 2000,

that won't. Once the trick of getting rich is known, as it now is, the world can't survive half rich and half poor. It's just not on." (p. 42)

Snow's scientistic optimism and gentlemanly sense of fair play ("its just not on") now seems touchingly naïve, and clearly he underestimated the complexity of economic and political factors underlying wealth creation. He was perhaps also overly romantic about the virtues of scientists: he thought that "scientists would do us good all over Asia and Africa;" he thought them "freer than most people from racial feeling," and in their internal culture "the breeze of equality of man hits you in the face" (p. 48).

For Snow and many of his literary antagonists, the epistemologies of science and literature were not a major issue. Science dealt with factual claims about the structure of the natural world, its laws and principles, and its objectivity was unquestionable. Literature dealt with the raw qualities of human experience, forging moral, social, and psychological insights and so exerting a normative influence on civilized behavior. The real issue was sociopolitical: the literati were too complacent, too right wing for Snow's liking, and too ignorant of science for the good of society. Yet when the fault line between the two cultures next became active, just over thirty years later, in an episode sometimes dubbed the Science Wars of the 1990s, all this was turned upside down. In this most recent manifestation of what increasingly looks like a dichotomy in Western culture, it was to be scientists who were targeted as the reactionary side by left-wing literary critics and humanities scholars who were claiming it was they who now championed liberal causes. Critics also went on to deny the objectivity and privileged epistemological status of science in explaining even the natural world. This strange inversion forms the subject of the next chapter.

Bibliographic Essay

The bibliographic essay for chapter four gives some further reading on Swift. A sophisticated treatment of Swift's aims in *The Battle of the Books* and *A Tale of a Tub* is to be found in Frank Boyle's *Swift as Nemesis* (Stanford CA: Stanford University Press, 2000). See especially chapter six. The dichotomy in Western culture between the sciences and the humanities is given an extended treatment in Stephen Jay Gould's *The Hedgehog, the Fox, and the Magister's Pox* (London: Jonathan Cape, 2003). The treatment is typical of Gould's style and quite personal but interesting also as his last book.

A good account of the early two cultures debate between Arnold and Huxley is given by David Daiches in "Literature and Science in 19th-Century England," which is chapter 15 of *The Modern World*, edited by Daiches and Thorlby (London: Aldus, 1972). Daiches explores the idea, also suggested in Abrams's *The Mirror and the Lamp* (see bibliographic essay for chapter five), that, post-Arnold, poetry became elevated to a type of religion. For Romantic conceptions of truth, an excellent work is once again Abrams's *The Mirror and the Lamp*.

On the subject of the Arnold-Huxley debate, the key speeches and essays were:

> Huxley's talk and essay, "A Liberal Education and Where to Find It," delivered at the South London Workingmen's College in 1868.
>
> Arnold's "Speech at Eton" on April 5, 1879.
>
> Huxley's address titled "Science and Culture," given on October 1, 1880, at the opening of Sir Josiah Mason's Science College in Birmingham.
>
> Arnold's speech of April 30, 1881, given before the Royal Academy of Arts in London.
>
> Arnold's Rede lecture, given at Cambridge on June 14, 1882, titled "Literature and Science," a lecture subsequently revised for his American tour of 1883.
>
> Huxley's speech "On Science and Art in relation to Education," given at the Liverpool Institute on February 16, 1883, and his speech given at the Royal Academy of Arts annual banquet on May 5, 1883.
>
> Finally, Huxley's own Rede lecture given at Cambridge on June 13, 1883.

Electronic versions of some of the speeches are now available. See, for example, *http://www.chass.utoronto.ca/~ian/huxley1.htm*.

An analysis of the Two Cultures debate of Arnold and Huxley and of Snow and Leavis, from a humanistic perspective, is given by Stanley Jaki, "A Hundred Years of Two Cultures" in *University of Windsor Review* 1975, vol. 11 (1) pp. 55–79. One of the best assessments of the Snow controversy is that by Lionel Trilling:, "Science, Literature and Culture: A Commentary on the Snow-Leavis Controversy," *Commentary* 33 (1962) pp. 461–477.

A book that followed closely after the Snow-Leavis debacle and gives a more balanced and measured assessment of the literary relations with science is Aldous Huxley's *Literature and Science* (London: Chatto and Windus, 1963).

12

Science Wars and Imperial Ambitions

John Cartwright and Brian Baker

Realism and Social Constructivism

Despite the fact that the history of science is littered with abandoned theories, scientists tend to assume that their ideas are getting better and going somewhere, that their theories are approaching closer to the truth and even occasionally succeed in capturing it. There is of course an ambiguity in the very word *theory.* Creationists are keen to insist, for example, that Darwinism is *only* a theory, carrying the implication that it might turn out to be false. But while scientists might concede that their ideas are provisional, they are also right to insist that well-established and time-honored theories are something more than mere hypotheses or speculative conjectures. Indeed, scientists would be the first to note that it is possible that erstwhile theories (such as the sphericity of the earth—a mere theory to the ancient Greeks) mature into the status of facts. Yet the ambivalence in the term, especially in the public mind, remains.

In the field of literary study (particularly in Anglo-American university English departments), "theory" arrived in the late 1960s, when French structuralist and post-structuralist literary theory and criticism began to be translated. (Both structuralism and post-structuralism have their roots in the linguistic theory of Saussure, who argued that language was a system of signs. How this sign system works—at a structural level or a textual level—is central to literary criticism of, and after, this period. Language as a sign-system—semiology—became the foundational assumption for the mainstream of literary criticism.) Attempts had been made before this to systematize literary study and make it less impressionistic, notably I. A. Richards's emphasis on close reading and the New Critics' bracketing off of the author and context in the name of close attention to the internal workings of the literary work itself. Post-structuralism achieves the same bracketing off of the author—such as in Roland Barthes's famous essay "The Death of the Author"—by emphasizing that each literary work—or text—is indivisible from the fabric of meanings produced whenever language is used. Meaning can then be produced in ways other than, or even in spite of, whatever the author may have intended. In the kind of critical work known as "deconstruction" (most closely associated with Jacques Derrida), an extremely close reading reveals the unacknowledged assumptions and gaps in the text being analyzed. It is here that such theoretical practice can dig up extremely revealing—and previously invisible—material about the culture that produces the text.

Science, too, is embedded in a wider fabric of cultural meaning, and the history and sociology of science has for many years successfully demonstrated the multifarious ways in which science is culturally situated. But one aspect of some contemporary cultural theories that arouses contempt among scientists is the idea that scientific knowledge is both relative and socially constructed. Such claims have resurfaced recently but actually go back a long way, to the time of the ancient Greeks. The sophist Protagoras (c.490–420 B.C.) was espousing relativism when he declared "mankind is the measure of all things." This is an ancient formulation of the idea that "beauty is in the eye of the beholder"—the view that the categories we sometime impose on the world (such as beauty) are not really in the world but are products of our own mind, and therefore their application may vary between cultures and individuals. Plato detested the sophists and argued for a realist view of human knowledge. In doing so, and in arguing for an absolutist conception of things like beauty and justice, he was forced to posit a transcendental realm where these "ideas" or "forms" reside (see also chapter five). In this view, knowledge becomes an apprehension of the real.

In opposition to this, relativism is the view that knowledge claims and their truth value cannot be judged outside of any particular social or intellectual context: there is no "privileged" vantage point, no Archimedian point for independent assessment. Relativism is sometimes a valid perspective, and a comparison with morality and social norms is instructive here. In most Western cultures it is illegal for a man to have (simultaneously) more than one wife, yet among the Kipsgis people of Kenya it is not only acceptable, but a high-status male with only one wife would be thought odd. In America and in the United Kingdom, blowing one's nose in public is acceptable (into a tissue at least); in Japan it would be seen as offensive. In both these cases a moral relativist would assert that there is no right way; acceptability is a function of the culture.

Social constructivism lends support to a relativistic view of knowledge by its suggestion that knowledge is constructed and fashioned according to the norms, concerns, and interests inherent in any given culture. Karl Marx gave an influential endorsement to this view, encapsulated in his aphorism that "being

"I KNOW THIS IS ALL NONSENSE, BUT THAT'S THE PARADIGM I'M STUCK WITH."

The importance of scientific paradigms. It was Thomas Kuhn who made the concept of paradigm widespread. Paradigms set a framework for scientific research, even though they sometimes turn out to be wrong. (©2005 by Sidney Harris)

determines consciousness." For Marx, the economic "substructure" in some way informed the "superstructure" of ideas (including, in some readings, science). The corollary of this was the notion that ideas (philosophical, political, ethical) were not objectively correlated with the external world but tended to be fashioned to support the interests of those promoting them—hence the observation that the ruling ideas of a given period were the ideas of the ruling class, a case of "they would say that wouldn't they."

But one does not have to be a Marxist to entertain the social construction of knowledge. Considerable authority was given to this perspective and its application to science in Thomas Kuhn's *The Structure of Scientific Revolutions* (1962), one of the most influential and commonly cited books of the last fifty years. Kuhn examined the actual historical practice of science and found it to be quite different from the logical and rational ideal as prescribed by philosophers such as Karl Popper. For Kuhn, the majority of scientists for most of their careers were engaged in puzzle solving within a specific paradigm, a paradigm being a cluster of ideas, theories, standard procedures, exemplars, and assumptions that provided an operating framework for the scientist. Scientists see and construct their worlds through and within particular paradigms. Eventually, however, such "normal" scientific activity gives way to a period of "revolutionary" science, when over a period of crisis the prevailing paradigm is abandoned and replaced by another. Examples of paradigm change are shown in the following table.

TABLE 8: EXAMPLES OF PARADIGM CHANGE IN THE NATURAL SCIENCES

Period over which change occurred	Old Paradigm	New Paradigm
1543–1650	Geocentric cosmology based on ideas of Aristotle and Ptolemy	Heliocentric cosmology based on work of Copernicus, Galileo, and Kepler
1770–1800	Theory of combustion based on phlogiston	French theory of oxygen
1840–1860	Static fixed species arranged along a chain of being	Species mutable, changed through evolution
c.1955–1970	Static view of continental land masses	Acceptance of continental drift and plate tectonics

Kuhn's crucial point was that an examination of any crisis period showed that the criteria for dropping one paradigm and switching to another were not entirely rational or objective. When a new paradigm does become triumphant its protagonists will always claim that progress has been made—a case of history being written by the victors. But, according to Kuhn, there is no theory-independent way to judge if the new paradigm is any nearer to reality or not.

Kuhn's ideas were truly shocking to a scientific community reared on the comfortable notion that its members were engaged in a steady journey toward the truth. His work was denounced as fallacious and irresponsible by some philosophers of science and scientists, and seized upon as a vital tool by sociologists. Whatever the strengths and weaknesses of Kuhn's model, his ideas have permeated the philosophy of science and have been taken up in other disciplines. Concepts such as "paradigm" and the "theory-laden" nature of facts have become standard tools of thought.

Parallels to this epistemological crisis of confidence occurred in the humanities, where the work of Michel Foucault has had a major influence. In *The Archaeology of Knowledge* (1966), Foucault suggested that (as in Kuhn's "paradigm") a culture in a given time period will have a set of unacknowledged assumptions and received ideas, which means that knowledge or understanding itself becomes skewed. Unconsciously, all texts, whether they are fictional, historical, sociological, or scientific, will reproduce these assumptions and will even avoid areas of enquiry that might bring these assumptions into question. For our own (Western) culture, for instance, Foucault was particularly interested in how the individual self is central to contemporary understanding of history, politics, and culture. This assumption of our own individual rights and autonomy, he suggested, was a construction, but one that is so central to our understanding of the world that it seems natural. Foucault's "archaeological" practice is to uncover what he calls the "episteme," the hidden structure of power in any given period. Like Kuhn's paradigm, the problem for Foucault's "episteme" is how this changes from period to period, what motivates the change, and whether the transition is a clean break or somewhat blurred. Later in his career, Foucault himself developed the idea of the "discourse" (a set of codes and practices inside a body of knowledge, discipline, or institution) that delimits what can and cannot be thought and said within it.

Following Kuhn there grew up a school of thought called the "strong program" in the sociology of knowledge, associated with such people as David Bloor, Harry Collins, Barry Barnes, Richard Rorty, and Bruno Latour. The word "strong" meant that both the direction of scientific research (i.e., the subjects under investigation, the allocation of grant money) and the content of the knowledge thereby produced could be analyzed and accounted for in terms of social factors. Collins, for example, made the astonishing remark that "The natural world has a small or nonexistent role in the construction of scientific knowledge" (Collins, 1981, p. 3). In France, Jean-Francois Lyotard referred to science as "just one language game among others." This was a radical manifesto. Everyone could agree that, while science had its own internal logic and momentum that helped determine the direction it took, society often set priorities for what it was prepared to fund and so shaped the type of science that was produced at any time. But scientists found it hard to swallow the idea that it was culture, and not the objective structure of the world, that determined the very content of science. The sociologists responded by saying that to talk of a correspondence between scientific concepts and the real objective world was meaningless, since we never have independent access to the objective world to make the comparison. In this view, science becomes not the objective search for the underlying laws and regularities of the exterior world but rather a sort of game where knowledge claims are made by social actors and accepted or rejected according to professional interests, power relations, or some other socially contingent criteria. Scientists such as Richard Dawkins responded with such common-sense observations as "show me a relativist at 30,000 feet (i.e., in a jet airliner) and I'll show you a hypocrite."

These social constructivist notions of science provided a way for some literary theorists to resist what they called the "hegemony" of natural science. If science was explicable as merely a social activity, then its privileged status and authority as both arbiter of truth claims and prime exemplar of the correct empirical way to generate knowledge (and by implication its favored position in the allocation of research money) could both be challenged. To be fair, there was also the genuine feeling that the use of linguistic, contextualist, and constructivist notions could genuinely illuminate the origination of scientific ideas and their interaction with literature. Table 9 provides a summary of the contrast between realist and constructivist approaches to scientific knowledge.

One of the more notable exemplars of this approach, and someone who has done much to explore the interpenetration of science and literature, is the American scholar George Levine. In tackling the relations between science and literature, Levine is concerned to show how the notion of "influence" works both ways, especially in the underexploited area of how scientists employ literary devices and literary imaginative constructions (drawn from a common culture) in their work. For Levine, the erosion of a realist view of scientific truth opens up science for cultural analysis. As he writes in *Darwin and the Novelists:*

> For the purposes of this volume, I, like Serres, consider science as an unprivileged form of cultural discourse . . ."a cultural formation equivalent to any other" but one that happens to have been privileged for much of its modern history. (Levine, 1998, p. 2)

Levine sees science as just one more "discourse" that "is no more grounded in a foundation of reality that gives special authority to its language than the language of literature" (Levine, 1987, 25). The variety of attacks on science from a whole range of literary theoretic perspectives will serve to demystify it:

> Different as they are, deconstructionist and reader response theories of literature (combined as they can be with Marxist and Freudian or Lacanian interpretation), Kuhnian theories of the history and philosophy of science,

TABLE 9: REALISM AND SOCIAL CONSTRUCTIVISM

Realist views of science	Constructivist views of science
An exterior world exists in which there are objects, entities, and processes that behave independently of our beliefs about them.	It is not helpful to talk about an exterior world, since we can never apprehend it directly except through language, texts, and symbols, which (to a debatable degree) structure the very reality we are trying to disguise. Facts are theory dependent or theory laden. Reality is always mediated by signs and conventions.
The aim of science is to give a factually and theoretically accurate account of the exterior world and so bare the laws of nature.	Science may claim the pursuit of realism to be its goal, but science is riddled with other values and interests. In the past, for example, science has been constructed and used to serve political interests such as those of racists and imperialists. It has been used to maintain existing power structures and corporate or gender interests. It is impossible for science to be disinterested.
Current scientific findings (facts, laws, principles, theories, etc.) bear some, albeit imperfect, correspondence to the world. Scientific knowledge is in many ways provisional and fallible. But over time, better procedures and more reliable theories and ideas are developed and selected into the scientific canon of approved knowledge. Few would now agree with naïve realists that scientific knowledge can provide a perfect map of the objective world; nevertheless, it is in some way "reality tracking."	The correspondence theory of truth has no validity. The world is always a theoretical construction. Scientific theories change, but there is no way of judging whether they are moving closer to a hypothetical reality.
Science exploits a variety of methods, which evolve over time, but their great strength lies in built-in checks (such as reproducibility, consistency, and peer review) to gauge if scientific knowledge is reliable.	Theories guide the interpretation of facts. The criteria scientists use to judge knowledge claims are in some ways arbitrary.
Scientific knowledge, like other forms, is guided by a whole network of assumptions, paradigms, frameworks, and values. However, such a framework does not predetermine the truth value of knowledge claims—beautiful theories can be slain by ugly facts. We can also, from time to time, break out of frameworks and replace them with better ones, ones that more closely resemble the external world.	We are prisoners of our intellectual frameworks, which are constructed by resources available in the cultural environment. Knowledge is thereby socially constructed, not "reality constructed." Scientific language, like that of other literature, is highly metaphorical. By demystifying scientific knowledge the power structures that it helps to buttress can be opened up and challenged.

developments in the sociology of science, philosophical hermeneutics—all
of these seem to participating in the same disruption (now we can call it
demystification) of the common sense notions (often condemned as posi-
tivist) according to which scientific propositions, or indeed propositions
carry their authority. (Levine, 1987, p. 13–14)

Gillian Beer is perhaps the foremost British-based literary critic who ana-
lyzes the interaction between literature and science. In *Darwin's Plots* (1983),
Beer looked at the way in which the "evolutionary narrative" can be found in the
nineteenth-century British novel (particularly in George Eliot). However, perhaps
the most challenging analysis she brings to bear is on Darwin's own use of language. What Beer demonstrates is that, particularly in the period before the "professionalization" of science in the mid- to late-nineteenth century, the division
between arts and science was blurred: Beer asserts that "scientists still shared a
common language with other educated readers and writers of their time" (1983,
p. 6). Scientists such as Darwin employed metaphor, analogy, and other literary
devices to shape their scientific "narratives." By analyzing Darwin's own use of
language, Beer investigates what she calls Darwin's "imaginative history," brought
forth through his theory of evolution. While her project is not to expose the dis-
cursive limitations of science, she does argue that science is not divorced from
culture, and especially in the mid-nineteenth century, interactions between literature and science are definitely two-way.

Human Nature and Human Knowledge:
The Allure of Social Constructivism

There is another, broader sense of social constructivism (sometimes called cultural or environmental determinism), which is the idea that the way humans
think, feel, and construct their world is directly determined by the culture they
live in. This too has a political dimension, and the idea that nurture and not
nature shapes our lives has always had an appeal to liberal and well-intentioned
reformers. The attraction is understandable. For a start, right-of-center ideo-
logues (the opposition) have often looked to a static human nature to support
their claims. The easiest way to justify unequal treatment of social groups and
the unequal distribution of wealth and power between different races, sexes, or
social classes, for example, is to argue that it reflects a fixed and so unchange-
able human nature. In much the same way, the Great Chain of Being (set up by
God and so unchallengeable) in the sixteenth and seventeenth centuries was
used to justify aristocratic privilege, the divine right of kings, and social hierar-

chies. At a deeper level, however, lies the often unquestioned assumption that if human vices are the product of social circumstances, then by changing the circumstances we can change human nature and the perfectibility of man becomes a real prospect. Similarly, feminists have often argued that the unequal distribution of power between the sexes, the differences in historical cultural achievements between men and women, gender stereotypes, and the "glass ceiling" are products not of biological differences between the sexes but of socialization in a patriarchal society. Change the society and we can change the roles.

The alternative to cultural determinism is of course the idea that there is something called human nature that is biologically shaped (in concert with environmental influences) through the maturation of each individual—a nature, moreover, that has been hewn by the long process of natural selection acting on our ancestors and inherited from them. Ironically, in the first half of the twentieth century, although the fusion of Mendelian genetics with the mechanism of natural selection added weight to the Darwinian paradigm—resulting in what was known as Neo-Darwinism—support for this biological conception of human nature gradually ebbed away. A Darwinian account of human behavior was seen to be tainted by association with Social Darwinism and more disturbingly the prescriptions of the eugenics movement. In its place there grew up what American psychologists John Tooby and Leda Cosmides have called the "standard social science model," a conception that dominated the social sciences and the humanities after the 1930s. The model, which has similarities to the blank slate metaphor of human perception developed by Locke (see chapter five), has several components. Firstly, it stresses the insignificance of intergroup variations in genetic endowment. In other words, people at birth across different races and cultures are by and large everywhere virtually the same. Secondly, since adult human behavior does vary across and within cultures, it must be culture itself that supplies the architecture of the adult mind, disposes it to think and behave in culturally specific ways, shapes adult behavior, and is responsible for the differences in achievement and temperament we see among individuals.

There is at least some internal coherence in this agenda, even if, as it now seems, the slate of the human mind is not a blank as it was supposed. If human nature has no fixed essence but is incredibly malleable, then social roles are similarly plastic, and inequalities and sexist divisions of roles can be challenged as no longer belonging to a natural order. Combine this with the idea that knowledge is also somehow socially constructed, and you have a potent mix. Any scientific challenge to the idea of a fluid human nature, such as the suggestion that there are real IQ differences between social groups or that the sexes are innately disposed to show behavioral differences, can be challenged as racist, sexist, classist, and generally ideologically contaminated and therefore flawed. A brilliant account of the rise and fall of this model of human nature is given by Steven Pinker in his *The Blank Slate* (2002).

Once science is conceived as just another form of discourse, no longer privileged by what some commentators would call its quaint and passé correspondence theory of truth, it becomes possible to use the tools of literary analysis to expose the gender and other biases in the very production of scientific knowledge. Examples of work adopting this approach include Luce Irigaray's *This Sex Which Is Not One* (1985), the work of Katherine Hayles on fluid mechanics and cybernetics (Hayles, 1992), and Donna Haraway (1989) on primatology. Each of these critics will have her own (not necessarily complete) understanding of the scientific principles she critiques, an understanding that may not stand up to very close scrutiny from within the scientific community. Such critique of the critique is, of course, entirely healthy if an analysis of the discourses of science is to have any validity, particularly to that skeptical scientific community.

The Counterattack

A book that signaled a counterattack by some scientists against the encroachments of cultural relativists was Norman Levitt's and Paul Gross's *Higher Superstition: The Academic Left and Its Quarrels with Science*, published in 1994. Levitt and Gross attacked what they saw as a concerted attack on science from cultural relativists, feminists, literary theorists, and left-wing academics in the humanities and social sciences. The subtitle was unfortunate, since it suggested that the entire academic left was antagonistic to science when in fact it was just some of its members. We should also remember that the political right, academic or otherwise, can also be hostile to science (as is the case in the opposition of Creationists to evolutionary biology) and many scientists (for example, Stephen Jay Gould, Steven Rose, Noam Chomsky) are proud to be allied with left-of-center social causes. *Higher Superstition* exposed what it took to be the sloppy and incoherent philosophy underpinning social constructivist, post-modernist, feminist, and deep ecological critiques of science. It saw such approaches as having no value for the hard sciences:

> It may be argued that in revolutionizing literary criticism, postmodernism will have created a valuable legacy, although many people (including students) who simply love literature and look to academic criticism for relevant inspiration and deeper insight about it have been cruelly disappointed. Still, the analysis of social questions may have benefited from postmodern intellectual strategies, however susceptible to subjectivism and giddy pontifica-

tions they may be. In the area of the hard sciences however (and we hold to the usage, anticipating the jeers of Derridean or Foucauldian sceptics), it has by now become clear, after a few short years, that criticism and analysis informed by postmodern attitudes has been, by and large, an irrelevant botch. (Gross and Levitt, 1994, p. 89)

Other scientists have shared the misgivings (and outrage) of Gross and Levitt. They view postmodernism with a mixture of bewilderment and dismay, and the division that has opened up between these two camps has been christened the "science wars." The suggestion that scientists, who regard themselves as laboring hard to understand how nature works, are really just social actors pouring out their prejudices of race, class, gender, and politics into a culturally fabricated vision of reality does not go down too well. The distinguished biologist E. O. Wilson (a passionate advocate of Enlightenment values) describes the situation as follows:

Postmodernism is the ultimate polar antithesis of the Enlightenment. The difference between the two extremes can be expressed roughly as follows: Enlightenment thinkers believe we can know everything, and radical post modernists believe we can know nothing. (Wilson, 1998, p. 40)

For Wilson, postmodernism is doomed to failure because it has detached itself from the biological view of human nature and those of any of the other sciences. Richard Dawkins is similarly critical: "The meaningless wordplays of modish francophone savants . . . seem to have no other function than to impress the gullible" (Dawkins, 1998, p. 41).

In viewing this exchange a host of questions arise. Are scientists ignorant of contemporary cultural theory, labeling any whiff of radicalism as beyond the pale postmodernism? Are these cultural theorists so ignorant of science that they fail to appreciate the considerable success of its results and the inbuilt checks and guards to ensure objectivity? It would also be wrong to suggest that all scientists are naïve realists and all literary scholars social constructivists. There are still "pragmatic critics" who retain a residual Arnoldian humanism and remain convinced that the canonical texts of Western literature embody a normative (i.e., standards to be followed) set of values and imaginative experiences. Harold Bloom is certainly of this camp and refers to these politically motivated cultural critics as the "School of Resentment." One of the most forceful critics of postmodernist tendencies of recent years has been the literary scholar Joseph Carroll. He chides the constructivists for inconsistency:

It is now the received wisdom that Western science and technology are merely hegemonic cultural constructions that should not be epistemologically privileged over any other form of discourse. If those who propound these views were to take their propositions seriously enough to live by them . . . the propositions themselves would soon disappear along with the observers. Medical science provides an obvious example. It is, I think, a safe assumption that the multitude of people like Ulin, Beer, Pitts, Barrish, Smith, Serres, Levine, Foucault, Bono, Hassan and Jameson . . . use antibiotics, visit the dentist regularly, and willingly undergo surgical procedures designed to save their lives. When they are sick, they do not go to a semiotician for a linguistic consultation; they do not submit their diseased bodies to literary colleagues for rhetorical analyses. (Carroll, 1995, p. 81)

Unfortunately, in picking a series of names from such a widely varied critical field to illustrate the same "tendency" toward ivory-tower "textualism," Carroll weakens his own argument. The work of Michel Foucault, when inspected, does not bear much relation to the work of Frederic Jameson. Carroll exhibits the backlash against theory, both from within and from without the English academic field, that has occurred in the last ten years or so. Humanist literary critics, long troubled by what they see as post-structuralism's assault on literary values, can now look toward the attack on (francophone or francophile) critical theory launched by scientists such as Wilson or Richard Dawkins. While the insights of critical discourse from within the humanities are, in a sense, fair game for critique from either scientific or humanist positions, it is necessary that they be evaluated with care and without caricature. All too often, this hasn't been the case.

Sokal's Modest Experiment

The shape that this cultural conflict between versions of scientific realism on the one hand and the varieties of cultural constructivism (labeled loosely—and its proponents would say unwisely—together as postmodernism) on the other took on by the late 1990s is indicated by the following three extracts that the reader is invited to study carefully:

Extract A

In quantum physics, Heisenberg's demon does not express the impossibility of measuring both the speed and the position of a particle on the grounds of a subjective interference of the measure with the measured, but it measures exactly an objective state of affairs that leaves the respective position of two of its particles outside of the field of its actualization, the number of independent variables being reduced and the values of the coordinates having the same probability. . . . Perspectivism, or scientific relativism, is never relative to a subject: it constitutes not a relativity of truth but, on the contrary, a truth of the relative, that is to say, of variables whose cases it orders according to the values it extracts from them in its system of coordinates.

Extract B

Finally, an exciting proposal has been taking shape over the past few years in the hands of an interdisciplinary collaboration of mathematicians, astrophysicists and biologists: this is the theory of the morphogenetic field. Since the mid-1980s evidence has been accumulating that this field, first conceptualized by developmental biologists, is in fact closely linked to the quantum gravitational field: (a) it pervades all space; (b) it interacts with all matter and energy, irrespective of whether or not that matter/energy is magnetically charged; and, most significantly, (c) it is what is known mathematically as a "symmetric second-rank tensor." All three properties are characteristic of gravity; and it was proven some years ago that the only self-consistent nonlinear theory of a symmetric second-rank tensor field is, at least at low energies, precisely Einstein's general relativity. Thus, if the evidence for (a), (b) and (c) holds up, we can infer that the morphogenetic field is the quantum counterpart of Einstein's gravitational field. Until recently this theory has been ignored or even scorned by the high-energy-physics establishment, who have traditionally resented the encroachment of biologists (not to mention humanists) on their "turf." However, some theoretical physicists have recently begun to give this theory a second look, and there are good prospects for progress in the near future.

Extract C

The main theme of the works of Gaiman is the common ground between society and class. It could be said that the premise of Debordist image states that discourse must come from the collective unconscious. The subject is interpolated into a dialectic paradigm of context that includes reality as a whole. Therefore, Derrida suggests the use of postsemanticist deconstruction to read and modify truth. Bataille uses the term "postdialectic discourse" to denote a textual paradox. But a number of narratives concerning the bridge between sexual identity and society exist. If Baudrillardist hyperreality holds, we have to choose between neosemantic Marxism and Marxist class. However, Lacan uses the term "the dialectic paradigm of context" to denote the role of the artist as writer. Lyotard promotes the use of textual nihilism to attack capitalism.

One of these is a computer generated piece of "post modernist" prose from a site designed by someone keen to mimic the style and phraseology of such writing (fresh versions of whole new essays are generated spontaneously each time anyone visits the site: http://www.elsewhere.org/cgi-bin/postmodern); one a serious piece of writing from two French thinkers; and one is a parody of such writing that was taken seriously enough by a critical theory journal to publish. The point is, of course, unless one is a scholar in the humanities, the three are difficult to tell apart. For our purposes the most interesting one to examine is the parody, one of the most decisive events in the science wars.

Shortly after Levitt's and Gross's *Higher Superstition* appeared, Alan Sokal, a physicist at New York University, hardly believing the description of postmodernist writers that Levitt and Gross were providing, decided to check the sources for himself. In his view, the situation was worse than he feared. He found a whole group of humanities scholars misappropriating ideas from physics and the philosophy of science and passing off their confused application as scholarly texts. So to test the intellectual standards of such scholarship he decided to perform a "modest experiment" in which he would send an article "liberally salted with nonsense" yet making the right ideological noises to a journal respected in the field of postmodern cultural theory. The test would be whether they would publish it; to their lasting embarrassment they did. The full title was "Transgressing the Boundaries: Towards a Transformative Hermeneutics of Quantum Gravity" (Sokal, 1996a). There is of course a certain irony in the title, since transgressing boundaries is precisely what Sokal did. His paper was published in a special edition of *Social Text* devoted to the subject of the science wars. The paper has a superficial plausibility, since it invokes the usual key words and phrases: "discourse," "post Enlightenment hegemony," "counter hegemonic narratives," "gender encoding," "marginalized communities," "Lacanian," "transgressive." It is a brilliant spoof, and extract B is taken from it (Sokal, 1996a, p. 223). Extract A is intended as a serious piece of writing from Deleuze and Guattari (1994, pp. 129–130), and C comes from the postmodern generator (http://www.elsewhere.org/cgi-bin/postmodern, 2003).

As Sokal said, any competent physicist or mathematician (or undergraduate physics or mathematics major) should have spotted the totally spurious basis to his article. In the previous extract, the ideas that a "morphogenic field" (a concept controversially suggested by Rupert Sheldrake and hardly accepted by any serious scientist) should be linked with quantum gravity or that matter can be "magnetically charged" are totally bizarre. Elsewhere in the article, Sokal suggests flatteringly that Derrida's grasp of general relativity enables us to perceive the "ineluctable historicity" of such constants as G and "the π of Euclid" (the idea that π changes through time is a wonderful piece of whimsy). The fact that the spoof is not so far from the sort of writing he was parodying is indicated by extract A above. Whatever the author's intention here, Heisenberg did not have a demon; they are confusing one formulation of his uncertainty principle with "Maxwell's demon." In addition, the explanation of the uncertainty principle is somewhat unclear.

The exposure of the hoax was followed by a mixed reaction of cheers and rebuke. Gary Kamiya, editor of the magazine *Salon*, for example, noted that: "Anyone who has spent much time wading through the pious, obscurantist, jargon filled cant that now passes for 'advanced' thought in the humanities knew it was bound to happen sooner or later." He notes that the editors (strictly an "editorial collective") of *Social Text* "must be now experiencing that queasy sensation that afflicted the Trojans the morning after they pulled that nice big gift horse into their city" (Kamiya, 1996). The British biologist Richard Dawkins was delighted and thought that Sokal had given a lead from the world of science to help "reclaim" the humanities for "genuine scholars" (Dawkins, 2003, p. 53). For others, however, the hoax left an unpleasant taste. Even Steven Jay Gould, a friend of Sokal, confessed to "very mixed feelings about this incident" (Gould, 2003, p. 100). Gould agreed with Sokal that some statements from the relativist camp were "truly silly and extreme . . . largely made by poseurs rather than genuine scholars" (Gould, 1993, p. 99). But his reservations are apposite:

> I, as a practicing scientist, happen to regard the vast bulk of scholarly work in the social analysis of science as not only important and respectable, but as immensely salutary for scientists who rarely think enough about the historical background and immediate social context of their research, and who would therefore greatly benefit from better understanding of these non-scientific influences upon their beliefs and practices. (Gould, 1993, p. 100)

The editors refused to publish Sokal's explanation of his hoax, but it did appear elsewhere. In face of the hostility from the editors he noted wryly: "If the *Social Text* editors find my arguments convincing, then why should they be disconcerted simply because I don't" (Sokal, 1996b, p. 64). Astonishingly, a few months after the hoax was exposed one of the editors remarked that "But we thought Sokal had a real argument, and we still do" (Robbins, 1996, p. 58).

So why did Sokal do it? His motives were far more serious than simply mischief. Sokal is politically left of center (he taught mathematics at the Universidad Nacional Autonoma de Nicaragua under the Sandinista government) and was alarmed that postmodernist nonsense would undermine liberal causes:

> But why did I do it? I confess that I'm an unabashed Old Leftist who never quite understood how deconstruction was supposed to help the working class. (Sokal, 1996c, p. 94)

He went on to say:

> But my main concern isn't to defend science from the barbarian hordes of lit crit (we'll survive just fine, thank you). Rather, my concern is explicitly political: to combat a currently fashionable postmodernist/poststructuralist/social-constructivist discourse—and more generally a penchant for subjectivism—which is, I believe, inimical to the values and future of the Left. (Sokal, 1996c, p. 94).

And he noted poignantly that if we give up the idea that statements can be objectively true independent of context and perspective then:

> Deny that non-context-dependent assertions can be true, and you don't just throw out quantum mechanics and molecular biology: you also throw out the Nazi gas chambers, the American enslavement of Africans. (Sokal 1996c, p. 96)

In subsequent articles Sokal has taken pains to emphasize the valuable role that historical and sociological analyses of science can play in clarifying economic and political issues surrounding science. (Sokal, http://www.physics.nyu.edu/faculty/sokal/reply.html, accessed March 15, 2004)

Although constructivist theorists often claim that their approach frees up discourse to engage with libertarian possibilities, Sokal was perhaps right to identify the reactionary implications of constructivism. As the distinguished Harvard physicist and historian of science Gerald Horton has shown, many leading Nazi's rejected the idea of an objective universal science. Hitler, for example, observed that "There is no truth, in either the moral or scientific sense. The concept of an independent Wissenschaft free of preconditions, could only emerge in the age of liberalism" (quoted in Horton, p. 75). Truth becomes what the state decrees.

Taking an overview of this unhappy episode in the history of ideas, when we examine the response of most scientists to the literary challenge to the very foundations of their work, the science wars begin to look more like a cold war than a full-blown conflict, for the simple reason that most scientists know nothing of the work of Kuhn, Derrida, or Foucault and pay no attention at all to social constructivism. It is difficult to sustain a war if one side refuses to turn up. Meanwhile, while some scientists were fighting off attacks on their epistemological high ground, others were busily tunneling into the enemy camp, purporting to show that the scientific method has a lot to offer literary theory.

Can Literature be Explored Scientifically?

Over the last two decades evolutionary psychology has mounted a withering attack on the blank slate view of the human mind and has helped reunite biological evolution with the study of human nature. So far this new discipline has had most success in the area of human mating behavior, mate choice, human conflict, and altruism toward kin and non-kin. It is also making inroads into such profound areas as human emotions, reasoning, and the evolution and function of language. If this approach proves successful, it promises to throw light on the origins and function of literature. The argument runs that since literature is the product of human brains, and human brains, like the rest of our bodies, have been shaped and wired by natural selection, then one way to understand literature (or at least one dimension of it) is through an analysis of how literature serves or once served adaptive ends. There is now a school of thought devoted to this aim, and this topic provides the most recent and possibly fruitful twist to the tangled tale of the literary relations of science.

E. O. Wilson and Consilience

Once leading protagonist in this new approach to the study of human behavior and culture has been the Harvard biologist E. O. Wilson. In *Sociobiology: The New Synthesis* (1975), Wilson speculated on the evolutionary origins and functions of art, aesthetics, and self-consciousness. He noted how natural selection would have shaped our hypothalamic and limbic systems, which then "flood our consciousness" with the emotions of hate, love, fear, and guilt that are then consulted by ethical philosophers. In *Biophilia* (1984) he extended his adaptive account of the origin of beauty. For Wilson, beautiful ideas, whether from the poet or the scientist, are those that provide elegant and cost-effective solutions to problems: "Mathematics and beauty are devices by which human beings get through life with the limited intellectual capacity inherited by the species" (Wilson, 1984, p. 61). In this sense, Wilson does not try to reduce poetry to science but seeks to explore their common origins. He suggests that mankind is the "poetic species" in that both science and art use metaphor and analogy to comprehend the world, science focusing on the external world and art the realm of experience and self-consciousness.

It was in *Consilience* (1998), however, that Wilson expressed his most deeply thought-out vision for the future dialogue between the arts and sciences. He begins by declaring his belief in the Enlightenment project of a unified world picture:

Edward O. Wilson (1929–)

Ed Wilson, as he is known to his colleagues, is one of the foremost living scientists in America. He was born in Birmingham, Alabama, and despite over forty years on the

faculty at Harvard, still retains his Alabama accent. He was educated at the University of Alabama at Tuscaloosa, earning both B.S. and M.A. degrees before relocating to Harvard for his Ph.D., which he gained in 1955. He became a professor in 1964 and was made curator of entomology at the Harvard Museum of Comparative Zoology in 1971. He received the National Medal of Science in 1976 and is today Pellegrino University Research Professor at Harvard, and is still attached to the museum.

E. O. Wilson. Edward Wilson is one of America's leading scientists. With books such as Sociobiology, On Human Nature, *and* Consilience *he has often set the agenda for debates and discussions about the role and nature of scientific thinking in relation to the human condition. Edward O. Wilson has written twenty books, won two Pulitzer prizes, and is a passionate conservationist. (Rick Friedman/Corbis)*

Wilson's primary area of specialization is entomology: the study of insects, and more specifically, social insects such as ants. His major publication on ants, *Insect Societies* (1971), was followed in 1991 by the Pulitzer Prize–winning *The Ants*. Wilson has in fact won the Pulitzer Prize twice; his other award came in 1979, for *On Human Nature*. The title of this book indicates the development of Wilson's thinking, on which his fame (and for a time, notoriety) outside the field of entomology rests. In *Sociobiology* (1975), Wilson proposed several

The greatest enterprise of the mind has always been and always will be the attempted linkage of the sciences and the humanities. The ongoing fragmentation of knowledge and the resulting chaos in philosophy are not reflections of the real world but artefacts of scholarship. (Wilson, 1998, p. 8)

To conceptualize this linkage he resurrects the term *consilience*, first used by the British philosopher of science William Whewell, which means roughly the use of a common and contiguous framework in which to locate ideas and knowledge. Whewell was a polymath and master of Trinity College, Cambridge. But his vision of consilience only went so far: as a deeply religious thinker, he refused to allow Darwin's *Origin of Species* in the Trinity College Library at Cambridge.

Wilson has been accused of crude reductionism. To be fair, however, his idea is not to reduce literature to biology but to be able to trace consistent threads linking cell chemistry, neurophysiology, and inherited mental circuitry.

mechanisms by which to explain the social behavior of a range of different species, behavior that, on the surface, may seem altruistic or self-sacrificing. Underlying these acts and social groupings, argued Wilson, are genetic and biologic motivations. Controversially, he connected human behavior to the same biological mechanisms.

For a time, Wilson became a highly controversial figure. He was attacked by left-leaning sociologists, who perceived a biological determinism in his work, and by colleagues such as Stephen Jay Gould and Richard Lewontin. In 1978, while giving a talk to the Association for the Advancement of Science, he was picketed by placard-wielding demonstrators and had a bucket of water dumped over his head. On the placards of the demonstrators were swastikas: Wilson's ideas had been perceived as right-wing, deterministic, even racist. Time has been kinder to Wilson and his ideas: the biological underpinning of human behavior is now a central tenet of evolutionary psychology.

Wilson is, in some senses, politically and philosophically complex and difficult to categorize. He is a Democrat, and he calls himself a deist, which he defines as "a person who's willing to buy the idea that some creative force determined the parameters of the universe when it began," though he counts himself skeptical about the existence of an interventionist God. In fact, although he was seen in the 1970s as preaching biological determinism, Wilson has demonstrated that contemporary scientists feel themselves called to be interventionists, to partake in the affairs of the wider world. Wilson is a passionate advocate of environmental and conservationist causes, and his 1990 Crafoord Prize (awarded by the Royal Swedish Academy of Science in areas not covered by their award of Nobel Prizes) was in recognition of his contribution to environmental science and environmental causes. With works such as *Consilience* (1998), Ed Wilson is still at the forefront of scientific thinking and of thinking about the role of science.

From an understanding of brain architecture and innate dispositions, a link can be made to the forms and functions of culture (including literature) and back again to examine the particular and singular resonance of great art with the brains of the humans that created it. At each level there will be a semi-autonomous set of laws and principles. Reductionism, then, properly conceived, does not, as Wilson says, "diminish the integrity of the whole," and "Scholars in the humanities should lift the anathema placed on reductionism. Scientists are not conquistadors out to melt the Inca gold" (Wilson, 1998, p. 211).

The key for Wilson is to place the humanities and the sciences on a common foundation. The appropriate foundation, ultimately, for the arts will be that of an evolved human nature:

> Artistic inspiration common to everyone in varying degrees rises from the
> artesian wells of human nature. It follows that even the greatest works of art

might be understood fundamentally with knowledge of the biologically evolved epigenetic rules that guided them. (Wilson, 1998, p. 213)

Wilson describes literature and its interpretation as a foray into the workings of the mind. In his view, literary theorists have fared so badly so far because they have had inadequate theories—such as Freudian psychoanalysis and "postmodern solipsism"—to guide them. As a more trustworthy guide Wilson proposes a model of gene-culture co-evolution whereby several million years of hominid evolution have molded the human genome to encode epigenetic rules "which are the inherited regularities of mental development that comprise human nature" (p. 214). Such rules then form the basis of a universal human psyche that biases the generation of culture (including the writing of literature) in biologically understandable ways.

From this perspective, Wilson sees the arts as an adaptive response of a highly intelligent organism to a complex and chaotic environment. The arts serve to simulate and model reality and pass on social learning. The oral tradition, for example, from which literature sprang, embodies generations of practical learning relevant to coping with the physical and, just as importantly for gregarious animals such as humans, the social environment. As the evolutionary psychologist Steven Pinker notes, "The technology of fiction delivers a simulation of life that an audience can enter in the comfort of their cave, couch, or theatre seat" (Pinker, 1997, p. 539). According to Pinker, fiction provides an experiment with characters that we can watch, experience, and learn from: "Fictional narratives supply us with a mental catalogue of the fatal conundrums we might face someday and the outcomes of strategies we could deploy in them" (Pinker, 1997, p. 543). Thus in Wilson's view, we can measure the quality of the arts by their "humaneness," by "the precision of their adherence to human nature. To an overwhelming degree that is what we mean when one speaks of the true and beautiful in the arts" (Wilson, 1998, p. 226).

Wilson insists, however, that the idea of the "biological origin of the arts" is a "working hypothesis and as such is meant to be testable, vulnerable and consilient with the rest of biology" (Wilson, 1998, p. 229). Testing these ideas is still in its infancy and is likely to encounter some understandable resistance from traditional literature departments.

One interesting feature of some of the works examined above, such as *Consilience* and *The Blank Slate*, is that they were works addressed to a wide readership, not just professional scholars. This has led some to suppose that we are witnessing the emergence of a third culture.

The Third Culture and Popularizations of Science

The Third Culture

When C. P. Snow published a second edition of his *Two Cultures* essay in 1963, he predicted the emergence of a third culture in which literary intellectuals and scientists could communicate with each other. This culture does not seem to have appeared in the form that Snow imagined. Indeed, Sokal, reflecting on his article, concluded that the "two cultures . . . are probably farther apart in mentality than at any time in the past 50 years" (Sokal, 1996c, p. 94). But the New York publisher and author John Brockman has commented on the massive growth in the consumption of popular science books over the last few decades and has concluded that we are witnessing the emergence of a third culture driven by scientist-humanists:

> The third culture consists of those scientists and other thinkers in the empirical world who, through their work and expository writing, are taking the place of the traditional intellectual in rendering visible the deeper meanings of our lives, redefining who and what we are. (Brockman, 1995, p. 17)

Such a phenomenon, he thinks, represents a shift in our culture's conception of important thought:

> What we are witnessing is a passing of the torch from one group of thinkers, the traditional literary intellectuals, to a new group, the intellectuals of the emerging third culture. (Brockman, 1995, p. 19)

These "new humanists" are not the third culture that Snow imagined, however:

> Literary intellectuals are not communicating with scientists. Scientists are communicating directly with the general public. (Brockman, 1995, p. 18)

Brockman sees a marked contrast between the science disciplines, with their expectation of systematic progress, and humanities disciplines that are "self-referential" and more often than not concerned with the "exegesis of earlier thinkers." To Brockman's mind, science finds answers and moves on; meanwhile "the traditional humanities establishment continues its exhaustive insular hermeneutics" (Brockman, 2003, p. 3).

Popular Culture and the Literature of Science

Many of the books that Brockman has in mind are shelved by bookstores under "popular science." But the word *popular* is not altogether apt: it suggests a watering down and simplification, whereas in actuality, although the technical content is restricted, such works often celebrate what the straightjackets of the traditional scientific paper or undergraduate text cannot: the excitement of discovery, the remarkable nature of the findings, the implications of the ideas for the human condition—in short, the cultural significance of science.

Identifying the genre is easy enough, but the books seem to defy a simple classificatory scheme, and scholarship on the phenomenon itself—the growth of popular science publishing—has hardly started. Some works, such as Dava Sobel's *Longitude*, are popular histories of science often employing a strong narrative plot replete with heroes and villains; some are popular expositions of recent developments or key ideas in science, such as Richard Dawkins's *The Selfish Gene*, or Steven Pinker's *The Language Instinct*; some, such as *Darwin* by Desmond and Moore, are popular biographies of famous scientists informed by a commitment to externalist or contextual history of science; some are autobiographical about a "life in science," such as *Trilobite* by Richard Fortey; some are serious works of synthesis addressed to fellow intellectuals and the general public, such as E. O. Wilson's *Consilience*. Viewing such works, the English critic John Carey thinks that they represent a "new kind of late twentieth century literature, which demands to be recognised as a separate genre" (Carey, 1995, p. xiv). The following list shows an attempt to classify some recent examples of science writing.

Popular History of Science

Longitude by Dava Sobel
Mendeleyev's Dream (2000) by Paul Strathern
Ever Since Darwin by Stephen Jay Gould
"The Revolutions in Science" series edited by Jon Turney, e.g., *Watt's Perfect Engine* by Ben Marsden (2002)

Expositions of Key or New Ideas

The Selfish Gene (1976) by Richard Dawkins
A Brief History of Time by Stephen Hawking
The Elegant Universe by Brian Greene

Synthesis of Ideas and Position Statements

The Moral Animal by Robert Wright
Steven Pinker's *The Blank Slate* and *How the Mind Works*

Biographies and Autobiographies

The Lunar Men by Jenny Uglow
Darwin by Adrian Desmond and James Moore

Compilations of Writings on or about Science

The Faber Book of Science edited by John Carey
The Longman Literary Companion to Science (1989) edited by Walter Gratzer

Plays and Poetry

Copenhagen by Michael Frayn
Oxygen (2001) by Carl Djerassi and Roald Hoffman
Square Rounds (1992) by Tony Harrison

Many of these books have sold extremely well, and whatever we think of Brockman's thesis, it is clear that there is a considerable public appetite for accessible works about science. Significantly, such works are not just non-technical simplifications. Some books are remarkable for the clarity of their exposition, such as Dawkins's *The Selfish Gene* (1976) and Brian Greene's *The Elegant Universe;* others, such as Pinker's *The Blank Slate* and *How the Mind Works*, are passionate accounts of trends in recent science (biology and psychology) and why they matter to us. Many show considerable historical and philosophical sophistication. In the play *Oxygen,* for example, the authors (two distinguished chemists) explore ethical issues of discovery and priority in science, the role of women, and epistemological issues about the nature of change in scientific theories. In *Copenhagen,* the novelist and playwright Michael Frayn examines the fateful meeting of Niels Bohr and Werner Heisenberg in 1941. The play examines the moral responsibility of scientists, the uncertainty of memory, and the perspectival nature of truth, playing at the same time on the metaphor of Heisenberg's famous uncertainty principle.

In other books, the use of history is less sophisticated. Dava Sobel achieved massive international sales of her book *Longitude* by taking the well-known tale of Harrison's marine chronometer and packaging it in the narrative format of the lonely journey of the hero. Professional historians were irritated by errors of fact and envious, no doubt, of its financial success. The subtitle, *The True Story of a Lone Genius Who Solved the Greatest Scientific Problem of His Time*, did not endear the volume to professional historians who had spent their careers trying to overcome such approaches. The success of *Longitude* stimulated a flood of books with a similar format, so much so that David Miller has described the phenomenon as the "Sobel Effect" or "The Amazing Tale of How Multitudes of Popular Writers Pinched All the Best Stories in the History of Science and became Rich and Famous while Historians Languished in Accustomed Poverty and Obscurity" (Miller, 2002, 185). Books that fall into this category are fond of using the possessive apostrophe. Hence we have *Mendeleyev's Dream*, *Boltzman's Atom*, *Galileo's Daughter*, and *Fermat's Enigma*. They also often make common assumptions about the nature of scientific discovery: that science is the product of an individual genius fighting against the odds but one who eventually triumphs and changes the world. In such works, hagiography and Whiggish approaches to history are alive and well.

Reviews of such works are revealing. A common pattern is that professional historians treat them critically and point to their limitations and their neglect of context; while practicing scientists rate them more highly. It is as if the institution of science itself approves stories of heroic discovery and the transforming power of science as part of its own means of justification. Despite these reservations, there are also highly readable and respectable examples of this genre such as Deborah Cadbury's *Dinosaur Hunters*, a book that was popular, accessible, and historically sophisticated without the encumbrance of dry and distracting scholarly apparatus or historiographical angst. As if to restate the expertise of professional historians, we also have the "Revolutions in Science" series, which so far has published over sixteen volumes in the history of science written by professional historians yet accessible to a popular market.

One lesson, then, from the boom in popular science publishing is that when scientists and others write books about science using crisp and well-turned prose, include a strong narrative format, are careful to capture the historical context of ideas, are not afraid to include biographical details of the personalities involved, and celebrate with conviction the importance of the central ideas, then such books are avidly consumed by the reading public. We might say that when science writing takes its cue from the humanities, then the result is an affection for science. This topic is explored in the epilogue.

Bibliographic Essay

A very readable and lucid guide to the debate between realist and constructivist views of science, part of the so-called science wars, is provided by James Brown's *Who Rules in Science* (Cambridge MA: Harvard University Press, 2001). The book is written in a student-friendly style, and philosophical terms are clearly defined. The special issue of the journal *Social Text* (Durham NC: Duke University Press, vol. 46–47, 1996) devoted to the issue of the science wars is worth reading, not only for Sokal's spoof, which appeared in this volume. Many of the articles are readable and make points worthy of consideration. Plenty of material on the science wars and the works of Sokal, Gross, and Levitt can be found attached to the science wars home page at http://members.tripod.com/ScienceWars/ (accessed February 20, 2004). Sokal gives a detailed account of his concerns in *Intellectual Impostures* (London: Profile Books, 2003) by Alan Sokal and Jean Bricmont. For an impassioned defense of scientific rationality and an exposé of the sloppy end of cultural contructivism see *Higher Superstition* by Paul Gross and Norman Levitt (Baltimore and London: John Hopkins University Press, 1994).

Also worth consulting is Stephen Jay Gould's last book (published after his death) *The Hedgehog, the Fox, and the Magister's Pox* (London: Jonathan Cape, 2003). This is Gould's last word on his vision of the relationship between the humanities and science. He takes issue with Wilson's notion of consilience and offers instead a suggestion that they represent alternative paths toward wisdom.

The Mating Mind by Geoffrey Miller (London: Heineman, 2000) is a readable account of sexual selection theory and its application to the arts. The evolutionary approach to understanding the human mind is discussed in two excellent books by Steven Pinker: *How the Mind Works* (New York: Penguin, 1997) and *The Blank Slate* (New York: Penguin, 2002). For further reading on evolutionary approaches to literature it is worth consulting a special issue of the journal *Philosophy and Literature*, Volume 25, October 2001, No. 2. It contains numerous articles on the value of evolution for literary studies. A good start in this volume would be Michelle Scalise Sugiyama's paper "Narrative Theory and Function: Why Evolution Matters." There are also plenty of articles by one of the leading exponents of this potentially highly fruitful line of inquiry, Joseph Carroll, at http://www.umsl.edu/~engjcarr/index/html (accessed February 20, 2004). For a detailed exposition of this line of theorizing consult Carroll's *Evolution and Literary Theory* (Columbia and London: University of Missouri Press, 1995). Another key work in this emerging area is Robert Storey's *Mimesis and the Human Animal: On the Biogenic Foundations of Literary Representations* (Evanston IL: Northwestern University Press, 1996). An accessible introduction, from an evolutionary perspective, into how male and female sexual psychologies may figure in literature is given in *Warrior Lovers: Erotic Fiction, Evolution and Female Sexuality* (London: Weidenfield and Nicolson, 2001) by Catherine Salmon and Donald Symonds. Also worth consulting is *Biopoetics: Evolutionary Explorations in the Arts* (Lexington KY: ICUS, 1999), edited by Brett Cooke and Frederick Turner

Gillian Beer discusses how science makes use of common cultural concepts and linguistic terms in her *Open Fields: Science in Cultural Encounter* (Oxford: Oxford University Press, 1996). Chapter eight, "Translation or Transformation," is a useful discussion of how the interchanges between science and literature can be conceptualized. For an application of literary approaches to the relationship between science and literature see *One Culture: Essays in Science and Literature* (Madison: University of Wisconsin Press, 1987), edited by George Levine.

For a discussion of the concept of the third culture see John Brockman's book *The Third Culture* (New York: Simon and Schuster, 1995). Brockman gives an introductory chapter to the concept, but the rest of the book consists of scientists' explanations of their area of work and its importance.

One of the few books dealing with popular scientific writing is *The Literature of Science*, edited by Murdo William McRae (Athens: University of Georgia Press, 1993). It includes a good assessment of Gould's work in a chapter by Louis P. Masur: "Stephen J. Gould's Vision of History." Some of the ways in which popular science deals with science are analyzed by Jon Turney in "More than Story Telling—Reflecting on Popular Science" in *Science Communication in Theory and Practice*, edited by Susan Stocklmayer, Michale Gore, and Chris Bryant (Dordrecht, The Netherlands: Kluer Academic Publishers, 2001). In the same volume is an interesting essay by Richard Eckerseley titled "Postmodern Science: The Decline or Liberation of Science" in which he suggests that postmodernism will be good for science. An excellent article on the rise of popular science narratives from the perspective of a professional historian is David Philip Miller's "The Sobel Effect" (*Metascience* 2002(11): 185–200). Miller is critical of the poor scholarship underlying some of these books but gives some interesting pointers as to how the phenomenon itself could be researched.

Epilogue

John Cartwright

In chapter eleven we explored the notion that science and literature lay either side of a fracture line that opened up in Western culture some 300 years ago. We have seen in this book that the situation is far more complicated and interesting. Yet there remains the nagging feeling that all is not well in the academy. It is not just that knowledge has become increasingly fragmented—specialization and the construction of a highly technical language within narrow discipline boundaries is an almost inevitable precondition for greater understanding. Indeed, it is no more reasonable to expect literary critics to converse on equal terms with quantum mechanicians or vice versa than to expect surgeons to fly passenger jets or airline pilots to perform kidney transplants. But what might be hoped for from all disciplines is an ability and inclination of its representatives to engage in wider cultural conversations about the nature of their work and a willingness to explore its significance and cultural import. We might also expect any discipline to remain open and responsive to influences and ideas from outside its boundaries, particularly from cognate disciplines. On both these scores many examples show that this is happening. The growth of popular science writing and the emergence of Darwinian aesthetics are just two examples. But there is also an insularity born of the very structure of academic life, where reputation is enhanced by publishing within a narrow range of expectations and to a familiar peer group that awards its honors for conforming to the party line. Such a system of rewards militates against cultural conversations between the realms of science and literature.

There is also an irony in the direction taken by some practitioners in the social studies of science. One of the genuine achievements of such studies over the last fifty years has been to show that ideological factors have often helped structure scientific knowledge. Soviet biology in the Lysenko period, Nazi racial science, and the diagnosis of female ailments by nineteenth-century male medics provide obvious examples of flawed Marxist, racist, and sexist science. The crucial point here, though, is that we must be aware of such influences, since they make for bad science. Instead, some cultural theorists seem to imagine that pursuing an overt political agenda will lead to a sounder grasp of culture. What the Sokal hoax teaches us is that in fact the opposite is likely to be the case.

Chapter twelve revealed some interesting parallels and contrasts in the story of how literature and science have negotiated their relationship. One can perhaps discern resisted bids for hegemony from both sides. When literary theorists assert that science is just another form of discourse, and one that should no longer be regarded as immune from literary, historical, and sociological analysis, we find howls of protest from scientists motivated by the conviction that they are laying out the laws of nature. When scientists such as evolutionary theorists approach literature and attempt to explain its function and forms from a naturalistic perspective, they are met with accusations of crude reductionism. Both responses are to be expected, of course, when professional interests and academic territories are jealously guarded. But on reflection, it begins to look as if both raids on the other camp have met with intellectual problems of a more substantial kind. The social constructivist approach to science, in its strong form, has failed lamentably to account for the enormous success of science (even on its own terms) in explaining, predicting, and controlling phenomena. Solipsism aside, the most parsimonious explanation for our experiences would seem to require the assumption of an objective world that behaves in ways independently of our wishes, desires, and by inference, social structures—a world that science, albeit imperfectly and in part, models and explains. The world is not created anew each morning, and its robust regularities are not plastic enough to sustain any interpretation. Aristotle was wrong, Galen was wrong, biblical chronology is wrong. However mediated the world is through our precepts and concepts, science has an uncanny knack of offering up reliable knowledge.

On the other hand, a scientific explanation of the deep structures of the human mind, apart from being in its infancy, still shows little prospect of explaining the content and enormous variety of cultural artifacts that the imagination creates. Science has a long way to go to interpret the complexities of cultural forms such as literature, but perhaps literary academics (and critical theorists) could profitably open themselves up to influences from mainstream science, even if they are suspicious of claims that science can present any kind of "truth" of the text. Similarly, even the most ardent searcher after consilience may have to face the possibility that culture moves according to its own mysterious laws and principles, not conjoined to the natural sciences.

At the level of education, perhaps literature and science can both gain something by comparing their traditions with one another. Even a cursory inspection reveals the stark contrast between the pedagogical methods of science and literature. Studying literature involves an examination of the history of literary production using a variety of techniques and perspectives. Such studies are sensitive to historical influences on genres, authors, and readers. In contrast, the natural sciences tend to ignore the historical and cultural contexts of their subject matter and train students with an eye to producing research practitioners rather than scientifically literate citizens. The remark by Thomas Kuhn that science education resembles finger exercise on the piano still has some truth.

It is not too unreasonable to suppose that most science graduates would benefit from an exposure to the methods and aims of the humanities applied to their own subject. Unless such students move into research careers, the sacrifice of knowing a little less depth in science for knowing more about science, and especially how it is embedded in social and historical contexts, would be a good one. One utilitarian justification might be that many contemporary social issues involving science are not soluble by scientific methods alone. The issues raised by such topics as animal welfare, global warming, genetically modified foods, environmental conservation, declining biodiversity, cloning, and so on have social, political, philosophical, ethical, and economic as well as scientific dimensions. Scientists who engage in problem solving in these areas might be better equipped by having some experience in the areas of thought—the social sciences and the humanities—where these perspectives are employed.

There is also a deeper rationale behind this call for a broadening of the science curriculum. Imagine for a moment if 100 years of educational tradition in the sciences and literature were to be inverted. That science undergraduates were barred from the laboratory and studied instead the great works of past masters: Galileo's *Starry Messenger*, Lavoisier's *Elements of Chemistry*, Newton's *Principia*, Darwin's *Origin of Species*, Watson and Crick's paper of 1953 on the structure of DNA, and so on. Meanwhile, at the other end of the campus, students of literature concentrated only on plays, poems, and novels of the last ten years; suffered long lectures on the textual mechanics of constructing a novel; learned about the fine details of poetic meter and the technology of stage lighting; and were dragooned at regular intervals into linguistic laboratories to turn out sonnets and one-act plays. Such an inversion is unthinkable and would clearly be at odds with the quite different aims and ambitions of the two disciplines. Literature students would have lost the history of their pursuit, and science students, having gained a history, would have lost the skills to participate in contemporary science. One thing the thought experiment does reveal, however, is that much current science teaching has indeed sacrificed its cultural heritage—those "monuments of unaging intellect"—to use Yeats's phrase—in favor of a heavy focus on contemporary science practice.

So perhaps in the last analysis science and literature still have something to learn from each other. With a bit of luck and persuasion the fashionable view that scientific knowledge is unprivileged text, and its grasp on the objective world just a social construction, will be seen as inadequate to explain the remarkable success of science in explaining and controlling the natural world. Conversely, perhaps science educators can be persuaded that science can be taught with tools sharpened by the humanities, that scientific inquiry is a cultural product with a human face and its history a rich source of inspiring, emotionally engaging, and morally edifying stories. There is of course a paradox here. The very process of popularizing and humanizing science, making it enjoyable, usually makes an appeal to the imaginative faculties of the reader. But targeting these subjective registers of experience could be viewed as a threat to the very values of objectivity and self-denial that underlie science. This paradox goes a long way to explaining the distrust that professional scientists have for those of their number that break rank and deign to popularize their subject matter. Resolving this tension is a necessary but difficult task.

Toward the end of *Two Cultures*, Snow spoke with wisdom when he warned about the implications of too wide a gap between science and the humanities: "When the two senses have grown apart, then no society is going to be able to think with wisdom" (p. 50). This was a view echoed by a much later representative of the fruitful fusion of the sciences and the humanities, the late S. J. Gould. In the very last sentence of his last (posthumously published) work, he echoed Benjamin Franklin ("our greatest Enlightenment hero"):

> As he stated for the people of America—and as I say for the wonderful and illuminating differences between the sciences and the humanities, all in the potential service of wisdom's one great goal—we had better hang together, or assuredly we will all hang separately. (S. J. Gould, 2003, p. 265)

Appendix

John Cartwright

Spherical Astronomy and "Saving the Appearances"

To really appreciate the medieval view of the cosmos it is best for contemporary readers to temporarily forget all they know about modern astronomy and cosmology and step back into the shoes of someone in the ancient or medieval world staring up at the night sky. A convenient way to start is to make a catalogue of the observations that such a keen-eyed observer could have made and then examine the various theories and models that were put forward by the Greeks and subsequent thinkers to explain these observations. It was these theories and models that became the bedrock for the medieval view of the universe. Forget, for a moment, that you believe we stand on a rocky planet some 6,000 miles in diameter rotating on its own axis once every day at the same time that it whirls about the sun at a speed of about 67,000 miles per hour, and consider only what you can actually observe. The telescope was not invented until about 1608, and so thinkers in the ancient and medieval periods had to construct their theories using naked-eye observations. The observations described below can still be made, of course, by anyone sufficiently interested. We will assume that the observer, like those living in the ancient civilizations of Babylon, Greece, Rome, and medieval Europe, resides in the northern hemisphere.

The Stars

The first thing anyone will notice spending even a short time looking at the sky at night is that the stars do not remain stationary. Instead, they can be seen to drift overhead moving from east to west, much as the sun does during the day. The next level of detail will reveal that one star does not move, but all the other stars appear to revolve around this star moving in a counterclockwise direction. This star is always found due north and is called the North Star or Polaris. It is the revolution of stars around this stationary object that gives rise to the appearance that some stars rise in the east and set in the west. In fact, some stars close to Polaris (so called circumpolar) never set and always remain above the horizon as they wheel around the North Star. The angle that the North Star makes to the northern horizon depends on the latitude of the observer, and it is easy to demonstrate that in the northern hemisphere, the latitude of the observer is the same as the angle of the star to the horizon. Hence, observers in Athens, London, and New York would see it 38 degrees, 51.5 degrees, and 40.5 degrees above the horizon, respectively. As well as revealing the latitude of the observer, the North Star has the obvious advantage of always hanging in the sky over geographical north. For this reason it became variously known as the Pole Star, the Steering Star, the Loadstar or Lodestar, and to the Anglo-Saxons, the Scip-steorra (ship star). Shakespeare's Helena in *A Midsummer Night's Dream* tells Hermia: "Your eyes are lodestars." Its constancy of position was also exploited by the ailing Keats when, aware of his own mortality, he wrote: "Bright star I would I were as steadfast as thou art." In Shakespeare's *Julius Caesar*, the resolve of Caesar is emphasized when he says

> I am as constant as the Northern Star
> Of whose true fixed and resting quality
> There is no fellow in the firmament.

So far we have imagined ourselves looking north at the stars on a piece of land of whose shape we have no notion. By the time of Aristotle, however, Greek natural philosophers widely accepted that the earth was a sphere. Around 140 B.C. the Alexandrian philosopher Eratosthenes measured the circumference of the earth and came up with a figure of 24,000 miles, very close to the modern figure.

Accurate timepieces did not exist in the Middle Ages, of course, but if a modern observer were to take a stopwatch out to examine the stars and time the period of revolution of any star around the pole, he or she would find it to be just under twenty-four hours: twenty-three hours fifty-six minutes and four seconds, to be more exact. The unfailing regularity of this motion obviously suggests a method for estimating the time at night, and before the advent of portable timepieces, this was a common way for country folk to estimate the time. The country characters that Thomas Hardy described were still using this method in the nineteenth century. In *Far from the Madding Crowd*, Hardy describes a scene involving the shepherd Gabriel Oak:

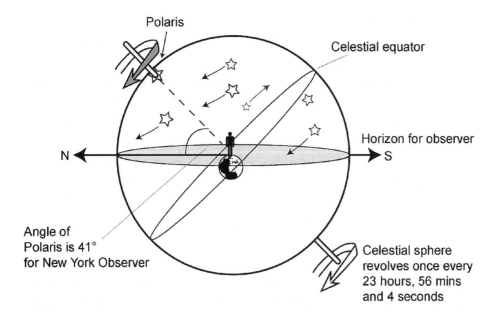

Figure 1: The celestial sphere conceived as a means of accounting for the rotation of the stars around Polaris. (A. Bell and G. Marin)

> The Dog-star and Aldebaran, pointing to the restless Pleiades, were halfway up to the Southern sky . . . . the barren and gloomy square of Pegasus was creeping around to the north west; far away through the plantation Vega sparkled like a lamp suspended amid the leafless trees, and Cassiopeia's chair stood daintily poised on the uppermost boughs. "One o' clock" said Gabriel. (*Far from the Madding Crowd*, 1889, p. 11–12)

It would seem reasonable to suppose that the stars we see set below the western horizon still exist when they are out of sight and are simply carried around to rise again the next day. It is easy to imagine, then, that the stars are embedded on some gigantic sphere that revolves around a stationary spherical earth. To account for the fact that the pole star does not move and yet points due north, we must assume that the whole axis of this sphere passes through the north pole of the earth (Figure 1). Dante notes how the stars closest to Polaris must of necessity move the slowest, since they have the shortest distance to travel:

> But my rapt gaze grew fixed in heaven where reel
> The slowest-gyring stars, as the wheel's gyre
> Is slowest near the axle of the wheel.
> (*Purgatory*, canto viii, l. 85)

This model, introduced here as a conceptual device for storing our observations, was taken to represent the physical reality of the stars by the time of Aristotle. Although we now have a completely different model of the cosmos to the Greeks, professional astronomers still employ the concept of the celestial sphere to divide up the sky and locate the positions of stars, planets, and galaxies. Its contemporary usefulness derives from the fact that although celestial objects are not located on a sphere at a fixed distance from the earth but are distributed at varying distances in space, their distances are so far from us that for most objects the parallax of observation is so small that it is both convenient and accurate enough to pretend they lie on a celestial sphere. Once we have grasped this concept, it becomes much easier to understand the much more complicated motions of the planets and the sun. This whole area of study is sometimes called spherical astronomy.

The next celestial object to understand is the motion of the sun. During the day the sun appears to rise somewhere in the east and set somewhere on the western horizon. The stars disappear at sunrise; they are still there, of course, on the celestial sphere, but the brightness of the sun is such that they are invisible to our eyes. At first inspection, the sun appears to be doing what all the other stars do: namely, moving from east to west on an axis centered on Polaris, taking about twenty-four hours to complete a circuit. A closer inspection, however, reveals a very real and important difference. If we were to time the motion of the sun, say from midday to the next midday, it would take on average (since this in itself varies slightly throughout the year) twenty-four hours, in other words four minutes longer than the rest of the stars. We now have, therefore, two concepts for the day: the solar day of twenty-four hours, and the sidereal (or star) day of twenty-three hours and fifty-six minutes. The stars are rotating faster than the sun and, like athletes running around a racing track, the faster stars will inevitable lap the slower sun. The most convenient way to describe this is to say that the sun has the same diurnal (from day to day) motion as the stars but has its own slower west to east motion superimposed on top of this.

If we perform a thought experiment and imagine that the sun is on the celestial sphere in the same area of the sky as, say, the constellation Taurus, then gradually the sun will move out of Taurus heading toward the east at a rate of about one degree per day (corresponding to the four minutes that the sun lags behind Taurus each day). Eventually, of course, the sun will move into other constellations, but after a period of time, as the faster stars lap the slower sun, the sun will reappear in Taurus once again. This time is exactly one year (365.25 days) and is the basis for defining a calendar year. If we could freeze temporarily the motion of the celestial sphere and simply let the sun perform its own movement, then we would see the sun move slowly across the sky along a pre-

THE STARS OF THE ZODIAC

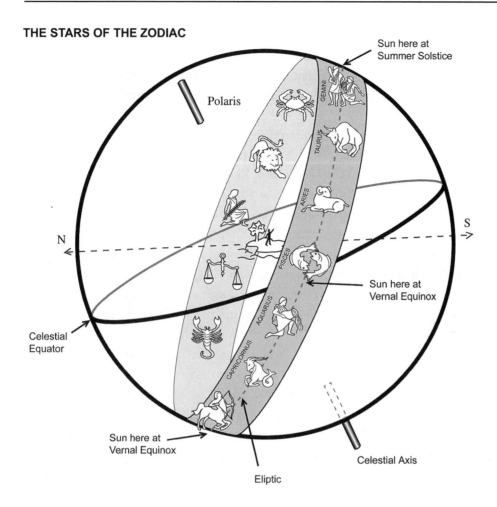

Figure 2: The zodiac and the ecliptic. The sun moves along the line of the ecliptic passing through the twelve constellations of the zodiac. The celestial equator runs around the celestial sphere perpendicular to the polar axis. The ecliptic is tilted 23° to this axis. (A. Bell and G. Martin)

cise line. It would be visible for six months of the year and below the horizon for another six months. This line is known as the ecliptic (see Figure 2).

Although the sun's motion might seem erratic, it remains on this line constantly and moves through the same constellations year after year. These constellations are those that lie in a band roughly six degrees either side of the ecliptic, and they are called the constellations of the zodiac. The word *zodiac* comes from a Greek phrase meaning circle of animals because, before the introduction of Libra as a zodiacal constellation, all the signs were those of animals (Pisces = fish, Taurus = bull, etc.). Originally the constellations occupied unequal spaces in the sky, but around 130 B.C., the Greek astronomer Hipparchos introduced more order by dividing the whole zodiac belt into equal parts of thirty degrees each and ensured that each part or sign corresponded to its appropriate constellation. Somewhat confusingly, and due to a phenomenon known as precession of the equinoxes, these signs are not now exactly coincident with constellations of the same name.

If we imagine the celestial sphere turning once every twenty-three hours and fifty-six minutes and pivoting on the pole star, then we can also conceive that this sphere could be given an equator line, the line dividing it into two hemispheres in the same fashion as the earth's equator (see Figure 2). Now as Figure 2 shows, the ecliptic is tilted from the celestial equator by about 23.5 degrees—the "obliquity of the ecliptic." This tilt has important implications, accounting for the seasons and the unequal length of day and night throughout the year. If we imagine the sun to be in the constellation of Gemini at midday on Figure 2, then as the whole celestial sphere turns, carrying the sun with it, the sun will set north of west and rise again some hours later north of east. Since the rotational speed of the sphere is constant (before the arrival of atomic clocks in the late twentieth century this was the most constant motion that humans knew), then the sun will spend more time above the horizon than below it. At midday it will also be high in the sky. The exact angle will of course depend upon the latitude of the observer, since this determines the angle of the axis of the whole sphere (through Polaris) above the horizon, but for someone in New York (latitude 40.5 degrees) the sun would reach 73 degrees above the horizon, and for someone in London (latitude 51.5 degrees) 62 degrees above the horizon. The time of year will be midsummer, days will be long, nights short, and, since the sun is high in the sky, the days will be warm.

As the months pass, the sun will move out of Gemini, through Cancer, Leo, and Virgo, and into Libra. Toward the end of September (usually September 21, plus or minus a day) the sun will be on the ecliptic at the point where this crosses the celestial equator. It is easy to see that at this point (if we let the celestial sphere revolve once again) the sun will rise due east and set due west. Moreover, day and night will be of equal length (twelve hours each)—hence the name equinox for this time of year. We will freeze the turning of the celestial sphere once more and let the sun drift day by day out of Libra, through Scorpio, and into Sagittarius. In Sagittarius, when the revolving celestial sphere brings the sun above the horizon it will rise south of east and set south of west. On or around December 21, we meet the winter solstice, when the angle of the sun in the sky at midday is the lowest it reaches: the days are short, the nights long, and we are in the depths of winter. Four months later, the sun will move into Aries and once again we have the sun rising due east and setting due west, giving twelve hours of daylight; we have reached the spring equinox. Three months after this and the sun is back in Gemini and we have completed a year.

The constellation in which the sun is to be found is therefore a way of calculating or indicating the month of the year. Chaucer uses this in a fairly standard allusion in the opening lines of *The Canterbury Tales* when he notes:

> When that April with his shoures soote
> The droghte of March hath perced to the roote
> and the yonge sonne
> Hath in the Ram his half cours y ronne.
> (CT l. 1,2.7,8)

In other words, the sun is about half way through the sign of Aries (the Ram) and so it is April. In *The Divine Comedy*, Dante always makes reference to time in terms of stellar configurations. In Hell, for example, Dante's guide, Virgil, urges him to depart with the words:

> Follow me now; I think we should depart;
> Horizon-high the twinkling Fishes swim
> And the Wain's right over Caurus.
> (l. 114)

Dante's readers, having already been told that the sun is in Aries, would instantly realize this is about two hours before daybreak, since if the constellation of Pisces is just over the horizon, then Aries (and so the sun) will rise about two hours later.

It is easy to see that the tilt of the ecliptic to the celestial equator is what gives rise to seasons. If the sun ran exactly along the celestial equator, or (to slip into modern parlance for any reader who still wants to root their understanding in modern science) if the axis of the earth's rotation was exactly 90 degrees to the plane of orbit around the sun), then day and night would always be twelve hours in duration, and the temperature during the day would be roughly the same at any time of the year. Well, the world is not like this, and this tilt has intrigued poets for centuries. In *The Divine Comedy*, for example, as Dante travels upward to the sphere of the sun he draws the attention of the reader to the deviation between the ecliptic (the line along which the planets and the sun move) and the celestial equator. The points where the two circles meet are in Aries and Libra. Dante provides a theological argument why the tilt (23.5 degrees) exists.

> For were their path not so tilted thus aside,
> Much heavenly power would go for naught,

While more or less than this if it should lie
Out of the straight, 'twould cause a grievous lack
Of order in the low world and the high.
(*Paradisio*, canto X, l. 16–21)

The heavenly power is that of the sun. If the sun moved exactly along the celestial equator, then there would be no seasons. If the tilt were greater than 23.5 degrees, however, the seasons would vary more dramatically and cause "a grievous lack of order." The reasoning of Dante here is typical of the teleological style of the Middle Ages. Things are as they are to satisfy some purpose; if things were different, then life would be less comfortable or harmonious.

The other obvious celestial object to record observations of is the moon, visible at night and sometimes during the day. If you watch the moon on any night, you will observe that it moves with all the other night sky objects across the sky from east to west, so it too is caught up with the diurnal motion of the celestial sphere. But the patient observer will notice that over the course of a few hours the moon moves slightly eastward relative to the stars around it. It appears that the moon is behaving like the sun, with its own slow eastward motion superimposed upon the more rapid circling of the celestial sphere. By the same time next evening, we would certainly notice that the moon has moved through the stars a considerable distance, about 13 degrees. Like the sun, the moon, by moving steadily eastward, will eventually return to its starting position. If we define the starting position by the stars (i.e., returning to roughly the same place on the celestial sphere), then the moon completes one complete orbit in twenty-seven days and eight hours. If we define its position in relation to the sun, then, since the sun is also moving slowly, it will take a little longer to return to its corresponding position: twenty-nine days and thirteen hours. It is from this period that the word *month* ("moonth") derives.

The other objects of interest to ancient and medieval astronomers are harder to observe. There are five other star-like objects that, while caught up in the great whirling of the celestial sphere rising and setting each day, also have their own steady eastward motion. The names they acquired by Roman times follow those of the gods: Mercury, Venus, Mars, Jupiter, and Saturn. Of these, Jupiter and Venus are the easiest to spot, since they are the brightest and usually brighter than any star. These objects were named wandering stars, or planets (from the Greek meaning wanderer). To most modern day observers, however, they would appear just like stars rising and setting with the rest. The crucial feature for the ancient astronomers, though, was that these objects wandered around the sky. The wandering was not entirely erratic: just as the sun wanders exactly along the line of the ecliptic, the other wandering stars keep close to the ecliptic and certainly never

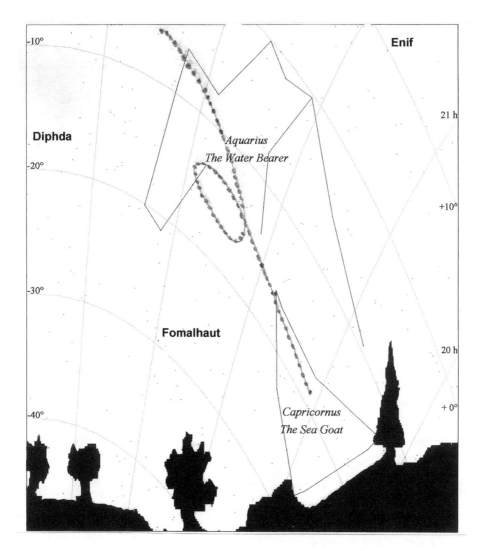

Figure 3: A loop of retrogression as followed by Mars over the period May 14 to December 6, 2003. The path shows successive positions of Mars as it moves across the background of fixed stars. It can be seen that a loop of retrogression occurred in the constellation of Aquarius. This was the closest approach of Mars to Earth over the last 60,000 years. (Path plotted by J. Cartwright using Voyager 3.2 software by Carina.)

leave the constellations of the zodiac. Their eastward motion periodically brings them back to the same region of sky. Table 10 shows these periods.

Table 10 shows that we have now included the moon and sun under the label *planet*. This was the case until the Copernican revolution in the seventeenth century (see chapter three). If we take the word *planet* to mean a star that wanders across the celestial sphere, then the sun and the moon must qualify. Certainly they look different than the other planets, but they are wanderers nevertheless.

**TABLE 10: APPROXIMATE PERIODS OF REVOLUTION
OF THE PLANETS SEEN FROM EARTH**

Planet	Period
Moon	About 28 days
Mercury	Just under 1 year
Venus	Just under 1 year
Sun	1 year
Mars	2 years
Jupiter	12 years
Saturn	29 years

There is one more set of observational facts we need to take cognizance of before we can proceed to the theories astronomers developed to explain them (and consider their use in medieval and later literature), and that is the phenomenon of retrograde motion. Although in time the wandering planet will return to that part of the zodiac it started from, the path through these constellations is not smooth and uniform. The speed of eastward motion varies, and sometimes the planets even stop and move westward for a while before resuming their journey toward the east. In others words, the planets loop their way through the zodiac. These loops are called loops of retrogression. The actual path of Mars from May 14 to December 6, 2003, is shown in Figure 3.

In *All's Well that Ends Well*, Shakespeare would have gotten a laugh from his audience by playing on this notion to describe the rather cowardly Parolles:

Helena: Monsieur Parolles, you were born under a charitable star.
Parolles: Under mars, I.
Helena: I especially think, under mars.
Parolles: Why under mars?
Helena: The wars hath so kept you under that you must needs be born
    under mars.
Parolles: When he was predominant.
Helena: When he was retrograde, I think, rather.
Paroles: Why think you so?
Helena: You go so much backward when you fight.
(Act I, scene i, l. 185-194)

Appearances Saved

Having recorded the phenomena, the obvious scientific question is: What is the real state of nature behind these appearances that can account for what we see?

What is the world really like such that we see these lights move across the sky in the way they do? It was the Greeks who first proposed answers to such questions. The dominant tradition among ancient astronomers was to assume that the earth was stationary and that the objects in Table 10 revolved around the earth. It was assumed that the order shown in Table 10 did represent the order of planets moving away from the earth. This was not simply a guess, since it could be seen that the moon, for example, moved in front of the sun during eclipses and occasionally moved in front of the stars and the other planets (lunar occultations). Intuitively, it was then reasoned that the slower the planet the more distant it would be, with the sphere of stars lying outside them all.

In the ancient world there were two basic types of models to account for the puzzling retrograde motion of the planets. Eudoxus (c. 400–347 B.C.) of Cnidus and Callipus of Cyzicus (370–300 B.C.) proposed a concentric sphere model of the heavens. Each planet was thought to be embedded in a series of spheres. Eudoxus proposed four each for Mercury, Venus, Mars, Jupiter, and Saturn, and three each for the sun and moon. The revolution of these spheres was adjusted to account for the motion of the planets across the heavens. The two innermost spheres (i.e., nearest the earth) revolved together to account for the retrograde motion of a planet; the next one accounted for its own motion through the zodiac (twenty-nine years for Saturn, twelve years for Jupiter, etc.); and the last one revolved every twenty-three hours and fifty-six minutes and accounted for the sidereal motion around Polaris. On the outside of the planetary spheres, a single sphere carried around the stars on an axis running through Polaris and the north pole of the earth. Callipus added seven more spheres to bring the model into closer alignment with the observations.

It is not clear whether Eudoxus really thought these spheres existed or whether they were just a mathematical exercise—merely a device to model the observations without suggesting some objective reality. Aristotle, however, wanted to bring astronomy in line with his system of physics, so the spheres for him had a physical reality. The initial problem was that since Saturn lay beyond Jupiter and was attached to its own innermost sphere, then this sphere would communicate its motion to the outer sphere of Jupiter; which would not do since the outer sphere, in the schemes of Eudoxus and Callipus, rotated once every sidereal day. To overcome this, Aristotle added four counter spheres to Mercury, Venus, the Sun, and Mars, and three counter spheres to Jupiter and Saturn. The purpose of the counter spheres was to lie beneath the innermost sphere of the planet above and effectively neutralize all but the sidereal motion. The moon obviously needed no counter spheres beneath it since it was the nearest planet to the earth. So, in the Aristotelian system fifty-five real ethereal spheres are required to account for planetary motion, topped by one more outer sphere carrying the stars. To an Aristotelian, a cross section of the universe would resemble a giant onion with layer nested upon layer, with each layer turning and sliding over the next carrying the planets around the stationary center of the earth.

One obvious question, among very many that will occur to the modern mind is what drives the spheres around? On this subject Aristotle left an ambiguous legacy. In *On the Heavens* he suggested that each celestial sphere moves in a circle "in virtue of its own nature"; but in his *Physics and Metaphysics* he suggests that each sphere is associated with an "intelligence" or spiritual power that has the ability to move the sphere while remaining unmoved itself. If we take Aristotle seriously, here we now require fifty-five "unmoved movers" for each of the planetary spheres and one unmoved mover for the stars. This last sphere had a special significance as The Prime Mover or primum mobile. Later commentaries on Aristotle speak as if this is the only mover of the heavens and from here all motion is transmitted downward. The idea of intelligences belonging to each sphere did, however, readily translate in Christendom into a role for angels (see Dante's *Paradise*).

Inevitably, as this incredibly complicated scheme was passed down to the Middle Ages there were revisions and simplifications. In popular accounts of the Aristotelian universe the subtlety of the various spheres was lost and one sphere was given for each planet—a maneuver that had an intuitive appeal but one that would hardly do to accurately explain the complex movements of the seven planets.

When the astronomers of the Middle Ages wanted to explain or predict the motions of the planets and stars more precisely, they turned to a rival scheme proposed by Ptolemy (c. 100–170 A.D.) in around 140 A.D. This scheme dispensed with the interlocking concentric spheres of Eudoxus, kept the same order of planets, but explained the puzzling retrograde motion using the idea of deferents and epicycles. Figure 4 shows the planet rotating on its epicycle while the center of the epicycle itself moves around a larger circle called the deferent. This scheme has the advantage of explaining the retrograde motion of a planet in terms of fewer spheres overall. In addition, the observational fact that a planet appears brighter to an earth-bound observer just in the middle of its retrograde loop—something totally inexplicable in Aristotle's scheme since the planet always remains the same distance away from the earth—is readily explained by Ptolemy's model. This scheme was wonderfully accurate at predicting the motions of the planets and was widely used by professional astronomers throughout the Middle Ages.

Another common notion in the Middle Ages was the belief in a profound connection between the motions of the spheres and musical harmony. The idea that the celestial spheres emitted musical notes as they turned goes back to the

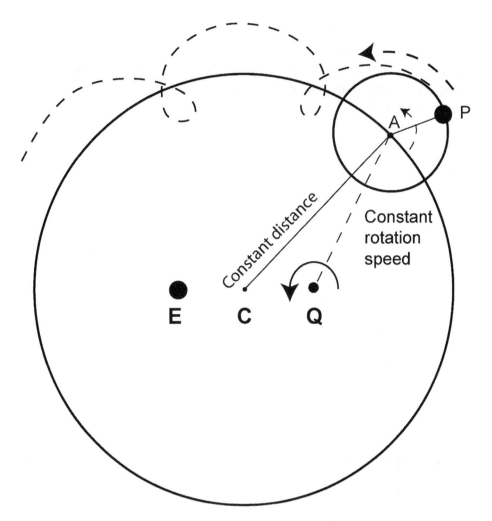

Figure 4: Ptolemy's Scheme to account for the retrograde and nonuniform motion of the planets. The planet P moves on an epicycle, the center of which (A) moves around a larger circle called the deferent, centered at C. The Earth (E) is slightly off center. The planet's rotational speed is constant about another point Q. (A. Bell and G. Martin)

Pythagoreans. Plato, in his *Republic,* also suggested a relationship between celestial motion and musical notes. Aristotle responded to the idea more literally and argued that no sound could be produced; otherwise it would be so loud as to shatter the crystalline spheres. The idea was carried on in Macrobius's *Dream of Scipio* (fifth century C.E.) and most importantly in *De musica* by Boethius (480–524). The "music of the spheres," as the idea came to be known, was taken by some to indicate that real sounds could be produced as the heavens turned, and by others as a poetic metaphor for a general harmony to be found in the laws of the universe.

In the late Middle Ages and the Renaissance, astronomy was an important part of the university curriculum. Moreover, in rural cultures such as Europe in this period, the observational facts of astronomy would have been much more widely known than they are today. In addition, most medieval thinkers really did think of heaven as just beyond the stars. It is not surprising, then, that the work of Dante and Chaucer is rich in astronomical imagery and that for them the heavens held a deep moral significance and exerted a powerful influence over human affairs.

Chronology of Significant Events

c. 450 B.C. Empedocles proposes his four-element theory of matter.

c. 330 B.C. Aristotle (384–322 B.C.) writes his major works on physics.

c. 140 A.D. Ptolemy (85–161 A.D.) publishes his major work *The Almagest*.

c. 1265 Roger Bacon (1214–1294) maintains that truth can be found in nature by observation and experiment as well as by consulting ancient texts.

Dante Alighieri born.

1300 Dante (1265–1321) begins his journey in the *Divine Comedy*.

1274 Death of Thomas Aquinas (1224–1274). Aquinas attempted to systematize Catholic theology and demonstrate its consistency with ancient science.

1348 First occurrence of the Black Death in England.

c. 1387 Geoffrey Chaucer (1340–1400) begins *The Canterbury Tales*.

1390–1393 John Gower publishes *Confessio Amantis*.

1516 Thomas Moore publishes *Utopia*.

1533–1535 Henry VIII excommunicated. Acts of Succession and Supremacy. Henry establishes himself as head of Church in England.

1536–1539 Abbeys suppressed in England. Breaking of religious images.

1543 Nicholaus Copernicus (1473–1543) publishes *De Revolutionibus*.

1543 Andreas Vesalius (1514–1564) of Brussels publishes his *De humani corporis fabrica* (*On the Structure of the Human Body*). It contains remarkably accurate descriptions of human anatomy.

1553 Agricola (1490–1555) publishes his *De re metallica*, the first systematic survey of mineralogy.

1558 Accession of Elizabeth I to throne in England.

1564 Birth of William Shakespeare.

Birth of Christopher Marlowe.

1572	Tycho Brahe observes a new star (super nova).
	Birth of Ben Jonson.
1577	Tycho Brahe (1546–1601) announces his Tychonic system of planetary orbits involving a stationary earth around which the sun moves but with the other planets orbiting the sun.
1588	Defeat of Spanish Armada.
1590	Spenser's *Faerie Queen* (Books I–III)
c. 1594	Shakespeare's Sonnets composed.
1598	Establishment of Gresham College in London.
1592–1599	Shakespeare's early plays, including *Henry VI, Richard II, Love's Labour's Lost.*
1600	William Gilbert (1540–1603) publishes *Concerning the Magnet* and proposes that the earth acts like a giant spherical magnet.
1604	First publication of Marlowe's *Faustus*, several years after its performance.
1605	Francis Bacon (1561–1626) publishes his *Advancement of Learning*. In this and subsequent works he discusses the rules of scientific procedure, arguing that knowledge comes from the study of nature not from pure deduction or copying the Ancients.
	Gunpowder plot by Jesuits to blow up English parliament.
	Shakespeare completes *King Lear.*
1607	English settlements established in Virginia.
1608	Lippershey and Jansen make the first telescope.
1609	Johannes Kepler (1571–1630) publishes his *Astronomia Nova* in which he presents his first two laws of planetary motion.
1610	Galileo Galilei (1564–1642) publishes his *Starry Messenger*, in which he describes his observations of the sun, the moon, and the planet Jupiter.
1616	Ben Jonson's *Works.*
1619	Johannes Kepler publishes his third law in *Harmonia Mundi.*
1620	*Novum Organum* by Bacon.
1621	Robert Burton's *Anatomy of Melancholy.*
1623	*The First Folio of Shakespeare* published.
1627	Bacon publishes *New Atlantis.*
1628	William Harvey (1578–1657) publishes *On the Motion of the Heart and Blood in Animals*, in which he shows that the blood circulates around the body.

1631 Death of John Donne. After his death Donne comes to be regarded as one of the leading metaphysical poets.

1632 Galileo publishes his book *Dialogue Concerning the Two Chief World Systems*.

1633 Galileo is put on trial for heresy.

1633 Donne's *Poems* published.

1637 Rene Descartes (1596–1650) publishes his *Discourse on Method*, in which he expounds the importance of deduction in science.

1642 Sir Thomas Browne's *Religio Medici*.

Civil war between king and parliament breaks out in Britain.

1644 Torricelli constructs a mercury barometer.

1649 Trial and execution of Charles I.

1649–1660 England becomes a republic under the protectorate of Oliver Cromwell.

1650 James Ussher publishes an estimate of the date of Creation as 4,004 B.C.

1651 *Leviathan* by Thomas Hobbes.

1660 Charles II restored. Theatres reopen.

1661 Robert Boyle publishes *The Sceptical Chemist*, a work that effectively demolished the medieval notion of the four elements—earth, air, fire, and water—and three principles—sulphur, salt, and mercury.

1662 The Royal Society of London receives its charter.

1665 Robert Hooke publishes *Micrographia*.

Great Plague in London.

1666 The French Academy of Science is founded.

Much of London destroyed in the Great Fire.

Margaret Cavendish publishes *Description of a New Blazing World*.

1667 John Milton (1608–1674) publishes his major work, *Paradise Lost*.

Margaret Cavendish makes a visit to the Royal Society.

Thomas Sprat publishes his *History of the Royal Society*.

1670 Dryden becomes poet laureate.

1671 Newton constructs a reflecting telescope.

1675 Foundation of Royal Observatory at Greenwich.

1676 *The Virtuoso* by Thomas Shadwell performed in London.

1687 Isaac Newton (1642–1727) publishes his *Principia Mathematica*.

1690   *Essay Concerning Human Understanding* by John Locke. In this influential work, Locke argues that mind is a product of matter and that knowledge is only acquired through the senses. He proposes the "blank slate" view of the mind.

William Temple publishes *Of Ancient and Modern Learning*, a milestone in the debate between advocates of ancient and modern learning.

1694   William Wotton publishes a reply to Temple's work of 1690 in the form of a book: *Reflections upon Ancient and Modern Learning*.

1703   Newton becomes president of the Royal Society.

1704   Newton publishes his *Optics*.

1704   Jonathan Swift publishes *Battle of the Books* and *A Tale of a Tub*.

1719   *Robinson Crusoe* by Daniel Defoe.

1726   *Gulliver's Travels* by Jonathan Swift.

1727   Death of Isaac Newton.

James Thomson publishes his ode *To the Memory of Isaac Newton*.

1730   *The Seasons* by James Thompson.

1732   Alexander Pope begins *An Essay on Man*.

1735   Carolus Linnaeus publishes his *Systema Naturae* and so begins the modern system of classification.

1739   David Hume's *Treatise of Human Nature*.

1743   Final version of Alexander Pope's *The Dunciad* published.

1752   Benjamin Franklin uses a kite to demonstrate the electrical nature of lightning.

1764   James Watt invents separate condenser, a device that enormously improves the efficiency of the steam engine.

1767   *Tristam Shandy* by Laurence Sterne.

1773   John Harrison is finally awarded the full prize for his chronometer that is accurate enough to solve the problem of longitude.

1774   Joseph Priestley discovers oxygen and terms it dephlogisticated air.

1776   American Declaration of Independence.

1781   William Herschel discovers Uranus.

Immanuel Kant publishes *Critique of Pure Reason*, in which he argues that the mind imposes order on experience (synthetic a priori judgments) in order to make sense of it. Many regard this as a Copernican revolution in philosophy.

1783   Blake's *Poetical Sketches.*

1787   Mary Wollstonecraft's *Thoughts on the Education of Daughters.*

1789   Antoine Lavoisier (1734–1794) publishes his *Traite Elementaire de Chimie* (*Elementary Treatise on Chemistry*), one of the main foundation blocks of modern chemistry.

Beginning of the French revolution: The Fall of the Bastille on July 14, Declaration of the Rights of Man, August 4.

1789   Gilbert White's *Natural History of Selborne.*

Erasmus Darwin publishes *The Loves of the Plants.*

1791   Galvani publishes his ideas on animal electricity.

1792   Mary Wollstonecraft publishes *A Vindication of the Rights of Woman.*

1793   Blake publishes *America* and *Visions of the Daughters of Albion.*

William Godwin publishes *Political Justice.*

1797   Death of Mary Wollstonecraft shortly after she gives birth to a daughter, the future Mary Shelley.

1798   *Lyrical Ballads* by William Wordsworth and Samuel Taylor Coleridge.

1798   Essay on the Principle of Population by Thomas Malthus.

William Godwin publishes *Memoirs of the Author of The Rights of Woman.*

1795   James Hutton publishes *Theory of the Earth.*

1800   Humphrey Davy discovers nitrous oxide, uses it to help him compose poetry, and suggests its use as an anaesthetic.

1802   William Paley publishes *Natural Theology.*

1807   Abolition of the slave trade in British Empire.

1808   John Dalton publishes his *Atomic Theory.*

1809   Jean Baptiste Lamarck publishes his speculations about the transmutation of species in *Philosophie zoologique.*

1812–1818   Lord Byron publishes *Childe Harold's Pilgrimage.*

1815   William Smith publishes his stratigraphic map of Britain.

1816   As a result of a volcanic explosion the previous year, this year is known as the year without a summer.

1817   *Poems* by Keats.

1818   Mary Shelley publishes *Frankenstein.*

1820   *Prometheus Unbound* by Shelley and *Lamia* by Keats.

1825	First steam locomotive railway, Stockton to Darlington in the United Kingdom.
1826	*The Last of the Mohicans* by James Fenimore Cooper.
1828	Friedrich Wohler synthesizes urea. His work helps break down vitalist approaches to organic chemistry.
1830–1833	Charles Lyell publishes his *Principles of Geology*, which argues that the earth's surface is the result of everyday effects acting over vast periods of time.
1831	Charles Darwin begins his voyage on *The Beagle*.
1840	Edgar Allan Poe, *Tales of the Grotesque and Arabesque*.
1844	*Vestiges* published anonymously by Chambers.
1850	Alfred Tennyson's *In Memoriam*.
1851	Herman Melville's *Moby-Dick*.
1853	Exhibition of the Industry of All Nations, New York.
1854	Auguste Comte's *Cours de philosophie positive* completed.
1854	Henry David Thoreau's *Walden*.
1855	Walt Whitman's *Leaves of Grass*.
1859	*On the Origin of Species by Natural Selection* published by Darwin.
1864	Jules Verne's *Journey to the Centre of the Earth*.
1865	Rudolph Clausius introduces the concept of entropy.
1865	Gregor Mendel publishes work on genetics but is largely ignored.
1866	Transatlantic telegraph begins operation.
1867	*New Poems* by Mathew Arnold.
1869	First transcontinental railway opens in United States.
	Jules Verne's *20,000 Leagues Under the Sea*.
1871	Darwin publishes *The Descent of Man*.
1871	*Middlemarch* by George Eliot.
1876	Telephone invented by Alexander Graham Bell.
1882	The printed version of Mathew Arnold's famous Cambridge Rede lecture published. In this lecture Arnold considers whether a curriculum should be based on the natural sciences or literature and the humanities. Arnold argues for the latter and so enters into a debate with T. H. Huxley.
1882	First generating station supplying electricity to customers opens in New York.

1886	*Strange Case of Dr Jekyll and Mr Hyde* by Robert Louis Stevenson.
1887	Albert Michelson and Edward Morley measure speed of light and conclude that the ether probably does not exist.
1887	First Sherlock Holmes mystery published.
1888	Hertz discovers radio waves.
1891	*Tess of the D'Urbervilles* by Thomas Hardy.
1895	*The Time Machine* by H. G. Wells.
1896	*The Island of Dr Moreau* by H. G. Wells.
1897	*The Invisible Man* by H. G. Wells.
1897	J. J. Thompson discovers the electron.
1900	Max Planck proposes his quantum theory.
	Guglielmo Marconi transmits radio waves across the Atlantic.
	Gregor Mendel's work on heredity rediscovered.
1902	Pierre and Marie Curie discover radium.
1903	Wright Brothers make first heavier-than-air flight.
1905	Albert Einstein publishes his theory of special relativity and his explanation of the photoelectric effect.
1908	Ford Model T introduced.
1909	Louis Bleriot makes first crossing of the English Channel in an aeroplane.
1912	Alfred Wegener proposes a theory of continental drift.
1913	Einstein's General Theory of Relativity.
1913	J. B. Watson founds the behaviorist school of psychology.
	Sigmund Freud publishes *Interpretation of Dreams*.
1914–1918	First World War.
1921	Karel Capek's R.U.R. performed in Prague.
1923	French physicist Louis de Broglie argues for the wave-like nature of particles.
1924	Edwin Hubble demonstrates that ours is not the only galaxy.
1925	Scopes "Monkey Trial": John T. Scopes convicted for teaching evolution in Tennessee.
1926	Hugo Gernsback launches *Amazing Stories*.
1927	Werner Heisenberg proposes the Uncertainty Principle.
	First Transatlantic flight by Charles Lindbergh.

1929	Hubble publishes paper indicating that galaxies moving away from our own ("red-shifted") move faster the farther away they are. This idea is fundamental to the acceptance of the theory of the Big Bang and the expanding Universe.
1930	Olaf Stapledon's *Last and First Men*.
1932	James Chadwick discovers the neutron, a particle predicted by Ernest Rutherford in 1920.
	Aldous Huxley's *Brave New World*.
1937	Theodore Dobzhansky publishes his *Genetics and the Origin of Species* and links Mendelian genetics with Darwinian evolution.
1938	John W. Campbell takes over as editor of *Astounding*.
1939	New York World's Fair.
	Neils Bohr predicts the fission of Uranium 235 by slow neutrons.
1939–1945	Second World War.
1941	Robert Heinlein's "By His Bootstraps."
	First of Isaac Asimov's robot stories.
1942	Enrico Fermi designs first atomic pile that is then brought into operation in Chicago.
1945	First atomic bombs exploded.
1947	John Bardeen, Walter Brattain, and William Shockley develop first transistor.
	First of the Macy conferences on cybernetics.
1952	American scientists explode the world's first fusion bomb.
1953	James Watson and Francis Crick explain the structure of DNA.
	Bernard Wolfe's *Limbo*.
1959	Charles Snow delivers his influential Cambridge Rede lecture on two cultures. Snow argues that a gulf has developed between the sciences and the humanities to the detriment of both.
1961	Edward Lorenz's computerized "toy weather" offers first insight into "chaotic" systems.
1962	First "live" telecast by satellite.
	Thomas Kuhn's *The Structure of Scientific Revolutions*.
1964	The British biologist William Hamilton provides a genetic explanation for the existence of altruism, a problem that Darwin never adequately solved. His work is an important foundation in the rise of sociobiology and what was later to become evolutionary psychology.

1964   Michael Moorcock takes over editorship of *New Worlds*.

1965   Arno Penzias and Robert Wilson discover uniform microwave radiation in the universe, providing evidence for the theory of the Big Bang and expanding universe.

1966   Thomas Pynchon's *The Crying of Lot 49*.

Michel Foucault's *Archaeology of Knowledge*.

1967   First human heart transplant.

Pamela Zoline's "The Heat Death of the Universe."

1968   Arthur C. Clarke's *2001: A Space Odyssey*.

1969   John Wheeler coins the term "black hole" to describe a collapsed star.

Neil Armstrong becomes the first human being to walk on the surface of another world, the moon.

1975   E.O. Wilson publishes *Sociobiology*.

1976   *The Selfish Gene* by Richard Dawkins.

1977   Russian scientist Ilya Prigogine wins Nobel Prize for his work on thermodynamics and "far from equilibrium" systems.

Benoit Mandelbrot publishes *The Fractal Geometry of Nature*.

1979   The American scientist Walter Alvarez detects the presence of a layer of iridium-rich material at the Mesozoic-Cenozoic boundary associated with the extinction of the dinosaurs, suggesting an asteroid impact.

1984   William Gibson's *Neuromancer*; coins word *cyberspace*.

1984   The Harvard biologist and conservationist Edward Wilson publishes his book *Biophilia*, in which he argues passionately for the need to conserve biodiversity. He suggests that a feeling for life in all its richness (biophilia) is a deep-seated human emotion.

1988   Stephen Hawking publishes *A Brief History of Time*.

1992   William Gibson and Bruce Sterling's *The Difference Engine*.

1994   An eleven-member jury in Anchorage awards $5 billion punitive damages against Exxon Corporation for the 1989 Exxon Valdez oil spill in Alaska. The damages are awarded on behalf of 12,000 people harmed by the 11-million-gallon oil spill in Prince William Sound that polluted the fishing grounds of Alaska and 1,500 miles of coastline.

1995   Stephen Baxter's *The Time Ships*.

1996   The New York physicist Alan Sokal publishes a hoax article in the journal *Social Text*.

1997   Scientists at the Roslin Institute in Edinburgh announce the world's first cloned sheep.

2000   Scientists in London and Washington, D.C., announce they have the first rough draft of the human genome.

General Bibliographic Essay

For the student of this field a most useful volume is *The Relations of Literature and Science: An Annotated Bibliography of Scholarship 1880–1980*, edited by W. Schatzberg, R. A. Waite, and J. K. Johnson (New York: Modern Languages Association of America). Sources are listed by century and by author, making this an invaluable research tool. Sadly the sources listed stop at 1980 and there has been no more recent edition of this work. For more recent work "The Relations of Literature and Science," a bibliography that appears annually in *Configurations: A Journal of Literature, Science, and Technology*, is useful. The website of The Society for Literature and Science (the organization behind *Configurations*) and from which resources can be located is http://sls.press.jhu.edu/info.html.

For literary extracts that pertain to science *The Faber Book of Science*, edited by John Carey (London and Boston: Faber and Faber, 1995), is quite useful. Carey provides a brief discussion before each extract. The extracts range from the Renaissance to the twentieth century. A similar volume is *The Longman Literary Companion to Science*, edited by Walter Gratzer (Harlow, Longman, 1989). This and the Carey book make an interesting contrast since Carey is a literary critic and Gratzer a scientist. Carey tends to choose extracts that show scientific writing at its best in terms of style and clarity, while Gratzer aims to provide material that also has social and historical interest. Douglas Bush gives an overview of the impact of science on English poetry in *Science and English Poetry 1590–1950* (New York: Oxford University Press, 1950). Bush details some useful points of contact, but his treatment is limited by his intention to show that science has somehow robbed man of his spiritual dimension.

For a readable and clear examination of how Western literature has represented scientists few books rival Roslynn Haynes's *From Faust to Strangelove* (Baltimore and London: The John Hopkins University Press, 1994). A valuable reference work is the *Encyclopedia of Literature and Science*, edited by Pamela Gossin (Westport: Greenwood Press, 2002). The contributors are experts in their field and although some of the entries are rather short there are several that give historical surveys or examine the state of theoretical thinking in this field. For a volume dealing explicitly with astronomical references in English literature see *The High Firmament*, by A. J. Meadows (Leicester: Leicester University Press, 1969).

An interesting treatment of the whole question of the "bridge" between the cultures of science and literature is given in the form of a dialogue between a scientist and a literary scholar in *Science and Literature: Bridging the Two Cultures* (Gainesville: University of Florida Press, 2001). The book is especially useful for characterizing the methods and approaches in current use in the sciences and the humanities and how these bear on works of literature that contain significant scientific content.

For a selection of primary sources covering the period 1660 to 1834 an excellent series of volumes has recently been published: (in four volumes) Literature and Science 1600–1834, edited by Judith Hawley (London: Pickering and Chatto, 2003). The texts are expensive but extracts deal with plants, animals, natural philosophy, chemistry, earth science, body and mind, and the culture of science.

Glossary

Alchemy: a pre-scientific mode of investigation of the natural world, often popularly understood as the search for a method of transmuting base metals into gold. The principle of transmutation is central to alchemy and stands as a figure for the transformation and enlightenment of the alchemist himself.

Allegory: a language use, or particularly a form of literature that depicts mythical or metaphysical relationships between things, people, or ideas in terms of a narrative or pictorial representation. An allegorical reading of Melville's *Moby-Dick*, for example, would see Captain Ahab's chase of the White Whale in terms of a sinful humanity challenging the order of God's creation.

Analogy: a way of thinking that understands a thing or concept in terms of another thing or object, in a relation of likeness. This method was common in pre-nineteenth-century scientific thinking.

Associationism: a way of thinking about how the mind collects and processes impressions of the external world. It described change in an individual's life as the outcome of past experience. Within this view, the associations of pleasure and pain with events and experience provided a vision of how humans and society as a whole could be improved. This early form of psychology was allied, therefore, with utilitarian social thought. It was popularized by David Hartley and exerted considerable influence over the early thought of Coleridge and Wordsworth.

Astrolabe: a portable instrument, usually between 10 and 20 cm in diameter, used to make observations in astronomy. It was popular in the Middle Ages, and European and Arabic versions exist. It could be used to measure the position of some major stars and the sun at various times of the year. It enabled the observer's latitude to be calculated. The poet Geoffrey Chaucer wrote a treatise on the astrolabe.

Atavism: a mode of thinking common in the late nineteenth century, which understood natural selection to occasionally produce retrogressive features. This was particularly important in the work of the Italian criminologist Cesare Lombroso, who catalogued "criminal types" in terms of the facial features and understood them to be "throwbacks" to a "less civilized" period of human development. See also degeneration.

Cartesian: an adjective that relates to the philosophy of Rene Descartes. Cartesian is usually taken to mean a form of dualism where matter and spirit are regarded as separate entities.

Catastrophism: one of the two contending theories of geology in the early nineteenth century. Opposed to uniformitarianism, catastrophism understood the geological and geographical formations of the world to be formed by a series of catastrophic events, such as floods, earthquakes, and vulcanism. One branch of catastrophism sought to reconcile science with the biblical narrative of the Flood. Later geological thinking brought the two opposing theories together.

Chaos theory: a branch of contemporary science that grew from fluid dynamics in the 1970s. It seeks to complicate the old opposition of "order" and "chaos" by suggesting that "far from equilibrium" systems actually conform to previously unacknowledged ordering principles, such as periodic frequency. It is also a term used, in the popular imagination, to indicate the kind of recursive mathematical structures known as fractals.

Consilience: a word made popular by William Whewell in the early nineteenth century and revived recently by E. O. Wilson. Consilience is a state of understanding such that all branches of knowledge are harmonious and share a common framework. In Wilson's view, consilience is a desirable goal for the humanities and the sciences.

Correspondences: an outlook on natural phenomena that supposed that events on one plane (e.g., the social) reverberated or were mirrored by events on another (e.g., the cosmic). Particularly associated with Elizabethan literature, correspondences provide detail on the linkages between the microcosm and the macrocosm.

Cybernetics: a science of information, most associated with the work of Norbert Wiener, author of *The Human Use of Human Beings*. In studying the workings of a computational device, cyberneticists assumed an analogy between a computer and the human brain, and therefore conceived of the human body as an organic machine.

Cyberpunk: a form of science fiction that came to prominence in the 1980s, most noticeably in the work of William Gibson. A hip, contemporary kind of fiction, usually set in a near-future dominated by corporations and computer technology, infused with references to popular culture and rock and roll, with outsider characters at the center of the narrative.

Cyborgs: in common terms, a figure that imagines the melding of the human body with technology. It has been used as a utopian figure, particularly in the work of Donna Haraway, in an attempt to rethink the body outside of received categories of gender, sexuality, and biology.

Deconstruction: a form of critical or literary theory most associated with the work of Jacques Derrida. While often caricatured as suggesting "there is nothing outside the text," deconstruction is a practice of close reading of texts that exposes the unacknowledged philosophical or cultural assumptions that inform its production.

Degeneration: a kind of popular discourse in the late nineteenth century that took natural selection and inverted it. Writers such as Max Nordau applied crude evolutionary theory to contemporary social and cultural upheavals to suggest that humanity was moving back "down the evolutionary ladder," becoming less "civilized" and more "savage."

Deism: a religious movement of thought (an unorthodox branch of Christianity) popular in the seventeenth and eighteenth centuries. Deists believed that God had supplied natural physical and moral laws but did not thereafter directly intervene in the affairs of the world. Voltaire was the best-known French advocate of deism. Many of the founding fathers of the United States, such as Benjamin Franklin and Thomas Jefferson were essentially deists. This line of thought fit well with the adulation of Newton (who had described God's laws) in the eighteenth century.

Dualism: a view that mind and matter are separate entities and not reducible to each other.

Dystopia: the inverse of utopia. An imagined place, society, or culture that is worse, more repressive, than the one that produced the dystopia. Typically, the dystopia imagines a totalitarian state where the citizens are de-individualized and the society is run on principles of efficiency or power. Key examples are George Orwell's *Nineteen Eighty-four* and Aldous Huxley's *Brave New World*. Dystopias are usually read as estranged versions of our own world.

Ecliptic: an imaginary line running across the celestial sphere (the sky) on which the sun moves throughout the year.

Elements: in older usage, this term referred to what was understood to be the four constituents of all matter: fire, air, earth, and water. In later usage, it refers to the indivisible atoms of matter that, in combination, form the basis of chemistry. They are catalogued in the Periodic Table.

Enlightenment: a term (from the German *Aufklärung*) that represents the dominant philosophical spirit of the eighteenth century, particularly in France and Germany (but also in Scotland). This period, known as the Age of Reason, is marked by scientific and rational enquiry and religious skepticism. The late eighteenth- and early nineteenth-century cultural phenomenon of Romanticism is often seen as a reaction to the rationalism of the Enlightenment.

Entropy: a term coined by Rudolph Clausius that refers to the amount of energy lost in any dynamic process, particularly important in thermodynamics. The entropic vision of the universe entails the "running down" of all energy systems to final "heat death." It was taken up by twentieth-century writers as a way of characterizing the increasing social dislocation, isolation, and fragmentation of contemporary life.

Epicycle: a geometric device used by early astronomers, particularly Ptolemy, to account for the retrograde motion of the planets as viewed from earth.

Epistemology: the branch of philosophical enquiry that deals with problems of knowledge. It is particularly concerned with how the mind is able to construct reliable knowledge of the external world.

Estrangement: in literary study, this usually means the process by which a literary text brings about in the reader (or in drama, in the audience) an awareness of the process of reading or spectating while the text is being read or performed. In the study of science fiction, it has been suggested that "estrangement" is the means by which the science fiction represents "our" world in other (alien) terms. See also dystopia.

Extrapolation: the way in which the science fiction text takes a "what if" scenario, or a scientific principle, and develops a coherent alternative world from that starting point.

Fall (the): the idea that following the original sin of Adam and Eve, humans fell from a state of grace to their vexed position today. The Fall was also thought to have affected the whole of creation—hence the idea that after the Fall some creatures became hostile to humans. Bacon thought that scientific knowledge could help redeem man from the Fall and help him to live more comfortably.

Fin-de-siècle: literally, "end of the century" in French. The century this refers to is the nineteenth, but the term refers to a "spirit" or "temper" rather than simply a period. Typically, fin-de-siècle texts were published in the 1880s and 1890s, but not all texts from this period come under this category. Themes of decadence, degeneration, monstrosity, altered states of being and consciousness, and a playfulness with regard to gender and sexuality can be found in such texts as Stoker's *Dracula* and Oscar Wilde's *The Picture of Dorian Gray*, and the pictures of Aubrey Beardsley.

Firmament: the sphere of fixed stars. Although the stars move across the night sky, they remain fixed in their relative positions to each other.

Frontier: literally, the barrier or border between two states or areas. In American culture, however, this refers to a mythical line between "civilization" and "savagery" in the western United States in the eighteenth and nineteenth centuries. It is usually invested with greater significance than simply a geographical boundary, indicating what the historian Frederick Turner (in 1893) argued was the birthplace of American individualism, self-sufficiency, and even democracy.

Geocentric: a view that the earth is the center of the universe. This was the common assumption from the time of the Greeks until the early seventeenth century.

Great Chain of Being: an idea that began with Plato and Aristotle and suggested that the universe was arranged hierarchically, with different classes of beings at each level. God was the highest level and man stood somewhere between the beasts and the angels.

Humanism: the view that human life and human nature is central rather than any religious or transcendental set of values. Renaissance humanism, however, was quite different from the modern form. It began with literary studies in the universities of Italy in the thirteenth and fourteenth centuries and was concerned with the translation and exegesis of ancient texts.

Humours: fluids or components of the human body. The four humours (yellow bile, black bile, blood, and phlegm) were thought to be linked with the four elements. Humoural theory was an early form of physiology that supposed that the humours were also under the influence of celestial objects and that illness was caused by an imbalance in the humours.

Heliocentric: a model of the universe that supposed that the sun and not the earth was central. Copernicus proposed a heliocentric view in 1543.

Imagination (Romantic): a faculty of the mind that was thought to have the power to apprehend reality in a more direct way than a mere passive acceptance of experience. The Romantic poets stressed the importance of the imagination in the mind's creative construction of reality.

Industrialism: a term, now usually used negatively, to describe the social and cultural changes brought about by the Industrial Revolution. This is connected to the massive growth in urbanization in the nineteenth century, and with the creation of a working class to populate the factories of the capitalist economies of Europe and America. Blake's "dark satanic mills" and Dickens's "Coketown" (from *Hard Times)* are the emblems of the dirtiness, oppressiveness, and spiritual emptiness of industrialism opposed by Romantic and Victorian critics.

Lamarkianism: a form of evolutionary theory that derived from the theories of the early-nineteenth-century scientist Jean-Baptiste Lamarck. Lamarck suggested in his *Philosophie Zoologique* (1809) that "transmutations" might occur where animal species adapt to a changing environment. He thought that no species became extinct: it "transmuted" into another form through the inheritance of "acquired characteristics" from one generation to the next. Rejected by T. H. Huxley and others, it survived in Soviet biology until the later twentieth century.

Macrocosm: the world at large that was supposed in Renaissance thought to both reflect and determine activities on a lower plane such as a political state or even the human body.

Materialism: a view that the primary stuff of being is matter, and that other apparently different forms, such as mind, are merely different manifestations of matter.

Medieval: usually refers to the European Middle Ages, between the eleventh and fifteenth centuries. The period before this, between the collapse of the Roman Empire and the end of the first millennium, is known as the Dark Ages, where the learning and scientific advances of the classical period were lost (though some were preserved, particularly in the Islamic world). The medieval period is characterized by a partial recovery of the means of scientific and philosophical enquiry, and politically by the beginnings of the European nation state.

Mephistophelean: refers to the figure of Mephistopheles, the diabolical tempter of Dr. Faustus in Christopher Marlowe's play *Dr Faustus*. Mephistopheles encourages the alchemical or magical overreaching of Faustus by offering him a bargain: all earthly knowledge and power in return for Faustus's eternal soul. Forerunner of the Frankenstein "mad scientist" who challenges both God and nature, the "Faustian bargain" reaffirms God's order by dooming the overreacher.

Metaphysics: literally "after physics," referring to the topics considered by Aristotle in books following his physics. Metaphysics is a concern with intangible ideas, the ultimate nature of reality, and hence a level of reality not easily apprehended or tested by ordinary experience. The metaphysical poets were so called because of their treatment of life, love, death, and faith.

Microcosm: see macrocosm and correspondences.

Modernism: a cultural and artistic movement driven by the changes in society in the first half of the twentieth century. Characterized by experimentation, a break from "classical" and "realist" modes of representation, and fragmentations in time and space, modernist art and texts both embodied and brought attention to the "shocks" of contemporary life. Typical modernist works include the subjectivism of Proust's *A la recherché du temps perdu*, Joyce's *Ulysses*, and Virginia Woolf's *To the Lighthouse*; the kaleidoscopic, fractured canvases and sculptures of cubism (Picasso and

Braque), dada (Duchamp) and futurism (Marinelli); and the montage cinema of Sergei Eisenstein.

Music of the spheres: a belief, initially suggested by the Pythagoreans, that the planets emit music as they move about the earth (or sun). The idea need not be taken literally and can also be used to refer to the suggestion that mathematical and quasi-musical harmonies govern the behavior of the heavens.

Naturalism: the position that all phenomena have natural (rather than supernatural or divinely driven) causes. It is a founding assumption of science that the world is governed by natural causes.

Natural selection: an idea advanced by Charles Darwin (and others such as Alfred Wallace) to explain how species diverge from one another and how species become adapted to their environments. It is a process by which those spontaneously arising variants in each generation will fare better or worse in leaving offspring according to whether their variations are favorable or unfavorable in a competitive environment. Favorable variations tend to be preserved and gradually become the norm. Unlike Lamarckianism, natural selection does not suppose that characteristics that are acquired by an animal by its own efforts are passed on to its offspring.

Natural theology: originally the title of a book by William Paley, natural theology celebrated Nature as bearing the signature of the divine hand. Paley's argument is the most recognizable form of the "argument from design." Paley suggested that if, while walking, you came across a rock, you would not necessarily think that the rock had been "made"; however, if you came across a watch, then you would certainly deduce a creator of that watch, because it cannot create itself. The world, or Creation in Paley's terms, by comparison is infinitely complex and diverse; therefore it implies the presence of an infinitely powerful creator.

Ontology: the branch of philosophical enquiry that deals with problems of "being," of what it is to exist.

Paradox: a proposition that seems to combine two absurdly contradictory elements or statements. It is often used to illuminate scientific or philosophical problems. Xeno's arrow, for instance, in flight, must travel from A (the bow) to B (the target); however, it must pass through midpoint C. To get to C, it must first travel through a point midway between A and C, point D. To get to this, however, it must first pass through a point midway between point A and point D, and so on to infinity. The paradox suggests, of course, against "common sense," that the arrow will never arrive.

Paradigm: this word has several meanings in literary studies. In relation to science, the word derives from Thomas Kuhn's usage in *The Structure of Sci-*

entific Revolutions. A paradigm is a set of assumptions, or an organizing intellectual framework, that determines the way in which scientific enquiry proceeds. These paradigms are periodic and subject to change, such as from geocentric (Earth-centered) to heliocentric (sun-centered) models of the solar system.

Phlebotomy: the medical practice of blood letting, a common procedure from the Middle Ages up to the nineteenth century.

Platonism: a school of thought following the ideas of the Greek philosopher Plato (c. 428–347 B.C.). Plato tended to reject what we would now call scientific rationalism (that is, the testing of ideas against experience) in favor of logical argument. For Plato and his followers, it was mind and not matter that was the fundamental entity in the universe. The world around us was merely an imperfect copy of abstract and eternal ideas or forms. Platonic teachings led, therefore, to a distrust of sensory experiences but valued the contribution of mathematics.

Postmodernism: a once fashionable term used to describe contemporary culture (in the 1980s and early 1990s), subject to a wide variety of possible interpretations. In the "science wars" of the later 1990s, and in some scientists' attack on literary theory, the word postmodernism comes to stand for a loss of rigor and values in the humanities, a catch-all for the importation of francophone linguistic and philosophical ideas into literary academia, which some have seen as detrimental to humanist study.

Prime Mover (*primum mobile*): an entity suggested by Aristotle as ultimately responsible for all motion in the universe. The Prime Mover exists outside of the sphere of stars and animates the whole universe such that the outer turning sphere communicates its motion downwards. In the late Middle Ages it was an easy step to identify the Prime Mover with God.

Promethean: in Greek mythology Prometheus stole fire from the gods to give to mankind and was punished for his efforts. By metaphorical extension, Promethean refers to that view of science that suggests that it exploits the forces of nature for human improvement.

Purgatory: in Dante's *Divine Comedy*, Purgatory is a mountain on the opposite side of the world from the entrance to Hell. After passing through the circles of Hell (in the *Inferno*), where he sees the figures of the damned (culminating in a vision of Satan and Judas), Dante must toil up the levels of the mountain of Purgatory and have his own sins removed so he can ascend to the divine vision of celestial spheres in *Paradiso*.

Puritan: a form of Protestant Christianity, particularly in sixteenth- and seventeenth-century England. Its members sought to further purge the English Church of what it believed to be unscriptural and corrupt (that is to say,

Catholic) practices. It reached its high-water mark in Cromwell's Commonwealth, but under the Restoration of King Charles II they found life in England increasingly intolerable. The Puritans were seen to be particularly important to the founding of the United States. As the "Pilgrim Fathers," the Puritan inheritance (especially in New England) is the subject of much historical debate and is central to Nathaniel Hawthorne's fiction.

Realism: a philosophical stance that supposes that human knowledge can be a true reflection of objective reality and not a mere subjective impression or cultural artifact.

Reformation: the religious and cultural movement by which the Protestant form of Christianity broke from Roman Catholicism, thereby precipitating centuries of conflict. It is central to the vital artistic and cultural legacy of the Renaissance.

Relativism: a philosophical position that supposes that human knowledge is relative to time, place, and agent, and that therefore it is unfixed and changing. Radical relativism would claim that it is meaningless to talk about any correspondence between knowledge and the external world.

Renaissance: a European cultural movement that originated in Italy in the fourteenth century. The term *renaissance* was applied to this period in the eighteenth century and meant a rebirth. The Renaissance continued in Western Europe until the seventeenth century. It was associated with new developments in art, architecture, science, biblical criticism, and the study of languages. Major figures of the Renaissance include the politician Machiavelli, the artists Michaelangelo and Raphael, writers such as Montaigne, Cervantes, Bacon, Marlowe, and Shakespeare, and scientists such as Galileo. One conservative aspect of Renaissance scholarship was its overriding concern to establish what the ancient authors had concluded rather than seeking fresh knowledge.

Restoration: In England, this refers to the reign of Charles II, son of the deposed and beheaded Charles I. After the English Civil War, Oliver Cromwell and Parliament ruled Britain until his death, a period in which the arts were suppressed, especially drama. The Restoration period is particularly connected to dramatic comedy in the arts, and the whole era is today identified with hedonism and license. However, this era saw the beginnings of modern commerce in London and is also the great birthplace of the scientific revolution in Britain. Charles II was highly interested in, and patronized, the sciences and, in the form of the Royal Society, gave them a legitimacy and a centrality they had not previously commanded.

Robot: a word coined by Czech writer Karel Capek in his play *R.U.R.* (Rossum's Universal Robots). The word usually refers to some kind of mechanical man, as opposed to the human-machine interface suggested by the word cyborg, or the computerized entity of the AI or artificial intelligence. The famous "Three Laws of Robotics" were proposed by Isaac Asimov in the short stories collected in *I, Robot*. Unlike the cyborg or AI, the robot is definitely less than human.

Romanticism: a very general term describing a Europe-wide cultural movement, largely reacting against the philosophical rationalism of the Enlightenment. The term covers a very wide set of literary figures, such as Schiller and Goethe in Germany, and Coleridge, Wordsworth, and Shelley in England, none of whom can be safely bracketed together in terms of their politics or even their poetic practice. However, what connects them is the centrality of feeling, communicated by a poetic language unconfined by classical forms or diction; the poet as dreamer, outsider, or "unacknowledged legislator" of the world and its sensibilities; and a connection with states of psychological "otherness," either in Coleridge's hallucinatory "Kubla Khan" or in Romanticism's dark double, the Gothic.

Scholasticism: a medieval form of scholarship that aimed to reconcile the teachings of Aristotle with Christian theology. One of the most important scholastic philosophers was Thomas Aquinas.

Science fiction: a form of popular fiction (and film) that represents beings, worlds, times, or states other than our own, but which makes us reconsider the assumptions we bring to our own world. See also estrangement.

Sexual selection: together with natural selection, a major plank in Darwin's account of the appearance and behavior of species. It is based on the idea that one sex will choose features that it prefers in a member of the opposite sex. Over time this choice will exert a selective force, so that animals will have attributes "designed" to please the opposite sex. The peacock's tail is one of the most extreme cases of how a female (the peahen) has driven males into producing extravagant features.

Social Darwinism: a form of thinking pioneered by Herbert Spencer that understood society in terms of species evolution. It was Spencer who coined the phrase "survival of the fittest," and in his hands "fittest" becomes not best adapted, but strongest. In Social Darwinism, the cultural organization of society directly corresponded to its intellectual, psychological, or "mental development." Evolution was also seen as taking place between the human "races" (ethnic groupings understood as species), which were in direct competition with each other. According to this version of Darwinism, the Caucasians would win the evolutionary battle, and others would necessarily perish. Social Darwinism reached its highpoint in the late nineteenth century, not coincidentally also the highpoint of imperialism.

Sublunary and superlunary: two regions of the universe below and above the sphere of the moon respectively. In Aristotelian thinking the division was important, since only below the sphere of the moon could change and decay occur. The appearance of new stars and comets above the moon, therefore, posed special problems. The idea of a fundamental distinction between these two areas began to disappear in the early seventeenth century.

Tabula rasa: literally an erased tablet. A view of the mind that suggests that at birth each human mind is a blank slate and only acquires form and shape through experience. It was initially thought to be a socially progressive notion, but research in biology and psychology over the last thirty years has shown its limitations.

Teleology: a way of thinking that understands a process in terms of an endpoint. In evolutionary theory, this would place humanity as the crowning achievement of evolution, the very purpose for which natural selection was designed. It is often connected to religious thinking.

Third culture: a view that scientists are now speaking to the public on a wide range of intellectual matters that once would have been thought to be the responsibility of intellectuals from the humanities. The term *third* is to suggest some breaking away from the two cultures division identified by C. P. Snow in 1959.

Transcendentalism: a particularly America literary movement, strongly influenced by Romanticism, including Thoreau, Emerson, and (more peripherally) Whitman. Essentially, the transcendentalists apprehended nature (and humanity's role in it, and relationship to it) as spiritual. The Divine, for them was not reachable through organized religion, but in everyday life, and through direct experience of nature.

Transmutationism: a term applied to that line of thought that suggested that species are not fixed but gradually change and evolve. It was the common term before the word evolution became popularly applied to nature in the middle of the nineteenth century.

Uniformitarianism: one of the two contending theories of geology in the early nineteenth-century. Opposed to catastrophism, uniformitarianism understood the geological and geographical formations of the world to be formed by the slow natural processes seen in the present: sedimentation, erosion, or glaciation. The case for uniformitarianism, whose most famous proponent was Charles Lyell, was strengthened by nineteenth-century datings of the earth's age at hundreds of millions, rather than mere thousands, of years. Such time scales allowed for slow processes (rather than catastrophes) to bring current geological formations into being. In turn, uniformitarian geology, because of its reliance on very long time scales, was more easily reconciled with Darwin's theory of natural selection.

Utopianism: the imagining of a better world than our own. The word *utopia* was coined by Thomas More, who derived it from two Latin words: *eutopos*, meaning "good place," and *outopos*, meaning "no place." Though literary in origin, utopian thinking had affected social thinkers and theorists by the nineteenth century, so that progressive figures such as Robert Owen attempted to create their own utopian communities, most of which were doomed to failure. In Ebenezer Howard's Garden City movement, or even in town planning, the utopian impulse lives on—even if literary utopias have long been displaced by dystopia.

Virtuoso: a common term for an amateur scientist in the seventeenth century. Satirists used the term critically to mean someone who was impractical and obsessed with trivial branches of learning and foolish schemes.

Primary Source Documents

The sources are presented in order of the chapters in the main text of the book to which they are most relevant and aligned.

Chapter 1

Extracts from La Vita Nuova (The New Life)

Taken from the translation by Sir Theodore Martin, 1893, *The Vita Nuova of Dante*, London: Blackwood and Sons

Some time in the 1280s Dante began writing the poems that he later assembled with a commentary by himself into La Vita Nuova (The New Life). The central theme of the poems is his love of Beatrice. What is particularly fascinating is that the poems give us a glimpse of the medieval mind at work. The selection here shows how features of the natural world (such as the number nine) had a highly symbolic function. The section headings have been added for clarity to Martin's translation.

Section II. The first meeting with Beatrice

Nine times already, since my birth, had the Heaven of light returned to well nigh the same point in its orbit when to my eyes was first revealed the glorious lady of my soul even she who was called Beatrice by many who wist not wherefore she was so called. She was then of such an age that during her life the starry heavens had advanced towards the East the twelfth part of a degree; so that she appeared to me about the beginning of her ninth year and I beheld her about the close of my own year. Her apparel was of a most noble colour, a subdued and becoming crimson and she wore a cincture and ornaments befitting her childish years. At that moment (I speak it in all truth) the spirit of life which abides in the most secret chamber of the heart began to tremble with a violence that showed horribly in the minutest pulsations of my frame; and tremulously it spoke these words: "*Ecce deus fortior me, qui veniens dominabitur nihi!* Behold a god stronger than I, who cometh to lord it over me!" And straitghway the animal spirit which abides in the upper chamber, whither all the spirits of the senses carry their perceptions began to marvel greatly and addressing itself especially to the spirits of vision, it spoke these words:—"*Apparuit jam betitudo vestra.* Now hath your bliss appeared." And straightway that natural spirit which abides in that part whereto our nourishment is ministered began to wail and dolorously it spoke these words—"*Heu miser! quia frequenter impeditus ero deinceps!* Ah wretched me for henceforth shall I be oftentimes obstructed" From that time shall I say that Love held sovereign empire over my soul which had upon the instant been betrothed unto him and through the influence lent to him by my imagination he at once assumed such imperious sway and masterdom over me that I could not choose but do his pleasure in all things. Oftentimes he enjoined me to strive if so I might behold this youngest of the angels; wherefore did I during my boyish years frequently go in quest of her and so praiseworthy was she and so noble in her bearing that of her might with truth be spoken that saying of the poet Homer –

"She is of god seemed born and not of mortal man."

And albeit her image which was evermore present with me might be Love's mere imperiousness to keep me in his thrall yet was its influence of such noble sort that at no time did it suffer me to be ruled by Love save with the faithful sanction of reason in all those matters wherein it is of importance to listen to her counsel. Were I to dwell upon all the passions and actions of this period of my youth they would appear like fables. On these therefore I shall not pause; but passing over many matters which may be conceived from the pattern of what I shall relate I will come to those words which are written in my memory in characters more conspicuous.

Section VI The List of Sixty Ladies

In this chapter Dante refers to a "screen"—that is, another lady that he pretended to love to hide his real love of Beatrice. He then considers the sixty most beautiful women in Florence and decides that of these Beatrice is the ninth.

I say then that during the time when this lady was the screen of a love which on my part was so great a which arose within me to record the name of that most gracious creature and to associate it with the names of many other ladies and in especial with hers of whom I have spoken; so taking the names of sixty of the most beautiful ladies of that city wherein the lady of my heart had been place by the Most High, I composed an epistle in the form of a serventese which I shall not transcribe here indeed I should not have made mention of it, but only to note what befell in marvellous wise in the composing thereof—namely that ninth in order and no otherwise would the name of my lady stand among the names of the ladies in question.

Chapter XXIX. The Number Nine

Dante now offers further thoughts on the significance of the number nine

Nevertheless as on several occasions in the preceding pages the number nine has occupied a place and apparently not without significance and as in her decease that number would seem to have filled an important place it may be right to say something here, which seems to be not irrelevant to the matter in hand. First, then, I will remark how it had a place in her decease, and then I will indicate a reason why this number was so propitious to her. I say then that according to the computation used in Italy her most noble spirit departed hence in the first hour of the ninth day of the month and according to the computation used in Syria she died in the ninth month of the year for there the first month is Tismim which is our October. And according to our computation she died in that year of our Lord to wit in which the perfect number was nine times completed within that century wherein she was born into the world she being a Christian of the thirteenth century. Why this number was so propitious to her may possibly be explained thus. According to Ptolemy and according to Christian truth the heavens that move are nine and according to the commonly received belief among astrologers these heavens exert a concurrent influence on mundane things each according to its peculiar position; so this number was propitious to her indicating as it did that at her birth all the nine moving heavens were in the most perfect conjunction. This is one reason but when the matter is scanned more closely and in conformity with infallible truth this number was her very self. I speak by way of similitude meaning thus: The number three is the root of nine because without any other number multiplied by itself it makes nine, it being obvious that three times three makes nine. If then three is by itself the efficient of nine and the Great Efficient of miracles is in Himself three, Father, Son and Holy Ghost, which are Three and One, this lady was accompanied by the number nine in order to show that she was a Nine in other words a Miracle whose only root is the adorable Trinity. A person more subtly-minded than myself might peradventure see some more subtle reason, but this is what I see in the matter and it is what pleases me best.

CHAPTER 2

Extract from Of the Laws of Ecclesiastical Polity *by Richard Hooker (1554–1600)*

After the English Church broke away from Rome it faced a crisis of justification. The Puritans argued that the only valid basis for the organization of the church was the Bible. If this were the case, then the whole hierarchical system of the Anglican Church, with its deacons, priests, and bishops, together with its rituals and liturgy, became invalid. Hooker defended the Anglican Establishment by employing the idea that God's creation is rational and governed by natural law. The Anglican Church, and hence Elizabethan society, could, therefore, look for its foundation in Scripture and natural law. In the passage that follows we are strongly reminded of the famous "degree" speech in Shakespeare's Troilus and Cressida *where the playwright justifies divisions of rank in society by reference to natural divisions in the heavens.*

III. [The law which natural agents have given them to observe, and their necessary manner of keeping it.]

I am not ignorant that by "law eternal" the learned for the most part do understand the order, not which God hath eternally purposed himself in all his works to observe, but rather that which with himself he hath set down as expedient to be kept by all his creatures, according to the several condition wherewith he hath endued them. They who thus are accustomed to speak apply the name of Law unto that rule only of working which superior authority imposeth; whereas we somewhat more enlarging the sense thereof term any kind of rule or canon, whereby actions are framed, a law. Now that law which, as it is laid up in the bosom of God, they call Eternal, receiveth according unto the different kinds of things which are subject unto it different and sundry kinds of names. That part of it which ordereth natural agents we call usually Nature's law; that which Angels do clearly behold and without any swerving observe is a law Celestial and heavenly; he law of Reason, that which bindeth creatures reasonable in this world, and with which by reason they may most plainly perceive themselves bound; that which bindeth them and is not known but by special revelation from God, Divine law; Human law, that which out of the law either of reason or of God men probably gathering to be expedient, they make It a law. All things therefore, which are as they ought to be, are conformed unto this second law eternal and even those things which to this eternal law are not conformable are notwithstanding in some sort ordered by the first eternal law. For what good or evil is there under the sun, what action or repugnant unto the law which God hath imposed upon his creatures, but in or upon it God doth work according to the law which himself hath eternally purposed to keep; that is to say, the first law eternal? So that a twofold law eternal thus made, it is not hard to conceive how they both take place in all things.

Wherefore to come to the law of nature: albeit thereby we sometimes mean that manner of working which God hath set for each created thing to keep; yet for as much as those things are termed most properly natural agents, which keep the law of their kind unwittingly, as the heavens and elements of the world, which can do no otherwise than they do; and forasmuch as we give unto intellectual natures the name of Voluntary agents, that so we may distinguish them from the other; expedient it will be, that we sever the law of nature observed by the one from that which the other is tied unto. Touching the former, their strict keeping of one tenure, statute, and law, is spoken of by all, but hath in it more than men have as yet attained to know; or perhaps ever shall attain, seeing the travail of wading herein is given of God to the sons of men, that perceiving how much the least thing in the world hath in it more than the wisest are able to reach unto, they may by this means learn humility. Moses, in describing the work of creation, attributeth speech unto God: "God said, Let there be light: let there be a firmament: let the waters under the heaven be gathered together into one place; let the earth bring forth: let there be lights in the firmament of heaven." Was this only the intent of Moses to signify the infinite greatness of God's power by the easiness of his accomplishing such effects, without travail, pain, or labour? Surely it seemeth that Moses had herein besides this a further purpose, namely, first to teach that God did not work as a necessary but a voluntary agent, intending beforehand and decreeing with himself that which did outwardly proceed from him: secondly, to shew that God did then institute a law natural to be observed by creatures, and therefore according to the manner of laws, the institution thereof is described, as being established by solemn injunction. His commanding those things to can be which are, and to be m such sort as they are, to keep that tenure and course which they do, importeth the establishment of nature's law. This world's first creation, and the preservation since of things created what is it but only so far forth a manifestation by execution, what the eternal law of God is concerning things natural? And as it cometh to pass in a kingdom rightly ordered, that after a law is once published, it presently takes effect far and wide, all states framing themselves thereunto; even so let us think it fareth in the natural course of the world: since the time that God did first proclaim the edicts of his law upon it, heaven and earth have hearkened unto his voice, and their labour hath been to do his will: He "made a law for the rain"; He gave his "decree unto the sea, that the water should not pass his commandment."

Now if nature should intermit her course, and leave altogether though it were but for a while observation of her own laws; if those principal and mother elements of the world, whereof all things in this lower world are made, should lose the qualities which now they have; if the frame of that heavenly arch erected over our heads should loosen and dissolve itself; if celestial spheres should forget their wonted motions, and by irregular volubility turn themselves any way as it might happen; if the prince of the lights of heaven, which now as a giant doth run his unwearied course should as it were through a languishing faintness begin to stand and to rest himself; if the moon should wander from her beaten way, the times and seasons of the year blend themselves by disordered and confused mixture, the winds breathe out their last gasp, the clouds yield no rain, the earth be defeated of heavenly influence, the fruits of the earth for pine away as children at the withered breasts of their mother no longer able to yield them relief: what would become of man himself, whom these things now do all serve? See we not plainly that obedience of creatures unto the law of nature is the stay of the whole world?

Notwithstanding with nature it cometh sometimes to pass as with art. Let Phidias have rude and obstinate stuff to carve, though his art do that it should, his work will lack that beauty which otherwise in fitter matter it might have had. He that striketh an instrument with skill may cause notwithstanding a very unpleasant sound, if the string whereon he striketh be uncapable of harmony. In. the matter whereof things natural consist, that of Theophrastus taketh place, Polu to ouc upakouon oude dexoeon to eu. "Much of it is oftentimes such as will by no means yield to receive that impression which were best and most perfect." Which defect in the matter of things natural, they who gave themselves unto the contemplation of nature amongst the heathen observed often: but the true original cause thereof; divine malediction, laid for the sin of man upon these creatures which God had made for the use of man, this being an article of that saving truth which God hath revealed unto his Church, was above the reach of their merely natural capacity and understanding. But howsoever these swervings are now and then incident into the course of nature, nevertheless so constantly the laws of nature are by natural agents observed that no man denieth but those things which nature worketh are wrought, either always or for the most part, after one and the same manner.

CHAPTER 3

Extract from The New Atlantis *(Internet Version—Details Below)*

From Ideal Commonwealths, P.F. Collier & Son, New York.
(c) 1901 The Colonial Press, expired.
Prepared by Kirk Crady from scanner output provided by Internet Wiretap.
This book is in the public domain, released August 1993.
Rendered into HTML by Jon Roland, Constitution Society

The New Atlantis *is a utopian vision writing written by Francis Bacon sometime around 1624. It was appended to a larger work,* The Sylva Sylvarum or The Natural History of Winds, *and published by Bacon's secretary Dr. Rawley in 1627 after the author's death. Bacon's* New Atlantis *describes the adventures of seamen who depart from Peru and come upon an ideal commonwealth on the island of Bensalem. Toward the end of the work, one of the travellers is introduced to Salomon's House, a place where Bacon outlines his vision of a research institution producing benefits for mankind. What is remarkable is the extent to which the activities, aspirations, and discoveries of the researchers accord with the modern world. It was Swift who satirized Bacon's vision in* Gulliver's Travels *(see extract for chapter four).*

WE sailed from Peru, where we had continued by the space of one whole year, for China and Japan, by the South Sea, taking with us victuals for twelve months; and had good winds from the east, though soft and weak, for five months' space and more. But then the wind came about, and settled in the west for many days, so as we could make little or no way, and were sometimes in purpose to turn back. But then again there arose strong and great winds from the south, with a point east; which carried us up, for all that we could do, toward the north: by which time our victuals failed us, though we had made good spare of them. So that finding ourselves, in the midst of the greatest wilderness of waters in the world, without victual, we gave ourselves for lost men, and prepared for death. Yet we did lift up our hearts and voices to God above, who showeth His wonders in the deep; beseeching Him of His mercy that as in the beginning He discovered the face of the deep, and brought forth dry land, so He would now discover land to us, that we might not perish.

And it came to pass that the next day about evening we saw within a kenning before us, toward the north, as it were thick clouds, which did put us in some hope of land, knowing how that part of the South Sea was utterly unknown, and might have islands or continents that hitherto were not come to light. Wherefore we bent our course thither, where we saw the appearance of land, all that night; and in the dawning of next day we might plainly discern that it was a land flat to our sight, and full of boscage, which made it show the more dark. And after an hour and a half's sailing, we entered into a good haven, being the port of a fair city.

The crew then land, meet the inhabitants, are entertained, and observe a "show" involving the passage of one of the "Father's of Salomon's House" through the street of a city. One of the travellers is then introduced to one of the Fathers of Salomon's House:

We found him in a fair chamber, richly hanged, and carpeted under foot, without any degrees to the state; he was set upon a low throne richly adorned, and a rich cloth of state over his head of blue satin embroidered. He was alone, save that he had two pages of honor, on either hand one, finely attired in white. His undergarments were the like that we saw him wear in the chariot; but instead of his gown, he had on him a mantle with a cape, of the same fine black, fastened about him. When we came in, as we were taught, we bowed low at our first entrance; and when we were come near his chair, he stood up, holding forth his hand ungloved, and in posture of blessing; and we every one of us stooped down and kissed the end of his tippet. That done, the rest departed, and I remained. Then he warned the pages forth of the room, and caused me to sit down beside him, and spake to me thus in the Spanish tongue:

"God bless thee, my son; I will give thee the greatest jewel I have. For I will impart unto thee, for the love of God and men, a relation of the true state of Salomon's House. Son, to make you know the true state of Salomon's House, I will keep this order. First, I will set forth unto you the end of our foundation. Secondly, the preparations and instruments we have for our works. Thirdly, the several employments and functions whereto our fellows are assigned. And fourthly, the ordinances and rites which we observe.

"The end of our foundation is the knowledge of causes, and secret motions of things; and the enlarging of the bounds of human empire, to the effecting of all things possible.

"The preparations and instruments are these: We have large and deep caves of several depths; the deepest are sunk 600 fathoms; and some of them are digged and made under great hills and mountains; so that if you reckon together the depth of the hill and the depth of the cave, they are, some of them, above three miles deep. For we find that the depth of a hill and the depth of a cave from the flat are the same thing; both remote alike from the sun and heaven's beams, and from the open air. These caves we call the lower region. And we use them for all coagulations, indurations, refrigerations, and conservations of bodies. We use them likewise for the imitation of natural mines and the producing also of new artificial metals, by compositions and materials which we use and lay there for many years. We use them also sometimes (which may seem strange) for curing of some diseases, and for prolongation of life, in some hermits that choose to live there, well accommodated of all things necessary, and indeed live very long; by whom also we learn many things . . .

"We have high towers, the highest about half a mile in height, and some of them likewise set upon high mountains, so that the vantage of the hill with the tower is in the highest of them three miles at least. And these places we call the upper region, account the air between the high places and the low as a middle region. We use these towers, according to their several heights and situations, for insulation, refrigeration, conservation, and for the view of divers meteors—as winds, rain, snow, hail, and some of the fiery meteors also. And upon them in some places are dwellings of hermits, whom we visit sometimes and instruct what to observe . . ..

"We have also a number of artificial wells and fountains, made in imitation of the natural sources and baths, as tincted upon vitriol, sulphur, steel, brass, lead, nitre, and other minerals; and again, we have little wells for infusions of many things, where the waters take the virtue quicker and better than in vessels or basins. And among them we have a water, which we call water of paradise, being by that we do it made very sovereign for health and prolongation of life.

"We have also great and spacious houses, where we imitate and demonstrate meteors—as snow, hail, rain, some artificial rains of bodies and not of water, thunders, lightnings; also generations of bodies in air—as frogs, flies, and divers others.

"We have also certain chambers, which we call chambers of health, where we qualify the air as we think good and proper for the cure of divers diseases and preservation of health.

"We have also fair and large baths, of several mixtures, for the cure of diseases, and the restoring of man's body from arefaction; and others for the confirming of it in strength of sinews, vital parts, and the very juice and substance of the body.

"We have also large and various orchards and gardens, wherein we do not so much respect beauty as variety of ground and soil, proper for divers trees and herbs, and some very spacious, where trees and berries are set, whereof we make divers kinds of drinks, beside the vineyards. In these we practise likewise all conclusions of grafting, and inoculating, as well of wild-trees as fruit-trees, which produceth many effects. And we make by art, in the same orchards and gardens, trees and flowers, to come earlier or later than their seasons, and to come up and bear more speedily than by their natural course they do. We make them also by art greater much than their nature; and their fruit greater and sweeter, and of differing taste, smell, color, and figure, from their nature. And many of them we so order as that they become of medicinal use . . .

"We have also parks, and enclosures of all sorts, of beasts and birds; which we use not only for view or rareness, but likewise for dissections and trials, that thereby may take light what may be wrought upon the body of man. Wherein we find many strange effects: as continuing life in them, though divers parts, which you account vital, be perished and taken forth; resuscitating of some that seem dead in appearance, and the like. We try also all poisons, and other medicines upon them, as well of chirurgery as physic. By art likewise we make them greater or smaller than their kind is, and contrariwise dwarf them and stay their growth; we make them more fruitful and bearing than their kind is, and contrariwise barren and not generative. Also we make them differ in color, shape, activity, many ways. We find means to make commixtures and copulations of divers kinds, which have produced many new kinds, and them not barren, as the general opinion is. We make a number of kinds of serpents, worms, flies, fishes of putrefaction, whereof some are advanced (in effect) to be perfect creatures, like beasts or birds, and have sexes, and do propagate. Neither do we this by chance, but we know beforehand of what matter and commixture, what kind of those creatures will arise . . .

"We have also sound-houses, where we practise and demonstrate all sounds and their generation. We have harmony which you have not, of quarter-sounds and lesser slides of sounds. Divers instruments of music likewise to you unknown, some sweeter than any you have; with bells and rings that are dainty and sweet. We represent small sounds as great and deep, likewise great sounds extenuate and sharp; we make divers tremblings and warblings of sounds, which in their original are entire. We represent and imitate all articulate sounds and letters, and the voices and notes of beasts and birds. We have certain helps which, set to the ear, do further the hearing greatly; we have also divers strange and artificial echoes, reflecting the voice many times, and, as it were, tossing it; and some that give back the voice louder than it came, some shriller and some deeper; yea, some rendering the voice, differing in the letters or articulate sound from that they receive. We have all means to convey sounds in trunks and pipes, in strange lines and distances.

"We have also perfume-houses, wherewith we join also practices of taste. We multiply smells which may seem strange: we imitate smells, making all smells to breathe out of other mixtures than those that give them. We make divers imitations of taste likewise, so that they will deceive any man's taste. And in this house we contain also a confiture-house, where we make all sweatmeats, dry and moist, and divers pleasant wines, milks, broths, and salads, far in greater variety than you have.

"We have also engine-houses, where are prepared engines and instruments for all sorts of motions. There we imitate and practise to make swifter motions than any you have, either out of your muskets or any engine that you have; and to make them and multiply them more easily and with small force, by wheels and other means, and to make them stronger and more violent than yours are, exceeding your greatest cannons and basilisks. We represent also ordnance and instruments of war and engines of all kinds; and likewise new mixtures and compositions of gunpowder, wild-fires burning in water and unquenchable, also fireworks of all variety, both for pleasure and use. We imitate also flights of birds; we have some degrees of flying in the air. We have ships and boats for going under water and brooking of seas, also swimming-girdles and supporters. We have divers curious clocks and other like motions of return, and some perpetual motions. We imitate also motions of living creatures by images of men, beasts, birds, fishes, and serpents; we have also a great number of other various motions, strange for equality, fineness, and subtilty . . .

"We have also houses of deceits of the senses, where we represent all manner of feats of juggling, false apparitions, impostures and illusions, and their fallacies. And surely you will easily believe that we, that have so many things truly natural which induce admiration, could in a world of particulars deceive the senses if we would disguise those things, and labor to make them more miraculous. But we do hate all impostures and lies, insomuch as we have severely forbidden it to all our fellows, under pain of ignominy and fines, that they do not show any natural work or thing adorned or swelling, but only pure as it is, and without all affectation of strangeness.

"These are, my son, the riches of Salomon's House."

Extract from The History of the Royal Society *by Thomas Sprat (1667)*

Sprat (1635–1713) was a clergyman, preacher, and man of letters. In 1684 he was made Bishop of Rochester. Sprat's history was written only a few years after the foundation of the Royal Society and serves as both a manifesto and justification for the new philosophy. One of the most interesting parts is where Sprat attacks what he sees as the meaningless verbosity of some writers and calls for a plainer and more direct way of writing. One can discern at this point a parting of the ways between the literature of science and the literature of humane learning. In the extract below "they" refers to the early fellows of the Royal Society.

Sect. XX. Their Manner of Discourse

Thus they have directed, judg'd, conjectur'd upon, and improved *Experiments.* But lastly, in these, and all other businesses, that have come under their care; there is one thing more, about which the *Society* has been most sollicitous; and that is, the manner of their *Discourse:* which, unless they had been very watchful to keep in due temper, the whole spirit and vigour of their *Design*, had been soon eaten out, by the luxury and redundance of *speech.* The ill effects of this superfluity of talking, have already overwhelm'd most other *Arts* and *Professions;* insomuch, that when I consider the means of *happy living*, and the causes of their corruption, I can hardly forbear recanting what I said before; and concluding, that *eloquence* ought to be banish'd out of all *civil Societies*, as a thing fatal to Peace and good Manners. To this opinion I should wholly incline; if I did not find, that it is a Weapon, which may be as easily procur'd by *bad* men, as *good:* and that, if these should onely cast it away, and those retain it; the *naked Innocence* of vertue, would be upon all occasions expos'd to the *armed Malice* of the wicked. This is the chief reason, that should now keep up the Ornaments of speaking, in any request: since they are so much degenerated from their original usefulness. They were at first, no doubt, an admirable Instrument in the hands of *Wise Men:* when they were onely employ'd to describe *Goodness, Honesty, Obedience;* in larger, fairer, and more moving Images: to represent *Truth,* cloth'd with Bodies; and to bring *Knowledg* back again to our very senses, from whence it was at first deriv'd to our understandings. But now they are generally chang'd to worse uses: They make the *Fancy* disgust the best things, if they come sound, and unadorn'd: they are in open defiance against *Reason;* professing, not to hold much correspondence with that; but with its Slaves, *the Passions:* they give the mind a motion too changeable, and bewitching, to consist with *right practice.* Who can behold, without indignation, how many mists and uncertainties, these specious *Tropes* and *Figures* have brought on our Knowledg? How many rewards, which are due to more profitable, and difficult *Arts*, have been still snatch'd away by the easie vanity of *fine speaking?* For now I am warm'd with this just Anger, I cannot with-hold my self, from betraying the shallowness of all these seeming Mysteries; upon which, *we Writers*, and *Speakers*, look so bigg. And, in few words, I dare say; that of all the Studies of men, nothing may be sooner obtain'd, than this vicious abundance of *Phrase*, this trick of *Metaphors*, this volubility of *Tongue*, which makes so great a noise in the World. But I spend words in vain; for the evil is now so inveterate, that it is hard to know whom to *blame*, or where to begin to *reform.* We all value one another so much, upon this beautiful deceipt; and labour so long after it, in the years of our education: that we cannot but ever after think kinder of it, than it deserves. And indeed, in most other parts of Learning, I look on it to be a thing almost utterly desperate in its cure: and I think, it may be plac'd amongst those *general mischiefs;* such, as the *dissention* of Christian Princes, the *want of practice* in Religion, and the like; which have been so long spoken against, that men are become insensible about them; every one shifting off the fault from himself to others; and so they are only made bare common places of complaint. It will suffice my present purpose, to point out, what has been done by the *Royal Society*, towards the correcting of its excesses in *Natural Philosophy;* to which it is, of all others, a most profest enemy.

They have therefore been most rigorous in putting in execution, the only Remedy, that can be found for this *extravagance:* and that has been, a constant Resolution, to reject all the amplifications, digressions, and swellings of style: to return back to the primitive purity, and shortness, when men deliver'd so many *things*, almost in an equal number of *words.* They have exacted from all their members, a close, naked, natural way of speaking; positive expressions; clear senses; a native easiness: bringing all things as near the Mathematical plainness, as they can: and preferring the language of Artizans, Countrymen, and Merchants, before that, of Wits, or Scholars.

CHAPTER 4

Extract from The Memoirs of Scriblerus

The Scriblerus Club was founded in 1713 and its members included Swift, Pope, Gay, Oxford, Parnell, and Arbuthnot. The idea was to produce a series of writings from an imaginary Martinus Scriblerus that ridiculed what the group saw as the abuses of learning and vulgar tastes of the day. The memoirs were written collaboratively and it is not certain who is the author of the extract below, although Swift and Arbuthnot are the most likely candidates. Swift's Gulliver's Travels *was a work originally intended to be part of Scriblerus's Memoirs. The group ceased to meet after about 1714.*

In the following extract, the character who has achieved such great things seems to be a composite of Newton, Boyle, Wilkins, Whiston, and in one place even Swift. The reference to the problem of longitude and proposed solutions such as "Bomb-Vessels" and the construction of "Two poles to the Meridian, with immense Light-houses on the top of them" is almost certainly a parody of the method advocated by William Whiston, Newton's successor at Cambridge. The problem of longitude was so acute for Britain in the early eighteenth century that the House of Commons passed a bill on July 13, 1714, offering a reward of £200,000 for anyone supplying a method accurate to within specified limits. The plan of William Whiston and Humphrey Ditton was that ships were to be anchored across the Atlantic at each degree of the meridian with instructions to set off canons and rockets at noon each day. The plan must have sounded as absurd to Swift and his circle as it does to the modern reader and served to provide another example of impractical science worthy only of satire.

Chapter XIV

Of the discoveries and works of the great Scriblerus, made and to be made, written and to be written, known and unknown.

Here therefore, at this great Period, we end our first Book. And here, O Reader, we entreat thee utterly to forget all thou hast hitherto read, and to cast thy eyes only forward, to that boundless field the next shall open unto thee; the fruits of which (if thine, or our sins do not prevent) are to spread and multiply over this our work, and over all the face of the earth.

In the mean time, know what thou owest, and what thou yet may'st owe, to this excellent Person, this Prodigy of our Age; who may well be called The Philosopher of Ultimate Causes, since by a Sagacity peculiar to himself, he hath discovered Effects in their very Cause; and without the trivial helps of Experiments, or Observations, hath been the Inventor of most of the modern Systems and Hypotheses.

He hath enrich'd Mathematicks with many precise and Geometrical Quadratures of the Circle. He first discover'd the Cause of Gravity, and the intestine Motion of Fluids.

To him we owe all the observations on the Parallax of the Pole-Star, and all the new Theories of the Deluge. He it was, that first taught the right use sometimes of the Fuga Vacui, and sometimes the Materia Subiilis, in resolving the grand Phcanomena of Nature.

He it was that first found out the Palpability of Colours; and by the delicacy of his Touch, could distinguish the different Vibrations of the heterogeneous Rays of Light.

His were the Projects of Perpelaum Mobiles, Flying Engines, and Pacing Saddles; the Method of discovering the longitude, by Bomb-Vessels, and of increasing the Trade-Wind by vast plantations of Reeds and Sedges.

I shall mention only a few of his Philosophical and Mathematical Works.

1. A compleat Digest of the Laws of Nature, with a Review of those that are obsolete or repealed, and of those that are ready to be renenv'd and put in force.

2. A Mechanical Explication of the Formation of the Universe, according to the Epicurean Hypothesis.

3. An Investigation of the Quantity of real Matter in the Universe, with the proportion of the specific Gravity of solid Matter to that of fluid.

4. Microscopical Observations of the Figure and Bulk of the constituent Parts of all fluids. A Calculation of the proportion in which the Fluids of the earth decrease, and of the period in which they will be totally exhausted.

5. A Computation of the Duration of the Sun, and how long it will last before it be bum'd out.

6. A method to apply the Force arising from the immense Velocity of Light to mechanical purposes.

7. An answer to the question of a curious Gentleman; How long a New Star was lighted up before its appearance to the Inhabitants of our earth? To which is subjoin'd a Calculation, how much the Inhabitants of the Moon eat for Supper, considering that they pass a Night equal to fifteen of our natural days.

8. A Demonstration of the natural Dominion of the Inhabitants of the Earth over those of the Moon, if ever an intercourse should be open'd between them. With a Proposal of a Partition-Treaty, among the earthly Potentates, in case of such discovery.

9. Tide-Tables, for a Comet, that is to approximate towards the Earth.

10. The Number of the Inhabitants of London determin'd by the Reports of the Gold-finders, and the tonnage of their Carriages; with allowance for the extraordinary quantity of the Ingesta and Egesta of the people of England, and a deduction of what is left under dead walls, and dry ditches.

It will from hence be evident, how much all his Studies were directed to the universal Benefit of Mankind. Numerous have been his Projects to this end, of which Two alone will be sufficient to show the amazing Grandeur of his Genius. The first was a Proposal, by a general contribution of all Princes, to pierce the first crust or Nucleus of this our Earth quite through, to the next concentrical Sphere: The advantage he propos'd from it was, to find the Parallax of the Fixt Stars; but chiefly to refute Sir Isaac Newton's Theory of Gravity, and Mr. Halley's of the Variations. The second was, to build Two Poles to the Meridian, with immense Lighthouses on the top of them; to supply the defect of Nature, and to make the longitude as easy to be calculated as the latitude. Both these he could not but think very practicable, by the Power of all the Potentates of the world. May we presume after these to mention, how he descended from the sublime to the beneficial parts of Knowledge, and particularly his extraordinary practice of physick? From the Age, Complexion, or Weight of the person given, he contrived to prescribe at a distance, as well as at a Patient's bed-side. He taught the way to many modem Physicians to cure their patients by Intuition, and to others to cure without looking on them at all. He projected a Menstruum to dissolve the Stone, made of Dr. Woodward's Universal Deluge-water. His also was the device to relieve consumptive or asthmatic persons by bringing fresh Air out of the Country to Town, by pipes of the nature of the Recipients of Air-pumps: And to introduce the Native air of a man's country into any other in which he should travel, with a seasonable Intromission of such Steams as were most familiar to him; to the inexpressible comfort of many Scotsmen, Laplanders, and white Bears.

In Physiognomy, his penetration is such, that from the Picture only of any person he can write his Life; and from the features of the Parents, draw the Portrait of any Child that is to be born. Nor hath he been so enrapt in these Studies as to neglect the Polite Arts of Painting, Architecture, Musick, Poetry, &c. It was he that gave the first hints to our modem Painters, to improve the Likeness of their Portraits by the use of such Colours as would faithfully and constantly accompany the Life, not only in its present state, but in all its alterations, decays, age, and death itself.

In Architecture, he builds not with so much regard to present symmetry or conveniency, as with a Thought well worthy of the lover of Antiquity, to wit, the noble effect the Building will have to posterity, when it shall fall and become a Ruin.

As to Musick, I think Heidegger has not the face to deny that he has been much beholden to his Scores. In Poetry, he hath appear'd under a hundred different names, of which we may one day give a Catalogue. In Politicks, his Writings are of a peculiar Cast, for the most part Ironical, and the Drift of them often so delicate and refin'd, as to be mistaken by the vulgar. He once went so far as to write a Persuasive to people to eat their own Children, which was so little under-stood as to be taken in ill part. He has often written against Liberty in the name of Freemen and Algernon Sydney, in vindication of the Measures of Spain under that of Raleigh, and in praise of Corruption under those of Cato and Publicola.

It is true, that at his last departure from England, in the Reign of Queen Anne, apprehending lest any of these might be perverted to the Scandal of the weak, or Encouragement of the flagitious, he cast them all, without mercy, into a Bog-house near St. James's. Some however have been with great diligence recov-er'd, and fish'd up with a hook and line, by the Ministerial Writers, which make at present the great Ornaments of their works. Whatever he judg'd beneficial to Mankind, he constantly communicated (not only during his stay among us, but ever since his absence) by some method or other in which Ostentation had no part. With what incredible Modesty he conceal'd himself, is known to numbers of those to whom he address'd sometimes Epistles, some- times Hints, sometimes whole Treatises, Advicei; to Friends, Projects to First Ministers, Letters to Mem-bers of Parliament, Accounts to the Royal Society, and innumerable others. All there will be vindicated to the true Author, in the course of these Memoirs. I may venture to say they cannot be unacceptable to any, but to those, who will appear too much concern'd as Plagiaries, to be admitted as Judges. Wherefore we warn the publick, to take particular notice of all such as manifest any indecent Passion at the appearance of this Work, as Persons most certainly involved in the Guilt.

Extract from Gulliver's Travels Part II: A Voyage to Laputa, Balnibarbi, Luggnagg, Glubbdubdrib, and Japan

Here Swift makes fun of a variety of aspects of the new philosophy, including its epistemology, its view of language, and the impracticality of its objectives. He visits the floating island of the Laputans and later is lowered down onto the island of the Balnibarbi, where he visits the Grand Academy of Lagredo.

Chapter II

The Humours and Dispositions of the Laputians described. An Account of their Learning. Of the King and his Court. The Author's Reception there. The Inhabi-tants subject to Fears and Disquietudes. An Account of the Women.

AT MY ALIGHTING I was surrounded by a Crowd of People, but those who stood nearest seemed to be of better Quality. They beheld me with all the Marks and Circumstances of wonder; neither indeed was I much in their Debt; having never till then seen a Race of Mortals so singular in their Shapes, Habits, and Countenances. Their Heads were all reclined either to the Right, or the Left; one of their Eyes turned inward, and the other directly up to the Zenith. Their outward Garments were adorned with the Figures of Suns, Moons, and Stars, interwoven with those of Fiddles, Flutes, Harps, Trumpets, Guittars, Harpsichords, and many more Instruments of Musick, unknown to us in *Europe*. I observed here and there many in the Habit of Servants, with a blown Bladder fastned like a Flail to the End of a short Stick, which they carried in their Hands. In each Bladder was a small Quantity of dried Pease, or little Pebbles, (as I was afterwards informed.) With these Bladders they now and then flapped the Mouths and Ears of those who stood near them, of which Practice I could not then conceive the Meaning. It seems the Minds of these People are so taken up with intense Speculations, that they neither can speak, nor attend to the Discourses of others, without being rouzed by some external Taction upon the Organs of Speech and Hearing; for which Reason those Persons who are able to afford it always keep a *Flapper* (the Original is *Climenole*) in their Family, as one of their Domesticks; nor ever walk abroad or make Visits without him. And the Business of this Officer is, when two or more Persons are in Company, gently to strike with his Bladder the Mouth of him who is to speak, and the right Ear of him or them to whom the Speaker addresses himself. This *Flapper* is likewise employed diligently to attend his Master in his Walks, and upon Occasion to give him a soft Flap on his Eyes; because he is always so wrapped up in Cogitation, that he is in manifest Danger of falling down every Precipice, and bouncing his Head against every Post; and in the Streets, of jostling others, or being jostled himself into the Kennel. . . .

Gulliver is then introduced to the King

My Dinner was brought, and four Persons of Quality, whom I remembered to have seen very near the King's Person, did me the Honour to dine with me. We had two Courses, of three Dishes each. In the first Course, there was a Shoulder of Mutton, cut into an AEquilateral Triangle; a Piece of Beef into a Rhomboides; and a Pudding into a Cycloid. The second Course was two Ducks, trussed up into the Form of Fiddles; Sausages and Puddings resembling Flutes and Haut-boys, and a Breast of Veal in the Shape of a Harp. The Servants cut our Bread into Cones, Cylinders, Parallelograms, and several other Mathematical Figures.

. . . .Those to whom the King had entrusted me, observing how ill I was clad, ordered a Taylor to come next Morning, and take my Measure for a Suit of Cloths. This Operator did his Office after a different Manner from those of his Trade in *Europe*. He first took my Altitude by a Quadrant, and then with Rule and

Compasses, described the Dimensions and Out-Lines of my whole Body; all which he entered upon Paper, and in six Days brought my Cloths very ill made, and quite out of Shape, by happening to mistake a Figure in the Calculation. But my Comfort was, that I observed such Accidents very frequent, and little regarded.

During my Confinement for want of Cloaths, and by an Indisposition that held me some Days longer, I much enlarged my Dictionary; and when I went next to Court, was able to understand many Things the King spoke, and to return him some Kind of Answers. His Majesty had given Orders that the Island should move North-East and by East, to the vertical Point over *Lagado*, the Metropolis of the whole Kingdom, below upon the firm Earth. It was about Ninety Leagues distant, and our Voyage lasted four Days and an Half. I was not in the least sensible of the progressive Motion made in the Air by the Island. On the second Morning, about Eleven o'Clock, the King himself in Person, attended by his Nobility, Courtiers, and Officers, having prepared all their Musical Instruments, played on them for three Hours without Intermission; so that I was quite stunned with the Noise; neither could I possibly guess the Meaning, till my Tutor informed me. He said, that the People of their Island had their Ears adapted to hear the Musick of the Spheres, which always played at certain Periods; and the Court was now prepared to bear their Part in whatever Instrument they most excelled. . . .

Their Houses are very ill built, the Walls bevil without one right Angle in any Apartment; and this Defect ariseth from the Contempt they bear to practical Geometry; which they despise as vulgar and mechanick, those Instructions they give being too refined for the Intellectuals of their Workmen; which occasions perpetual Mistakes. And although they are dextrous enough upon a Piece of Paper in the Management of the Rule, the Pencil, and the Divider, yet in the common Actions and Behaviour of Life, I have not seen a more clumsy, awkward, and unhandy People, nor so slow and perplexed in their Conceptions upon all other Subjects, except those of Mathematicks and Musick. They are very bad Reasoners, and vehemently given to Opposition, unless when they happen to be of the right Opinion, which is seldom their Case. Imagination, Fancy, and Invention, they are wholly Strangers to, nor have any Words in their Language by which those Ideas can be expressed; the whole Compass of their Thoughts and Mind, being shut up within the two forementioned Sciences.

Most of them, and especially those who deal in the Astronomical Part, have great Faith in judicial Astrology, although they are ashamed to own it publickly. . . .

These People are under continual Disquietudes, never enjoying a Minute's Peace of Mind; and their Disturbances proceed from Causes which very little affect the rest of Mortals. Their Apprehensions arise from several Changes they dread in the Celestial Bodies. For Instance; that the Earth by the continual Approaches of the Sun towards it, must in Course of Time be absorbed or swallowed up. That the Face of the Sun will by Degrees be encrusted with its own Effluvia, and give no more Light to the World. That, the Earth very narrowly escaped a Brush from the Tail of the last Comet, which would have infallibly reduced it to Ashes; and that the next, which they have calculated for One and Thirty Years hence, will probably destroy us. For, if in its Perihelion it should approach within a certain Degree of the Sun, (as by their Calculations they have Reason to dread) it will conceive a Degree of Heat ten Thousand Times more intense than that of red hot glowing Iron; and in its Absence from the Sun, carry a blazing Tail Ten Hundred Thousand and Fourteen Miles long; through which if the Earth should pass at the Distance of one Hundred Thousand Miles from the *Nucleus* or main Body of the Comet, it must in its Passage be set on Fire, and reduced to Ashes. That the Sun daily spending its Rays without any Nutriment to supply them, will at last be wholly consumed and annihilated; which must be attended with the Destruction of this Earth, and of all the Planets that receive their Light from it.

They are so perpetually alarmed with the Apprehensions of these and the like impending Dangers, that they can neither sleep quietly in their Beds, nor have any Relish for the common Pleasures or Amusements of Life. When they meet an Acquaintance in the Morning, the first Question is about the Sun's Health; how he looked at his Setting and Rising, and what Hopes they have to avoid the Stroak of the approaching Comet. This conversation they are apt to run into with the same Temper that boys discover, in delighting to hear terrible Stories of Sprites and Hobgoblins, which they greedily listen to, and dare not go to Bed for fear.

Chapter V

The Author permitted to see the grand Academy of *Lagado*. The Academy largely described. The Arts wherein the Professors employ themselves.

THIS ACADEMY is not an entire single Building, but a Continuation of several Houses on both Sides of a Street; which growing waste, was purchased and applyed to that Use.

I was received very kindly by the Warden, and went for many Days to the Academy. Every Room hath in it one or more Projectors; and I believe I could not be in fewer than five Hundred Rooms.

The first Man I saw was of a meager Aspect, with sooty Hands and Face, his Hair and Beard long, ragged and singed in several Places. His Cloathes, Shirt, and Skin were all of the same Colour. He had been Eight Years upon a Project for extracting Sun-Beams out of Cucumbers, which were to be put into Vials hermetically sealed, and let out to warm the Air in raw inclement Summers. He told me he did not doubt in Eight Years more he should be able to supply the Governors Gardens with Sun-shine at a reasonable Rate; but he complained that his stock was low, and intreated me to give him something as an Encouragement to Ingenuity, especially since this had been a very dear Season for Cucumbers. I made him a small Present, for my Lord had furnished me with Money on Purpose, because he knew their Practice of begging from all who go to see them.

I went into another Chamber, but was ready to hasten back, being almost overcome with a horrible Stink. My Conductor pressed me forward, conjuring me in a Whisper to give no Offence, which would be highly resented; and therefore I durst not so much as stop my Nose. The Projector of this Cell was the most ancient Student of the Academy. His Face and Beard were of a pale Yellow; his Hands and Clothes daubed over with Filth. When I was presented to him, he gave me a close Embrace (a Compliment I could well have excused.) His Employment from his first coming into the Academy, was an Operation to reduce human Excrement to its original Food, by separating the several Parts, removing the Tincture which it receives from the Gall, making the Odour exhale, and scumming off the Saliva. He had a weekly Allowance from the Society, of a Vessel filled with human Ordure about the Bigness of a *Bristol* Barrel.

I saw another at work to calcine Ice into Gunpowder; who likewise shewed me a Treatise he had written concerning the Malleability of Fire, which he intended to publish.

There was a most ingenious Architect who had contrived a new Method for building Houses, by beginning at the Roof, and working downwards to the Foundation; which he justified to me by the like Practice of those two prudent Insects, the Bee and the Spider.

There was a Man born blind, who had several Apprentices in his own Condition: Their Employment was to mix Colours for Painters, which their Master taught them to distinguish by feeling and smelling. It was indeed my Misfortune to find them at that Time not very perfect in their Lessons; and the Professor himself happened to be generally mistaken: This Artist is much encouraged and esteemed by the whole Fraternity.

In another Apartment I was highly pleased with a Projector, who had found a Device of plowing the Ground with Hogs, to save the Charges of Plows, Cattle, and Labour. The Method in this: In an Acre of Ground you bury at six Inches Distance, and eight deep, a Quantity of Acorns, Dates, Chestnuts, and other Maste or Vegetables whereof these Animals are fondest; then you drive six Hundred or more of them into the Field, where in a few Days they will root up the whole Ground in search of their Food, and make it fit for sowing, at the same time manuring it with their Dung. It is true, upon Experiment they found the Charge and Trouble very great, and they had little or no Crop. However, it is not doubted that this Invention may be capable of great Improvement.

I went into another Room, where the Walls and Ceiling were all hung round with Cobwebs, except a narrow passage for the Artist to go in and out. At my Entrance he called aloud to me not to disturb his Webs. He lamented the fatal Mistake the World had been so long in of using Silk-Worms, while we had such plenty of domestick Insects, who infinitely excelled the Former, because they understood how to weave as well as spin. And he proposed farther, that by employing Spiders, the Charge of dying Silks should be wholly saved; whereof I was fully convinced when he shewed me a vast Number of Flies most beautifully coloured, wherewith he fed his Spiders; assuring us, that the Webs would take a Tincture from them; and as he had them of all Hues, he hoped to fit every Body's Fancy, as soon as he could find proper Food for the Flies, of certain Gums, Oyls, and other glutinous Matter to give a Strength and Consistence to the Threads.

There was an Astronomer who had undertaken to place a Sun-Dial upon the great Weather-Cock on the Town-House, by adjusting the annual and diurnal Motions of the Earth and Sun, so as to answer and coincide with all accidental Turnings of the Wind.

I was complaining of a small fit of the Cholick; upon which my Conductor led me into a Room, where a great Physician resided, who was famous for curing that Disease by contrary Operations from the same Instrument. He had a large Pair of Bellows with a long slender Muzzle of Ivory. This he conveyed eight Inches up the Anus, and drawing in the Wind, he affirmed he could make the Guts as lank as a dried Bladder. But when the Disease was more stubborn and violent, he let in the Muzzle while the Bellows were full of Wind, which he discharged into the Body of the Patient, then withdrew the Instrument to replenish it, clapping his Thumb strongly against the Orifice of the Fundament; and this being repeated three or four Times, the adventitious Wind would rush out, bringing the noxious along with it (like Water put into a Pump), and the Patient recover. I saw him try both Experiments upon a Dog, but could not discern any Effect from the former. After the latter, the Animal was ready to burst, and made so violent a Discharge, as was very offensive to me and my Companions. The Dog died on the Spot, and we left the Doctor endeavouring to recover him by the same Operation.

I visited many other Apartments, but shall not trouble my Reader with all the Curiosities I observed, being studious of Brevity. . . .

We next went to the School of Languages, where three Professors sate in Consultation upon improving that of their own country.

The first Project was to shorten Discourse by cutting Polysyllables into one, and leaving out Verbs and Participles, because in reality all things imaginable are but Nouns.

The other, was a Scheme for entirely abolishing all Words whatsoever; and this was urged as a great Advantage in Point of Health as well as Brevity. For it is plain, that every Word we speak is in some Degree a Diminution of our Lungs by Corrosion, and consequently contributes to the shortning of our Lives. An Expedient was therefore offered, that since Words are only Names for *Things*, it would be more convenient for all Men to carry about them, such *Things* as were necessary to express the particular Business they are to discourse on. And this Invention would certainly have taken Place, to the great Ease as well as Health of the Subject, if the Women in conjunction with the Vulgar and Illiterate had not threatned to raise a Rebellion, unless they might be allowed the Liberty to speak with their Tongues, after the manner of their Ancestors; such constant irreconcilable Enemies to Science are the common People. However, many of the most Learned and Wise adhere to the New Scheme of expressing themselves by *Things*, which hath only this Inconvenience attending it, that if a Man's Business be very great, and of various kinds, he must be obliged in Proportion to carry a greater bundle of *Things* upon his Back, unless he can afford one or two strong Servants to attend him. I have often beheld two of those Sages almost sinking under the Weight of their Packs, like Pedlars among us; who, when they met in the Streets, would lay down their Loads, open their Sacks, and hold Conversation for an Hour together; then put up their Implements, help each other to resume their Burthens, and take their Leave.

CHAPTER 5

Extract from Preface to Lyrical Ballads, *by William Wordsworth (1800)*

This extract is from the Preface to the second edition of Lyrical Ballads. *Here Wordsworth outlines his views on poetry and its relationship to science.*

THE FIRST volume of these Poems has already been submitted to general perusal. It was published, as an experiment, which, I hoped, might be of some use to ascertain, how far, by fitting to metrical arrangement a selection of the real language of men in a state of vivid sensation, that sort of pleasure and that quantity of pleasure may be imparted, which a Poet may rationally endeavour to impart. . . .

It is supposed, that by the act of writing in verse an Author makes a formal engagement that he will gratify certain known habits of association; that he not only thus apprises the Reader that certain classes of ideas and expressions will be found in his book, but that others will be carefully excluded. This exponent or symbol held forth by metrical language must in different eras of literature have excited very different expectations: for example, in the age of Catullus, Terence, and Lucretius, and that of Statius or Claudian; and in our own country, in the age of Shakespeare and Beaumont and Fletcher, and that of Donne and Cowley, or Dryden, or Pope. I will not take upon me to determine the exact import of the promise which, by the act of writing in verse, an Author in the present day makes to his reader: but it will undoubtedly appear to many persons that I have not fulfilled the terms of an engagement thus voluntarily contracted. They who have been accustomed to the gaudiness and inane phraseology of many modern writers, if they persist in reading this book to its conclusion, will, no doubt, frequently have to struggle with feelings of strangeness and awkwardness: they will look round for poetry, and will be induced to inquire by what species of courtesy these attempts can be permitted to assume that title. I hope therefore the reader will not censure me for attempting to state what I have proposed to myself to perform; and also (as far as the limits of a preface will permit) to explain some of the chief reasons which have determined me in the choice of my purpose: that at least he may be spared any unpleasant feeling of disappointment, and that I myself may be protected from one of the most dishonourable accusations which can be brought against an Author, namely, that of an indolence which prevents him from endeavouring to ascertain what is his duty, or, when his duty is ascertained, prevents him from performing it.

The principal object, then, proposed in these Poems was to choose incidents and situations from common life, and to relate or describe them, throughout, as far as was possible in a selection of language really used by men, and, at the same time, to throw over them a certain colouring of imagination, whereby ordinary things should be presented to the mind in an unusual aspect; and, further, and above all, to make these incidents and situations interesting by tracing in them, truly though not ostentatiously, the primary laws of our nature: chiefly, as far as regards the manner in which we associate ideas in a state of excitement. . . .

A sense of false modesty shall not prevent me from asserting, that the Reader's attention is pointed to this mark of distinction, far less for the sake of these particular Poems than from the general importance of the subject. The subject is indeed important! For the human mind is capable of being excited without the application of gross and violent stimulants; and he must have a very faint perception of its beauty and dignity who does not know this, and who does not further know, that one being is elevated above another, in proportion as he possesses this capability. It has therefore appeared to me, that to endeavour to produce or enlarge this capability is one of the best services in which, at any period, a Writer can be engaged; but this service, excellent at all times, is especially so at the present day. For a multitude of causes, unknown to former times, are now acting with a combined force to blunt the discriminating powers of the mind, and, unfitting it for all voluntary exertion, to reduce it to a state of almost savage torpor. The most effective of these causes are the great national events which are daily taking place, and the increasing accumulation of men in cities, where the uniformity of their occupations produces a craving for extraordinary incident, which the rapid communication of intelligence hourly gratifies. . . .

Nor let this necessity of producing immediate pleasure be considered as a degradation of the Poet's art. It is far otherwise. It is an acknowledgement of the beauty of the universe, an acknowledgement the more sincere, because not formal, but indirect; it is a task light and easy to him who looks at the world in the spirit of love: further, it is a homage paid to the native and naked dignity of man, to the grand elementary principle of pleasure, by which he knows, and feels, and lives, and moves. We have no sympathy but what is propagated by pleasure: I would not be misunderstood; but wherever we sympathize with pain, it will be found that the sympathy is produced and carried on by subtle combinations with pleasure. We have no knowledge, that is, no general principles drawn from the contemplation of particular facts, but what has been built up by pleasure, and exists in us by pleasure alone. The Man of science, the Chemist and Mathematician, whatever difficulties and disgusts they may have had to struggle with, know and feel this. However painful may be the objects with which the Anatomist's knowledge is connected, he feels that his knowledge is pleasure; and where he has no pleasure he has no knowledge. What then does the Poet? He considers man and the objects that surround him as acting and re-acting upon each other, so as to produce an infinite complexity of pain and pleasure; he considers man in his own nature and in his ordinary life as contemplating this with a certain quantity of immediate knowledge, with certain convictions, intuitions, and deductions, which from habit acquire the quality of intuitions; he considers him as looking upon this complex scene of ideas and sensations, and finding everywhere objects that immediately excite in him sympathies which, from the necessities of his nature, are accompanied by an overbalance of enjoyment.

To this knowledge which all men carry about with them, and to these sympathies in which, without any other discipline than that of our daily life, we are fitted to take delight, the Poet principally directs his attention. He considers man and nature as essentially adapted to each other, and the mind of man as naturally the mirror of the fairest and most interesting properties of nature. and thus the Poet, prompted by this feeling of pleasure, which accompanies him through the whole course of his studies, converses with general nature, with affections akin to those, which, through labour and length of time, the Man of science has raised up in himself, by conversing with those particular parts of nature which are the objects of his studies. The knowledge both of the Poet and the Man of science is pleasure; but the knowledge of the one cleaves to us as a necessary part of our existence, our natural and unalienable inheritance; the other is a personal and individual acquisition, slow to come to us, and by no habitual and direct sympathy connecting us with our fellow-beings. The Man of science seeks truth as a remote and unknown benefactor; he cherishes and loves it in his solitude: the Poet, singing a song in which all human beings join with him, rejoices in the presence of truth as our visible friend and hourly companion. Poetry is the breath and finer spirit of all knowledge; it is the impassioned expression which is in the countenance of all Science. Emphatically may it be said of the Poet, as Shakespeare hath said of man, 'that he looks before and after.' He is the rock of defence for human nature; an upholder and preserver, carrying everywhere with him relationship and love. In spite of difference of soil and climate, of language and manners, of laws and customs: in spite of things silently gone out of mind, and things violently destroyed; the Poet binds together by passion and knowledge the vast empire of human society, as it is spread over the whole earth, and over all time. The objects of the Poet's thoughts are everywhere; though the eyes and senses of man are, it is true, his favourite guides, yet he will follow wheresoever he can find an atmosphere of sensation in which to move his wings. Poetry is the first and last of all knowledge—it is as immortal as the heart of man. If the labours of Men of science should ever create any material revolution, direct or indirect, in our condition, and in the impressions which we habitually receive, the Poet will sleep then no more than at present; he will be ready to follow the steps of the Man of science, not only in those general indirect effects, but he will be at his side, carrying sensation into the midst of the objects of the science itself. The remotest discoveries of the Chemist, the Botanist, or Mineralogist, will be as proper objects of the Poet's art as any upon which it can be employed, if the time should ever come when these things shall be familiar to us, and the relations under which they are contemplated by the followers of these respective sciences shall be manifestly and palpably material to us as enjoying and suffering beings. If the time should ever come when what is now called science, thus familiarized to men, shall be ready to put on, as it were, a form of flesh and blood, the Poet will lend his divine spirit to aid the transfiguration, and will welcome the Being thus produced, as a dear and genuine inmate of the household of man. It is not, then, to be supposed that any one, who holds that sublime notion of Poetry which I have attempted to convey, will break in upon the sanctity and truth of his pictures by transitory and accidental ornaments, and endeavour to excite admiration of himself by arts, the necessity of which must manifestly depend upon the assumed meanness of his subject.

CHAPTER 6

Extract from Ralph Waldo Emerson, "The American Scholar" (1837)

Collected in *English Traits, Representative Men and Other Essays* (London: J.M. Dent, 1908)

Ralph Waldo Emerson is best known for his connection to the Transcendentalists, and his essays on Nature and Representative Men. Emerson's "The American Scholar," a radical document at the time, challenges the "rote learning" then current in schools and colleges and opens up a debate about the principles of what is taught and learned, and how people should be educated.

Mr. President and Gentlemen,

I greet you on the re-commencement of our literary year. Our anniversary is one of hope, and, perhaps, not enough of labor. We do not meet for games of strength or skill, for the recitation of histories, tragedies, and odes, like the ancient Greeks; for parliaments of love and poesy, like the Troubadours; nor for the advancement of science, like our contemporaries in the British and European capitals. Thus far, our holiday has been simply a friendly sign of the survival of the love of letters amongst a people too busy to give to letters any more. As such, it is precious as the sign of an indestructible instinct. Perhaps the time is already come, when it ought to be, and will be, something else; when the sluggard intellect of this continent will look from under its iron lids, and fill the postponed expectation of the world with something better than the exertions of mechanical skill. Our day of dependence, our long apprenticeship to the learning of other lands, draws to a close. The millions, that around us are rushing into life, cannot always be fed on the sere remains of foreign harvests. Events, actions arise, that must be sung, that will sing themselves. Who can doubt, that poetry will revive and lead in a new age, as the star in the constellation Harp, which now flames in our zenith, astronomers announce, shall one day be the pole-star for a thousand years?

In this hope, I accept the topic which not only usage, but the nature of our association, seem to prescribe to this day,—the AMERICAN SCHOLAR. Year by year, we come up hither to read one more chapter of his biography. Let us inquire what light new days and events have thrown on his character, and his hopes.

It is one of those fables, which, out of an unknown antiquity, convey an unlooked-for wisdom, that the gods, in the beginning, divided Man into men, that he might be more helpful to himself; just as the hand was divided into fingers, the better to answer its end.

The old fable covers a doctrine ever new and sublime; that there is One Man,—present to all particular men only partially, or through one faculty; and that you must take the whole society to find the whole man. Man is not a farmer, or a professor, or an engineer, but he is all. Man is priest, and scholar, and statesman, and producer, and soldier. In the *divided* or social state, these functions are parcelled out to individuals, each of whom aims to do his stint of the joint work, whilst each other performs his. The fable implies, that the individual, to possess himself, must sometimes return from his own labor to embrace all the other laborers. But unfortunately, this original unit, this fountain of power, has been so distributed to multitudes, has been so minutely subdivided and peddled out, that it is spilled into drops, and cannot be gathered. The state of society is one in which the members have suffered amputation from the trunk, and strut about so many walking monsters,—a good finger, a neck, a stomach, an elbow, but never a man.

Man is thus metamorphosed into a thing, into many things. The planter, who is Man sent out into the field to gather food, is seldom cheered by any idea of the true dignity of his ministry. He sees his bushel and his cart, and nothing beyond, and sinks into the farmer, instead of Man on the farm. The tradesman scarcely ever gives an ideal worth to his work, but is ridden by the routine of his craft, and the soul is subject to dollars. The priest becomes a form; the attorney, a statute-book; the mechanic, a machine; the sailor, a rope of a ship.

In this distribution of functions, the scholar is the delegated intellect. In the right state, he is, *Man Thinking.* In the degenerate state, when the victim of society, he tends to become a mere thinker, or, still worse, the parrot of other men's thinking.

In this view of him, as Man Thinking, the theory of his office is contained. Him nature solicits with all her placid, all her monitory pictures; him the past instructs; him the future invites. Is not, indeed, every man a student, and do not all things exist for the student's behoof? And, finally, is not the true scholar the only true master? But the old oracle said, 'All things have two handles: beware of the wrong one.' In life, too often, the scholar errs with mankind and forfeits his privilege. Let us see him in his school, and consider him in reference to the main influences he receives.

I. The first in time and the first in importance of the influences upon the mind is that of nature. Every day, the sun; and, after sunset, night and her stars. Ever the winds blow; ever the grass grows. Every day, men and women, conversing, beholding and beholden. The scholar is he of all men whom this spectacle most engages. He must settle its value in his mind. What is nature to him? There is never a beginning, there is never an end, to the inexplicable continuity of this web of God, but always circular power returning into itself. Therein it resembles his own spirit, whose beginning, whose ending, he never can find,—so entire, so boundless. Far, too, as her splendors shine, system on system shooting like rays, upward, downward, without centre, without circumference,—in the mass and in the particle, nature hastens to render account of herself to the mind. Classification begins. To the young mind, every thing is individual, stands by itself. By and by, it finds how to join two things, and see in them one nature; then three, then three thousand; and so, tyrannized over by its own unifying instinct, it goes on tying things together, diminishing anomalies, discovering roots running under ground, whereby contrary and remote things cohere, and flower out from one stem. It presently learns, that, since the dawn of history, there has been a constant accumulation and classifying of facts. But what is classification but the perceiving that these objects are not chaotic, and are not foreign, but have a law which is also a law of the human mind? The astronomer discovers that geometry, a pure abstraction of the human mind, is the measure of planetary motion. The chemist finds proportions and intelligible method throughout matter; and science is nothing but the finding of analogy, identity, in the most remote parts. The ambitious soul sits down before each refractory fact; one after another, reduces all strange constitutions, all new powers, to their class and their law, and goes on for ever to animate the last fibre of organization, the outskirts of nature, by insight.

Thus to him, to this school-boy under the bending dome of day, is suggested, that he and it proceed from one root; one is leaf and one is flower; relation, sympathy, stirring in every vein. And what is that Root? Is not that the soul of his soul?—A thought too bold,—a dream too wild. Yet when this spiritual light shall have revealed the law of more earthly natures,—when he has learned to worship the soul, and to see that the natural philosophy that now is, is only the first gropings of its gigantic hand, he shall look forward to an ever expanding knowledge as to a becoming creator. He shall see, that nature is the opposite of the soul, answering to it part for part. One is seal, and one is print. Its beauty is the beauty of his own mind. Its laws are the laws of his own mind. Nature then becomes to him the measure of his attainments. So much of nature as he is ignorant of, so much of his own mind does he not yet possess. And, in fine, the ancient precept, "Know thyself," and the modern precept, "Study nature," become at last one maxim.

II. The next great influence into the spirit of the scholar, is, the mind of the Past,—in whatever form, whether of literature, of art, of institutions, that mind is inscribed. Books are the best type of the influence of the past, and perhaps we shall get at the truth,—learn the amount of this influence more conveniently,—by considering their value alone.

The theory of books is noble. The scholar of the first age received into him the world around; brooded thereon; gave it the new arrangement of his own mind, and uttered it again. It came into him, life; it went out from him, truth. It came to him, short-lived actions; it went out from him, immortal thoughts. It came to him, business; it went from him, poetry. It was dead fact; now, it is quick thought. It can stand, and it can go. It now endures, it now flies, it now inspires. Precisely in proportion to the depth of mind from which it issued, so high does it soar, so long does it sing.

Or, I might say, it depends on how far the process had gone, of transmuting life into truth. In proportion to the completeness of the distillation, so will the purity and imperishableness of the product be. But none is quite perfect. As no air-pump can by any means make a perfect vacuum, so neither can any artist entirely exclude the conventional, the local, the perishable from his book, or write a book of pure thought, that shall be as efficient, in all respects, to a remote posterity, as to cotemporaries, or rather to the second age. Each age, it is found, must write its own books; or rather, each generation for the next succeeding. The books of an older period will not fit this.

Yet hence arises a grave mischief. The sacredness which attaches to the act of creation,—the act of thought,—is transferred to the record. The poet chanting, was felt to be a divine man: henceforth the chant is divine also. The writer was a just and wise spirit: henceforward it is settled, the book is perfect; as love of the hero corrupts into worship of his statue. Instantly, the book becomes noxious: the guide is a tyrant. The sluggish and perverted mind of the multitude, slow to open to the incursions of Reason, having once so opened, having once received this book, stands upon it, and makes an outcry, if it is disparaged. Colleges are built on it. Books are written on it by thinkers, not by Man Thinking; by men of talent, that is, who start wrong, who set out from accepted dogmas, not from their own sight of principles. Meek young men grow up in libraries, believing it their duty to accept the views, which Cicero, which Locke, which Bacon, have given, forgetful that Cicero, Locke, and Bacon were only young men in libraries, when they wrote these books.

Hence, instead of Man Thinking, we have the bookworm. Hence, the book-learned class, who value books, as such; not as related to nature and the human constitution, but as making a sort of Third Estate with the world and the soul. Hence, the restorers of readings, the emendators, the bibliomaniacs of all degrees.

Books are the best of things, well used; abused, among the worst. What is the right use? What is the one end, which all means go to effect? They are for nothing but to inspire. I had better never see a book, than to be warped by its attraction clean out of my own orbit, and made a satellite instead of a system. The one thing in the world, of value, is the active soul. This every man is entitled to; this every man contains within him, although, in almost all men, obstructed, and as yet unborn. The soul active sees absolute truth; and utters truth, or creates. In this action, it is genius; not the privilege of here and there a favorite, but the sound estate of every man. In its essence, it is progressive. The book, the college, the school of art, the institution of any kind, stop with some past utterance of genius. This is good, say they,—let us hold by this. They pin me down. They look backward and not forward. But genius looks forward: the eyes of man are set in his forehead, not in his hindhead: man hopes: genius creates. Whatever talents may be, if the man create not, the pure efflux of the Deity is not his;—cinders and smoke there may be, but not yet flame. There are creative manners, there are creative actions, and creative words; manners, actions, words, that is, indicative of no custom or authority, but springing spontaneous from the mind's own sense of good and fair.

On the other part, instead of being its own seer, let it receive from another mind its truth, though it were in torrents of light, without periods of solitude, inquest, and self-recovery, and a fatal disservice is done. Genius is always sufficiently the enemy of genius by over influence. The literature of every nation bear me witness. The English dramatic poets have Shakspearized now for two hundred years.

Undoubtedly there is a right way of reading, so it be sternly subordinated. Man Thinking must not be subdued by his instruments. Books are for the scholar's idle times. When he can read God directly, the hour is too precious to be wasted in other men's transcripts of their readings. But when the intervals of darkness come, as come they must,—when the sun is hid, and the stars withdraw their shining,—we repair to the lamps which were kindled by their ray, to guide our steps to the East again, where the dawn is. We hear, that we may speak. The Arabian proverb says, "A fig tree, looking on a fig tree, becometh fruitful."

It is remarkable, the character of the pleasure we derive from the best books. They impress us with the conviction, that one nature wrote and the same reads. We read the verses of one of the great English poets, of Chaucer, of Marvell, of Dryden, with the most modern joy,—with a pleasure, I mean, which is in great part caused by the abstraction of all *time* from their verses. There is some awe mixed with the joy of our surprise, when this poet, who lived in some past world, two or three hundred years ago, says that which lies close to my own soul, that which I also had wellnigh thought and said. But for the evidence thence afforded to the philosophical doctrine of the identity of all minds, we should suppose some preestablished harmony, some foresight of souls that were to be, and some preparation of stores for their future wants, like the fact observed in insects, who lay up food before death for the young grub they shall never see.

I would not be hurried by any love of system, by any exaggeration of instincts, to underrate the Book. We all know, that, as the human body can be nourished on any food, though it were boiled grass and the broth of shoes, so the human mind can be fed by any knowledge. And great and heroic men have existed, who had almost no other information than by the printed page. I only would say, that it needs a strong head to bear that diet. One must be an inventor to read well. As the proverb says, "He that would bring home the wealth of the Indies, must carry out the wealth of the Indies." There is then creative reading as well as creative writing. When the mind is braced by labor and invention, the page of whatever book we read becomes luminous with manifold allusion. Every sentence is doubly significant, and the sense of our author is as broad as the world. We then see, what is always true, that, as the seer's hour of vision is short and rare among heavy days and months, so is its record, perchance, the least part of his volume. The discerning will read, in his Plato or Shakspeare, only that least part,—only the authentic utterances of the oracle;—all the rest he rejects, were it never so many times Plato's and Shakspeare's.

Of course, there is a portion of reading quite indispensable to a wise man. History and exact science he must learn by laborious reading. Colleges, in like manner, have their indispensable office,—to teach elements. But they can only highly serve us, when they aim not to drill, but to create; when they gather from far every ray of various genius to their hospitable halls, and, by the concentrated fires, set the hearts of their youth on flame. Thought and knowledge are natures in which apparatus and pretension avail nothing. Gowns, and pecuniary foundations, though of towns of gold, can never countervail the least sentence or syllable of wit. Forget this, and our American colleges will recede in their public importance, whilst they grow richer every year.

III. There goes in the world a notion, that the scholar should be a recluse, a valetudinarian,—as unfit for any handiwork or public labor, as a penknife for an axe. The so-called 'practical men' sneer at speculative men, as if, because they speculate or *see*, they could do nothing. I have heard it said that the clergy,—who are always, more universally than any other class, the scholars of their day,—are addressed as women; that the rough, spontaneous conversation of men they do not hear, but only a mincing and diluted speech. They are often virtually disfranchised; and, indeed, there are advocates for their celibacy. As far as this is true of the studious classes, it is not just and wise. Action is with the scholar subordinate, but it is essential. Without it, he is not yet man. Without it, thought can never ripen into truth. Whilst the world hangs before the eye as a cloud of beauty, we cannot even see its beauty. Inaction is cowardice, but there can be no scholar without the heroic mind. The preamble of thought, the transition through which it passes from the unconscious to the conscious, is action. Only so much do I know, as I have lived. Instantly we know whose words are loaded with life, and whose not.

The world,—this shadow of the soul, or *other me*, lies wide around. Its attractions are the keys which unlock my thoughts and make me acquainted with myself. I run eagerly into this resounding tumult. I grasp the hands of those next me, and take my place in the ring to suffer and to work, taught by an instinct, that so shall the dumb abyss be vocal with speech. I pierce its order; I dissipate its fear; I dispose of it within the circuit of my expanding life. So much only of life as I know by experience, so much of the wilderness have I vanquished and planted, or so far have I extended my being, my dominion. I do not see how any man can afford, for the sake of his nerves and his nap, to spare any action in which he can partake. It is pearls and rubies to his discourse. Drudgery, calamity, exasperation, want, are instructers in eloquence and wisdom. The true scholar grudges every opportunity of action past by, as a loss of power.

It is the raw material out of which the intellect moulds her splendid products. A strange process too, this, by which experience is converted into thought, as a mulberry leaf is converted into satin. The manufacture goes forward at all hours.

The actions and events of our childhood and youth, are now matters of calmest observation. They lie like fair pictures in the air. Not so with our recent actions,—with the business which we now have in hand. On this we are quite unable to speculate. Our affections as yet circulate through it. We no more feel or know it, than we feel the feet, or the hand, or the brain of our body. The new deed is yet a part of life,—remains for a time immersed in our unconscious life. In some contemplative hour, it detaches itself from the life like a ripe fruit, to become a thought of the mind. Instantly, it is raised, transfigured; the corruptible has put on incorruption. Henceforth it is an object of beauty, however base its origin and neighborhood. Observe, too, the impossibility of antedating this act. In its grub state, it cannot fly, it cannot shine, it is a dull grub. But suddenly, without observation, the selfsame thing unfurls beautiful wings, and is an angel of wisdom. So is there no fact, no event, in our private history, which shall not, sooner or later, lose its adhesive, inert form, and astonish us by soaring from our body into the empyrean. Cradle and infancy, school and playground, the fear of boys, and dogs, and ferules, the love of little maids and berries, and many another fact that once filled the whole sky, are gone already; friend and relative, profession and party, town and country, nation and world, must also soar and sing.

Of course, he who has put forth his total strength in fit actions, has the richest return of wisdom. I will not shut myself out of this globe of action, and transplant an oak into a flower-pot, there to hunger and pine; nor trust the revenue of some single faculty, and exhaust one vein of thought, much like those Savoyards, who, getting their livelihood by carving shepherds, shepherdesses, and smoking Dutchmen, for all Europe, went out one day to the mountain to find stock, and discovered that they had whittled up the last of their pine-trees. Authors we have, in numbers, who have written out their vein, and who, moved by a commendable prudence, sail for Greece or Palestine, follow the trapper into the prairie, or ramble round Algiers, to replenish their merchantable stock.

If it were only for a vocabulary, the scholar would be covetous of action. Life is our dictionary. Years are well spent in country labors; in town,—in the insight into trades and manufactures; in frank intercourse with many men and women; in science; in art; to the one end of mastering in all their facts a language by which to illustrate and embody our perceptions. I learn immediately from any speaker how much he has already lived, through the poverty or the splendor of his speech. Life lies behind us as the quarry from whence we get tiles and copestones for the masonry of to-day. This is the way to learn grammar. Colleges and books only copy the language which the field and the work-yard made.

But the final value of action, like that of books, and better than books, is, that it is a resource. That great principle of Undulation in nature, that shows itself in the inspiring and expiring of the breath; in desire and satiety; in the ebb and flow of the sea; in day and night; in heat and cold; and as yet more deeply ingrained in every atom and every fluid, is known to us under the name of Polarity,—these "fits of easy transmission and reflection," as Newton called them, are the law of nature because they are the law of spirit.

The mind now thinks; now acts; and each fit reproduces the other. When the artist has exhausted his materials, when the fancy no longer paints, when thoughts are no longer apprehended, and books are a weariness,—he has always the resource *to live*. Character is higher than intellect. Thinking is the function. Living is the functionary. The stream retreats to its source. A great soul will be strong to live, as well as strong to think. Does he lack organ or medium to impart his truths? He can still fall back on this elemental force of living them. This is a total act. Thinking is a partial act. Let the grandeur of justice shine in his affairs. Let the beauty of affection cheer his lowly roof. Those 'far from fame,' who dwell and act with him, will feel the force of his constitution in the doings and passages of the day better than it can be measured by any public and designed display. Time shall teach him, that the scholar loses no hour which the man lives. Herein he unfolds the sacred germ of his instinct, screened from influence. What is lost in seemliness is gained in strength. Not out of those, on whom systems of education have exhausted their culture, comes the helpful giant to destroy the old or to build the new, but out of unhandselled savage nature, out of terrible Druids and Berserkirs, come at last Alfred and Shakspeare.

I hear therefore with joy whatever is beginning to be said of the dignity and necessity of labor to every citizen. There is virtue yet in the hoe and the spade, for learned as well as for unlearned hands. And labor is everywhere welcome;

always we are invited to work; only be this limitation observed, that a man shall not for the sake of wider activity sacrifice any opinion to the popular judgments and modes of action.

I have now spoken of the education of the scholar by nature, by books, and by action. It remains to say somewhat of his duties.

They are such as become Man Thinking. They may all be comprised in self-trust. The office of the scholar is to cheer, to raise, and to guide men by showing them facts amidst appearances. He plies the slow, unhonored, and unpaid task of observation. Flamsteed and Herschel, in their glazed observatories, may catalogue the stars with the praise of all men, and, the results being splendid and useful, honor is sure. But he, in his private observatory, cataloguing obscure and nebulous stars of the human mind, which as yet no man has thought of as such,—watching days and months, sometimes, for a few facts; correcting still his old records;—must relinquish display and immediate fame. In the long period of his preparation, he must betray often an ignorance and shiftlessness in popular arts, incurring the disdain of the able who shoulder him aside. Long he must stammer in his speech; often forego the living for the dead. Worse yet, he must accept,—how often! poverty and solitude. For the ease and pleasure of treading the old road, accepting the fashions, the education, the religion of society, he takes the cross of making his own, and, of course, the self-accusation, the faint heart, the frequent uncertainty and loss of time, which are the nettles and tangling vines in the way of the self-relying and self-directed; and the state of virtual hostility in which he seems to stand to society, and especially to educated society. For all this loss and scorn, what offset? He is to find consolation in exercising the highest functions of human nature. He is one, who raises himself from private considerations, and breathes and lives on public and illustrious thoughts. He is the world's eye. He is the world's heart. He is to resist the vulgar prosperity that retrogrades ever to barbarism, by preserving and communicating heroic sentiments, noble biographies, melodious verse, and the conclusions of history. Whatsoever oracles the human heart, in all emergencies, in all solemn hours, has uttered as its commentary on the world of actions,—these he shall receive and impart. And whatsoever new verdict Reason from her inviolable seat pronounces on the passing men and events of to-day,—this he shall hear and promulgate.

These being his functions, it becomes him to feel all confidence in himself, and to defer never to the popular cry. He and he only knows the world. The world of any moment is the merest appearance. Some great decorum, some fetish of a government, some ephemeral trade, or war, or man, is cried up by half mankind and cried down by the other half, as if all depended on this particular up or down. The odds are that the whole question is not worth the poorest thought which the scholar has lost in listening to the controversy. Let him not quit his belief that a popgun is a popgun, though the ancient and honorable of the earth affirm it to be the crack of doom. In silence, in steadiness, in severe abstraction, let him hold by himself; add observation to observation, patient of neglect, patient of reproach; and bide his own time,—happy enough, if he can satisfy himself alone, that this day he has seen something truly. Success treads on every right step. For the instinct is sure, that prompts him to tell his brother what he thinks. He then learns, that in going down into the secrets of his own mind, he has descended into the secrets of all minds. He learns that he who has mastered any law in his private thoughts, is master to that extent of all men whose language he speaks, and of all into whose language his own can be translated. The poet, in utter solitude remembering his spontaneous thoughts and recording them, is found to have recorded that, which men in crowded cities find true for them also. The orator distrusts at first the fitness of his frank confessions,—his want of knowledge of the persons he addresses,—until he finds that he is the complement of his hearers;—that they drink his words because he fulfils for them their own nature; the deeper he dives into his privatest, secretest presentiment, to his wonder he finds, this is the most acceptable, most public, and universally true. The people delight in it; the better part of every man feels, This is my music; this is myself.

In self-trust, all the virtues are comprehended. Free should the scholar be,—free and brave. Free even to the definition of freedom, "without any hindrance that does not arise out of his own constitution." Brave; for fear is a thing, which a scholar by his very function puts behind him. Fear always springs from ignorance. It is a shame to him if his tranquillity, amid dangerous times, arise from the presumption, that, like children and women, his is a protected class; or if he seek a temporary peace by the diversion of his thoughts from politics or vexed questions, hiding his head like an ostrich in the flowering bushes, peeping into microscopes, and turning rhymes, as a boy whistles to keep his courage up. So is the danger a danger still; so is the fear worse. Manlike let him turn and face it. Let him look into its eye and search its nature, inspect its origin,—see the whelping of this lion,—which lies no great way back; he will then find in himself a perfect comprehension of its nature and extent; he will have made his hands meet on the other side, and can henceforth defy it, and pass on superior. The world is his, who can see through its pretension. What deafness, what stone-blind custom, what overgrown error you behold, is there only by sufferance,— by your sufferance. See it to be a lie, and you have already dealt it its mortal blow.

Yes, we are the cowed,—we the trustless. It is a mischievous notion that we are come late into nature; that the world was finished a long time ago. As the world was plastic and fluid in the hands of God, so it is ever to so much of his attributes as we bring to it. To ignorance and sin, it is flint. They adapt themselves to it as they may; but in proportion as a man has any thing in him divine, the firmament flows before him and takes his signet and form. Not he is great who can alter matter, but he who can alter my state of mind. They are the kings of the world who give the color of their present thought to all nature and all art, and persuade men by the cheerful serenity of their carrying the matter, that this thing which they do, is the apple which the ages have desired to pluck, now at last ripe, and inviting nations to the harvest. The great man makes the great thing. Wherever Macdonald sits, there is the head of the table. Linnaeus makes botany the most alluring of studies, and wins it from the farmer and the herb-woman; Davy, chemistry; and Cuvier, fossils. The day is always his, who works in it with serenity and great aims. The unstable estimates of men crowd to him whose mind is filled with a truth, as the heaped waves of the Atlantic follow the moon.

For this self-trust, the reason is deeper than can be fathomed,—darker than can be enlightened. I might not carry with me the feeling of my audience in stating my own belief. But I have already shown the ground of my hope, in adverting to the doctrine that man is one. I believe man has been wronged; he has wronged himself. He has almost lost the light, that can lead him back to his prerogatives. Men are become of no account. Men in history, men in the world of to-day are bugs, are spawn, and are called 'the mass' and 'the herd.' In a century, in a millennium, one or two men; that is to say,—one or two approximations to the right state of every man. All the rest behold in the hero or the poet their own green and crude being,—ripened; yes, and are content to be less, so *that* may attain to its full stature. What a testimony,—full of grandeur, full of pity, is borne to the demands of his own nature, by the poor clansman, the poor partisan, who rejoices in the glory of his chief. The poor and the low find some amends to their immense moral capacity, for their acquiescence in a political and social inferiority. They are content to be brushed like flies from the path of a great person, so that justice shall be done by him to that common nature which it is the dearest desire of all to see enlarged and glorified. They sun themselves in the great man's light, and feel it to be their own element. They cast the dignity of man from their downtrod selves upon the shoulders of a hero, and will perish to add one drop of blood to make that great heart beat, those giant sinews combat and conquer. He lives for us, and we live in him.

Men such as they are, very naturally seek money or power; and power because it is as good as money,—the "spoils," so called, "of office." And why not? for they aspire to the highest, and this, in their sleep-walking, they dream is highest. Wake them, and they shall quit the false good, and leap to the true, and leave governments to clerks and desks. This revolution is to be wrought by the gradual domestication of the idea of Culture. The main enterprise of the world for splendor, for extent, is the upbuilding of a man. Here are the materials strown along the ground. The private life of one man shall be a more illustrious monarchy,—more formidable to its enemy, more sweet and serene in its influence to its friend, than any kingdom in history. For a man, rightly viewed, comprehendeth the particular natures of all men. Each philosopher, each bard, each actor, has only done for me, as by a delegate, what one day I can do for myself. The books which once we valued more than the apple of the eye, we have quite exhausted. What is that but saying, that we have come up with the point of view which the universal mind took through the eyes of one scribe; we have been that man, and have passed on. First, one; then, another; we drain all cisterns, and, waxing greater by all these supplies, we crave a better and more abundant food. The man has never lived that can feed us ever. The human mind cannot be enshrined in a person, who shall set a barrier on any one side to this unbounded, unboundable empire. It is one central fire, which, flaming now out of the lips of Etna, lightens the capes of Sicily; and, now out of the throat of Vesuvius, illuminates the towers and vineyards of Naples. It is one light which beams out of a thousand stars. It is one soul which animates all men.

But I have dwelt perhaps tediously upon this abstraction of the Scholar. I ought not to delay longer to add what I have to say, of nearer reference to the time and to this country.

Historically, there is thought to be a difference in the ideas which predominate over successive epochs, and there are data for marking the genius of the Classic, of the Romantic, and now of the Reflective or Philosophical age. With the views I have intimated of the oneness or the identity of the mind through all individuals, I do not much dwell on these differences. In fact, I believe each individual passes through all three. The boy is a Greek; the youth, romantic; the adult, reflective. I deny not, however, that a revolution in the leading idea may be distinctly enough traced.

Our age is bewailed as the age of Introversion. Must that needs be evil? We, it seems, are critical; we are embarrassed with second thoughts; we cannot enjoy any thing for hankering to know whereof the pleasure consists; we are lined with eyes; we see with our feet; the time is infected with Hamlet's unhappiness,—

"Sicklied o'er with the pale cast of thought."

Is it so bad then? Sight is the last thing to be pitied. Would we be blind? Do we fear lest we should outsee nature and God, and drink truth dry? I look upon the discontent of the literary class, as a mere announcement of the fact, that they find themselves not in the state of mind of their fathers, and regret the coming state as untried; as a boy dreads the water before he has learned that he can swim. If there is any period one would desire to be born in,—is it not the age of

Revolution; when the old and the new stand side by side, and admit of being compared; when the energies of all men are searched by fear and by hope; when the historic glories of the old, can be compensated by the rich possibilities of the new era? This time, like all times, is a very good one, if we but know what to do with it.

I read with joy some of the auspicious signs of the coming days, as they glimmer already through poetry and art, through philosophy and science, through church and state.

One of these signs is the fact, that the same movement which effected the elevation of what was called the lowest class in the state, assumed in literature a very marked and as benign an aspect. Instead of the sublime and beautiful; the near, the low, the common, was explored and poetized. That, which had been negligently trodden under foot by those who were harnessing and provisioning themselves for long journeys into far countries, is suddenly found to be richer than all foreign parts. The literature of the poor, the feelings of the child, the philosophy of the street, the meaning of household life, are the topics of the time. It is a great stride. It is a sign,—is it not? of new vigor, when the extremities are made active, when currents of warm life run into the hands and the feet. I ask not for the great, the remote, the romantic; what is doing in Italy or Arabia; what is Greek art, or Provencal minstrelsy; I embrace the common, I explore and sit at the feet of the familiar, the low. Give me insight into to-day, and you may have the antique and future worlds. What would we really know the meaning of? The meal in the firkin; the milk in the pan; the ballad in the street; the news of the boat; the glance of the eye; the form and the gait of the body;—show me the ultimate reason of these matters; show me the sublime presence of the highest spiritual cause lurking, as always it does lurk, in these suburbs and extremities of nature; let me see every trifle bristling with the polarity that ranges it instantly on an eternal law; and the shop, the plough, and the leger, referred to the like cause by which light undulates and poets sing;—and the world lies no longer a dull miscellany and lumber-room, but has form and order; there is no trifle; there is no puzzle; but one design unites and animates the farthest pinnacle and the lowest trench.

This idea has inspired the genius of Goldsmith, Burns, Cowper, and, in a newer time, of Goethe, Wordsworth, and Carlyle. This idea they have differently followed and with various success. In contrast with their writing, the style of Pope, of Johnson, of Gibbon, looks cold and pedantic. This writing is blood-warm. Man is surprised to find that things near are not less beautiful and wondrous than things remote. The near explains the far. The drop is a small ocean. A man is related to all nature. This perception of the worth of the vulgar is fruitful in discoveries. Goethe, in this very thing the most modern of the moderns, has shown us, as none ever did, the genius of the ancients.

There is one man of genius, who has done much for this philosophy of life, whose literary value has never yet been rightly estimated;—I mean Emanuel Swedenborg. The most imaginative of men, yet writing with the precision of a mathematician, he endeavored to engraft a purely philosophical Ethics on the popular Christianity of his time. Such an attempt, of course, must have difficulty, which no genius could surmount. But he saw and showed the connection between nature and the affections of the soul. He pierced the emblematic or spiritual character of the visible, audible, tangible world. Especially did his shade-loving muse hover over and interpret the lower parts of nature; he showed the mysterious bond that allies moral evil to the foul material forms, and has given in epical parables a theory of isanity, of beasts, of unclean and fearful things.

Another sign of our times, also marked by an analogous political movement, is, the new importance given to the single person. Every thing that tends to insulate the individual,—to surround him with barriers of natural respect, so that each man shall feel the world is his, and man shall treat with man as a sovereign state with a sovereign state;—tends to true union as well as greatness. "I learned," said the melancholy Pestalozzi, "that no man in God's wide earth is either willing or able to help any other man." Help must come from the bosom alone. The scholar is that man who must take up into himself all the ability of the time, all the contributions of the past, all the hopes of the future. He must be an university of knowledges. If there be one lesson more than another, which should pierce his ear, it is, The world is nothing, the man is all; in yourself is the law of all nature, and you know not yet how a globule of sap ascends; in yourself slumbers the whole of Reason; it is for you to know all, it is for you to dare all. Mr. President and Gentlemen, this confidence in the unsearched might of man belongs, by all motives, by all prophecy, by all preparation, to the American Scholar. We have listened too long to the courtly muses of Europe. The spirit of the American freeman is already suspected to be timid, imitative, tame. Public and private avarice make the air we breathe thick and fat. The scholar is decent, indolent, complaisant. See already the tragic consequence. The mind of this country, taught to aim at low objects, eats upon itself. There is no work for any but the decorous and the complaisant. Young men of the fairest promise, who begin life upon our shores, inflated by the mountain winds, shined upon by all the stars of God, find the earth below not in unison with these,—but are hindered from action by the disgust which the principles on which business is managed inspire, and turn drudges, or die of disgust,—some of them suicides. What is the remedy? They did not yet see, and thousands of young men as hopeful now crowding to the barriers for the career, do not yet see, that, if the single man plant himself indomitably on his instincts, and there abide, the huge world will come round to him. Patience,—patience;—with the shades of all the good and great for company; and for solace, the perspective of your own infinite life; and for work, the study and the communication of principles, the making those instincts prevalent, the conversion of the world. Is it not the chief disgrace in the world, not to be an unit;—not to be reckoned one character;—not to yield that peculiar fruit which each man was created to bear, but to be reckoned in the gross, in the hundred, or the thousand, of the party, the section, to which we belong; and our opinion predicted geographically, as the north, or the south? Not so, brothers and friends,—please God, ours shall not be so. We will walk on our own feet; we will work with our own hands; we will speak our own minds. The study of letters shall be no longer a name for pity, for doubt, and for sensual indulgence. The dread of man and the love of man shall be a wall of defence and a wreath of joy around all. A nation of men will for the first time exist, because each believes himself inspired by the Divine Soul which also inspires all men.

CHAPTER 7

Extract from Vestiges of The Natural History of Creation *by Robert Chambers*

First edition, 1844; London/John Churchill, Princes Street, extract taken from pp. 250 to 276.

When this book was published, anonymously, it caused a sensation.
Tennyson acquired many of his ideas about evolution from this work.
Here Chambers discusses the position of man and ends with the idea
that higher races may one day evolve.

The general conclusions regarding the geography of organic nature, may be thus stated. (1.) There are numerous distinct foci of organic production throughout the earth. (2.) These have everywhere advanced in accordance with the local conditions of climate &c., as far as at least the class and order are concerned, a diversity taking place in the lower gradations. No physical or geographical reason appearing for this diversity, we are led to infer that, (3,) it is the result of minute and inappreciable causes giving the law of organic development a particular direction in the lower subdivisions of the two kingdoms. (4.) Development has not gone on to equal results in the various continents, being most advanced in the eastern continent, next in the western, and least in Australia, this inequality being perhaps the result of the comparative antiquity of the various regions, geologically and geographically.

It must at the same time be admitted that the line of organic development has nowhere required for its advance the whole of the families comprehended in the two kingdoms, seeing that some of these are confined to one continent, and some to another, without a conceivable possibility of one having been connected with the other in the way of ancestry. The two great families of quadrumana, cebidæ and simiadæ, are a noted instance, the one being exclusively American, while the other belongs entirely to the old world. There are many other cases in which the full circular group can only be completed by taking subdivisions from various continents. This would seem to imply that, while the entire system is so remarkable for its unity, it has nevertheless been produced in lines geographically detached, these lines perhaps consisting of particular typical groups placed in an independent succession, or of two or more of these groups. And for this idea there is, even in the present imperfect state of our knowledge of animated nature, some countenance in ascertained facts, the birds of Australia, for example, being chiefly of the suctorial type, while it may be presumed that the observation as to the predominance of the useful animals in the Old World, is not much different from saying that the rasorial type is there peculiarly abundant. It does not appear that the idea of independent lines, consisting of particular types, or sets of types, is necessarily inconsistent with the general hypothesis, as nothing yet ascertained of the Macleay system forbids their having an independent set of affinities. On this subject, however, there is as yet much obscurity, and it must be left to future inquirers to clear it up. . . .

A question of a very interesting kind will now probably arise in the reader's mind—*What place or status is assigned to man in the new natural system?* Before going into this inquiry, it is necessary to advert to several particulars of the natural system not yet noticed.

It is necessary, in particular, to ascertain the grades which exist in the classification of animals. In the line of the aves, Mr. Swainson finds these to be nine, the species pica, for example, being thus indicated:—

Kingdom	Animalia.
Sub-kingdom	Vertebrata.
Class	Aves.
Order	Incessores.
Tribe	Conirostres.
Family	Corvidæ.
Sub-family	Corvinæ.
Genus	Corvus.
Sub-genus, or species	Pica. . . .

That man's place is to be looked for in the class mammalia and sub-kingdom vertebrata admits of no doubt, from his possessing both the characters on which these divisions are founded. When we descend, however, below the *class*, we find no settled views on the subject amongst naturalists. Mr. Swainson, who alone has given a review of the animal kingdom on the Macleay system, unfortunately writes on this subject in a manner which excites a suspicion as to his judgment. His arrangement of the first or typical order of the mammalia is therefore to be received with great hesitation. It is as follows:—

Typical	Quadramana	Pre-eminently organized for grasping
Sub-typical	Feræ	Claws retractile; carnivorous
Natatorial	Cetacæ	Pre-eminently aquatic; feet very short
Suctorial	Glires	Muzzle lengthened and pointed
Rasorial	Ungulata	Crests and other processes on the head

He then takes the quadrumana, and places it in the following arrangement:—

Typical	Simiadæ	(Monkeys of Old World.)
Sub-typical	Cebidæ	(Monkeys of New World.)
Natatorial	Unknown.	
Suctorial	Vespenilionide	(Bats.)
Rasorial	Lemuridæ	(Lemurs.)

He considers the simiadæ as a complete circle, and argues thence that there is no room in the range of the animal kingdom for man. Man, he says, is not a constituent part of any circle, for, if he were, there ought to be other animals on each hand having affinity to him, whereas there are none, the resemblance of the orangs being one of mere analogy. Mr. Swainson therefore considers our race as standing apart, and forming a link between the unintelligent order of beings and the angels! And this in spite of the glaring fact that, in our teeth, hands, and other features grounded on by naturalists as characteristic, we do not differ more from the simiadæ than the bats do from the lemurs—in spite also of that resemblance of analogy to the orangs which he himself admits, and which, at the least, must be held to imply a certain relation. He also overlooks that, though there may be no room for man in the circle of the simiadæ, (this, indeed, is quite true.) there may be in the order, where he actually leaves a place entirely blank, or only to be filled up, as he suggests, by mermen! Another argument in his arrangement is, that it leaves the grades of classification very much abridged, there being at the most seven instead of nine. But serious argument on a theory so preposterous may be considered as nearly thrown away. I shall therefore at once proceed to suggest a new arrangement of this portion of the animal kingdom, in which man is allowed the place to which he is zoologically entitled.

I propose that the typical order of the mammalia should be designated cheirotheria, from the sole character which is universal amongst them, their possessing hands, and with a regard to that pre-eminent qualification for grasping which has been ascribed to them—an analogy to the perching habit of the typical order of birds, which is worthy of particular notice. The tribes of the cheirotheria I arrange as follows:—

Typical	Bimana.
Sub-typical	Simiadæ.
Natatorial	Vespertilionidæ.
Suctorial	Lemuridæ.
Rasorial	Cebidæ.

Here man is put into the typical place, as the genuine head, not only of this order, but of the whole animal world. The double affinity which is requisite is obtained, for here he has the simiadæ on one hand, and the cebidæ on the other. The five tribes of the order are completed, the vespertilionidæ,æbeing shifted (provisionally) into the natatorial place, for which their appropriateness is so far evidenced by the aquatic habits of several of the tribe, and the lemuridæ into the suctorial, to which their length of muzzle and remarkable saltatory power are highly suitable. At the same time, the simiadæ are degraded from the typical place, to which they have no sort of pretension, and placed where their mean and mischievous character seem to require; the cebidæ again being assigned that situation which their comparatively inoffensive dispositions, their arboreal habits, and their extraordinary development of the tail, (which with them is like a fifth hand,) render so proper. . . .

Man, then, considered zoologically, and without regard to the distinct character assigned to him by theology, simply takes his place as the type of all types of the animal kingdom, the true and unmistakable head of animated nature upon this earth. It will readily occur that some more particular investigations into the ranks of types might throw additional light on man's status, and perhaps his nature; and such light we may hope to obtain when the philosophy of zoology shall have been studied as it deserves . . ..

It may be asked,—Is the existing human race the only species designed to occupy the grade to which it is here referred? Such a question evidently ought not to be answered rashly; and I shall therefore confine myself to the admission that, judging by analogy, we might expect to see several varieties of the being, homo. There is no other family approaching to this in importance, which presents but one species: The corvidæ, our parallel in aves, consist of several distinct genera and sub-genera. It is startling to find such an appearance of imperfection in the circle to which man belongs, and the ideas which rise in consequence are not less startling. Is our race but the initial of the grand crowning type? Are there yet to be species superior to us in organization, purer in feeling, more powerful in device and act, and who shall take a rule over us! There is in this nothing improbable on other grounds. The present race, rude and impulsive as it is, is perhaps the best adapted to the present state of things in the world; but the external world goes through slow and gradual changes, which may leave it in time a much serener field of existence. There may then be occasion for a nobler type of humanity, which shall complete the zoological circle on this planet, and realize some of the dreams of the purest spirits of the present race.

From Thomas Hardy, A Pair of Blue Eyes (1873), Chapter 22

This is the famous cliff-hanging scene where Hardy places an amateur geologist, Knight, hanging over a cliff contemplating his own destiny whilst he meditates on the extinction of fellow creatures such as trilobites. Knight's hopes lie in the hands of his female companion Elfride.

Haggard cliffs, of every ugly altitude, are as common as sea-fowl along the line of coast between Exmoor and Land's End; but this outflanked and encompassed specimen was the ugliest of them all. Their summits are not safe places for scientific experiment on the principles of air-currents, as Knight had now found, to his dismay.

He still clutched the face of the escarpment—not with the frenzied hold of despair, but with a dogged determination to make the most of his every jot of endurance, and so give the longest possible scope to Elfride's intentions, whatever they might be.

He reclined hand in hand with the world in its infancy. Not a blade, not an insect, which spoke of the present, was between him and the past. The inveterate antagonism of these black precipices to all strugglers for life is in no way more forcibly suggested than by the paucity of tufts of grass, lichens, or confervae on their outermost ledges.

Knight pondered on the meaning of Elfride's hasty disappearance, but could not avoid an instinctive conclusion that there existed but a doubtful hope for him. As far as he could judge, his sole chance of deliverance lay in the possibility of a rope or pole being brought; and this possibility was remote indeed. The soil upon these high downs was left so untended that they were unenclosed for miles, except by a casual bank or dry wall, and were rarely visited but for the purpose of collecting or counting the flock which found a scanty means of subsistence thereon.

At first, when death appeared improbable, because it had never visited him before, Knight could think of no future, nor of anything connected with his past. He could only look sternly at Nature's treacherous attempt to put an end to him, and strive to thwart her.

From the fact that the cliff formed the inner face of the segment of a huge cylinder, having the sky for a top and the sea for a bottom, which enclosed the cove to the extent of more than a semicircle, he could see the vertical face curving round on each side of him. He looked far down the facade, and realized more thoroughly how it threatened him. Grimness was in every feature, and to its very bowels the inimical shape was desolation.

By one of those familiar conjunctions of things wherewith the inanimate world baits the mind of man when he pauses in moments of suspense, opposite Knight's eyes was an imbedded fossil, standing forth in low relief from the rock. It was a creature with eyes. The eyes, dead and turned to stone, were even now regarding him. It was one of the early crustaceans called Trilobites. Separated by millions of years in their lives, Knight and this underling seemed to have met in their death. It was the single instance within reach of his vision of anything that had ever been alive and had had a body to save, as he himself had now.

The creature represented but a low type of animal existence, for never in their vernal years had the plains indicated by those numberless slaty layers been traversed by an intelligence worthy of the name. Zoophytes, mollusca, shell-fish, were the highest developments of those ancient dates. The immense lapses of time each formation represented had known nothing of the dignity of man. They were grand times, but they were mean times too, and mean were their relics. He was to be with the small in his death.

Knight was a geologist; and such is the supremacy of habit over occasion, as a pioneer of the thoughts of men, that at this dreadful juncture his mind found time to take in, by a momentary sweep, the varied scenes that had had their day between this creature's epoch and his own. There is no place like a cleft landscape for bringing home such imaginings as these.

Time closed up like a fan before him. He saw himself at one extremity of the years, face to face with the beginning and all the intermediate centuries simultaneously. Fierce men, clothed in the hides of beasts, and carrying, for defence and attack, huge clubs and pointed spears, rose from the rock, like the phantoms before the doomed Macbeth. They lived in hollows, woods, and mud huts—perhaps in caves of the neighbouring rocks. Behind them stood an earlier band. No man was there. Huge elephantine forms, the mastodon, the hippopotamus, the tapir, antelopes of monstrous size, the megatherium, and the myledon—all, for the moment, in juxtaposition. Further back, and overlapped by these, were perched huge-billed birds and swinish creatures as large as horses. Still more shadowy were the sinister crocodilian outlines—alligators and other uncouth shapes, culminating in the colossal lizard, the iguanodon. Folded behind were dragon forms and clouds of flying reptiles: still underneath were fishy beings of lower development; and so on, till the lifetime scenes of the fossil confronting him were a present and modern condition of things. These images passed before Knight's inner eye in less than half a minute, and he was again considering the actual present. Was he to die? The mental picture of Elfride in the world, without himself to cherish her, smote his heart like a whip. He had hoped for deliverance, but what could a girl do? He dared not move an inch. Was Death really stretching out his hand? The previous sensation, that it was improbable he would die, was fainter now.

However, Knight still clung to the cliff.

To those musing weather-beaten West-country folk who pass the greater part of their days and nights out of doors, Nature seems to have moods in other than a poetical sense: predilections for certain deeds at certain times, without any apparent law to govern or season to account for them. She is read as a person with a curious temper; as one who does not scatter kindnesses and cruelties alternately, impartially, and in order, but heartless severities or overwhelming generosities in lawless caprice. Man's case is always that of the prodigal's favourite or the miser's pensioner. In her unfriendly moments there seems a feline fun in her tricks, begotten by a foretaste of her pleasure in swallowing the victim.

Such a way of thinking had been absurd to Knight, but he began to adopt it now. He was first spitted on to a rock. New tortures followed. The rain increased, and persecuted him with an exceptional persistency which he was moved to believe owed its cause to the fact that he was in such a wretched state already. An entirely new order of things could be observed in this introduction of rain upon the scene. It rained upwards instead of down. The strong ascending air carried the rain-drops with it in its race up the escarpment, coming to him with such velocity that they stuck into his flesh like cold needles. Each drop was virtually a shaft, and it pierced him to his skin. The water- shafts seemed to lift him on their points: no downward rain ever had such a torturing effect. In a brief space he was drenched, except in two places. These were on the top of his shoulders and on the crown of his hat.

The wind, though not intense in other situations was strong here. It tugged at his coat and lifted it. We are mostly accustomed to look upon all opposition which is not animate, as that of the stolid, inexorable hand of indifference, which wears out the patience more than the strength. Here, at any rate, hostility did not assume that slow and sickening form. It was a cosmic agency, active, lashing, eager for conquest: determination; not an insensate standing in the way.

Knight had over-estimated the strength of his hands. They were getting weak already. 'She will never come again; she has been gone ten minutes,' he said to himself.

This mistake arose from the unusual compression of his experiences just now: she had really been gone but three.

'As many more minutes will be my end,' he thought.

Next came another instance of the incapacity of the mind to make comparisons at such times.

'This is a summer afternoon,' he said, 'and there can never have been such a heavy and cold rain on a summer day in my life before.'

He was again mistaken. The rain was quite ordinary in quantity; the air in temperature. It was, as is usual, the menacing attitude in which they approached him that magnified their powers.

He again looked straight downwards, the wind and the water-dashes lifting his moustache, scudding up his cheeks, under his eyelids, and into his eyes. This is what he saw down there: the surface of the sea—visually just past his toes, and under his feet; actually one-eighth of a mile, or more than two hundred yards, below them. We colour according to our moods the objects we survey. The sea would have been a deep neutral blue, had happier auspices attended the gazer it was now no otherwise than distinctly black to his vision. That narrow white border was foam, he knew well; but its boisterous tosses were so distant as to appear a pulsation only, and its plashing was barely audible. A white border to a black sea—his funeral pall and its edging.

The world was to some extent turned upside down for him. Rain descended from below. Beneath his feet was aerial space and the unknown; above him was the firm, familiar ground, and upon it all that he loved best.

Pitiless nature had then two voices, and two only. The nearer was the voice of the wind in his ears rising and falling as it mauled and thrust him hard or softly. The second and distant one was the moan of that unplummetted ocean below and afar—rubbing its restless flank against the Cliff without a Name.

Knight perseveringly held fast. Had he any faith in Elfride? Perhaps. Love is faith, and faith, like a gathered flower, will rootlessly live on.

Nobody would have expected the sun to shine on such an evening as this. Yet it appeared, low down upon the sea. Not with its natural golden fringe, sweeping the furthest ends of the landscape, not with the strange glare of whiteness which it sometimes puts on as an alternative to colour, but as a splotch of vermilion red upon a leaden ground—a red face looking on with a drunken leer.

Most men who have brains know it, and few are so foolish as to disguise this fact from themselves or others, even though an ostentatious display may be called self-conceit. Knight, without showing it much, knew that his intellect was above the average. And he thought—he could not help thinking—that his death would be a deliberate loss to earth of good material; that such an experiment in killing might have been practised upon some less developed life.

A fancy some people hold, when in a bitter mood, is that inexorable circumstance only tries to prevent what intelligence attempts. Renounce a desire for a long-contested position, and go on another tack, and after a while the prize is thrown at you, seemingly in disappointment that no more tantalizing is possible.

Knight gave up thoughts of life utterly and entirely, and turned to contemplate the Dark Valley and the unknown future beyond. Into the shadowy depths of these speculations we will not follow him. Let it suffice to state what ensued.

At that moment of taking no more thought for this life, something disturbed the outline of the bank above him. A spot appeared. It was the head of Elfride.

Knight immediately prepared to welcome life again.

CHAPTER 8

Extract from Bram Stoker's Dracula

Source: Project Gutenberg, www.gutenberg.net

Bram Stoker, in Dracula, *displays his awareness of the "criminal anthropology" studies of Cesare Lombroso, and Max Nordau's theories of degeneration, in his representation of the vampire's monstrosity. While the vampire-hunter Van Helsing cites both authorities later in the novel, here we can see Jonathan Harker's first meeting with the Count, whose face bears all the marks of the "higher" degenerate.*

Within, stood a tall old man, clean shaven save for a long white moustache, and clad in black from head to foot, without a single speck of colour about him anywhere. He held in his hand an antique silver lamp, in which the flame burned without a chimney or globe of any kind, throwing long quivering shadows as it flickered in the draught of the open door. The old man motioned me in with his right hand with a courtly gesture, saying in excellent English, but with a strange intonation.

"Welcome to my house! Enter freely and of your own free will!" He made no motion of stepping to meet me, but stood like a statue, as though his gesture of welcome had fixed him into stone. The instant, however, that I had stepped over the threshold, he moved impulsively forward, and holding out his hand grasped mine with a strength which made me wince, an effect which was not lessened by the fact that it seemed cold as ice, more like the hand of a dead than a living man. Again he said,

"Welcome to my house! Enter freely. Go safely, and leave something of the happiness you bring!" The strength of the handshake was so much akin to that which I had noticed in the driver, whose face I had not seen, that for a moment I doubted if it were not the same person to whom I was speaking. So to make sure, I said interrogatively,

"Count Dracula?"

He bowed in a courtly way as he replied, "I am Dracula, and I bid you welcome, Mr. Harker, to my house. Come in, the night air is chill, and you must need to eat and rest." As he was speaking, he put the lamp on a bracket on the wall, and stepping out, took my luggage. He had carried it in before I could forestall him. I protested, but he insisted.

"Nay, sir, you are my guest. It is late, and my people are not available. Let me see to your comfort myself." He insisted on carrying my traps along the passage, and then up a great winding stair, and along another great passage, on whose stone floor our steps rang heavily. At the end of this he threw open a heavy door, and I rejoiced to see within a well-lit room in which a table was spread for supper, and on whose mighty hearth a great fire of logs, freshly replenished, flamed and flared.

The Count halted, putting down my bags, closed the door, and crossing the room, opened another door, which led into a small octagonal room lit by a single lamp, and seemingly without a window of any sort. Passing through this, he opened another door, and motioned me to enter. It was a welcome sight. For here was a great bedroom well lighted and warmed with another log fire, also added to but lately, for the top logs were fresh, which sent a hollow roar up the wide chimney. The Count himself left my luggage inside and withdrew, saying, before he closed the door.

"You will need, after your journey, to refresh yourself by making your toilet. I trust you will find all you wish. When you are ready, come into the other room, where you will find your supper prepared."

The light and warmth and the Count's courteous welcome seemed to have dissipated all my doubts and fears. Having then reached my normal state, I discovered that I was half famished with hunger. So making a hasty toilet, I went into the other room.

I found supper already laid out. My host, who stood on one side of the great fireplace, leaning against the stonework, made a graceful wave of his hand to the table, and said, "I pray you, be seated and sup how you please. You will I trust, excuse me that I do not join you, but I have dined already, and I do not sup."

I handed to him the sealed letter which Mr. Hawkins had entrusted to me. He opened it and read it gravely. Then, with a charming smile, he handed it to me to read. One passage of it, at least, gave me a thrill of pleasure.

"I must regret that an attack of gout, from which malady I am a constant sufferer, forbids absolutely any travelling on my part for some time to come. But I am happy to say I can send a sufficient substitute, one in whom I have every possible confidence. He is a young man, full of energy and talent in his own way, and of a very faithful disposition. He is discreet and silent, and has grown into manhood in my service. He shall be ready to attend on you when you will during his stay, and shall take your instructions in all matters."

The count himself came forward and took off the cover of a dish, and I fell to at once on an excellent roast chicken. This, with some cheese and a salad and a bottle of old tokay, of which I had two glasses, was my supper. During the time I was eating it the Count asked me many questions as to my journey, and I told him by degrees all I had experienced.

By this time I had finished my supper, and by my host's desire had drawn up a chair by the fire and begun to smoke a cigar which he offered me, at the same time excusing himself that he did not smoke. I had now an opportunity of observing him, and found him of a very marked physiognomy.

His face was a strong, a very strong, aquiline, with high bridge of the thin nose and peculiarly arched nostrils, with lofty domed forehead, and hair growing scantily round the temples but profusely elsewhere. His eyebrows were very massive, almost meeting over the nose, and with bushy hair that seemed to curl in its own profusion. The mouth, so far as I could see it under the heavy moustache, was fixed and rather cruel-looking, with peculiarly sharp white teeth. These protruded over the lips, whose remarkable ruddiness showed astonishing vitality in a man of his years. For the rest, his ears were pale, and at the tops extremely pointed. The chin was broad and strong, and the cheeks firm though thin. The general effect was one of extraordinary pallor.

Hitherto I had noticed the backs of his hands as they lay on his knees in the firelight, and they had seemed rather white and fine. But seeing them now close to me, I could not but notice that they were rather coarse, broad, with squat fingers. Strange to say, there were hairs in the centre of the palm. The nails were long and fine, and cut to a sharp point. As the Count leaned over me and his hands touched me, I could not repress a shudder. It may have been that his breath was rank, but a horrible feeling of nausea came over me, which, do what I would, I could not conceal.

The Count, evidently noticing it, drew back. And with a grim sort of smile, which showed more than he had yet done his protruberant teeth, sat himself down again on his own side of the fireplace. We were both silent for a while, and as I looked towards the window I saw the first dim streak of the coming dawn. There seemed a strange stillness over everything. But as I listened, I heard as if from down below in the valley the howling of many wolves. The Count's eyes gleamed, and he said,

"Listen to them, the children of the night. What music they make!"

Seeing, I suppose, some expression in my face strange to him, he added, "Ah, sir, you dwellers in the city cannot enter into the feelings of the hunter." Then he rose and said,

"But you must be tired. Your bedroom is all ready, and tomorrow you shall sleep as late as you will. I have to be away till the afternoon, so sleep well and dream well!" With a courteous bow, he opened for me himself the door to the octagonal room, and I entered my bedroom.

I am all in a sea of wonders. I doubt. I fear. I think strange things, which I dare not confess to my own soul. God keep me, if only for the sake of those dear to me!

Extract from Sir Arthur Conan Doyle, "The Final Problem," The Memoirs of Sherlock Holmes

Source: Project Gutenberg, www.gutenberg.net

As in Stoker's Dracula, *Sir Arthur Conan Doyle's Sherlock Holmes stories also exhibit a knowledge of the latest "scientific" speculations of the last decade of the nineteenth century. Here, Holmes describes his encounter with the "higher degenerate" Professor Moriarty to the faithful Watson. This story, "The Final Problem," saw Conan Doyle's famous (and unsuccessful) attempt to kill off his creation at the Reichenbach Falls.*

"As you are aware, Watson, there is no one who knows the higher criminal world of London so well as I do. For years past I have continually been conscious of some power behind the malefactor, some deep organizing power which forever stands in the way of the law, and throws its shield over the wrong-doer. Again and again in cases of the most varying sorts—forgery cases, robberies, murders—I have felt the presence of this force, and I have deduced its action in many of those undiscovered crimes in which I have not been personally consulted. For years I have endeavored to break through the veil which shrouded it, and at last the time came when I seized my thread and followed it, until it led me, after a thousand cunning windings, to ex-Professor Moriarty of mathematical celebrity.

"He is the Napoleon of crime, Watson. He is the organizer of half that is evil and of nearly all that is undetected in this great city. He is a genius, a philosopher, an abstract thinker. He has a brain of the first order. He sits motionless, like a spider in the center of its web, but that web has a thousand radiations, and he knows well every quiver of each of them. He does little himself. He only plans. But his agents are numerous and splendidly organized. Is there a crime to be done, a paper to be abstracted, we will say, a house to be rifled, a man to be removed—the word is passed to the Professor, the matter is organized and carried out. The agent may be caught. In that case money is found for his bail or his defence. But the central power which uses the agent is never caught—never so much as suspected. This was the organization which I deduced, Watson, and which I devoted my whole energy to exposing and breaking up.

"But the Professor was fenced round with safeguards so cunningly devised that, do what I would, it seemed impossible to get evidence which would convict in a court of law. You know my powers, my dear Watson, and yet at the end of three months I was forced to confess that I had at last met an antagonist who was my intellectual equal. My horror at his crimes was lost in my admiration at his skill. But at last he made a trip—only a little, little trip—but it was more than he could afford when I was so close upon him. I had my chance, and, starting from that point, I have woven my net round him until now it is all ready to close. In three days—that is to say, on Monday next—matters will be ripe, and the Professor, with all the principal members of his gang, will be in the hands of the police. Then will come the greatest criminal trial of the century, the clearing up of over forty mysteries, and the rope for all of them; but if we move at all prematurely, you understand, they may slip out of our hands even at the last moment.

"Now, if I could have done this without the knowledge of Professor Moriarty, all would have been well. But he was too wily for that. He saw every step which I took to draw my toils round him. Again and again he strove to break away, but I as often headed him off. I tell you, my friend, that if a detailed account of that silent contest could be written, it would take its place as the most brilliant bit of thrust-and-parry work in the history of detection. Never have I risen to such a height, and never have I been so hard pressed by an opponent. He cut deep, and yet I just undercut him. This morning the last steps were taken, and three days only were wanted to complete the business. I was sitting in my room thinking the matter over, when the door opened and Professor Moriarty stood before me.

"My nerves are fairly proof, Watson, but I must confess to a start when I saw the very man who had been so much in my thoughts standing there on my threshhold. His appearance was quite familiar to me. He is extremely tall and thin, his forehead domes out in a white curve, and his two eyes are deeply sunken in this head. He is clean-shaven, pale, and ascetic-looking, retaining something of the professor in his features. His shoulders are rounded from much study, and his face protrudes forward, and is forever slowly oscillating from side to side in a curiously reptilian fashion. He peered at me with great curiosity in his puckered eyes.

"'You have less frontal development that I should have expected,' said he, at last. 'It is a dangerous habit to finger loaded firearms in the pocket of one's dressing-gown.'

"The fact is that upon his entrance I had instantly recognized the extreme personal danger in which I lay. The only conceivable escape for him lay in silencing my tongue. In an instant I had slipped the revolved from the drawer into my pocket, and was covering him through the cloth. At his remark I drew the weapon out and laid it cocked upon the table. He still smiled and blinked, but there was something about his eyes which made me feel very glad that I had it there.

"'You evidently don't now me,' said he.

"'On the contrary,' I answered, 'I think it is fairly evident that I do. Pray take a chair. I can spare you five minutes if you have anything to say.'"

Conan Doyle's "The Creeping Man"

The Case-Book of Sherlock Holmes (1927) (London: Penguin, 1951), now out of copyright. This text from http://infomotions.com/etexts/literature/english/1800-1899/doyle-case-381.txt.

In a later Sherlock Holmes story, "The Creeping Man," Holmes and Watson attend "Camford University" to investigate the mystery of a strange quasi-human being seen near one of the colleges. In this story, we see the influence of degenerationist discourses, and of evolutionary theory, as late as the 1920s.

Mr. Sherlock Holmes was always of opinion that I should publish the singular facts connected with Professor Presbury, if only to dispel once for all the ugly rumours which some twenty years ago agitated the university and were echoed in the learned societies of London. There were, however, certain obstacles in the way, and the true history of this curious case remained entombed in the tin box which contains so many records of my friend's adventures. Now we have at last obtained permission to ventilate the facts which formed one of the very last cases handled by Holmes before his retirement from practice. Even now a certain reticence and discretion have to be observed in laying the matter before the public.

It was one Sunday evening early in September of the year 1903 that I received one of Holmes's laconic messages:

Come at once if convenient—if inconvenient come all the same. S. H.

The relations between us in those latter days were peculiar. He was a man of habits, narrow and concentrated habits, and I had become one of them. As an institution I was like the violin, the shag tobacco, the old black pipe, the index books, and others perhaps less excusable. When it was a case of active work and a comrade was needed upon whose nerve he could place some reliance, my role was obvious. But apart from this I had uses. I was a whetstone for his mind. I stimulated him. He liked to think aloud in my presence. His remarks could hardly be said to be made to me—many of them would have been as appropriately addressed to his bedstead—but none the less, having formed the habit, it had become in some way helpful that I should register and interject. If I irritated him by a certain methodical slowness in my mentality, that irritation served only to make his own flame-like intuitions and impressions flash up the more vividly and swiftly. Such was my humble role in our alliance.

When I arrived at Baker Street I found him huddled up in his armchair with updrawn knees, his pipe in his mouth and his brow furrowed with thought. It was clear that he was in the throes of some vexatious problem. With a wave of his hand he indicated my old armchair, but otherwise for half an hour he gave no sign that he was aware of my presence. Then with a start he seemed to come from his reverie, and with his usual whimsical smile he greeted me back to what had once been my home.

"You will excuse a certain abstraction of mind, my dear Watson," said he. "Some curious facts have been submitted to me within the last twenty-four hours, and they in turn have given rise to some speculations of a more general character. I have serious thoughts of writing a small monograph upon the uses of dogs in the work of the detective."

"But surely, Holmes, this has been explored," said I. "Bloodhounds—sleuthhounds—"

"No, no, Watson, that side of the matter is, of course, obvious. But there is another which is far more subtle. You may recollect that in the case which you, in your sensational way, coupled with the Copper Beeches, I was able, by watching the mind of the child, to form a deduction as to the criminal habits of the very smug and respectable father."

"Yes, I remember it well."

"My line of thoughts about dogs is analogous. A dog reflects the family life. Whoever saw a frisky dog in a gloomy family, or a sad dog in a happy one? Snarling people have snarling dogs, dangerous people have dangerous ones. And their passing moods may reflect the passing moods of others."

I shook my head. "Surely, Holmes, this is a little far-fetched," said I.

He had refilled his pipe and resumed his seat, taking no notice of my comment.

"The practical application of what I have said is very close to the problem which I am investigating. It is a tangled skein, you understand, and I am looking for a loose end. One possible loose end lies in the question: Why does Professor Presbury's wolfhound, Roy, endeavour to bite him?"

I sank back in my chair in some disappointment. Was it for so trivial a question as this that I had been summoned from my work? Holmes glanced across at me.

"The same old Watson!" said he. "You never learn that the gravest issues may depend upon the smallest things. But is it not on the face of it strange that a staid, elderly philosopher—you've heard of Presbury, of course, the famous Camford physiologist?—that such a man, whose friend has been his devoted wolfhound, should now have been twice attacked by his own dog? What do you make of it?"

"The dog is ill."

"Well, that has to be considered. But he attacks no one else, nor does he apparently molest his master, save on very special occasions. Curious, Watson—very curious. But young Mr. Bennett is before his time if that is his ring. I had hoped to have a longer chat with you before he came."

There was a quick step on the stairs, a sharp tap at the door and a moment later the new client presented himself. He was a tall, handsome youth about thirty, well dressed and elegant, but with something in his bearing which suggested the shyness of the student rather than the self-possession of the man of the world. He shook hands with Holmes, and then looked with some surprise at me.

"This matter is very delicate, Mr. Holmes," he said. " Consider the relation in which I stand to Professor Presbury both privately and publicly. I really can hardly justify myself if I speak before any third person."

"Have no fear, Mr. Bennett. Dr. Watson is the very soul of discretion, and I can assure you that this is a matter in which I am very likely to need an assistant."

"As you like, Mr. Holmes. You will, I am sure, understand my having some reserves in the matter."

"You will appreciate it, Watson, when I tell you that this gentleman, Mr. Trevor Bennett, is professional assistant to the great scientist, lives under his roof, and is engaged to his only daughter. Certainly we must agree that the professor has every claim upon his loyalty and devotion. But it may best be shown by taking the necessary steps to clear up this strange mystery."

"I hope so, Mr. Holmes. That is my one object. Does Dr. Watson know the situation?"

"I have not had time to explain it."

"Then perhaps I had better go over the ground again before explaining some fresh developments."

"I will do so myself," said Holmes, "in order to show that I have the events in their due order. The professor, Watson, is a man of European reputation. His life has been academic. There has never been a breath of scandal. He is a widower with one daughter, Edith. He is, I gather, a man of very virile and positive, one might almost say combative, character. So the matter stood until a very few months ago.

"Then the current of his life was broken. He is sixty-one years of age, but he became engaged to the daughter of Professor Morphy, his colleague in the chair of comparative anatomy. It was not, as I understand, the reasoned courting of an elderly man but rather the passionate frenzy of youth, for no one could have shown himself a more devoted lover. The lady, Alice Morphy, was a very perfect girl both in mind and body, so that there was every excuse for the professor's infatuation. None the less, it did not meet with full approval in his own family."

"We thought it rather excessive," said our visitor.

"Exactly. Excessive and a little violent and unnatural. Professor Presbury was rich, however, and there was no objection upon the part of the father. The daughter, however, had other views, and there were already several candidates for her hand, who, if they were less eligible from a worldly point of view, were at least more of an age. The girl seemed to like the professor in spite of his eccentricities. It was only age which stood in the way.

"About this time a little mystery suddenly clouded the normal routine of the professor's life. He did what he had never done before. He left home and gave no indication where he was going. He was away a fortnight and returned looking rather travel-worn. He made no allusion to where he had been, although he was usually the frankest of men. It chanced, however, that our client here, Mr. Bennett, received a letter from a fellow-student in Prague, who said that he was glad to have seen Professor Presbury there, although he had not been able to talk to him.

Only in this way did his own household learn where he had been.

"Now comes the point. From that time onward a curious change came over the professor. He became furtive and sly. Those around him had always the feeling that he was not the man that they had known, but that he was under some shadow which had darkened his higher qualities. His intellect was not affected. His lectures were as brilliant as ever. But always there was something new, something sinister and unexpected. His daughter, who was devoted to him, tried again and again to resume the old relations and to penetrate this mask which her father seemed to have put on. You, sir, as I understand, did the same—but all was in vain. And now, Mr. Bennett, tell in your own words the incident of the letters."

"You must understand, Dr. Watson, that the professor had no secrets from me. If I were his son or his younger brother I could not have more completely enjoyed his confidence. As his secretary I handled every paper which came to him, and I opened and subdivided his letters. Shortly after his return all this was changed. He told me that certain letters might come to him from London which would be marked by a cross under the stamp. These were to be set aside for his own eyes only. I may say that several of these did pass through my hands, that they had the E. C. mark, and were in an illiterate handwriting. If he answered them at all the answers did not pass through my hands nor into the letter-basket in which our correspondence was collected."

"And the box," said Holmes.

"Ah, yes, the box. The professor brought back a little wooden box from his travels. It was the one thing which suggested a Continental tour, for it was one of those quaint carved things which one associates with Germany. This he placed in his instrument cupboard. One day, in looking for a canula, I took up the box. To my surprise he was very angry, and reproved me in words which were quite savage for my curiosity. It was the first time such a thing had happened, and I was deeply hurt. I endeavoured to explain that it was a mere accident that I had touched the box, but all the evening I was conscious that he looked at me harshly and that the incident was rankling in his mind." Mr. Bennett drew a little diary book from his pocket. "That was on July 2d," said he.

"You are certainly an admirable witness," said Holmes. "I may need some of these dates which you have noted."

"I learned method among other things from my great teacher. From the time that I observed abnormality in his behaviour I felt that it was my duty to study his case. Thus I have it here that it was on that very day, July 2d, that Roy attacked the professor as he came from his study into the hall. Again, on July 11th, there was a scene of the same sort, and then I have a note of yet another upon July 20th. After that we had to banish Roy to the stables. He was a dear, affectionate animal—but I fear I weary you."

Mr. Bennett spoke in a tone of reproach, for it was very clear that Holmes was not listening. His face was rigid and his eyes gazed abstractedly at the ceiling. With an effort he recovered himself.

"Singular! Most singular!" he murmured. "These details were new to me, Mr. Bennett. I think we have now fairly gone over the old ground, have we not? But you spoke of some fresh developments."

The pleasant, open face of our visitor clouded over, shadowed by some grim remembrance. "What I speak of occurred the night before last," said he. "I was lying awake about two in the morning, when I was aware of a dull muffled sound coming from the passage. I opened my door and peeped out. I should explain that the professor sleeps at the end of the passage—"

"The date being?" asked Holmes.

Our visitor was clearly annoyed at so irrelevant an interruption.

"I have said, sir, that it was the night before last—that is, September 4th."

Holmes nodded and smiled.

"Pray continue," said he.

"He sleeps at the end of the passage and would have to pass my door in order to reach the staircase. It was a really terrifying experience, Mr. Holmes. I think that I am as strong-nerved as my neighbours, but I was shaken by what I saw. The passage was dark save that one window halfway along it threw a patch of light. I could see that something was coming along the passage, something dark and crouching. Then suddenly it emerged into the light, and I saw that it was he. He was crawling, Mr. Holmes—crawling! He was not quite on his hands and knees. I should rather say on his hands and feet, with his face sunk between his hands. Yet he seemed to move with ease. I was so paralyzed by the sight that it was not until he had reached my door that I was able to step forward and ask if I could assist him. His answer was extraordinary. He sprang up, spat out some atrocious word at me, and hurried on past me, and down the staircase. I waited about for an hour, but he did not come back. It must have been daylight before he regained his room."

"Well, Watson, what make you of that?" asked Holmes with the air of the pathologist who presents a rare specimen.

"Lumbago, possibly. I have known a severe attack make a man walk in just such a way, and nothing would be more trying to the temper."

"Good, Watson! You always keep us flat-footed on the ground. But we can hardly accept lumbago, since he was able to stand erect in a moment."

"He was never better in health," said Bennett. "In fact, he is stronger than I have known him for years. But there are the facts, Mr. Holmes. It is not a case in which we can consult the police, and yet we are utterly at our wit's end as to what to do, and we feel in some strange way that we are drifting towards disaster. Edith—Miss Presbury—feels as I do, that we cannot wait passively any longer."

"It is certainly a very curious and suggestive case. What do you think, Watson?"

"Speaking as a medical man," said I, "it appears to be a case for an alienist. The old gentleman's cerebral processes were disturbed by the love affair. He made a journey abroad in the hope of breaking himself of the passion. His letters and the box may be connected with some other private transaction—a loan, perhaps, or share certificates, which are in the box."

"And the wolfhound no doubt disapproved of the financial bargain. No, no, Watson, there is more in it than this. Now, I can only suggest—"

What Sherlock Holmes was about to suggest will never be known, for at this moment the door opened and a young lady was shown into the room. As she appeared Mr. Bennett sprang up with a cry and ran forward with his hands out to meet those which she had herself outstretched.

"Edith, dear! Nothing the matter, I hope?"

"I felt I must follow you. Oh, Jack, I have been so dreadfully frightened! It is awful to be there alone."

"Mr. Holmes, this is the young lady I spoke of. This is my fiancee."

"We were gradually coming to that conclusion, were we not, Watson?" Holmes answered with a smile. "I take it, Miss Presbury, that there is some fresh development in the case, and that you thought we should know?"

Our new visitor, a bright, handsome girl of a conventional English type, smiled back at Holmes as she seated herself beside Mr. Bennett.

"When I found Mr. Bennett had left his hotel I thought I should probably find him here. Of course, he had told me that he would consult you. But, oh, Mr. Holmes, can you do nothing for my poor father?"

"I have hopes, Miss Presbury, but the case is still obscure. Perhaps what you have to say may throw some fresh light upon it."

"It was last night, Mr. Holmes. He had been very strange all day. I am sure that there are times when he has no recollection of what he does. He lives as in a strange dream. Yesterday was such a day. It was not my father with whom I lived. His outward shell was there, but it was not really he."

"Tell me what happened."

"I was awakened in the night by the dog barking most furiously. Poor Roy, he is chained now near the stable. I may say that I always sleep with my door locked; for, as Jack—as Mr. Bennett—will tell you, we all have a feeling of impending danger. My room is on the second floor.

It happened that the blind was up in my window, and there was bright moonlight outside. As I lay with my eyes fixed upon the square of light, listening to the frenzied barkings of the dog, I was amazed to see my father's face looking in at me. Mr. Holmes, I nearly died of surprise and horror. There it was pressed against the windowpane, and one hand seemed to be raised as if to push up the window. If that window had opened, I think I should have gone mad. It was no delusion, Mr. Holmes. Don't deceive yourself by thinking so. I dare say it was twenty seconds or so that I lay paralyzed and watched the face. Then it vanished, but I could not—I could not spring out of bed and look out after it. I lay cold and shivering till morning. At breakfast he was sharp and fierce in manner, and made no allusion to the adventure of the night. Neither did I, but I gave an excuse for coming to town—and here I am."

Holmes looked thoroughly surprised at Miss Presbury's narrative.

"My dear young lady, you say that your room is on the second floor. Is there a long ladder in the garden?"

"No, Mr. Holmes, that is the amazing part of it. There is no possible way of reaching the window—and yet he was there."

"The date being September 5th," said Holmes. "That certainly complicates matters."

It was the young lady's turn to look surprised. "This is the second time that you have alluded to the date, Mr. Holmes," said Bennett. "Is it possible that it has any bearing upon the case?"

"It is possible—very possible—and yet I have not my full material at present."

"Possibly you are thinking of the connection between insanity and phases of the moon?"

"No, I assure you. It was quite a different line of thought. Possibly you can leave your notebook with me, and I will check the dates. Now I think, Watson, that our line of action is perfectly clear. This young lady has informed us—and I have the greatest confidence in her intuition—that her father remembers little or nothing which occurs upon certain dates. We will therefore call upon him as if he had given us an appointment upon such a date. He will put it down to his own lack of memory. Thus we will open our campaign by having a good close view of him."

"That is excellent," said Mr. Bennett. "I warn you, however, that the professor is irascible and violent at times."

Holmes smiled. "There are reasons why we should come at once—very cogent reasons if my theories hold good. To-morrow, Mr. Bennett, will certainly see us in Camford. There is, if I remember right, an inn called the Chequers where the port used to be above mediocrity and the linen was above reproach. I think, Watson, that our lot for the next few days might lie in less pleasant places."

Monday morning found us on our way to the famous university town—an easy effort on the part of Holmes, who had no roots to pull up, but one which involved frantic planning and hurrying on my part, as my practice was by this time not inconsiderable. Holmes made no allusion to the case until after we had deposited our suitcases at the ancient hostel of which he had spoken.

"I think, Watson, that we can catch the professor just before lunch. He lectures at eleven and should have an interval at home."

"What possible excuse have we for calling?"

Holmes glanced at his notebook.

"There was a period of excitement upon August 26th. We will assume that he is a little hazy as to what he does at such times. If we insist that we are there by appointment I think he will hardly venture to contradict us. Have you the effrontery necessary to put it through?"

"We can but try."

"Excellent, Watson! Compound of the Busy Bee and Excelsior. We can but try—the motto of the firm. A friendly native will surely guide us."

Such a one on the back of a smart hansom swept us past a row of ancient colleges and, finally turning into a tree-lined drive, pulled up at the door of a charming house, girt round with lawns and covered with purple wistaria. Professor Presbury was certainly surrounded with every sign not only of comfort but of luxury.

Even as we pulled up, a grizzled head appeared at the front window, and we were aware of a pair of keen eyes from under shaggy brows which surveyed us through large horn glasses. A moment later we were actually in his sanctum, and the mysterious scientist, whose vagaries had brought us from London, was standing before us. There was certainly no sign of eccentricity either in his manner or appearance, for he was a portly, large-featured man, grave, tall, and frock-coated, with the dignity of bearing which a lecturer needs. His eyes were his most remarkable feature, keen, observant, and clever to the verge of cunning.

He looked at our cards. "Pray sit down, gentlemen. What can I do for you?"

Mr. Holmes smiled amiably.

"It was the question which I was about to put to you, Professor."

"To me, sir!"

"Possibly there is some mistake. I heard through a second person that Professor Presbury of Camford had need of my services."

"Oh, indeed!" It seemed to me that there was a malicious sparkle in the intense gray eyes. "You heard that, did you? May I ask the name of your informant?"

"I am sorry, Professor, but the matter was rather confidential. If I have made a mistake there is no harm done. I can only express my regret."

"Not at all. I should wish to go further into this matter. It interests me. Have you any scrap of writing, any letter or telegram, to bear out your assertion?"

"No, I have not."

"I presume that you do not go so far as to assert that I summoned you?"

"I would rather answer no questions," said Holmes.

"No, I dare say not," said the professor with asperity. " However, that particular one can be answered very easily without your aid."

He walked across the room to the bell. Our London friend Mr. Bennett, answered the call.

"Come in, Mr. Bennett. These two gentlemen have come from London under the impression that they have been summoned. You handle all my correspondence. Have you a note of anything going to a person named Holmes?"

"No, sir," Bennett answered with a flush.

"That is conclusive," said the professor, glaring angrily at my companion. "Now, sir"—he leaned forward with his two hands upon the table—" it seems to me that your position is a very questionable one."

Holmes shrugged his shoulders.

"I can only repeat that I am sorry that we have made a needless intrusion."

"Hardly enough, Mr. Holmes!" the old man cried in a high screaming voice, with extraordinary malignancy upon his face. He got between us and the door as he spoke, and he shook his two hands at us with furious passion. "You can hardly get out of it so easily as that." His face was convulsed, and he grinned and gibbered at us in his senseless rage. I am convinced that we should have had to fight our way out of the room if Mr. Bennett had not intervened.

"My dear Professor," he cried, "consider your position! Consider the scandal at the university! Mr. Holmes is a wellknown man. You cannot possibly treat him with such discourtesy."

Sulkily our host—if I may call him so—cleared the path to the door. We were glad to find ourselves outside the house and in the quiet of the tree-lined drive. Holmes seemed great!y amused by the episode.

"Our learned friend's nerves are somewhat out of order," said he. "Perhaps our intrusion was a little crude, and yet we have gained that personal contact which I desired. But, dear me, Watson, he is surely at our heels. The villain still pursues us."

There were the sounds of running feet behind, but it was, to my relief, not the formidable professor but his assistant who appeared round the curve of the drive. He came panting up to us.

"I am so sorry, Mr. Holmes. I wished to apologize."

"My dear sir, there is no need. It is all in the way of professional experience."

"I have never seen him in a more dangerous mood. But he grows more sinister. You can understand now why his daughter and I are alarmed. And yet his mind is perfectly clear."

"Too clear!" said Holmes. "That was my miscalculation. It is evident that his memory is much more reliable than I had thought.

By the way, can we, before we go, see the window of Miss Presbury's room?"

Mr. Bennett pushed his way through some shrubs, and we had a view of the side of the house.

"It is there. The second on the left."

"Dear me, it seems hardly accessible. And yet you will observe that there is a creeper below and a water-pipe above which give some foothold."

"I could not climb it myself," said Mr. Bennett.

"Very likely. It would certainly be a dangerous exploit for any normal man."

"There was one other thing I wish to tell you, Mr. Holmes. I have the address of the man in London to whom the professor writes. He seems to have written this morning, and I got it from his blotting-paper. It is an ignoble position for a trusted secretary, but what else can I do?"

Holmes glanced at the paper and put it into his pocket.

"Dorak—a curious name. Slavonic, I imagine. Well, it is an important link in the chain. We return to London this afternoon, Mr. Bennett. I see no good purpose to be served by our remaining. We cannot arrest the professor because he has done no crime, nor can we place him under constraint, for he cannot be proved to be mad. No action is as yet possible."

"Then what on earth are we to do?"

"A little patience, Mr. Bennett. Things will soon develop. Unless I am mistaken, next Tuesday may mark a crisis. Certainly we shall be in Camford on that day. Meanwhile, the general position is undeniably unpleasant, and if Miss Presbury can prolong her visit "

"That is easy."

"Then let her stay till we can assure her that all danger is past. Meanwhile, let him have his way and do not cross him. So long as he is in a good humour all is well."

"There he is!" said Bennett in a startled whisper. Looking between the branches we saw the tall, erect figure emerge from the hall door and look around him. He stood leaning forward, his hands swinging straight before him, his head turning from side to side. The secretary with a last wave slipped off among the trees, and we saw him presently rejoin his employer, the two entering the house together in what seemed to be animated and even excited conversation.

"I expect the old gentleman has been putting two and two together," said Holmes as we walked hotel-ward. "He struck me as having a particularly clear and logical brain from the little I saw of him. Explosive, no doubt, but then from his point of view he has something to explode about if detectives are put on his track and he suspects his own household of doing it. I rather fancy that friend Bennett is in for an uncomfortable time."

Holmes stopped at a post-office and sent off a telegram on our way. The answer reached us in the evening, and he tossed it across to me.

Have visited the Commercial Road and seen Dorak. Suave person, Bohemian, elderly. Keeps large general store.

MERCER.

"Mercer is since your time," said Holmes. "He is my general utility man who looks up routine business. It was important to know something of the man with whom our professor was so secretly corresponding. His nationality connects up with the Prague visit."

"Thank goodness that something connects with something," said I. "At present we seem to be faced by a long series of inexplicable incidents with no bearing upon each other."For example, what possible connection can there be between an angry wolfhound and a visit to Bohemia, or either of them with a man crawling down a passage at night? As to your dates, that is the biggest mystification of all."

Holmes smiled and rubbed his hands. We were, I may say, seated in the old sitting-room of the ancient hotel, with a bottle of the famous vintage of which Holmes had spoken on the table between us.

"Well, now, let us take the dates first," said he, his fingertips together and his manner as if he were addressing a class. "This excellent young man's diary shows that there was trouble upon July 2d, and from then onward it seems to have been at nine-day intervals, with, so far as I remember, only one exception. Thus the last outbreak upon Friday was on September 3d, which also falls into the series, as did August 26th, which preceded it. The thing is beyond coincidence."

I was forced to agree.

"Let us, then, form the provisional theory that every nine days the professor takes some strong drug which has a passing but highly poisonous effect. His naturally violent nature is intensified by it. He learned to take this drug while he was in Prague, and is now supplied with it by a Bohemian intermediary in London. This all hangs together, Watson!"

"But the dog, the face at the window, the creeping man in the passage?"

"Well, well, we have made a beginning. I should not expect any fresh developments until next Tuesday. In the meantime we can only keep in touch with friend Bennett and enjoy the amenities of this charming town."

In the morning Mr. Bennett slipped round to bring us the latest report. As Holmes had imagined, times had not been easy with him. Without exactly accusing him of being responsible for our presence, the professor had been very rough and rude in his speech, and evidently felt some strong grievance. This morning he was quite himself again, however, and had delivered his usual brilliant lecture to a crowded class. "Apart from his queer fits," said Bennett, "he has actually more energy and vitality than I can ever remember, nor was his brain ever clearer. But it's not he—it's never the man whom we have known."

"I don't think you have anything to fear now for a week at least," Holmes answered. "I am a busy man, and Dr. Watson has his patients to attend to. Let us agree that we meet here at this hour next Tuesday, and I shall be surprised if before we leave you again we are not able to explain, even if we cannot perhaps put an end to, your troubles. Meanwhile, keep us posted in what occurs."

I saw nothing of my friend for the next few days, but on the following Monday evening I had a short note asking me to meet him next day at the train. From what he told me as we travelled up to Camford all was well, the peace of the professor's house had been unruffled, and his own conduct perfectly normal. This also was the report which was given us by Mr. Bennett himself when he called upon us that evening at our old quarters in the Chequers. "He heard from his London correspondent to-day. There was a letter and there was a small packet, each with the cross under the stamp which warned me not to touch them. There has been nothing else."

"That may prove quite enough," said Holmes grimly. "Now, Mr. Bennett, we shall, I think, come to some conclusion tonight. If my deductions are correct we should have an opportunity of bringing matters to a head. In order to do so it is necessary to hold the professor under observation. I would suggest, therefore, that you remain awake and on the lookout. Should you hear him pass your door, do not interrupt him, but follow him as discreetly as you can. Dr. Watson and I will not be far off. By the way, where is the key of that little box of which you spoke?"

"Upon his watch-chain."

"I fancy our researches must lie in that direction. At the worst the lock should not be very formidable. Have you any other able-bodied man on the premises?"

"There is the coachman, Macphail."

"Where does he sleep?"

"Over the stables."

"We might possibly want him. Well, we can do no more until we see how things develop, Good-bye—but I expect that we shall see you before morning."

It was nearly midnight before we took our station among some bushes immediately opposite the hall door of the professor. It was a fine night, but chilly, and we were glad of our warm overcoats. There was a breeze, and clouds were scudding across the sky, obscuring from time to time the half-moon. It would have been a dismal vigil were it not for the expectation and excitement which carried us along, and the assurance of my comrade that we had probably reached the end of the strange sequence of events which had engaged our attention.

"If the cycle of nine days holds good then we shall have the professor at his worst to-night," said Holmes. "The fact that these strange symptoms began after his visit to Prague, that he is in secret correspondence with a Bohemian dealer in London, who presumably represents someone in Prague, and that he received a packet from him this very day, all point in one direction. What he takes and why he takes it are still beyond our ken, but that it emanates in some way from Prague is clear enough. He takes it under definite directions which regulate this ninth-day system, which was the first point which attracted my attention. But his symptoms are most remarkable. Did you observe his knuckles?"

I had to confess that I did not.

"Thick and horny in a way which is quite new in my experience. Always look at the hands first, Watson. Then cuffs, trouser-knees, and boots. Very curious knuckles which can only be explained by the mode of progression observed by—" Holmes paused and suddenly clapped his hand to his forehead. "Oh, Watson, Watson, what a fool I have been! It seems incredible, and yet it must be true. All points in one direction. How could I miss seeing the connection of ideas? Those knuckles how could I have passed those knuckles? And the dog! And the ivy! It's surely time that I disappeared into that little farm of my dreams. Look out, Watson! Here he is! We shall have the chance of seeing for ourselves."

The hall door had slowly opened, and against the lamp-lit background we saw the tall figure of Professor Presbury. He was clad in his dressing gown. As he stood outlined in the doorway he was erect but leaning forward with dangling arms, as when we saw him last.

Now he stepped forward into the drive, and an extraordinary change came over him. He sank down into a crouching position and moved along upon his hands and feet, skipping every now and then as if he were overflowing with energy and vitality. He moved along the face of the house and then round the corner. As he disappeared Bennett slipped through the hall door and softly followed him.

"Come, Watson, come!" cried Holmes, and we stole as softly as we could through the bushes until we had gained a spot whence we could see the other side of the house, which was bathed in the light of the half-moon. The professor was clearly visible crouching at the foot of the ivy-covered wall. As we watched him he suddenly began with incredible agility to ascend it. From branch to branch he sprang, sure of foot and firm of grasp, climbing apparently in mere joy at his own powers, with no definite object in view. With his dressing-gown flapping on each side of him, he looked like some huge bat glued against the side of his own house, a great square dark patch upon the moonlit wall. Presently he tired of this amusement, and, dropping from branch to branch, he squatted down into the old attitude and moved towards the stables, creeping along in the same strange way as before. The wolfhound was out now, barking furiously, and more excited than ever when it actually caught sight of its master. It was straining on its chain and quivering with eagerness and rage. The professor squatted down very deliberately just out of reach of the hound and began to provoke it in every possible way. He took handfuls of pebbles from the drive and threw them in the dog's face, prodded him with a stick which he had picked up, flicked his hands about only a few inches from the gaping mouth, and endeavoured in every way to increase the animal's fury, which was already beyond all control. In all our adventures I do not know that I have ever seen a more strange sight than this impassive and still dignified figure crouching frog-like upon the ground and goading to a wilder exhibition of passion the maddened hound, which ramped and raged in front of him, by all manner of ingenious and calculated cruelty.

And then in a moment it happened! It was not the chain that broke, but it was the collar that slipped, for it had been made for a thick-necked Newfoundland. We heard the rattle of falling metal, and the next instant dog and man were rolling on the ground together, the one roaring in rage, the other screaming in a strange shrill falsetto of terror. It was a very narrow thing for the professor's life. The savage creature had him fairly by the throat, its fangs had bitten deep, and he was senseless before we could reach them and drag the two apart. It might have been a dangerous task for us, but Bennett's voice and presence brought the great wolf-hound instantly to reason.

The uproar had brought the sleepy and astonished coachman from his room above the stables. "I'm not surprised," said he, shaking his head. "I've seen him at it before. I knew the dog would get him sooner or later."

The hound was secured, and together we carried the professor up to his room, where Bennett, who had a medical degree, helped me to dress his torn throat. The sharp teeth had passed dangerously near the carotid artery, and the haemorrhage was serious. In half an hour the danger was past, I had given the patient an injection of morphia, and he had sunk into deep sleep. Then, and only then, were we able to look at each other and to take stock of the situation.

"I think a first-class surgeon should see him," said I.

"For God's sake, no!" cried Bennett. "At present the scandal is confined to our own household. It is safe with us. If it gets beyond these walls it will never stop. Consider his position at the university, his European reputation, the feelings of his daughter."

"Quite so," said Holmes. "I think it may be quite possible to keep the matter to ourselves, and also to prevent its recurrence now that we have a free hand. The key from the watch-chain, Mr. Bennett. Macphail will guard the patient and let us know if there is any change. Let us see what we can find in the professor's mysterious box."

There was not much, but there was enough—an empty phial, another nearly full, a hypodermic syringe, several letters in a crabbed, foreign hand. The marks on the envelopes showed that they were those which had disturbed the routine of the secretary, and each was dated from the Commercial Road and signed "A. Dorak." They were mere invoices to say that a fresh bottle was being sent to Professor Presbury, or receipt to acknowledge money. There was one other envelope, however, in a more educated hand and bearing the Austrian stamp with the postmark of Prague. "Here we have our material!" cried Holmes as he tore out the enclosure.

HONOURED COLLEAGUE [it ran]:

Since your esteemed visit I have thought much of your case, and though in your circumstances there are some special reasons for the treatment, I would none the less enjoin caution, as my results have shown that it is not without danger of a kind.

It is possible that the serum of anthropoid would have been better. I have, as I explained to you, used black-faced langur because a specimen was accessible. Langur is, of course, a crawler and climber, while anthropoid walks erect and is in all ways nearer.

I beg you to take every possible precaution that there be no premature revelation of the process. I have one other client in England, and Dorak is my agent for both.

Weekly reports will oblige.

Yours with high esteem,

H. LOWENSTEIN.

Lowenstein! The name brought back to me the memory of some snippet from a newspaper which spoke of an obscure scientist who was striving in some unknown way for the secret of rejuvenescence and the elixir of life. Lowenstein of Prague! Lowenstein with the wondrous strength-giving serum, tabooed by the profession because he refused to reveal its source. In a few words I said what I remembered. Bennett had taken a manual of zoology from the shelves. " 'Langur.' " he read. " 'the great black-faced monkey of the Himalayan slopes, biggest and most human of climbing monkeys. Many details are added. Well, thanks to you, Mr. Holmes, it is very clear that we have traced the evil to its source."

"The real source," said Holmes, "lies, of course, in that untimely love affair which gave our impetuous professor the idea that he could only gain his wish by turning himself into a younger man. When one tries to rise above Nature one is liable to fall below it. The highest type of man may revert to the animal if he leaves the straight road of destiny." He sat musing for a little with the phial in his hand, looking at the clear liquid within. "When I have written to this man and told him that I hold him criminally responsible for the poisons which he circulates, we will have no more trouble. But it may recur. Others may find a better way.

There is danger there—a very real danger to humanity. Consider, Watson, that the material, the sensual, the worldly would all prolong their worthless lives. The spiritual would not avoid the call to something higher. It would be the survival of the least fit. What sort of cesspool may not our poor world become?" Suddenly the dreamer disappeared, and Holmes, the man of action, sprang from his chair. "I think there is nothing more to be said, Mr. Bennett. The various incidents will now fit themselves easily into the general scheme. The dog, of course, was aware of the change far more quickly than you. His smell would insure that. It was the monkey, not the professor, whom Roy attacked, just as it was the monkey who teased Roy. Climbing was a joy to the creature, and it was a mere chance, I take it, that the pastime brought him to the young lady's window. There is an early train to town, Watson, but I think we shall just have time for a cup of tea at the Chequers before we catch it."

Extract: The "Final Vision" from H. G. Wells's The Time Machine

Source: Project Gutenberg, www.gutenberg.net

H. G. Wells trained with T. H. Huxley, and himself wrote an introductory text-book on biology for school pupils. He is most famous, of course, for his "scien-tific romances." In this first extract from The Time Machine, *the Traveller journeys to the very end of the Earth itself, and experiences a bleak, chilling vision of the cosmic degeneration at work in fin-de-siècle culture.*

XI

I have already told you of the sickness and confusion that comes with time trav-elling. And this time I was not seated properly in the saddle, but sideways and in an unstable fashion. For an indefinite time I clung to the machine as it swayed and vibrated, quite unheeding how I went, and when I brought myself to look at the dials again I was amazed to find where I had arrived. One dial records days, and another thousands of days, another millions of days, and another thousands of millions. Now, instead of reversing the levers, I had pulled them over so as to go forward with them, and when I came to look at these indicators I found that the thousands hand was sweeping round as fast as the seconds hand of a watch—into futurity.

As I drove on, a peculiar change crept over the appearance of things. The palpitating greyness grew darker; then—though I was still travelling with prodigious velocity—the blinking succession of day and night, which was usually indicative of a slower pace, returned, and grew more and more marked. This puzzled me very much at first. The alternations of night and day grew slower and slower, and so did the passage of the sun across the sky, until they seemed to stretch through centuries. At last a steady twilight brooded over the earth, a twilight only broken now and then when a comet glared across the darkling sky. The band of light that had indicated the sun had long since disappeared; for the sun had ceased to set—it simply rose and fell in the west, and grew ever broader and more red. All trace of the moon had vanished. The circling of the stars, growing slower and slower, had given place to creeping points of light. At last, some time before I stopped, the sun, red and very large, halted motionless upon the horizon, a vast dome glowing with a dull heat, and now and then suffering a momentary extinction. At one time it had for a little while glowed more brilliantly again, but it speedily reverted to its sullen red heat. I perceived by this slowing down of its rising and setting that the work of the tidal drag was done. The earth had come to rest with one face to the sun, even as in our own time the moon faces the earth. Very cautiously, for I remembered my former headlong fall, I began to reverse my motion. Slower and slower went the circling hands until the thousands one seemed motionless and the daily one was no longer a mere mist upon its scale. Still slower, until the dim outlines of a desolate beach grew visible.

I stopped very gently and sat upon the Time Machine, looking round. The sky was no longer blue. North-eastward it was inky black, and out of the blackness shone brightly and steadily the pale white stars. Overhead it was a deep Indian red and starless, and south-eastward it grew brighter to a glowing scarlet where, cut by the horizon, lay the huge hull of the sun, red and motionless. The rocks about me were of a harsh reddish colour, and all the trace of life that I could see at first was the intensely green vegetation that covered every projecting point on their south-eastern face. It was the same rich green that one sees on forest moss or on the lichen in caves: plants which like these grow in a perpetual twilight.

The machine was standing on a sloping beach. The sea stretched away to the south-west, to rise into a sharp bright horizon against the wan sky. There were no breakers and no waves, for not a breath of wind was stirring. Only a slight oily swell rose and fell like a gentle breathing, and showed that the eternal sea was still moving and living. And along the margin where the water sometimes broke was a thick incrustation of salt—pink under the lurid sky. There was a sense of oppression in my head, and I noticed that I was breathing very fast. The sensation reminded me of my only experience of mountaineering, and from that I judged the air to be more rarefied than it is now.

Far away up the desolate slope I heard a harsh scream, and saw a thing like a huge white butterfly go slanting and flittering up into the sky and, circling, disappear over some low hillocks beyond. The sound of its voice was so dismal that I shivered and seated myself more firmly upon the machine. Looking round me again, I saw that, quite near, what I had taken to be a reddish mass of rock was moving slowly towards me. Then I saw the thing was really a monstrous crablike creature. Can you imagine a crab as large as yonder table, with its many legs moving slowly and uncertainly, its big claws swaying, its long antennae, like carters' whips, waving and feeling, and its stalked eyes gleaming at you on either side of its metallic front? Its back was corrugated and ornamented with ungainly bosses, and a greenish incrustation blotched it here and there. I could see the many palps of its complicated mouth flickering and feeling as it moved.

As I stared at this sinister apparition crawling towards me, I felt a tickling on my cheek as though a fly had lighted there. I tried to brush it away with my hand, but in a moment it returned, and almost immediately came another by my ear. I struck at this, and caught something threadlike. It was drawn swiftly out of my hand. With a frightful qualm, I turned, and I saw that I had grasped the antenna of another monster crab that stood just behind me. Its evil eyes were wriggling on their stalks, its mouth was all alive with appetite, and its vast ungainly claws, smeared with an algal slime, were descending upon me. In a moment my hand was on the lever, and I had placed a month between myself and these monsters. But I was still on the same beach, and I saw them distinctly now as soon as I stopped. Dozens of them seemed to be crawling here and there, in the sombre light, among the foliated sheets of intense green.

I cannot convey the sense of abominable desolation that hung over the world. The red eastern sky, the northward blackness, the salt Dead Sea, the stony beach crawling with these foul, slow-stirring monsters, the uniform poisonous-looking green of the lichenous plants, the thin air that hurts one's lungs: all contributed to an appalling effect. I moved on a hundred years, and there was the same red sun—a little larger, a little duller—the same dying sea, the same chill air, and the same crowd of earthy crustacea creeping in and out among the green weed and the red rocks. And in the westward sky, I saw a curved pale line like a vast new moon.

So I travelled, stopping ever and again, in great strides of a thousand years or more, drawn on by the mystery of the earth's fate, watching with a strange fascination the sun grow larger and duller in the westward sky, and the life of the old earth ebb away. At last, more than thirty million years hence, the huge red-hot dome of the sun had come to obscure nearly a tenth part of the darkling heavens. Then I stopped once more, for the crawling multitude of crabs had disappeared, and the red beach, save for its livid green liverworts and lichens, seemed lifeless. And now it was flecked with white. A bitter cold assailed me.

Rare white flakes ever and again came eddying down. To the north-eastward, the glare of snow lay under the starlight of the sable sky and I could see an undulating crest of hillocks pinkish white. There were fringes of ice along the sea margin, with drifting masses further out; but the main expanse of that salt ocean, all bloody under the eternal sunset, was still unfrozen.

I looked about me to see if any traces of animal life remained. A certain indefinable apprehension still kept me in the saddle of the machine. But I saw nothing moving, in earth or sky or sea. The green slime on the rocks alone testified that life was not extinct. A shallow sandbank had appeared in the sea and the water had receded from the beach. I fancied I saw some black object flopping about upon this bank, but it became motionless as I looked at it, and I judged that my eye had been deceived, and that the black object was merely a rock. The stars in the sky were intensely bright and seemed to me to twinkle very little.

Suddenly I noticed that the circular westward outline of the sun had changed; that a concavity, a bay, had appeared in the curve. I saw this grow larger. For a minute perhaps I stared aghast at this blackness that was creeping over the day, and then I realized that an eclipse was beginning. Either the moon or the planet Mercury was passing across the sun's disk. Naturally, at first I took it to be the moon, but there is much to incline me to believe that what I really saw was the transit of an inner planet passing very near to the earth.

The darkness grew apace; a cold wind began to blow in freshening gusts from the east, and the showering white flakes in the air increased in number. From the edge of the sea came a ripple and whisper. Beyond these lifeless sounds the world was silent. Silent? It would be hard to convey the stillness of it. All the sounds of man, the bleating of sheep, the cries of birds, the hum of insects, the stir that makes the background of our lives—all that was over. As the darkness thickened, the eddying flakes grew more abundant, dancing before my eyes; and the cold of the air more intense. At last, one by one, swiftly, one after the other, the white peaks of the distant hills vanished into blackness. The breeze rose to a moaning wind. I saw the black central shadow of the eclipse sweeping towards me. In another moment the pale stars alone were visible. All else was rayless obscurity. The sky was absolutely black.

A horror of this great darkness came on me. The cold, that smote to my marrow, and the pain I felt in breathing, overcame me. I shivered, and a deadly nausea seized me. Then like a red-hot bow in the sky appeared the edge of the sun. I got off the machine to recover myself. I felt giddy and incapable of facing the return journey. As I stood sick and confused I saw again the moving thing upon the shoal—there was no mistake now that it was a moving thing—against the red water of the sea. It was a round thing, the size of a football perhaps, or, it may be, bigger, and tentacles trailed down from it; it seemed black against the weltering blood-red water, and it was hopping fitfully about. Then I felt I was fainting. But a terrible dread of lying helpless in that remote and awful twilight sustained me while I clambered upon the saddle.

CHAPTER 9

Extract from H. G. Wells, The Time Machine

In this second extract from The Time Machine, *which takes place at the beginning of the novel, the Traveller explains the principle of time travel to a group of skeptical male friends, including the Provincial Mayor and Filby.*

'Really this is what is meant by the Fourth Dimension, though some people who talk about the Fourth Dimension do not know they mean it. It is only another way of looking at Time. THERE IS NO DIFFERENCE BETWEEN TIME AND ANY OF THE THREE DIMENSIONS OF SPACE EXCEPT THAT OUR CONSCIOUSNESS MOVES ALONG IT. But some foolish people have got hold of the wrong side of that idea. You have all heard what they have to say about this Fourth Dimension?'

'*I* have not,' said the Provincial Mayor.

'It is simply this. That Space, as our mathematicians have it, is spoken of as having three dimensions, which one may call Length, Breadth, and Thickness, and is always definable by reference to three planes, each at right angles to the others. But some philosophical people have been asking why THREE dimensions particularly—why not another direction at right angles to the other three?—and have even tried to construct a Four-Dimension geometry. Professor Simon Newcomb was expounding this to the New York Mathematical Society only a month or so ago. You know how on a flat surface, which has only two dimensions, we can represent a figure of a three-dimensional solid, and similarly they think that by models of three dimensions they could represent one of four—if they could master the perspective of the thing. See?'

'I think so,' murmured the Provincial Mayor; and, knitting his brows, he lapsed into an introspective state, his lips moving as one who repeats mystic words. 'Yes, I think I see it now,' he said after some time, brightening in a quite transitory manner.

'Well, I do not mind telling you I have been at work upon this geometry of Four Dimensions for some time. Some of my results are curious. For instance, here is a portrait of a man at eight years old, another at fifteen, another at seventeen, another at twenty-three, and so on. All these are evidently sections, as it were, Three-Dimensional representations of his Four-Dimensioned being, which is a fixed and unalterable thing.

'Scientific people,' proceeded the Time Traveller, after the pause required for the proper assimilation of this, 'know very well that Time is only a kind of Space. Here is a popular scientific diagram, a weather record. This line I trace with my finger shows the movement of the barometer. Yesterday it was so high, yesterday night it fell, then this morning it rose again, and so gently upward to here. Surely the mercury did not trace this line in any of the dimensions of Space generally recognized? But certainly it traced such a line, and that line, therefore, we must conclude was along the Time-Dimension.'

'But,' said the Medical Man, staring hard at a coal in the fire, 'if Time is really only a fourth dimension of Space, why is it, and why has it always been, regarded as something different? And why cannot we move in Time as we move about in the other dimensions of Space?'

The Time Traveller smiled. 'Are you sure we can move freely in Space? Right and left we can go, backward and forward freely enough, and men always have done so. I admit we move freely in two dimensions. But how about up and down? Gravitation limits us there.'

'Not exactly,' said the Medical Man. 'There are balloons.'

'But before the balloons, save for spasmodic jumping and the inequalities of the surface, man had no freedom of vertical movement.' 'Still they could move a little up and down,' said the Medical Man.

'Easier, far easier down than up.'

'And you cannot move at all in Time, you cannot get away from the present moment.'

'My dear sir, that is just where you are wrong. That is just where the whole world has gone wrong. We are always getting away from the present moment. Our mental existences, which are immaterial and have no dimensions, are passing along the Time-Dimension with a uniform velocity from the cradle to the grave. Just as we should travel DOWN if we began our existence fifty miles above the earth's surface.'

'But the great difficulty is this,' interrupted the Psychologist. 'You CAN move about in all directions of Space, but you cannot move about in Time.'

'That is the germ of my great discovery. But you are wrong to say that we cannot move about in Time. For instance, if I am recalling an incident very vividly I go back to the instant of its occurrence: I become absent-minded, as you say. I jump back for a moment. Of course we have no means of staying back for any length of Time, any more than a savage or an animal has of staying six feet above the ground. But a civilized man is better off than the savage in this respect. He can go up against gravitation in a balloon, and why should he not hope that ultimately he may be able to stop or accelerate his drift along the Time-Dimension, or even turn about and travel the other way?'

'Oh, THIS,' began Filby, 'is all—'

'Why not?' said the Time Traveller.

CHAPTER 11

Extract from The Belfast Address *by John Tyndall*

London: Longmans, Green, and Co., 1874, pp. 59–63

In 1874, the physicist John Tyndall chose the occasion of his presidential address to the British Association for the Advancement of Science to express his vision of New Nature and the role of the scientists. Since the British Association was founded with the aim of popularizing science, large numbers of the public attended its meetings and were eager to sample the latest controversies. Tyndall's address is a powerful piece of writing that caused great consternation at the time. Some suggested he had abused his office or that he might be culpable of blasphemy. The address was printed in The Times *and provided fuel for many condemnatory sermons the following Sunday.*

It was a similar meeting of the British Association where Huxley clashed with Wilberforce in the heart of the Anglican establishment at Oxford. Tyndall was no doubt conscious of the significance of the venue at Belfast for his speech. The Irish Catholic hierarchy had just rejected a plan to include physical science in the curriculum of the Catholic University. To Tyndall this must have seemed like the repressive theology of the middle ages in its antagonism to science. In his view of the historical development of science it is now known that Tyndall was heavily influenced by John William Draper, a professor of chemistry in New York, who, in 1862, presented a paper to the British Association that depicted the progressive force of science at war with a reactionary set of religious beliefs. Draper's "warfare" metaphor greatly influenced some natural scientists.

Further, the doctrine of evolution derives man in his totality from the interaction of organism and environment through countless ages past. The Human

Understanding, for example—that faculty which Mr. Spencer has turned so skil-fully round upon its own antecedents-is itself a result of the play between organ-ism and environment through cosmic ranges of time. Never surely did prescrip-tion plead so irresistible a claim. But then it comes to pass that, over and above his understanding, there are many other things appertaining to man whose per-spective rights are quite as strong as those of the understanding itself. It is a result, for example, of the play of organism and environment that sugar is sweet and that aloes are bitter, that the smell of henbane differs from the perfume of a rose. Such facts of consciousness (for which, by the way, no adequate reason has yet been rendered) are quite as old as the understanding; and many other things can boast an equally ancient origin. Mr. Spencer at one place refers to that most powerful of passions-the amatory passion—as one which, when it first occurs, is antecedent to all relative experience whatever; and we may pass its claim as being at least as ancient and valid as that of the understanding. Then there are such things woven into the texture of man as the feeling of Awe, Reverence, Wonder—and not alone the sexual love just referred to, but the love of the beau-tiful, physical, and moral, in Nature, Poetry, and Art. There is also that deep-set feeling which, since the earliest dawn of history, and probably for ages prior to all history, incorporated itself in the Religions of the world. You who have escaped from these religions into the high-and-dry light of the intellect may deride them; but in so doing you deride accidents of form merely, and fail to touch the immovable basis of the religious sentiment in the nature of man. To yield this sentiment reasonable satisfaction is the problem of problems at the present hour. And grotesque in relation to scientific culture as many of the reli-gions of the world have been and are dangerous, nay destructive, to the dearest privileges of freemen as some of them undoubtedly have been, and would, if they could, be again—it will be wise to recognize them as the forms of a force, mis-chievous, if permitted to intrude on the region of *knowledge*, over which it holds no command, but capable of being guided to noble issues in the region of *emo-tion*, which is its proper and elevated sphere.

All religious theories, schemes and systems, which embrace notions of cos-mogony, or which otherwise reach into the domain of science, must, *in so far as they do this*, submit to the control of science, and relinquish all thought of con-trolling it. Acting otherwise proved disastrous in the past, and it is simply fatu-ous to-day. Every system which would escape the fate of an organism too rigid to adjust itself to its environment must be plastic to the extent that the growth of knowledge demands. When this truth has been thoroughly taken in, rigidity will be relaxed, exclusiveness diminished, things now deemed essential will be dropped, and elements now rejected will be assimilated. The lifting of the life is the essential point; and as long as dogmatism, fanaticism, and intolerance are kept out, various modes of leverage may be employed to raise life to a higher level. Science itself not unfrequently derives motive power from an ultra-scientific source. Whewell speaks of enthusiasm of temper as a hindrance to science; but he means the enthusiasm of weak heads. There is a strong and resolute enthusiasm in which science finds an ally; and it is to the lowering of this fire, rather than to the diminution of intellectual insight, that the lessening productiveness of men of science in their mature years is to be ascribed. Mr. Buckle sought to detach intellectual achievement from moral force. He gravely erred; for without moral force to whip it into action, the achievements of the intellect would be poor indeed.

It has been said that science divorces itself from literature; but the statement, like so many others, arises from lack of knowledge. A glance at the less technical writings of its leaders—of its Helmholtz, its Huxley, and its Du Bois-Reymond—would show what breadth of literary culture they command. Where among modern writers can you find their superiors in clearness and vigour of literary style? Science desires not isolation, but freely combines with every effort towards the bettering of man's estate. Single-handed, and supported not by outward sympathy, but by inward force, it has built at least one great wing of the many-mansioned home which man in his totality demands. And if rough walls and protruding rafter-ends indicate that on one side the edifice is still incomplete, it is only by wise combination of the parts required with those already irrevocably built that we can hope for completeness. There is no necessary incongruity between what has been accomplished and what remains to be done. The moral glow of Socrates, which we all feel by ignition, has in it nothing incompatible with the physics of Anaxagoras which he so much scorned, but which he would hardly scorn to-day.

And here I am reminded of one amongst us, hoary, but still strong, whose prophet-voice some thirty years ago, far more than any other of this age, unlocked whatever of life and nobleness lay latent in its most gifted minds—one fit to stand beside Socrates or the Maccabean Eleazar, and to dare and suffer all that they suffered and dared fit, as he once said of Fichte, 'to have been the teacher of the Stoa, and to have discoursed of Beauty and Virtue in the groves of Academe.' With a capacity to grasp physical principles which his friend Goethe did not possess, and which even total lack of exercise has not been able to reduce to atrophy, it is the world's loss that he, in the vigour of his years, did not open his mind and sympathies to science, and make its conclusions a portion of his message to mankind. Marvellously endowed as he was—equally equipped on the side of the Heart and of the Understanding—he might have done much towards teaching us how to reconcile the claims of both, and to enable them in coming times to dwell together in unity of spirit and in the bond of peace.

"Science and Culture" by Thomas Henry Huxley

From *Collected Essays*, 9 vols. London: Methuen, 1893–1902.

At the opening of a new science college in Birmingham, England,
Huxley took the opportunity to advance his views on the role of science
and the humanities in a balanced education.

Science and Culture

We may take it for granted then, that, in the opinion of those best qualified to judge, the diffusion of thorough scientific education is an absolutely essential condition of industrial progress; and that the College which has been opened today will confer an inestimable boon upon those whose livelihood is to be gained by the practice of the arts and manufactures of the district. . . .

Sir Josiah Mason, without doubt most wisely, has left very large freedom of action to the trustees, to whom he proposes ultimately to commit the administration of the College, so that they may be able to adjust its arrangements in accordance with the changing conditions of the future. But, with respect to three points, he has laid most explicit injunctions upon both administrators and teachers.

Party politics are forbidden to enter into the minds of either, so far as the work of the College is concerned; theology is as sternly banished from its precincts; and finally, it is especially declared that the College shall make no provision for "mere literary instruction and education."

It does not concern me at present to dwell upon the first two injunctions any longer than may be needful to express my full conviction of their wisdom. But the third prohibition brings us face to face with those other opponents of scientific education, who are by no means in the moribund condition of the practical man, but alive, alert, and formidable.

It is not impossible that we shall hear this express exclusion of "literary instruction and education" from a College which, nevertheless, professes to give a high and efficient education, sharply criticized. Certainly the time was that the Levites of culture would have sounded their trumpets against its walls as against an educational Jericho.

How often have we not been told that the study of physical science is incompetent to confer culture; that it touches none of the higher problems of life; and, what is worse, that the continual devotion to scientific studies tends to generate a narrow and bigoted belief in the applicability of scientific methods to the search after truth of all kinds ? How frequently one has reason to observe that no reply to a troublesome argument tells so well as calling its author a "mere scientific specialist." And, as I am afraid it is not permissible to speak of this form of opposition to scientific education in the past tense; may we not expect to be told that this, not only omission, but prohibition, of "mere literary instruction and education" is a patent example of scientific narrow-mindedness?

I am not acquainted with Sir Josiah Mason's reasons for the action which he has taken; but if, as I apprehend is the case, he refers to the ordinary classical course of our schools and universities by the name of "mere literary instruction and education," I venture to offer sundry reasons of my own in support of that action.

For I hold very strongly by two convictions: The first is, that neither the discipline nor the subject-matter of classical education is of such direct value to the student of physical science as to justify the expenditure of valuable time upon either; and the second is, that for the purpose of attaining real culture, an exclusively scientific education is at least as effectual as an exclusively literary education.

I need hardly point out to you that these opinions, especially the latter, are diametrically opposed to those of the great majority of educated Englishmen, influenced as they are by school and university traditions. In their belief, culture is obtainable only by a liberal education; and a liberal education is synonymous, not merely with education and instruction in literature, but in one particular form of literature, namely, that of Greek and Roman antiquity. They hold that the man who has learned Latin and Greek, however little, is educated; while he who is versed in other branches of knowledge, however deeply, is a more or less respectable specialist, not admissible into the cultured caste. The stamp of the educated man, the University degree, is not for him.

I am too well acquainted with the general catholicity of spirit, the true sympathy with scientific thought, which pervades the writings of our chief apostle of culture to identify him with these opinions; and yet one may cull from one and another of those epistles to the Philistines, which so much delight all who do not answer to that name, sentences which lend them some support.

Mr. Arnold tells us that the meaning of culture is "to know the best that has been thought and said in the world." It is the criticism of life contained in literature. That criticism regards "Europe as being, for intellectual and spiritual purposes, one great confederation, bound to a joint action and working to a common result; and whose members have, for their common outfit, a knowledge of Greek, Roman, and Eastern antiquity, and of one another. Special, local, and temporary advantages being put out of account, that modern nation will in the intellectual and spiritual sphere make most progress, which most thoroughly carries out this program. And what is that but saying that we too, all of us, as individuals, the more thoroughly we carry it out, shall make the more progress?"

We have here to deal with two distinct propositions. The first, that a criticism of life is the essence of culture; the second, that literature contains the materials which suffice for the construction of such criticism.

I think that we must all assent to the first proposition. For culture certainly means something quite different from learning or technical skill. It implies the possession of an ideal, and the habit of critically estimating the value of things by comparison with a theoretic standard. Perfect culture should supply a complete theory of life, based upon a clear knowledge alike of its possibilities and of its limitations.

But we may agree to all this, and yet strongly dissent from the assumption that literature alone is competent to supply this knowledge. After having learned all that Greek, Roman, and Eastern antiquity have thought and said, and all that modern literature have to tell us, it is not self-evident that we have laid a sufficiently broad and deep foundation for that criticism of life, which constitutes culture.

Indeed, to any one acquainted with the scope of physical science, it is not at all evident. Considering progress only in the "intellectual and spiritual sphere," I find myself wholly unable to admit that either nations or individuals will really advance, if their common outfit draws nothing from the stores of physical science. I should say that an army, without weapons of precision and with no particular base of operations, might more hopefully enter upon a campaign on the Rhine, than a man, devoid of a knowledge of what physical science has done in the last century, upon a criticism of life. . . .

It is, happily, no new thing that Englishmen should employ their wealth in building and endowing institutions for educational purposes. But, five or six hundred years ago, deeds of foundation expressed or implied conditions as nearly as possible contrary to those which have been thought expedient by Sir Josiah Mason. That is to say, physical science was practically ignored, while a certain literary training was enjoined as a means to the acquirement of knowledge which was essentially theological. . . .

The representatives of the Humanists, in the nineteenth century, take their stand upon classical education as the sole avenue to culture, as firmly as if we were still in the age of Renascence. Yet, surely, the present intellectual relations of the modern and the ancient worlds are profoundly different from those which obtained three centuries ago. Leaving aside the existence of a great and characteristically modern literature, of modern painting, and, especially, of modern music, there is one feature of the present state of the civilized world which separates it more widely from the Renascence, than the Renascence was separated from the middle ages.

This distinctive character of our own times lies in the vast and constantly increasing part which is played by natural knowledge. Not only is our daily life shaped by it; not only does the prosperity of millions of men depend upon it, but our whole theory of life has long been influenced, consciously or unconsciously, by the general conceptions of the universe, which have been forced upon us by physical science.

In fact, the most elementary acquaintance with the results of scientific investigation shows us that they offer a broad and striking contradiction to the opinion so implicitly credited and taught in the middle ages.

The notions of the beginning and the end of the world entertained by our forefathers are no longer credible. It is very certain that the earth is not the chief body in the material universe, and that the world is not subordinated to man's use. It is even more certain that nature is the expression of a definite order with which nothing interferes, and that the chief business of mankind is to learn that order and govern themselves accordingly. Moreover this scientific "criticism of life" presents itself to us with different credentials from any other. It appeals not to authority, nor to what anybody may have thought or said, but to nature. It admits that all our interpretations of natural fact are more or less imperfect and symbolic, and bids the learner seek for truth not among words but among things. It warns us that the assertion which outstrips evidence is not only a blunder but a crime. . . .

Thus I venture to think that the pretensions of our modern Humanists to the possession of the monopoly of culture and to the exclusive inheritance of the spirit of antiquity must be abated, if not abandoned. But I should be very sorry that anything I have said should be taken to imply a desire on my part to depreciate the value of classical education, as it might be and as it sometimes is. The native capacities of mankind vary no less than their opportunities; and while culture is one, the road by which one man may best reach it is widely different from that which is most advantageous to another. Again, while scientific education is yet inchoate and tentative, classical education is thoroughly well organized upon the practical experience of generations of teachers. So that, given ample time for learning and estimation for ordinary life, or for a literary career, I do not think that a young Englishman in search of culture can do better than follow the course usually marked out for him, supplementing its deficiencies by his own efforts.

But for those who mean to make science their serious occupation; or who intend to follow the profession of medicine; or who have to enter early upon the business of life; for all these, in my opinion, classical education is a mistake; and it is for this reason that I am glad to see "mere literary education and instruction" shut out from the curriculum of Sir Josiah Mason's College, seeing that its inclusion would probably lead to the introduction of the ordinary smattering of Latin and Greek.

Nevertheless, I am the last person to question the importance of genuine literary education, or to suppose that intellectual culture can be complete without it. An exclusively scientific training will bring about a mental twist as surely as an exclusively literary training. The value of the cargo does not compensate for a ship's being out of trim; and I should be very sorry to think that the Scientific College would turn out none but lopsided men. . . .

In conclusion, I am sure that I make myself the mouthpiece of all present in offering to the venerable founder of the Institution, which now commences its beneficent career, our congratulations on the completion of his work; and in expressing the conviction, that the remotest posterity will point to it as a crucial instance of the wisdom which natural piety leads all men to ascribe to their ancestors.

Literature and Science *by Matthew Arnold (1883)*

Arnold published his reply to Huxley's speech in 1882 (published in The Nineteenth Century, *August 1882). The version shown below is that modified slightly for Arnold's American tour of 1883.*

The usual education in the past has been mainly literary. The question is whether the studies which were long supposed to be the best for all of us are practically the best now, whether others are not better. The tyranny of the past, many think, weighs on us injuriously in the predominance given to letters in education. The question is raised whether, to meet the needs of our modern life, the predominance ought not now to pass from letters to science; and naturally the question is nowhere raised with more energy than here in the United States. The design of abasing what is called "mere literary instruction and education," and of exalting what is called "sound, extensive, and practical scientific knowledge," is in this intensely modern world of the United States, even more perhaps than in Europe, a very popular design, and makes great and rapid progress.

I am going to ask whether the present movement for ousting letters from their old predominance in education, and for transferring the predominance in education to the natural sciences, whether this brisk and flourishing movement ought to prevail, and whether it is likely that in the end it really will prevail. An objection may be raised which I will anticipate. My own studies have been almost wholly in letters and my visits to the field of the natural sciences have been very slight and inadequate, although those sciences have always strongly moved my curiosity. A man of letters, it will perhaps be said, is not competent to discuss the comparative merits of letters and natural science as means of education. To this objection I reply, first of all that his incompetence, if he attempts the discussion but is really incompetent for it, will be abundantly visible; nobody will be taken in he will have plenty of sharp observers and critics to save mankind from that danger. But the line I am going to follow is, as you will soon discover, so extremely simple, that perhaps it may be followed without failure even by one who for a more ambitious line of discussion would be quite incompetent.

Some of you may possibly remember a phrase of mine which has been the object of a good deal of comment, an observation to the effect that in our culture, the aim being *to know ourselves and the world*, we have, as the means to this end, *to know the best which has been thought and said in the world.* A man of science, who is also an excellent writer and the very prince of debaters, Professor Huxley, in a discourse at the opening of Sir Josiah Mason's college at Birmingham laying hold of this phrase, expanded it by quoting some more words of mine, which are these: "The civilised world is to be regarded as now being, for intellectual and spiritual purposes, one great confederation, bound to a joint action and working to a common result, and whose members have for their proper outfit a knowledge of Greek, Roman and Eastern antiquity, and of one another. Special local and temporary advantages being put out of account, that modern nation will in the intellectual and spiritual sphere make most progress, which most thoroughly carries out this programme."

Now on my phrase, thus enlarged, Professor Huxley remarks that when I speak of the above-mentioned knowledge as enabling us to know ourselves and the world, I assert *literature* to contain the materials which suffice for thus making us know ourselves and the world. But it is not by any means clear, says he, that after having learnt all which ancient and modern literatures have to tell us, we have laid a sufficiently broad and deep foundation for that criticism of life, that knowledge of ourselves and the world, which constitutes culture. On the contrary, Professor Huxley declares that he finds himself "wholly unable to admit that either nations or individuals will really advance, if their outfit draws nothing from the stores of physical science. An army without weapons of precision, and with no particular base of operations, might more hopefully enter upon a campaign on the Rhine, than a man, devoid of a knowledge of what physical science has done in the last century, upon a criticism of life."

This shows how needful it is for those who are to discuss any matter together, to have a common understanding as to the sense of the terms they employ,—how needful, and how difficult. . . .

When I speak of knowing Greek and Roman antiquity, therefore, as a help to knowing ourselves and the world, I mean more than a knowledge of so much vocabulary, so much grammar, so many portions of authors in the Greek and Latin languages. I mean knowing the Greeks and Romans, and their life and genius, and what they were and did in the world; what we get from them, and what is its value. That, at least, is the ideal; and when we talk of endeavouring to know Greek and Roman antiquity, as a help to knowing ourselves and the world, we mean endeavouring so to know them as to satisfy this ideal, however much we may still fall short of it.

The same also as to knowing our own and other modern nations with the like aim of getting to understand ourselves and the world. To know the best that has been thought and said by the modern nations, is to know, says Professor Huxley, "only what modern *literatures* have to tell us; it is the criticism of life contained in modern literature." And yet "the distinctive character of our times," he urges, "lies in the vast and constantly increasing part which is played by natural knowledge." And how, therefore, can a man, devoid of knowledge of what physical science has done in the last century enter hopefully upon a criticism of modern life?

Let us, I say, be agreed about the meaning of the terms we are using. I talk of knowing the best which has been thought and uttered in the world; Professor Huxley says this means knowing *literature*. Literature is a large word; it may mean everything written with letters or printed in a book. Euclid's *Elements* and Newton's *Principia* are thus literature. All knowledge that reaches us through books is literature. But by literature Professor Huxley means *belles lettres*. He means to make me say, that knowing the best which has been thought and said by the modern nations is knowing their *belles lettres* and no more. And this is no sufficient equipment, he argues, for a criticism of modern life. But as I do not mean, by knowing ancient Rome, knowing merely more or less of Latin *belles lettres*, and taking no account of Rome's military, and political, and legal, and. administrative work in the world; and as, by knowing ancient Greece, I understand knowing her as the giver of Greek art, and the guide to a free and right use of reason and to scientific method, and the founder of our mathematics and physics and astronomy and biology,—I understand knowing her as all this, and not merely knowing certain Greek poems, and histories, and treatises, and speeches,—so as to the knowledge of modern nations also. By knowing modern nations, I mean not merely knowing their *belles lettres*, but knowing also what has been done by such men as Copernicus, Galileo, Newton, Darwin. "Our ancestors learned," says Professor Huxley, "that the earth is the centre of the visible universe, and that man is the cynosure of things terrestrial; and more especially was it inculcated that the course of nature had no fixed order but that it could be, and constantly was, altered." But for us now continues Professor Huxley, "the notions of the beginning and the end of the world entertained by our forefathers are no longer credible. It is very certain that the earth is not the chief body in the material universe, and that the world is not subordinated to man's use. It is even more, certain that nature is the expression of a definite order, with which nothing interferes." "And yet," he cries, "the purely classical education advocated by the representatives of the humanists in Our day gives no inkling of all this!" The great results of the scientific investigation of nature we are agreed upon knowing, but how much of our study are we bound to give to the processes by which those results are reached? The results have their visible bearing on human life. But all the processes, too, all the items of fact, by which those results are reached and established, are interesting. All knowledge is interesting to a wise man, and the knowledge of nature is interesting to all men. It is very interesting to know, that, from the albuminous white of the egg, the chick in the egg gets the materials for its flesh, bones, blood, and feathers; while, from the fatty yolk of the egg, it gets the heat and energy which enable it at length to break its shell and begin the world. It is less interesting, perhaps, but still it is interesting, to know that when a taper burns, the wax is converted into carbonic acid and water. Moreover, it is quite true that the habit of dealing with facts, which is given by the study of nature, is, as the friends of physical science praise it for being, an excellent discipline. The appeal, in the study of nature, is constantly to observation and experiment; not only is it said that the thing is so, but we can be made to see that it is so. Not only does a man tell us that when a taper burns the wax is converted into carbonic acid and water, as a man may tell us, if he likes, that Charon is punting his ferry-boat on the river Styx, or that Victor Hugo is a sublime poet, or Mr. Gladstone the most admirable of statesmen; but we are made to see that the conversion into carbonic acid and water does actually happen. This reality of natural knowledge it is, which makes the friends of physical science contrast it, as a knowledge of things, with the humanist's knowledge, which is, say they, a knowledge of words. And hence Professor Huxley is moved to lay it down that, "for the purpose of attaining real culture, an exclusively scientific education is at least as effectual as an exclusively literary education." And a certain President of the Section for Mechanical Science in the British Association is, in Scripture phrase, "very bold," and declares that if a man, in his mental training, "has substituted literature and history for natural science, he has chosen the less useful alternative." But whether we go these lengths or not, we must all admit that in natural science the habit gained of dealing with facts is a most valuable discipline, and that every one should have some experience of it.

More than this, however, is demanded by the reformers. It is proposed to make the training in natural science the main part of education, for the great majority of mankind at any rate. And here, I confess, I part company with the friends of physical science, with whom up to this point I have been agreeing. In differing from them, however, I wish to proceed with the utmost caution and diffidence. The smallness of my own acquaintance with the disciplines of natural science is ever before my mind, and I am fearful of doing these disciplines an injustice. The ability and pugnacity of the partisans of natural science make them formidable persons to contradict. The tone of tentative inquiry, which befits a being of dim faculties and bounded knowledge, is the tone I would wish to take and not to depart from. At present it seems to me, that those who are for giving to natural knowledge, as they call it, the chief place in the education of the majority of mankind, leave one important thing out of their account: the constitution of human nature. But I put this forward upon the strength of some facts not at all recondite, very far from it; facts capable of being stated in the simplest possible fashion, and to which, if I so state them, the man of science will, I am sure, be willing to allow their due weight. . . .

Experience shows us that the generality of men will find more interest in learning that, when a taper burns, the wax is converted into carbonic acid and water, or in learning the explanation of the phenomenon of dew, or in learning how the circulation of the blood is carried on, than they find in learning that the genitive plural of pais and pas does not take the circumflex on the termination. And one piece of natural knowledge is added to another, and others are added to that, and at last we come to propositions so interesting as Mr. Darwin's famous proposition that "our ancestor was a hairy quadruped furnished with a tail and pointed ears, probably arboreal in his habits." Or we come to propositions of such reach and magnitude as those which Professor Huxley delivers, when he says that the notions of our forefathers about the beginning and the end of the world were all wrong, and that nature is the expression of a definite order with which nothing interferes.

Interesting indeed, these results of science are, important they are, I and we should all of us be acquainted with them. But what I now I wish you to mark is, that we are still, when they are propounded to us and we receive them, we are still in the sphere of intellect and knowledge. And for the generality of men there will be found, I say, to arise, when they have duly taken in the proposition that their ancestor was "a hairy quadruped furnished with a tail and pointed ears, probably arboreal in his habits," there will be found to arise an invincible desire to relate this proposition to the sense in us for conduct, and to the sense in us for beauty. But this the men of science will not do for us, and will hardly even profess to do. They will give us other pieces of knowledge, other facts, about other animals and their ancestors, or about plants, or about stones, or about stars; and they may finally bring us to those great "general conceptions of the universe, which are forced upon us all," says Professor Huxley, "by the progress of physical science." But still it will be *knowledge* only which they give us, knowledge not put for us into relation with our sense for conduct, our sense for beauty, and touched with emotion by being so put; not thus put for us, and therefore, to the majority of mankind, after a certain while, unsatisfying, wearying. . . .

I once mentioned in a school-report, how a young man in one of our English training colleges having to paraphrase the passage in *Macbeth* beginning,

Can'st thou not minister to a mind diseased?

turned this line into, "Can you not wait upon the lunatic?" And I remarked what a curious state of things it would be, if every pupil of our national schools knew, let us say, that the moon is two thousand one hundred and sixty miles in diameter, and thought at the same time that a good paraphrase for

Can'st thou not minister to a mind diseased?

was, "Can you not wait upon the lunatic?" If one is driven to choose, I think I would rather have a young person ignorant about the moon's diameter, but aware that "Can you not wait upon the lunatic?" is bad, than a young person whose education had been such as to manage things the other way. . . .

If then there is to be separation and option between humane letters on the one hand, and the natural sciences on the other, the great majority of mankind, all who have not exceptional and overpowering aptitudes for the study of nature, would do well, I cannot but think, to choose to be educated in humane letters rather than in the natural sciences. Letters will call out their being at more points, will make them live more. . . .

And so we at last find, it seems, we find flowing in favour of the humanities the natural and necessary stream of things, which seemed against them when we started. The "hairy quadruped furnished with a tail and pointed ears, probably arboreal in his habits," this good fellow carried hidden in his nature, apparently, something destined to develop into a necessity for humane letters. Nay, more; we seem finally to be even led to the further conclusion that our hairy ancestor carried in his nature, also, a necessity for Greek.

And therefore, to say the truth, I cannot really think that humane letters are in much actual danger of being thrust out from their leading place in education, in spite of the array of authorities against them at this moment. So long as human nature is what it is, their attractions will remain irresistible. . . .

Bibliography

Abrams, M. H. 1953. *The Mirror and the Lamp.* Oxford and New York: Oxford University Press.

Abrams, M. H., and Greenblatt, S. J., eds. 1993. *The Norton Anthology of English Literature.* New York: Norton.

Adler, Bill, Jr., ed. 1998. *Time Machines: The Best Time Travel Stories Ever Written.* New York: Carroll and Graf.

Aldiss, B., with D. Wingrove. 1986. *Trillion Year Spree.* London: Gollancz.

Aldiss, B. 1973. *Billion Year Spree.* London: Weidenfeld and Nicholson.

Allen, R. H. 1963 (reprint of 1899). *Star Names: Their Lore and Meaning.* New York: Dover.

Arnold, M. 1882. "Literature and Science," in *The Norton Anthology of English Literature (vol 2,* 1993). M. H. Abrams and Greenblatt, S. J., eds. New York: Norton.

Asimov, I. 1996. *I, Robot.* London: Voyager.

Batchelor, J. 1995. *H. G. Wells.* Cambridge: Cambridge University Press.

Baxter, S. 1995. *The Time Ships.* London: Voyager.

Beer, G. 1983. *Darwin's Plots: Evolutionary Narrative in Darwin, George Eliot and Nineteenth Century Fiction.* London and Boston: Routledge and Kegan Paul.

———. 1990. "Science and Literature." In *Companion to the History of Science,* edited by R. C. Olby, G. N. Cantor, J. R. R., Christie, and M. J. S. Hodge. London: Routledge.

———. 1996. *Open Fields: Science in Cultural Encounter.* Oxford: Oxford University Press.

Benedikt, M., ed. 1991. *Cyberspace: First Steps.* Cambridge, MA and London: MIT Press.

Bergonzi, B. 1961. *The Early H. G. Wells: A Study of the Scientific Romances.* Manchester: Manchester University Press.

Bewley, M., ed. 1966. *John Donne: Selected Poetry.* New York: The New American Library.

Bloom, H., ed. 1986. *Thomas Pynchon*. New York: Chelsea House.

Boorstin, D. *The Americans: The National Experience*. London: Phoenix.

Borges, J. L. 1962. *Ficciones*. New York: Grove.

———. 1970. *Labyrinths*. Harmondsworth, UK: Penguin.

Bowler, P. J. 1992. *The Fontana History of The Environmental Sciences*. London: Fontana.

Brockman, J. 1995. *The Third Culture*. New York and London: Simon and Schuster.

———. 2003. *The Third Culture*. http://www.edge.org/3rd_culture/brockman/brockman_print.html (accessed February 25, 2003).

Brown, J. R. 2001. *Who Rules in Science? An Opinionated Guide to the Science Wars*. Cambridge, MA: Harvard University Press.

Burkhart, F., and S. Smith, eds. 1997. *The Correspondence of Charles Darwin*, Vol 7 1858–1859. Cambridge: Cambridge University Press.

Bush, D. 1950. *Science and English Poetry*. New York: Oxford University Press.

Byard, M. 1977. "Poetic Responses to the Copernican Revolution." *Scientific American*, June 1977: 121–129.

Bynum, W. F. 1994. *Science and the Practice of Medicine in the Nineteenth Century*. Cambridge and New York: Cambridge University Press.

Cameron, S. 1981. *The Corporeal Self: Allegories of the Body in Melville and Hawthorne*. Baltimore and London: Johns Hopkins University Press.

Carey, J. 1995. *The Faber Book of Science*. London: Faber and Faber.

———. 1990. *John Donne: Life, Mind and Art*. London: Faber and Faber.

Carroll, J. 1995. *Evolution and Literary Theory*. Columbia: University of Missouri Press.

Chase, R. 1957. *The American Novel*. New York: Doubleday.

Christie, J., and S. Shuttleworth. 1989. *Nature Transfigured*. Manchester: University of Manchester Press.

Clarke, A. C. 1999. *Greetings, Carbon-based Bipeds!: A Vision of the Twentieth Century As It Happened*. Ian T. Macauley, ed. London: Voyager.

———. 2001. *2001: A Space Odyssey*. London: Orbit.

Clarke, G. 1991. *Edgar Allan Poe: Critical Assessments*. Mountfield, East Sussex: Helm Information.

Coburn, K. 1973. "Coleridge, a Bridge Between Science and Poetry: Reflections on the Bicentenary of his Birth." *Proceedings of the Royal Institution of Great Britain* 46: 45–63.

Coffin, C. M. 1958. *John Donne and the New Philosophy*. New York: Humanities Press.

Collins, Harry, "Stages in the Empirical Programme of Relativism," *Social Studies of Science* 11 (1981): 3–10.

Conn, P. 1990. *Literature in America: An Illustrated History.* London and New York: Guild.

Cook, E. T. and A. Wedderburn. 1909. *The Works of Ruskin*, 39 vols. London: G. Allen.

Cooke, B. 1999. "Biopoetics: The New Synthesis. " In B. Cooke and F. Turner, *Biopoetics: Evolutionary Explorations in the Arts.* Lexington, KY: ICUS (International Conference on the Unity of the Sciences).

Cosslett, T. 1982. *The Scientific Movement in Victorian Literature.* Brighton: Harvester Press.

Cunliffe, M. 1982. *The Literature of the United States.* Harmondsworth: Penguin.

Curry, W. C. 1960. *Chaucer and the Medieval Sciences.* London: George Allen and Unwin.

Daiches, D. 1972. Literature and Science in 19th-Century England in Daiches, D. and Thorlby, A. *The Modern World*, vol. 5 of *Literature and Western Civilization.* London: Aldus.

Daly, M., and M. Wilson. 1988. *Homicide.* Hawthorne, NY: Aldine de Gruyter.

Darwin, C. 1859. *On the Origin of Species by Means of Natural Selection.* London: John Murray.

———. 1874. *The Descent of Man.* London: John Murray.

Darwin, F., ed. 1929. *Autobiography of Charles Darwin.* London: Watts.

Dawkins, R. 1998. *Unweaving the Rainbow.* London: Penguin.

———. 2003. *The Devil's Chaplain.* London: Weidenfield and Nicolson.

Deleuze, G., and F. Guattari. 1994. *What Is Philosophy?*, trans. Hugh Tomlinson and Graham Burchell. New York: Columbia University Press.

Delillo, D. 2002. *White Noise.* London: Picador.

Dennett, D. C. 1995. *Darwin's Dangerous Idea.* New York: Simon and Schuster.

Dick, P. K. 1990. *Martian Time-Slip.* London: Gollancz.

———. 1969. *Do Androids Dream of Electric Sheep?* London: Grafton.

Digdae, J. 1990. *Thomas Pynchon: Allusive Parables of Power.* Basingstoke: Macmillan.

Doyle, Sir A. C. 1951. "The Creeping Man." In *The Case-Book of Sherlock Holmes.* London: Penguin. 162–185.

———. 1981. "The Empty House." In *The Return of Sherlock Holmes.* London: Penguin. 7–30.

———. 1992. "The Final Problem." In *The Adventures of Sherlock Holmes.* London: Wordsworth. 435–446.

Emerson, R. W. 1908. "The American Scholar." In *English Traits, Representative Men and Other Essays.* London: J. M. Dent. 293–310.

Gardner, J. 1967. "The Canon's Yeoman's Prologue and Tale: An Interpretation." *Philological Quarterly* 46, January 1967: 1–17.

Gibson, W. 1987. *Count Zero*. London: Grafton.

———. 1988a. "Johnny Mnemonic." In *Burning Chrome*. London: Grafton. 14–36.

———. 1988b. *Mona Lisa Overdrive*. London: Grafton.

———. 1995. N*euromancer*. London: Voyager.

Gibson, W., and B. Sterling. 1991. *The Difference Engine*. London: Gollancz.

Gleick, J. 1998. *Chaos*. London: Vintage.

Gliserman, S. 1975. "Early Victorian Science Writers and Tennyson's 'In Memoriam': A Study in Cultural Exchange." *Victorian Studies*, March 1975: 277–308.

Gould, S. J. 2003. *The Hedgehog, the Fox and the Magister's Pox*. London: Jonathan Cape.

———. 1980. *Ever Since Darwin*. London: Penguin.

———. 1990. *Time's Arrow, Time's Cycle: Myth and Metaphor in the Discovery of Geological Time*. London: Penguin.

Green, M. 1964. *Science and the Shabby Curate of Poetry*. London: Longmans, Green.

Greenland, C. 1983. *The Entropy Exhibition: Michael Moorcock and the British "New Wave" in Science Fiction*. London: Routledge and Kegan Paul.

Greenslade, W. 1994. *Degeneration, Culture and the Novel, 1880–1940*. Cambridge: Cambridge University Press.

Gribbin, J. 2002. *Science: A History 1543–2001*. London: Allen Lane.

Griswold, R. W. 1873. *The Prose Works of John Milton*. Philadelphia: J. W. Moore.

Gross, P. and Levitt, N. 1994. *Higher Superstition: The Academic Left and Its Quarrels with Science*. Baltimore and London: John Hopkins University Press.

Haller, J. S., Jr. 1995. *Outcasts from Evolution: Scientific Attitudes of Racial Inferiority, 1859–1900*. 2nd. ed. Carbondale and Edwardsville: Southern Illinois University Press.

Hankins, J. 1978. *Backgrounds of Shakespeare's Thought*. Hassocks, Sussex: Harvester Press.

Hardy, T. 1975 (1874). *Far from the Madding Crowd*. London: Macmillan.

Hardy, T. 1978. *Tess of the d'Urbervilles*. London: Penguin.

Hawking, S. 1988. *A Brief History of Time*. London: Bantam.

Hawthorne, N. 1974a. *Mosses from and Old Manse*. Columbus: Ohio State University Press.

———. 1974b. *The Snow Image*. Columbus: Ohio State University Press.

Hayles, N. K. 1992. "Gender Encoding in Fluid Mechanics: Masculine Channels and Feminine Flows." *Differences: A Journal of Feminist Cultural Studies* 4(2): 16–44.

————. 1999. *How We Became Posthuman.* Chicago and London: University of Chicago Press.

Heath, S. "Psychopathia Sexualis: Stevenson's Strange Case." *Critical Quarterly* 28, nos. 1–2 (Spring/Summer 1986): 93–108.

Heath-Stubbs, J., and P. Salaman, eds. 1984. *Poems of Science.* London: Penguin.

Heinlein, R. 1979. "By His Bootstraps." In *Classic Science Fiction: The First Golden Age,* edited by Terry Carr. n.p.: Robson, 279–343.

Hillegas, M. 1967. *The Future as Nightmare: H. G. Wells and the Anti-Utopians.* New York: Oxford University Press.

Horton, G. 2002. "The Rise of Post-Modernism and the "End of Science," in *Post-Modernisms,* edited by Claudio Veliz. Boston: Boston University Press.

Hughes, R. 1997. *American Visions: The Epic History of Art in America.* London: Harvill.

Hurley, K. 1996. *The Gothic Body: Sexuality, Materialism, and Degeneration at the Fin de Siècle.* Cambridge: Cambridge University Press.

Huxley, A. 1963. *Literature and Science.* London: Chatto and Windus.

————. 1994. *Brave New World.* London: Flamingo.

Huxley, T. H. 1993 (1880). "Science and Culture." In M. H. Abrams and Greenblatt, S. J., eds. *The Norton Anthology of English Literature. Vol. 2.* New York: Norton.

Irigaray, L. 1985. *The Sex Which Is Not One,* trans. Catherine Porter and Carolyn Burke. Ithaca: Cornell University Press.

James, E. 1994. *Science Fiction in the Twentieth Century.* Oxford and New York: Oxford University Press.

Jardine, L. 2003. *The Curious Life of Robert Hooke: The Man Who Measured London.* London: Harper Collins.

Johnson, M. L., and J. E. Grant, eds. 1979. *Blake's Poetry and Designs: Authoritative Texts, Illumination in Colour and Monochrome, Related Prose, Criticism.* New York: Norton.

Jones, W. P. 1966. *The Rhetoric of Science.* London: Routledge and Kegan Paul.

Jordanova, L., ed. 1986. *Languages of Nature.* London: Free Association Books.

Kamiya, G. 1996. *Transgressing the Transgressors: Towards a Transformative Hermeneutics of Total Bullshit.* Salon. Retrieved from http://www.salon.com/media/media960517.html on December 5, 2003.

Keynes, G. 1966. *The Complete Writings of William Blake.* Oxford: Oxford University Press.

Kinghorn, A. M. 1971. *The Chorus of History: Literary-Historical Relations in Renaissance Britain, 1485–1558.* London: Blandford Press.

Kipperman, M. 1998. "Coleridge, Shelley, Davy, and Science's Millenium." *Criticism* 40 (3): 409–436.

Kumar, K. 1987. *Utopia and Anti-Utopia in Modern Times*. New York and Oxford: Blackwell.

Lambourne, R., M. Shallis, and M. Shortland. 1990. *Close Encounters? Science and Science Fiction*. Bristol and New York: Adam Hilger.

Lankester, E. R. 1888. *Degeneration: An Essay in Darwinism*. London: Macmillan.

Leavis, F. R., and M. Yudkin. 1962. *Two Cultures? The Significance of C. P. Snow*. New York: Pantheon Books.

Lederer, S. E. 2002. *Frankenstein: Penetrating the Secrets of Nature*. New Brunswick: Rutgers University Press.

Ledger, S., and R. Luckhurst, eds. 2000. *The Fin-de-Siècle: A Reader in Cultural History, 1880–1900*. Oxford: Oxford University Press.

Levine, G. 1988. *Darwin and the Novelists: Patterns of Science in Victorian Fiction*. Chicago: University of Chicago Press.

———. 1996. "What Is Science Studies For and Who Cares?" *Social Text* 46/47, (1 & 2): 113–127.

Levine, G., ed. 1987. *One Culture: Essays in Science and Literature*. Madison: University of Wisconsin Press.

Levine, G., and U. C. Knoepflmacher, eds. 1982. *The Endurance of Frankenstein: Essays on Mary Shelley's Novel*. Berkeley: University of California Press.

Levitt, N., and P. Gross. 1994. *Higher Superstition: The Academic Left and Its Quarrels with Science*. Baltimore, MD: John Hopkins University Press.

Limon, J. 1990. *The Place of Fiction in the Time of Science: A Disciplinary History of American Writing*. Cambridge: Cambridge University Press.

Lindberg, D. C. 1992. *The Beginning of Western Science*. Chicago: University of Chicago Press.

Macdonald, D. L., Scherf, K. eds. 2001. *Frankenstein by Mary Shelley*. Letchworth, Hertfordshire: Broadview Literary Texts.

Macklem, M. 1958. *The Anatomy of the World: Relations between Natural and Moral Law from Donne to Pope*. Minneapolis: University of Minnesota Press.

Mattes, E. 1973. "Further Reassurances in Herschel's Natural Philosophy and Chamber's Vestiges of Creation." In R. H. Ross, *In Memoriam by Alfred, Lord Tennyson*. New York: W. W. Norton.

McCaffrey, L., ed. 1991. *Storming the Reality Studio*. Durham, NC: Duke University Press.

McHale, B. 1992. *Constructing Postmodernism*. London: Routledge.

McKenzie, A. E. E. 1960. *The Major Achievements of Science*. Cambridge: Cambridge University Press.

McNeil, M. 1986. "The Scientific Muse: The Poetry of Erasmus Darwin." In *Languages of Nature*, edited by L. Jordanova. London: Free Association Books.

Meadows, A. J. 1969. *The High Firmament: A Survey of Astronomy in English Literature*. Leicester: Leicester University Press.

Melville, H. 1987. *Moby-Dick*. London: Penguin.

Mighall, R. 1999. *A Geography of Victorian Gothic Fiction: Mapping History's Nightmares*. Oxford: Oxford University Press.

Miller, D. M. 2002. "The Sobel Effect." *Metascience* 11: 185–200.

Miller, G. 1998. "How Mate Choice Shaped Human Nature: A Review of Sexual Selection and Human Evolution." In *Handbook of Evolutionary Psychology*, edited by C. Crawford and D. L. Krebs. Mahwah, NJ: Lawrence Erlbaum Associates.

———. 2000. *The Mating Mind*. London: William Heinemann.

Morton, P. 1984. *The Vital Science: Biology and the Literary Imagination, 1860–1900*. London: George Allen and Unwin.

Moylan, T. 1986. *Demand the Impossible: Science Fiction and the Utopian Imagination*. New York and London: Methuen.

———. 2000. *Scraps of the Untainted Sky: Science Fiction, Utopia, Dystopia*. Boulder and Oxford: Westview Press.

Mullen, R. D., et al., eds. 1992. *On Philip K. Dick: 40 Articles for Science Fiction Studies*. Terre Haute, IN: TH-SFS (Terre Haute-Science Fiction Studies).

Nicolson, M. H. 1946. *Newton Demands the Muse: Newton's Optics and the Eighteenth Century Poets*. Princeton, NJ: Princeton University Press.

———. 1960. *The Breaking of the Circle: Studies in the Effect of the New Science upon Seventeeth-Centruy Poetry*. New York: Columbia University Press.

Nicolson, M. J., and D. S. Rodes, eds. 1966. *Thomas Shadwell, The Virtuoso*. London: Edward Arnold.

Nordau, M. 1993. *Degeneration*. Lincoln: University of Nebraska Press.

North, J. D. 1988. *Chaucer's Universe*. Oxford: Oxford University Press.

Olby, R. C., G. N. Cantor, J. R. R. Christie, and M. J. S. Hodge, eds. 1990. *Companion to the History of Modern Science*. London and New York: Routledge.

Oldroyd, D. R. 1980. *Darwinian Impacts*. Milton Keynes: Open University Press.

Orr, M. A. 1969 (1913). *Dante and the Early Astronomers*. Port Washington, NY: Kennikat Press.

Otis, L., ed. 2002. *Literature and Science in the Nineteenth Century: An Anthology*. Oxford: Oxford University Press.

Owen, W. J. B., and Worhtington Smyser, eds. 1974. *The Prose Works of William Wordsworth*, Vol. 1. Oxford: Clarendon Press.

Paradis, J., and T. Postlewait, eds. 1985. *Victorian Science and Victorian Values: Literary Perspectives*. New Brunswick, NJ: Rutgers University Press.

Parrinder, P. 1995. *Shadows of the Future: H. G. Wells, Science Fiction and Prophecy*. Liverpool: Liverpool University Press.

Patey, D. G. 2002 (1991). "Swift's Satire on 'Science' and the Structure of *Gulliver's Travels*." In *Jonathan Swift: Gulliver's Travels*, edited by A. J. Rivero. New York and London: W. W. Norton.

Pick, D. 1996. "'Terrors of the Night': *Dracula* and 'Degeneration' in the Late Nineteenth Century." In *Reading Fin de Siècle Fictions*, edited by Lyn Pykett. London and New York: Longman, 149–165.

———. 1993. *Faces of Degeneration: A European Disorder, c.1848–1918*. Cambridge: Cambridge University Press.

Pinker, S. 1997. *How the Mind Works*. London and New York: Penguin.

Poe, E. A. 1980a. "The Facts in the Case of M. Valdemar." In *Selected Tales*. Oxford and New York: Oxford Classics, 269–277.

———. 1980b. "Some Words with a Mummy." In *Selected Tales*. Oxford and New York: Oxford Classics, 248–262.

Porter, R. 1999. *The Greatest Benefit to Mankind: A Medical History of Humanity from Antiquity to the Present*. London: Fontana.

Porush, D. "Prigogine, Chaos and Contemporary Science Fiction." *Science Fiction Studies* 18: 55, November 1991. 367–386.

———. 1985. *The Soft Machine: Cybernetic Fiction*. New York: Methuen.

Prigogine, I., and I. Stengers. 1985. *Order Out of Chaos*. London: Flamingo.

Pyenson, L., and S. Sheets-Pyenson. 1999. *Servants of Nature: A History of Scientific Institutions, Enterprises and Sensibilities*. London: Fontana.

Pynchon, T. 1979. *The Crying of Lot 49*. London: Picador.

———. 1998. "Entropy." In *The Norton Anthology of American Literature*, 5th edition, edited by Nina Bawm et al. New York: W. W. Norton, 2180–2190.

Richardson, A. 2000. "Rethinking Romantic Incest: Human Universals, Literary Representation, and the Biology of the Mind." *New Literary History* 31: 553–572.

Ricks, C., ed. 1980. *A. E. Houseman: Collected Poems and Selected Prose*. London: Allen Lane.

Robbins, B. 1996. "Anatomy of a Hoax." *Tikkun*, September–October 1996: 58–59.

Roberts, Adam. 2000. *Science Fiction*. London and New York: Routledge.

Rogers, J. 1996. *The Matter of Revolution: Science, Poetry and Politics in the Age of Milton*. Ithaca: Cornell University Press.

Rollins, H. E., and H. Baker. 1954. *The Renaissance in England*. Boston: D.C. Heath.

Rudd, G. 2001. *The Complete Critical Guide to Geoffrey Chaucer*. London and New York: Routledge.

Sayers, D. L., and B. Reynolds, eds. 1962. *The Comedy of Dante Alighieri, Paradise*. London: Penguin.

Scott, J. A. 1983. "Dante Alighieri: *The Divine Comedy*." In *Medieval Literature Part Two, The European Inheritance*, edited by B. Ford. London: Pelican.

Seed, D. 1988. *The Fictional Labyrinths of Thomas Pynchon*. Basingstoke: Macmillan.

———, ed. 1995. *Anticipations: Essays on Early Science Fiction and Its Precursors*. Liverpool: Liverpool University Press.

Shannon, C., and W. Weaver. 1949. *The Mathematical Theory of Communication*. Urbana: Illinois University Press.

Slotkin, R. *1973 Regeneration Through Violence: The Mythology of the American Frontier, 1600–1860*. Norman: University of Oklahoma Press.

Slusser, G., and T. Shippey, eds. 1992. *Fiction 2000: Cyberpunk and the Future of Narrative*. Athens: University of Georgia Press.

Smith, E. E. "Doc." 1972. *Triplanetary*. London: Panther.

Smith, H. N. 1950. *Virgin Land: The American West as Symbol and Myth*. Cambridge, MA and London: Harvard University Press.

Snow, C. P. 1959. *The Two Cultures and the Scientific Revolution*. Cambridge and New York: Cambridge University Press.

Sokal, A. 1996c. "Transgressing the Boundaries: An Afterword." *Dissent* 43 (4): 93–99.

———. 1996b. "A Physicist Experiments with Cultural Studies." *Lingua Franca* May–June 1996: 62–64.

———. 1996a. "Transgressing the Boundaries: Towards a Transformative Hermeneutics of Quantum Gravity." *Social Text* 46/47 (1–2): 217–252.

———. 2004. http://www.physics.nyu.edu/faculty/sokal/reply.html (accessed March 15, 2004).

Sokal, A., and J. Bricmont. 1998. *Intellectual Impostures*. London: Profile Books.

Sprat, T. 1667. *History of the Royal Society*. London: Routledge, Kegan and Paul.

Stapledon, O. 1999. *Star Maker*. London: Millenium.

———. 2000. *Last and First Men*. London: Millenium.

Stevenson, R. L. 1999. *Strange Case of Doctor Jekyll and Mr Hyde*, Martin A. Danahay, ed. Peterborough, OH: Broadview.

Stoker, B. 1992. *Dracula*. Kerry, Eire: Brandon.

Sutherland, J. 1996. *The Literary Detective*. Oxford: Oxford University Press.

Sutin, L. 1991. *Divine Invasions: A Life of Philip K. Dick*. London: Paladin.

Suvin, D. 1988. *Positions and Presuppositions in Science Fiction*. Basingstoke: Macmillan.

———. 1979. *Metamorphoses of Science Fiction: On the Poetics and History of a Literary Genre*. New Haven, CT and London: Yale University Press.

Swirski, P. 2000. *Between Literature and Science: Poe, Lem and Explorations in Aesthetics, Cognitive Science, and Literary Knowledge*. Montreal: McGill-Queens University Press.

Tanner, T. 1971. *City of Words: American Fiction 1950–1970*. London: Jonathan Cape.

———. 2000. *The American Mystery: American Literature from Emerson to Delillo*. Cambridge: Cambridge University Press.

Thomas, W. K., and W. U. Ober. 1989. *A Mind Forever Voyaging*. Edmonton: University of Alberta Press.

Thoreau, H. D. *Walden*. 1992. New York: W. W. Norton.

Tillyard, E. M. W. 1943. *The Elizabethan World Picture*. London: Chatto and Windus.

Toulmin, S. 1990. *Cosmopolis*. Chicago: University of Chicago Press.

Tyndall, J. 1874. *Address delivered before The British Association assembled at Belfast*. London: Longman, Green.

Umland, S. J., ed. 1995. *Philip K. Dick: Contemporary Critical Interpretations*. Westport, CT and London: Greenwood Press.

Verne, J. 1993. *Twenty Thousand Leagues Under the Sea*. London: Everyman.

———. 1996. *Journey to the Centre of the Earth*. Ware, UK: Wordsworth.

Wells, H. G. 1911. *The Time Machine*. London: Heinemann.

Wiener, N. 1954. *The Human Use of Human Beings: Cybernetics and Society*. Garden City, NY: Doubleday.

Wiley, B. 1934. *The Seventeenth Century Background*. London: Chatto and Windus.

Wilson, E. O. 1984. *Biophilia*. Cambridge, MA: Harvard University Press.

———. 1998. *Consilience*. New York: Alfred A. Knopf.

Wilson, F. 1989. "Wordsworth and the Culture of Science." *Centennial Review* 33 (4): 322–392.

Winny, J. 1968. "Chaucer's Science." In M. Hussey, A. C. Spearing, and J. Winny, *An Introduction to Chaucer*. Cambridge: Cambridge University Press.

Wolfe, B. *Limbo* 1987. New York: Carroll and Graf.

Zoline, P. 1983. "The Heat Death of the Universe," *New Worlds* 173, July 1967; Reprint, Michael Moorcock, ed. (1983), *New Worlds: An Anthology*. London: Flamingo, 148–159.

Index

About the Authors

John Cartwright is a senior lecturer in Science and teaching fellow at the University of Chester. He holds degrees in natural science and the history and philosophy of science. At Chester he teaches courses in Darwinian approaches to understanding human behavior and the history of science. His research interests lie in two areas: Darwinism and the relationship between science and literature. He has previously published books and articles in both these areas. More generally he is motivated by the conviction that the sciences and the humanities would benefit from a closer alliance and that each has something to learn from the other. He hopes that *Literature and Science* is a step in this direction.

Brian Baker is a senior lecturer in Literature and Film in the English department of University of Chester. He has published on British and American science fiction, and is currently writing a book-length study of the contemporary British novelist Iain Sinclair for the Manchester University Press's Contemporary British Novelists series. He is also completing a book-length project on screen masculinities, entitled *Masculinities in Fiction and Film: Representing Men in Popular Genres 1945–2000*, for Continuum.